Political Economy

Christian A. Conrad

Political Economy

An Institutional and Behavioral Approach

 Springer Gabler

Christian A. Conrad
University of Applied Sciences
Saarbrücken, Germany

ISBN 978-3-658-30883-4   ISBN 978-3-658-30884-1   (eBook)
https://doi.org/10.1007/978-3-658-30884-1

Bei diesem Buch handelt es sich um eine überarbeitete und erweiterte Übersetzung des 2020 bei Springer Gabler erschienenen Buches „Wirtschaftspolitik. Eine praxisorientierte Einführung", 2. Aufl.

This Springer Gabler imprint is published by the registered company Springer Fachmedien Wiesbaden GmbH part of Springer Nature.
The registered company address is: Abraham-Lincoln-Str. 46, 65189 Wiesbaden, Germany

Preface

This book is the culmination of my research stay at Georgetown University and the EC Commission and my time as an Assistant Professor in the Department of Economics at the University of Tübingen, Germany. I have also amassed more than 12 years of professional experience in a large German bank, where I often worked with the management of international companies as a business consultant. The time period of this experience included the boom and crash at the beginning of the new millennium and the financial crisis. As a result, I have held seminars on political economy in the bachelor's and master's degree programs at the University of Applied Science HTW in Saarbrücken. This teaching experience as well as an extensive literature study has been incorporated into this book.

Finally, I would like to thank Ms. Danica Webb (USA) for the translation of the major part of this book and Prof. Starbatty, Prof. Hartherz, and the asset manager Dr. Markus Stahl for their support.

Saarbrücken, Germany   Christian A. Conrad
May 2020

Contents

Abbreviations

C	consumption
c	consumption rate
c`	marginal consumption rate
Cap	capital
D	deficit (state budget deficit) or demand
d	marginal change of a variable (like dC/dY = marginal consumption rate)
Ex	exports
ER	exchange rate
G	government or government expenditures
I	investment demand
Im	imports
i	nominal or real interest rate
k	cash holding coefficient
L	liquidity (money demand)
M	nominal money supply
N	number (number of hours worked)
P	prices (general price level)
S	savings or supply (offer)
T	taxes
ToT	terms of trade
v	velocity of money
w	wages (general wage level)
Y	Yielt (income or national product)

List of Figures

Introduction

Economics uses quantitative models to describe the behavior of economic agents and the development of the economy as a process. Models require deterministic behavior. The results must be reproducible. To preserve scientific accuracy, economics chose the homo-oeconomicus as a representation of human behavior.

This book takes with its behavioral orientation a different approach than economics. Instead of assuming rational deterministic behavior in order to derive quantitative models, it analyzes human behavior in order to derive incentives for welfare-maximizing behavior of economic agents. To achieve this goal, it combines the well-known non-quantitative approach of political economy with the findings of behavioral science. The knowledge of political economy is presented topic oriented and supplemented by the insights of behavioral science.

This book refers to newer research results from behavioral economics, but also from other disciplines such as psychology and sociology, thus leading to new conclusions for economic science. How people behave and how such behavior can be guided towards moral welfare for everyone will be examined within the context of this book. The knowledge relevant to the students is first derived scientifically then the results are presented as summarized. Students are also introduced to economic behavior using behavioral games.

If irrational behavior is not the exception, models based on rational behavior can no longer be a rule, but can at best describe optimal behavior or average behavior by which the irrational behavior shows deviations. If people do not behave predictably like natural laws, then at best we can set a framework to direct behavior with incentives and sanctions. The economy then consists mainly of institutional regulations, a regulatory framework (See Fig. 1.1). One goal of this book is to create a state control framework as an institution for economical optimal behavior.

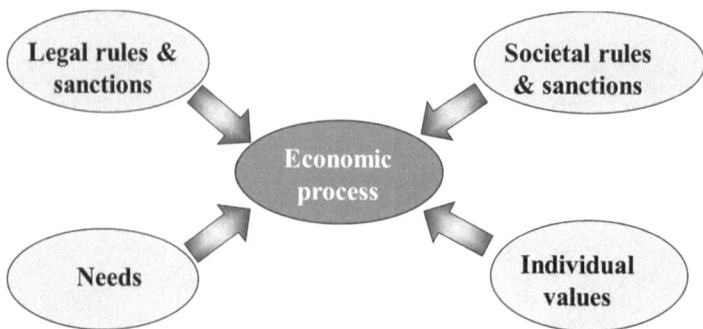

Fig. 1.1 Economy as institutional regulations

Political economy as a behavioral approach, based on the findings of behavioral economics, sociology, social psychology and psychology, develops an institutional and organizational framework to ensure the desired optimal behavior of economic agents and thus the desired economic development. Thus, the behavioral political economy builds on German order policy and institutional economics. The result is an incentive economy.

Economic policy includes the political shaping of the economy and intervention in it. The target audience for this textbook are students of political economy, economics, political science and governmental studies. Economic policy is intended to supplement the more theoretical disciplines of micro- and macroeconomics by addressing concrete economic problems and their solutions. Focus of this book are issues of national economics that must be verbally analyzed because they are qualitative and thus quantitative models do not apply.

We will answer the central question of economics, whether and how the state should intervene in the economy to increase the welfare of society. We are primarily concerned with the interplay between a democratic society and the economy. Which incentives have a political and economic impact and influence the outcome of economic policy? This is where the findings of behavioral economics and new institutional economics are to be incorporated into political economy.

We will also analyze the extent to which ethics plays a role in the economic processes and the achievement of optimum welfare. Moral values and concepts of justice are closely linked to this analysis, and theories of justice will be used to explain questions of distributive justice such as taxation. In our efforts to understand how people are behaving ethically or unethically and how this affects the economy we will apply research findings from economics, psychology and behavioral economics.

Chapter 2 analyses the weaknesses in economics and economic education that have to be addressed by political economy. Chapter 3 continues by defining terms and delineating objectives of political economy. Modeling the image of Man is the next Chap. 4. Here we will deal with man and his behavior. What motivates him? To what extent is it ethically oriented? Is there a sense of justice? This is the background for deriving economic incentives.

Economic policy is tasked with explaining the market economy, how markets and competition function, as well as centralized economies and social market economies. Chapter 5 analyses the functioning of market and competition. What are the advantages and disadvantages of the various economic systems and which one is the best? We will answer these questions in this book in Chap. 6 using institutional economics to design the economic framework.

Market economy has established itself as the economic system, but this does not mean that the market is infallible. Market failure occurs whenever market functions do not deliver socially desired results. If the market does not work properly the state must intervene, which is why market failure gives rise to the need for political economy interventions. This is the focus of Chap. 7. Individual policy areas such as environmental policy and labor market policy are thus due to market failure.

How does the political system work? When the political system does not work properly we find policy failures in Chap. 8. One reason for failures is the political voting procedure. There is no actor to optimally aggregate the will of the people and take it to the political decision-makers. Market functions must be supplemented by competition in order to produce optimal results, yet competition only works optimally with a state competition policy. Our next step is then in Chap. 9 to find out what state intervention must include by examining restrictions of competition such as monopolies, cartels and the like. We then analyze the challenges of an international competition policy. The next topic of political economy, industrial policy in Chap. 10, shows us policies through which economic structures and research are influenced by financial contributions.

Economic fluctuations, particularly those of demand, are a major economic and business problem that political economy can influence only to a very limited extent. Chapter 11 outlines the causes and effects of inflation in order to understand the ECB's primary objective of ensuring price level stability. The chapter is dedicated to the euro. How did the common currency euro come about and what are the pros and cons? An introduction to the monetary policy of the ECB completes the chapter. The following Chap. 12 analyzes the economic phenomenon of business cycles and its effects on the economy. The reasons behind cyclical fluctuations are explained using the leading economic theories. Next we will deal in Chap. 13 with the international financial markets and analyse the reasons for the latest financial crisis which had nearly caused a depression like in 1929. Are the reforms sufficient or is a crisis still possible? In the following, we will then take a closer look at monetary policy.

As globalization progresses international economic relationships are becoming increasingly important to managers. The last Chap. 14 explains the basic determinants of foreign trade, international capital movements and exchange rates. Finally Chap. 15 contains the solutions to the exercise.

Weaknesses in Economics and Economic Education

2

What Follows Why?
Quantitative oriented economics up to this point has described the behavior of economic agents and the development of the economy as a process by means of models. Quantitative models presuppose deterministic behavior. The results must be reproducible. In order to preserve such scientific accuracy, economics chose homo economicus to represent human behavioral patterns. This assumption has since been refuted in numerous experiments. In the following chapter we want to ask to what extent the quantitative economics can grasp the economic reality and thus come to the right conclusions.
    Learning Goals
    You should be able to assess the limitations of quantitative economics in describing reality.

2.1 Cultural and Institutional Factors in Economics

An article in the German newspaper Handelsblatt titled, "Economic Culture Revolution." describes the self-recognition that economics "was ignorant for a long time about cultural factors." Representing the ignorant "traditional" economy, the assertion of Nobel laureates George Stigler and Gary Becker was quoted from the end of the 1970s: "Economists who argue with cultural factors are just disguising the failure of their analysis." According to the article this verdict remained the dominant opinion until the late 1990s. American researchers were able to prove the influence of culture with a valid methodological effort.

Professor Raquel Fernández from New York University, together with her colleague Alessandra Fogli, was able to separate cultural factors from classical economic factors of influence. They made use of a medical research approach called the epidemiological approach. When American doctors want to filter out environmental influences as the cause of, for example, heart attacks in Japanese, they compare the heart attack rates for Japanese patients who have emigrated to the USA with their genetically similar counterparts living in Japan. The economic scientists compared the tendency to engage in a particular profession for women born in the USA, but whose parents came from different countries. The political and economic conditions were the same for all subjects, yet they showed great occupational differences. The greater the participation in employment of the family's original country, the more likely the daughters born later in the USA were working.[1] Another research group, Guiso, Sapienza and Zingales were able to prove that the normative, positive formation of thriftiness was just as important in explaining country-to-country differences in thriftiness as the economic factors of influence.[2] Another study by Andrea Ichino and Giovanni Maggi confirmed that regional culture differences formed the economic behavior of people. They investigated for a large Italian bank why southern Italians took more sick leave than their northern counterparts. They discovered that the place of birth had a significant influence on calling in sick. Italians born in the south had significantly higher absentee rates, even if they worked for years in the north.[3]

What conclusions can be drawn from these new revelations of economics? First of all, they are not new revelations, they are at best merely statistic confirmation. The sociologist Max Weber had already shown the importance of culture in economic development in "The Protestant Ethic and the Spirit of Capitalism" in 1905.[4] Before that there were already references made to the idea. Cultural influences were, and are, the basis for cultural sciences such as sociology or behavioral research. Many of the new statistic revelations made with such effort can be derived logically through common sense and may even be called banal.

What is in fact new is the alarming admission of economics to have ignored cultural factors for decades. It shut out all of the influencing factors in its observable world that it could not examine and proove with quantitative factors. It simply ignored their existence and all economists who wanted to include them despite their incalculability were denounced and banned, as was expressed in the statement of the two Nobel laureates.

In the modern, free society, everyone should have the chance to develop however they desire. Everyone should at least have the chance to work their way up to being a millionaire, which is a central incentive for performance in the market economy. National

---

[1] See *Fernández, Raquel/Fogli, Alessandra* (2005), pp. 552–561.

[2] See *Guiso, Luigi/Sapienza, Paola/Zingales, Luigi* (2006), pp. 23–48.

[3] See Ichino, Andrea/Maggi, Giovanni (1999), p. 1057–1090 and Handelsblatt dated 19.02.07, p. 9.

[4] See Weber, Max (1905). For the critique of sociology on the onesidedness of economics see Maurer, Andrea/Schmid, Michael (2010), pp. 194.

wealth is then not statically in the hands of the few. According to the enlightenment all people are equal, at least in their basic rights, which makes the solution relatively simple in that the freedoms of one individual end where those of the others begin. If we were to leave it at that, this would be an idealistic illusion, leading neither to a functional nor a humane society. There would only be individualists who maximize their benefits and freedoms within the limits determined by the rights of others. Each person would create their own island of freedom and benefits. The result would be just millions of little islands of freedom and egoists. Society as a continuous entity, a community, would not exist. No one would do anything useful to others for the common good. No one would sacrifice himself for his family; no one would care for their parents in old age out of gratitude, or care for their children. Volunteer work necessary for a community would no longer be performed. Politicians would use their positions just to maximize their own benefit. No one would engage themselves for the good of the community, society, state or nation.

All modern societies have institutions and organizations, giving them order, and instilling discipline in their citizens to behave in the manner socially desired. As we have already shown however, this is not sufficient. For a society to function and for productive forces to develop, the appropriate social capital for the type of system order and economic stage of development must be available. This depends greatly on the attitudes of people required for societal or community cooperation. Norms, values and morality are important here, including attitudes towards the political and economic system.

It is clear that it really must be the opposite, and that the more freedom individuals have, the greater their morality must be. When political leaders and church no longer sanction people in relation to their moral behavior or missteps and when there are few predetermined rules, people must have already internalized socially desirable behavior, possessing inner values and social capital. The more modern the economy, the more important morals and values are for the development of productive forces.

The Sociologist Max Weber had already noted in 1905 that the source of a positive economic development in Switzerland, the Netherlands, England and parts of Germany was a Protestant or Calvinist influence.[5] The attitudes of people in a society towards economically relevant activities have been paid as little attention by economic science as the existence of general economic knowledge. What does it help in the case of Russia that a market economy system was introduced, if the people still behave as they did in the communist, planned economy? What does it help if a framework, such as a legal system with legislative and executive branch, if the judges can be bribed because they are not remunerated adequately? What does it help if a democratic framework is created like in Russia at the end of the 1980s and in Germany in the 1920s if people are politically passive and desire a strong leadership that takes care of their problems? If a system of order is neither accepted nor understood it has no future.

---

[5]See Weber, Max (1905); Ulrich, P. (1993), pp. 1168 and Noll, Bernd (2002), p.166.

Cultural terms are not always exact, and are surely not solely responsible for an economic development. There are many cultural values that influence productivity, and on the other hand institutional framework conditions, or political order, play a role just as much as do macroeconomic variables such as monetary and human capital. One must therefore avoid normative conclusions from quantitative investigations and statements such as "the labor productivity of people A is greater than that of people B because people A are more willing to make an effort or work harder." The universal applicability claimed by this kind of statistic must be questioned, even if there is significance for a factor. Many factors are usually ignored, and it is meaningful to know how many people were questioned over what time frame. Associations are also problematic, since "not willing to perform" can be equated with "lazy," for example.

Ultimately the goal is to recognize the importance of such soft facts, bringing the qualitative factors into a logical connection with other factors to affect higher productivity. Company management and state government must implement morals and ethics, as well as propagate and exemplify values for each individual. Opinion surveys can offer an indication, but no more than that, although they do show where improvement is needed. This should be easier for companies than a national economy. Economics is not an exact science, but we may hope that at least more value will be place on ethics, morals and norms. This hope may be deceiving, however. Because a quantitative proof was provided it has now been admitted that cultural values have an effect on the economy, but which values exactly and how the values coincide will remain unknown based on purely quantitative analysis. With even the most refined quantitative analysis there will always be many influential factors and connections, ethics in particular, that will not be included. Thinking and deriving in contextual forms remains impossible.[6]

The significance of a legal framework has often been discussed. Without ethical rules, thus the laws or the norms of a scociety we have anarchy which allows now economic productivity. We call these ruels institutions. They have evolved over time to overcome social dilemma structures. Institutions are made up by the society and thus have a strong cultural infuence. They regulate interpersonal coexistence, in which they place appropriate incentives, for example laws and penal sanctions in the event of an offense. Economists like Marshal have stated that the institutional structure exerts an important influence on economic behavior. There has been a renaissance of institutional thinking with the New

---

[6]"Business scholars could take a lesson from their colleagues in the discipline of psychology, which was stifling under the scientific model three or four decades ago. Psychological research then was dominated by rigorous, but ultimately unproductive, studies of reaction time. As long as psychology professors labored within a small area, they learned little that was of value to anyone. It was only after they began to apply their imaginations—and rigor—to much boarder problems that psychology began to make enormous strides. Not until respected psychologists dared to ask questions that mattered, whether or not they could be quantified in traditional ways, were groundbreaking studies undertaken, such as the Nobel Price—winning work of Daniel Kahneman and the late Amos Tversky on how people make financial decisions". Bennis, Warren G./O'Toole, James (2005), p. 4.

Institional Economic in the nineties but its meaning in economics is still much to low. The reason might be simple as some economists tried to transform the social science economics to a hard science.[7]

"In the project of turning economics into a hard science could succeed, it would be worth doing ... Ther are, however, some reasons for pessimism about the project."[8]

2.2   Economics as a Natural Science?

The most striking thing about mathematics is that it always delivers precise results from the model assumptions and the model construction, and these results are evidence. The first economic pioneer to develop economic science into a scientific/mathematical discipline such as mechanics or hydrodynamics was Léon Walras (1834–1910) with his general theory of equilibrium. After the Second World War the later American Nobel laureates Paul Samuelson, Gérad Debruie and Kenneth Arrow ensured the breakthrough of mathematics in economics. This seemingly scientific precision was apt for a social science and continued to prevail in the following years. The mathematical trend was perfected in the USA in the following decades. With the gigantic further development of computer computing, enormous amounts of numbers were processed. It also allowed statistics as so-called econometrics to move into the economics sciences. In 1940, in the prestigious "American Economic Review" 3% of the pages were filled with mathematical formulas, today it is about 50%.[9] This did not, however, increase the practical significance of the essays. A well-respected CEO described the economics publications as a "vast wasteland."[10] Meanwhile even in the USA, the pioneers of this orientation are critical. For Alan Binder, professor at the famous Princeton University, economics has become more mathematical than physics and the Nobel laureate for economics, Roland Coase, considers economic science to have been degraded to

a theoretical system floating in the air with hardly any connection to what is happening in the real world."[11] Or "As a method of economic analysis, econometrics are a childish game with figures that does not contribute anything to the elucidation of the problems of economic reality.[12]

---

[7]See Furobotn, Erik G./Richter, Rudolf (2005), p. 1.

[8]Solow, R. M. (1979), pp. 328–331, p. 331.

[9]See Wirtschaftswoche vom 9.02.2006, p. 31.

[10]Quoted from Bennis, Warren G./O'Toole, James (2005), p. 90.

[11]See Wirtschaftswoche vom 9.02.2006, p. 31, translated into English.

[12]"Deluded by the Idea that the science of human action must ape the technique of the natural sciences, host of authors are intent upon a quantification of economics. They think that economics ought to imitate chemistry, which progressed from a qualitative to a quantitative state. Their motto is the positivistic maxim: Science is measurement. Supported by rich funds, they are busy reprinting and rearranging statistical data provided by governments, by trade associations, and by corporations and

This is where economic science strives to conceal its socio-scientific roots and to give itself the appearance of an exact science. Whatever is not measurable and calculable does not exist. Factors of influence such as qualitative soft facts are usually ignored. There is no gray area, just black or white. A lack of new discoveries, or only imprecise insights, is not something that can be marketed. What science wants to be constantly displaying its limits or inabilities? Professorships are not awarded for saying that one does not know. Whoever is searching for economic realities, for the truth, has a hard time of it on the job market for economic scientists. Technicians who show an exact science are in demand. Here it becomes clear how economic science attempts to hide its social science roots and appear as an exact natural science. Bennis and O'Toole talk of a "scientific model" that the social scientific economic science has borrowed from the natural sciences due to its "physics envy."

> The scientific model, as we call it, is predicated on the faulty assumption that business is an academic discipline like chemistry or geology. In fact, business is a profession, akin to medicine and the law, and business schools are professional schools—or should be.[13]

This is why the economic scientists think that the more complicated and complex the arithmetic model the better. The spread of computers and their calculation capacities has only augmented the trend. Meanwhile a verbal, logical, deductive thought process has no place in economic science and is scorned as unscientific. The increasing complexity has caused increased specialization. In order to present something new the models must be more complex. In order to achieve and to process this complexity, the new generation of economic scientists is forced to concentrate on a very narrow subject area and to present it repeatedly in minute variations. There has been no place at universities for a while now for generalists, in particular verbal generalists.

> In fact, management professors seem to have an almost morbid fear of being damned as popularizers. Do they believe that the regard of their peers is more important than studying what really matters to executives who can put their ideas into practice? Apparently so. . . .

---

other enterprises. They try to compute the arithmetical relations among various of these data and thus to determine what they call, by analogy with the natural science, "correlations" and "functions" do not describe anything else than what happened at a definite instant of time in a definite geographical area as the outcome of the actions of a definite number of people. As a method of a economic analysis econometric is a childish play with figures that does not contribute anything to the elucidation of the problems of economic reality." Mises, Ludwig van (1978): The Ultimate Foundation of Economic Science, Jim Fedako: Correlating nonsense, http://antipositivist.blogspot.com/2007/02/correating-nonsence.html

[13] And further: "Like other professions, business calls upon the work of many academic disciplines. For medicine, those disciplines include biology, chemistry, and psychology; for business, they include mathematics, economics, psychology, philosophy, and sociology." Bennis, Warren G./ O'Toole, James (2005), p. 2.

Today it is possible to find tenured professors of management who have never set foot inside a real business, except as customers.[14]

In the meantime economics as a science has increasingly excluded the uncountable, qualitative implications of economic action because of the strong model orientation, and has separated itself from society as a self-contained discipline. There is little room for non-quantitative business ethics. Weber already criticized this tendency as a "fiction useful for theoretical purposes," which can not be made "the basis of practical evaluations of real facts." The economic instruments are multifaceted and, as a rule, "in another respect which is potentially important for human interests."[15]

Numbers are facts. However, this does not correspond to economic reality, since the economy is made by people. As we have seen, people do not always behave rationally, often emotionally and sometimes wrongly. Economic science is therefore not an exact deterministic science, but a spiritual and social science. Also, the inclusion of non-rational behavior in models does not alter the non-predictability.

Here follows one example of misinterpretation and judgement problems due to economic calculation methods. Much empirical research has already been conducted in order to analyze how speculation affects commodity and especially food prices. According to the scientists of the Raiffeisen Association the majority of empirical studies show no verifiable connection between stock volumes and the price increase.[16] The NGO WEED disagrees and lists over 100 empirical studies that are critical of speculation.[17] The economic ethicist Pies examined 35 studies and concluded that no negative effect from commodity speculation could be proven.[18] WEED accuses Pies of not examining important studies critiquing speculation and having biased criticism against the methodology used in studies critical of speculation.[19]

Within the discussion both sides criticize one another's methodological weaknesses in econometric studies based primarily on Granger. Irwin and Sanders' results are criticized based on the fact that the Granger test is not an appropriate method with highly volatile

---

[14]Bennis, Warren G./O'Toole, James (2005), p. 4.

[15]See Weber, Max (1968), p. 529...

[16]"Ganz im Gegenteil kommt die weit überwiegende Mehrzahl der bis dato zu diesem Thema verfassten empirischen Arbeiten—allerdings ebenfalls auf dem Boden der suboptimalen Terminmarktdatensätze—zu dem Ergebnis, dass kein nachweisbare Kausalzusammenhang zwischen Anlagevolumina und Preisanstiegen besteht." Translation: "Quite the opposite, the large majority of papers written on this topic to date—though also based on suboptimal futures market data sets—come to the conclusion that there no causal connection exists between stock volumes and price increases." Petersen, V. J./ Herlinghaus, A./Menrad, M. (2012), p. 14.

[17]See http://www2.weed-online.org/uploads/evidence_on_impact_of_commodity_speculation.pdf (Stand 26. November 2013, 04/01/2014).

[18]See Pies, Ingo/Prehn, Sören/Glauben, Thomas/Will, Matthias Georg (2013).

[19]See Henn, Markus (2013).

variables, thus distorting results.[20] The problem is of a more fundamental nature, however. If causal variables are not eliminated, false correlations can show up in Granger tests (spurious regression). The same is true for purely coincidental correlations, which can show up particularly in short time periods of observation.

As we have already shown, many speculation proponents argue that the greatly increased demand for commodities from China, India and other emerging economies, interruptions in oil production, less consumer demand elasticity and US monetary policy were all responsible for the price increases. Increased biofuel production and weather were considered to have caused the price increases.[21] If so many factors were truly affecting prices the Granger test would not have been applicable due to multi-causality. The same is true for the effects of weather, since the required stationarity of variables would not be given.[22] Highly volatile variables such as stock prices or commodities were also determined to have insufficient covariant stationarity, thus the requirement for the regression of time series is not met.[23]

Both positions are in fact supportable using the empirical studies that have been conducted. One part of the studies shows that speculation has influenced commodity prices and the other part proves the opposite. We see here the dilemma of econometric research. There is no proof of causality, as there can be many factors behind a correlation.[24]

Therefore the Popper criterion is not fuilfilled. According to Karl Popper, who founded the Critical Rationalism school of thought, the universal validity of scientific hypotheses must be refutable, thus falsifiable. The original purpose of Popper's falsificationism was to provide a demarcation criterion for which of the actual activities of investigation count as real, empirical sciences.[25]

Also the Popper criterion is also not fulfilled if the assumptions are not in line with reality.

With the model-based statistics, called econometrics in economic science, many connections can be calculated with a great degree of effort and make a grand impression, depending on the sample with its respective probability. It does not matter if there is no real economic sense from these calculations. The senselessness is sometimes apparent: "the level of beauty in high schools has an effect on criminal propensity 7–8 years later."[26] In 1929, Yule found a correlation of 0.95 between the ratio of marriages in the Church of England to all marriages and the death rate for the years 1866–1911. Henry developed was

---

[20]For a critique of Irwin and Sanders see Frenk, David et al. (2011), pp. 43–49.

[21]See Irwin, Scott H./Sanders, Dwight R. (2010), p. 4.

[22]See Schulze, Peter M. (2004), p. 17; Hassler, Uwe (2003), pp. 811–816, p. 813.

[23]See Pagan, A./Schwert, C. (1990), pp. 165–170; Phillips, P./Loretan, M. (1990), p. 45.

[24]See Conrad, Christian A. (2014), pp. 58–64.

[25]See Popper, Karl (1958), pp. 34–9 and Suikkanen, Jussi (2017).

[26]See Mocan, Naci/Tekin, Erdal (2006) and Fedako, Jim (2007).

he later jokingly referred to as a new theory of inflation in 1980, in which he showed the correlation between rainfall in the UK and development of price levels.[27]

The obviously false conclusions of these models are much more dangerous, however. They can originate in a sequence of numbers that lead to false correlations, incorrect model assumptions or unrealistic model constructions, or just forgotten factors of influence. These weaknesses can also have mathematical model constructions. Here is one example from the German economic newspaper Handelsblatt about economic models.[28]

> Economists show with a theoretical model that it can make sense for a company owner to do without strict controls on managers. When a manager is constantly kept under watch his risk of losing his job increases. He must also give up some of his authority. In compensation he demands more money and is tempted to manipulate his information to the supervisory board. [Authors of the model: Benjamin Hermalin (University of California) and Michael Weisbach (University of Illinois)[29]]

Let us discuss the logical content of this model. Too strict of controls (whatever that means) is not possible unless the company owners follow a manager's every move. Controls per se have nothing to do with a manager's risk of losing his position unless the manager is bent on cheating the company. The authors of this model also assume that managers are bad people in principle. Why else would they assume that managers would react to controls by manipulating information? Manipulation of company information in such a case is not created by the controls, it is made more difficult. Why should the "bad" managers demand the maximum salary independent of their authority? It is more likely that managers find it easier to obtain advantages (salary and other benefits) when they are controlled less.

In addition, the results can be influenced not only in the selection of assumptions, but also through the construction of the models, but this is not obvious to non-statisticians, such as journalists.[30] Other researchers have simply miscalculated. Results may be considered scientifically proven for years if other researchers do not decide to follow the calculations in detail, which would otherwise have made the errors known. Harvard professor Martin Feldstein showed in 1974 in the renowned "Journal of Political Economy" that the increases in social benefits in the USA since 1937 had displaced the tendency to save money in private persons. Six years later Dean Leimer and Selig Lesnoy showed that Feldstein had miscalculated.[31] The thesis from Levitt and Donohue from 2001 suffered a

---

[27]See Zorita, E. (2006).

[28]Handelsblatt dated 04/03/06, p. 11, translated into English.

[29]See Hermalin, Benjamin E./Weisbach, Michael p. (2007), pp. 1–26.

[30]Anyone who would like to see an example of this can take a look at the website http://timlambert. org/2003/09/0910/. Here the author of a statistical model proving that broad ownership of guns leads to less crime is accused of manipulation.

[31]"This paper uses an extended life-cycle model to analyse the impact of social security on the individual's simultaneous decision about retirement and saving Economic evidence, using an

similar fate. They had said that the main reason for a drop in criminality rates in USA since the early 1990s was the legalization of abortion in 1973. They maintained that unwanted children are raised in conditions that increase the probability that they will become criminals. Four years after the publication in the renowned Quarterly Journal of Economics, in 2005, two economists of the Federal Reserve Bank of Boston discovered their mistaken calculations.[32]

The worst thing about mathematics is that it almost always provides exact and clear results, thus proof, based on the model assumptions and design. Business science seems to have given in to the same temptation as economic science with the increasing popularity of financial mathematics. Numbers are facts. This is not economic reality however, since people make up the economy. People do not always act rationally; they are in fact often emotional and sometimes wrong. "Figures are facts, but people are not." Economic science cannot be an exact, deterministic natural science, but a social science. Including irrational behavior in model does not change the incalculable nature. There is a good reason why the economists often argue in public over the best method, which encourages some people to participate even if they have no background in economics. The progress made in academics through economic science and progress applicable in practice has been very slight in comparison to the natural sciences. It is very difficult to objectively evaluate the value of research contributions in a social science. Alfred Nobel most likely considered economic science as part of the social sciences, and therefore did not make a separate prize for it. The prize often called the Nobel Prize for Economics, awarded at the same time as the Nobel Prize, is from the Swedish National Bank. The attempt by economics to conduct experiments like those in the natural sciences at great expense have failed through their lack of comparability between situations, and the interchangeability of actors. Let us remember that the innumerable environmental influences that are constantly changing and the incalculable factor of humans only allow the identification of economic development trends. Hayek recognized this, and said that only pattern predictions can be seriously considered.[33] The future us never like the past. National economies and companies are not calculable. In the best case central factors such as money, and conditions such as state and competition can be observed and regulated, but the rest happens of its own accord through the human productive forces. We don't need so many calculations for this, it is sufficient to train and educate the humans so that they can work within the framework (economic order) with the right incentives, and to structure the framework so that the human productive forces can develop for the good of the community.

This book makes clear that incentives for better institutions and morality are a prerequisite for economic efficiency. The economy can only work with people if the person is the

---

estimated time series of "social security wealth," indicates that social security depresses personal savings by 30–50 percent." Feldstein, Martin (1974), p. 90.

[32]"We offer evidence that legalized abortion has contributed significantly to recent crime reductions" Donohue, John J./Levitt, Steven D. (2001), p. 379 see also Handelsblatt dated 04/30/07, p. 9.

[33]See Hayek, Friedrich August von (1974).

center of attention. Economic laws and human characteristics must both be taken into account, with the economy as the sum of man-made, economically relevant institutions and organizations serving the human being. It is only in this way that it can be useful and gives meaning.

Ultimately the goal is to recognize the importance of soft facts, bringing the qualitative factors into a logical connection with other factors to affect higher productivity. Company management and state government must implement morals and ethics, as well as propagate and exemplify values for each individual. Opinion surveys can offer an indication, but no more than that, although they do show where improvement is needed. This should be easier for companies than a national economy. Economics is not an exact science, but we may hope that at least more value will be placed on ethics, morals and norms. This hope may be deceiving, however. Because a quantitative proof was provided it has now been admitted that cultural values have an effect on the economy, but which exact values and how the values coincide will remain unknown based on purely quantitative analysis. With even the most refined quantitative analysis there will always be many influential factors and connections, ethics in particular, that will not be included. Thinking and deriving in contextual forms remains impossible.[34]

Economics has isolated people and reality with its envy of hard sciences. To deny academic disciplines such as law and to discard interdisciplinary cooperation leads to economics becoming less relevant and economists less likely to be heard. The British Queen's accusatory question about the reasons for the failure of economics in the financial crisis has put the company's doubts in a nutshell. If there is no opening up of economics, fewer students and financial contributions must be expected.

The legitimacy of economics through elaborate mathematical or statistical methods is a mistake, as long as it does not lead to more economic insights. Scale must be the economic reality and not the maximum degree of abstraction and formalization as evidence of apparent scientific accuracy. Why should it make sense that theorists make assumptions if the know they are not accurate descriptions of reality?

---

[34]"Business scholars could take a lesson from their colleagues in the discipline of psychology, which was stifling under the scientific model three or four decades ago. Psychological research then was dominated by rigorous, but ultimately unproductive, studies of reaction time. As long as psychology professors labored within a small area, they learned little that was of value to anyone. It was only after they began to apply their imaginations—and rigor—to much boarder problems that psychology began to make enormous strides. Not until respected psychologists dared to ask questions that mattered, whether or not they could be quantified in traditional ways, were groundbreaking studies undertaken, such as the Nobel Prize-winning work of Daniel Kahneman and the late Amos Tversky on how people make financial decisions". Bennis, Warren G./O'Toole, James (2005), p. 4.

2.3   Ethics in Economic Education

A common feature of the financial crises and others was the immoral enrichment of managers at the expense of their companies and the system and thus the society. But the way the world is viewed is also influencing people's behavior. Ideas and attitudes, including moral values, must be demonstrated and educated. The early socialization phase plays an important role in the moral behavior of a person. For example, schooling has had a great influence on the ethical-cognitive development of human beings as has been empirically proven.[35] In this respect, economic academies have a special responsibility.

There are those who blame management training for catastrophes such as Enron, the subprime crisis etc. Thomas Lindsay, once Dean of the University of Dallas, points to studies before Enron that prove managers rarely fail economically or morally because of a lack of professional knowledge. What they are generally missing is what Aristotle calls "wisdom," to be understood as interpersonal capabilities and practical knowledge. In Lindsay's opinion the American education for managers is excessively subject-oriented, and the moral capabilities of the students is almost completely lost through unadulterated profit maximization. Aristotle said that true leadership is based on the ability to recognize and serve the good of the community. To train these abilities one needs much more than a professional education, one needs instruction in history, philosophy, literature, theology and logic.[36]

In this context, international criticism of economic education at universities is increasing. Göbel, for example, argues that it is all too often suggested that "one can put oneself on a purely economic standpoint and hide everything else."[37] At universities, therefore, a rethink is necessary. Ethical considerations must not be excluded from the economic education.

With this background the internationally renowned business schools are in the defensive. Students, companies and the media blame the university for their graduates no longer being able to solve the complex, multidisciplinary problems of today's economy due to the wrong education. The universities fail to equip their students with useful abilities, to prepare them adequately as future managers and give them norms for ethical behavior, they say. Critique comes from within the university staff as well, such as from the Dean of the renowned Kellog School of Management at Northwestern University. Professor Mintzberg from the Canadian McGill University accuses the business schools of lesson plans unconnected to practical needs. According to Warren G. Bennis and James O'Tool from the Marshall School of Business at the University of Southern California, number games and simulations are used more in the universities to give the education a scientific

---

[35] See Lind, Georg (1989), p. 311.

[36] See Bennis, Warren G./O'Toole, James (2005), p. 95.

[37] Göbel, Elisabeth (2010), p. 256.

touch, and simultaneously neglects a broad, practical training.[38] The columnist David Brooks thus complains:

> ...our universities operate too much like a guild system, throwing plenty of people with dissertations at students, not enough with practical knowledge. Why aren´t there more scholars ... who teach students to be generalists, to see the great connections?[39]

As early as 1988, a commission of the American Economic Association for the assessment of the graduate education program feared that the programs would produce "idiot savants" who had no knowledge of the real economic problems.[40]

Behavioral Economics experiments show that economics students are less cooperative from the beginning. In Ultimatum Game, they spend less and accept smaller amounts, so expect less cooperative behavior from the others.[41] As early as 1993, Frank, Gilovich and Regan found out from the economics study they examined that economics lessons in particular, which are based on the economic self-interest model, have cooperation-reducing effects.[42,43]

The economics theory chose homo oeconomicus as a simplified model of thought. The Homo Oeconomicus, like the computer, is like the machine a purely rational being. Starting from a given information level, this creature always decides for the benefit-maximizing action and can thus be mathematically calculated. This gives students the impression that they have to maximize their own benefits, in order to be good, socially desirable. If households maximize their benefits and companies profit, this behavior is at the same time economically efficient and is therefore also a benchmark for economic education. Subcontractors always behave to maximize profits. Anyone who wants to become a successful entrepreneur should behave accordingly. Households make choices that follow benefit maximizing, as microeconomics teaches us. So this is the normal behavior as a private person.

This is the world that conveys economic science to young students in the Western industrialized countries. Many will say the world, and the people, are recklessly benefit maximizing. But what if men are neither good nor bad, and they are told to behave badly? Then the world would be worse than it could be.

---

[38]See Bennis, Warren G./O'Toole, James (2005). See auch Mintzberg, H./Gosling, J. (2004).

[39]Bennis, Warren G./O'Toole, James (2005), p. 5.

[40]See Hodgson, Geoffrey M. (2009), p. 1210.

[41]See Carter, John R.; Irons, Michael (1991), pp. 171–177; Marwell, Gerald; Aimes, Ruth (1981), pp. 306.

[42]See Frank, Robert; Gilovich, Thomas; Regan, Dennis (1993), pp. 159–171. Beck 278.

[43]It was interesting to see that in the ultimatum games students who had the course microeconomic before and therefore knew the experiment for showing not rational behavior gave only one of the ten chewing gums to the second person. Their argument was that they wanted to behave rational and the other person should be grateful to receive anything.

Bad examples also corrode morals as well. It can be dangerous to continue to preach utility maximization with model thinking and to represent this as the only rational behavior. The consequence will be that people orient themselves towards these maxims of action and suppress their positive human qualities, such as compassion, willingness to help, general sacrifice and selflessness. Management education in particular must therefore ask whether it did not create these immoral managers, even indirectly, perhaps not even adversely affecting social development as a whole.

Many organizations are now active in the field of business ethics. For instance the Netzwerk Wirtschaftsethik (Network Economic Ethics) was founded in 1993, in which the churches, as well as representatives of business, politics and science, took part.[44] On the part of the students the demand for business ethics has intensified. This development is due to the immoral developments in the economy, which have been highlighted in the Enron scandal and the financial crisis. The Student Network for Ethics in Economics and Practice was founded by the students. The aim is to promote economic and business ethics in society and science, as well as to promote sustainable economics in theory and practice.[45] "Sneep would like to encourage students, doctoral candidates, apprentices, as well as apprentices of all kinds, to think outside the boundaries of a "classical economy" and thus to show opportunities for business in the 21st century." Sneep called on the rectors of the German business schools to add business ethics as a compulsory lecture in the curriculum. The UN (Global Compact) launched an initiative in 2007 to stimulate research and teaching on business ethics, which has already signed nearly 500 universities around the world, with its Principles for Responsible Management Education (PRME).[46]

Harvard Business School formulates their community values:

At Harvard Business School we believe that leadership and values are inseparable. The teaching of ethics here is explicit, not implicit, and our Community Values of mutual respect, honesty and integrity, and personal accountability support the HBS learning environment and are at the heart of a school-wide aspiration: to make HBS a model of the highest standards essential to responsible leadership in the modern business world. Our values are a set of guiding principles for all that we do wherever we are and with everyone we meet.[47]

Despite all these initiatives, business ethics is still not an integral part of economic science education.

What about management training in companies? Can an ethical behavior be created here? The mediation of ethical knowledge and awareness of the consequences of one's own actions are possible within the framework of seminars. Analytic capacity is not the problem among executives and the majority of employees.[48] It is questionable, however, whether

---

[44]See http://www.dnwe.de/Ueberblick.html (3.05.2013).

[45]http://www.sneep.info/sneep (3.05.2013). (author's translation).

[46]See http://www.unprme.org (5.05.2013).

[47]https://www.hbs.edu/mba/student-life/Pages/community-values.aspx (03/07/2018).

[48]See Göbel, Elisabeth (2010), p. 259.

the ethical motivation can be changed or produced. A problem arises from the market economy. The market only knows the do-it-yourself mentality, i.e. reciprocity and a demand-driven efficiency or market fairness. According to the Kohlberg scheme, this corresponds to the second stage. The market is partly immoral. In the case of external effects, market failures occur, and the effects of economic trade on the welfare of an uninvolved third party. In addition to this, many companies have a strong hierarchy on the basis of orders and obedience, as well as a social appreciation of the company in the hierarchy. Against this background, Oppenrieder considers that it is possible for individuals to become negatively socialized with the entry into professional life and to re-develop in their moral consciousness.[49] A quotation from a board shows the discrepancy between ethical claim and reality:

> But inside the executives are aware of their ethical values, but they are often no longer able to get them out through the appliances. The companies have become appliances. The managers ... are often driven by their system.[50]

This quotation also shows that, from the point of view of leadership, that the economic environment has become more unethical. From this point of view, the current problem of ethics cannot be solved with ethics seminars alone. It requires the use of all ethics tools in the company, an ethically oriented legislation and jurisprudence as well as a critical public. The companies are part of the nation. Politicians, too, must therefore be aware of their ethical social role.

Conclusion

All modern societies have institutions and organizations, giving them order, and instilling discipline in their citizens to behave in the manner socially desired. As we have already shown however, this is not sufficient. For a society to function and for productive forces to develop, the appropriate social capital for the type of system order and economic stage of development must be available. This depends greatly on the attitudes of people required for societal or community cooperation. Norms, values and morality are important here, including attitudes towards the political and economic system. The attitudes of people in a society to the economically relevant activities have been paid as little attention by economic science as the existence of general economic knowledge.

The way the world is viewed also influences people's behavior. Ideas and attitudes, including moral values, must be demonstrated and educated. The early

(continued)

---

[49]See Oppenrieder, Bernd (1986), p. 38 and Göbel, Elisabeth (2010), p. 256.

[50]Statement in the framework of an empirical study on the value propositions of top managers. See Buß, Eugen Buß (2009).

socialization phase plays an important role in the moral behavior of a person. For example, schooling has had a great influence on the ethical-cognitive development of human beings, as has been empirically proven. In this respect, economic academies have a special responsibility.

Comprehension Questions

1. What are the limitations of quantitative economics in describing reality?
2. Why are social aspects often not taken into account by economics?
3. Have moral aspects been sufficiently taken into account in your business education?
4. What would you suggest to foster ethical behaviour of managers?

References

Bennis, W. G., & O'Toole, J. (2005). Was ist die Managementausbildung noch wert? *Harvard Business Manager, 2005*(27), 8–97.

Buß, E. (2009). *Die soziale Kennkarte und Moral der deutschen top-manager. Befunde einer empirischen Erhebung. Vortragsmanuskript, Eugen Gutmann Gesellschaft.* Accessed March 26, 2009, from www.eugen-gutmann-gesellschaft.de/upload/vortrag_buss.pdf

Carter, J. R., & Irons, M. (1991). Are economists different, and if so, why? *Journal of Economic Perspectives, 5*, 171–177.

Conrad, C. A. (2014). Commodity and food speculation, is there a need for regulation? A discussion of the international research. *Applied Economics and Finance, 1*(2), 58–64.

Cowles Foundation for Economic Research at Yale University New Haven Conneticut 1990, p. 45. Accessed April 4, 2014, from http://www.matthias-schlecker.de/kointegrationsanalyse-stationaritaet-und-augmented-dickey-fuller-test.

Donohue, J. J., & Levitt, S. D. (2001). The impact of legalized abortion on crime. *The Quarterly Journal of Economics, CXVI*(2), 379–420.

Fedako, J. (2007). *Correlating nonsense.* Accessed February 18, 2007, from http://antipositivist.blogspot.com

Feldstein, M. (1974). Social security, induced retirement, and aggregate capital accumulation. *The Journal of Political Economy, 82*, 905–926.

Fernández, R., & Fogli, A. (2005). Fertility: The role of culture and family experience. *Journal of the European Economic Association, 4*(2-3), 552–561.

Frank, R., Gilovich, T., & Regan, D. (1993). Does studying economics inhibit cooperation? *Journal of Economic Perspectives, 7*, 159–171.

Frenk, D. et al. (2011). *Review of Irwin and Sanders 2010 OECD Report.* In Institute for Agriculture and Trade Policy (Hrsg.). Excessive Speculation in Agriculture Commodities, Selected writings from 2008-2012, pp. 43–49. Accessed from http://www.iadb.org/intal/intalcdi/PE/2011/08247.pdf

Furobotn, E. G., & Richter, R. (2005). *Institutions & economic theory* (Vol. 2005, 2nd ed., p. 1). Ann Arbor: The University of Michigan Press.

Göbel, E. (2010). *Unternehmensethik.* Stuttgart: UTB.

Guiso, L., Sapienza, P., & Zingales, L. (2006). Does culture affect economic outcomes? *Journal of Economic Perspectives, 20*(2), 23–48.

Hassler, U. (2003). Zeitabhängige Volatilität und instationäre Zeitreihen. *Wirtschaftsdienst, 12,* 811–816.

Henn, M. (2013). *Kommentar zum Literaturüberblick zur Spekulation mit Agrarrohstoffen von Will et al., WEED.* Accessed March 14, 2013, from http://www2.weed-online.org/uploads/kommentar_literaturueberblick_agrarspekulation.pdf

Hermalin, B. E., & Weisbach, M. S. (2007). *Transparency and corporate governance*, pp. 1–26. Accessed from http://ssm.com/abstract=958628

Hodgson, G. M. (2009). The great crash of 2008 and the reform of economics. *Cambridge Journal of Economics, 33,* 1205–1221.

Ichino, A., & Maggi, G. (1999). Work environment and individual background: Explaining regional shirking differentials in a large Italian firm. *Quarterly Journal of Economics, 115,* 1057–1090.

Irwin, S. H., & Sanders, D. R. (2010). *The impact of index and Swap Funds on commodity future markets.* OECD Food, Agriculture and Fisheries Working Papers, No. 27, Paris.

Lind, G. (1989). Moralische Entwicklung in betrieblichen Organisationen. In H. Steinmann & A. Löhr (Eds.), *Unternehmensethik* (pp. 299–314). Stuttgart: Schaeffer Poeschel.

Marwell, G., & Aimes, R. (1981). Economists free ride, does anyone else? *Journal of Public Economics, 1981,* 295–310.

Maurer, A., & Schmid, M. (2010). *Erklärende Soziologie* (1st ed.). Wiesbaden: Springer.

Mintzberg, H., & Gosling, J. (2004). Die fünf Welten eines Managers. *Harvard Business Manager, 2004*(26), 46–59.

Noll, B. (2002). *Wirtschafts- und Unternehmensethik in der Marktwirtschaft.* Stuttgart: Kohlhammer.

Oppenrieder, B. (1986). *Implementationsprobleme einer Unternehmensethik, Diskussionsbeiträge, Heft 34 des Lehrstuhls für allgemeine Betriebswirtschaftslehre und Unternehmensführung der Universität Erlangen-Nürnberg,* Prof. Dr. Horst Steinmann, Nürnberg.

Pagan, A., & Schwert, C. (1990). Testing for covariance stationarity in stock market data. *Economics Letters, 33*(2), 165–170. https://doi.org/10.1016/0165-1765(90)90163-U.

Petersen, V. J., Herlinghaus, A., & Menrad, M. (2012). *Risikomanagement auf globalen Agrarmärkten, Deutscher Raiffeisenverband e.V.,* DZ Bank 2012. Accessed from http://www.raiffeisen.de/wp-content/uploads/downloads/2012/11/DRV-Brosch-Risiko_10_02.pdf

Phillips, P., & Loretan, M. (1990). Testing covariance stationarity under moment condition failure with an application to common stock returns, Discussion Paper No. 947.

Pies, I., Prehn, S., Glauben, T., & Will, M. G. (2013). *Kurzdarstellung Agrarspekulation, Diskussionspapier Nr. 2013-2, des Lehrstuhls für Wirtschaftsethik an der Martin-Luther-Universität Halle-Wittenberg, hrsg.* Halle: von Ingo Pies.

Popper, K. (1958). *The logic of scientific discovery.* New York: Harper Torchbooks.

Schulze, P. M. (2004, August). *Granger-Kausalitätsprüfung – Eine Anwendungsorientierte Darstellung.* Institut für Statistik und Ökonometrie, Johannes Gutenberg-Universität Mainz, Arbeitspapier Nr. 28.

Suikkanen, J. (2017). *Ethics of justification: A defence of contractualism.* Philosophical Studies from the University of Helsinki 17. Accessed from https://helda.helsinki.fi/bitstream/handle/10138/21756/ethicsof.pdf?sequence=2&isAllowed=y

Ulrich, P. (1993). Unternehmerethos. In U. A. Enderle (Ed.), *Lexikon der Wirtschaftsethik* (pp. 1165–1175). Freiburg: Herder.

Weber, M. (1905). *Die protestantische Ethik und der "Geist" des Kapitalismus, Tübingen 1905 (Faksimile-Ausgabe der in Tübingen erschienenen Erstausgabe),* Düsseldorf 1992.

Weber, M. (1968). Der Sinn der "Wertfreiheit" der soziologischen und ökonomischen Wissenschaften. In M. Weber (Ed.), *Gesammelte Aufsätze zur Wissenschaftslehre* (3rd ed., pp. 489–540). Tübingen: J. C. B. Mohr.

Zorita, E. (2006). Interactive comment on "on the verification of climate reconstructions" (G. Bürger, & U. Cubach, Eds.). Accessed from https://www.clim-past-discuss.net/2/S153/2006/cpd-2-S153-2006.pdf

Basics of Political Economy

3

> **What Follows Why?**
> This chapter will give an overview of the basic problems facing the practical
> discipline of political economy and represents the goal of optimum economic
> allocation.

3.1 Why Political Economy?

▶ **Definition** Political economy is the sum of all actions that regulate or control the
economic process.

Political economy also exists as a science. The goal of both is to provide policy
recommendations based on economic theory.

Seen in this way, there is no dispute over methodology, as it was discussed in Germany
in 2009 after the financial crisis, but economic policy always came after the economic
theory as an application-oriented discipline. It is therefore neutral in value and un-biased,
drawing on all theories in the derivation of suitable policy recommendations. These include
the macroeconomics, the miroeconomics and econometrics, but also the
Odnungsökonomik or institutional economics as a qualitative exploration of the economic
order.[1]

---

[1] See Feld, L. P., & Köhler, E. (2011).

Why does the state have to intervene in the economic process or set and optimize a business environment at all? The realization that the market cannot be left to its own devices was the result of trial and error through history. Social problems became apparent in the labor market early on in the Industrial Revolution. The first stock market crashes and economic fluctuations we already happening in the nineteenth century. By the end of the nineteenth century there was already a strong concentration of economic power in trusts (a contractually agreed merger of several companies), which showed the importance of political economy.

The biggest global crisis occurred in the twentieth century, with the Great Depression of 1929, which demonstrated global interdependence and the political effects of economic upheavals. In fact, governments were able to draw on these experiences and the resulting Keynesian theory to prevent an economic collapse like in 1929 during the next global economic crisis in this century, Historical experiences are always an occasion to revise and expand economic theory.

One of the last great realizations of the twentieth century, which still needs to be better understood, was that the economy is having a strong negative impact on the environment. This has caused environmental theory and the resulting political economy to become environmental policy.

While economic theory seeks to disclose cause-and-effect relationships, political economy makes statements about target-means relationships. It has a direct application reference and is therefore the more pragmatic part of the economic disciplines. Here she complements the business administration in the macroeconomic issues and the international and inter-enterprise approach.

▶ **Definition** Economic policy can be subdivided into institutional policy and process policy. Institutional policy includes all state measures to influence economic conditions, in particular the maintenance, adaptation and improvement of the economic order.

Political goals can only be achieved by legal regulations that provide incentives.

▶ **Definition** Process policy is for direct intervention in economic processes to achieve political goals directly.

Social benefits to disabled citizens are an example of process-related measures that correct the market mechanism, since these people are not able to receive market income from the labor market. Process policy is implemented primarily by the government, while institutional policy is implemented by the legislature (see Fig. 3.1).

The state tries to influence the quantitative results of the economic process in the given economic order according to its goals. Governments, authorities, central banks, antitrust authorities, etc. as the main process-policy makers usually operate with a short to medium

Political Economy		
	Institutional Economics	**Process policy**
Objective	shaping the framework of the economy	controlling the economic process by interventions
Goals	qualitative	quantitative
Actor	parliament	government
Instruments	Economic constitution like the monetary order, company laws, social and environmental laws, financial market regulation, trading law such as GATT	budgetary policies like taxes, subsidies, government bonds, social policy, social benefits infrastructure policies like investments, competition policies like maximum prices for monopolies, labor market policies like minimum wages, monetary policies like key interest rate, open market policy

Fig. 3.1 Structure of political economy

time frame. They attempt to exert influence by locking in or varying quantitative measures such as key interest rates, tax and customs duties, subsidy payments, fixed prices or production quotas, which cause changes in individual economic planning.

3.2   Value Judgement Problems and Conflicting Goals

The economy is predominantly determined by people. There are some irrefutable laws such those of mathematical science, but the essential part an economy cannot be predetermined because it is defined by human behavior. This makes economics a social science. An economy is also resistant to mathematical determination because it consists of an infinite number of components that could not be captured in a single model. We derive and formulate many hypotheses in political economy verbally, yet we need clarity and objectivity comparable to mathematics. It is also a challenge for us that, unlike in natural science, economics uses colloquial speech and may potentially involve emotions. For these reasons economics has agreed on some rules for the so-called value judgment problem.

By scientific statements we mean non-trivial statements that are verifiable by everyone in the same way, that is, with the same methods. This means that emotions are not scientific statements because they are subjective and not verifiable by a third person. It is therefore also particularly important to make the way in which the statement is made transparent to others so that they can verify it. Scientific methods on how to arrive at the statements are empirical, as well as statistics and rules of logic. For example, if $A > B$ and $B > C$ then $A > C$.

We also distinguish between deductive and inductive conclusions. If one draws a conclusion from the general to the specific it is called deductive and from the specific to the general inductive. For example, all trees are green in summer. If one concludes from this that a particular tree that one has not seen must also be green, because it is a tree in July, this would be deductive. Induction would be to conclude from a green tree in July, that all other trees are also green. The deductive method is more scientifically accepted because it is more likely that an object will be the same as a group of others than to find a single object so representative that all others will be the same.

According to Karl Popper, who founded the Critical Rationalism school of thought, the universal validity of scientific hypotheses must be refutable, thus falsifiable. For example, the statement that all swans are white is a universalizing sentence. This hypothesis is refuted as soon as black swan is found. Therefore, in principle, hypotheses cannot be verified. It is not possible to check all the swans for color, let alone the unborn. Furthermore, tautologies are not permissable scientific statements. Tautologies are statements that are always true because they include all possibilities. A tautology would be, for example: "When the rooster crows on the dung heap, the weather will either change or stays as it is."

Political economy must define its objectives clearly and concretely (quantifiable), and identify conflicting objectives and their influence on each other so that a net social benefit can be found.[2]

Political economics must define its objectives in such a way that it is possible to test whether or not they have been achieved. Success must be verified to make the costs and benefits of the policy transparent. Politicians who prefer to avoid scrutiny tend not to follow these value judgements, by making statements that are unclear or impractical. The following discussion exercise illustrates this point.

Groupwork: Goals for Modern Democracies

Imagine that a politician promises voters the following: 1. Freedom, 2. Equality, 3. Security, 4. Prosperity and 5. Justice. Would you vote for them? What do you understand each of these goals to mean? How would you define them for yourself?

Results

One way to define the goals would be as follows:

Freedom = self-determination. The freedom of the individual is limited by the rights of others.

Prosperity = material freedom to choose actions

Security = no changes, no risk

Justice = equality? What is justice? As a rule, people always demand justice when they feel worse than others. The reverse is rare.

Conclusion: These ideals make great campaign promises because they are universally desired but are not clearly defined. Everyone has their own understanding of the

---

[2]See Popper, Karl (1958).

terms making them unfeasable. This means a politician can promise these things without having to worry that they must very verify their achievement of the goals.

Conflicting goals

Differing goals will come into conflict with each other whenever the achievement of one goal is possible only at the expense of others. The solution to this conflict is often only possible through economic policy compromises.

Groupwork

Discuss the following conflicting goals:

1. Equality versus justice
2. Security versus wealth
3. Freedom versus security
4. Justice based on merit versus justice based on needs

Solutions:

1. Neither are all people nor their economic outputs the same. Therefore, equal pay would not be fair.
2. Without change and the willingness to take risks there is security, but no growth from technical progress and generally no improvements. If you try new things you run the risk of failure. The entrepreneur who invests in a new product or a new production process runs the risk of losing his capital but also of achieving wealth.
3. Freedom means taking responsibility for oneself, but then you lose the security guarantee of third parties. Think about when you were still living at home with your parents. Did you have security?—Yes. Did you have freedom?—Only very limited, because your parents were only willing to take responsibility for you if they could tell you what you were allowed to do (for example, not to stay out later than 2 am).
4. Should one be paid according to their needs or their performance?

Conclusion: Political economy takes place somewhere between the economic and political spheres.

3.3   Optimum Welfare as a Political Economy Goal

Originally, the economy and ethics were interconnected. According to Aristotle, the purpose of economics as an art of household management was to provide the means to enable a happy life for man. The economics should solve the problem of scarce resources, which means to ensure their efficient use so that the welfare could be maximized, thus enabling a life to unfold human potential. This was the ethical purpose, and thus the goal of economics. Prosperity was not an end in itself.[3] The long-term maximization of profit was the first step towards the development of business economics as a separate discipline. Added to this was the maximization of the shareholder valuation. It was thus left to the remaining national economics (national economy) to ensure that the maximization of profits also leads to a welfare maximization. According to Aristotle the "art of gainfulness" and "the pursuit of maximum wealth" explicitly do not belong to economics.[4] Aristotle does not see the goal of "increasing money to the infinite"[5] as a meaningful, happy, human goal.[6]

What should be the goal of an economic policy? What goals should a state achieve for its citizens? To maximize people's happiness would be the obvious answer, because our happiness is the ultimate goal of our lives. Everybody strives for this all their lives and thus this would also be the maximum goal for a state. This is where modern happiness research comes in. It tries to measure the subjective happiness of people through questioning and medical tests. The problem with this approach, however, is that human happiness is highly volatile and exposed to many influencing factors, of which economics can only affect some.[7]

In general, it is assumed that maximizing gross domestic product, ie growth, will lead to a corresponding increase in income and hence also to a lucky profit. But that does not have to be like the Easterlin paradox. In the last 50 years, real national product has risen in the United States, but population satisfaction has remained constant as American average happiness has remained almost constant. This relationship has been reviewed by other studies. It is undisputed that satisfaction increases with increasing income, but with decreasing intensity.[8] There are many explanations for this result. For example, income distribution may have become more unjust, environmental pollution or job risk may have increased, but also non-economic influences such as lower internal or external security or reduced social contacts could be the root cause. Objectively, people are better off in terms of size of GDP. Or is relative income in relation to fellow citizens more important than the absolute? This is called a status effect. Luttmer showed that finding happiness is most likely when the income of neighbors decreases.[9]

Or are we just not built to be permanently happy? We know that the moment of happiness from the consumption of goods is brief. This seems true for income as well. We feel better and happier in the short term, but we get used to it, so we need even more

---

[3]See Aristoteles (1991a), pp. 22 or 1258a,b, 1059b and Aristoteles (1960), pp. 5 or 1094a,b, 1095a.
[4]See Aristoteles (1991a), p. 27 or 1258b.
[5]See Aristoteles (1991a), p. 26 or 1258b.
[6]See Aristoteles (1991a), pp. 22 or 1257b and 1258b.
[7]See Diener, E. (1984), pp. 542–575.
[8]See Deaton, Angus (2010), pp. 235–263.
[9]See Luttmer, Erzo (2005).

income to maintain the sense of happiness. Studies have shown that lottery winners do not have a permanently higher feeling of happiness compared to non-lottery winners.[10] Clark, Frijters, Shields, found that the increased happiness from an increase of income was just approx. 40% and beyond that just 13% of the feeling of happiness lasted long-term.[11]

The Kingdom of Bhutan has introduced a gross national happiness index with 33 weighted indicators in nine different areas to capture the well-being of its citizens.[12] Bhutan does exaggerate its efforts to make his citizens happy, however. For example, the sale of tobacco and smoking in non-smoking areas is prohibited and punished with up to 3 years in prison.[13] There is thus a risk that a "happyness dictatorship" will occur, in which the lucky researchers and the state will decide what makes the citizens happy.[14]

It should also be remembered that happiness as an exclusive goal for civilization and evolution is not appropriate. In order for us to evolve there must be an urge for change and, therefore, a degree of dissatisfaction. In the short term, happiness as a political goal can even be dangerous if long-term, important unpopular reforms are omitted, and here, as behavioral economics shows, man is naturally inclined not to think about the future, but rather of his short-term happiness. And who doesn't want to look back at their life and things they have done that demanded self sacrifice? The meaning of life is more than happiness. Ultimately, everyone has to find their own happiness over a life span while taking the happiness of others into consideration. A feeling of happiness is subjective. Only usefulness is objectively verifiable, which we will discuss later. Thus happiness remains too diffuse of a measurement for economics.

Consider: What is the fundamental human problem in this world?

Answer: The Earth's resources are limited and we humans have unlimited needs. Even when we are no longer concerned about securing our survival, we will always find new needs. We can often find ourselves trying to decide what we want to have next once the first object of our desire has been obtained. We humans are not programmed to be content. On the up side, we never stop improving our existence by developing our technology and civilization.

▶ **Definition Allocation (Latin: Place)**   Allocation of scarce resources to the various uses in production.

▶ **Definition Distribution**   Distribution of goods directly or indirectly to individuals via incomes.

---

[10]See Brickman, Philip, Dan Coates, and Ronnie Janoff-Bulman (1978).

[11]See Clark, Andrew E., Frijters, Paul, Shields, Michael A. (2007), p. 19.

[12]See Ura, Karma; Alkire, Sabina; Zangmo, Tshoki (2012).

[13]See Wangdi, Kencho (2011).

[14]See Ura, Karma; Alkire, Sabina; Zangmo, Tshoki (2012).

Human economic activity is necessary because we must try to produce as many high-quality goods as possible from the scarce resources available. To maximize welfare we must also create products that maximize the benefits of society. Our goal is allocative efficiency, which we understand as the use of resources in the form that brings the highest benefit to society.

Let us consider the following questions:

1. Which and how many products should be produced for whom? (Allocation and distribution problem)
2. How can we produce as many high quality goods as possible? (Production problem)
3. How do we get maximum benefit for the whole society? (Goals in all economic systems or social systems)

▶ **Definition** The term "economical"refers here to the optimal use of resources. We define economically (efficient):

    (a) achieving a specified goal with minimum effort or
    (b) realizing a maximum goal with a specific level of effort.

We maximize production output using given resources to maximize the benefits for society. This productive efficiency is the goal of human effort regardless of the state form or era.

How Do We Measure Social Benefit?

Our goal must be to increase the benefits for everyone up to the point that they cannot be further increased without impinging on the benefits to others. This is the Pareto efficiency that we are striving for.

▶ **Definition** A situation is pareto-efficient when benefits cannot be increased any further for one person without reducing the benefits to others. This is as far as we go as economists. Increasing the value of some people at the expense of others is a societal decision, not for market economics with its system based on choice.

▶ **Definition** Allocative efficiency is the use of resources in such a way that they provide maximum benefit.

Figures 3.2, 3.3, 3.4, 3.5, 3.6, and 3.7 illustrate allocative economic production.

The convex maximized transformation curve in Fig. 3.2 shows the efficient economics of production. The transformation curve represents the maximum possible production

Fig. 3.2 Efficient production

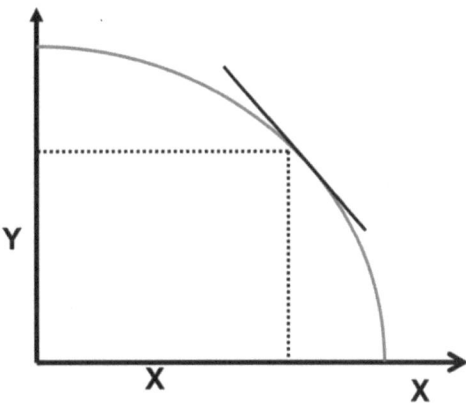

Fig. 3.3 Indifference curve

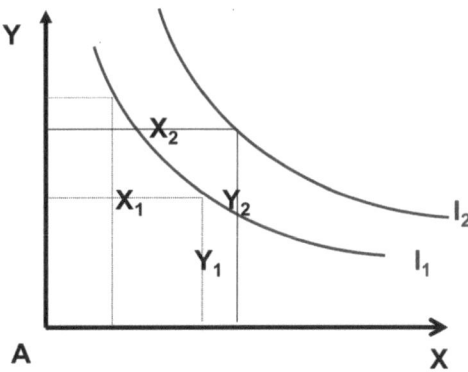

Fig. 3.4 Exchange optimum in
the Edgeworth box

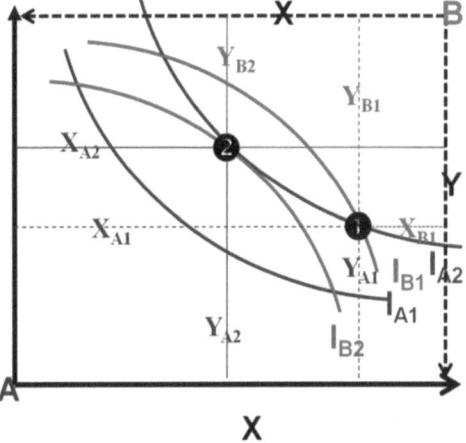

Fig. 3.5 Pareto-efficient optima

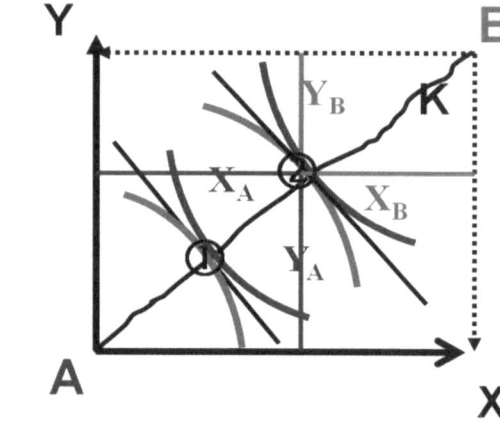

Fig. 3.6 Pareto-efficient exchange points. K = contract curve: all pareto-efficient exchange points

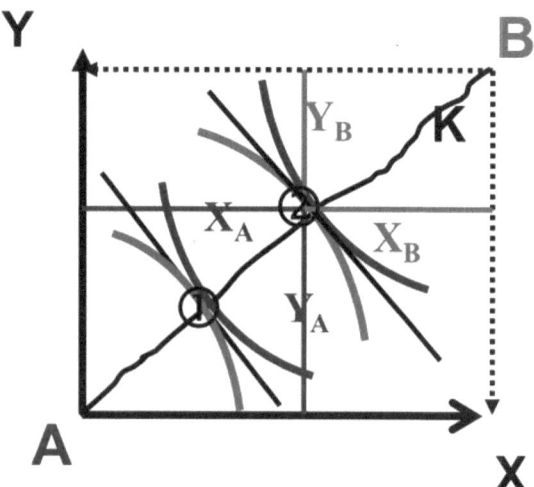

quantity of goods X or Y under optimal, thus efficient, use of the available resources. In such cases resources are optimally distributed to companies and optimally used in production. As an example one could take the products wine for Y and beer for X. Starting from the origin, the green curve represents the maximum possible combination of wine and beer, signaling that it is produced efficiently. In the tangent, the marginal rate of the transformation dY/dX results as a negative slope, indicating how much Y I have to give for an X. The angle of the curve shows that the more you want from one product, the less you will have from the other, meaning the negative marginal rate of transformation increases.

In the next graph (Fig. 3.3) I1 and I2 are indifference or isoquant curves of A.

For A, the question arises: which goods combination provides the highest benefit?

Fig. 3.7 The welfare optimum

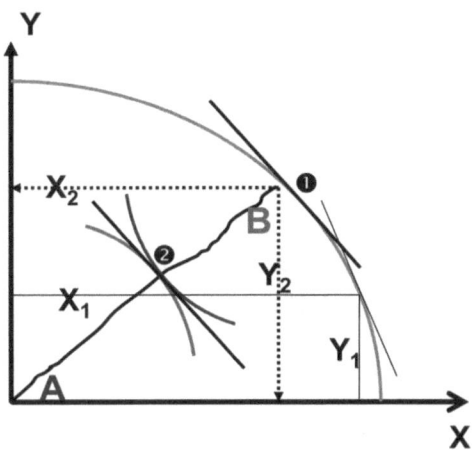

All goods combinations of X (e.g., beer) and Y (e.g., wine) on the indifference curves are equivalent for A, with I2 being more valuable for A because it has more of X and Y at each point.

In the market economy welfare is achieved through voluntary exchange. People exchange their goods or services through markets, until no one can increase their own benefit without reducing the benefit of another. This is how Pareto efficiency is achieved. Exchange continues until the pareto-efficient state has been reached. When it will be reached depends on the initial distribution of income and wealth. The more income or wealth a person has, the more goods they can acquire. If you buy a good for money, the benefit from this good must be higher than the alternative benefit from the consumption of another good (opportunity benefit).

Fraud is reduced by way of the welfare system, because the benefit expected by the exchange partner being deceived is not gained after the exchange, and thus Pareto efficiency is not achieved. Moral behavior, on the other hand, would guarantee Pareto efficiency.

In Fig. 3.4, A and B have different goods combinations so they can be found on indifference or isoquant curves that are different from the original. ❶ The utility of B can be increased with the same benefit to A, if A of good X is B, and B gets more Y. This will lead to an exchange. In ❷ there is a pareto-efficient state, since the utility of A cannot be increased without decreasing that of B and vice versa. This makes for a voluntary exchange: both have benefits (free lunch) until the pareto-efficient state is reached. Here the indifference curves of A and B are affected. The utility of A cannot be increased without the benefit of B being reduced. This corresponds to an efficient exchange: both have exchanged goods for as long as both can no longer gain an advantage through an exchange. The tangent at the point of intersection then has the substitution dY/dX and the slope is the marginal rate of the exchange.

This does not address the distribution of benefits between A and B, however. From Pareto combination 1, B has a relatively higher benefit than for A and 2 is better for A (see Fig. 3.5).

Fraud is deceptive promise of benefit to the other party in a voluntary exchange, which turns out to be non-existent. Thus the pareto-efficient optimum cannot be achieved.

Results from the last graphic: Pareto efficiency indifference curves for A and B are tangents. The benefits of A cannot be increased without reducing the benefits of B. This reflects an efficient exchange: both have exchanged goods until neither can gain an advantage through further exchanges.

The slope of the tangent at the intersection indicates the marginal rate of exchange, the substitution dY/dX, yet this says nothing about the distribution of benefits (distribution) between A and B. Let's take a look at Fig. 3.6. B has a relatively higher benefit than A from Pareto combination ❶ while ❷ is better for A than ❶, and vice versa for B. This is due to the different initial distribution of the goods X and Y. Asset and income distribution varies within our economy as well. For example, A could be a worker in a Russian vodka factory and B the owner of the factory. K is the contract curve with all possible Pareto-efficient exchange points.

In Fig. 3.7, an arbitrary Pareto-efficient state has been created. No further benefit is to be had through exchange. A curve has a different slope at each point. Only if the slope of the tangent of the transformation curve is equal to the slope of the tangent of the indifference curves, will exactly the amount required for X and Y be produced. The societal allocation optimum or welfare optimum (allocative efficiency, overall economic efficiency) is thus present if the limit of the ❶ exchange dY/dX is equal to the marginal rate of the ❷ technical production transformation dY/dX, because then the ratio of X and Y is produced as X2 and Y2 that meets the needs of A and B, making it pareto efficient. The Pareto-optimal amount will be produced. It can neither be better produced nor better exchanged. The benefits of society can no longer be increased. This optimum level of exchange and production is provided by the market, as we will see in the next chapter.

Although the combination of X1 and Y1 may produce efficiently, it is not the amount A and B need to realize their pareto-efficient exchange optimums. In this case, a company would offer a lot on the market that does not meet the needs of Demand A and B and could not sell it. There would be, for example, too much beer and too little wine.

Conclusion
Political Economy tries to implement social goals by using economic theories and taking economic conditions into account. This places it right between business and politics. Happiness is inappropriate as a civilizing and evolutionary goal because only added benefit is objectively verifiable.

Comprehension Questions

1. What is the fundamental human problem in this world?
2. Explain the welfare optimum. What conditions must be fulfilled?
3. What is meant by the Easterlin paradox and the status effect?
4. Why is happiness unsuitable as a civilizing and evolutionary goal?

References

Brickman, P., Coates, D., & Janoff-Bulman, R. (1978). Lottery winners and accident victims: Is happiness relative? *Journal of Personality and Social Psychology, 36*(8), 917–927.

Clark, A. E., Frijters, P., & Shields, M. A. (2007, June). *Relative income, happiness, and utility: An explanation for the Easterlin paradox and other puzzles,* Institute for the Study of Labor (IZA), Discussion Paper No. 2840.

Deaton, A. (2010). Income, aging, health and well-being around the world: Evidence from the Gallup World Poll. In D. A. Wise (Ed.), *Research findings in the economics of aging* (pp. 235–263). Chicago, IL: The University of Chicago Press.

Diener, E. (1984). Subjective well-being. *Psychological Bulletin, 95,* 542–575.

Feld, L. P., & Köhler, E. (2011). Ist die Ordnungsökonomik zukunftsfähig? *Zeitschrift für Wirtschafts- und Unternehmensethik, 12*(2), 173–195. https://nbn-resolving.org/urn:nbn:de:0168-ssoar-349165.

Luttmer, E. (2005). Neighbours as negatives, relative earnings and well-being. *QuarterlyJournal of Economics, 120*(3), 963–1002.

Popper, K. (1958). *The logic of scientific discovery.* New York: Harper Torchbooks.

Ura, K., Alkire, S., & Zangmo, T. (2012). Case study: Bhutan. Gross National Happiness and the GNH Index. In J. Helliwell, R. Layard, & J. Sachs (Eds.), *World happiness report.* Columbia: Columbia University.

Wangdi, K. (2011). Do Bhutan's anti-smoking laws go too far? *Time Magazine.* Accessed May 11, 2019, from http://content.time.com/time/world/article/0,8599,2057774,00.html

Modeling the Image of Man

4

What Follows Why?

This chapter analyzes human behavior in the economy. What motivates people, what goals do they pursue and what makes them happy? We need the insights gained to explain unethical behavior and to move people to ethical behavior.

Here we will examine the image of man in the economic sciences, along with recent interdisciplinary research. First we will analyze the economic science postulation of Homo economicus as a benefit-maximizing selfish individual, and challenge Adam Smith's "Invisible Hand" assumption of selfish utility maximization. Subsequently, recent experimental findings describe humans as social beings and we will then challenge both the economic-scientific behavioral assumption of egoism and benefit maximization. Finally, in conclusion, the results of recent research are contrasted with the behavioral assumptions of economics and summarized into a new idea of man.

Learning Goals

You should be able to describe the fundamentals of human behavior in your own words.

© The Editor(s) (if applicable) and The Author(s), under exclusive license to Springer Fachmedien Wiesbaden GmbH, part of Springer Nature 2020
C. A. Conrad, *Political Economy*,
https://doi.org/10.1007/978-3-658-30884-1_4

4.1   The Classical View of Man: Homo Economicus

Macroeconomics uses a simplified model of humanity to represent economic actors, namely homo economicus, an egoistic creature.[1] According to F. A. Hayek the term homo economicus goes back to John Stuart Mill[2] and Utilitarianism.[3] Homo economicus is like a computer, or a being that only acts rationally (principle of rationality) as a machine would. This ideal actor is attributed preferences, and thus a constant utility function. Such assumptions have the advantage that human behavior would change only if the basic parameters for a decision changed.[4] Assuming a given degree of information, they would always choose the option that maximizes their gain (principle of the individual), making their decisions mathematically predictable.[5] On the other hand, it means that homo economicus not only leaves the benefit to others out of the equation but that he would even commit amoral acts to achieve his goal of maximizing his own advantage, including lying, betraying and other immoral acts.[6]

The theoretical homo economicus is a shallow image. When societal influences are not part of the equation, such an actor is represented as being purely psychological, not sociological. Mill considered people sociological, however.[7] If we take societal mores for human behavior into consideration, the resulting decisions change. These mores are societal norms that dictate to the members of a society how they should act in order to

---

[1] Weber explains the reduction to rational goal-oriented action as simplified behavioral assumptions by giving examples of exceptions to rational behavior, such as stock market panic. See Weber, Max (1922), p. 16.

[2] "It is concerned with him solely as a being who desires to possess wealth, and who is capable of judging of the comparative efficacy of means for obtaining that end. It predicts only such of the phenomena of the social state as take place in consequence of the pursuit of wealth. It makes entire abstraction of every other human passion or motive;" Mill, John Stuart (1844), See p. 38.

[3] See Hayek, F. A. (1971), p. 77.

[4] See Franz, Stephan (2004) and Göbel, Elisabeth (2010), p. 52.

[5] See Erlei, Mathias/Leschke, Martin/Sauerland, Dirk (1999), p. 2. Current economic thinking handles market failure as a human failure only marginally, if it means rejecting the Rationality Theory of homo-oeconomicus. But even then human behavior is deterministic based on the assumptions of how they behave irrationally.

[6] See Milgrom, Roberts (1992).

[7] "The deeply rooted conception which every individual even now has of himself as a social being, tends to make him feel it one of his natural wants that there should be harmony between his feelings and aims and those of his fellow creatures. If differences of opinion and of mental culture make it impossible for him to share many of their actual feelings—perhaps make him denounce and defy those feelings—he still needs to be conscious that his real aim and theirs do not conflict; that he is not opposing himself to what they really wish for, namely their own good, but is, on the contrary, promoting it. This feeling in most individuals is much inferior in strength to their selfish feelings, and is often wanting altogether. But to those who have it, it possesses all the characters of a natural feeling." Mill, John Stuart (1863), p. 267.

benefit the society and not harm it. Societal norms and values can be chosen consciously by the individuals or inculcated socially. Societal sanctions in the case of norm infractions can make certain decision alternatives seem to be more utility maximizing even if they bring fewer individuals more advantage than others.[8] The term gain is to be understood as net individual advantage, in other words profitable gain reduced by losses from social sanctions. On the flip side, sanctions prevent decision alternatives that would maximize the individual's gain at the cost of society. Sociology refers to motive/norm conflicts in this context, because an individual's need conflicts with the norm. Societal norms have rarely been taken into consideration by economic science, if at all.

The same is true for ethical values, although the term "gain" applies even less. The need that many people feel to do good for other people only indirectly provides a gain, by satisfying an existing subjective need. Everything that a person wants and gets could be described as a gain,[9] but additional benefit must also be objectively comprehensible to a third party. The fairy tale "Hans in Luck" by the Grimm Brothers[10] illustrated how a person can feel better subjectively, even though their objective gain has diminished. The term "gain" in this context is really too restrictive, as one can really only speak of fulfilling a need. Economic decision-making theory needs to be expanded to include this concept. To sacrifice something for others may be rare, but it is a very well-known human phenomenon. To sacrifice would then indicate following the dictates of a need to help others, even if it reduces one's own objective advantage. This is exactly what earns our admiration and what many religions, including Christianity, demand of people; "It is better to give than to receive." The moral of the fairy tale is that Hans minimizes his objective gain and maximizes his subjective benefit, or better his happiness. We need to speak more generally of happiness maximization when examining human motivations. The idea that having goods from the economy alone does not bring happiness is clear once goods have been acquired. That happy feeling does not usually last very long, and in the end the goods only fulfill material needs.

The Prospect Theory of Kahnemann and Tversky provides an empirical approach for measuring subjective benefit based on decision-making behavior under uncertainty. The problem, however, is the different risk behavior of humans, which is why no clear reproducible utility function can result. Human behavior is not deterministic.[11]

Jeremy Bentham, James Mill and his son John Stuart Mill, the main founders of Utilitarianism, grew apart over time. Utility maximization is now understood exclusively in relation to material gain. Happiness is closer to Bentham's thinking, as he considered

---

[8]See Föhr, Silvia/Lenz, Hansrudi (1992), p. 153.

[9]See Hausmann, Daniel M./McPherson, Michael (2006), p. 79.

[10]See http://www.authorama.com/grimms-fairy-tales-2.html

[11]See Kahneman, Daniel/Tversky, Amos (1979) and Kahneman, Daniel; Tversky, Amos (1984).

pain and pleasure.[12] For Bentham, happiness could arise from things such as sensory pleasure, a good reputation, wealth, power, or charitableness, but also negatively connoted traits such as malevolence. Pain might result from privation, a bad reputation, enemies, but potentially also from charitableness, piety or malevolence. John Stuart Mill includes not only desire in the pursuit of happiness but also the pursuit of honor, duty, and morality. Whoever rejects Utilitarianism because they reject the pursuit of happiness underestimates humanity. People search for happiness through their desires, but also through dignity.[13] A person's self interest, thus the basis for being happy, can be found in the pleasure derived from understanding and morality. According to Mill, there are moral and immoral pleasures or perceptions of happiness, which is why people must question their interests and adjust their motives to their ethical views.[14] Utility maximization must therefore be understood as pleasure maximization and not solely as the maximization of material gain.

As opposed to the economic theory of homo economicus the information processor, social psychology considers people to be decision-making problem simplifiers. To this end people use patterns, created from their impressions and experiences. Social psychology has used several interesting experiments to show the influence of patterns. Pre-determined thought structures and ways to solve problems (behaviors) help to call up patterns and information quickly. Over-confidence can also be an issue with thinking. It has been shown that people do not have the abilities of a homo economicus.[15] New Behavioral Finance agrees.[16]

The simplified human model of homo economicus is legitimate. Rational, informed and balanced action generally does bring advantages. The assumptions behind homo

---

[12]"Nature has placed mankind under the governance of two sovereign masters, pain and pleasure. It is for them alone to point out what we ought to do, as well as to determine what we shall do. On the one hand the standard of right and wrong, on the other the chain of causes and effects, are fastened to their throne. They govern us in all we do, in all we say, in all we think: every effort we can make to throw off our subjection, will serve but to demonstrate and confirm it. In words a man may pretend to abjure their empire: but in reality he will remain subject to it all the while. The principle of utility recognizes this subjection, and assumes it for the foundation of that system, the object of which is to rear the fabric of felicity by the hands of reason and of law." Bentham, Jeremy (1789), first chapter.

[13]". . . but its most appropriate appellation is a sense of dignity, which all human beings possess in one form or other, and in some, though by no means in exact, proportion to their higher faculties, and which is so essential a part of the happiness of those in whom it is strong. . ." Mill, John Stuart (1863), p. 10. See Mill, John Stuart (1992), p. 86.

[14]See Mill, John Stuart (1992), pp. 86 and 90.

[15]See Jonas K./Stroebe, W./Hewstone M. (2007), p. 374; Fehr, Ernst/Fischbacher, Urs (2003), p. 786 and Fehr, Ernst/Gächter, Simon/Fischbacher, Urs (2001); Frank, Robert H. (2004); Frank, Robert H. (1988) and Gürerk, Özgür/Irlenbusch, Bernd/Rockenbach, Bettina (2006).

[16]See Conrad, Christian A. (2005), p. 391.

economicus become problematic when economic science forgets that they are dealing with a model[17] and treat it as reality.[18]

4.2 Falsely Understood Egoism

Perhaps the lack of ethics and morals of many managers comes from a false understanding of the economic bible "Wealth of Nations," by Adam Smith, or at least a very abbreviated and thus misleading representation of his ideas as presented in economic education. The brilliant idea of Adam Smith was how human self-interest is directed toward the common good through the "invisible hand" of the market. Even bad people thus serve the common good, as Hume commented. The law of the market functions as an ethical guideline thus[19]:

> ...it is not from the benevolence of the butcher, the brewer, or the baker, that we expect our dinner, but from their regard to their own interest.[20]
>
> By pursuing his own interest he frequently promotes that of the society more effectually than when he really intends to promote it.[21]

It almost seems as though many managers take this as a free pass to limitless pursuit of their own interest, as though they understood it as egoism at the cost of others. The second central work of the Scottish moral philosopher Adam Smith, "Theory of Moral Sentiments" is almost never mentioned. Here we find quite different quotes:

> How selfish soever man may be supposed, there are evidently some principles in his nature, which interest him in the fortune of others, and render their happiness necessary to him, though he derives nothing from it except the pleasure of seeing it.[22]

---

[17]"Not that any political economist was ever so absurd as to suppose that mankind are really thus constituted, but because this is the mode in which science must necessarily proceed." Mill, John Stuart (1844), V 38.

[18]An interesting neurological experiment was conducted in 2003 that showed *homo-economicus* to be a fiction, and the press gave its conclusions much attention. The ultimatum game was conducted in the laboratory of Princeton University by Alan Sanfeys. See Sanfey, Alan et al. (2003) and Handelsblatt vom 03/23/06, p. 11.

[19]See Starbatty, Joachim (1999), p. 17.

[20]Smith, Adam (1776), Paragraph I, p. 82. The idea of an invisible hand can be traced back to Mandevilles bee fable. "The worst of all the Multitude Did something for the Common Good." Mandeville, Bernard de (1732) p. 9. Mandeville had already seen the danger than self-interest can pose to society: "So vice is beneficial found, when it's by justice lopt, and bound; Nay the people would be great; as necessary to the state; As hunger is to make them eat; Bare virtue can't make nations live; In Splendor; they, that would revive A Golden Age must be as free For Acorns, as for Honesty." Mandeville, Bernard de (1732) p. 24.

[21]Smith, Adam (1776), Book IV, Chap. II, p. 489.

[22]Smith Adam (1759), Part I, Chap. I.

According to Smith, people have a highly developed conscience that functions as an internal moral judge. Like Schopenhauer and Hume,[23] he accords people the capacity of compassion and sympathy with other people. They can empathize with the interests and needs of their fellow humans, and must therefore weigh them in their conscience against their own self-interest. They are helped in this by an imaginary, objective third-person opinion derived from the question of how an impartial third party would decide. The principle of rational thinking is the basis for weighing the various interests. This capacity of a human conscience is generally credited to God or generally to human rationality. The individual is part of the natural whole and responsible for his or her own decisions. Responsibility and freedom are natural and God-given. Smith believes a truly uninvolved and objective third party's opinion is necessary to determine whether an action is morally and ethically acceptable. This impartial observer takes on the task of social corrective, which is comparable to Immanuel Kant's categorical imperative. Always act in such a way, that the basis for decisions could be the principle behind a general rule, the behavior could always be acted upon by all people and for the good of society.[24]

Empathy has meanwhile been detected as human compassion in the region of the brain called the insula. As a rule, it also leads to altruistic helpfulness.[25]

Adam Smith was aware that the invisible hand is not sufficient to protect the common good from damage done by an individual. He stressed the need for an economic and structural system that included protection for the common good. Enrichment of the individual at the expense of the common good cannot be tolerated by a society for various reasons. Besides the damage sustained by the national economy, such behavior supplants the system. According to Smith, trade can develop via markets to the benefit of all people, thus creating wealth, only when the legal system is functional and there is trust in the supremacy of the state.[26]

4.3   Behavior in Groups

▶ **Definition** Groups arise when several people feel that they belong to each other.

Groups are economically relevant both as companies and as societies of states. Only a common stay such as in a waiting room is not enough. However, if it comes to a delay of an aircraft, but there may be a solidarity effect through the shared delay. Groups have

---

[23]"We are certain, that sympathy is a very powerful principal in human nature." Hume, David (1739), p. 667. See Schopenhauer, Arthur (1840), § 15–18.

[24]See Nass, Elmar (2002), p. 47.

[25]See Singer, T., & Lamm, C. (2009), pp. 81–96.

[26]See Smith, Adam (1776), chap. III, first paragraph.

similar knowledge, describe themselves in a similar way and follow similar rules, norms.[27]

▶ **Definition** Norms are social behavioral guidelines.

For instance: Do not smoke if others are eating. Respect the property of others, etc. The elementary norms are incorporated into the laws of a society. Empirical studies show that apart from the damage caused by an action, the social norms, or the ethical consensus, are decisive for whether a person behaves ethically or unethically.[28]

For sociology, norms are the unwritten rules that make the conflict-free coexistence of many people in a society possible. Unclear or missing norms lead to anomie-producing situations, meaning a lack of social integration. Too much or too restrictive of norms cause special stress situations and contradictory norms create norm conflicts. If a society has many different groups or sub-societies (pluralistic society), it will also have many different and conflicting norms, as each sub-society has its own norms. If a person moves in different sub-groups he must inevitably violate the behavior norms of the sub-groups. This applies not only to immigration but also between generations. A youth must behave according to the rules of his age group in order to be recognized there, but he is also dependent on the acceptance of his parents. And there are other norms of behavior. In contrast to norms, conventions are voluntary agreements between people, for instance the terms for objects in a language, or shaking hands with greetings.

According to Darwin's theory of evolution, the sociobiological concept emphasizes the adaptive value, thus the value-generating value of group formation. In the group, people could hunt better, raise children and support each other in emergencies. The evolutionary advantage favored people who could socialize in groups, and as a stimulus created the need for group affiliation. They survived and reproduced and the group orientation has been passed on. And indeed, group orientation is found in all human cultures, which is an indication of an evolutionary context.[29]

The stronger the identification with a group, the more members conform in their behavior. This is called self-stereotyping. Individuals are at least partially absorbed in the collective by behaving in accordance with the prototypes of the group that demonstrate the group's characteristics, rules, standards, and ideals. Addressing a group membership reinforces this behavior, as demonstrated by psychologists who became more empathic when they were reminded of their professional orientation.[30]

---

[27]See Kessler, Thomas/Fritsche, Immo (2018).

[28]See Singhapakdi, A./Vitell, S. J./Kraft, K. L. (1996); Frey, B. F. (2000) and Butterfield, K. D./ Treviño, L. K./Weaver, G. R. (2000).

[29]See Bowlby, J. (1958); Baumeister, R. F., & Leary, M. R. (1995) and Jonas, Klaus/Stroebe, Wolfgang /Hewstone, Miles (Hrsg.), p. 441.

[30]See Turner, J. C., Oakes, P. J., Haslam, S. A., & McGarty, C. (1994) and Hogg, M. A., & Turner, J. C. (1987) and Kessler, Thomas/Fritsche, Immo (2018), p. 117.

The identification of individuals with the group can be enhanced by initiation rites. Gerard and Mathewson divided four groups. Two were given weak electric shocks and two were given strong shocks. Half of the group was also told that the electric shocks are a condition to be included in a discussion group. It turned out that the subjects who received strong jolts to join the discussion group rated them the most positive and found the other members most attractive.[31] The harder or more expensive admission into the group is, the higher the individual rated the group affiliation. Gangs or religions, therefore, usually have tough induction rituals because they want to achieve strong group cohesion and subordination of the individual to group norms. Rituals, shared prayers and dance also reinforce the sense of community among religions and the coordination of the group. The higher the identification of the individuals with the group, the smoother the coordination of joint actions. Expectations as reliance on the behavior of the other group members are stabilized.[32]

What sanctions can groups use to force an individual to comply with the group norms? They range from the withdrawal of recognition by the group, to mobbing to exclusion. Exclusion is the hardest sanction. During simulated exclusion, reactions in the pain center of the brain have been detected.[33]

People rely on social contact to be happy. Everyone needs social acceptance. According to various studies the presence of other people contributes to a feeling of wellbeing, especially if they are familiar people with whom a social relationship already exists. Everyone needs social belonging. There are several studies showing that positive social relationships even promote good health. Berkman and Syme, for example, used a random sample of the population (nearly 7000 inhabitants of Alameda, California) or people with positive social relationships and found a survival probability two to three times greater (2.3 in men and 2.8 in women) after 9 years.[34] This is currently justified in the literature by an evolutionary advantage. People who could rely on the support of others have survived and have been able to reproduce.[35] Here one differentiates between emotional and instrumental social support.[36]

Schachter simulated group socialization processes by inserting dissenters. Since they did not adapt their opinion to the group, they were first marginalized, no longer talked to and ignored. Finally, they were excluded.[37]

---

[31] See Gerard, H. B., & Mathewson, G. C. (1966).

[32] See Platow, M. J., Foddy, M., Yamagishi, T., Lim, L., & Chow, A. (2012). See Kessler, Thomas/ Fritsche, Immo (2018).

[33] See Richman, L., & Leary, M. R. (2009), pp. 365–383; Eisenberger, N. I., Lieberman, M. D., & Williams, K. D. (2003), pp. 290–292 and Kessler, Thomas/Fritsche, Immo (2018).

[34] See Berkman, L. F., & Syme, S. L. (1979) and Karremans, Johan C./Finkenauer, Catrin (2014).

[35] See Baumeister, R. F., & Leary, M. R. (1995), p. 499.

[36] See Karremans, Johan C./ Finkenauer, Catrin (2014), p. 403.

[37] See Schachter, S. (1951) and Karremans, Johan C./ Finkenauer, Catrin (2014), p. 451.

As early as 1954, Berkowitz showed in an experiment that the enforcement of norms in this case specifically motivates and thus the performance capacity depends positively on the group feeling of belonging, the so-called group cohesion. Four groups were to produce ashtrays with three tasks in a division of labor (cutting, painting and pasting together). He manipulated the group affiliation feeling by suggesting to the groups that the psychological tests had shown that they fit well or not well together and measured the performance after 12 min each. In the next step he faked messages from group members to establish norms. There were standards with high performance standards: "Let's try to set a new record!", "Let's keep up a fast, steady clip!" And weak performance standards: "You are getting way ahead of me relax," "Take it easy, I'm tired!". Both types of norms affected group performance relative to baseline performance, but only if the group was highly cohesive. With low cohesion there was no influence.[38]

What pay best motivates groups? Rosenbaum et al. (1980) showed that competition within small groups can be counterproductive. They had teams of three build towers with building blocks and varied the payoffs from cooperative (everyone gets the same amount) and only the best gets a reward. The amount of blocks built was decisive. With cooperative reward the group members got the same amount and in the case of pure competition the best member was rewarded for all built blocks. An intermediate solution would be, for example, that 50% of the bricks are credited to all and 50% to the best. It showed that as more competition was brought into the group, the result became worse and worse. The group members did not cooperate anymore by taking turns in setting the blocks and got negative attitudes towards the other group members. Finally, the towers collapsed more often as competition increased.[39]

In the case of individually identifiable and non-interdependent tasks, however, a productivity-increasing competition was also identified. The individuals try to outdo each other in group performance (social competition, interpersonal competition).[40] Hüffmeier and Hertel showed this on the basis of the relay swimming. Here, the individual performance is very transparent and their importance increases the later they start in the group. It turns out that thanks to this motivational effort, the group performance is well above the sum of the individual performances.[41] In terms of transparency of performance, there is also the Köhler effect, in which the weaker group members work harder to not be responsible for poor group performance.[42] Finally, there is social compensation where the stronger group members try to compensate for the lower performance of the weaker

---

[38]See Berkowitz, L. (1954).

[39]See Rosenbaum, M. E., Moore, D. L., Cotton, J. L., Cook, M. S., Hieser, R. A., Shovar, M. N., et al. (1980), pp. 626–642.

[40]See Stroebe, W., Diehl, M., & Abakoumkin, G. (1996).

[41]See Hüffmeier, J., & Hertel, G. (2011).

[42]See Köhler, O. (1926), pp. 274–282 and Witte, E. H. (1989).

group members. Social compensation occurs when the group goals are accepted by everyone, as Williams and Karau have shown.[43]

James and Greenberg, however, showed that competition between groups increases performance. They allowed groups of different universities to solve anagram problems, once independently and again by emphasizing direct comparison and group affiliation. The group performance without this emphasis was much lower.[44] This corresponds to the market competition between companies as groups. Businesses can thus increase their productivity by increasing group cohesion and ensuring the acceptance of corporate goals.

The presence of other people can be performance enhancing (so-called social relief) or inhibiting. As studies have shown, this depends on whether there is a valuation expectation, and whether the actor thus feels dependent on the judgment of others. If the work is difficult, observation by others tends to be detrimental to performance but more stimulating in simple activities.[45]

The performance of groups is influenced by coordination and motivation. In addition to the sense of group cohesion (see above), motivation is influenced by the awareness of one's own significance for group performance. Thus, a football team classified clearly lower can win against the favorites, because here the players think that their performance contributions are necessary (free-riding). On the other hand, social loafing is when the group members limit their performance because they can hide in the group. Decisive here is to make the individual's contribution in the group transparent and to sanction free-riding as shown in the public good games (see above). Coordination losses occur when the performance of the individual group members cannot be optimally aggregated, such as in tug of war, if not all use their power simultaneously.

However, the nature of the group performance is also crucial to the optimal organization of the group. There are tasks with a positive interdependence of group performance, because you can only succeed together as a group, such as in a football team (one wins or loses together). This promotes cooperation, whereas being negatively interdependent means the contribution of the individual without the team is what brings success.

For example, in tug-of-war or building a tower of building blocks as discussed above, we have an additive performance, while in team tasks the weakest group member determines group performance (eg mountaineering). Here it is advisable as far as possible not to form a single large group, but several small ones. For example, a group of powerful mountain climbers could push ahead. In disjunctive tasks, the performance of the best group member is the most important, such as for solving math problems.[46]

---

[43]See Williams, K. D., & Karau, S. J. (1991).

[44]See James, K., & Greenberg, J. (1989), pp. 604–616.

[45]See Kessler, Thomas/Fritsche, Immo (2018), pp. 123.

[46]See Kessler, Thomas/Fritsche, Immo (2018), pp. 125 and Karremans, Johan C./Finkenauer, Catrin (2014), p. 474.

It is easy to describe the impact on group performance using the example of brainstorming groups. According to Osgood and others, groups should be able to generate more effective ideas than individuals because they creatively stimulate each other. However, experiments showed that the group members can generate about twice as many ideas individually as in the group. Diel and Stroebe showed that performance reduction is multi-causally conditioned by both motivation and coordination. They found social loafing a group that was to told only the group performance counted and compared those results with a group in which the individual performance was recorded. They also examined the influence of rating anxiety by filming a group in brainstorming and announcing that they would be showing the film to fellow students. The filmed group created far fewer ideas than the unfilmed ones. Diel and Stroebe then studied coordination effects by gradually adjusting the conditions of the individuals (nominal group) to those of the brainstorming group by using microphones. When participants had to wait to contribute their ideas until the others had made their contributions the results were very similar to that of the brainstorming group, which shows that the contributions of the group ultimately interfere with each other and brainstorming should be a phase with individual idea generation before discussing the results in the group. Diel and Stroebe discovered that brainstorming gives the impression of a high level of mutual creative stimulation because the group members themselves in the discussion also take the ideas of others into account.[47]

Moods and emotions are transmitted in groups. Barsade had an actor in a group transmit moods through facial expressions and accents. When communicating positive emotions, the group behaved more cooperatively, and there were fewer conflicts. Sy, Coté, and Saavedra came to the same conclusion, letting a group leader transmit emotions. Here the group performance increases when the group leader exhibits positive emotions.[48]

How does competition affect the relationship between groups? Sherif and Campbell developed the theory of realistic group conflict. This theory is based on maximizing utility and rational behavior in individuals, but more on the specific characteristics of individuals. In order to maximize its utility for public goods, division of labor (emergence), or in conflicts, individuals need groups. The achievement of goals depends on other individuals (interdependence).

There is a positive interdependence when other individuals contribute positively or are necessary to achieving one's goals, and negative when others are against one's goals because they pursue other conflicting goals. Attitudes to the other individuals and groups are developed from these interdependencies. Anyone who can be used to further ones's goal becomes the object of positive feelings, while those who are not helpful are seen negatively.

---

[47]See Osgood, C. E., Suci, G., & Tannenbaum, P. (1957); Diehl, M., & Stroebe, W. (1987); Stroebe, W., & Diehl, M. (1994) and Kessler, Thomas/Fritsche, Immo (2018), p. 127.

[48]See Barsade, S. G. (2002), pp. 644–675; Sy, T., Coté, S., & Saavedra, R. (2005), pp. 295–305.

Sheriff and others tested the theory of realistic group conflict as part of vacation camps for children ages 10–12. They formed groups of children who did not know each other or where influences of origin, personality, or interpersonal attraction would not be factors. Group norms, structures, loyalty, and positive attitudes quickly developed among the group members. In the best-known Robbers Cave study, they engaged the groups in competitive situations with a prize awarded for the best group. Thus, all actions that contributed to the success of one's own group were bad for the success of the other groups. The tensions between the groups became so strong that the groups yelled at each other and threw apples at each other or tore the tents of the other group. Then the game leaders gave the groups tasks that they could only solve together, cooperatively. For example they were to pull out a truck with food that was allegedly stuck in the mud, or repair the pipes for water supply. As a result, the conflicts and negative attitudes between the groups diminished and even friendships between the groups developed.[49] This shows the importance of common economic interests and projects in international understanding. Global trade, and customs and economic unions in particular, can reduce the negative attitudes between national groups. Here it is important that the benefits are shared with the group members as well. European integration would be an example of such an approach to international understanding.

Henri Tajfel et al. studied group relationships without interdependence by arbitrarily forming groups randomly and not providing group members with information about the other group members. There was also no interaction between the group members. The subjects should now distribute money among the trial participants. The subjects preferred the members of their own group. Even the knowledge of belonging to a group leads to behavioral changes, by favoring one's own group members. The subjects were even willing to give up money for their own group, if they could distinguish their group from the other group. Giving rewards to the subjects was not influenced by the profit for all participants, but only based on group success.[50]

Experiments showed that people have a need for self-determination. They want the freedom to take their destiny into their own hands and react to restrictions of this freedom with resistance (so-called reactance).[51]

In 1974 Zanna and Cooper had a group of students voluntarily write an essay against freedom of expression, and forced another group to do so. The assessment of a ban on freedom of expression was much more positive for the voluntary group, thus the resistance (reactance) to write something that was not their own opinion was lower because they were willing to do it. There was cognitive dissonance involved in writing the essay, so

---

[49]See Sherif, M. (1966), p. 71; Sherif, M., Harvey, O. J., White, B. J., Hood, W. R., & Sherif, C. W. (1961).

[50]See Tajfel, H., Billig, M. G., Bundy, R. P., & Flament, C. (1971), pp. 149–178 and Kessler, Thomas/Fritsche, Immo (2018), p. 161.

[51]See Brehm, p. S., & Brehm, J. W. (1981).

participants adapted their attitude to avoid an unpleasant feeling about acting contrary to their own opinion. A group that had been given a placebo tablet that supposedly caused negative emotions did not adjust their attitudes because they attributed the negative sense of cognitive dissonance to the tablet.[52] The state must therefore guarantee the freedom of its citizens. Freedom also becomes an independent value in economic activity.

Comprehension Questions

1. When do people orient their behavior to groups?
2. What remuneration criteria work in and between groups?
3. How to prevent social loafing (free riding) in groups?
4. Why does brainstorming reduce group performance?

4.4   Individualism Versus Collectivism

Rolegame Individualism Versus Collectivism
Each participant gets 7 clothespins. The goal is to attach as many clothespins as possible to the other participants. After 30 s play stops and clothespins are counted. Round 2 follows with the aim of removing as many clothespins as possible from the others. The participants fight for the clothespins. After 30 s again play is stopped and clothespins counted. The game host now asks the participants why they fought against each other. He never said anything about competition. Through cooperation, they would have progressed much further (The game was explained in a talk by Dirk von Vopelius at the IHK in Nuremberg on June 10th 2015).

Social morality, or better ethos, as moral behavior in practice, is a public good in economic terms. The benefits of cooperative, considerate, and polite behavior of a society benefit all who are a part of it. The benefit is arbitrarily divisible, so not rival, and no one can be excluded. This also applies to teamwork. There is a free-rider problem, however. There is an incentive not to participate in the group performance because one cannot be excluded from the group's success.

Rational utility maximization, however, does not necessarily mean harm to third parties. For example, in game theory multi-round games show that decision-makers learn from their decisions and take into account the other's harmful counter-reaction, which is why they no longer maximize their usefulness in the short term. From a game theory point of view, games over several rounds have shown behavior to be profit-maximizing if one behaves first cooperatively and only if the other does not cooperate, to counter this with a likewise uncooperative behavior (trigger or tit-for-tat strategy).

---

[52]See Zanna, M. P., & Cooper, J. (1974), pp. 703–709, pp. 140.

The trigger or tit-for-tat games describe the underlying conflict between individual and collective rationality. In the prisoner's dilemma, maximizing individual utility at the cost of third parties is in direct opposition to collective benefit through social gains, e.g. access to collective goods such as a clean environment. In the 60s, Anatol Rapoport and Albert Chammah used experiments to show that cooperation begins if games such as the prisoner's dilemma are played repeatedly. Based on computer simulations, Robert Axelrod later analyzed the conditions under which cooperation comes into being. In this context the tit-for-tat strategy suggested by Rapoport maximized results. This strategy has its strengths and weaknesses. The strategy says to play fair and never fleece or injure your opponent. Only if your opponent behaves uncooperatively, should you do the same. This strategy maintains the possibility for opponents to gain more only as long as they behave cooperatively, and to gain less if they are uncooperative. The motivation is thus to be cooperative and receive sanctions if you are not. The regulated sanctions would be the norms of the game. Exploitative strategies harm one's self and the other, because the gains from cooperation disappear. In the end, maximizing individual gain at the cost of another party means less net utility. Rapoport calls the principle behind this strategy "in weakness is strength," and recommends it as a leitmotif in his studies on arms races and conflict avoidance.[53] But this is only true for smaller groups. The more players are in the game the less they can see the connection between their (un-) cooperative behaviour and the reaction of the others.

The issue of cooperation benefits from public goods can also be illustrated with a game. A **public goods game** consists of say 5 people who must each pay 10$ into a pot. If everyone pays in, the money in the pot doubles, which is meant to represent the added value of public goods. If not everyone pays in, the public good is not created and the sum is divided by five and paid back out. In the worst case scenario a player could pay in 10$ and get back 2$.

Game 1: Public Goods Game

Play the public goods game with chewing gum.

Give at least three people 2 pieces of chewing gum each. Tell them if they all put the chewing gum in a pot or in a cap below the table then you will give them an additional chewing gum each. If there are not two from each person in the pot all the chewing gum is distributed equally between the players.

The experiment shows that in the case of public goods made available, the initial trust decreases over several rounds of play because of the free-rider issue.[54] The player does not know how the others behave. Best case: he does not pay but he gets 1.3 pieces of chewing gum (3 players) and does not risk anything. Worst case: he gives 2 pieces and all others do not, then he gets 0.30 pieces back.

---

[53] See Rapoport, Anatol /Chammah, Albert M. (1970); Axelrod, Robert (1987) and Schwaninger, Markus (2008).

[54] See Holzmann, Robert (2015), p. 131.

In a public goods game, 40–60% of players are cooperative at the beginning. This behavior decreases when they notice that they are hurting themselves and the cooperative good is not being created. They then play up to ten rounds of anonymous play cooperatively and then become uncooperative.[55] There is always a base group of players who insist on being uncooperative and try to maximize their gain to the detriment of the other players. These free riders make up about one third of players. Altruistic rewards and punishments, which are also at the cost of the participants, can discipline the free riders into more cooperative behavior, which can allow the public good to be created to everyone's benefit.[56]

Fehr, Fischbacher, Gürerk et al. emphasize the role of so-called "strong reciprocators," meaning players that punish uncooperative free riders even though it is to their detriment.[57] Emotions motivate the strong reciprocators to set the norms despite the loss they may suffer. Altruistic sanctioning of uncooperative behavior can be motivated by gratefulness, or a desire for retaliation. Without emotions no one would punish another to their own detriment. Getting upset over uncooperative behavior creates a sense of gratification and thus a net benefit for inflicting the punishment, which makes altruistic punishments possible.[58] Fehr and Fischbacher showed that over 60% of neutral third parties will intervene in the case of game behavior perceived as unfair and uncooperative to impose fairness and cooperation even if it puts them at a disadvantage.[59] We are talking about the sense of justice that makes us human. The sense of justice is why cooperative behavior in a group gets enforced. There are sanctions meted out, even though doing so requires effort and the sense of justice unites the group in its behavior.

The strong reciprocity goes far beyond the reciprocal altruism, because no countervailing countermeasures can be expected in the future, but the individual harms himself for the system. The group interest is placed above the individual interest.

These games also show the importance of societal sanctions (norms) and learning/socialization. The great majority of players enter the game in a spirit of cooperation, but they are willing to change that behavior if the advantages of cooperating turn to disadvantages. Such an experience is also part of the learning process, such as the role that reputation plays. If there is an option to switch to a game where sanctions are possible, it will be taken in order enjoy public goods. With time the players are able to establish

---

[55]See Fehr, Ernst/Fischbacher, Urs (2003), p. 786.

[56]See Fehr, Ernst/Fischbacher, Urs (2003), p. 786 and Fehr, Ernst/Gächter, Simon/Fischbacher, Urs (2001). Fehr, E., & Gächter, p. (2000), pp. 980–994.

[57]"Strong reciprocators bear the cost of rewarding or punishing even if they gain no individual economic benefit whatsoever from their acts." Fehr, Ernst/Fischbacher, Urs (2003), p. 785. See Gürerk, Özgür/Irlenbusch, Bernd/Rockenbach, Bettina (2006). In the games they can pay for the punishment of the freerides.

[58]See Föhr, Silvia/Lenz, Hansrudi (1992), pp. 153 and Frank, Robert H. (1988) and Frank, Robert H. (2004).

[59]See Fehr, Ernst/Fischbacher, Urs (2003).

norms, allowing punishments to diminish greatly.[60] The tit-for-tat strategy was observed during these games as well. Thus most players saw their cooperative contribution increase along with that of the other players.[61]

It maximizes one's advantage to be uncooperative when playing just one round of the game, yet cooperative if playing several rounds. In other words, if the other players can neither defend themselves nor retaliate it is advantageous to fleece one's opponents, behaving unethically to the detriment of others, but not if they are able to defend their interests.

It is therefore not surprising that many ethical misdeeds have taken place within the finance sector within the last few years, since the games are generally played with just one round. No one even knows their business partner on the stock market. The bad subprime credits were mostly sold through the stock markets. If the buyer could have prosecuted the seller, the worthless sales would never have reached such a level because it would not have maximized utility to do so. Anywhere there is a long-term business relationship, or legal damage compensation is easy to obtain, it is not utility maximizing to injure a business partner.

We can observe however, that business is sometimes conducted such that this utility-maximizing strategy is contradicted. There are fields of u-pick flowers, and self-serve newspaper kiosks in the city, where one can cut flowers or take a paper without paying for it. Not paying would be the rational utility maximization strategy, since the "buyer" would not fear any reprisal. These offers exist nonetheless, which means that many people behave ethically and socially, instead of rationally utility-maximizing.

There have been several studies on human behavior using errant pieces of mail. Letters with postage were tossed into a mailbox at a rate of almost 80%. If the letter contained money, still more than 50% were forwarded.[62] In an experiment in which a wallet was placed in the letter, passersby in New York forwarded untouched wallets at a rate of almost 50%.[63] Gneezy's sender-receiver game experiment using students showed[64] that many people tend towards the truth, even if they do worse because of it. Asymmetrical information is thus not always used to one's advantage.

The results of these experiments can be explained by altruism, honesty as a human character trait or by corresponding social norms. That the addressees of the letter were unknown, and thus the finder could not identify with them, speaks for the explanation that moral behavior derives from norms.[65] On the other hand, there are no sanctions in this example that would create the norms, since the behavior was believed to be unobserved.

---

[60] See Fehr, Ernst/Fischbacher, Urs (2003).

[61] See Falk, Armin (2003), p. 147 and Fehr, Ernst/Gächter, Simon/Fischbacher, Urs (2001).

[62] See Lück, Helmut E./Manz, Wolfgang (1973).

[63] See Hornstein, Harvey A./Fisch, Elisha/Holmes, Michael (1968).

[64] See Gneezy, Uri (2005), p. 387.

[65] See Hausmann, Daniel M./McPherson, Michael (2006), p. 86.

The individual becomes part of the collective as soon as he or she assumes a social role. The deindividuation through role assignments and social norms is made clear in the "Stanford Prison Experiment" by Haney, Banks and Zimbardo.[66] Stanford University researchers built a prison in the basement of the Psychological Institute and assigned 24 "normal, average and healthy" students the roles of prison guards and inmates. The experiment took 2 weeks but had to be stopped after 6 days because the guards tortured the prisoners too much.

Guards and prisoners wore different clothes and got so deep into their roles that the sense of individual identity and responsibility got lost (deindividuation). New behavioral norms developed, although there had been no explicit influence from the experimenter. The experiment recalls the treatment of Iraqi prisoners in Abu Ghraib prison in 2003.[67]

In 1955 Solomon E. Asch showed through an experiment in which individuals must say which of three lines is the longest that approx. 37% opted for the wrong group opinion if it was presented sufficiently strongly and dominantly. With the Asch Conformity Experiment, Asch proved that individuals can adapt to wrong group opinions if the group is self-assured.[68]

The larger the group, the stronger its influence on opinion if it represents the majority. Asch later showed that the pressure to conform wears off as soon as the majority opinion is contrasted with a contradictory opinion. Having social support for correct judgment is not the crucial factor, but whether there are other opinions at all. For example, Asch had an assistant give a second false opinion, which led to more subjects being willing to stand up for their correct opinion.[69]

Allen and Levine noted that influencing opinion also depends on the acceptance of opinion leaders in the group (social support), and Bond and Smith (1996) found in a meta-study that collectivist cultures tend to be more opinion-conformant than individualistic cultures.[70]

Three reasons are given to explain the tendency of individuals to adjust their assessment to that of the group opinion. First, only the group can effectively pursue a goal, so the group members must agree in their assessment. Second, due to uncertainty, the individual may question their opinion (informative influence) and correct it, and thirdly adapt to be accepted by group members (normative influence).[71]

All the influences on group decisions that lead to an informative exchange being compromised, so that informational rather than normative decisions will be made, are

---

[66]See Haney, C., Banks, C., & Zimbardo, P. (1973), pp. 69–97; Zimbardo, P. G. (2006), pp. 47–53 and Zimbardo, P. G., Maslach, C., & Haney, C. (2000), pp. 193–237).

[67]See Hewstone, Miles/Martin, Robin (2014), p. 278

[68]See Asch, Solomon E. (1951) and Jonas K./Stroebe, W./Hewstone M. (2007), pp. 9, 379.

[69]See Asch, p. E. (1987), p. 477.

[70]See Allen, V. L., & Levine, J. M. (1971) and Bond, R., & Smith, P. B. (1996).

[71]See Hewstone, Miles/Martin, Robin (2014), p. 283.

called groupthinks. The group members strive for conformity at the expense of a realistic appraisal of alternative courses of action.[72]

Conclusion
Based on the examples, we can see that an individual can be in conflict with the collective, or other people, and yet that individual is dependent on others in the pursuit of their own interests, if those interests must be realized in a group. Dependency on other people does automatically limits one's freedom, however. Group-dependent goals cannot be achieved without considering the interests of other group members, which to a certain extent subordinates the individual to the collective, in order to benefit from the group goods. The desirability of the goods, as well as the necessity of individual adaptation, will tend to increase along with the cultural division of labor (emergence).

Group adaptation behavior can become market-relevant if market participants have social contact and identify themselves as a group. This is possible in financial centers or online chat platforms, where market participants can exchange their opinions and adapt them to each other. Here too, in the sense of groupthink, false dominant market opinions can arise. This is what New Behavioral Finance calls herding behavior.

4.5   Fairness as Motivation

Alan Sanfeys conducted the "ultimatum game" in the laboratory at Princeton University.[73] Two subjects are told to divide $10 amongst themselves. The first (proposer) get the whole amount and can decide how much he gives the other. The second (responder) can then decide whether he accepts or rejects the portion he is offered. If he rejects the offer, neither gets anything.

Game 2: Ultimatum Game
Two students are to split 10 pieces of chewing gum. The first one receives everything and can determine how much he gives to the second. The second can then decide whether to accept or reject the gift. If he does not accept the money, they both get nothing.

The ultimatum game is normally played with 10$ instead of chewing gum. Rational behavior would dictate that the second subject agree to any amount offered. Regardless of how much he is given, he would still be better off than if he were to reject it and both get nothing. People apparently behave quite differently, however. If the offer is seen as too

---

[72]See Hewstone, Miles/Martin, Robin (2014), p. 302.

[73]See Sanfey, Alan G.; Rilling, James K.; Aronson, Jessica A.; Nystrom, Leigh E; Cohen, Jonathan D. (2003).

low, many subjects rejected the offer completely and preferred to have nothing.[74] Brain activity values (MRT) showed that the lower the offer was, the more the prefrontal cortex (PFC), responsible for rational thinking, was overshadowed by the Insula, responsible for emotions. The interpretation of this experiment indicates that the positive decision to gain money was increasingly superimposed by the negative feeling of being treated badly by the other subject.[75]

This interesting neurological experiment from 2003 was lauded by the press for the realization that homo economicus is a fiction, yet the experiment can be interpreted differently if we take into account that humans are social animals, as Aristotle suggested.[76] We can interpret the second subject's rejection of an offer felt to be too low as an expression of the sense of fairness. It seems obvious that $10 should be split evenly among equals with $5 each. If we assume that humans are social animals descended from apes, we can call the behavior of rejecting a low offer irrational, yet goal-oriented and effective. How would such a group experiment play out in real life? By rejecting the offer, the second subject signals that he rejects the social behavior of the first subject as unfair. He is also showing the proposer that his behavior can have negative consequences for him in the group if the other members agree that he has violated a social norm, namely how sustenance is divided within a group. This behavior is programmed into us as humans and could not be denied in another experiment with different parameters. The refusal to accept the amount could alternatively mean that the second subject wishes to signal the first that he is not willing to be disparaged in the group with a lesser share of sustenance, and that the first subject has maneuvered himself into a conflict situation with his offer and the second subject will get him back at the next opportunity regardless of the experiment.[77]

Therefore, the Proposer's knowledge of the distribution is also crucial to the Responder. It has been shown that the responder accepts lower bids if he believes the Proposer unconsciously treats him unfairly.[78] In contrast, the amount of the amounts to be distributed has no influence on the behavior of the subjects since the same experiments in poorer cultures did not lead to substantially different results. Rather, the contributions depended on the civilizational development of the cultures. The more interactive, dependent and the more divided the labor of society was, the more was given.[79]

---

[74]The ultimatum game was adapted and executed under competitive conditions with a proposer and several responders. Only the first responder to accept the proposer's offer received a payout. The responders accepted even very low offers in this situation. See Holzmann, Robert (2015), p. 130 and Roth, A. E./Prasnikar, V./Okuno-Fujiwara, M./Zamir, p. (1991). Such a something or nothing situation is not comparable to the competition based on performance as per the do-ut-des principle of the markets.

[75]See Sanfey, Alan et al. (2003). The ultimatum game has existed since the 1980s. See Güth, W./ Schmittberger R./Schwarze, B. (1982).

[76]See Aristoteles (1944), 1253a.

[77]See Conrad, Christian A. (2010), pp. 125 and Fehr, Ernst/Fischbacher, Urs (2003), pp. 785.

[78]See Kagel, John H, Kim; Moser, Donald (1996), pp. 100–110.

[79]See Henrich, Joseph, et al. (2005) and Beck, H. (2014), p. 279.

Therefore, the Proposer's knowledge of distribution is also crucial for the Responder. It has been shown that the Responder accepts lower bids if he believes the Proposer unconsciously treats him unfairly.[80] In contrast, the amounts to be distributed have no influence on the behavior of the subjects.[81]

A variant of the ultimatum game is the dictator game.

Game 3: Dictator Game

Two students are to split 10 pieces of chewing gum. The first one receives everything and can determine how much he gives to the second. The second has to accept the offer.

In this game the second subject has no influence on the final distribution, rather he must accept what the first subject gives him. Here it would rationally maximize one's utility for the first subject to keep everything. The dictator game is normally played with 10$ instead of chewing gum. The experiment shows however, that on average about 30% is given to the second subject, again showing an altruistic sense of justice.[82]

Research on primates has also concluded that fairness is a central principle for creating cooperation in a group. Frans de Waal and Sarah Brosnan at Emory University in Atlanta conducted experiments with capuchin monkeys, in which different rewards—a grape or a cucumber—were given for the same effort. The monkeys refused the cucumber as a lesser reward for the same effort, leading De Waal and Brosnan to conclude that primates have an innate sense of fairness that has evolved to develop cooperation. Susan Perry from the Max Planck Institute for Evolutionary Anthropology in Leipzig also did experiments with capuchin monkeys and arrived at similar conclusions.[83]

The experiment also shows the influence of group behavior on economic decisions, which has been heretofore neglected in economic science. Fairness as an ethical value has concerned people as long as they have existed. Fairness, or justice, is the objective of the basic normative principle of human co-habitation (principle of social behavior).[84] This is the prerequisite for an individual to participate in the division of labor of a group. The individual will only adapt to group's demands and work cooperatively if his share from the labor distribution is felt to be fair. Without fairness there is no added value from labor distribution for our society and civilization (emergence). That means for a company as the group with which he earns his livings the employee will adapt to supervisors demands and work cooperatively if his share from the labor distribution is felt to be fair. If not he will stop cooperation, which is important information for leadership theory. To be successful

---

[80] See Kagel, John H, Kim; Moser, Donald (1996), pp. 100–110.

[81] See Henrich, Joseph, et al. (2005) and Beck, H. (2014), pp. 279.

[82] See Holzmann, Robert (2015), p. 129 and Kessler, Thomas/Fritsche, Immo (2018), p. 101.

[83] See Brosnan, Sarah F./de Waal, Frans B. M. (2003); Perry, Susan (2003) and Brosnan, Sarah F./de Waal, Frans B. M. (2014).

[84] See Höffe, Otfried (1997), p. 91.

the leader has to explain this distribution share to each individual in order to create motivation to work in a group.

Yaari and Bar-Hillel[85] had young volunteers distribute 12 grapefruits and 12 avocados between Jones and Smith. The only important factor is how many vitamins both can gain from the fruits. Due to their differing nutritional predispositions, the doctors say that Jones can gain 100 mg of vitamins from each grapefruit but none from avocados, but Smith can get 50 mg from each fruit. If you wanted to maximize welfare, Jones would have to get all Grapefruits and Smith all of the avocados (Jones): 1200 mg + Smith 600 mg = 1800 mg of vitamins. Only 2% decided to do so while 82% of the subjects wanted to give the same benefits to both: Jones gets 8 grapefruit (800 mg) and Smith 4 grapefruit and all 12 avocados (800 mg, so together 1600 mg of vitamins).

People do not seem to strive for welfare maximization, but for equal distribution. As a compromise, the primary economic policy objective is to maximize gross domestic product in order to have a greater amount for redistribution via the secondary income distribution.

The desire for justice is so strong in people that they are willing to make sacrifices for it. This is shown by Fehr and Fischbacher's third-party punishment game. A gets a sum and should divide it between herself and B. C also gets a sum and can use it to correct the division by three units downwards if he thinks that A did not split up fairly. He can thus reduce A's self-assigned amount by 3 if he is ready to give up one unit. Roughly 60% of the subjects make use of it in unfair distribution and thus sacrifice for the benefit of others for the sake of justice. However, this sacrifice for B tends to decrease sharply if C is included in A's original distribution. Above all, what counts is what C receives.[86]

There are further developments of the Ultimatum Game and the Dictator Game, which explore the human notions of fair distribution in more detail. Bolton and Ockenfels hereby determine an orientation of the subjects to an average payout, namely that people do not want to be worse off than the average. Fehr and Schmidt as well as Engelmann and Strobel determined that any kind of deviations of the distributions is not accepted.[87] Other studies have shown that the Unltimatum Game depends on the relative proportion of the amount to be distributed. The more the amount approaches half, which is considered fair, the more positive reactions can be detected in the brain (ventral striatum).[88] The Ultimatum Game shows sanctions for unequal distribution and the Dictator Game the willingness to surrender. Everyone preferred equal distribution.[89] These games, however, all refer to arbitrary distributions among objectively equal persons.

---

[85]See Yaari, M. E.; Bar-Hillel, M. (1984).

[86]See Fehr, Ernst/Fischbacher, Urs (2004).

[87]See Bolton, Gary E; Ockenfels, Axel (2000); Fehr, Ernst; Klaus M. Schmidt (1999), p. 275 and Engelmann, Dirk; Strobel, Martin (2000).

[88]See Golnaz, T., Satpute, A.B., and Lieberman, M.D. (2007), pp. 339–347.

[89]See Bolton, Gary E; Ockenfels, Axel (2000), pp. 166–193; Fehr, Ernst; Klaus M. Schmidt (1999), pp. 817–868 and Engelmann, Dirk; Strobel, Martin (2000).

Fershtman, Gneezy and List test the tendency to equal distribution based on the dictator game. The dictator should decide if he gives himself $11 and the second player $2 or if each player gets $8.75% preferred equal distribution, although they waived $3. This could be interpreted as needs-based, since the candidates had to assume the same needs.

Fershtman, Gneezy and List then introduced a performance and competitive component. The subjects had to do a GMAT test or tick off individual letters from a series of letters. If the dictator won the test, he got $11 and the second player only two dollars, if he lost, each player got back the same $8, so he would have equalized without effort. However, the participants struggled to win and get the $11, thus declining an equal distribution without effort.[90] To make sure that the reward incentive and not the fun of competitive play was the motivation, Fershtman, Gneezy and List turned the pay rule into a control group, giving the dictator, like the second player, $8 if the dictator won, but then the participants no longer made an effort. Apparently they refused an equal distribution on the basis of different performance. The idea of performance justice was already shown in 1987 by Yamagishi. Thus, unequal distributions are considered to be acceptable if the payouts for all depend on the total service provided, but not if they are independent of the service.[91]

Fershtman, Gneezy and List explain the behavior as social norms, one for equal distribution and one for performance-based pay. The results in anonymous dictator games would seem to confirm their hypothesis. If the players know that neither the teammates nor the game leaders know how much they are giving away, the sharing rate drops to 10.5% (from 23.3%).[92]

List simulated the behavior in markets conducted as Gift Exchange Game. He first ran the sale of baseball cards in the lab and then on an anonymous market. The sellers were expected to deliver the lowest quality for profit maximization and the buyers were expectected to maximize their gain by paying the lowest price. In the laboratory the participants could be observed, but not in the market. The result was that sellers in the lab offered better quality and customers paid more. In the markets they felt unobserved and sold the customers low quality at high prices.[93] We are generally born with this social behavior preprogrammed, as even small children share more when they feel they are being watched.[94] In spite of everything, equality remains a human need, albeit a minor one. It has been shown that rising inequality leads to less happiness, but more so in Europe than in the US.[95]

---

[90]See Fershtman, Chaim; Gneezy, Uri; List, John A. (2012), pp. 131–144 and Beck, H. (2014), p. 275.

[91]See Yamagishi, T. (1987).

[92]See Smith, Vernon (2002).

[93]See List, John A. (2006).

[94]See Leimgruber, Kristin L.; Shaw, Alex; Santos, Laurie R.; Olson, Kristina R. (2012).

[95]See Alesina, A.; Di Tella, Rafael; MacCulloch, Robert J. (2004) and Beck, H. (2014), pp. 283 and 319.

Whether one had to earn the money is decisive for the willingness to share, apart from the observation by third parties. Cherry, Frykblom and Shogren distributed $10 and $40 at first without work, and then the dictators made them work for it. Then the dictators were again asked if and how much they would give to the second player who had not worked. Only the administrator knew how much they gave, not the players. The dictators that gave nothing rose from 19% (or 15% at $40) to 79% (70% at $40) percent. Now, when not even the person administering the test knew whether the dictator shared, the percentage of dictators sharing nothing rose to 95% at 10€ and 97% at $40.[96]

Levine et al. tested to what extent group affiliation plays a role in helping to emphasize different social identities. Manchester United's football fans wrote one essay on how they like to be fans of Manchester United and another on why they like being football fans. Then they let the fans help injured spectators and found that after the first essay they were more likely to help the spectators with Manchester united jerseys and after the second essay people in all jerseys with club names were helped, including Liverpool fans, whereas spectators with jerseys not bearing a team name were helped less. So social identity is crucial and it can be influenced.[97]

Hein et al. found that willingness to help someone of one's own group correlated with activation in the anterior insula, a brain region activated by empathy, whereas the nucleus accumbens was activated when those outside of the group was not helped. This part of the brain is known to be activated when people enjoy the misfortune of others. Hein et al. also noted that the empathy-based insula was activated (identification) when an outsider was seen positively, making it likely that they would receive help despite belonging to another group.[98]

Singer et al. tested subjects' responses to fair and unfair behavior in connection with punishment. Punishments of fair individuals produced empathy (compassion) in the corresponding brain areas (fronto-insular and anterior cingulate cortices), whereas this pity greatly diminished for the punishment of people being unfair in males and activated brain hemispheres responsible for rewarding revenge feelings. This confirms the empirical studies on altruistic punishers (strong reciprocators). Other studies using fMRI brain scanners also showed neural rewards for punishing unfair behavior.[99]

The greater the identification, the more likely and more strongly one is to adopt group behavior and to favor one's own group members in resource distribution. According to Tajfel, identification with a group is defined as social identity is "that part of an individual's

---

[96]See Cherry, Todd L.; Frykblom, Peter; Shogren, Jason F. (2002) and Beck, H. (2014), p. 277.

[97]See Levine, M., Prosser, A., Evans, D., & Reicher, p. D. (2005), pp. 443–453.

[98]See Hein, G., Silani, G., Preuschoff, K., Batson, C. D., & Singer, T. (2010), pp. 149–160; Singer, T., & Lamm, C. (2009); Singer, T., Seymour, B., O'Doherty, J. P., Stephan, K. E., Dolan, R. J., & Frith, C. D. (2006) and Jonas, Klaus/Stroebe, Wolfgang /Hewstone, Miles (Hrsg.), p. 393.

[99]See DeQuervain, D., et al. (2004) and Singer, T., et al. (2006), pp. 466–469 and Fehr, E., & Camerer, C. F. (2007).

self-concept which derives from his knowledge of his membership of a social group (or groups) together with the emotional significance attached to that membership".[100]

Conversely, an identification increases the willingness to work for the group and to share with the group members. This should be taken into account in taxation and redistribution within national groups. A country where citizens identify strongly with each other can redistribute more because the willingness to share with other group members is greater. Thus it can be assumed that in states such as the USA, which have a relatively heterogeneous society, the willingness to co-finance a social system through taxes will be lower.

Conclusion

Altruism and compassion do exist. A limited amount of redistribution can thus be justified, because it enhances welfare. As the differences between public and non-public behavior show, here too the social norms that can also differ culturally are decisive. If there is no income, people tend to regard equal distribution as fair. However, the willingness to pay something from earned income is much lower and there is a conflict of interest regarding willingness to perform. The willingness to work with equal distribution for income is very low.

Subjectively, fairness is understood as an ethical value. The classical world considered it a fundamental virtue as well as a guiding principle for action, which prevented any overreaching one's fellow humans. Even though there are no sanctioned norms, a righteous person behaves ethically by not taking advantage of others even when he has the opportunity; he in fact gives others their share.

People strive for equal distribution, especially when they identify with other group members. But they reject an equal distribution with different performance of the group members. The performance motivation decreases with equal distribution, which redistributive policy must take into account. It is therefore not advisable to compensate for income differences caused by performance. The purpose of this is to maximize the gross domestic product as a distribution mass. A progressive income tax must not reduce the achievement motivation so much that welfare losses occur. Not only would this not be considered fair, it would also reduce the redistributive mass.

Comprehension Questions

1. What function do fairness and justice have for the cooperation of humans?
2. Which experiments prove altruism and compassion?
3. Which distribution do people consider fair? What influences her attitude? Justify your assessment with the experiments presented above.
4. Why are rules with sanctions important for human co-operative living?
5. What is the function of strong reciprocators?

---

[100]See Tajfel, H. (1978), p. 69.

4.6   The Cultural Impact

▶ **Definition** Culture are all norms, values and attitudes that define the behavior of people as a group.

Culture unites the members of a social system in terms of the meaning and interpretation of what is going on around them, which encourages similar behaviors. Culture thus gives identity to the group members. The concept of culture can be applied to families, teams, organizations and countries. Culture develops society as a group when society tries to respond to external influences using optimal adaptation. Climate, landscape and natural resources all lead to economic activities such as agriculture, hunting and mining. Conflicts with other groups often lead to to military actions. This results in social best practices in family structure, intergroup relationships, gender roles that are conveyed through socialization processes such as parenting, schooling, and occupational socialization, which in turn leave behind psychological footprints such as cognitive styles, values, beliefs, and behaviors as a culture that binds society together.[101]

Empirical studies confirm a familiar basic principle of raising children, or human socialization in general. Social, or more exactly, moral and ethical behavior can be taught and learned.[102] The reverse conclusion is that moral behavior weakens whenever it is no longer taught or demonstrated. For this reason there is a duty to educate children and socialize members of a society in all areas. If this does not take place, or only poorly, the effects will be felt in all areas, in companies and in national economies. The effects are gradual, noticeable only over the longer term, similar to the effects of pollution in the environment. It often pays off for individuals to violate social rules as long as others keep to them. There is also the fact that socialization as a practiced social behavior and moral values can be lost. Like a young cat dependent on the role model of its mother to catch mice despite its hunting instinct, humans need role models, guidelines and education, including punitive measures for moral transgressions. This allows them to become functional members of the human community in a positive sense. If values are not passed on and socialization does not occur, this human capital, the experiences of living together, is lost and cannot be given to the next generation.

Morality and customs of managers are also products of each respective society. Morality of the individual is partially inherent and partially trained through the social and familial socialization process.[103] According to David Hume, Stinchcombe and Friedrich A. von Hayek there is also a cultural development process. Sociology calls this the process of

---

[101] See Smith, P. B., Bond, M. H., & Kağıtçıbaşı, Ç. (2006) and Smith, Peter B. (2014), p. 569.

[102] One study was conducted in Germany with craftsmen and one in the USA with students (lecture "business ethics"). See See Steinmann, H./Löhr, A. (1994), pp. 174, 190 and Noll, Bernd (2002), p. 144.

[103] See Wiswede, Günther (1985), p. 195.

natural selection. The unsuitable behavioral patterns and rules (institutions) die out with the groups that have selected them. Cultural development is a process of trial and error, with uncertain results. Legal constructs (institutional rules) such as private property, money and credit, even the market economy itself, are discoveries that brought benefits to groups that initiated them. Forms of social life and societal organization are tried out and taken on if they provide economic success and social acceptance, and rejected if they do not. If a society does not behave in this manner, it risks going under in the competition with other societies with its poorer organization, which is the explanation for such a developmental process.[104] One could argue, for example, that when the Socialist and Communist systems collapsed, private property had instituted itself. The process of natural selection takes place through a very slow process of selection. The decisive factor is selection through human thought and learning from experience (trial and error). This applies especially for the creation of economic order and in general of social order.

The social evaluation of good and evil is also subjected to this principle of cultural selection. A society defines what is good and bad for itself, just as does every individual. Society develops norms for its protection and welfare. If it develops the wrong norms it can cause its destruction. This awareness is very broad and is not applicable only to moral norms, but to all behavioral guidelines.

People orient themselves by other people. If traditional values are rejected, in youth for example, or by influential social classes, first a trend is created as a new mainstream culture. We may refer to this as the zeitgeist, which represents the temporary nature of this trend. A regeneration is then already almost impossible, if the old values no longer reflect common sense in the society. If the moral values are no longer common sense, or dominant, there are no longer sanctions from the society for moral missteps. At some point the values are forgotten. The respective social culture is then lost forever, it dies out, like so many cultures of the native peoples in earlier colonies during the European socialization. We are not talking about the natural questioning of parental values during one's youth and the process of constant rejuvenation that results for social orientation and values, but of massive cultural ruptures. A rupture of this kind can be brought about by exceptional events, such as a war. Families are torn apart in war, which impedes the natural process of passing on values. Social values are particularly called into question when a war is lost and the dominant social and power structures collapse. Not only is an authority vacuum created, but there seems to be a tendency to take on the social norms and values of the superior, victorious society.

How does culture affect the economic behavior of people?

Henrich, Joseph, et al. noted that the willingness to contribute was culturally different in the public good games and the ultimatum games.[105]

---

[104]See Wiswede, Günther (1985), p. 195, Hayek, Friedrich August von (1976), p. 39, 40 und 59; Hayek, Friedrich August von (1979), pp. 154 and 167 and Noll, Bernd (2002), p. 29.

[105]See Henrich, Joseph, et al. (2005), p. 814.

In the early 1980s, Hofstede described the connection between the general culture of a country and the behavior of the people in the company by interviewing IBM employees in 71 countries with a questionnaire on their behavior for 10 years. He showed that the behavior of managers is strongly influenced by their culture, which is particularly reflected in their leadership and the organization of the company process.[106]

From the answers Hofstede developed four cultural dimensions for describing cultures:

1. an individualistic versus a collectivist culture, in which the American corporate cultures are given an individualistic character and the Japanese a collectivist.
2. a different acceptance of status differences (power-distance)
3. a different risk assessment or uncertainty avoidance (uncertainty avoidance)
4. more male or female dominated cultures (masculinity/femininity)

Schwartz conducted similar transnational studies in 1994 and 2004, which essentially confirmed Hofstede's findings.[107] Bond and Smith (1996) applied Asch's Conformity Experiment to those countries that also examined Hofstede and Schwartz and found higher conformity in collectivist countries.[108]

Many more studies have been done, but they did not give a consistent picture of other properties. It is very difficult to find further significant and stable differences between national cultures.[109] However, further distinctions can be deduced from the difference between cultures oriented towards collectivist or individualist styles.

Earley tested the collectivist and individual orientation of 45 Israelis, 60 mainland Chinese and 60 Americans and then tested their performance individually and within groups, whereby one group would seem homogeneous and similar to the participants (self group) and the other group would be different (foreign group). Then all test subjects were asked to solve tasks on their own, whereby the individual task was to solve a box filled with 20 tasks and the two other groups were said to have a total of 200 tasks to solve. The individualists were predominantly Americans and solved significantly fewer tasks in one of the seemingly collective conditions as opposed to individually. Conversely, the collectivists - mostly Chinese - were much more productive when they thought they were working in an in-house group.[110]

Weber described the economic ascent after the Reformation as a result of a Protestant ethic, which enhanced performance motivation by permanently shaping the attitudes of entrepreneurs and workers. This is a form of one "gets nothing out of this wealth for himself, except the irrational sense of having done his job well".[111]

---

[106]See Hofstede, Geert/Hofstede, Gert Jan/Minkov, Michael (2010).

[107]See Schwartz, S. H. (1994), pp. 85–119 and Schwartz, S. H. (2004).

[108]See Bond, R., & Smith, P. B. (1996).

[109]See Smith, Peter B. (2014), p. 574.

[110]See Earley, P. C. (1993), pp. 319–348 and J Smith, Peter B. (2014), p. 591.

[111]See Weber, M. (1905).

McClelland was inspired by Weber and suggests that Protestant values in education have promoted the achievement motive. Values such as personal responsibility and hard work lead to more entrepreneurial activity and thus to an economic upswing.

McClelland developed a performance index in 1961 by evaluating historical textual sources of various kinds for performance motives (eg fairy tales, poems, speeches or textbook texts) and compared them to the economic development of the respective cultures. For ancient Greece, late medieval Spain, England in the fifteenth to nineteenth centuries, and the United States for the period between 1800 and 1950, he was able to show that periods of economic upturn had been preceded by an increase in the national index of performance indices, whereas an economic decline was preceeded by a decrease. This is a connection but not necessarily proven a causality.[112] In 2009 there was a comparable analysis in relation to two German states, which confirmed the result of McClelland.[113]

Conclusion

Culture is a productive factor as the identity of society. In collectivist cultures, incentives work differently than in individualistic cultures. Max Weber (Protestant Ethics) was correct. Cultural achievement motives (eg fairy tales, poems, speeches or textbook texts) influence economic development.

Economic policy should be geared towards positively assessing performance in society or as a group norm. On the other hand, there are limits to individual freedom and, more generally, to the human rights of the individual to be respected. On the other hand, social recognition and identity, which a society can give as a group, are contrasted with negative group actions in the case of standard infringement.

4.7   Economic Behavior Motivation

What motivates living beings to become economically active and perform well?

Perin and Williams explored this in rats. The longer they were deprived of their food (between 3 and 23 h) and the more often they had to press a lever to get food (incentive) (between 5 and 90 times), the stronger their resistance to giving up (reaction potential) when there was no longer a reward for lever pressing. It was measured how often the lever was pressed until the test animals persisted for at least 5 min without any reaction in the experimental apparatus.[114]

This means that living beings are motivated by deprivation of their basic needs, which would explain that cultures that had suffered very hard deprivations were subsequently

---

[112]See McClelland, D. C. (1961) and Brandstätter, Veronika/ Schüler, Julia/Puca, Rosa Maria/Lozo, Ljubica (2018), p. 35.

[113]See Engeser, S., Rheinberg, F., & Möller, M. (2009).

[114]See Perin, C. I. (1942) and Williams, p. B. (1938).

very economically engaged. Provided they have had the positive experience of economic behavior that they can alleviate their misery.

Based on the experiments of Perin and Williams, Hull found in 1952 that the motivation is also positively dependent on the quality of the reward offered as an incentive. The behavioral theory of Hull determined a behavioral tendency as follows:

Behavioral tendency $=$ habit $\times$ drive $\times$ incentive.[115]

Need-induced instincts generate a pressure to act (push), while situational incentives created by the environment of the individual trigger a certain behavior in order to satisfy the pressure to act and to bring about satisfaction (pull).[116]

The economy can influence incentives. The rules of the game that lead to rewards or sanctions form the institutional framework for behavior.

There are three incentive classes, which can be assigned to three motivational topics and are treated separately in later chapters. These incentive classes are

1. Achievement motive, that is, to master challenges. In behavior that is oriented towards achievement, the actor's goal is to be economically productive. Performance motivation reflects the need for fair performance competition in the market economy.
2. Affiliation motive, ie socializing and maintaining social contacts.[117] The pursuit of interpersonal satisfying relationships was of great importance in evolutionary biology. Bonding with peers and coexistence in groups was central to ensuring the survival of individual.

   This poses a special challenge in the computer age. The workplace of humans should still allow social contacts to meet the needs of the people.
3. Power motivation, so other people influence or impress.

   The power motive is defined as the tendency to draw satisfaction from the physical, mental or emotional influence on others.[118] This plays a role in the motivation of politicians and managers.

In motivational research, it was shown that motives measured indirectly thus unconsious by pictorial stories and recorded openly via the self-report differed from one another, ie did not correlate with each other.[119]

---

[115]See Hull, C. L. (1952), pp. 140.

[116]See Brandstätter, Veronika/ Schüler, Julia/Puca, Rosa Maria/Lozo, Ljubica (2018), pp. 18.

[117]For the affiliation motive see the study of Atkinson et al. See Atkinson, J. W., Heyns, R. W., & Veroff, J. (1954), pp. 405–410.

[118]See Schultheiss, O. C. (2008).

[119]See deCharms, R., Morrison, H. W., Reitman, W., & McClelland, D. C. (1955) and McClelland, D. C., Atkinson, J. W., Clark, R. A., & Lowell, E. L. (1953).

This is because there are conscious (intrinsic) and unconscious motives "self-imposed motives" (explicit motives or self-attributed motives) for human action.[120]

The implicit motives arise from past affective experiences (affect-driven needs) that enter the subconscious mind, whereas the explicit motives consciously question the advantageousness of one's own action, even though they are less spontaneous. Here social structures in the form of social incentives flow into this.

In the power motive, the positive affective experiences are decisive as the feeling of being able to empower others to feel strong. The attachment motivation comes from the feelings of social harmony, if one experiences affection and sympathy from other people. From these experiences, preferences for certain actions form.[121]

In addition, one distinguishes between intrinsic and extrinsic motives. In the case of intrinsic motives, the incentive for action is internal, whereas stimuli such as rewards or sanctions are behavior-inducing for external motivation.[122]

The theory of basic needs explains how intrinsic motivation arises. It distinguishes three basic psychological needs: autonomy, competence and social inclusion. These were universally proven for different types of people (women, men, workers, managers, etc.) and cultures (individualistic Western and collectivist Eastern cultures).

- Autonomy can be characterized as self-determination. It is defined as need. Man wants to experience himself as autonomous in his actions so that he can adapt them to his values and interests. Studies show that extrinsic motivational tools such as control, sanctions, rewards, but also more subtle manipulations such as controlling language ("Thou shalt" rather than "You can") and the generation of guilt, reduce intrinsic motivation.
- Competency experience means the need to experience oneself as competent and effective in the pursuit of goals. This includes the need for clear structures that reveal the effect of one's own actions.
- Social inclusion is the need not only to be socially recognized, but also to be associated and connected with other people or groups (partners, family, friends, work colleagues).

To achieve social inclusion, a warm and inclusive social environment is important. A distant and indifferent environment causes the opposite. Received emotional social support has a positive effect because it stimulates behavior oriented towards reinforcing that support.

---

[120]See McClelland, D. C., Koestner, R., & Weinberger, J. (1989) and Brandstätter, Veronika/ Schüler, Julia/Puca, Rosa Maria/Lozo, Ljubica (2018).

[121]See Schultheiss, O. C. (2008); McClelland, D. C., Koestner, R., & Weinberger, J. (1989) and Brandstätter, Veronika/ Schüler, Julia/Puca, Rosa Maria/Lozo, Ljubica (2018), p. 81.

[122]See Brandstätter, Veronika/Schüler, Julia/Puca, Rosa Maria/Lozo, Ljubica (2018), p. 113 and Deci, E. L., & Ryan, R. M. (2000), p. 233.

Basic needs are basic human needs such as eating and sleeping. When they are met one has intrinsic motivation, well-being and personal development. If they are not satisfied, the result is demotivation and malaise.[123]

Economic goals can be derived from these needs: the state must guarantee the economic freedom of the individual, but must also make social contact possible. In addition, the state structures, in particular those with direct citizen contact must remain small enough to be personal.

Meyer et al. tested the theory of basic needs of professional fashion and photo models with two studies. Their hypothesis was that they would have to be dissatisfied because they have little influence on their success (competence), they are judged (autonomy) on superficial values (of their beauty) and they have relatively few opportunities for deep interpersonal relationships due to work-related travel. The models reported low life satisfaction, low emotional well-being, and low self-esteem.[124]

Conclusion

Living beings are motivated by deprivation of their basic needs, which would explain why cultures that had suffered very hard deprivations were subsequently very economically engaged.

The motives of autonomy and competence show that people actively deal with the challenges of life and want to understand the effects of their actions.

Freedom of design and achievement motivation are central human needs. They are thus overarching goals of the state, which the state must take into account in its organization and institutions. This inevitably leads to the desire for free-market freedom and a decentralized organization of the economy. The goal of the actor to be economically productive reflects the need for fair competition in the market economy.

Need-induced drives generate a push of action, while situational incentives created by the environment of the individual trigger a certain behavior.

The economy can influence the incentives. The rules of the game that lead to rewards or sanctions form the institutional framework for behavior. The state must guarantee the economic freedom of the individual, but must also enable social contact in order to take account of the attachment motivation (motive of social inclusion). In addition, the state structures, especially for the authorities with citizen contact, must be kept accessible and be able to waive regulations and taxation, insofar as they complicate the economic processes for the actor and thus make processes opaque (social inclusion).

The tendency to draw satisfaction from physical, mental or emotional influence on others (power motivation) must be taken into account when assessing the behavior of politicians.

---

[123] See Deci, E. L., & Ryan, R. M. (2000), 227–268 and Brandstätter, Veronika/Schüler, Julia/Puca, Rosa Maria/Lozo, Ljubica (2018), p. 117.

[124] See Meyer, B., Enström, M. K., Harvstveit, M., Bowles, D. P., & Beevers, C. G. (2007), pp. 2–17.

4.8   Emotions

Evolutionary theory assumes that emotions have a function because they have prevailed and been passed on. They have an adaptive function in enabling adaptation to the environment, thus ensuring their survival and reproductive success. Emotions are a genetically rooted position that a being has to its environment. Situations are evaluated and serve the preparation of action and communication. The fear of unknown situations may have helped survival just as much as positive feelings from social confirmation and the pride of coping with a challenge or important task. Emotional evaluations occur unconsciously in the amygdala, situated in the deeper brain regions, whereas the conscious emotional evaluations happen in the cerebrum. The unconscious emotional assessment is faster than the conscious and initiates physiological responses before the assessment becomes conscious and thus controllable.[125] Emotions such as fear or anger usually set in quickly and uncontrollably, allowing a quick reaction to new environmental impressions. Here the most important advantage is speed. Since the emotional center of the brain causes the action, often without allowing a rational check of the action, it can also lead to wrong behavior.

Emotions have a negative connotation for us because they are not rational behaviors, but they can be efficiency-enhancing. Damasio tested people with damage to the prefrontal cortex compared to people without damage in the emotional center. They were asked to draw from four piles of cards, with two stacks holding poor cards that caused a corresponding loss. The emotionally-responsive candidates behaved irrationally, because they had negative emotional reactions from repeatedly pulling from the poor pile. The emotionally injured behaved just the opposite. They had no emotional reactions and continued to move evenly from all four piles, resulting in corresponding losses. The same applies vice versa. It has been observed that in lotteries with a positive expectation the subjects with functional emotion center play too little due to loss aversion and then perform worse.[126] Emotions like fear superimpose thinking in order to escape quickly. This will have proven beneficial in evolution. Seen in this light one can differentiate between short-term and long-term human decisions, according to Kahnemann. Short-term decision-making behavior is about speed. Heuristics and emotions are dominant. Only when we consciously think about problems does rational thinking dominate.[127] Neuroscience speaks of controlled and automatic brain processes.[128]

---

[125]See Schneider, K. (1992), p. 407 and Brandstätter, Veronika/ Schüler, Julia/Puca, Rosa Maria/ Lozo, Ljubica (2018), p. 169.

[126]See Shiv Baba, Loewenstein George, Bechara Antoine (2005) and Damasio, Antonio (2006), p. 212.

[127]See Kahneman, Daniel (2011) and Beck, H. (2014), p. 13.

[128]See Camerer, Colin; Loewenstein, George; Prelec, Drazen (2005).

McClure et al. determined that different areas of the brain were activated depending on the time horizon and complexity of the decision. For short-term simple decisions and rewards, the beta region (ventral striatum, medial orbifrontal cortex, medial prefrontal cortex) and, in the case of difficult decisions, the delta region (prefrontal and parietal cortex, lateral prefrontal cortex and posterior parietal cortex) were used.[129]

For short-term decision-making behavior, one can also count the so-called good feeling (somatic marker hypothesis). The somatic marker is an emotion that unconsciously gives us the green light in our decisions or warns us of negative consequences.[130] Emotions strongly influence our decisions, but they are difficult to measure and explain because people react differently in the same situations and everyone reacts differently.

4.9   Human Intelligence

What abilities are decisive in life? What makes it possible for people to cope with the challenges from their environment? What makes people successful? These are questions about human intelligence. Today intelligence is mainly defined as the correctness and speed with which unknown tasks are solved.[131] There used to be three forms of intelligence identified. The ones necessary here are the mathematical, spatial and linguistic intelligence, whereby the mathematical is the most well-known. Mathematics is understood here to be the pure form of abstract and logical thought. People gifted with this intelligence are able to use chains of proof and rules that can be recorded with figures. Mathematics is considered nature's blueprint because many laws of nature can be represented mathematically. The most famous of those with this feature of intelligence was Albert Einstein, the founder of the Theory of Relativity. The second, spatial intelligence, allows three-dimensional comprehension and processing of the environment as forms, spaces or objects. The embodiment of this form of intelligence is considered to be Michelangelo Buonarotti with his statue of David and the images in the Sistine Chapel with perfect perspective. The third traditional form of intelligence is a gift with languages. This allows hearing through words, written and verbal expression and independent reflection through writing. An example here would be Johann Wolfgang von Goethe with a vocabulary of around 90,000 words. The average person has between 2000 and 5000 words. These three traditional forms of intelligence have determined the way human capabilities are perceived and perhaps their valuation for decades. The explanatory power of these gifs for success in solving tasks in life is quite limited, however. According to the Harvard Professor for Psychology Howard Gardner, in the best case these three traditional forms of intelligence could only predict scholastic success to a certain extent. According to Gardner there are some careers whose demands are concentrated in these forms of intelligence, such as lawyers through

---

[129]See McClure, Samuel; Laibson, David I.; Loewenstein, George; Cohen, Jonathan (2004).

[130]See Damasio, Antonio (2006) and Pham, Michel T. (2007) and Beck, H. (2014), p. 292.

[131]See http://wirtschaftneudenken.blogspot.de/2010/09/abschied-vom-iq.html

formulations and verbal arguments, physicists who work with mathematical formulas or pilots who must think spatially. For most other careers however, such as managers, politicians, musicians etc., these criteria are not suited to determining potential. This fact caused the Gardner to investigate other forms of intelligence. In the 1980s he developed his radical concept of multiple types of intelligence, in which he included four additional gifts. In the meanwhile research has identified a total of ten forms of intelligence.

First there are the special forms of intelligence, such as the naturalist, musical and kinesthetic intelligence. Naturalist intelligence refers to a particular comprehension of nature and its products. Foresters, biologists, veterinarians and top chefs would be careers for this group. Alexander von Humboldt, who discovered and explained many interconnections with his field research would a prime example of naturalist intelligence. The first example to come to mind for musical intelligence is the genius Wolfgang Amadeus Mozart. Kinesthetic intelligence is relatively unknown. Science considers it to be the ability to use one's body to complete tasks. A famous kinesthetic genius would be the silent film actor Charlie Chaplin.

The four most important forms of intelligence to have been recently identified are the existential, interpersonal, intrapersonal and emotional intelligence. Relationships between people, social competence or soft-facts had been completely neglected by the traditional forms of intelligence. Interpersonal intelligence allows one to recognize and understand the motives and desires of other people. In particular teachers, politicians and sales people need this kind of empathic ability. Only someone who can put him or herself in the shoes of others can motivate and recognize both strengths and weaknesses to then best apply, encourage and demand them, developing them optimally, as an ideal manager does. Another example is politicians who must recognize the desires of their voters in order to be successful.

The transitions between the abilities are fluid however, and there are many overlaps depending on the type of demands made. Thus rhetorical abilities belong to linguistic abilities as well as to interpersonal intelligence, since a good speaker must gauge what the listeners are receiving and react rhetorically to their reactions. Overlaps are particularly numerous for interpersonal relationships. This is how the American Daniel Goleman developed the concept of emotional intelligence in the mid-90s. He considers this to be not only recognizing and dealing with the feelings of others, but applies this to one's own feelings as well. Emotional intelligence is thus located between the interpersonal and intrapersonal intelligence as the capacity to deal with human emotions. Mahatma Gandhi represents an excellent example of emotional intelligence. He was able to judge the feeling of his compatriots, influence them and channel them into passive resistance as well as to control his own feelings in an exemplary manner, making him an excellent leader. He was a model for his compatriots in suffering. The nickname Gandhi translates as "large spirit." The intrapersonal capacity to understand one's self makes it possible to differentiate between realistic goals and personal dreams, an ability not to underestimated, as it is then possible to achieve an inner balance at live with inner harmony. In 1896 Sigmund Freud described scientifically for the first time how self-knowledge is the basis for human existence on earth, and inner peace. Internal balance and finding the right relationship between reality and a person's capacities and desires is the basis for internal force and perseverance, and thus for a person's long-term success.

The last three forms of intelligence for social competence are not only determining factors for managers, but also for the successful integration in a team. Only he who knows himself and understands others can offer his strengths and weaknesses to the team in a way that increases the team's ability to perform. The last of the new forms of intelligence is the existential intelligence. It is attributed mostly to philosophers, priests and authors, because they are capable of addressing the fundamental questions about the world and humanity. Immanuel Kant is our example here, who significantly contributed to modern thinking with his work "Critique of pure reason" (1781) and his categorical imperative,[132] as well as his thoughts on enlightenment. This intelligence can generally be characterized as the capacity to get to the source the past and future of things, or to put social or environmental observations into a larger perspective. This form of intelligence is therefore important when addressing that big picture of human structures. This also applies for economic science as the science of people in economic interconnections.[133]

For the question of the extent to which man behaves ethically, compassion, that is, sympathy with other people, plays an outstanding role. This is an emotion. In principle, it is therefore necessary to distinguish between a rational impact assessment and emotion-driven compassion. This also occurs in two separate brain areas, as the case of the railway worker Phineas Gage showed. In an accident, an iron rod, 1 m long and 3 cm wide, had been shot through his head. He survived this and, surprisingly, the basic cognitive basic functions were unaffected as perception (except for the loss of an eye), intelligence, memory and speech. Only his social intelligence seemed to be impaired. Before, he was a popular, prudent and successful personality, after the accident he had problems, long-term decisions and social contacts. It turned out in a later investigation that especially brain regions had been damaged, which are added to the processing of emotions.[134] As in experiments where the brain activity was measured by means of functional magnetic resonance tomographs (fMRI), emotional inhibitions occurred in subjects especially when: (1) a personal responsibility (ME) was (2) for direct physical damage (HURT) (3) A physically present or alive person (YOU) was present (MeHurtYou).[135]

Haidt et al. succeeded in demonstrating the influence of emotions caused by norms, in particular, on moral decisions by placing people before decision—making alternatives which did not result in objective harm but were morally problematic, such as the eating

---

[132]People need to select maxims to guide their actions, which can simultaneously function as general laws.

[133]See Gardner, Howard (1983); Gardner, Howard/Kornhaber, Mindy L. (1996); Gardner, Howard (1999) and Schlesinger, Christian (2006).

[134]See Holzmann, Robert (2015), p. 117.

[135]See Greene, Joshua D./Nystrom, Leigh E./Engell, Andrew D./Darley, John M. (2004).

of the deceased dog before the Background that dog meat should taste good or use a bust American flag to wipe the toilet.[136]

Where do we place the character of morality with the background described above? Morality, like all characteristics, is partially inherent and can be helpful in solving unknown tasks in life, just like the forms of intelligence. It belongs to the social abilities, or more exactly to interpersonal intelligence. As we have already shown, morality is the basis for trust and thus also for productive human social existence. Repeated moral behavior inspires others to do the same, to compromise in transactions, to invest for example, and to trust in the later reciprocal action of a business partner, which leads moral people to experience more interpersonal success than immoral people. There is a negative form of interpersonal intelligence, which we call cleverness. We understand cleverness to be the ability to enrich one's self immorally at the cost of others, to gain advantages, without being discovered. This ability is unfortunately often a key to success in life. From the perspective of the society, this success should be prevented because it damages individuals and the system as a whole.

Pure altruism can be associated with empathy (empathy-altruism hypothesis). Batsons u.a. experimented with pity in 1981 using an electric shock experiment. They tested the extent to which the subjects were willing to accept the electric shocks as substitutes for a subject Elaine, if this signaled extreme suffering. The subjects were divided into four groups, for one group a similarity to Elaine was established and then it was open as to wheter the subject could leave after two rounds of watching the electric shock or if they had to watch even longer. The possibility of leaving was only entertained by subjects who did not identify with Elaine. If the test subjects were very similar to Elaine they stayed and were in large part ready to receive the electric shocks on her behalf.[137]

It seems that people can empathize with the suffering of other people (empathic emotion) when they take on the perspective of a suffering person or they perceive themselves as similar to the other person. Then they want to improve the other's situation. This behavior shows man as a social being. Since this behavior has asserted itself through evolution, it must not only have produced benefits in the group, but also favored the individual in reproduction at the very least.[138]

Studies showed that altruistic behavior is associated with specific intrinsic rewards, as various studies have shown that charitable donations are activate areas of the brain that exhibit a high degree of overlap with areas (eg, strata) that are activated when people receive positive social or financial rewards.[139]

---

[136]See Haidt, J./Koller, S./Dias, M. (1993).

[137]See Batson, C. D., Duncan, B. D., Ackerman, P., Buckley, T., & Birch, K. (1981) and Batson, C. D., & Shaw, L. L. (1991), pp. 107–122.

[138]See Campbell, D. T. (1965) and Brewer, M. B., & Caporael, L. R. (2006), pp. 143–161) and Kessler, Thomas/Fritsche, Immo (2018), pp. 99.

[139]See Moll, J., et al. (2006); Harbaugh, W.T., Mayr, U., and Burghart, D.R. (2007); Fehr, E., & Camerer, C. F. (2007), pp. 419–427 and Levine, Mark und Manning, Rachel (2014), p. 392.

The conclusions on can draw from these new findings are quite reassuring. When someone has not scored well in the traditional three forms of intelligence, it neither means that they will be unsuccessful, nor that they are dumb. Intelligence as the capacity to be successful in life is as complex and diverse as the challenges of life itself. Analysis and problem simplification can be trained with a study in an orchestra score. In order to be successful in a group, one needs both interpersonal and emotional intelligence. There are many overlapping abilities, so that it seems almost impossible to definitively classify a person's intelligence or to evaluate someone in relation to their chances in life. Everyone has strengths and weaknesses that are often balanced, even at extremes. All too often we find engineers who cannot use their ingenious inventions because they lack the ability to sell it. Intelligence can also be learned to a certain degree. The fundamental abilities are inherited, but they can be increased by around 15% through training.

From the various forms of intelligence one can conclude that people are able to understand the effect of their behavior on the welfare of third parties and to feel compassion. Furthermore, they show that human nature goes far beyond the homo oeconomicus.

On the whole, it may be doubted that all the intelligentsia worked out by Gardner can be proved empirically. Up to now, social intelligence has been isolated and empirical proof has been given of a connection with the success of personal influence on people. In addition, links between the academic degree as well as age and social intelligence were identified.[140]

Comprehension Questions

1. How can one explain altruism and compassion? What are the requirements for this?
2. What are the central motivations for human behavior?
3. What functions have emotions? How can this be economical relevant?
4. How could be explained why cultures that had suffered very hard deprivations were subsequently very economically engaged.
5. Which forms of intelligence are important for moral thinking and decision making?
6. Which forms of intelligence are important for a successful life?

4.10   Further Deviations from Rational Behavior

Heuristics are simplified rules of behavior that people use to respond quickly and easily. They are mainly based on experience. One could speak of prejudice, for example. People are more likely to recognize events when they can remember or see things more often, which is called availability heuristics. Also, the effort to get to the information affects the assessment. For example, Schwartz and Vaughn a.o. found that respondents rated

---

[140]See Eshghi, Parto/Arofzad, Shahram /Hosaini, Taghi Agha (2013) and Diskussion See Gardner, Howard /Moran, Seana (2006).

themselves as less assertive when they had to write down 12 situations in which they succeeded instead of just 6. They then felt the situations they were able to remember were too few.[141] In response to this observation, the concept of bounded rationality was developed, implying limited information processing capacities as opposed to complete rationality. A decision is then rationally limited if, taking account of information access and processing effort, the decision that maximizes utility is chosen.[142] From this, the so-called Nugdes were derived.

▶ **Definition** Nugdes are an instrument for influencing decision-makers behavior by directing them towards higher benefit using simplified access.

For example, healthy food is placed at eye and grasp level and unhealthy food is to be located on the bottom of the shelf in supermarkets.[143]

The Prospect Theory of Kahnemann and Tversky not only provides an empirical approach on how to measure subjective benefit, but also incorporates irrational behaviors. After using heuristics, various irrational behaviors are included that have been empirically determined. Probabilities and payouts are not valued linearly. Thus, the valuation of profits and losses is distorted by previous gains and losses as reference points. The perceived gain or loss decreases with its amount, which means decreasing marginal utility or damage.

In 1992, Kahnemann and Tversky determined loss aversion. Losses are thus rated more heavily than comparable profits. They also found a non-linear probability estimation. Small probabilities are rated higher than large ones. Kahnemann and Tversky also found, in addition to the loss average and the reference points, that the presentation and formulation of questions affects the decision of subjects.

▶ **Definition** Influencing decisions through representation of the problem of decision-making has since been called framing.[144]

The best way to explain framing is the Asian disease problem of Kahnemann and Tversky. There is an epidemic and 600 vulnerable people. Subjects should choose between two alternative therapies that are presented in different ways:

---

[141]See Schwarz, Norbert; Vaughn, Leigh Ann (2002) and Schwarz, Norbert/Bless, Herbert/Starck, Fritz/Klumpp, Gisela/ Rittenauer-Schatka, Helga/Simons, Annette (1991).

[142]See Simon, Herbert A. (1959), p. 262 f.

[143]See Thaler, Richard H., Sunstein, Cass R. (April 8, 2008); Thaler, Richard H., Sunstein, Cass R. and Balz, John P. (2010); Sunstein, Cass (2009); Wright, Joshua; Ginsberg, Douglas (2012).

[144]See Kahneman, Daniel; Tversky, Amos (1981); Kahneman, Daniel; Tversky, Amos (1982); Kahneman, Daniel; Tversky, Amos (1984). Kahneman, Daniel; Tversky, Amos (1986). Kahneman, Daniel; Knetsch, Jack; Thaler, Richard (1991), pp. 193–206.

1. Presentation

   In therapy A, 200 people die. In therapy B, 600 people are treated with a 1/3 chance of survival. There is a 2/3 chance that no one will be saved.

2. Presentation

   In therapy A, 400 people are saved. In therapy B, there is a probability of 33% that nobody will die. There is a 66% chance that 600 people will die. Although both representations are equivalent in their result. In presentation 1 the majority (72%) chose A and in the second presentation a majority (78%) opted for B.

Kahnemann and Tversky explain this with a positive reference point in the first presentation, because it puts in the foreground that people are saved. In the positive area people are risk-averse. They do not want to endanger the rescued people and opt for safe rescue. In the second presentation, both times the loss is emphasized. Here people want to minimize the loss (loss aversion), avoid alternative A as a worst case reference point and are prepared for higher risks.

Framing can be used to manipulate decisions to the benefit or disadvantage of the decider. For example, you may be more likely to encourage people to take a health check-up by telling them the risks of illness if they fail to get a check-up than by emphasizing the opportunities for early discovery and recovery.[145]

The Prospect theory has since been relativized. Thus, the decision of the subjects in the Asian Disease Problem is also due to incomplete information. Kühberger showed that the decisions are balanced, so the framing effect disappears, if you supplement the missing information in alternative A: "200 people are saved, 400 people are not saved" for variant A and "400 people will die and 200 people will not die "for variant B. Kühberger changed the wording in the first version of A to "400 people are not saved" for variant A and in the second presentation to "200 people will not die" for variant A. Now the subjects decided exactly vice versa. In the first representation B was preferred and in the second representation A. The framing effect reversed. There was a willingness for risk with the profit formulation and risk aversion in the loss formulation. What remains is the framing effect in general, since the decision alternatives were still equivalent.[146]

Overconfidence is the overestimation of one's abilities that has been demonstrated in numerous experiments as early as the 1970s. Studies established a subjective favorable judgment of one's self. Subjects regularly overestimate their own knowledge, their control options, their abilities as well as their achievements.[147]Lichtenstein and Fischhoff found that the overestimation decreases as more tasks are solved correctly. The harder the tasks, the greater the overconfidence.[148]

---

[145]See Meyerowitz, Beth E.; Chaiken, Shelly (1987) and Beck, H. (2014), p. 154.

[146]See Kühberger, Anton (1995), pp. 230–240 and Beck, H. (2014), p. 162.

[147]See Metcalfe, Janet (1998).

[148]See Lichtenstein, Sarah, Fischhoff, Baruch, Phillips, Lawrence D. (1982).

Weinstein tested students and found that they overestimate their positive outcomes and underestimate their negative outcomes. They estimated the likelihood of earning more than $10,000 as their starting salary, 41.5% higher than their fellow students, and the likelihood of a heart attack before the age of 40, 38.4% lower than their peers.[149] Overconfidence increases with the difficulty level of the tasks. It is also subject to experts who feel that they are better informed.[150] This is also a problem in economic consulting, which Hayek called the presumption of knowledge. Confirmation bias reinforces the problem.

The confirmation bias describes how people process facts in a way that confirms their own opinions. Contradictory facts are not taken into account or are subordinate.[151] These include:

– Pseudo-diagnostics: Humans tend to favor their own hypotheses rather than weighing them objectively critically against others. Doctors should not commit themselves so early to their diagnosis, for example.[152]
– Belief Perservance: In order not to have to change their opinion, hypotheses are maintained even when they have already been refuted.[153]

Added to this is the illusion of control as an overestimation of one's own influence on processes, such as throwing dice to influence the outcome or selecting a winning ticket. Experiments showed that test takers overestimate their dice skills if they were lucky in the beginning[154] and that test takers are willing to buy the more expensive tickets if they can choose the numbers themselves.[155] Thus, there is a tendency to rate more expensive products as higher quality, although the correlation is very weak. And the willingness to pay a higher price for a product increases when it externally resembles a quality product.

People shy away from change when they cannot assess how they are affected. The status quo is preferred over another alternative (status quo bias). Samuelson and Zeckhauser found that the majority of test subjects do not change their investment portfolio in the case of inheritance. The subjects retained the shares they had inherited or did not buy any shares in cash.[156] In principle, sticking to the status quo can be a rational and efficient approach.

---

[149] See Weinstein, Neil D. (1980).

[150] See Angner, E. (2006) and Russo, J. Edward; Schoemaker, Paul J. H. (1992).

[151] See Wason, Peter C. (1960), pp. 129–140; Nickerson, Raymond P (1998), pp. 175–220.

[152] See Doherty, Michael E.; Mynatt, Clifford R.; Tweney, Ryan D.; Schiavo, Michael D. (1979).

[153] See Ross, Lee; Lepper, Mark R.; Hubbard, Michael (1975).

[154] See Langer, Ellen J./Roth, Jane (1975).

[155] See Langer, Ellen J. (1975).

[156] See Samuelson, William; Zeckhauser, Richard (1988), pp. 12 and Kahneman, Daniel; Knetsch, Jack; Thaler, Richard (1991), pp. 193–206. Beck, H. (2014), pp. 164.

Boxall, Adamowicz and Moon found that the status quo bias increases the more complex and time-consuming the decision-making process is.[157] Another explanatory approach is the regret aversion. To revise a decision that has already been made means, on the one hand, that one has to admit to having made a mistake. This generates regret and negative emotions.[158]

The status quo bias is reinforced by the omission bias.[159] People rate negative results from active actions higher than negative results resulting from non-actions, ie omissions. Kahneman and Tversky showed as early as 1982 that the losses on an equity investment are considered to be more negative if they were created through active buying than by neglecting to sell.[160] Ritov and Baron show that parents refrain from vaccination even if the risk of disease is 5/10,000 lower than that of non-vaccination at 10/10,000.[161]

When valuing goods, people tend to value the benefits higher than when they do not have them, which can make sales more difficult. This is called an endowment effect.[162] The effect is more pronounced in long-lived household goods which are rarely bought. The use of consultants (eg estate agents) can reduce this effect.[163]

Decisions are not always logically and rationally linked or their results connected to each other. In decision-making situations people form accounts in which they allocate losses and profits (mental accounting).[164]

Experiments show that the future benefit does not decrease continuously. This is called hyperbolic discounting. Thaler asked subjects what interest rate they demand-ed in order to accept a decrease in value of $15. It turned out that they required a much higher value for short periods of time than for long periods: For 1 month, they demanded $20 (345%), $50 (120%) and $1 for a year 10 years $ 100 (19%).[165] This explains why people renounce a benefit compensation for saving as a short-term consumption in the form of the interest demand.

You can also explain that people plan a lot of good things for the long term, but then do not implement them when the time comes. We want to lose weight, for example, but then when it's time to start the diet we weaken and eat the wrong things.[166] To overcome this weakness, we develop self-imposed limitations. Beck cites as an example the so-called

---

[157] See Boxall, Peter; Adamowicz, W. L. (Vic); Moon, Amanda (2009) and Beck, H. (2014), p. 167.

[158] See Bell, David E. (1982) and Loomes, Graham; Sudgen, Robert (1982), pp. 805–824.

[159] See Ritov, Illana/Baron, Jonathan (1992) and Spranca, Marc; Minsk, Elisa; Baron, Jonathan (1991) and Beck, H. (2014), p. 168.

[160] See Kahneman, Daniel; Tversky, Amos (1982), p. 173.

[161] See Ritov, Illana; Baron, Jonathan (1992).

[162] See Kahneman, Daniel; Knetsch, Jack; Thaler, Richard (1991), pp. 193–206.

[163] See Marshall, J.D.; Knetsch, J.; Sinden, J.A. (1986).

[164] See Kahneman, Daniel; Tversky, Amos (1984), p. 160.

[165] See Thaler, Richard H. (1981) and Beck, H. (2014), p. 215.

[166] See Beck, H. (2014), p. 214.

Christmas clubs in the US, where you can deposit money that is paid out again just before Christmas. This is meant to counteract temptation to spend it on other things.[167]

Comprehension Questions

1. Explain the status quo bias. How can this influence economic behavior?
2. Is the confirmation bias a problem for science? Should scientists control themselves? How could they do that?
3. Is framing dangerous? Discuss the advantages and disadvantages.
4. Why do people use heuristics?

Conclusion and Summary

What motivation for ethical behavior do we have? There are many people who selflessly do good deeds and feel better for doing so, not worse. This gives us a selfless motivation that contradicts the theory of utility maximization, or the concept of homo economicus. The fact that selfless, or even self-sacrificing, acts exists shows that such an ethic is not unrealistic. Volunteer work and individuals like Mother Theresa are clear examples. This behavior can be explained by a more general theory of maximizing happiness, which is behind theories like the Happiness Theory from Bentham and Mill. Many people are generally good, which is to say they have an ethical disposition.

Selfless acts generally garner prestige in a society, presenting another motivation for ethical behavior. Both motivations are bases for behavior relevant to the satisfaction of a person's basic needs, according to Maslow's[168] hierarchy of needs. Beyond maximizing one's advantage, people need to feel a purpose in life. There are people who measure their benefit or value as a person by how beneficial they are to others. Behavioral theories have given too little consideration to intrinsic motivations until now. Here we are looking at an enlightened human ethos. People consciously behave ethically because they understand the importance of such behavior to society, or because they empathize with other people. Normally these motivations only become meaningful after all of one's basic needs have been met, and they cannot be presupposed for every person. Nonetheless, such ethical motivations must not be disregarded. Our representative democracy in fact demands altruistic behavior from people as a prerequisite to allowing delegates to represent the voter's interests. This expanded theory allows us to explain altruism, helping others and sympathy.

(continued)

---

[167]See Beck, H. (2014), pp. 171, 234.

[168]See Maslow, A. H. (1943).

The genetic predisposition to cooperative behavior we have described is not sufficient on its own, however. Hobbes recognized that cooperative behavior must be worthwhile for the individual, who must also be able to count on it from others, since we would otherwise have anarchy. Luhmann considers trust to be a tool used to reduce the complexity of social interactions.[169] Trust can only be ensured by a society rewarding cooperative behavior and punishing non-cooperative behavior. Without controls and sanctions there is no guarantee of fair, thus economically ethical, behavior.

Therefore moral hazards are extremely dangerous. The existing asymmetries of bonus compensation schemes have led to a divergence of interests between employees on the one hand and the health of financial institutions and other companies at large on the other hand. Remuneration and bonuses depend on short-term profitability, which increases share prices in the short-term, but not the long-term health of the company. In the financial system, investment managers increased the risks for their employer by buying highly profitable but risky assets and were rewarded with high bonuses, which led to the financial crisis in the long term. Without accountability variable compensation schemes become unilateral bonus maximation schemes with negative effects for the company and the principal. It means risking other people's money which will generally be abused unethically.[170]

Moreover people are influenced in their behavior by their view of the world. Ideas and attitudes, or moral values, must be shown by example and included in education. This makes schools of economic science particularly important. There are those who blame management training for catastrophes such as Enron, the subprime crisis etc. Thomas Lindsay, once Dean of the University of Dallas, points to studies before Enron that prove managers rarely fail economically or morally because of a lack of professional knowledge. What they are generally missing is what Aristotle calls "wisdom," to be understood as interpersonal capabilities and practical knowledge. In Lindsay's opinion the education for managers was excessively subject-oriented, and the moral capabilities of the students are almost completely lost through unadulterated profit maximization. Aristotle said that true leadership is based on the ability to recognize and serve the good of the community. To train these abilities one needs much more than a professional education, one needs instruction in history, philosophy, literature, theology and logic.[171]

(continued)

---

[169] See Luhmann, Niklas (2000).
[170] See Conrad, Christian A. (2015).
[171] See Bennis, Warren G./O'Toole, James (2005), p. 95.

If households maximize their benefits and companies maximize their profits, it is economically efficient and economic science would consider this a goal for orientation. Good businessmen always act to maximize profit. Whoever wants to be a good businessman should act accordingly. Good households also act to maximize benefits. Thus private persons should also act to maximize benefits. This is the world being taught to young students of economic science in the Western industrial countries. Many would say that this is how the world is, and people ruthlessly maximize their benefits. What about the idea that people are neither wholly good nor wholly bad - as this paper has shown - but they were only told to behave badly? The world would be worse than it had to be.

In the company, management must consider the employees' strong sense of justice. The distribution of income in the company must be explained to the employees so that it is accepted and the employee remains motivated. In addition, a key task of management is to ensure that the company is also justified among the employees.

According to social psychology, cultural/societal influences inform human behavior, which deviates from the homo economicus stereotype. Examples include various gestures and the strongly self-centered Western cultures as opposed to Asian cultures. It is also important to know how people adapt to cognitive dissonance, which might be created by an immoral environment. The Ash Conformity Experiment proved that individuals even adopt a false group opinion if the group presents its view with self-confidence. We humans therefore tend to over evaluate the way something is being presented. This also explains why managers who are so self-confident that they do not question themselves and never admit mistakes are more successful than those that correct themselves. However, this also results in more mistakes.

Groups are economically relevant both as companies and as societies of states. People take on roles within groups that influence their behavior. Individuals adapt to the group in order to gain social recognition (social comparison process or aspiring to conformity). It is assumed on the other hand, that only the individual influences the behavior of homo economicus. Norms create moral behavior, as has been shown in experiments.[172] However, the presented behavioral studies show also that human beeings are not social oriented enough for an economic altruism as a socialistic or communistic system demands.

(continued)

---

[172]See Jonas K./Stroebe, W./Hewstone M. (2007), pp. 374; Fehr, Ernst/Fischbacher, Urs (2003), p. 786 and Fehr, Ernst/Gächter, Simon/Fischbacher, Urs (2001); Frank, Robert H. (2004); Frank, Robert H. (1988) and Gürerk, Özgür/Irlenbusch, Bernd/Rockenbach, Bettina (2006).

Man is a social being. Social rewards have a positive effect in the brain (dorsal or ventral striatum).[173] Withdrawal of social inclusion, recognition and empowerment causes pain and even damage to health.

The economics, with their focus on a pure objective utility maximization, are far from human reality. Although an exclusively objective benefit allows for measurability and thus the use of deterministic decision-making models, they lead to the wrong results. There are three systematic errors:

1. Economic sciences are exclusively psychologically oriented. People decide in a social environment, which is why sociology is at least as important for behavior as psychology. Motives such as social rewards or sanctions are not taken into account. For instance is acceptance by others is a very important behavioral incentive.
2. Taking the objective as the basis for human decision-making, the influence of the group (the company) or society must also be taken into account. Norms that are sanctioned reduce payouts and are critical to decision-making.
3. Finally, the objective benefit is not decisive but the subjectively perceived. However, this is difficult to measure from the outside. However, decision models that build on only objective material utility are misrepresentative and cannot explain many human motives, such as emotions, envy, sense of justice, and compassion. Man is stunted with the homo oeconomicus. It would therefore be more realistic to base the explanation of human behavior on the maximization of happiness as on benefit maximization.

People should be motivated to work happily and efficiently in such a way that they use their skills to maximize the company's participation in the production process. That's how they benefit others. This is best ensured by freedom and competition in decentralized decision-making and market coordination. Quantitative economics should be supplemented in this book by the findings of behavioral sciences.

If irrational behavior is not the exception, models based on rational behavior can no longer be a rule, but can at best describe optimal behavior or average behavior by which the irrational behavior shows deviations. If people do not behave predictably like natural laws, then at best we can set a framework to direct behavior with incentives and sanctions. The economy then consists mainly of institutional regulations, a regulatory framework.

The Prospect theory complements the previous behavioral models based on rational behavior and thus moves a step closer to reality. However, as expected,

(continued)

---

[173]See Fehr, E., & Camerer, C. F. (2007).

this increases the complexity of the models. This was the very reason for the simplistic assumption of the homo oeconomicus. The problem, however, is the different risk behavior and irrational behavior of humans, which is why no clear, reproducible utility function can result. Human behavior does not remain deterministic.

Why should markets be rational if their human participants are not?

Comprehension Questions

1. Describe the characteristics of homo oeconomicus. Is that image of human beings realistic? Draw your own image of man.
2. What importance do societal norms have for society?
3. Why have many ethical misdeeds taken place especially within the finance sector?
4. What functions have emotions? Is irrational behavior a disadvantage in terms of economic success?

References

Alesina, A., Tella, D., Rafael, & MacCulloch, R. J. (2004). Inequality and happiness: Are Europeans and Americans different? *Journal of Public Economics, 88*(2004), 2009–2042.

Allen, V. L., & Levine, J. M. (1971). Social support and conformity: The role of independent assessment of reality. *Journal of Experimental Social Psychology, 7*, 48–58.

Angner, E. (2006). Economists as experts: Overconfidence in theory and practice. *Journal of Economic Methodology., 13*, 1–24.

Aristoteles. (1944). *Politics.* Accessed from http://www.perseus.tufts.edu/hopper/text?doc=Perseus: text:1999.01.0058:book=1:section=1253a

Asch, S. E. (1951). Effects of group pressure upon the modification and distortion of judgments. In H. Guetzkow (Ed.), *Groups, leadership and men; research in human relations* (pp. 177–190). Oxford: Carnegie Press.

Asch, S. E. (1987). *Social psychology.* New York: Oxford University Press.

Atkinson, J. W., Heyns, R. W., & Veroff, J. (1954). The effect of experimental arousal of the affiliation motive on thematic apperception. *Journal of Abnormal and Social Psychology, 49*, 405–410.

Axelrod, R. (1987). *Die evolution der Kooperation*, Munich.

Baba, S., George, L., & Antoine, B. (2005). The dark side of emotions? When individuals with decreased emotional reactions make advantageous decisions. *Cognitive Brain Research, 23*, 85–92.

Barsade, S. G. (2002). The ripple effect: Emotional contagion and its influence on group behavior. *Administrative Science Quarterly, 47*, 644–675.

Batson, C. D., & Shaw, L. L. (1991). Evidence for altruism: Toward a pluralism of prosocial motives. *Psychological Inquiry, 2*, 107–122.

Batson, C. D., Duncan, B. D., Ackerman, P., Buckley, T., & Birch, K. (1981). Is empathic emotion a source of altruistic motivation? *Journal of Personality and Social Psychology, 40*, 290–302.

Baumeister, R. F., & Leary, M. R. (1995). The need to belong: Desire for interpersonal attachments as a fundamental human motivation. *Psychological Bulletin, 117*, 497–529.

Beck, H. (2014). *Behavioral economics: Eine Einführung.* (1 Aufl., p. 214) Wiesbaden: Springer

Bell, D. E. (1982). Regret in decision making under uncertainty. *Operations Research, 1982*(30), 961–981.

Bennis, W. G., & O'Toole, J. (2005, May). How business schools lost their way. *Harvard Business Review*, pp. 1–9. Accessed from https://hbr.org/2005/05/how-business-schools-lost-their-way

Bentham, J. (1789). Introduction to the principles of morals and legislation (1780, published 1789). In J. H. Burns & H. L. A. Hart (Eds.), *The collected works of Jeremy Bentham* (2nd ed.). Oxford: Oxford University Press.

Berkman, L. F., & Syme, S. L. (1979). Social networks, host resistance, and mortality: A nine year follow-up study of Alameda County residents. *American Journal of Epidemiology, 109*, 186–204.

Berkowitz, L. (1954). Group standards, cohesiveness, and productivity. *Human Relations, 7*, 509–519.

Bolton, G. E., & Ockenfels, A. (2000). ERC: A theory of equity, reciprocity, and competition. *American Economic Review, 90*(1), 166–193.

Bond, R., & Smith, P. B. (1996). Culture and conformity: A meta-analysis of studies using Asch's (1952b, 1956) line judgment task. *Psychological Bulletin, 119*, 111–137.

Bowlby, J. (1958). The nature of the child's tie to his mother. *International Journal of Psychoanalysis, 39*, 350–373.

Boxall, P., Adamowicz, W. L., & Moon, A. (2009). Complexity in choice experiments: Choice of the status quo alternative and implications for welfare measurement. *The Australian Journal of Agricultural and Resource Economics, 53*, 503–519.

Brandstätter, V., Schüler, J., Puca, R. M., & Lozo, L. (2018). *Motivation und emotion.* Wiesbaden: Springer.

Brehm, S. S., & Brehm, J. W. (1981). *Psychological reactance. A theory of freedom and control.* New York: Academic.

Brewer, M. B., & Caporael, L. R. (2006). An evolutionary perspective on social identity: Revisiting groups. In M. Schaller, J. A. Simpson, & D. T. Kenrick (Eds.), *Evolution and social psychology* (pp. 143–161). New York: Psychology Press.

Brosnan, S. F., & de Waal, F. B. M. (2003). Monkeys reject unequal pay. *Nature, 425*, 297–299.

Brosnan, S. F., & de Waal, F. B. M. (2014). Evolution of responses to (un) fairness. *Science, 346* (6207), 314–320.

Camerer, C., Loewenstein, G., & Prelec, D. (2005). Neuroeconomics: How neuroscience can inform economics. *Journal of Economic Literature, XLIII*, 9–64.

Campbell, D. T. (1965). Ethnocentric and other altruistic motives. In D. Levine (Ed.), *Nebraska symposium on motivation* (Vol. 13). Lincoln: University of Nebraska Press.

Cherry, T. L., Frykblom, P., & Shogren, J. F. (2002). Hardnose the dictator. *American Economic Review, 92*(4), 1218–1221.

Conrad, C. A. (2010). *Morality and economic crisis - Enron, subprime & co.* Hamburg: disserta Verlag.

Conrad, C. A. (2015). Incentives, risk and compensation schemes: Experimental evidence on the importance of risk adequate compensation. *Applied Economics and Finance, 2*(2), 50–55.

Damasio, A. (2006). *Descartes' error: Emotion, reason and the human brain.* New York: Vintage.

deCharms, R., Morrison, H. W., Reitman, W., & McClelland, D. C. (1955). Behavioral correlates of directly and indirectly measured achievement motivation. In D. C. McClelland (Ed.), *Studies in motivation* (pp. 414–423). New York: Appleton-Century-Crofts.

Deci, E. L., & Ryan, R. M. (2000). The "what" and "why" of goal pursuits: Human needs and the self-determination of behavior. *Psychological Inquiry, 11*, 227–268.

DeQuervain, D., et al. (2004). The neural basis of altruistic punishment. *Science, 305*(5688), 1254–1258.

Doherty, M. E., Mynatt, C. R., Tweney, R. D., & Schiavo, M. D. (1979). Pseudodiagnosticitiy. *Acta Psychologica, 1979*, 111–121.

Earley, P. C. (1993). East meets west meets Mideast: Further explorations of collectivistic versus individualistic work groups. *Academy of Management Journal, 36*, 319–348.

Eisenberger, N. I., Lieberman, M. D., & Williams, K. D. (2003). Does rejection hurt? An fMRI study of social exclusion. *Science, 302*, 290–292.

Engelmann, D., & Strobel, M. (2000). *An experimental comparison of the fairness models by Bolton and Ockenfels and by Fehr and Schmidt*, Discussion Papers, Interdisciplinary Research Project 373: Quantification and Simulation of Economic Processes, No. 2000, 28, urn:nbn:de:kobv:11-10047345. Accessed from http://hdl.handle.net/10419/62222

Engeser, S., Rheinberg, F., & Möller, M. (2009). Achievement motive imagery in German schoolbooks: A pilot study testing McClelland's hypothesis. *Journal of Research in Personality, 43*, 110–113.

Erlei, M., Leschke, M., & Sauerland, D. (1999). *Neue Institutionenökonomik*. Stuttgart.

Falk, A. (2003). Homo oeconomicus versus Homo recipocans: Ansätze für ein neues Wirtschaftspolitisches Weltbild? *Perspektiven der Wirtschaftspolitik, 4*(2003), 141–172.

Fehr, E., & Camerer, C. F. (2007). Social neuroeconomics: The neural circuitry of social preferences. *Trends in Cognitive Sciences, 11*, 419–427.

Fehr, G., & Fischbacher, U. (2001). Are people conditionally cooperative? Evidence from a public goods experiment. *Economics Letters, 71*, 397–404.

Fehr, E., & Fischbacher, U. (2003). The nature of human altruism. *Nature, 425*(23), 785–791.

Fehr, E., & Fischbacher, U. (2004). Third party punishment and social norms. *Evolution and Human Behavior, 25*, 63–87.

Fehr, E., & Gächter, S. (2000). Cooperation and punishment in public goods experiments. *The American Economic Review, 90*, 980–994.

Fehr, E., & Schmidt, K. M. (1999). A theory of fairness, competition and cooperation. *Quarterly Journal of Economics, 1999*, 817–868.

Fershtman, C., Gneezy, U., & List, J. A. (2012). Equity aversion: Social norms and the desire to be ahead. *American Economic Journal: Microeconomics, 4*(4), 131–144.

Föhr, S., & Lenz, H. (1992). Unternehmenskultur und ökonomische Theorie. In W. H. Staehle & P. Conrad (Eds.), *Managementforschung* (pp. 111–162). Berlin: De Gruyter.

Frank, R. H. (1988). *Passion within reason. The strategic role of the emotions*. New York: Norton.

Frank, R. H. (2004). *What price the moral high ground?* Princeton, NJ: Princeton Univesity Press.

Franz, S. (2004). Grundlagen des ökonomischen Ansatzes: Das Erklärungskonzept des Homo Oeconomicus, *Working Paper der Universität Potsdam*. 2004-02. Accessed from www.uni-potsdam.de/u/makrooekonomie/docs/studoc/stud7.pdf

Gneezy, U. (2005). Deception: The role of consequences. *American Economic Review, 95*(1), 384–394.

Göbel, E. (2010). *Unternehmensethik*. Stuttgart: UTB.

Golnaz, T., Satpute, A. B., & Lieberman, M. D. (2007). The sunny side of fairness. Preference for fairness activates reward circuitry. *Psychological Science, 19*(4), 339–347.

Grimm Brothers. (1819). *Hans in luck*. Accessesed from http://www.authorama.com/grimms-fairy-tales-2.html

Gürerk, Ö. I., & Rockenbach, B. (2006). The competitive advantage of sanctioning institutions. *Science, 312*(April), 108–111.

Güth, W., Schmittberger, R., & Schwarze, B. (1982). An experimental analysis of ultimatum bargaining. *Journal of Economic Behavior and Organization, 3*(4), 367–388.

Haney, C., Banks, C., & Zimbardo, P. (1973). Interpersonal dynamics in a simulated prison. *International Journal of Criminology and Penology, 1,* 69–97.

Harbaugh, W. T., Mayr, U., & Burghart, D. R. (2007) Neural responses to taxation and voluntry giving reveal motives for charitable donations. *Science, 316,* 1622–1625; Fehr, E., & Camerer, C. F. (2007), pp. 419–427.

Hausmann, D. M., & McPherson, M. (2006). *Economic analysis, moral philosophy, and public policy* (2nd ed.). Cambridge: Cambridge University Press.

Hein, G., Silani, G., Preuschoff, K., Batson, C. D., & Singer, T. (2010). Neural responses to ingroup and outgroup members' suffering predict individual differences in costly helping. *Neuron, 68,* 149–160.

Henrich, J., et al. (2005). "Economic man" in cross-cultural perspective: Behavioral experiments in 15 small-scale societies. *Behavioral and Brain Sciences, 28*(2005), 795–855.

Hewstone, M., & Martin, R. (2014). Sozialer Einfluss. In K. Jonas, W. Stroebe, & M. Hewstone (Eds.), *Sozialpsychologie, 6, vollständig überarbeitete Auflage* (pp. 269–314). Berlin: Springer.

Höffe, O. (1997). *Lexikon der Ethik* (5th ed.). Munich: C.H. Beck.

Hofstede, G. (2010). *Hofstede, Gert Jan, Minkov, Michael (2010), cultures and organizations – Software of the mind: Intercultural cooperation and its importance for survival.* New York: McGraw-Hill Education.

Hogg, M. A., & Turner, J. C. (1987). Intergroup behaviour, self-stereotyping and the salience of social categories. *British Journal of Social Psychology, 26,* 325–340.

Holzmann, R. (2015). Wirtschaftsethik. *Wiesbaden, 2015.*

Hornstein, H. A., Fisch, E., & Holmes, M. (1968). Influence of a model's feeling about his behavior and his relevance as a comparison other on observers' helping behavior. *Journal of Personality and Social Psychology, 10*(3), 222–226.

Hüffmeier, J., & Hertel, G. (2011). When the whole is more than the sum of its parts: Group motivation gains in the wild. *Journal of Experimental Social Psychology, 47,* 455–459.

Hull, C. L. (1952). *A behavior system: An introduction to behavior theory concerning the individual organism.* Westport, CT: Greenwood Press.

James, K., & Greenberg, J. (1989). In-group salience, intergroup comparison, and individual performance and self-esteem. *Personality and Social Psychology Bulletin, 15,* 604–616.

Jonas, K., Stroebe, W., & Hewstone, M. (2007). *Sozialpsychologie, Eine Einführung* (5th ed.). Heidelberg: Springer.

Jonas, K., Stroebe, W., & Hewstone, M. (Eds.). (2014). *Sozialpsychologie, 6, vollständig überarbeitete Auflage.* Heidelberg: Springer.

Kagel, J. H., & Kim, M. D. (1996). Fairness in ultimatum games with asymmetric information and asymmetric payoffs. *Games and Economic Behavior, 13,* 100–110.

Kahneman, D., & Tversky, A. (1979). Prospect theory: An analysis of decision under risk. *Econometrica, 47*(2), 263–292.

Kahneman, D., & Tversky, A. (1981). The framing of decisions and the psychology of choice. *Science, 211,* 453–457.

Kahneman, D., & Tversky, A. (1982). The psychology of preferences. *Scientific American, 146,* 160–173.

Kahneman, D., & Tversky, A. (1984). Choices, values and frames. *American Pschologist, 39*(4), 342–350.

Kahneman, D., & Tversky, A. (1986). Rational choice and the framing of decisions. *Journal of Business, 59*(4), 5251–5278.

Kahneman, D., Knetsch, J., & Thaler, R. (1991). Anomalies: The endowment effect, loss aversion and status quo Bias. *The Journal of Economic Perspectives, 5*(1), 193–206.

Kahneman, D. (2011). *Thinking, fast and slow.* London: Allen Lane.

Karremans, J. C., & Finkenauer, C. (2014). Affiliation, zwischenmenschliche Anziehung und enge Beziehungen. In K. Jonas, W. Stroebe, & M. Hewstone (Eds.), *Sozialpsychologie, 6., vollständig überarbeitete Auflage* (pp. 401–438). Berlin: Springer.

Kessler, T., & Fritsche, I. (2018). *Sozialpsychologie*. Wiesbaden: Springer.

Köhler, O. (1926). Kraftleistungen bei Einzel- und Gruppenarbeit. *Industrielle Psychotechnik, 3*, 274–282.

Kühberger, A. (1995). The framing of decisions: A new look at old problems. *Organizational Behaviour and Human Decision Processes, 62*(2), 230–240.

Langer, E. J. (1975). The illusion of control, in. *Journal of Personality and Social Psychology, 32*(2), 311–328.

Langer, E. J., & Roth, J. (1975). Heads I win, tails it's chance: The illusion of control as a function of the sequence of outcomes in a purely chance task. *Journal of Personality and Social Psychology, 32*(6), 951–955.

Leimgruber, K. L., Shaw, A., Santos, L. R., & Olson, K. R. (2012). Young children are more generous when others are aware of their actions. *PLoS One, 7*(10), e48292. https://doi.org/10.1371/journal.pone.0048292.

Levine, M., & Manning, R. (2014). Prosoziales Verhalten. In K. Jonas, W. Stroebe, & M. Hewstone (Eds.), *Sozialpsychologie, 6., vollständig überarbeitete Auflage* (pp. 357–400). Berlin: Springer.

Levine, M., Prosser, A., Evans, D., & Reicher, S. D. (2005). Identity and emergency intervention: How social group membership and inclusiveness of group boundaries shape helping behavior. *Personality and Social Psychology Bulletin, 31*, 443–453.

Lichtenstein, S., Fischhoff, B., & Phillips, L. D. (1982). Calibration of probabilities: The state of art to 1980. In D. Kahneman, P. Slovic, & A. Tversky (Eds.), *Judgment under uncertainty: Heuristics and biases* (pp. 306–334). Cambridge: Cambridge University Press.

List, J. A. (2006). The behavioralist meets the market: Measuring social preferences and reputation effects in actual transactions. *Journal of Political Economy, 114*(1), 1–37.

Loomes, G., & Sudgen, R. (1982). Regret theory: An Alternative theory of rational choice under uncertainty. *The Economic Journal, 92*(368), 805–824.

Lück, H. E., & Manz, W. (1973). Die Technik der verlorenen Briefe – Ein neues Instrument verhaltensbezogener Einstellungsmessung? *Zeitschrift für Soziologie, 2*(4), 352–365.

Luhmann, N. (2000). *Vertrauen: Ein Mechanismus der Reduktion sozialer Komplexität*, Stuttgart.

Mandeville, Bernard de (1732). *The fable of the bees; or, private vices, public benefits*. London 1714 (first edition 1714).

Marshall, J. D., Knetsch, J., & Sinden, J. A. (1986). Agents evaluations and the disparity in measures of economic loss. *Journal of Economic Behavior and Organization, 7*, 115–127.

Maslow, A. H. (1943). A theory of human motivation. *Psychological Review, 50*(4), 370–396.

McClelland, D. C. (1961). *The achieving society*. Princeton, NJ: Van Nostrand.

McClelland, D. C., Atkinson, J. W., Clark, R. A., & Lowell, E. L. (1953). *The achievement motive*. New York: Appleton-Century-Crofts.

McClelland, D. C., Koestner, R., & Weinberger, J. (1989). How do self-attributed and implicit motives differ? *Psychological Review, 96*(4), 690–702.

McClure, S., Laibson, D. I., Loewenstein, G., & Cohen, J. (2004). Separate neural systems value immediate and delayed monetary rewards. *Science, 306*, 503–507.

Metcalfe, J. (1998). Cognitive optimism: Self-deception or memory-based processing heuristic? *Personality and Social Psychology Review, 2*(2), 100–110.

Meyer, B., Enström, M. K., Harvstveit, M., Bowles, D. P., & Beevers, C. G. (2007). Happiness and dispair on the catwalk: Need satisfaction, well-being, and personality adjustment among fashion models. *The Journal of Positive Psychology, 2*(1), 2–17.

Meyerowitz, B. E., & Chaiken, S. (1987). The effect on message framing on breast-self-examination attitudes, intentions and behavior. *Journal of Personality and Social Psychology, 52,* 500–510.

Milgrom, P., & Roberts, J. (1992). *Economics, organization & management.* Upper Saddle River, NJ, Prentice Hall.

Mill, J. S. (1844). *Essays on some unsettled questions of political economy,* London. Accessed April 25, 2015, from http://www.econlib.org/library/Mill/mlUQP5.html

Mill, J. S. (1863). Utilitarism. In J. S. Mill (Ed.), *The basic writings of John Stuart Mill: On liberty, the Subjection Of Women And Utilitarianism.* New York: Random House.

Mill, J. S. (1992). Utilitarismus. In O. Höffe (Ed.), *Einführung in die utilitaristische Ethik* (pp. 84–97). Tübingen: Klassische und zeitgenössische Texte.

Moll, J., et al. (2006). Human fronto-mesolimbic networks guide decisions about charitable donation. *Proceedings of the National Academy of Sciences of the United States of America, 103,* 15623–15628.

Nickerson, R. S. (1998). Confirmation bias: An ubiquitous phenomen in many guises. *Review of general Psychology, 2*(2), 175–220.

Osgood, C. E., Suci, G., & Tannenbaum, P. (1957). *The measurement of meaning.* Urbana: University of Illinois Press.

Perin, C. I. (1942). Behavior potentiality as a joint function of the amount of training and the degree of hunger at the time of extinction. *Journal of Experimental Psychology, 30,* 93–113.

Perry, S. (2003). Social conventions in wild white-faced capuchin monkeys: Evidence for traditions in a neotropical primate. *Current Anthropology, 44*(2), 241–268.

Pham, M. T. (2007). Emotion and rationality: A critical review and interpretation of empirical evidence. *Review of General Psychology, 11*(2), 155–178.

Platow, M. J., Foddy, M., Yamagishi, T., Lim, L., & Chow, A. (2012). Two experimental tests of trust in in-group strangers: The moderating role of common knowledge of group membership. *European Journal of Social Psychology, 42,* 30–35. https://doi.org/10.1002/ejsp.852.

Rapoport, A., & Chammah, A. M. (1970). *Prisoner's dilemma – A study in conflict and cooperation* (2nd ed.). University of Michigan Press: Ann Arbor.

Richman, L., & Leary, M. R. (2009). Reactions to discrimination, stigmatization, ostracism, and other forms of interpersonal rejection: A multimotive model. *Psychological Review, 116,* 365–383.

Ritov, I., & Baron, J. (1992). Status-quo bias and omission-bias. *Journal of Risk and Uncertainty, 1992*(5), 49–61.

Rosenbaum, M. E., Moore, D. L., Cotton, J. L., Cook, M. S., Hieser, R. A., Shovar, M. N., et al. (1980). Group productivity and process: Pure and mixed reward structures and task interdependence. *Journal of Personality and Social Psychology, 39,* 626–664.

Ross, L., Lepper, M. R., & Hubbard, M. (1975). Perseverance in self perception and social perception: Biased attributional processes in the debriefing paradigm. *Journal of Personality and Social Psychology, 1975,* 880–892.

Roth, A. E., Prasnikar, V., Okuno-Fujiwara, M., & Zamir, S. (1991). Bargaining and market behavior in Jerusalem, Ljubljana, Pittsburgh, and Tokyo: An experimental study. *American Economic Review, 81*(5), 1068–1095.

Russo, J. E., & Schoemaker, P. J. H. (1992). Managing overconfidence. *Sloan Management Review, 33,* 7–17.

Sanfey, A. G., Rilling, J. K., Aronson, J. A., Nystrom, L. E., & Cohen, J. D. (2003). The neural basis of economic decision-making in the ultimatum game. *Science, 300*(13), 1755–1758.

Schachter, S. (1951). Deviation, rejection, and communication. *Journal of Abnormal and Social Psychology, 46,* 190–207.

Schneider, K. (1992). Emotionen. In H. Spada (Ed.), *Lehrbuch allgemeine Psychologie* (2nd ed., pp. 403–449). Bern: Huber.

Schopenhauer, A. (1840). *Preisschrift über die Grundlage der moral*. Hamburg: Meiner.

Schultheiss, O. C. (2008). Implicit motives. In O. P. John, R. W. Robins, & L. A. Pervin (Eds.), *Handbook of personality: Theory and research* (3rd ed., pp. 603–633). New York: Guilford.

Schwaninger, M. (2008). Anatol Rapoport (May 22, 1911–January 20, 2007). Pioneer of systems theory and peace research, mathematician, philosopher and pianist. *Systems Research and Behavioral Science, 24*(6), 655–658.

Schwartz, S. H. (1994). Beyond individualism and collectivism: New cultural dimensions of values. In U. Kim, H. C. Triandis, Ç. Kağitçibaşi, S. C. Choi, & G. Yoon (Eds.), *Individualism and collectivism: Theory, method and applications* (pp. 85–119). Thousand Oaks, CA: Sage.

Schwartz, S. H. (2004). Mapping and interpreting cultural differences around the world. In H. Vinken, J. Soeters, & P. Ester (Eds.), *Comparing cultures: Dimensions of culture in a comparative perspective* (pp. 43–73). Leiden, NL: Brill.

Schwarz, N., & Vaughn, L. A. (2002). The availability heuristic revisited: Ease of recall and content of recall as distinct sources of information. In T. Gilovich, D. W. Griffin, & D. Kahneman (Eds.), *Heuristics and Biases: The psychology of intuitive judgment* (pp. 103–119). Cambridge: Cambridge University Press.

Schwarz, N., Bless, H., Starck, F., Klumpp, G., Rittenauer-Schatka, H., & Simons, A. (1991). Ease of retrieval as information: Another look at the availability heuristic. *Journal of Personality and Social Psychology, 61*(2), 195–202.

Sherif, M. (1966). *In common predicament. Social psychology of intergroup conflict and cooperation*. Boston, MA: Houghton Mifflin.

Sherif, M., Harvey, O. J., White, B. J., Hood, W. R., & Sherif, C. W. (1961). *Intergroup conflict and cooperation. The robbers cave experiment*. Norman: University of Oklahoma Press.

Simon, H. A. (1959). Theories of decision-making in economics and behavioral science. *The American Economic Review, 49*(3), 253–283.

Singer, T., & Lamm, C. (2009). The social neuroscience of empathy. *Annals of the New York Academy of Sciences, 1156*, 81–96.

Singer, T., Seymour, B., O'Doherty, J. P., Stephan, K. E., Dolan, R. J., & Frith, C. D. (2006). Empathic neural responses are modulated by the perceived fairness of others. *Nature, 439*, 466–469.

Smith, A. (1759). *The theory of the moral sentiments*. Edinburgh.

Smith, A. (1776). *An inquiry into the nature and causes of the wealth of nations*, Edinburgh. Accessed from http://www.econlib.org/library/Smith/smWN8.html

Smith, V. (2002). *Constructivist and ecological rationality in economics; Nobel Prize Lecture*, December 8, 2002; printed in The American Economic Review June 2003. Accessed from https://s3.amazonaws.com/academia.edu.documents/39690274/Constructivist_and_Ecological_Rationality_in_Economics.pdf?AWSAccessKeyId=AKIAIWOWYYGZ2Y53UL3A&Expires=1557228716&Signature=JGGEiHTSNscHsGWEJZ94uSZIHLc%3D&response-content-disposition=inline%3B%20filename%3DConstructivist_and_Ecological_Rationalit.pdf. pp. 465-508.

Smith, P. B. (2014). Sozialpsychologie und kulturelle Unterschiede. In K. Jonas, W. Stroebe, & M. Hewstone (Eds.), *Sozialpsychologie, 6, vollständig überarbeitete Auflage* (pp. 565–606). Berlin: Springer.

Smith, P. B., Bond, M. H., & Kağıtçıbaşı, Ç. (2006). *Understanding social psychology across cultures: Living and working in a changing world*. London: Sage.

Starbatty, J. (1999). Das Menschenbild in den Wirtschaftswissenschaften. *Tübinger Diskussionsbeiträge der Wirtschaftswissenschaftlichen Fakultät, 176*. Accessed from https://publikationen.uni-tuebingen.de/xmlui/handle/10900/47437

Stroebe, W., & Diehl, M. (1994). Why groups are less effective than their members: On productivity losses in idea-generating groups. In W. Stroebe & M. Hewstone (Eds.), *European review of social psychology* (Vol. 5, pp. 271–303). London: Wiley.

Stroebe, W., Diehl, M., & Abakoumkin, G. (1996). Social compensation and the Köhler effect: Toward a theoretical explanation of motivation gains in group productivity. In E. H. Witte & H. Davis (Eds.), *Understanding group behaviour: Small group processes and interpersonal relations* (Vol. 2, pp. 37–65). Hillsdale, NJ: Erlbaum.

Sunstein, C. (2009). *Going to extremes: How like minds unite and divide*. Oxford: Oxford University Press.

Sy, T., Coté, S., & Saavedra, R. (2005). The contagious leader: Impact of the leader's mood on the mood of group members, group affective tone, and group processes. *Journal of Applied Psychology, 90*, 295–305.

Tajfel, H. (1978). Social categorization, social identity and social comparison. In H. Tajfel (Ed.), *Differentiation between social groups: Studies in the social psychology of intergroup relations* (pp. 65–93). London: Academic Press.

Tajfel, H., Billig, M. G., Bundy, R. P., & Flament, C. (1971). Social categorization and intergroup behaviour. *European Journal of Social Psychology, 1*, 149–178.

Thaler, R. H. (1981). Some empirical evidence on dynamic inconsistency. *Economic Letters, 8*, 201–207.

Thaler, R. H., & Sunstein, C. R. (2008, April 8). *Nudge: Improving decisions about health, wealth, and happiness*. London: Yale University Press.

Thaler, R. H., Sunstein, C. R., & Balz, J. P. (2010, April 2). Choice architecture. doi:https://doi.org/10.2139/ssrn.1583509.

Turner, J. C., Oakes, P. J., Haslam, S. A., & McGarty, C. (1994). Self and collective: Cognition and social context. *Personality and Social Psychology Bulletin, 20*, 454–463.

Wason, P. C. (1960). On the failure to eliminate hypothesis in a conceptual task. *Quarterly Journal of Experimental Psychology, 1960*, 129–140.

Weber, M. (1905). *The protestant ethic and the spirit of capitalism*, chapter 4. Accessed from https://www.marxists.org/reference/archive/weber/protestant-ethic/ch02.htm. Deutsches Original: Weber, M. (1904). Die protestantische Ethik und der Geist des Kapitalismus. Archiv für Sozialwissenschaft und Sozialpolitik.

Weber, M. (1922). *Wirtschaft und Gesellschaft, Grundriss der verstehenden Soziologie*. Tübingen: von Johannes Winckelmann.

Weinstein, N. D. (1980). Unrealistic optimism about future life events. *Journal of Personality and Social Psychology, 39*, 806–457.

Williams, S. B. (1938). Resistance to extinction as a function of the number of reinforcements. *Journal of Experimental Psychology, 23*, 506–521.

Williams, K. D., & Karau, S. J. (1991). Social loafing and social compensation: The effects of expectations of co-worker performance. *Journal of Personality and Social Psychology, 61*, 570–581.

Witte, E. H. (1989). Köhler rediscovered: The anti-Ringelmann effect. *European Journal of Social Psychology, 19*, 147–154.

Wright, J., & Ginsberg, D. (2012, February 16). Free to err?: Behavioral Law and economics and its implications for liberty. *Library of Law & Liberty*. Accessed from https://www.lawliberty.org/liberty-forum/free-to-err-behavioral-law-and-economics-and-its-implications-for-liberty/

Yaari, M. E., & Bar-Hillel, M. (1984). On dividing justly. *Social Choice and Welfare, 1*(1), 1–24.

Yamagishi, T. (1987). Interpersonal conflicts in reward allocation and their resolution. *Japanese Journal of Psychology, 58*, 78–83. (in Japanese).

Zanna, M. P., & Cooper, J. (1974). Dissonance and the pill: An attribution approach to studying the arousal properties of dissonance. *Journal of Personality and Social Psychology, 29*, 703–709.

Zimbardo, P. G. (2006). On rethinking the psychology of tyranny: The BBC prison study. *British Journal of Social Psychology, 45*, 47–53.

Zimbardo, P. G., Maslach, C., & Haney, C. (2000). Reflections on the Stanford prison experiment: Genesis, transformations, consequences. In T. Blass (Ed.), *Obedience to authority: Current perspectives on the Milgram paradigm* (pp. 193–237). Mahwah, NJ: Erlbaum.

The Functioning of Market and Competition

5

What Follows Why?

After familiarizing ourselves with the image of man and the basic tenets of political economy, we will now analyze the functions of the market and competition as the basis of our market system. We will show that the market and competition provide an allocation-efficient result and thus a welfare optimum.

What is the system as a whole? Which rules apply in the so-called market economy? We will address these questions in the following.

Learning Goals

You should be able to

1. explain why the market and competition provide an allocation-efficient result and.
2. explain the competition functions by means of examples.

5.1 Economy and Freedom: A Historical Overview

What did economy and society look like a few hundred years ago? In the middle ages the economic and social form of organization was feudalism. These two forms were interdependent even then, whereby the technological-economic developments determined the social form. The societies that adapted to these new developments applied the technological progress and the subsequent productivity advantages the best.

In feudalism the society was hierarchically centrally organized corresponding to the economic structure. The economy was particularly determined by the agrarian sector.

© The Editor(s) (if applicable) and The Author(s), under exclusive license to Springer
Fachmedien Wiesbaden GmbH, part of Springer Nature 2020
C. A. Conrad, *Political Economy*,
https://doi.org/10.1007/978-3-658-30884-1_5

Simple tasks were required for agriculture and the distribution of labor was slight. There were few products that had to be produced. The simple tasks to be executed were easy to supervise. Whether or not a laborer picked the fields was easy to see. The aristocracy and the church had power concentrated in their hands. The prince assured internal order and external security and there was no separation of powers. Legislative and executive powers were held by the same person. The individual had to subjugate himself and submit. In the towns the people were unconditionally at the mercy of the prince. In addition to the harsh early rules of the prince, there were also strict moral rules from the church. The punishment for disobedience could reach all the way to eternal hellfire. Life for people at that time was very constricted, there was hardly any individual freedom. The fact that these societal structures were determined by the economy is clear in the saying of the time that "city air makes you free by year and day." [1]

In the so-called free cities it was at least possible to work as an independent handyman or salesman, allowing a certain amount of self-determination in life. The amount possible was determined by the guilds, the self-government of the cities. The guilds embodied the economic order of the time. Within their framework the individual could move freely, be active in the guilds and even participate in determining the city policies depending on one's fortune, such as in a city council. The cities were created with the development of differentiate crafts and the blossoming of trade. Later the manufacturers came and with them a new economic level with the corresponding power. The level of welfare that could then be obtained created power, which the princes repeatedly tried to obtain for themselves over the next few centuries, but which they never could. On the contrary, the new bourgeoisie demanded with the economic power increasing distribution of power in feudalism and ended up stripping the power of aristocracy. [2] The technology determined the economy, and the economy determined the society.

The economy continued to develop. With technological progress people were increasingly replaced by machines for simple tasks. The people were needed for planning, building and operating. Fewer and fewer people were needed in agriculture. The labor saved by technological progress could then be used to produce new products, which increased the general welfare or could be used as leisure time. The time this freed up allowed a broad populace to achieve a basic education. With the shift in the national economic production from agriculture to the continual industrial manufacturing of new goods, the rules of a market economy gained new importance. Whereas the agricultural system allowed centralized, top-down planning, implementation and supervision, more complex production of an increasing number of goods had to be coordinated. This was only possible through the decentralized price mechanism of the market. More and more markets for more and more products and preliminary products were created and controlled the production, sales, investment and consumption plans of people. The structure of the

---

[1] See Mitteis, Heinrich (1976) and Hühns, Erik /Hühns, Ingeborg (1963), pp.123.
[2] See Schäfer, Michael (2009).

products and thus their production process were increasingly complex, and the variety of products increased as well. Thus the distribution of labor and specialization also increased. This trend is very visible in new training and study courses.

The tendency towards more complex structures demanded an increasing level of self-responsible behavior from people, thus an increasing level of freedom. The strong incorporation of the individual in the village community and extended family as well as the subjugation to the power of the prince and the church were replaced over time with more freedom for the individual. After the industrial revolution the service sector rose to the fore, and then came the computer age, which brought new demands for the people in the economic process once again. The tendency moved away from physical activities towards metal activities. If there were still many simple tasks in industry before the computer age, now the manufacturing robots have taken over the simple assembly line jobs. The machines were mostly controlled by calculating machines, the computers. With the progressing industrialization not only the market economy but also the individual had a completely different value. The actions that were simple for supervisors to control, within the hierarchy, became fewer, while being a self-starter and having self-responsibility became more important. The computer age increased this trend. The companies had to grant their employees more space and responsibility. The strictly hierarchical control through supervision of the employees was not as well-suited to assure optimal manufacturing processes. Instead, the companies increasingly turned to setting targets and a sliding scale for wages. Technical progress determined the economic and thus the political development. Thus if an economic system of market and competitive freedom is to function with the level of technology we have today, the individual must be free. A system that tries to separate economic from political freedom will not last, as history as shown. Over the long term economic power has always acquired political power. In the end the economic power makes decisions about the options to politically assert itself. This applies to countries as well. Economically developing countries have always demanded political power abroad over the long or short term. One could compare the foreign policy power of the USA now with 200 years ago.

The decentralized economic activity of the market economy on the other hand, has remained just as important, with a high level of individual freedom. This is why democracy and market economies are interdependent, since democracy promises the maximum possible political influence for the individual as a form of political freedom. For a modern market economy system to function the individual must be free. Technological development determines the economic structure, which in turn determines the societal structure. The stages of economic development and the political system are interdependent if the strengths of the respective economic system are to be realized.

The agrarian sector does not need the individuals involved to develop independently. A feudalistic social system is thus possible and fitting for the organizational needs. Cultivation of fields can be planned and controlled centrally. The optimal economic system appropriate for the modern production technology is the market economy and the appropriate political system is democracy. A centralized, dictatorial system would be contradictory. Considering this the USSR could never have won the arms race because the political system did not fit the economic requirements of the second half of the twentieth century. It was destined to lose for evolutionary reasons. This does not necessarily mean that the society must unconditionally subordinate itself to the economy. The law of economy must be used for the good of humanity, just like the law of nature. Freedom is connected to the possibility for individuals to gain property through their performance in the market. Owning property is the central motivation in a market economy, although it also contains the respective power of disposal over the resources and thus rights and power.

Market economy needs self-determined entrepreneurs as a personality type, like Schumpeter's pioneer entrepreneur.[3] This type of person must be able to develop freely. It is not sufficient to liberate those who are not free. When people grow up in bondage of any kind, no one can expect them to behave creatively and self-responsibly when they suddenly gain freedom. Even if people have a basic tendency to be entrepreneurial, they must reorient themselves to the new freedom and the new market system. Experience in a market economy is only gained through trial and error, which needs time.

For instance there is a great gap between the economic and the political freedom in China, which historically always let to a political emancipation of the citizens.

The tendency towards the separation of the individual from society induced through technology, thus the tendency towards increasing freedom of the individual from social constraints, still exists. The enlightenment with its freedom and participation demands the consequences resulting from the technological developments that have changed economic and social structures. The consequent application of the market economy rules is also the consequence of the optimal adaptation to the predetermined technical conditions.

How does this tendency affect individual freedom?

In 1989, Kerber found that the young leaders were inclined to opportunism and accepted immoral and often criminal behavior when material success was achieved. Slogans like "Everyone is the next one", "One hand washes the other" or "To achieve a higher goal, sometimes wrong can not be circumvented" were popular. Kerber summarized the trend as follows:

> The tendency seems to be a stronger ego-orientation and more attention to success, material goods and enjoyment.[4]

At the beginning of the 1990s there was a trend away from duties such as order, discipline, loyalty, thoroughness and reliability to so-called unfolding values such as independence, self-responsibility, participation and creativity.[5]

---

[3] See Schumpeter, Joseph Alois (1911).
[4] Kerber, Walter p. J. (1989), p. 280.
[5] See Dahm, Karl-Wilhelm (1993), pp. 4.

A tendency towards individualization has been confirmed by the consulting company Hay Group - in a joint study ("Leadership-2030") with the company Z-Punkt. They also refer to the impact on employee motivation:

> Individualization has a strong impact on the loyalty and willingness of employees, who often attach greater importance to 'soft factors' such as recognition, self-development, self-responsibility, value-driven commitment and work-life balance than traditional factors such as payment and promotion.[6]

Many authors see the way into the "post-material evolutionary development" not only positively. They point out that a society can not exist without obligations. Many problems cannot not be solved through self-realization, pleasure, and embarrassment, but would only be talked away.[7]

In modern free society everyone should have the opportunity to develop as he wishes. Everyone should at least have the chance to work their way up to become a millionaire, which is the central stimulus of the market economy. According to the Enlightenment, all human beings are at least equal to their basic rights, which is why a problem-solving approach suggests that the freedom of the individual ceases where the other begins. If left aside, this would be a very idealistic illusion which would lead neither to a functioning nor a humane society. There were only individualists who would maximize their usefulness, their freedom within the boundaries defined by the rights of others. A society as a coherent whole, a community would not exist. No one would do something useful, something charitable, for others. No one would sacrifice himself for his family, no one would nurture or support his parents in old age, or strive to educate his children. Socially necessary honorary offices would no longer be accepted. Politicians would only use their offices to maximize their own benefit. For the benefit of the community, society, the state, or the nation, no one would stand.

Conclusion and Summary

The view that honesty is stupidity seems not only to have established itself in the economy, but throughout the society. "You have to be able to afford morality" and "you have to watch out for your own," are common phrases. Public spirit and a willingness to make sacrifices have been replaced by a thoughtless benefit maximization. Social education is subject to variations, which we called zeitgeist. If there were ideologies at the beginning of the twentieth century that demanded self-sacrifice for the supposed general good, today the individual and its benefit maximization is the dominant idea. People had the same predispositions over the past few centuries as

(continued)

---

[6]See Hay-Group (2011), p. 8.
[7]See Leisinger, Klaus M. (1997), p. 144.

they do today. Immorality was always rife, and after a time a cultivated civilization developed morally, then often fell back into the middle ages.[8] Still, there were other, more moral times and societies. How can these moral changes be explained? Morality is above all a social problem, and has always been so, at least since people have been dependent on one another in groups. The church had a monopoly on interpreting morality for the last 2000 years, or at least until the enlightenment. Whether the result was morally irreproachable is another issue. According to Immanuel Kant, enlightenment is a person leaving the nonage they themselves are responsible for. This sounds well enough, like freedom and escaping moral slavery, but it is also like a second expulsion from the Garden of Eden. A shortcoming of the modern age is that people are left to their own conscience, and must make the choice between good and evil on their own. It is the "you mayest" of the American author John Steinbeck, who expresses the ability to choose even as the meaning of life. For an average person this balancing act between good and evil is almost impossible without help from outside. Leaving the self-imposed nonage has led to a certain loss of orientation.

This disorientation is not unproblematic. It is probably the tree of knowledge in fact, from which Adam and Eve ate the apple. They can distinguish between good and bad actions, which means they have the fundamental aptitude of conscience. The right path is not handed to people without their own effort, however. They must work for it, or to put it another way, people are not born good, but they can improve. This can take place internally through increasing mental maturity or externally. This phenomenon is called socialization, and is the forming of human behavior patterns through rewards or negative sanctions and role models. We could also call this one's upbringing. Parents are not the only ones to educate their children, rather the whole society influences people through these mechanisms.

On the way to total freedom, more and more rules and norms are abandoned, more and more taboos are broken. This trend, however, should be questioned by society, because it is also a way to total individualism. Does this route offer more advantages than disadvantages for society? Does the trend have to be steered into the socially desired pathways?It becomes clear that due to the technically driven economic and social changes, we can assume less and less duty ethics combined with social control. To this extent, we agree to the statement of Homann, but we arrive at other conclusions than the moral economy. It must be the other way round: the greater the freedom of the individual, the greater the morality of man. If the prince and the church no longer sanction men for moral misconduct, if there are little or no

(continued)

---

[8]Such as in Germany during the time of National Socialism

pre-determined rules, then the individual must have internalized the socially desirable behavior by inner values, so called ethos. The more modern the economy is, the more important are morality and values for the development of the productive forces.[9]

A total state control of human behavior is both impossible and undesirable, because individual behavioral freedom should be abandoned. This also applies to the control of employees in companies. This gap must close moral, ethical behavior, and business ethics also applies to the economic sector. It has to influence the behavior of the people in the economy in such a way that the company productivity and the common good are maximized.

In conclusion, many authors point to a tendency towards individualism and materialism. It is a question of a "change in values", a neglect of the classical class and profession ethos, as well as an erosion of traditional values such as honesty, justice and solidarity.[10] In the following, we will ask ourselves what business ethics can change in this environment.

Comprehension Questions

1. What is meant by so-called individualization?
2. What are the reasons for this?
3. What is the significance of this development for business ethics?

5.2   Basic Conceptions of the Market

The worldview that stressed individual freedom and responsibility, and encouraged individuals to pursue their own self interest made its way into economics via Adam Smith (1723–1790). A division of labor increases productivity, and a strict system of competition prevents monopolies. The unifying idea of the classical school, its liberalism influenced by the Enlightenment, is that self-interest within the context of competition works in the interest of the economy as a whole (Invisible Hand).

The socio-political, legal and economic concepts of liberalism are:

1. Democracy
2. Rule of law
3. Market economy

---

[9]See auch Dahm, Karl-Wilhelm (1993), p. 8.
[10]See Pritzl, Rupert F. J./Schneider, Friedrich (1999), p. 327.

In the so-called free market economy, self-determined, self-responsible individuals with private property act in their own interest and pursue individual goals (pursuit of happiness). Everyone is trying to increase their own welfare. If there is competition in the market, this can only be achieved by above-average performance at below-average costs. If man wants to improve his fate, he must work hard to provide the market with a desirable product. This is how the self-interest of people through the market as an institution becomes a productive force for the community.

According to David Hume, Stinchcombe and Friedrich A. von Hayek, there is also a cultural development process.[11] Sociology calls this the process of natural selection. Unsuitable patterns of behavior and rules (institutions) will fail along with the groups that have chosen them. Cultural development is thus process of trial and error with an uncertain outcome. Legal constructions (institutional arrangements) such as private property, as well as money and credit, and even the market economy itself have benefited the groups that introduced them. Forms of social coexistence and social organization are tried out and adopted if they garner economic success and social acceptance, and are otherwise discarded. If a society does not choose its structure this way it risks losing in competition with the other societies, which also describes a cultural development process. For example, one could argue that with the collapse of socialist and communist systems, the private property form of ownership prevailed. However, the process of natural selection by elimination is very slow. More crucial is the selection through human thinking and learning from experience (trial and error). This is especially true for the design of economic systems and general social order.

Group Work Transfer the economic thinking of Adam Smith into our time:

- Which political party in your country best represents the position of liberalism?
- What do you understand by democracy and the rule of law?

Solution
A democracy includes freedom of expression, freedom of the press, and freedom of assembly. Policy is largely determined by the people (demos), be it directly through voting or in representative democracy through elected representatives.

The rule of law requires a legal system, laws to which everyone is subject, including the state. Citizens must be protected against encroachments from the state by a constitutional organ, in our case the Federal Constitutional Court. The judges must be independent and incorruptible. In addition, there must be a separation of powers (concept of the french philosopher Montesquieu); independent judiciary, legislative and executive. In Germany,

---

[11]See Wiswede, Günther (1985), p. 195, Hayek, Friedrich August von (1976), p. 39, 40 and 59; Hayek, Friedrich August von (1979), p. 154ff and 167 and Noll, Bernd (2002), p. 29.

the division of authority by the appointment or promotion of judges by the Ministry of Justice is slightly limited.

→ Give examples of countries where all three criteria exist and countries where this is not the case?

We sum it up:

▶ **Definition** The basic ideas of the free market economy are that self-determined, self-responsible individuals enjoy private ownership, act in their self-interest and pursue individual goals (pursuit of happiness), while their decisions are coordinated anonymously and powerlessly over markets where contractual freedom prevails.

In general, the polypol is cited as a perfect market. Here special conditions apply.

Assumptions of a polypol as the perfect market:

1. Homogeneous goods
2. Perfect information
3. Prices adjust with infinite speed.
4. Suppliers and buyers are not able to influence the price (price taker).

→ The supply of companies will be extended until the price equals the marginal cost.

The market coordinates the plans of supply and demand. Price is the controlling instrument. It signals shortages as profit potential and overproduction as loss potential (information function) and thus enables companies to make the desired offer available.

The equilibrium prices, as marginal cost prices, reflect the efficiency of the market and the competition. As a social benefit they lead to the maximum social surplus in the form of producer and consumer surpluses. As long as there is competition, the market mechanism produces equilibrium prices and quantities. These are pareto and production efficient because at the equilibrium price in a polypoly the marginal utility is equal to the marginal cost. It is then not possible to produce goods cheaper or more efficiently (see Fig. 5.1). All economic subjects have exchanged and reached a pareto optimal state. Households either exchanged their products with each other by means of money or bought the products of

Fig. 5.1 Stable market clearing at the equilibrium price. For p * applies: limits of buyer's willingness to pay = price in monetary units = marginal production costs

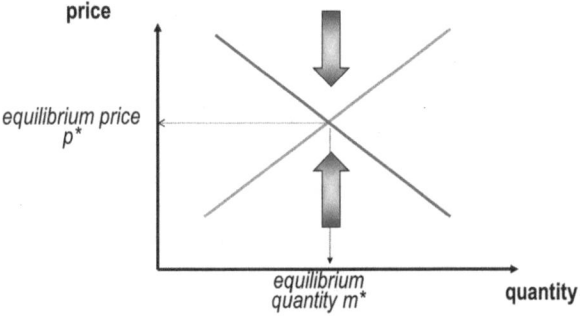

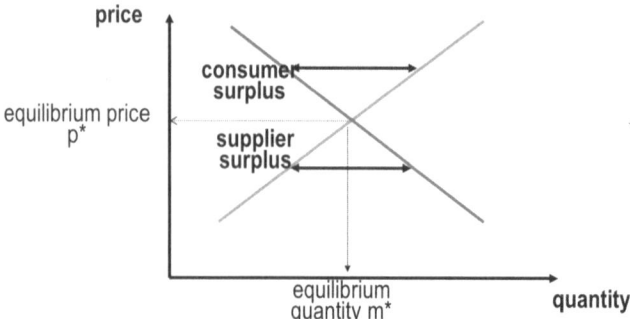

Fig. 5.2 The Marshall supply and demand cross

companies and therefore have maximum benefits. The companies are at the profit maximum, the profit representing a benefit maximum for the company owner.

Prices set too high lead to an oversupply. As companies compete for customers the price drops until it just covers the extra cost per product, and consumer surplus rises at the same time. The equilibrium price is equal to the marginal cost of the last company offering. If the company sold cheaper, it would lose money. For the household, the same applies. If the price is too low, not all buyers will get a product. However, the marginal utility of the buyers is higher, so they will offer a higher price in order to obtain the goods. They increase the price until it is equal to their marginal utility. If they were to buy more products, the benefit from the price of the good would be higher than the benefit of the purchase. With the money for the purchase, the household could have bought a good with a higher benefit. Outbidding raises the price and thus the producer's income (see Fig. 5.2), which maximizes consumer and employee benefits as well. The plans of vendors and buyers are matched by p, which is also a signal for the new plans.

5.3   How Does the Market Economic System Work?

The market economy is described by many authors as being driven by common sense, using morality, social values and even solidarity. Starbatty contradicts Dietzfelbinger that morality and market economy have different rationalities, that is, the market can be immoral, but he believes that these are two ethical designs. Molitor sees the market economy as a moral institution, because it has the prosperity of all as its goal and it achieves best results. Here, he compares the pure market economy with the central administration economy. For him the higher productivity and the higher degree of freedom for the individual are an ethical advantage of the market economy. He sees the central social ethical justification in its orientation to the wishes of the consumers, as the prosperity of all. The market economy is considered to be ethically superior to alternatives such as a planned economy (central administration).[12] In principle, the Catholic Church is in favor of this assessment:

> "At the national level of the individual nations as well as those of international relations, the free market appears to be the most effective instrument for the creation of resources and for the best satisfaction of needs."[13]

However, the Catholic Church does not see the market economy as sufficient to satisfy all human needs. For a Christian ethic, the basic statement of the pastoral autonomy of the Second Vatican Council is that man is the author, the center and the goal of all economics. This essentially corresponds to Kant's rules for reasoning.

5.3.1   Functions of Competition

What comprises the system as a whole? What rules apply in the so-called market economy? What does market economy have to do with morality? Or, to ask it a different way, do market forces encourage or hinder moral and ethical behavior? We examine these questions in the following sections.

Because of its various forms, there is no generally accepted definition of "competition."[14] The core of the market economy competition could be seen as at least two market participants who compete with each other on the supply side and the demand side. In a market economy the decentralized decisions are made by individuals and coordinated via the market. Each participant is responsible for their own economic plans and decisions, and is then rewarded or punished by the market. The strength of the market economy is that all the productive forces of individual people are stimulated and coordinated. The limit is only human potential and their creativity or inventiveness and their level of education. The basic prerequisite for the development of market economic forces is competition with transparency in what is offered on the markets. Private property and the improved economic situation it brings for the individual is the main incentive of the market economy. Markets and competition fulfill various functions together.

The ethical result of the market economy can be attributed to competition functions.[15] The market provides the basis for the elementary competition functions with the price signals and the market mechanism. Prices indicate scarcity, costs, profit potentials and benefits (opportunity utilization). Without market competition, however, the market does not provide any allocation-efficient results.

---

[12]See Molitor, Bruno (1989), pp. 71.

[13]See Max, Reinhard/Wulsdorf, Helge (2002), p. 290.

[14]See Herdzina, Klaus (1984), p. 9.

[15]See Conrad, Christian A. (2005), pp. 23.

There is no universally accepted definition of competition because of the many forms it can take.[16] The basic character of competition in a market economy can be understood as the contention between at least two participants on the supply side and those on the demand side.

Static Competition Functions
Static competition functions have a short-term effect, dynamic competition functions long-term. If you want to get a rough idea of the length of this short term, you could imagine a period of up to 2 years.

1. Steering function
   Competition forces companies to adjust their supply to correspond to the wishes and needs of their consumers (Consumer sovereignty). A supplier who is not oriented to the wishes of the customer will sell nothing, thus fail in the market.
2. Incentive function
   The reward (profit) in competition is the motivation to perform well, which is the basic requirement for productivity. This reflects Adam Smith's idea that people perform for the market in competition to improve their own lives, their well-being.
3. Sanction function
   Competition ensures that only those companies that use their resources efficiently (productive efficiency) and are guided by market requirements can remain in the market. The entrepreneur who does not produce what the market (consumers) wants or who does not use resources efficiently in production is sanctioned. Here, the sanctions emphasize loss of income or even exclusion from the market, which is the livelihood and wealth of the company. Here the liability for misconduct in the market has the greatest effect.
   Incentive and sanction function are the two sides of competition; reward for market orientation and punishment for long-term disregard. A monopolist exists outside of these rules, however. If he wants to increase profit, he only has to increase prices depending on the price elasticity of demand.
4. Distribution function
   Competition leads to fair market remuneration and thus provides motivation for good performance, which is in turn the basic requirement for productivity.
   Competition leads to a marketable, performance-based pay. The market, and more specifically the people as market participants, reward performance via their willingness to pay and through the conditions of competition.
5. Allocation function
   In a national economic system the desire to maximize profit produces the dynamic in which the raw materials with the best value are used in production. As we have already seen, striving to maximize profit guarantees that the raw materials to offer the best

---

[16]See Herdzina, Klaus (1999), p. 9.

quality for the lowest price are the ones used (*1st allocation function*). In addition, the most cost-effective company has the highest demand and can attract more production because it has the most room to maneuver with its prices (*2nd allocation function*).[17]

Companies achieve optimal success when their costs equal the profits from an additional unit of production. When they have enough influence, in other words a lack of competition such as in a monopoly, entrepreneurs will set a price far above their costs. Competition forces prices down towards the production costs through dispersed market power. Lower prices are then charged for a higher quality product, both for finished products and raw materials. This increases consumer profit in the case of finished products and the international competitiveness of a country for raw materials, thus indirectly also affecting employment. Competition guarantees that over the longer term only companies using their resources efficiently (*productive efficiency*) can stay on the market (*sanctioning function*). Trying to keep a step ahead of one's competitors prevents resources from being wasted and encourages relative prices to be corrected for production factors.

6. Freedom function

   Competition provides a lot of leeway for those participating in the market to develop their potential. Companies can decide how to make profit but also take responsibility for their decisions, workers can change their employment, and consumers have the freedom to choose between many different offers.[18] Everybody is free to make their own decisions but also resposible for them.

   As we discussed in Chap. 3, freedom for people is a value in itself. Behavioral experiments showed that people have a need for self-determination. They want to have the freedom to take their destiny into their own hands and react to restrictions of this freedom with resistance (so-called reactance).

7. Control function

   The competition of many players for buyers or suppliers automatically ensures a limitation of economic power. Dominant positions cannot exist in competition and thus have no power over market participants.

Dynamic Competition Functions

1. Adaptation function

   The competition we have described thus far is in reference to a point in time and is thus referred to as static competition. The dynamic character of competition is especially

---

[17] According to empirical estimations, in a polypoly – as opposed to a monopoly - the static welfare gains in one period alone constitute 10% of the GDP. This is assuming there are no secondary effects. See Scherer, F. M. (1997), p. 11.

[18] See Berg, Hartmut (1999), p. 233. The Freiburger School sees the equivalent of democracy in individualistically oriented competition, and thus the prevention of a dictator.

important for the growth process of an economy, however.[19] Successful companies must also continually try to gain a competitive advantage over their competitors by offering new products and new production techniques (*adaptation function*).

If companies do not continuously adjust their production to market requirements in response to changing demand structures, optimal international division of labor or other external influences, they will be sanctioned by the market. For example, labor-intensive products such as textiles or toys are manufactured today in Eastern Europe or Asia. The reason for this is the lower labor costs there and the sharp drop in transport costs in recent decades. German companies that did not relocate their production to these countries lost their market position and with it the sales of these products.

Friedrich August von Hayek portrayed dynamic competition as a process of search and discovery, through which things are discovered that would otherwise have remained unknown or at least not made use of. Competition is evolutionary for Hayek,[20] which applies to both product and process innovation. Innovation can be understood in this context as the economic application of a discovery, in other words invention. In the expectation of above-average rewards from the market an entrepreneur is always searching for cost-effective methods of production and new products for which there is a potential market demand. The entrepreneur conducts risk assessment at their own cost or analyzes external research results. The market decides the success of an innovation and thus in the end the consumer or producer that further refines a product has the last say (*innovation function*). Should an entrepreneur decide not to bother with innovation and invention, they will be pushed off the market by their competitors (see adaptation and sanction function). It is clear that the functions of competition and adaptation are closely connected with each other. If companies fail to adapt their products to the demand structures on the market and international division of labor, they will also be sanctioned by the market.

2. Innovation function

   According to Friedrich August von Hayek, dynamic competition is a process of search and discovery.[21] Hayek characterizes competition as a process for the discovery of facts (process or product innovations) that would either remain unknown or at least not be used if there were no competition. These facts enable pioneer profits and a place in the competition.

   The successful innovation of the pioneering entrepreneur gives him a competitive advantage in the marketplace over the entrepreneurs who have retained their old production structure. For Hayek, competition is above all evolutionary. At some point, all products and production processes were once an innovation. For example, Apple's iPhone was launched as a product innovation on the market. This was the

---

[19]See Heuß, Ernst (1968), pp. 29 for the importance of competition for the growth process.

[20]See Hayek, Friedrich August von (1969), p. 249 and Starbatty, Joachim (1987), p. 164.

[21]Hayek, Friedrich August von (1969).

combination of known techniques to create a new product. Traditional cell phones like those from Nokia did not have the iPhone features. Apple was a pioneer and got the monopoly profits as a reward for the market for innovation. When Samsung phones came out with their smart phone, prices fell. Here the imitation function starts as a competition function.

3. Imitation function

According to Joseph Schumpeter,[22] competition is a process of innovation and subsequent imitation (*imitation function*). The successful innovation on the part of the pioneering company proves a competitive advantage over other companies on the market that have maintained their old production structures. Above-average profits are won from this advantage, which in turn makes other companies want to copy the invention, or even forces them to do so if they do not want to be pushed off the market. This is how the new, resource saving methods of production come about, and thus brings about widespread technological progress and production growth.[23] Innovation and sanction functions thus support each other in dynamic competition.

Having explained the central static and dynamic functions of competition we can now derive the **criteria of market conformity,** which has been developed by ordoliberalism (see Sect. 8.1.1). All market interventinons of governments have to be market conform, thus they must not impede the functions of competition. Otherwise the productivity-enhancing impact of the functions is reduced. We will apply this criteria to the central administration economy in Sect. 5.9 and to the industrial policy in Chap. 9.

From the perspective of the individual companies it would be positive to restrict competition. For one thing, when a company profits from an increase in its market power, such as those from a monopoly, it reaps the benefits without having to work for it. Competition is also a nuisance, in that it forces companies to constantly better their performance. If they do not adapt to the market and innovate they must face losses or may even have to withdraw from the market altogether.[24] The state must protect competition in order to make sure that companies cannot elude the competition functions. Are these functions applicable at the international level, though?

The competition forces companies to continually try to gain competitive advantage through new products or production processes, or at the very least to catch up with the competitors' competitive advantages. On the one hand, this reduces the use of resources and, on the other hand, adapts to changes in the relative prices of production factors.

---

[22]See Schumpeter, Joseph Alois (1911).

[23]For an explanation of "Schumpeter's entrepreneur" see Dürr, Ernst (1987), pp. 245 and Vickers, John (1993), pp. 17.

[24]See Drude, Michael (1991), p. 7.

This principle must be the same internationally,[25] though there are country-specific absolute and comparative cost advantages (Ricardo's Theory of Comparative Cost Advantage). According to Ricardo even a unilateral liberalization of foreign trade would give the importing country an advantage. Scarce production factors in individual countries would balance out internationally, which would in turn lead to higher total productivity.[26]

The largest part of world trade takes place inter-sectorally, which means within a branch and between the western industrial nations that have similar cost and demand structures such as capital and labor provisions. How does foreign trade come about even when there are identical cost and demand structures? This can be explained by the specialization of the producers to various demands. Foreign trade as cross-border competition forces the suppliers to orient themselves to the international demands and or to qualify themselves for a market niche. The broad pallet of products to result from this process is also a gain in welfare. Gains are also possible digressively, in other words with a reduced amount of production within the framework of international specialization. With the increased demand corresponding to the world market, production amounts increase and thus unit costs decrease.[27]

In principle then, globalization as national markets growing closer together into one national market leads to an overall higher level of welfare. How the benefits are distributed is another question. This is mostly because with changes in international production the jobs are shifted and cause short-term structural unemployment.

Unfortunately the advantages and functions of the market and competition are not public goods, which is surely the main source of the rejection and hate directed at the market, and at the international market in particular. The willingness of states to explain and educate is desperately needed.

Can the market process really regulate everything based on human egotism? Does the market really need morality? Is it really true that the more profit companies make, the more immorally they behave? Do the laws of the market even allow companies to act morally?

5.3.2   A Free-Market without Social Rules?

An extreme free-market orthodoxy is considered as one of the causes for the subprime crisis. A spoke word of the investment bankers is "rules are for fools". Greenspan and many U.S. politicians such as Reagan were against rules for the economy. Rather, they wanted to

---

[25]Empirical proof of the positive effects from import competition on productivity can be found in MacDonald, Porter, Baily, and Gernsbach as well as in the studies from the EU-Commission on gains in welfare within the European domestic market. See Baily, Martin/Gernsbach, Hans (1995); Commission of the European Communities (1988); MacDonald, James M. (1994); Porter, Michael (1990) and Scherer, F. M. (1997).

[26]See Conrad, Christian A. (2003a).

[27]See *Conrad, Christian, A.* (2005) and Bender, Dieter (1992), pp. 419-448.

unleash the market forces in order to create more growth. Continental Europe, however, demanded stronger regulation of financial markets. The reason are different conceptions of economics. As Fox points out:

> Europeans tend to be less hostile to government as regulator and more sceptical of private cooperation as servant of the public interest.[28]

In Continental Europe the most spread economic concept is the Ordoliberalism. It does not share the optimism that the market would develop perfectly without state intervention, however, since it might be in the interest of companies to rid themselves of irksome competition, such as price agreements, mergers, vertical restraints etc., and secure profits through a monopoly.[29] The individual freedom in the market is a competition policy goal for ordoliberalism inasmuch as the assumption holds that companies will try to abuse their freedom at the cost of others within competition processes.[30] Thus a strong state is necessary to channel the behavior of market participants through laws and prevent or remove restrictions to competition through intervention.

Adam Smith was aware that the invisible hand alone is not sufficient to protect the common good from damage by individuals. He stressed the necessity of an economic system and a system to keep order, which did not exclude intervention to protect the common good. An individual enrichment at the cost of the common good cannot be tolerated by a society for several reasons. Besides the damage that is done to the national economy, such behavior has a degenerative effect on the system. Only if the legal system functions well and there is "trust in the sovereignty of the state" can trade on markets develop to the advantage of people, according and create welfare. Smith also identifies the most important components of order to be internal security, jurisprudence, infrastructure, educational institutions and national defense.[31] Adam Smith had already differentiated between an economy and an economic system. The economic system must set the framework for economic behavior in such a way that the invisible hand of the market and competition can develop optimally, meaning that the actions of people determined by their own interests are channeled for the common good. The economic system has the task of setting and implementing the rules for competition and the markets. Adam Smith was thus the first theoretician of order. Unfortunately he did not analyze the importance of the framework for economic order in depth.

The opposite view is represented for instance by Milton Friedman. An extreme belief in the market is expressed for instance in the answer Friedman gave in reaction to the balance

---

[28]See *Fox, Eleanor M.* (1986), p. 983.

[29]See Starbatty, Joachim (1983), pp. 570.

[30]See *Starbatty, Joachim* (1983), p. 569 and *Hildebrand, Doris* (2002), p. 160.

[31]See Smith, Adam (1776), chap. III, first paragraph.

sheet scandal in the USA at the beginning of this decade. He said, "Don't do anything, the market will regulate itself!"[32] Is that really the case?

5.3.3   Moral Goals and Market Economy

The market cannot solve all human problems. The solution that the market has developed is that each person pays for the performance they want. The problem creates a demand that creates its own supply. The market only knows the principle "due ut des" as the principle for trade. This mechanism often functions, but not always. The reach of market forces is limited. Superordinate and subordinate relationships have always exited. In every group of apes or humans there is a social order. There are also different mental and physical capabilities and different access to resources, especially in humans, which determines power, dependencies and hierarchies. For example, the resource distribution in Latin America and many developing countries cripples their economic development. Whoever was able to grab something now owns it. Lands and assets have often been inherited within the same family for centuries. Like noble titles, the children of these families have inherited the fortunes of these families without any effort of their own. They have the capital for worthwhile investments, however. Distribution of assets and welfare are therefore set, just like the hierarchical relationships. Anyone without land must work for the others as a dependent employee. In order to change anything in the order and the distribution of wealth, one must have power and even use violence. If this is the case, power through strength or access to resources is a central factor in the social order, which is much stronger than the market mechanism. The given factors of power make the question of whether spontaneous market mechanisms and their ability to fix themselves are sufficient, or whether the state must provide an additional framework with its order and even directly intervene in the market mechanism obsolete. The voluntary, mutual, advantageous exchange of goods is more of the exception. The market mechanism can only ever control a small part of the societal exchange process, so it is more of a question really of how much and which system of order, and when the market mechanism is appropriate and when it is not. This question is settled to a large degree by the social framework conditions, as will make clear with the example of Russia.

A lack of property means dissatisfaction, since threatened survival means having to enter into dependent employment, or the rental of one's own time and labor. The distribution of income in a market economy is only oriented towards performance to a certain extent, since the initial distribution of wealth is differently inherited. However a market economy system with the correct conditions provides for a distribution of income based on performance, and thus leads to a more balanced equity distribution with time.

---

[32]See Schwarz, Gunter Christian/Holland, Björn (2002), p. 1672.

Business ethics places people above the economy, and assumes that the economy should serve the people. There are other perspectives on this, whereby economic success justifies the means. Economics would then be placed above morality. According to Calvinism, economic success is s sign of God's benediction. Economic success is thus not only morally legitimized, but those with success have been chosen by God. There can hardly be a greater incentive to strive to earn more. Hard work and asceticism are then the fundamental characteristics of a successful Calvinistic enterprising personality.[33]

This idea contradicts the original Christian belief of justified wealth. This has been expressed in sayings such as "it is easier for a camel to go through the eye of a needle, than for a rich man to enter the kingdom of heaven."[34] Theologians from the middle ages demanded that no Christian work as a salesman, since breaches in loyalty, honor and virtue would result from exchange with the promise of profit in the spirit of greed.[35] Market prices were felt to be unfair (Thomas von Aquinas (1224/25–1274 A.D.) or generally the income distribution of the market, because it was not based only on performance and it completely neglected human needs. The Christian economy was to be a responsible and thus free proposition and establishment of as many individuals as possible for the good of everyone.[36] Adam Smith (1723–1790), shared this view with his "invisible hand" of the market that led to the benefit of everyone.

The moral expectations confronting economy is ancient. Aristotle (384–322 b.c.) had already differentiated between the art of naturally acquiring or procuring and the art of enrichment (chrematistic) which he condemned because it did not naturally occur but was rooted in the weakness of mankind. Striving after money becomes an end in and of itself, which distances man from his natural purpose, namely satisfying the elementary needs for a good life. Aristotle places virtue above economics because man can only achieve happiness by exercising his virtues. The perfect virtue for Aristotle is justice, which serves as a norm for the economy. He does not understand distributional justice as the equity of needs as did Socialism, but rather equal for the equal and unequal for the unequal. According to this principle from Aristotle there must also be a redistributive justice, which balances out unjust distribution results such as those from fraud.[37]

Moral Property
The human factor as individuals is the central actor in the market economy. In a market economy the market mechanism coordinates the plans of individuals through the market

---

[33]Max Weber had already recognized the source of the positive economic developments in Switzerland, the Netherlands, England and parts of Germany as being from the Protestant or Calvinist influence. See Ulrich, P. (1993), Sp. 1168f and Noll, Bernd (2002), p. 166.

[34]See Schwarze, Gunter (2007).

[35]See Wilkening, Hans-Rüdiger (2004), p. 61.

[36]See Beutter, Friedrich (1989), pp. 56–75.

[37]See Schefold, Bertram (1989), pp. 19–55.

price which matches supply and demand. The basic prerequisite for a total economy to develop optimally is that competition dominates the markets. Private property and its augmentation are the main incentive for individual economic activity. More is required than just the free interaction of supply and demand for such a complex system to function, however. For example, to transform a socialist planned economy into a market economy, allowing free price-setting and creating private property is not sufficient. What good is property if it is not protected or acquiring it is not regulated? The market economy conditions are thus much more extensive than those according to the theory of order from Walter Eucken, and include a functional legal system, among other things. Insufficient attention was given to the necessary conditions in the consultation for the countries leaving Socialism or Communism, as we saw in the example of Russia. With the currently dominant mathematical and quantitative perspective being taught, the market is assumed to function ideally. The human factor is systematically ignored because it cannot be put into deterministic models due to its often irrational nature. People are equal in their rights, but not in their behavior. Thus the market economy could not be successfully established in Russia. People are formed and socialized by their environment from birth. Market economy behavior must be practiced. The market economy demands a different behavior from individuals than planned economies do, such as individual responsibility. An abrupt changeover from planned to market economy is like suddenly demanding a spoiled housecat go catch its own dinner. It is not possible to just switch from a feudal agrarian system or a tribal or clan system to a market economy with individuals that can hardly be controlled without going through an adjustment process.

For the mendicant from the Dominican order, Thomas von Aquinas, all goods are God-given. They are only entrusted to people for their earthly use. Like Aristotle he rejects ownership as an end in itself. Property should serve the good of humankind. He rejects common property as well, since no one would feel responsible for it. According to the idea that "property binds," those who have possessions should give some to those in need. Property is generally to be used with consideration for others.[38]

Even without using God as an argument the question of justifying the use of property arises. Property can serve a single individual or the community. If an economy is to serve the good of the community, property may only be obtained through participation in the economic process. Performance on the market, thus evaluated by other people, contributes the most to the general good via the rules of the market and competition. Deceit or theft is obtaining services or property from others without reciprocation, which is usually only possible through devious means or the use of force.

Moral values are expressed e.g. through "fair competition". This includes the moral demand that the fruit of the market, income, should only be received by those who contribute, in other words those who outdo their competition through an exchange of effort on the market and open competition and not through advantages. Whenever assets are not

---

[38] See Beutter, Friedrich (1989), pp. 56–75.

earned through effort, the community will not accept an unequal distribution. In extreme cases assets are immoral, when they are obtained through theft and fraud. Societal approval as a motivation to perform well disappears in such cases. The motivating model of the American dishwasher who worked his way up no longer has any effect, since effort does not pay off. Property is therefore above all a motivation to perform well. Adam Smith was the one to recognize its importance the most comprehensively. On the other hand, as Smith considers the cause, or driving force, behind the development process to be the constant striving of people to improve their material situation, those who are "satisfied" and those who are hungry but cannot amass assets are hardly motivated to make an effort. The development of productive forces thus requires equitable rewards for performance as the distribution principle for income and assets, which the market evaluates as the location of all material needs of the community.

It is of no importance for the market and the general good whether the performance comes from the necessity to meet one's basic needs or from limitless greed, glamour and power. The market is only interested in the performance, not the motivation. The individuals bear the consequences, not the community. Each person has just one life and must decide how to invest his energy during his lifetime and for what ends, insofar as conditions allow. However, for the community it can be a problem if too many individuals make egotistical economic gain their life goal, seeing ruthless property maximization as an end in and of itself.

Independent of subjective assessments, the economy may not be its own end, which applies for all instruments used by people to survive since they have existed. The economy must serve people, not the other way around. This statement is always universally valid, including this era of globalization.

What role should money play in a market economy as property? Money functions as an exchange and value retention device, as well as a unit of calculation with all of the price signal and competition functions connected with it. Money is of central importance in a market economy. Because of its value retention function, money represents purchasing power and thus power. The market mechanism consciously relies upon egotism and the human striving to enrich themselves, and money is the means to do so. Money makes it possible for the market economy incentives and thus Smith's invisible hand to function fully. Money should always be a means to an end however, not as a dominant societal goal in and of itself that replaces other important goals including social morality. For example, if we assume that the end justifies the means, it would mean that every damaging action for other people or the community would be justified. The top manager who sold his stock to others even though he knew his company would do poorly would be a societal role model just because he got rich. Social morality is thus an important corrective in a market economy. If a market economy works for the advantage of the community, the community must condemn immoral, damaging behavior through legal punishments or social exclusion.

For Kant, the market has its limits where dignity is at stake and therefore there can be no price:

In the realm of purposes, everything has either a price, or a dignity. What has a price, in its place can be put something else as equivalent; which, on the other hand, is superior to all price, and therefore does not allow any equivalent, that has a dignity.[39]

For the market and for the general good, however, it is irrelevant whether the service meets a necessity for the satisfaction of basic needs or arises from boundless greed, courage and power. Only the performance on the market counts, not the motivation. Individuals must bear the consequences in this case, not the community. Everyone has only one life and, as far as possible he has to consider precisely towards what goals he uses his life and energy. For society, however, it can become a problem if not only a few individuals, but many see their life purpose exclusively in the selfish economy, that is, in the unqualified property maximization as self-purpose.

Moral values can be found, for example, in the term "fair performance competition". This implies that the moral demand that only those who perform well receive the fruits of the market, the income, that they not disadvantage competitors in the market and that they succeed in fair competition through their own efforts. If assets are not earned through performance, there is also a lack of public acceptance for unequal distribution. Or, in the extreme case, wealth is even immoral if it is acquired by robbery and fraud. Performance motivation, social recognition, then ceases to be effective. The motivating role of the American dishwasher, who has worked hard, is missing. Performance is not worth it. If an immoral success without performance becomes the rule, performance is no longer worthwhile and the productivity of the market system decreases. The same applies if the property acquired through performance is regularly robbed or taxed too high.

Property is therefore primarily a means of motivation. This was recognized as early as Aristotle.[40] Adam Smith recognized its importance most extensively. Conversely, when Smith sees the cause or driving force that determines the process of development in the constant striving of man to improve his material situation, people who are "full" and people who are hungry, but cannot acquire property, are little motivated to perform. The unfolding of productive forces therefore presupposes a fairness of the distribution of the income and wealth. It has been shown in Chap. 3 that people demand a fair distribution of the collective gains in order to participate in group performance.

What forms of justice are there? We differentiate between (1) Justice of performance, (2) Justice of exchange, (3) Justice of distribution, (4) Justice of needs and (5) Social justice.

1. Justice of performance

   The basis for remuneration is productivity in the company. What added value does the employee provide? Here the result decisive, not the effort. If the results of individual

---

[39]See Kant, Immanuel (1785), p. 434.
[40]See Aristoteles (1991), p. 17 or 1263a.

employees cannot be measured, as in large corporations, the effort and willingness to commit (commitment) are often chosen as a reward criteria. It can be advantageous for the employee to stay longer in the office, even if he does not do any productive work.

2. Justice of exchange

Is assumed for voluntary exchanges as both parties agree only if the exchanged benefits are beneficial for both and seen as fair.

3. Justice of distribution

Distribution is a relative measure and refers here to income and other rewards. There is a distribution within the company and a distribution of income in the economy. Both distributions are perceived as being justified only if they are transparent and their criteria are recognized.

4. Justice of needs

Justice based on need is different from just exchange because entitlement to benefits based on need or urgency is considered just.

Karl Marx proposed the quality of necessity ("each according to his needs"). This is about the urgency with which an individual needs an income. For example, a single-parent unemployed mother is in a state of emergency. In this respect, it would be more appropriate to give more to her than to a high-income woman without family obligations.

5. Social justice

The goal here is that all individuals in society have the same income chances. For example, Workers are to waive wage increases in order to employ others.

The market distribution is not just based on performance. The remuneration for value is determined by the market (also called market fairness) such as when the market compensates scarcity. Here it is not based on effort, but on the result and the evaluation by the market. The reward is based on competitive conditions and people's preferences in the marketplace. This becomes clear in fashion and art objects. Here, the performance can be completely irrelevant if everyone wants to own the output of a popular painter or fashion designer.

Competition can only assure a fair outcome in the markets if it is not limited, for example by monopolies, cartel agreements, or corruption. The same applies to the cases that are regulated in the law against unfair competition, such as misleading buyers about product characteristics, exploitation of inexperience, and other forms of fraud.

Justice of exchange is often assumed in market transactions to be voluntary. If both improve their position in the exchange, the welfare of all is improved (Pareto efficiency or overall economic optimum, see Sect. 4.1.1). However, consideration must be given to whether there were dependencies or power positions. Rawls speaks of procedural justice in this context. Economic procedures should lead to fair distribution results. For example, competition on the markets as a procedure ensures a fair result only if it is not limited by monopolies, cartel agreements or the like, or eliminated by corruption.[41] The competition thus legitimates the market economy as an ethical process. In order to ensure fair competition, there are competition authorities and laws regulating how unfair competition law is regulated, such as misleading buyers about product properties, fraud, and exploiting inexperience, etc.

For example, if the employee is dependent on the employer to ensure his/her survival, it can not be assumed that the "voluntarily" accepted wage is just because it corresponds to the employee's performance. In this context, the unions are important in order to establish a fair method. They have the task of bundling the interests of employees into a negotiating position, thus balancing the unequal distribution of the economic power of many "small" workers (suppliers) against a large monopolist labor market (bilateral monopoly).

The justice of needs is a contrast to the justice of exchange, since a claim is regarded as just if it is based not on a performance but on a need. For example, Pope Leo XIII said in the social encyclica "Rerum novarum" that a worker must be able to earn with his wages, his livelihood.[42] But we do not find any need for justice in the market economy.

In the case of the justice as regards performance, remuneration is based on the performance as assessed on the market. Productivity is the basis for this assessment. The value added is generated by the employee or the company. This does not depend on the effort made, but on the result and the evaluation by the market, which is measured as demand.

Ultimately justice is considered very subjective. For example, equal pay for equal work was demanded by the East German workers after reunification. Objectively, however, due to the old economic system the East German workers were less productive than the West German workers. The well-known principle of equality by Aristotle is therefore: "The same is to be treated equally and unequal unequally."

Despite evaluations being subjective, one thing must be said about the economy that applies to all the instruments that have been used by man since his existence to secure his survival. The economy is not self-serving, it has to serve man and not vice versa. This statement is always and universally applicable.

Conclusion
Market and competition together provide an allocation-efficient result. While the market provides the information, the competitive features ensure the best possible involvement of the market players. At first glance, competition is a zero-sum game: one person can only increase their degree of achievement if the target achievement of

(continued)

---

[41]See Rawls, John (1999), pp. 73 and 240.
[42]See Papst Leo XIII. (1891), No. 34; Höffe, Ottfried (1997a), p. 93; Schmidt, Heinrich (1982), p. 225 and Göbel, Elisabeth (2010), pp. 152.

at least one other person decreases, It's just like a sport in which everyone struggles to finish ahead of the other competitors.

The winner gets the prize and maybe there will be a reward for the second and third places. It has been shown that as a whole society profits from the competition of companies. Yet competition also encourages individuals to perform and rewards them, making competition worthwhile for the individual as well as companies. There are losers in competition too, in which cases society is obliged to secure at least the survival of the losers using welfare gained by the competition. This will be shown later in the chapter on Social Market Economy.

Exercises

1. What is meant by the sanction function?
2. Describe the allocation function.
3. Why are the three dynamic competitive functions important? Explain briefly how it works.
4. Assign the examples below to the respective competition functions. The examples may fit several competition functions.
   (a) The invention of of the assembly line and serial production by Henry Ford at the beginning of the previous century (Ford model-T) lowered production costs and allowed Ford to make so-called pioneering profits. He was the first to use process innovation, which allowed him to undercut the competition. The competitors were also forced to introduce series production. Ford was not able to hold on to its pioneering profits thanks to the existing competition and had to lower prices in favor of its customers. A broad range of people could then afford a car.
   (b) An entrepreneur produces 2 million pink rubber boots for the German market but nobody wants them.
   (c) Consumers do not have to buy the pink boots, but the producer can offer them if they want to. People are free in their decisions, but they have to bear the consequences.
   (d) Competition allows independence for supply and demand. If there are several competing textile producers, the textile workers can apply elsewhere if they are treated badly.
   (e) A textile producer buys his yarn from his brother in Germany. The market for textile products is opened to foreign competition. The foreign price is about 20% below the German price. Competition forces the textile producer to purchase the cheaper yarn from abroad.
   (f) The textile producer who cannot sell the pink rubber boots suffers a loss and must leave the market.

(g) Steel was the most important raw material until the 1970s. In addition, after the Second World War there was an over-demand for steel to rebuild European industry. The market price showed this through a high profit margin on the manufacturing costs, which is why many companies invested in the expansion of their steel capacities. There was a massive overproduction crisis in the Seventies and the price of steel fell drastically. Many steelworkers lost their jobs, and some companies had to close or merge. In this adjustment process, capacities were adjusted to demand again.

(h) A textile producer uses a computer-controlled fabric punching machine to produce shirts with less fabric than the competitors, making them 20% cheaper. As a result, they undercut their competitors by 10%, allowing them to sell more shirts cheaper.

(i) Our company succeeds in turning the pink rubber boots into a lifestyle product within the framework of a skilful advertising campaign and thus generating demand that far exceeds supply. The entrepreneur could thus sell the entire lot far above production costs.

(j) A dynamic young entrepreneur sells his house to build his idea of a recruitment agency on the Internet. He works proverbially day and night and is very successful and after 3 years can buy a new house twice as big.

(k) A manager takes over an ailing company (management buy-in) from his boss. He works day and night and creates a turnaround.

References

Aristoteles. (1991). *Politik II, Werke Band 9/II*. Darmstadt.
Berg, H. (1999). Wettbewerbspolitik. In D. Bender et al. (Eds.), *Vahlens Kompendium der Wirtschaftstheorie und Wirtschaftspolitik, Bd. 2, 7. Überarb. Und erw* (pp. 299–362). Munchen: Auflage.
Beutter, F. (1989). Klassiker des ökonomischen Denkens. In J. Starbatty (Ed.), *Thomas von Aquin* (pp. 56–75). Munich: Beck.
Conrad, C. A. (2005). *Die Notwendigkeit, die Möglichkeiten und die Grenzen einer internationalen Wettbewerbsordnung – Reformansätze vor dem Hintergrund derzeitiger außenwirtschaftlicher Problemfelder und der Doha-Welthandelsrunde*. Berlin: Dunckner & Humblot.
Göbel, E. (2010). *Unternehmensethik*. Stuttgart: UTB.
Herdzina, K. (1999). *Wettbewerbspolitik* (5th ed.). Stuttgart: UTB.
Kant, I. (1785). Grundlegung zur Metaphysik der Sitten, (A). In W. von Wilhelm (Ed.), *Werksausgabe Band VII*. Frankfurt: Suhrkamp, 1974, first edition 1785 Internet-edition (B). Accessed April 17, 2015, from http://www.korpora.org/kant/aa04.html
Leisinger, K. M. (1997). *Unternehmensethik, Globale Verantwortung und modernes Management*, Munich 1997.
Leo XIII (1891). *Über die Arbeiterfrage, Enzyklika RERUM NOVARUM*. Accessed April 4, 2015, from www.christusrex.org/www1/overkott/rerum.htm
Mitteis, H. (1976). Über den Rechtsgrund des Satzes "Stadtluft macht frei". In E. Kunz (Hrsg.), Festschrift Edmund E. Stengel zum 70. Geburtstag am 24. Dezember 1949 dargebracht von

Freunden, Fachgenossen und Schülern. Böhlau, Münster u. a. 1952, S. 342–358, (Auch in: Carl Haase (Hrsg.), Die Stadt des Mittelalters. Band 2: Recht und Verwaltung. 2. Auflage, Darmstadt 1976, ISBN 3-534-04680-3, (= Wege der Forschung 244), S. 182–202 Berlin, 1963).

Noll, B. (2002). *Wirtschafts- und Unternehmensethik in der Marktwirtschaft.* Stuttgart: Kohlhammer.

Rawls, J. (1999). *A theory of justice* (Harvard University Press, Cambridge (revised edition 1999)). Accessed March 4, 2015, from http://www.univpgri-palembang.ac.id/perpus-fkip/Perpustakaan/American%20Phylosophy/John%20Rawls%20-%20A%20Theory%

Schäfer, M. (2009). *Geschichte des Bürgertums.* UTB: Köln.

Schefold, B. (1989). Klassiker des ökonomischen Denkens. In J. Starbatty (Ed.), *Platon (428/427–348/347) und Aristoteles (384–322).* Munich: C.H. Beck.

Schmidt, H. (1982). Technik. In G. von Schischkoff (Ed.), *Philosophisches Wörterbuch* (21st ed.). Stuttgart: Kröne.

Schumpeter, J. A. (1911). *Theorie der wirtschaftlichen Entwicklung. Eine Untersuchung über Unternehmergewinn, Kapital, Kredit, Zins und den Konjunkturzyklus* (München und Leipzig: Duncker & Humboldt, München, 1911).

Schwarze, G. (2007), *Gibt es gerechten Reichtum? oder Wie kommt das Kamel durch's Nadelöhr?* In Von einer Tagung in Brandenburg, Morgenandacht. Accessed from www.oekonomie-und-kirche.de/diskussion/Kamel.pdf

von Hayek, F. A. (1969). Freiburger Studien. In F. A. von Hayek (Ed.), *Der Wettbewerb als Entdeckungsverfahren.* Tübingen: Mohr (Siebeck).

von Hayek, F. A. (1976). *Law, legislation and liberty. The mirage of social justice* (Vol. 2). Chicago: University of Chicago Press.

von Hayek, F. A. (1979). *Law, legislation and liberty. The political order of free people* (Vol. 3). Chicago: University of Chicago Press.

Wilkening, H.-R. (2004). Competitiveness und Ethik, Herausforderungen an das Management. In R. Berndt et al. (Eds.), *Wirtschaft und Ethik – aktueller denn je!* (pp. 59–75). Zurich: Schriftenreihe der Graduate School of Business Administration Bd. 11.

Wiswede, G. (1985). *Soziologie* (1st ed.). Landsberg am Lech: Verlag Moderne Industrie AG.

Theory of Economic Systems

6

What Follows Why?

After discussing the functioning of markets and competition and showing that they achieve our desired welfare optimum, let us now turn to the institutional framework of the two alternative economies within market economy and central administration. Like our social market economy, most economies in the real world are hybridized to these two alternatives.

Learning Goals

You should be able to explain the functions, advantages and disadvantages as well as the essential differences between the two systems in your own words.

6.1 Theories of Justice

What ideas were there to regulate social coexistence and economic activities and the distribution of the resulting goods? What is meant by a just social order?

It was Thomas Hobbes who defined justice in 1651 independently of God and thus provided the first scientific theory of justice in his main work "Leviathan". He imagines a natural state of people without state order. The consequence would be anarchy as a state without property and legitimacy. His image of man is not just a utility maximizer, but a wolf. "Homo homini lupus est",[1] so that the abolition of the state order would result in war of everyone against everyone, "Bellum omnium contra omnes". Man is not fair, because he

---

[1] Hobbes dedication in his work "De Cive" an William Cavendish, den Grafen von Devonshire.

© The Editor(s) (if applicable) and The Author(s), under exclusive license to Springer Fachmedien Wiesbaden GmbH, part of Springer Nature 2020
C. A. Conrad, *Political Economy*,
https://doi.org/10.1007/978-3-658-30884-1_6

pursues only his own interests, with which he comes into conflict with the interests of others. For reasons of humanity, therefore, man decides to restrict his natural freedom by, in the context of a social contract, entrusting to a sovereign the task of enforcing peace and justice by force. Justice is then expressed through the treaties and the legislature of the sovereign.[2]

For David Hume, 1748, justice is not logically grounded, but a value-judgment that has emerged as a habit. But justice is also the virtue that ensures order in human life. Extreme deficiency leads to a collapse of social justice, because only those who act egoistically can survive. Based on a shortage of everyday necessities, there can be no need-based justice. Only in a land of milk and honey can everyone get what they want. Like Adam Smith, he sees equality of justice as central justice, because it best promotes society's well-being.[3] He rejects the original natural state described by Hobbes as false, because the family stood as a community before the state formation by larger groups. There were already rules and education, but also a caring love that can not be transferred to larger groups. States can only be formed if there are already social orders.[4]

In contrast to Hobbes, in 1823 John Locke developed the idea of a divine right of nature that was given to man by the Creator. These are life, freedom and possessions. Citizens assign the task of enforcing or protecting natural law to the state. Unlike Hobbes, the articles of association can be recalled at any time if the state does not adequately represent the will of the citizens. Locke developed law enforcement (Judiciary, Executive and Legislature) as an instrument to control the power of the government. The legislature is elected by the people and is bound by a constitution. The government is also bound by the laws.[5]

Rousseau also starts from a natural state. Man was not originally selfish, but peaceful, self sufficient, and compassionate. The fruits of nature belonged to all humans and the soil to no one. Only through the development of agriculture did property become property. Labor-acquired property is beneficial to Rousseau, but not the property that enhances inequality, for the rich as through agriculture, because it increases wealth through the work of the poor. Freedom and equality are lost and greed and domination gain the upper hand. A way out of this unjust society is only offered by a social contract (contrat sociale) in which citizens transfer their rights to the state. It then has to represent the interests of the community. The interests of the community are not identical with the sum of the individual

---

[2]See Hobbes, Thomas (1651), Chaps. 13–31 and Ebert, Thomas (2015), pp. 130.
[3]See Hume, David (1748).
[4]See Ebert, Thomas (2015), pp. 143.
[5]See Locke, John (1823).

interests, since these are only for themselves. Starting from his postulate of equality,[6] he calls for social redistribution by the state in order to restore social justice.[7]

> Enlightenment is man's release from his self-incurred tutelage. Tutelage is man's inability to make use of his understanding without direction from another. Self-incurred is this tutelage when its cause lies not in lack of reason but in lack of resolution and courage to use it without direction from another. Sapere aude! 'Have courage to use your own reason!'—that is the motto of enlightenment.[8]

For Kant equality, freedom and respect for the rights of others result from reason. The personality and dignity of man must be respected. Through reason, for example, he develops the categorical imperative, which can be regarded as an essential basis for human coexistence and thus also for jurisprudence.[9]

The categorical imperative:

> Only act according to the maxim that you can make a universal law.[10]

For Kant, maxims are guidelines that people give themselves. In addition, there are generally applicable human laws, which therefore absolutely apply categorically.[11] And the practical imperative:

> Act in the way that you use humanity, both in your person and in the person of each other, at any time not just as means but also as a purpose.[12]

How do my actions affect people? The purpose of my action should be to do good, or at least not to harm anyone.

The sociological institutional theories go back to Durkheim and Weber. Because man is free in his actions, social rules are needed to avoid damaging others. Therefore, even interests cannot lead to stable social relationships or orders. For this purpose, the morality of a group (Durkheim) requires legitimate systems of order (Weber).[13] "I can only be free to the extent that someone else is prevented from exploiting his physical, economic, or

---

[6] *"L'homme est né libre, et partout il est dans les fers." Rousseau, Jean-Jaques* (1762b), *Du contracts social ou principles du droit polititiques, Livre 1, capitre 1.1,* https://www.rousseauonline.ch/pdf/rousseauonline-0004.pdf, *english:* "Man is born free and everywhere he is in chains".

[7] See Rousseau, Jean-Jacques (1755), p. 117 and Rousseau, Jean-Jacques (1762a).

[8] Kant, Immanuel (1784), pp. 481–494.

[9] See Ebert, Thomas (2015), pp. 177.

[10] See Kant, Immanuel (1797a), (C), p. 421.

[11] See Schmidt, Walter (1986), p. 47.

[12] Kant, Immanuel (1797a), (C), p. 429.

[13] See Weber, Max (1980/1922), pp. 16; and Maurer, Andrea (2017), p. 135.

other superiority, which he holds in order to suppress my freedom; only social rules can prevent abuse of power."[14]

Karl Marx sees the dependence of labor on capital, that is, the ownership of factories, as the reason for the injustice in income distribution. Only when property belongs to everyone in communism can one say: "Everyone according to their abilities, each according to his needs."[15]

For Hayek, there is a legal and political equality of people, but not economic. Hayek emphasizes that the rules of the game are given by the market and that changing the rules of the game only worsens productivity. If the game's rules are followed, the result is fair. Hayek is, however, in favor of a social security at subsistence level. It is therefore possible to have an adequate life, but no distribution justice in the sense of equal distribution. A social policy that conforms to the market does not change the rules of the game, but it can increase the satisfaction and security of society and thus the productivity of the economy.[16]

For Rawls, a social order has the task of overcoming conflicts and harmonizing citizens' interests. The social institutions are formed according to the social ideas of justice. Institutions such as the rule of law, private property, competition rules, etc. enable welfare profits for all involved. There is a primitive state in which the members of the society, who are entitled to equal rights, commit themselves to a basic order which everyone considers to be just. They do this to benefit from the collaborative gains (e.g., Prisoner's Dilemma Game). These are therefore the public goods which only a state as an organized community can make available to the individual. In doing so, a veil of ignorance helps to establish the principles in which no one knows what role he will play under what conditions and qualifications. According to Rawls, those involved will then agree on basic human rights such as equality before the law, democratic freedoms, the rule of law, human rights, and so on. Central to all concerned is equality of opportunity. Inequalities are only allowed if they bring about an advantage for the least favored person (principle of difference). Rawls is therefore committed to a market economy with a welfare state with a social redistribution, especially in the education sector (egalitarian liberalism). A high savings rate should increase the fairness between the generations.[17]

In 1986 Gauthier developed a morale based on utility-maximizing rationality. Moral behavior is chosen when it benefits the individual. According to this, moral behavior of not cheating one's competition, that is to say cooperation, brings cooperation gains over several rounds in the theoretical prisoner's dilemma. Prerequisite for a stable cooperation solution is mutual trust, because otherwise people would protect themselves from cheating by non-cooperation. In addition, imperfect market conditions must be replaced by a fair,

---

[14]See Durkheim, Émile (1988) and Büttner, Sebastian M. (2017), pp. 47.

[15]See. Marx, Karl (1972) and Ebert, Thomas (2015), pp. 230.

[16]Vgl. Hayek, Friedrich August von (1971); Hayek, Friedrich August von (1981), p. 112 and Ebert, Thomas (2015), p. 327.

[17]Vgl. Rawls, John (1971) and Ebert, Thomas (2015), pp. 291.

negotiated solution. For this it is important that fair starting conditions for negotiations are created. There must be enough rationality that the negotiated solution does not fail due to unrealistic maximum demands. Everyone has to be better off with the negotiated solution and it is optimal if the cooperation achieves a maximum result with minimum concessions that are the same for each one (justice as a minimax principle).[18] This approach thus corresponds to the image of man of homo oeconomicus and of economics[19] as a justification for morality.

Scanlon takes up the rationality of Kant and derives principles of justice from a universal balance. In terms of content, the postulates must be recognized by other persons, in other words the society, as undeniable (**contractualism**). On this basis, he advocates egalitarianism. Gross status differences lead to humiliation, which is why human equality should be improved. In what he calls equal opportunity, power should be limited in the economic system, as it leads to an unequal income distribution. Economic freedom limits economic power. Redistribution is intended to improve the situation of people in great need, but people have to shape their own lives and are responsible for their own quality of life.[20]

Habermas rejects legal positivism, natural law and reason as justifications for societal regulations, ie institutions such as law. Laws cannot be derived from higher principles, because the complexity of society would cause them to fail. Since religious and metaphysical legitimacy are no longer effective in modern society, social norms must be accepted by society. Law and morality as social ideas belong together and are subject to social change. For this purpose, the individual must be convinced of the correctness of the rules, consider them to be just because he was involved in their determination, understands himself as a "reasonable author of these norms". The law thus obtains legitimacy through a social discourse on the structure of the rules, in which all concerned must be involved. Democracy, the rule of law and public free opinion forming an important basis for this.[21]

Starting from Hegel, Honneth develops a theory of justice that emphasizes intersubjective relationship, social interaction and recognition. It is not about isolated individual ideas of freedom of the liberal justice theories, but about equal rights in the form of recognition of

---

[18]See Gauthier, David (1986); Heil, Joachim (2005), pp. 197 and Herlinde Pauer-Studer, (2015),pp. 75.

[19]A moral framework should be designed in such a way that self-interest becomes socially productive. Homann transfers the utility maximization from Adam Smith to all spheres of life, referring to the economist G. S. Becker. See K. Homann (1999), pp. 322–343, pp. 335 and Conrad, Christian, A. (2018), pp. 32.

[20]See Scanlon, Thomas M. (1998); Wallace, R. Jay (2002), pp. 429–470; Wallace, R. Jay (2002), pp. 429–470; Scanlon, Thomas M. (2018) and Weisshaar, Kenneth R. (2018).

[21]See Habermas, Jürgen (1992); Mazouz, Nadia (2009, pp. 263 and Goppel Anna/Mieth, Corinna/ Neuhäuser, Christian (2016), pp. 236.

equal rights by the other fellow citizens. Justice is thus not primarily the distribution of goods, but the distribution of rights and duties among each other. In this way, Honneth sees distributive justice and needs-based justice derived from charity, as well as the performance justice derived from the fair division of labor and an expression of social esteem.[22]

For Sen, prosperity is less about material wealth, but about freedom of design, which allows people to shape their lives according to their own needs. Freedom is thus a value in itself. A society is fairer the more self-realization opportunities it offers people. Sen includes political and economic freedoms, equal opportunities, freedom of expression and the press and social security, such as social assistance in such opportunities. For Sen, the social institutions must promote justice. Sen has developed this approach together with the UN, which has been an international standard for capturing the evolution of states.[23] He sees utilitarianism and Kant's ethics of reason as an approach to global justice. Global justice in terms of equal opportunities could—as Sen critically notes—only be enforced by a world government, which he considers unrealistic.[24]

Conclusion

Kant's principles of reason, democracy, and the separation of powers have largely prevailed. Equality, freedom and respect for the rights of others arise from reason. The personality and dignity of man are reflected in human rights. Hume is right to say that the scarcity of goods requires economic activity in the form of labor, which goes hand in hand with deprivation. It is not the desire for organized work that determines occupations, but the shortages or the needs of the people. There can therefore be no need-based justice, but a compensatory social redistribution that protects against unfair acts of fate and makes possible a humane life in the interest of human dignity. The redistribution must be made by others who are willing to do so, otherwise they will emigrate.

As we discussed in Sect. 4.5 on the topic of fairness, people on a non-performance based income tend to regard equal distribution as fair. However, the willingness to give up earned income is much lower. And there is a conflict of interest regarding willingness to perform. The willingness to work in equal distribution for income is very low.

This requires a social discourse that weighs the balances sacrifices and needs against each other and a democratic decision-making process, which is supported by all citizens. However, this does not require a veil of ignorance, but the recognition of

(continued)

---

[22]See Honneth, Axel (2007); Axel Honneth (2011); Baschek, Nicklas (2012) and Horn, Anita (2018), pp. 16–40.

[23]See Sen, Amartya (2000, 2001, 2003, 2009).

[24]See Sen, Amartya (2001); Böhler, Thomas (2004) and Dierksmeier, Claus (2013).

one's own position in the common system. It must be made clear to what extent the individual benefits from the state and what he has to do for it. For this purpose, trust of the citizen in the machinations of the state with its rights and contributions is required. In order to finance social compensation and livelihood security, it is necessary for citizens to realize that they themselves can get into such a situation, then they would see the contributions as an insurance premium. As the presented behavioral studies on groups have shown, it is additionally beneficial for citizens to identify with each other, since compassion favors the willingness to make a donation.

Justice thus results from social discourse. Inheritance tax increases equality of opportunity when used to finance a public education system.

Civilization is the central strength of humanity. By sharing work in a large group, productivity benefits can be realized. For the organization of this division of labor states were founded and the "natural rights" were transferred to the state. The financing and provision of public goods is the central task of the state. These benefits are for anyone who submits to the rule of the state.

Even Durkheim and Weber see the need for rules. Recognized institutions must be enforced by the state to protect the individual and enable civilization. Society must agree on morality and give itself group rules.

Following the rules of the market maximizes the social return from the division of labor. Imperfect market conditions must be supplemented socially or corrected by the state. Competition limits power and increases freedom. Freedom is seen by humans as a value in itself. The state institutions must provide the framework for economic and social freedom.

Justice is an order that is socially accepted. Prerequisite is the freedom to choose between the social roles, ie duties and rights. Changes can often be brought about only by revolutions. According to Hayek, society evolves evolutionarily. Social market economy increases productivity and the technical development of the economy determines social roles.

Global justice in the sense of equal rights can only exist in public goods, to which all people have the same claim. All other goods were taken over by the settlement and agriculture and historically fought or defended. Global justice will therefore only be able to refer to behavior towards each other. In the sense of universal human rights, the rights of others must be respected. Help in times of need will therefore always be voluntary.

Social decisions are not unproblematic as group decisions. They do not automatically lead to the best decision for a society. The influences on group decisions that cause the informative exchange to be impaired, leading to decisions that are normative based instead of informationally based (groupthink), must be prevented. In addition, even public good games have shown that group interests and individual

(continued)

interests can diverge. Only if everyone participates in the financing of a public good such as a legal system or infrastructure, the public goods come about. Individual interests can also directly oppose this, if, for example, a highway is to be built for the community, but to do so a property must be expropriated or lose its value due to external effects. For this reason, no social rules can arise from individual interests. Individual interests would always try to achieve personal gain, but never weigh the personal interests up with conflicting other individual interests and they would never represent the overriding group interests. So you need a social discourse about the common rules and the form of fairness that the group wants and enforces against individual interests. The result is democracy as the rule of the group. Alternatively, you can hire a third party to represent the common interests, a monarch, but then the group must control the pursuit of common interests.

Comprehension Questions

1. What is meant by "homo homini lupus est"?
2. Why is there no need for justice, according to Hume?
3. What problems does Rousseau associate with property?
4. Why cannot there be economic equality, according to Hayek? What does he offer as a solution?
5. From what does Honneth derive performance justice and needs justice?
6. Why are the self-development opportunities of people so important to Sen?

6.2   Constitutional Economics

Constitutional economics examines the rules, the constitution of the economy in its functioning, with the aim of shaping them so that they serve the interest of the affected individuals. The consent of the individual applies as an objective evaluation criterion. The order is considered legitimated when all indivuals agree (methodological individualism).[25] What is problematic here is that individuals agree on their own with regard to their preferences and goals, with which the subjective interests of individuals become the basis of legitimation (normative individualism). Objective function criteria or superordinate common interests are not considered.

"The critical normative presupposition on which the whole contractarian construction stands or falls is the location of value exclusively in the individual human being".[26]

---

[25]See Vanberg, V. J. (1997), 707–726; p. 713; Vanberg, V. J. (1998), p. 70.
[26]Brennan, G./Buchanan, J. M. (1985), p. 25.

However, an agreement of all individuals means unanimity, whereby a design or change of the rules only succeeds if all individuals have the same interests and a decision is organisationally possible.[27] Vanberg deduces the constitutional economic importance of consumer sovereignty from the precedence of the citizen's interests where individual benefit is greatest. Entrepreneurial interests are then subordinate. Consumer sovereignty is best supported by a performance competition that comes from the school's public policy free school.[28]

Buchanan broadens economics by the rules that bring people economic and political benefits.

> My argument was that economics, as a social science, is or should be about trade, exchange, and the many and varied institutional forms that implement and facilitate trade, including all of the complexities of modern contracts as well as the whole realm of collective agreement on the constitutional rules of political society.[29]

According to Buchanan, traditional economics deals with the voluntary relationships between economic agents. Constitutional Economics examines the institutional framework in the form of rules that organize economic and social coexistence. People subject themselves to rules, thus voluntarily restricting their freedom in order to benefit from those rules. While traditional economics examines and attempts to optimize the behavior of economic agents within the given institutional framework, Constitutional Economics addresses the effects and optimization of the institutional framework, including the political framework.[30]

Constitutional economics, like the Freiburg School, places the shaping of the economic order in the foreground and looks for optimal rules, but more specifically, voluntariness places citizens' approval of the rules in the foreground.[31] The Freiburger Schule, however, saw welfare maximization of the population as a central goal. If one supplements the main principles of competitive order as per Eucken with the principle of the ability to assent and adds consumer sovereignty to citizen's sovereignty, Order Theory becomes Constitution Theory.[32]

---

[27]See Vanberg, V. J. (2004a), p. 4; Vanberg, V. J. (1997), pp. 707–726; pp. 713.

[28]See Vanberg, V. J. (2004a), p. 19; Vanberg, V. J. (1997), pp. 707–726; pp. 721; Feld, L. P., & Köhler, E. (2011), pp. 180.

[29]Buchanan, James M. (1991), pp. 31.

[30]See Buchanan, James M. (1991), pp. 81; Buchanan, James M. (1979), pp. 17 and Vanberg, V. J. (2004a), pp. 5.

[31]See Vanberg, V. J. (1988), p. 27.

[32]See Feld, L. P., & Köhler, E. (2011), p. 182.

6.3   Parts of a Market Economic System

What constitutes an economy? How is everything related? Let's begin with the building blocks of a market economy.

1. **Legal protection of private property**

   Property is the basis of a market economy and must therefore be anchored in the constitution of a country. Without ownership there can be no incentive function from competition. Without ownership of the means of production, there is no pursuit of profit and no liability for errors in competition, thus eliminating all competitive functions but the freedom and control functions. The Invisible Hand cannot fulfill its role. Ownership of goods is also the basis for the purchasing power of money and thus for capital and thus also for saving and investing.

2. **Constituent and formative company laws**

   Business laws are necessary, such as bankruptcy law, competition law, HGB, Stock Corporation Act etc. They are the basis for liability and contractual freedom.

3. **Tax Law**

   To finance the state or community you also need a tax law.

4. **Institutions or organizations for law enforcement**

   An executive is necessary to enforce the law. A multi-level legal system with independent judges is required to ensure legal certainty. Defendants must be able to have a judgment reviewed by another judge to prevent arbitrariness and dependency. Of course the judges must not be corrupt, so that fair judgments are given. Here again, separation of powers is a necessary condition. The judiciary and the executive should be separate and there should be no dependencies between them. Seen in this way, it is not in the interest of a meaningful separation of powers that the judges are not appointed by the Ministry of Justice in Germany. Other necessary enforcement bodies are the police and competition oversight (see Chap. 9).

   Secure framework conditions for business transactions reduce the risk, and hence the hedging costs, of business transactions (see Sect. 7.6). This is one competitive advantage of the FRG compared to other countries. Transactions are safer in Germany than in many other countries.

5. **Financial system**

   We also need a two-tier banking system with profit-driven private banks and a non-profit independent central bank (e.g. ECB). The role of private commercial banks is to ensure efficient capital allocation as financial intermediaries. Banks must look for profit-driven investment opportunities in the economy that offer high returns relative to risk. This function can only be carried out by commercial banks. They collect the capital (capital collection points) and thereafter ensure the efficient allocation of that capital. They are liable for mistakes they make even if this means the bankruptcy of one's own company, which is associated with a high loss of assets. If there is no liability, there are moral hazard issues. As in the financial crisis, there is a risk that profits will be privatized and losses will be socialized. An efficient supply of capital also requires a scarce supply of money. If money is made abundantly available by the central bank, it will not be carefully distributed and efficient capital allocation will not be achieved. For this purpose, a potential-oriented monetary policy is required, which means that only so much money may be circulated by the central bank since the production potential develops as a measure of the quantity of goods. If the money supply rises faster than the quantity of goods it causes inflation (see also the equation of quantity in Chap. 11).

The value retention function of money must be unimpaired in order to preserve confidence in the currency. The ban on financing public deficits and the independence of the central bank are important prerequisites in this context in order to create confidence in a policy of the central bank aimed at price stability. For this reason, a central bank is not allowed to work for profit, but can only be committed to the goal of price stability. A central bank makes profits primarily by providing liquidity. The central bank or another independent organization also has the task of supervising the commercial banks. It must monitor the implementation of financial market laws and prevent excessive risk positions (cluster risks).

From an institutional order perspective the central bank is part of the governmental system, which is why it is not allowed to buy private or state bonds on the capital market or even worse shares in private companies.

(a) The state must decide on an exchange rate system, such as flexible or fixed exchange rates. If necessary it can fix its currency to another or join the European Monetary System.
(b) Finally, domestic and foreign convertibility must be defined. This means that domestic and foreign parties can buy or sell unlimited currencies of any origin at the existing (fixed or floating) exchange rate (monetary convertibility). Restrictions may relate to a specific group of persons (national/foreign convertibility) as well as to the underlying transactions (performance/capital transactions).

6.4 Institutional Economics: Elements of the Economy

- What is the economy made of?
- How is everything related?
- Why are there companies and contracts?

From the perspective of institutional economics, economic actions are not just technical processes of production or the transfer of goods. Rather, they are transactions, thus transfers of property rights on goods.

Transaction cost theory[33]: Representatives: Oliver E. Williamson (1975–1996) and Ronald Coase (1937).

Economic decisions are implemented by market participants through transactions.

▶ **Definition** Transactions are all transfers of property rights for goods and services. The transfer of services also includes, for example, the employment activity in a company.

▶ **Definition** Under transaction costs we understand all costs that are directly or indirectly caused by the transactions.

The transfer of goods and services is associated with many costs: information, negotiation, control and enforcement costs and, in a broader sense, transport costs. For example, inspection and enforcement costs can be caused by the lack of a legal system in the buyer country for exports.

According to transaction cost theory, transaction partners choose the contractual relationship that best minimizes transaction costs. The reason for institutions like contracts is then to minimimize the transaction costs if the market solution is more expensive.

For a company, the question is: make-or-buy? Also called insourcing or outsourcing. Threecriteria of the transaction influence the optimization calculus according to Williamson:

1. frequency (is it worth it),
2. uncertainty (ie the risk to the company associated with the price management) and
3. specificity (of investment) or complexity (increase with adaptation). The more specific, regular, and uncertain a transaction is, the more it speaks for an internal, "hierarchical" coordination. According to the respective combination of transaction frequency and specific investments, one can differentiate between three types of contracts:

1. **Classic contracts**

   The interaction is clearly defined by scope and time. The risk of poor execution of the contract is limited. No party expects a subsequent adjustment to the contract. For example, buying a newspaper in the supermarket is a classic contract.

   There is no risk or complexity associated with the transaction of acquiring a newspaper for either transaction partner. It is only when the buyer decides to buy the newspaper

---

[33] See Williamson, O. E. (1979), p. 18ff and Williamson, O. E. (1985) and Furubotn, Eirik G./Richter, Rudolf (2005), pp. 47.

every day that it is worthwhile for both parties to conclude a long-term contract in the form of a subscription. A subscription contract minimizes transaction costs.

2. **Long-term contracts**

A contract cannot include all possible conditions for a transaction, so some adjustment is to be expected. Security, adjustment and warranty clauses serve this purpose. For example, building a home is a complex transaction thatalso carries some risks. The buyer cannot be sure that the transaction will be implemented to his satisfaction. During the construction, adjustments and changes to the transaction may occur. Some defects show up only long after the completion of the house. Guarantee clauses are just as necessary here as they are for long-lived assets such as machines. The more frequently a transaction takes place, the more it pays off to hire employees for this and to promote them in the company. Employee contracts are long-term contracts, but frequency has an effect on transactions outside the company as well.

3. **Relational contractual relations**

Relationship-based transactions are long-term and complex. Common decisions and adjustments are expected, such as occurs throughout a project, which is why the work takes place in organizations such as companies. For example, the production or distributionof complex products are best handled internally. The quality and development of the product cannot be controlled and monitored by other companies. In sales, the commitments and negotiations must be tailored to the product. The company is not only liable for mistakes, but the customer relationship is also endangered.

Here is an example scenario: a bank outsourced its securities settlement for cost reasons but the implementation was very flawed, and customers complained. They could not submit their tax return. The board explained the problem to the head of the company, but he did not have any influence on the operation because it had not taken place within the company. The available options would be to terminate the contract with the outside company or sue for damages, but neither would directly improve the situation.

In addition to the transactions, there are relationships between people, the actors who work together. Optimization approaches have evolved over time for this as well. In the next section of this chapter we will look at organizations, institutions cooperative networks and human capital. We will then be able to answer the following questions:

- What is the economy made of?
- How is everything related?
- Why are there companies?

6.5   The Economic Division of Labor

The decisive question is thus which soft facts are relevant for productivity in a company and national economy and how they can be used. To be more exact, how can the natural tendencies, motivations and desires of employees be applied for the good of the company and other employees? What would this kind of management or company approach look like? First we want to define a company more precisely however, what its functions and special features are. Let us consult academic science. Institutional economics defines a company as "a coalition of resource owners bound by a nexus of contractual relations that is governed by a contract decision and monitory agent—the entrepreneur."[34] This definition describes the composition of a company, but does not really address its core. According to Coase, the function of a company is to avoid transaction costs. This would make companies a unit that regulates repetitive transactions internally and externally through relational long-term contracts, which would then save transaction costs. Adam Smith recognized companies as a means of organizing labor distribution and thus taking advantage of the learning process, which simplifies production and using the individual strengths of the employees. Alchian and Demsetz later stress this aspect and identify team production as the main function of a company, as did Wieland.

An important task of a company is thus to enforce cooperative behavior in the context of prisoner mentality and thus to prevent free riding.[35]

The decisive characteristic of a company is neither long-term contracts nor team production, but organization in and of itself. A company does not have to produce in a team to make profits. A bus company for example, is made up of many individually operating transportation units that are completely independent of one another. There is no team production here. The important value creation in this case is the organization of buses or bus routes.

▶ **Definition** We define organization as the systematic assignment of functions into a whole capable of action.

In our example this would be the assignment of routes to the individual buses and drivers, thus assigning functions to people and machines. Within the framework of the company organization the employees receive tasks and decision-making powers. This organization of productive forces provides productivity, from which comes the added value of the organizational form "company." The art is thus in an optimal assignment of functions to employees and machines. The productive force of the company is hidden here.

---

[34]Quoted from Novac, Eric (1997), p. 22.

[35]See Alchian, A. A./Demsetz, H. (1972); Novac, Eric (1997), S 19ff and Wieland, Josef (1999b), pp. 54.

For example this is why job descriptions in a company (tasks and abilities) must be matched with the capabilities of the employees.[36]

Why is there human culture? Only because the mathematical principle of $A + B + C = 1 \times (A + B + C)$ is disproved by life in human communities. If a group of people join forces for a common task the result of the common action is greater than the sum of the individual actions (emergence). The sum is greater than its parts, which is a human wonder because it contradicts mathematical law. In the end organizations are nothing else but societal solutions to problems that they have developed in answer to external demands and conditions. Over time social constructs come into being, which create added value through the cooperation of different people. For these people to create an added value cooperatively, several challenges must be overcome. Suitable rules for potential conflicts must be found. In companies this often takes the form of the long-term contracts mentioned. Not only do they reduce transaction costs by regulating performance and compensation between the employer and employee of the long term, which encompasses the social inclusion of the actors in team production, but they also regulate the power to make decisions and thus all internal rights and duties including the distribution of added value created in the company as income.

With cooperation people can realize as society gains from devision of labor, economies of large scale and specialization. Organised groupwork allows to combine the strength of each individual and thus to overcome the weaknesses of each individual. The types of intelligence show us the diversity of human abilities.

Social rules are called institutions in Sociology. In contrast to the organization, an institution does not create direct added value, but it is an important requirement to do so. Institutions have been created over time to overcome societal dilemma structures, such as the state legal system. A social dilemma comes from the fact without a state framework for order, it would be worth enriching one's self at the cost of others. For example, not even a bridge could be built with the guarantee of ownership, because the construction site would be constantly plundered. If only the law of the strongest applied, property would not be obtainable through labor, or at least one could not keep it, which removes a central motivation to work. Without institutions many added social values would not be obtainable.

Another social construction that creates added value is cooperative networks. These are practiced forms of cooperation or generally supportive interactions amongst many people, which create added value. Every team is a cooperative network; repetitive labor is delegated within a team and practiced in cooperation together, for example. Every team member knows what output is received from each partner. The decisive factor is the added value possible through this cooperation. The cooperation between the network members can also include the exchange of information. The added value then comes from decisions made that are more in touch with reality.

---

[36]See Vahs, Dietmar (2001), p. 62 and Conrad, Christian A. (2010).

Companies are generally made up of several interactively cooperating networks that are included in the organization as an assignment of functions. Cooperative networks also exist outside of companies however. The first such networks was probably founded in hunting groups in the Stone Age. Only together was it possible to herd wild animals or kill a large beast. A soccer team is another example of a cooperative network that is not a company. A soccer team can be created spontaneously, which makes clear that long-term contracts are not imperative for cooperative networks. An informal, mutual agreement is sufficient. Since most cooperative networks are designed to be long term, such contracts are the rule. For all social constructs based on mutuality, at least an informal agreement is required for cooperation. Otherwise the members of the network would not agree to advance concessions with their cooperation, since they are usually expecting compensation. Let us resume: Cooperative networks are social constructs, just like institutions and organizations that have been created in the society over time to create more added value through group cooperation. Cooperative networks are the first level of cooperation if measured by complexity. Organizations give structure to cooperation, putting the cooperative networks in a more complex order and hierarchy, so that more complex processes can be structured securely over the long term. Long-term contracts are necessary for this. Institutions make cooperation possible as rules that provide a framework. In principle this is nothing more than the best possible application of all productive forces, the combination of humans and machines. With this background the necessity for hierarchies is given for purely functional reasons, to coordinate processes from above and to bundle the flow of information from below upwards.

There is no corresponding example in nature for the differentiated labor distribution in human culture. Take the comparison with ants. Ants do not have differentiated possibilities for communication, nor do they have a central decision-making body that can collect and evaluate information in order to make decisions for the group. Despite these differences, the following has been observed in ant colonies: (a) they raise and milk aphids, (b) they grow trees suitable for their housing by destroying the seedlings of other trees (c) they collectively build bridges over rivers and (d) together they build living rafts in case of a flood. These are also repetitive behaviors, yet they are not consciously designed and then practiced. They must be the product of evolution. Certain inborn behaviors offered survival advantages over other species, and with this programming they were able to solve problems in a decentralized manner and were able to gain the evolutionary advantage compared to other insects. All of the estimated 10 trillion ants, including 12,000 species, amount to as much biomass as the humans living on earth.[37] Recent observations have even led to the supposition that ants have at least a certain degree of cognitive abilities. There is one species of ants for example, in which it was observed that the older ants showed the younger ants the way to food sources.[38] We can conclude from this that decentralized

---

[37] See Handelsblatt dated September 14th 2006, p. 9.
[38] See Handelsblatt dated January 26th 2006, p. 15.

solutions to complex tasks, or decision-making at lower levels taking superior company goals into consideration is indeed possible without consulting a higher instance. This assumes however, that the employees have a character like that of the ants. This would include knowing the goals of the company and the morality, or better said the willingness to follow them without supervision.

We have now worked out two important components of companies, first cooperative networks that are, second, embedded in an organization. Another important component is the human capital of the employees. If one put together a company with just any employees without paying attention to their characteristics, it would not be functional. Human capital can be understood here as all of the prerequisites and potential for added value creation in which people are involved and incorporated as productive forces. We can differentiate here between social capital and individual capital.

Social capital is all of the prerequisites for productivity a person has, but only in a group, thus social in the sense that they can only be realized within a society. The practiced cooperative and informative behavior of members in cooperative networks is social capital, because it can only provide an added value through the interaction with other people. Another example for social capital is practiced social behavior, including virtues, morals and politeness.[39] The social added value that is only created with others comes from a reduction in the transaction and control costs of all social activities. The so-called honorable salesman used to know the basic principle of "good faith." If everyone behaved perfectly morally, most legal costs and other expenses created by the implementation of rights would be done away with. Of course the problem of defining correct moral behavior and delimitation of individual rights would not be solved. The most extensive certainty of the law coming from moral behavior from individuals would stimulate many economic decisions, in particular investment decisions that would otherwise not be made due to insecurity about the behavior of others and the rights to investment profits. More productive forces would be developed and social product and welfare would increase. Morality as social capital makes decisions that are good for everyone possible, and thus increases the productivity of the company and national economy. For instance researchers at the University of Bern in Switzerland found out that rats selflessly help even unknown members of their species if they had been helped in their own past. This allows us to assume that a willingness to help proved beneficial to evolutionary goals. The more help the rat had experienced, the more help it was willing to give.[40] Individual capital on the other hand is all of the prerequisites the individual has in order to produce added value, creating value without the community or third parties. Education as a goldsmith is an example of individual capital.

---

[39]For the impact of social capital as norms on crime rates see Buonanno, Paolo; Montolio, Daniel; Vanin, Paolo (2009), pp. 145–170.

[40]See Weltkompakt dated July 3th 2007, p. 25.

Each person has various abilities as a social being and individual. An efficient business organization seeks to combine these useful qualities through a structured assignment of function—through the inclusion of real capital, for example by bringing together machinery and patents—to create a greater synergistic whole and thereby the optimal creation of value. Human capital (through individual and social capital) and real capital create for the firm the maximum benefit, or greatest possible combined interaction of assets.[41]

Is social capital created without costs? Of course not. Just like for individual capital, it needs investments over longer time periods. Cooperation for networks must be practiced, for example. This means that every member practices their function in the network and learns who can give them what information or performance, and who to delegate to. Organizations, such as companies whose design and continuation create costs, are also social capital because they assign functions and structure a whole unit capable of making decisions and taking action, including practicing processes. Except for the costs of company excursions, the costs of social capital are not included in the controlling and national economy calculations. In fact, the labor time to create cooperative networks, in other words training cooperation, should also be measured and evaluated. Forgetting this fact, and because it is perhaps only difficult or quite costly to capture it in detail, a value estimate of this capital is neglected. Unfortunately the benefits reaped from the social capital are not attributed to social capital. In general only a small part of human capital is registered, with the corresponding distortions in the allocations of resources. With the costs to build up human capital, just the costs for education or training is registered, but even so, the value created or the individual and social capital do not appear as an asset. An employee who has been trained for a task in a company has human capital, be it more individual or social capital depending on the task envisioned. If the employee is incorporated into the company for this task, additional social capital is created. His "value" for the company is realized when applied for the good of the company, just like for a machine, and corresponds to the cash value of the added value from production minus the wage expenses and the expenses of the job. Human capital in positions filled is taken all too seldom into consideration, although the company is interested specifically in the optimal development of productive forces. Analyses of employee potential, in which the companies identify the maximum contribution an employee can make to value creation are thus invaluable in order to avoid poor resource allocation.

The costs of the cooperative networks and a large part of the organizational costs for a company are recorded just as little as the company added value, which means that there is de facto no value approach. How can one explain the difference between the liquidation value of a company, thus the value of the net assets (value of the non human capital minus the liabilities) and the present value of the cash flow (or the shareholder value) as the net value creation of a company? Only through the added value that the organization, institutions and cooperative networks create via the productive combination of human

---

[41] See Conrad, Christian A. (2010).

and non-human capital. Alternatively formulated, if the cash value of the cash flow drops below the net asset value, it is often because of a poor combination of productive forces. The same applies of course in general for national economic systems as a whole and even for states. The state is also an organization, comparable to a company with branches with a systematic assignment of functions into a functional whole. Organizations, institutions and cooperative networks create added value in states as well, through the productive combination of human and non-human capital. Just like in companies, this added value is the difference between the value of a national economy's capital stock, or assets, and the cash value of the future GDP.

There are studies on the importance of social capital as common group knowledge, the so-called transactive memory. Moreland and Myaskovsky had three different types of groups assemble a radio. The groups were trained differently for this. In the first group the members were only individually trained, in the second the individuals were given information about the task-related knowledge of others and in the third group the members were trained together as a group. The result of the last two groups was significantly better than that of the group in which the members were individually trained. The most productive (measured by the number of errors) was the group with shared group training. In the experiment, the implementation was additionally evaluated according to the three criteria for a transactive memory: specialization, coordination and trust. Specialization was understood as the application of one's own expert knowledge, coordination as an optimal assignment of tasks to the respective abilities of the group members and trust in the expert knowledge of the other as fewer disputes about the assignment of tasks.[42]

Improving productive forces is about the best possible assignment and structuring of organizations, institutions and cooperative networks. This is a science of order. Seen in this light it is possible to compare order using business science and economic science to find out what combinations of organizations, institutions and cooperative networks have had the best results or which deficits have been found. Human capital varies from country to country and is difficult to capture. This is a decisive factor to develop productive forces however, and therefore for the development of a country as well. These factors are more qualitative than they are quantitative. Despite the unpredictability, at least tendencies can be identified. An ideal order like a blueprint to guide companies or the national economy does not exist, and will never exist. The most that can be hoped for is the optimization of order as a framework for a company or economy and for a certain point in time.

The Incomputability is also the main reason for the previous neglect of qualitative factors. Despite this unpredictability however, there is not only an influence from these factors, this influence is so lasting that it would be negligence not to include it in calculations. Quantitative economic science does not explain why, for example, many Asian countries that were at a similar level of affluence to African countries were able to

---

[42]See Hollingshead, A. B. (1998); Moreland, R. L. (1999); Moreland, R. L., & Myaskovsky, L. (2000), pp. 117–133 and Jonas, Klaus/Stroebe, Wolfgang /Hewstone, Miles (Hrsg.), pp. 459.

achieve economic prosperity in the last few centuries and many African countries have been fighting starvation despite development aid. The limited ability to predict and plan macroeconomic indicators is generally made clear by the different development in planned and market economic systems. The differences in the development between West and East Germany or North and South Korea after the war can only be explained qualitatively, thus by comparing the systems of order. On the other hand, Communism and Socialism were able to get many people to work until physically exhausted or to sacrifice themselves. Wages do not exist in these cases as an incentive, and the willingness to sacrifice oneself cannot be explained only through the threat of totalitarian measures of oppression. There must therefore have been an immaterial, intrinsic incentive. Why are there countries that develop into prosperous and dominant countries seemly out of nothing, increasing their capital stock many fold, just to then become meaningless and poor again without outside influence? Human capital is not a static factor. Also the institutions and organizations change.

Communism and Fascism are ideologies. Like religions, they give people clear moral values and behavioral guidelines. They give actions a purpose. Human behavior is given a value that goes above and beyond the material value, and it thus becomes a value in and of itself. Apparently many people want to believe in something good, something they can apply themselves to. They want to feel they are part of something bigger than themselves. One's personal benefit is at least partially subjugated to the greater good because individuals define benefit differently, and they feel better because of their activities for the group. Of course ideologies and religions are often abused and there tends to be a danger of being manipulated. We do not wish to preach an economic ideology, just to determine the importance of moral values as motivations for actions and behavior, and thus for the development of productive forces. Values as human capital can also advance societies as well as in particular companies and national economies by stimulating the productive forces of its people.

Humans aren't machines, and almost all of them question the sense in their existence either consciously or unconsciously. Considered in this way moral values are like the oil in the machinery, if we want to stick with the machine metaphor. If the values are lost, the engine grinds. The gears no longer catch for the functioning of the system as a whole, and take on a life of their own. People maximize their own benefit at the cost of the whole system. Such behavior was one reason of the Enron crisis and the subprime crisis. This is not the maximization of one's interests that encourages general welfare, as Adam Smith had in mind. The invisible hand cannot do anything against corruption and embezzlement. Profit and morality are not in conflict, as is often assumed. There can be no profit without morals, either in companies or national economies.

A survey of 400 German executives showed that the majority of problem-solving competencies are seen in self-organizing networks. Because of the collective intelligence, more creative impulses, higher innovative power, acceleration of processes and reduction of complexity can be expected by this organizational form than by others.[43]

Conversely, immoral behavior diminishes the added value of organizational forms. Let us assume that employees are distrustful and do not help each other anymore. If they do not exchange information among themselves or inform themselves wrongly, the added value they can reach through division of labor and cooperation will decrease.

Immoral behavior from top managers has the greatest negative effect on stakeholders and shareholders. The company's success is endangered by immoral behavior. Moral, ethical behavior is thus very important for companies, and the same applies among the companies and in competition. As we have already described, only fair competition for performance assures an optimal allocation of resources and thus an efficient economic production. Immoral behavior damages the society as a whole, beginning with market process, internal company processes and all the way down to interpersonal relationships.

The genetic disposition towards cooperative behavior we have already described is unfortunately insufficient. Hobbes had already recognized that cooperative behavior must be worth it for the individual, and that he must be able to trust in it, because otherwise we would have anarchy. How can this be achieved? Only if society encourages cooperative behavior by rewarding it and by sanctioning uncooperative behavior. Economic laws, courts and supervision are absolutely necessary for this reason. They have the task of acting as referee for behavior in accordance with competition, so they must be able to control competitive actions and sanction missteps. Without controls and sanctions there is no assurance of fair, thus economically ethical behavior. Cooperative behavior is the same as moral/ethical behavior. People will only trust the cooperative behavior of others if they can presume moral/ethical behavior, thus morality as a social standard to measure actions that must be practiced and trained (socialization).

The disparity described somewhat provocatively at the beginning between private, rewarded morality on the one hand and societal and politically unsanctioned immorality on the other hand is a basic evil that need not exist. The society must find appropriate conditions for moral behavior, which must be worth the effort in politics and economics. This is even true for a community of apes, where deceit, such as stealing bananas or beating weaker apes in the group is addressed and usually punished.[44]

---

[43]See Initiative Neue Qualität der Arbeit (2012), p. 7.

[44]See Handelsblatt, dated 8th december 2005, p. 8.

Conclusion

Morality complements the positive effects of the market. The results of the market correspond only partially to our ideas of what is right. In case of market failure, morality ensures that third parties are not harmed. Against this background, the social market economy is entering the market and changing the distribution results. Social morality is an important corrective factor in the market economy. If a market economy is to be an advantage for society, society must discourage immoral, damaging behavior through legal penalties or social exclusion. In addition, it must promote voluntary ethical behavior through the provision of values.

In order for a society to function and to develops its productive forces, there is still the ethics of social capital which has to be in line with the orders, the system, and the economic stage of development. In this context, the attitudes of the people are particularly important for society, thus the community, and social cooperation. The norms, values and morality as well as the attitudes to the political and economic system are important.

Comprehension Questions

1. Define a company. What makes a company and what creates added value?
2. Define organization, institution, human and social capital.
3. To what extent is morality necessary for the functioning of an organization?

6.6   Institutional Challenges in Specific Game Situations

6.6.1   The Ethical Prisoner Dilemma

If all competitors behave morally it creates a fair performance competition from which all parties profit. It has already been established that the economic order has to exhibit moral behavior. If it is advantageous for a company to behave immorally, it may be forced to do so in order to remain competitive. Market advantages can result from unfair competition such as deceptive advertising, libel, etc. At the very least the trust of the consumer in the product is lost. Due to intransparency he will not buy the product from any company. This is a prisoner's dilemma.[45] Even if the company were to behave morally, it does not know how the other companies will behave, and therefore must assume immoral behavior and behave immorally in order to ensure its survival. There is a risk of an unfair predatory competition by means of concealed immoral means. The economic welfare potential cannot be achieved. The problem of ethical imprisonment always arises when no moral rules are enforced. The ethical prisoner dilemma is not just true for companies in

---

[45]See Kirchgässner, Gebhard (1991), pp. 51.

Fig. 6.1 Payout matrix of fair competition in the ethical prisoner dilemma. *Nash equilibrium is the worst case for all (Nash: No one can unilaterally improve through another strategy)

payment	B behaves morally	B behaves im- morally
A behaves morally	(5, 5)	0, 6
A behaves im- morally	6, 0	1, 1*

competition but also for companies with unethical business cultures and for the employees themselves. This also applies to the internal competition of employees within the company. Here an employee can gain a career advantage by lying. Unethical companies cannot realize the collective best case with high productivity if the employees do not behave morally. Like with Enron, the employees compete internally and do not cooperate. The return of teamwork cannot be realized.

The ethical prisoner dilemma for a fair competition is as follows (see Fig. 6.1): The worst case for a company manager A is if he behaves morally, but the company manager of another company B does not and the best case for A is if A behaves immorally, but B does not. B is in the same decision-making situation. The result is the combination in which both companies operate unfairly, thus the worst case for all (Nash equilibrium). Without ethical rules, such as law enforcement when the ethical prisoner dilemma arises, a company finds itself in the worst-case situation if it behaves ethically.

In the context of such a distorted situation, companies have the opportunity to approach the government and request a change to the regulatory framework. Unfortunately, such attempts to change regulations are rarely successful. Rather, many companies try to delay ethically motivated regulations for as long as possible. For example, Ford's self-defeating lobbying delayed Ford's security measures for 8 years to avoid the additional $11 of the plastic buffer on the petrol tank. Accident victims were accepted as a liability.[46] The egg industry, which defends the agonizing mass management of laying hens, is another good example.[47] This is due to the fact that the decision-making structure for A and B changes as a result of the company having to bear only a part of the costs of a decision in the case of decisions made at the expense of third parties (external effects, see Sect. 7.1). The payouts for third parties are therefore listed separately in Fig. 6.2. In the case of the environment, the cost of pollution is borne by the public, whose health and quality of life are adversely

---

[46]See Wörz, M. (1994), p. 22.

[47]See Göbel, Elisabeth (2010), p. 183.

Fig. 6.2 Payout matrix; Decisions on third parties in the ethical prisoner dilemma. *Nash equilibrium is equivalent to the worst case for all. The morphological/moral combination is pareto-efficient

payment A/B/third parties	B behaves morally	B behaves immorally
A behaves morally	[1, 1, (0)] **	0, 5
A behaves immorally	5, 0	[3, 3 (-10)] *

affected (negative external effects). In the case of work safety, the company can save costs at the expense of employees. In our examples above, the health risk affected Ford's customers or laying hens.

An empirical study has shown that managers are only willing to stick to moral standards when they believe their business partners are sticking to them.If this is not so, they are not willing to behave morally, even if they consider the rules to be important and meaningful.[48] In the case of the prisoner's dilemma, there is uncertainty about the conduct of the other companies. Even if they all wanted to behave ethically, they could not, because there was then the risk of coming into the worst-case situation. The solution to this problem is:

1. Educating A and B about the added value of moral behavior so that the incentive to behave morally is increased. One can, for example, appeal to the altruistic conscience or use-oriented arguments. In game theory, it could be shown in games over several rounds that it is result-maximizing if one behaves cooperatively at first, and only if the other does not behave cooperatively to counter this with an equally uncooperative behavior (trigger or tit-for-tat- Strategy, see Chap. 4.4). With many players, however, this reciprocity goes under. Here it depends on the so-called "strong reciprocators" to punish unfair behavior. Motives for the altruistic punishment of uncooperative behavior are emotions such as gratitude, desire for revenge and the pursuit of retribution. Without the feelings, no one would punish others to their own disadvantage. Getting angry about uncooperative behavior brings satisfaction and thus also a benefit if punishment has been carried out. This is the only way to succeed in altruistic punishments because there is a positive net benefit. However, this behavior can only be assumed for family businesses. In public companies, shareholders will not accept personal goals such as altruistic punishment for unfair behavior.

---

[48] See Blickle, Gerhard (1996), p. 116.

2. Moral behavior is rewarded by incentives (morality must be worthwhile) z. B. An ethical consumer awareness leads to increased sales of ethical products. Immoral behavior must not pay off for companies. Moral violations must be made known so that the actors can be socially sanctioned. This is where the non-governmental organizations (NGO) come in. The media also have a special responsibility here.
3. Binding contracts with sanction options: laws, state control and sanctions in the event of misconduct (institutions).

6.6.2 Games of the Gender Struggle Type

There are also gender-based games where there is no reward for cooperative behavior in the first round, but only a dilemma (see Fig. 6.3). The woman wants to go to the opera and the man to a soccer game. Only when the two go together do the benefits come from the evening together. Here, however, cooperative behavior is the prerequisite for any additional benefit to be achieved. The solution is that the spouses take turns fulfilling the other's wishes.[49]

This game represents the compromise. Only if you give, do you get something. Such games are always found in mutual dependence without dominance in the pursuit of different goals in politics, which is why a vote exchange takes place. Mutual dependence is the basis of human coexistence. The gains are realized in organisations like companies or states which use regulations to organize the do ut des (institutions). People accept these institutional arragements as compromise in order to get the gains.

Fig. 6.3 Payout matrix gender struggle

Woman Man	Soccer	Theatre
Soccer	3, 1	0, 0
Theatre	0, 0	1, 3

---

[49]Vgl. Kirchgässner, Gebhard (1991), pp. 52.

6.6.3 Insurance or Trust Game

Another variant of the game was already used by Rousseau for the derivation of the necessity of social contracts. Two persons A and B can form a hunting group to kill a deer (see Fig. 6.4). Each can also kill a hare alone. Now they both want to meet in the forest, but do not know if the other one is going to keep the meeting or has killed a hare to be on the safe side. There are two Nash balances as positions from which one cannot improve one-sidedly.[50] The players can contractually agree in advance to take a deer together. To enforce this penalties are required. Or they can observe the behavior of the other, and if it repeatedly comes to stag hunting, the game stabilizes, as trust is created. Like the gender struggle and the prisoner mentality, this game is the starting point for international cooperation in specific policy areas. Only together can they take down a deer, thus achieving added value. The EU Treaties are an example of this.

Which distribution results will arise from these games? With the same distribution of power, the same results tend to be had, while unequal distribution of power tends to create unequal results, which is also accepted by the players.[51] However, it will not be the case that the losing position gets nothing. This is shown by the ultimatum games. If there is too much deviation from the equal distribution, the weaker players react irrationally and the result is rejected so that the superior player receives nothing.

Conflicting Strategies, the Chicken Game, Negative Payouts
The Chicken Game (see Fig. 6.5) belongs to the Hawks and Doves Games and deals with conflict situations. The situation became known through the film "Rebel Without a Cause" with James Dean. Two people want to find out who of them is the "chicken", or the coward. They drive towards each other with two cars and whoever swerves first is the "chicken". In

Fig. 6.4 Payout matrix
Stag Hunt

B A	Stag	Hare
Stag	4, 4*	0, 3
Hare	3, 0	3, 3*

---

[50]See Rousseau, Jean-Jacques (1988/1755), pp. 233; Maurer, Andrea/Schmid, Michael (2010), pp. 221.
[51]See Maurer, Andrea/Schmid, Michael (2010), pp. 253.

Fig. 6.5 Payout matrix
Chicken Game

	A behaves cooperatively	A behaves conflictory
A behaves cooperatively	-100, -100	10, -10
A behaves conflictory	-10, 10	0, 0

the narrower sense, there is nothing to gain here, since it involves a relative change in the positions between two players (see chart).[52]

Players can strengthen their position by bluffing or self-restriction. These would be threatening gestures to display aggression and irrationality in order to make conflictual action credible. Self-restraint would be like tying a rope to the steering wheel while driving. There is also a time pressure to be the first to take the superior conflictual position to force the other to the lower position. As a solution to conflict games, it is a good idea to involve a third party as a mediator, who provides a stable distribution compromise. However, such credibility enhancement of the conflicting strategy can be used by both parties, increasing the potential for maximum damage to both. Conversely, in multi-round games there is a risk of yielding, or cooperative behavior, such as a lastingposition in a game of chicken, in which aggressive behavior no longer seems credible to the other player.

Application examples would be warlike conflicts, such as between the US and North Korea. Here, North Korean dictator Kim Jong-un managed to connect an irrational image with nuclear weapons, bringing the US to the negotiating table even as an insignificant state. The chicken game leads to divorce in many marriages, if irrationally no one wants to yield to the other,. Divorce is the crash with maximum loss for both sides. This is also the peculiarity of the game. In the non-cooperative situation there are extremely negative payouts for both players. You can win if you simulate the conflict behavior in order to bring the other player into the worse position of the "chicken". In marriage, that would be: "I will get a divorce if you do not give me that and that". Of course, this inevitably leads to the loss of a basis of trust and makes cooperation profits difficult. Therefore, in the end, such a strategy is only advisable if there are no joint cooperative gains. In the economic area, a competitor could threaten to introduce a product to prevent the introduction of a

---

[52]See Dawkins, R. (1978), pp. 83.; Gramms, T. (1999), Von Helden, Feiglingen und Anderen. http://www2.hs-fulda.de/~grams/OekoSimSpiele/Helden.html; Presteich K. N. (1999), Explanation of the Hawks and Doves Game. http://college.holycross.edu/faculty/kprestwi/behavior/ESS/HvD_intro.html; Theodor W. May (1983) and Maurer, Andrea/Schmid, Michael (2010), pp. 218.

competitor's product, or threaten to penetrate into competitor's markets with both a ruinous dumping competition. An employer might face dismissal, although it is legally difficult and involves high costs to force the employee into desired behavior or wage loss.

How should the distribution of income within a company be organized? Labor and capital benefit from division of labor as a product of the company as an organization because the assignment of functions creates an actionable whole. The employee must be able to harm the employer to avoid pushed to a disadvantageous position. If there is no coordination of all workers through unions, no strikes are possible and the worker must accept an inferior position in the distribution or leave the company (see Sect. 7.10).

Both players can avoid a negative game like in the game of chicken, in which they convince themselves to behave cooperatively, thus not to play the game. Alternatively, a third party can enforce cooperative behavior, so for example, the state can prohibit conflict behavior. And finally, morality and ethics can prevent damaging behavior, thus creating cooperative play.

As a social solution to conflictual and non-conflictual games, institutions have established themselves as social rules that are enforced through sanctions. Stabilizing behavioral expectations can prevent damage in conflictual games, while cooperation gains can be safely realized in non-conflictual games. The resulting benefits move the individual to join society and submit to the institutions, at least as long as the benefits outweigh the disadvantages. As the public good games without sanction show, the willingness to behave cooperatively decreases greatly after a few negative distribution experiences, which is why the games then collapse without sanctions. Switching to other games with sanction options, ie standards, are used by the players to increase their own benefits.[53]

6.7   Ethical Institutions and Organizations

The significance of an ethical framework has often been discussed. Without an ethical rule, thus laws which are also enforced, an ethical problem arises in which the company comes into the worst-case situation, which is unethical. Of course, positive incentives such as environmental subsidies can also help escape the ethical prisoner dilemma. After all, the state can counteract unethical behavior by trying to develop social morality and thus shape employees either before they enter the company or create a more ethical environment for the company. Ultimately, all citizens are asked to act ethically in their environment (duty ethics).

Institutions have evolved over time to overcome social dilemma structures, such as the state legal system. Institutions are made up of people who serve people. They regulate

---

[53]See Falk, Armin (2003), p. 147; Fehr, Ernst/Fischbacher, Urs (2003) and Fehr, Ernst/Gächter, Simon/Fischbacher, Urs(2001).

interpersonal coexistence, in which they place appropriate incentives, for example laws and penal sanctions in the event of an offense. Ethics, which is concerned with moral institutions, is called institutional ethics, social ethics, or even order ethics.[54]

Insofar as we are not dealing with a dictatorship, institutional ethics derives from collective ethics. All social regulations are developed and implemented by the community. An institution such as the legal system must be morally recognized by society. It is only through compulsion and control that institutions cannot go against the will of the individual. The institutions also shape the individuals who live with them. Together with non-legislative collective ethics (norms) and parents, institutions determine the socialization of individuals. Ultimately, the institutions, such as the legal system, determine the consequences of moral actions and thereby set the incentives to behave in certain ways. If there is no employment law and a prohibition of association, the employee is not only at the mercy of the employer (institutional ethics), but another employer is also hard-pressed to make concessions to his employees as he has to fear competitive disadvantages. Moral behavior is thereby made more difficult. Institutions such as democracy, with all the legal regulations on the division of powers, make it possible to exercise equitable, and thus moral, discourse ethics.

In a study that investigated why people obey laws, it turned out to be crucial for most people that they are convinced that the laws are ethical and legitimate. Furthermore, most people feel a strong commitment to follow laws that address education and protect the environment. Penalties are necessary for a minority, excessive penalties in case of violation of regulations can have a counterproductive effect.[55]

Social moral norms and values emerge in a trial and error process: a cultural evolution. They express what behavior is desired by society because it benefits society and its members. This behavior that a company considers positive is rewarded by social recognition. Conversely, negative and thus societally damaging, behavior is sanctioned by social exclusion or even by the judiciary as a social organization. We refer to people as good when they are positive for others and vice versa. Ultimately, the categorical imperative of Kant expresses exactly this: always act so that your action could be the basis of a general law, or as per the saying "what you do not want done to yourself, do not do to others." Ultimately, laws are valid for everyone and represent a social rule that should be valid for all. Equality before the law should always apply.[56]

Legitimacy derives from what reason, conscience, and public discourse recognize as justifiable interests. Legitimacy does not necessarily follow legality. Laws can also be immoral, such as the laws on racial segregation in the US and South Africa. Economic activities can be legal but unethical, such as child labor in some countries. Finally, many

---

[54]See Göbel, Elisabeth (2010), p. 34.
[55]See Tyler, Tom E. (1990) and Paine, Lynn Sharp (1994), p. 111.
[56]See also Habermas, Jürgen (1975), p. 72

unethical practices are not punishable, because a court action is often not worthwhile or the injured parties lack the necessary financial resources.

An example of the difference between legality and legitimacy from the company's point of view is the case of the 1991 Salomon Brothers. Four top managers were reported for legally non-conformist behavior at the trading table for government bonds. They had their legal department check whether they were obliged to publish the lapse, and they were not. However later, when the incident came to the public, their silence led to a massive breach of trust that led to an estimated loss of 1 billion US dollars due to customer or contract losses and higher legal and refinancing costs.[57]

The state regulates the company's dealings with its stakeholders through laws and regulations. Of particular importance are the following:

(A) Employee protection rights
(B) Protection of consumers (starting with the general terms and conditions of business, the regulation of prices, the food regulation and the Unfair Competition Law).
(C) Investor protection (from the Investment Protection Act to the Securities Trading Act)
(D) Environmental protection legislation (covers waste disposal, noise protection, air pollution, water protection and landscape protection)
(E) Animal welfare laws and regulations

6.8   Is the State of Law Sufficient?

The economy produces goods for the community to consume and invest in. This is necessary for the survival of the community, but there are also other products that the community needs. These include inner stability, including internal security, low crime rates, a general harmony amongst its members and thus a smooth functioning of societal and economic processes. There are many prerequisites for this to happen, including societal rules and laws and thus institutions and organizations to implement them. These alone are not sufficient, however. Social morality, good behavior and politeness are additional prerequisites for societal processes to run smoothly. The state as an organization cannot control, monitor and implement everything. Even if one were to attempt to do so, the expense would be enormous. On the other hand, if social rules were not adhered to by anyone the social system would collapse. Machiavelli had already realized this in his Discorsi: "Just as. . . laws are necessary to maintain manners, good morals are necessary to respect the laws."[58] This interconnection also applies to the economy, since the economy is part of the society, but we will address this in more detail later on. Good manners, morality or more generally, behavior in conformance with the community, is mostly transmitted

---

[57]See Paine, Lynn Sharp (1994), p. 110.
[58]Machiavelli, Nicola (1977), p. 64.

through social education. This basis for behavior is another good needed for the society to survive, and which must be produced by the people themselves. It is not just a question of rules and control. For instance, you cannot make a functioning company out of a prison full of criminals. Even if the criminals are controlled as well as possible, the outcome will be miserable without motivation and morality.

Market failure would occur without these laws. For example, some companies in Germany use the fact that the packaging sizes are no longer regulated by law. Price increases are hidden by a smaller packaging content. The consumer only sees that the packaging costs the same as before. Such packaging tricks are unethical because they change the exchange to the disadvantage of the customer, without informing them about what is actually fraud in the broader sense.[59]

Laws are a necessary prerequisite for the functioning of an economic and social system but not sufficient. Without morality it does not work. Laws can be ignored because either control is incomplete or the punishment is not dissuasive. Thus, it becomes worthwhile for long-haul drivers not to comply with legally prescribed rest periods and to accept a fine. And in the construction industry the legal minimum wages are undermined. Laws can be circumvented. Since children's programs are not allowed to show advertising blocks, the channels broadcast the programs as a "family program." Laws are inaccurate or leave a great deal of room for interpretation because they must be universal and cannot anticipate every individual case. For example, there are interpretable terms such as "faithfulness and faith," "carefulness," or "reasonable compensation." The Act on the Appropriateness of the Management Board Remuneration (VorstAG) merely states that the remuneration of the Management Board should be proportionate to the tasks and performance of the Management Board, the Company's position and the usual remuneration.

There is, for example, a problem of law enforcement in the economy. Economic deprivation is seldom uncovered in comparison with other illegal acts, and even more rarely punished. In relation to the consequences and the likelihood of being discovered, the penalties for economic crime are far too small. For a long time economic science has been calling for a tightening of economic criminal law. For example, the economist Gary S. Becker claims that the penalties are based on the consequential damages and the probability of discovery. The aim is that the expected value of the sentence is not less than the consequential damages for society. For example, if the impact of an action is €1 million and the probability of detection is 10%, the penalty would be €10 million.[60]

In order to comply with these laws, the acting norms and customs also need their own morality. Furthermore, society, economy and technology are developing, so that laws have yet to be enacted for many immoral acts. An example is the Internet and the mobile phone

---

[59]See Göbel, Elisabeth (2010), pp. 287.
[60]See Becker, Gary S./Becker, Guity Nashat (1998), pp. 173.

sector with new possibilities to take advantage of customers. Laws usually end at the borders of a country, which is why regulatory arbitrage occurs. By way of example, shipping companies bypass the safety regulations of their home countries by sailing under the flag of a country without regulations.[61] In general, morality or ethical awareness is the prerequisite for the emergence of laws and jurisprudence. In the case of legislation, the judge is bound to his conscience, as is the judge in case law. There can be no laws and no jurisprudence without morality.

You can also see it reversed. It is not the order that matters, but what people make of it. Here Johann Heinrich Pestalozzi can be cited as a representative of the people who believe that people can be influenced by education: "He has learned that all forms of government are of no use when people are no good".[62]

Conclusion

The economy produces consumer goods and capital goods for society. This is vital for society, but there are also other products that society needs. This is above all inner stability, which is to be understood not only as internal security, but above all a low crime rate, in general the harmonization of the citizens and thus the smooth running of social (also economic) processes. For this, there are many prerequisites: above all, social rules, laws and institutions, and the organizations to enforce them, but these prerequisites are not enough. Social morality, good manners or courtesy are further prerequisites for the smooth running of social processes. The institutions and organizations cannot control, monitor and enforce everything. If, on the other hand, no social rules were respected by anyone, the social system would collapse immediately. Where laws and control cease, morality begins. Morality regulates human behavior so as to prevent social harm.

Comprehension Questions

1. Explain the ethical prisoner's dilemma in fair competition and at the expense of third parties. What are the possible solutions?
2. Why is there a difference between legality and legitimacy?
3. Explain the extent to which morality is necessary for the functioning of a legal system.

---

[61] See Göbel, Elisabeth (2010), pp. 289.

[62] http://haus-des-verstehens.ch/tagebuch-blog/636-johann-heinrich-pestalozzi-und-rosa-luxemburg.html

6.9   Central Administration Economy

In principle, there are two ways to organize an economy: decentralized via markets or centrally via a planning authority. We call these two basic forms of economic systems the market economy and central administration economy.

▶ **Definition of Central Economy** (planned economy) the economy is planned ex ante (from the earlier point of view) centrally (a plan).

▶

▶ **Definition of the Market Economy** People plan themselves ex ante decentrally and the plans are coordinated via markets ex post (from a retrospective perspective) (many plans).

Historical examples of states in which the central administration economy was used are the GDR (German Democratic Republic), the USSR and China. They still exist in North Korea and Cuba. In times of war intermediate forms often developed, in which the state determined who produced what, however there was still private property.

Characteristics of the Central Administration Economy

1. Only ex-ante planning, no ex-post coordination of the plans. An extensive, hierarchically organized bureaucracy aggregates people's needs in the form of one to five-year plans (bottom-up) and then determines production, including resource allocation, giving top-down specifications, Companies are asked what capacity they have and what resources they need for production.
2. Planning via production balances, adjustment of plans by force
   Then they are assigned the production of end products and delivery of pre-production materials to other companies by the central planning office. The production and distribution of goods and services must be organized by a bureaucracy. To this end, the authority must be able to assess people's needs and control the optimal use of resources. Property rights must be severely encroached upon to get this control.
3. No private ownership of the means of production
   That means that there can be no private property. Companies belong to the state. In this sense, all people work for the state and, in the communist sense, for the community, ie only indirectly for themselves.
4. Prices are only politically assigned values
   There are no markets and no market prices. The prices for production are planned in such a way that they should cover the costs for the companies or are determined according to political criteria. For example, books and housing were subsidized by the state in the GDR.

This was touted to have led to advantages over the market economy solution. The main criticism of capitalism was that goods or asset distribution was seen to be unjust.

Advantages of the Central Administration Economy Compared to the Market Economy

The industrial revolution led to extreme income differences between workers and factory owners, the so-called capitalists. The market mechanism led to extremely low wages and thus to the so-called "impoverishment of the proletariat" with the excess supply of labor caused by the population explosion (see Sect. 7.10). Ownership of the means of production was considered problematic. The market only pays for things when there is a demand (and perhaps values enhanced by scarcity). The market as an institution is neither humane nor social.

The distribution of goods according to need and diminishing the power of capital was seen as a solution to this problem (see the writings of Karl Marx, and as precursors of the state designs Plato or the book Utopia by Thomas More). We saw this idea after the October Revolution in Russia first and then implemented the USSR, which led to a social form of communism in which private property no longer existed.

If the state, in other words society, owns the means of production, there are theoretically some advantages.

1. Planning security for companies and workers, no unemployment
   If all production is planned with the available workers, there is no unemployment. If there are no planning errors, there are also
2. No business cycles or economic crises.
3. Theoretically there are also no problems with microeconomic conflicts of interest, such as pollution from production, since all business decisions are ultimately made by the state, and thus welfare-oriented.

How was this approach implemented in practice?
To answer this question, let's look at the example of the GDR.

Case Study: Life in the GDR
Group work: Read the article about the GDR. What do you notice? What are the advantages and disadvantages compared to your experience with the market economy?
1 article: Impressions of the GDR central administration economy
Conversation with Marion Blumeyer, saleswoman
For years, Marion Blumeyer was a meat specialist in the deli of a consumer department store.
MDR: Ms Blumeyer, was everything delivered that you ordered?
Marion Blumeyer: No. Pork fillet, pork chops, roulades were barely delivered, the items we sold with "no". Schnitzel, pork belly and offal were always available—but who always wanted to eat those? In order to avoid misunderstandings: In the GDR nobody had to

starve. If there were no pork chops, then there was schnitzel on the lunch table—if asparagus didn't happen to be in season. Not the quantity, but the selection was rather small.

How often did people come to your department store and ask, "Do you have. . .?"

That happened all day long. It was really like families sending their grandma out to find out where there was something to be had. So this grandma came to us four or five times a day and asked. So we also knew our regular customers well and could set our clocks by their visits. This did not work for bananas and the like, because they were given only against the presentation of an identity card, on which the number of children was noted. The more children, the more bananas. But the few bananas were never enough for all the customers anyway. Customers stood in line forever and when it was finally their turn there were no bananas left. There were always short tempers.

Speaking of scarce goods like bananas, how about "under the counter"?

When coveted goods arrived, usually a quarter was withheld and distributed among us buyers. Our boss, on the other hand, even had a store room of her own, and when canned peaches or pineapples came at Christmas, everything went straight to her stocks, and even we saleswomen could only beg to see if we could get a can. We put the rest in small bags with price tags, so it did not stand out. But I think every customer knew exactly what was in the bags.

Who did you hold those things for?

On the one hand for acquaintances and relatives. For example, my grandfather got a bottle of brandy every Friday and three boxes of filter cigarettes of a certain brand. I always gave him that in a bag. On the other hand, we were approached by our customers: "We're having a party and would like to have cooked ham or bacon, and if you need an anorak, then you come to me." One knew their clientele.

Have you never had problems with customers who came away with nothing?

Of course. Some customers were sad, others became aggressive. They then shoved each other's shopping carts into each other's heels and got into fistfights over certain rare things. Every Saturday morning we sold the remnants of the Friday delivery and when we opened at 7 am, the customers were already in a really long queue at 6:30 waiting for us to open. Everyone wanted to be first and they shoved and jostled until it got ugly. If there were any bananas, people were queuing up in front of the empty fruit stand before we knew a delivery was on the way.

They saw the car and they all ran to us. Then they knocked on the window and got downright pushy. They never actually robbed the trucks or anything, but the people have always stood in a disciplined line.

Did the supply situation improve over time or not?

It got steadily worse. In the 70s we were still able to sell fruit, but later we had it almost exclusively on public holidays. In the last few years before the wall fell, we had to stretch our product supply further and further just so that we could fill the shelves. In other words, we were always expanding the space for jam, flour, rice and pasta because we no longer had enough baking mixes, peas, lentils, waffles or even ketchup bottles.

Given the constant worsening, would you have called yourself a saleswoman or a distributor?

I was a saleswoman! Despite the shortage, we had a set sales target and to achieve this we had to talk up our goods, to make people want the unpopular items. There were also real billboards or special events such as "in-house slaughter days" or the like. None of our stuff ever spoiled.

Were you happy in your job?

Yes, I was a happy saleswoman for 20 years.

(Conversation with Marion Blumeyer, saleswoman, 2013, translation by the author)

2 Article: Economy of the GDR

Consumption Policy|Shortage economy|Economic policy

War damage in the production plants, reparation payments to the Soviet Union and the economy destroyed throughout Europe—after World War II and well into the 1950s, the main goal of the GDR's economic policy was to reach the pre-war levels of food supply and consumer goods.

It was not until 1958 that the last rations on everyday commodities could be abolished (meat, butter, shoes, etc.). The political systembore most of the responsibility for the "long post-war period" in comparison with West Germany and the "stable" lack of critical goods. From the very beginning, competition between economic reason and political-ideological maxims impeded economic development. Economically necessary measures were regularly prevented or weakened to maintain the ruling party or its main convictions.

Stable prices through subsidies

Attempting to achieve social justice, consumption for all, and stable prices with a central plan instead of cautiously directing the free market required so much state intervention that it overburdened the administration and hampered economic productivity. Thus the predetermined stable and low prices for basic foodstuffs, housing rents, heating led to increasingly horrendous subsidy amounts, which could only be financed by over-taxing other products (such as technical devices and "luxuries") or by lending. At the end of its history the GDR faced bankruptcy, unable to meet its financial obligations either internally or externally.

Although the population, the "ruling class of workers and peasants", was otherwise rarely asked their views, the concerns of ordinary people as regarded living standards were watched attentively. What the disappointed and enraged people were capable of when cheated out of their wages had been demonstrated on June 17, 1953.

"How we work today, we will live tomorrow"

Ever new initiatives and solutions were created from the activist movement following Adolf Hennecke (from 1948). To get the people to increase production with promises of a rosy future as a reward for current deprivations, easy explanations for the permanent lacks there were formulas such as "How we work today, we will live tomorrow" and propaganda lies of sabotage by enemy forces.

(Source: Central German Broadcasting, http://www.mdr.de/heute-im-osten/index.html and http://www.mdr.de/damals/lexikon/artikel75416.html, Economy of the GDR, translation by the author)

The example of the GDR shows that the central administration economy did not work in some areas. In the following, we will analyze these areas to explain what these problems are.

Phenomena of the Central Administration Economy

1. **Long lines**

   How can you explain so many lines? Lines are an expression of scarcity. People are not getting the goods they want. Due to low productivity, too little was produced or the wrong products were produced, which nobody wanted. There has to be store guards. In the market economy the market mechanism balances supply and demand. If there are too few goods, the price increases and with it the profit margin of the producers. To increase profits production is expanded.and it becomes worth importing goods from abroad. In a central economy prices are fixed, which is why the market mechanism cannot work. On the contrary, black markets with flexible prices form and offer the desired goods at higher prices.

2. **Black markets**

   The black markets are expressions of good shortages, wrong prices and bad money. There was too much currency in Ostmark in relation to goods. Some goods were scarce, so you could not buy it at the government-fixed prices in the shop, but only on the black markets. On the black markets, therefore, foreign exchange was usually used or a much higher price in Ostmark than the state-fixed one.

3. **Money surplus (hidden inflation)**

   Money surplus is an expression of money overproduction, lack of productivity or lack of value to customers. Money has to be scarce, so that the money has purchasing power and supply aligns to demand (for example, German currency reform in 1948 led to supply.). The money surplus led to hidden inflation. The people hoarded their earned money because they did not find the products they wanted, or there were just too few goods. However, the companies continued to pay wages. If they did not sell their products they took a loss, but this was offset by the state, which printed more money. This was called soft budgets for the companies.The people were all busy and no one was unemployed, at least not in the sense of not being assigned to a company as a worker.

4. **Hidden unemployment** means a lack of productivity. Although everyone had jobs, they were not all productive. Unemployment is also an expression of a delayed adaptation to structural change. This was also a reason for the low productivity of East Germany. Structural change was delayed, especially in heavy industry, i.e. coal and steel.

5. **Hidden goods distribution** according to the access to power. Not every East German citizen suffered the shortage of goods. Heads from supermarkets always had a full range

of food choices. They had the right of first access. Those who could get to the goods first did so in the shops and in the companies. Even more important was the political power that allowed production to be channeled and used. Politicians used the system to their advantage and took advantage of what they wanted.

The increasing diversification of the economy (products and production) was increasingly difficult to control centrally despite the use of computers. Why was it that the central administration economy failed, especially economically?

Systemic Errors of the Central Administration Economy

1. Welfare losses due to extensive bureaucracy

It is obvious that the planning of an entire economy is laborious down to the last detail. More elaborate than when people plan decentrally because the plan does not have to be brought together and aggregated through a bureaucracy. In addition, as a result of product innovations, there were more and more products that needed to be planned. The increasing diversification of the economy (products and production) was increasingly difficult to control centrally despite the use of computers.

In order to analyze the malfunctioning of the central administration economy, we will now go into the question of how competition functions in the central administration economy, thus how functions are performed.

Disadvantages of a Central Administration Economy

A. **Static competitive functions**

The authorities have an information deficit (from Hayek, von Mises[63]), as there are no market prices (**information function**). If many consumers want a product, the price goes up. The increased price signals an increased profit margin for companies, which is why they expand production. Conversely, low prices for primary products and production processes signal increased profit margins. The producers optimize production and make the desired offer available. Since prices are fixed in the central administration economy, the planning authority lacks this information.

The authorities cannot know everyone's needs. The bureaucracy of planning is time-consuming and inflexible, which is why they can't react to short-term changes, in needs or scarcities, for example. Lack of competition for demand and lack of incentive leads to lower quality and wasted resources. Plan fulfillment through quantity, because quality is not measurable (Control function).

---

[63]See *Hayek, Friedrich August von* (1975) and Mises, Ludwig (1920).

Neither can the authorities know the abilities of people, all production methods, or availabilities of resources, nor do they have profit incentive (1. Allocation function). Without flexible prices, even the cheapest supplier cannot attract the most demand (second allocation function) and would not be interested in it without ownership and profit.

Without ownership, competition and existential risk, there is a lack of significant performance incentive, which reduces productivity. Absolute control does not exist. Corruption and laziness are frequent. Community ownership belongs to everyone and no one. Nobody cares about the property because it belongs to nobody in particular, but to everyone. The same phenomenon can be observed in the shared ownership of student dormitories. Everyone wants to use the dishes, but nobody wants to wash them. Lack of liability and a lack of property rights lead to waste (**incentive function**).

Since companies do not have to fear bankruptcy, there is no incentive to operate efficiently (**sanction function**). The state must be responsible for losses of the companies. To finance this, it prints more money (alimentation by government money supply, soft budgets).

The authorities must determine the needs of people, their labor input and the distribution of goods, which is why the consumer sovereignty of the market economy becomes the political sovereignty of the planned economy (**freedom function**). Central administrations must therefore be dictatorships. The need-oriented distribution (**better political allocation**) of the goods is ultimately no fairer than the performance-oriented in the market system. Politicians can maximize their own benefits in the system by having access to the means of production through political power (**Distribution function**).

As a rule, the state combined the production of goods in order to exploit the economies of scale. Without competition, companies will behave like monopolists and artificially tighten supply in order to impose higher prices on the planning authority. They will try to hide capacities in order to have production for themselves and reserves for the fulfillment of the plan (**control function**).

B. Functions of dynamic competition

Lack of competition and lack of incentive lead to less technical progress, because innovations are not worthwhile (**innovation function**). The dynamic entrepreneur (Schumpeter) cannot develop within the rigid planning bureaucracy. Imitating innovations is not worthwhile for lack of ownership (profit) and is not necessary due to the soft budget (**imitation function**).

There is no further incentive to adapt quickly to other economic conditions (adjustment function) when companies do not have to fear bankruptcy because of the soft budgets. The many identified functional disadvantages of the central administration economy caused the cultural and social advantages of communism to be replaced by inefficiencies and statism; everyone was equally poor. The economic situation of the population deteriorated more and more and the distance to the western market economy systems increased. The population wanted a system change that politicians could not stop from happening. Russia opted for a market economy.

Is it possible for a society to develop without any social values, democratic knowledge or economic understanding? If we are looking for an example to analyze this question we can look at Russia. There can hardly be a more fascinating country than Russia, an empire that determined world politics in the last few decades together with the USA and which is an example for the attempt to find an alternative to the market economy system through socialism and communism. In the end Russia decided to return to a market economy. This transformation policy made Russia in the 90s into an example of an ***unsocial and badly constructed*** market economy ("predatory capitalism").

From November 1991 to January 1994, Åslund worked with Jeffrey Sachs and David Lipton as a senior advisor to the Russian reform government under President Boris Yeltsin.

6.10   Russia's Transformation into a Market Economy with a Poor Economic System

After Glasnost and Perestroika and after Yeltsin and part of the army held off the communist putsch, there was a historically unique chance for Russia at the end of the 1980s to make a fresh start economically and politically. Russia called in one of the most internationally renown economic scientists, such as the American Geoffrey Sachs, and thus representatives of the quantitative research trend of the period. The USSR was economically finished for good, not least of all because of the arms race with the USA, and discredited morally as a totalitarian system among a large portion the Russian population. Russia thus seemed to be a unique chance to apply economic theory in a practical setting and to create a flourishing landscape with the market system the theorists had dreamt up. Using a quantitative model Sachs found it reasonable to apply the elementary point of departure to Russia, and thus the functional prerequisites of the model, namely private property, contractual freedom and free prices all introduced overnight as a so-called shock therapy. The Russian economy did not develop as the model had predicted however, but fell apart visibly with the raw material sector being the only exception. Per capital real income fell to a third of its previous value. Unemployment, which had not occurred directly in socialism, became a mass phenomenon, and those who were lucky enough to have a job were often not paid. Many of the proud middle class in the USSR, the intellectual elite such as researchers, teachers, engineers and doctors were poverty-stricken or emigrated, as did the employees of the state such as judges and police officers. The educational system, social system and internal security all collapsed, including basic medical care for the population, all of which were quite obviously a public good in the USSR. The UN Human Development Report placed Russia in the early 1990s among the developed nations with a high standard of living. The system collapse after the shock therapy threw Russia back to the dark ages in a catastrophe of biblical proportions. The average life expectancy for the population dropped from 69.3 years in 1986 to 63.4 in 1994, being just 57.6 years for men. Illnesses that had been long forgotten, such as tuberculosis and cholera appeared again. Alcoholism and other diseases of addiction also spread. More than 2 million children were homeless, much more than during the Russian civil war and World War II. Another 2 million children did not attend school. Criminality increased dramatically, with politically and economically motivated murders a daily occurrence. 10–15% of the population clearly benefited from the reforms, but 60% were made poor. What happened? It had nothing to do with the expected adjustment process to the new market economy framework. Were these the promised benefits of a market economy? Were these the flourishing landscapes?

Surely not. Where then, was the mistake? There were two elementary mistakes. The first mistake was that the shock therapy destroyed the existing economic and social institutions and organizations without creating new ones. The reforms were purely quantitative, which means that the specific qualitative conditions in Russia were not taken into consideration. The second grave mistake was to conduct the privatization from a regime that was not democratic. The two mistakes together meant that assets were distributed according the law of the fittest. Power and influence in the political cadres and access to resources combined with unscrupulous brutality set up the new distribution. 40–45% of the capital used to acquire assets is thought to have been from criminal activities.[64] The public legal and security systems were overwhelmed, incapacitated or were corrupt or disorientated due to a lack of political guidelines. New democratic or market economy structures such as institutions and organizations were nonexistent. According to the Analytical Center of Russian Academy of Science, 55% of company capital and 80% of voting rights in the public companies were acquired by Russian and foreign criminals. 85% of public property was sold at a low nominal value. In the end the American consultant Geoffrey Sachs distanced himself from the Russian market reform. In his opinion the Russian leadership had exceeded the worst prejudices of Marxists about the capitalistic system by understanding their function or goal as achieving private enrichment at the cost of the general population. The criminal circles did not hesitate to engage in murder in order to remove adversaries and resistance. We must fear that in the meanwhile large portions of the Russian economy and politics are in their hands. The illegal economy was neither recorded by the state nor controlled by the official economy, and probably accounted for around 40% of GDP at that time. It was impossible for an independent, innovative middle class to develop in this environment. Performance was never established as a criterion for economic success. Within 7 years between $300 and 400 billion in private funds was transferred to foreign banks. With this background it is not a surprise that in 1997 only 8% of Russians said they were better off than before the economic reform. When asked what was responsible for the "new Russians" doing so well, 39% was speculation, 34% theft from state

---

[64]See Yurlov, Felix N. (1999); Åslund, Anders (2007) and Weigl, Tobias (2008).

assets and 17% the use of criminal funds.[65] This is what one would call predatory capitalism, an anarchistic capitalism at its extreme.

Tests for the success of the market economy reforms thus came back with disastrous results. The market economy system and so-called neoliberalism have not only been discredited, but have a negative association and not just since the subprime crisis. As a result of the unethical und disastrous Russian transformation they have been equated with social injustice, mass poverty, exploitation, hunger and impoverishment. Russia's experiences with a market economy were not seen in isolation, but have been transferred to the discussion on globalization. The idea that the market, competition and liberalism are able to bring welfare to everyone was doubted. The representatives of liberalism have been dubbed market fundamentalists by their new critics.[66]

Of course it is easy to criticize something after the fact. On the other hand, we would always be repeating the same mistakes if we were not prepared to learn from them. One of the main reasons for the failure of market economy reforms is the lack of attention given to the initial cultural and social situations, in other words the qualitative factors. What was the qualitative situation? Firstly, a functional market economy was as nonexistent in Russia as was democracy. There was thus neither a middle class that had arisen out of the enlightenment and industrial revolution, nor was there practiced market economy and democratic behavior available as human capital, which would have come from knowledge of market economic functions and individual behavior optimally adapted to market economic conditions or social capital[67] such as the function and practice of common behavior among supply and demand on markets. This may sound banal, but is it not banal in any way. When one must present themselves to an employer in competition with others, the way one must strive to attract customers, what customers should expect from a seller, that one must compare and deal over prices and quality are not abilities one is born with. A moral code for delivery and payment must also be learned. Paying bills on time is in principle a difficult thing for any customer, but he must learn that if he does not pay on time he will have to pay additional fees or face a lawsuit. This is necessary in the market economy system, since the supplier would otherwise have liquidity costs or might even go bankrupt, leaving other creditors all the way down to the employees without compensation. All of these examples are human experiences, rules of behavior that must be learned through practice in the market economy. These games must be played over several rounds so that people can see how they must behave in the market economy. The invisible hand of Adam Smith must be practiced. Behavior in economic freedom must be learned as much as behavior within political freedom.

---

[65]See Lapidus, Gail Warshofsky (1995), Åslund, Anders (2007), Marsh, Christopher (2005) and Yurlov, Felix N. (1999), p. 5.

[66]See Yurlov, Felix N., (1999), p. 5

[67]For the expressions individual capital and social capital see Sect. 6.5.

The same applies for the system of political freedom, democracy. Market economy and democracy presuppose the existence of active, self-confident and responsible citizens, and democracy also demands an active, selfless political participation. Those people driving the economy and citizens must be informed and know what they want and actively work towards achieving it based on that information. Even an optimal market economy and democratic system as institution and organization will not inspire the desired behaviors in people, at least not at the beginning. First people have to learn the rules of the game in order to follow them, and they will not immediately behave in such a way in the newly created organizations that they would carry out their assigned functions optimally. To fully develop the productive forces the human capital in a market economy is required beyond just the organizations and institutions. Democratic human capital is necessary for a functioning democracy. There was no human capital (social capital) for the market economy in Russia, which is why the transformation to a market economy had to fail as shock therapy. The same applies to the transformation into a democracy.

Because Russia was lacking both political and economic frameworks as well as human capital, the old social structures have taken hold in a new guise, the same structures that formed people during the time of the Czars, and which only nominally changed power holders during Communism. A small group of beneficiaries surrounded a dominant leader who got rich ruthlessly at the cost of the Russian people. At least under Communism the people received basic provisions. This is still no longer provided and the difference in wealth gets constantly larger. If this continues a new socialist revolution may result. Neither is the social situation endurable for the population, nor the distribution of assets acceptable, since it is based on immoral behavior instead of performance. The only chance for the new upper class, the so-called "new Russians" would be to create a new social market economy based on the existing property distribution and hope that the people forget the where the distribution originated. A functional tax system without a shadow economy, with which public goods such as education could be socially redistributed and financed would be a basic prerequisite.

To bring it all together we want to look for the lessons to be learned from the greatest national economic experiment of all time. A much-discussed and fundamental question of transformation theory is whether shock therapy or gradualism is preferable. The question can now be answered. A shock therapy, the short-term changes to all institutions and organizations from planned to market economy, or Socialism to Capitalism, can only work in exceptional cases such as after German reunification where an economically and politically stable country economically controls and socially cushions the change of a smaller country. In all other cases only gradualism is an option, as seen in the context of Russia's example. In fact Russia's experiences may well have moved China to decide in favor of a gradual release or changeover in its economy and ownership structures. Russia would have been better off importing human capital, in particular executives on a large scale from a country in considered suitable, as Peter the Great did in his reforms. This human capital, appointed to the most important political and economic functions, would have provided a gradual but constant dissemination and implementation of the necessary knowledge behind market economies and democratic systems.

If Geoffrey Sachs had predicted this development he would have given a different consultation, or perhaps none at all. Admittedly a consultant cannot be held responsible for a development over which he has no influence. Be he is responsible for the advice he has given. The project to transform Russia will always be connected to his name. A consultant always has the option of distancing himself from the project if his advice is not followed, but this only applies if the action is not taken at the important crossroads. The quantitative American line of research was simply overwhelmed due to its simplicity and was not qualified for a consultation on a practical economic and political order.

Geoffrey Sachs is a phenomenon who represents the current state of national economic science. He was and is one of it's largest figureheads. At 30 he was already a Professor at Harvard and meanwhile receives a salary from three departments at Columbia University in New York. Having been brought up and educated in a mathematical form of thought, it was easy for him to reach clear statements and recommendations. The models have another advantage in that they can be applied to any countries. Mathematics and econometric models are universally applicable and transferable. A model has variables, which can take on the respective quantitative country values. This is how Sachs managed to advise at least 75 countries. Did he know any of them? In Russia he later said that the corruption "was surprising" for him and that he had underestimated how much Russia was hindered by the lack of a functioning citizenry. Today he expresses doubt about the dominant economy, the standard education "has little use" and hardly any connection to the public.[68]

Admittedly the economic performance has improved in Russia. From 1999 to 2005 Russia's economy experienced an average rate of 5.5% real growth and the per capita income more than doubled from 2001 to 2005 to around $5250. Be that as it may, it could have been quite a different story. This economic growth is mostly due to the significant increase of raw material prices. The raw material price index CRB increased by around 81.6% from 2001 to 2005 and the price of oil by around 90%. Distortions caused by ruble to dollar conversions mean that we can only make approximations for the share raw material price developments had in Russia's economic upswing. For example, the oil price increased by 40% in 2005, but real oil production only by 2.2%. The CRB increased by around 23% in 2005, and Russia's exports in dollars increased by around 33% to approx. $241 billion, whereby raw materials comprised 67% of this, or around $161 billion. The exports minus imports were $36.8billion, which increased GDP by around 4.8% to $766 billion. If we also consider the multiplier effects for the Russian domestic demand due to increased income from the higher raw material prices, we may conclude that the Russian growth is at least mostly due to the raw material price increases.

---

[68]See Heuser, Uwe Jean: Die Wandlung des Jeffrey Sachs, in: Die Zeit, no. 38, 2003.

What is more, the majority of the population has barely profited from the positive development. We should wish for Russia that it finds a way to use the billions earned from raw materials for social security and education for the general population, which would provide a step towards long-term stabilization of a modern national economy.[69]

Conclusion

As the example of Russia shows, the twentieth century was the century of competition between systems. Different economic systems were attempted. The market economy was able to establish itself as the basic principle of order. Socialism seemed to be the answer to many ethical problems created by the industrial revolution at first. Here we should mention the pauperization of the working class or the lower classes that were poorly educated or impoverished. Market and morality were considered opposites. Socialism considered the basis of the evil to be distribution of wealth via the central function of capital in the market economy as well as market mechanisms felt to be unfair and held responsible for the inequity of needs met. By removing private property and with the central coordination of production plans in the planned economy, a method was devised to better satisfy the needs of the society. Socialism, or Communism, was unable to develop the productive forces. The gulf in the standard of living between the capitalistic and socialist countries grew until it caused the socialist system to collapse. What remains however, are several questions about the market economy system that have gone unanswered. We have examined company crises and the errors in company organization. A lack of moral values or a code of ethics was determined to be a central cause for the crises as much as the one-sided focus on figures or quantitative facts. We have also analyzed Russia as an example for an unethical market economy and an example of quantitative economic consultation.

The subprime crisis has shown that a market system without rules and controls can not function. Although capitalism or better to say the market economy is responsible for many crises, it remains with its growth and individual freedom the best of all possible economic systems. Crucial is much more that rules and controls exist to prevent damaging individual behavior. The regulatory concept of ordoliberalism has prevailed against the laissez-faire liberalism. Additionally the society has to implement moral responsibility in order to get a functioning market system.

---

[69]For details about the Russian transformation see Weigl, Tobias (2008); Åslund, Anders (2007); Lapidus, Gail Warshofsky (1995); Grabrisch, Hubert/Holscher, Jens (2007); Javlinskij, Grigorij A. (1994), Der Spiegel, no. 39 (2007), p. 82 and Yurlov, Felix N., (1999), p. 7.

6.11   Social Market Economy

The market and competition offer great advantages, expressed in the market functions already described. Other social or humanitarian goals such as a margin of subsistence or the compensation of market power between employer and employee cannot be explained through the market and competition, however. Other institutions and organizations are necessary for such goals, and are incorporated into the economic order. The market only considers interests important if they have market power. An employee who cannot find a demand for his skills on the labor market because of an overabundance of competitors with his job qualifications will not receive compensation from the market. On the other hand, the employer can afford to treat the employees he already has poorly, since they are so easily replaceable, a behavior that would otherwise be punished via the market.

Market sanctions are moody and sometimes unfair. The market rewards luck, such as those who already have a scarce resource with market condition profits, or a scarcity benefit. Real estate speculators for example, count on the real estate supply being limited with an increasing demand. Hard work itself is not a value for the market. Hard work is rewarded only if labor leads to something others are willing to pay for. In other words, without a product for which there is a demand, there is no reward from the market, which can mean starvation. There is no such thing as compensation according to need in the market system. The criticism from Karl Marx regarding the market economy system is thus justified. Charity and sympathy are foreign concepts to the market. Market and competition are instruments to achieve only some of humanity's goals, and they must be supplemented by other social regulations. This is where the social market economy comes in. It differentiates between primary and secondary income distribution, which closes the gap between economic and social goals. Since there is no intervention in the primary income distribution of the market, such as price or competition-distorting subsidies, the market and competition continue to function. The subsequent control of income created allows a certain amount of social goals to be realized, such as securing a margin of subsistence. Social market economy does not mean interfering in the market mechanisms for social purposes, as it is often misunderstood. Social means societal, not socialist. Applied correctly, the concept of a social market economy is preferable to all other forms.

This statement may cause objection at first, but it will be understandable when we remember all of the things that the market cannot provide. We already identified securing a margin of subsistence. What would the advantages of this be? The first may be the avoidance of social unrest. A person who fears for their existence may be prepared to do anything including criminal activities. The willingness of market participants to take risks may well be much higher if they know that should their investment or founding of a company fail, their physical survival will still be secure. This would encourage enterprising or innovative behavior. Securing a level of subsistence also guarantees human capital for the economic process. A policy of financed education through redistribution can be justified economically as an investment in human capital. The productivity of those who have been supported increases, thus increasing economic power and income through taxes for the country. A good basic education also strengthens democracy, since citizens no longer believe unbalanced, one-sided arguments so easily. On the other hand, support for primary and university education exclusively through private scholarships will not provide a broad system of human capital. Procuring external knowledge is an alternative for the national economy and for companies. The international competition between states and companies for resources is not just over capital, but also over human capital.

It would be a fallacy to think that the community, the state, could provide for all the responsibilities in caring for people and perhaps even raising children. It must intercede where there are no family members, but the idea that people only behave egotistically and hand over all duties and responsibilities to the state is contrary to human nature and is simply impracticable. Not even the Socialism that existed went so far.

How can we explain that in reality countries that call their form of economy a social market economy, e.g. Germany, are not necessarily superior in economic productivity to exclusively market economies such as the USA? Most countries have a mixed form. Even the arch-capitalistic USA often demonized by socialists is not a purely market economy, since it has social security, even if not very much. An active social education policy is not implemented, but they do use clever lures for human capital, in particular through the elite American universities. Germany refuses to take this path in the belief that an active educational policy is sufficient. Most European universities are no competition for American universities in the international human capital market due to the lower salaries.

▶ **Definition** Under a social market economy we understand the combination of free market with social compensation.

This is where the concept of the social market economy begins. It distinguishes between primary and secondary distribution of income, thus balancing between economic and social goals. Since the primary income distribution of the market is not influenced, for example through subsidies that distort prices or distort competition, the market and competition remain functional. The subsequent taxation of income generated can be influenced to a certain extent by social objectives, such as securing the subsistence minimum.

The term "social market economy" was introduced by Ludwig Erhard, who was the first Federal Minister of Economics of the Federal Republic of Germany from 1949 to 1963. The term was first mentioned by Erhard's comrade-in-arms Alfred Müller-Armack, who was head of the Economic Policy Department in the ministry of economic since 1952, in his book "Wirtschaftslenkung und Marktwirtschaft".[70]

Social market economy, therefore, does not mean to enter the market mechanism socially, as is often misunderstood. Social is not socialist but societal. Properly

---

[70]See Müller-Armack, Alfred (1947), p. 88; Zweynert, Joachim (2008) and Bundesministerium für Wirtschaft und Technologie (2013).

implemented, the concept of social market economy must be superior to all other economic contexts because it balances the disadvantages of market and competition through additional regulations.[71]

This statement is likely to produce a contradiction, but becomes understandable when one realizes what the market cannot afford. We have already mentioned the protection of the subsistence minimum. What is the benefit of this? We first think of the prevention of social unrest. A person who has to fear for his existence is willing to do anything in order to survive and will likely not shy even from criminal acts. However, the risk attitude of the market participants is also likely to be higher if they know that in the event of a failure of their investment or business start-up, at least their physical continuity is guaranteed. This should encourage entrepreneurial or innovative behavior. In addition, by simply safeguarding livelihoods the human capital for the economic process is preserved. An education policy financed by redistribution can also be justified economically as an investment in human capital. The productivity of the beneficiaries increases, and thus also the economic power and the tax revenue of the affected country. Good general education also strengthens democracy, because citizens are no longer so easily exposed to unbalanced one-sided arguments. An exclusive promotion of school and university education with private scholarships will not be able to guarantee a broad range of human capital. An alternative here is the acquisition of external knowledge for the national economy as well as for companies. The international competition of states and enterprises for resources includes not only capital, but also human capital.

The main structural building blocks of a social market economy are social, pension, unemployment and health insurance, a free educational system and a progressive tax system.[72] This results in ethical advantages, inasmuch as a benefit is generated for people. A secure existence and health care regardless of income, as well as equality of opportunity through free education, are important prerequisites for a good and meaningful human life according to Aristotle. However, there are also economic advantages. Social market economy pays off. The main economic advantages are:

1. Development of human capital through a government financed education system
    Educating the population increases productivity. Employees with better skills earn more. Due to technical progress the demands on the qualification of workers are increasing. A high human capital is once again the prerequisite for innovations, ie

---

[71] In a sense, Aristotle already foresaw the social market economy in which he wished to make use of the advantages of private property but also wanted to make private property available to the community: "On the other hand, an order of property which follows the custom and which is characterized by habitual behavior and the Order of proper laws is a great advantage: it should combine the advantage of both orders-by this I mean the advantage of common property and of private property."

Aristoteles (1991), pp. 17 or 1263a. (author's translation).

[72] See Bundesministerium für Wirtschaft und Technologie (2013).

technical progress. And innovations increase the productivity, competitiveness and profits of the industry of a country. Well-paid jobs are created. This all leads to significantly higher tax revenues. Investment in the human capital of the population thus pays off in many ways.

2. Greater equality of opportunity and thus better economic use of human capital

The education that a person receives should not depend on the income of his parents, but on his abilities. If education has to be paid for, there will always be people whose skills could not be developed because they could not afford the training.

3. Preservation of human capital by statutory health insurance

It makes little sense to invest in human capital and then let it be destroyed by illness. Even well-trained workers can become unemployed. If they can no longer pay for their health care, the human capital is lost.

4. Social peace through a state guarantee of the subsistence minimum and a redistribution in the form of progressive taxation.

Anyone afraid for his existence is ready for violence. A market economy is more likely to be accepted as an economic form if the inequality of the distribution results is mitigated. Not least of all, the distribution results of the markets are not just based on performance and are sometimes perceived as unjust.

The principle of assistance for self-help applies. This principle of subsidiarity derives from Catholic social doctrine.[73] The social market economy also corresponds to Rawl's principle of justice. Everyone can be freed from their interests by moving into a primitive state, without social differences, in order to ensure procedural fairness when establishing social institutions. Out of a veil of ignorance the citizens do not know their fate and must fend for themselves in the worst case.[74] However, if they do not know whether they are born poor or rich or have health problems, they need social security and basic care. They would, therefore, opt for a social market economy with social redistribution as an insurance against the worst case scenario.

But how do we explain that in reality, countries that characterize their economic form as a social market economy, such as Germany, are not necessarily superior to the other almost exclusive market economies, such as the US, in the productivity of the economy? Most countries are mixed forms. Even the US is not a pure market economy, but has a social security, albeit a small one. An active social education policy is not being pursued, but the skillful abolition of human capital, especially by American elite universities. Germany, for example, renounces this in the belief that an active education policy alone is sufficient. However, due to lower salaries for professors, most European universities are not able to

---

[73]See Schulte, Bernd (2000) and http://www.uni-muenster.de/Geschichte/SWG-Online/sozialstaat/glossar_subsidiar.htm

[74]See Rawls, John (1979), p. 158ff and 341, and in the original Rawls, John (1971), p. 10ff, 12, 139f.

compete with the US in the international competition for human capital. The term "socialized market economy" also applies to Germany as a "social market economy". On the one hand, a large number of economic sectors were directly involved, with the result that competition and market functions were disrupted. On the other hand, taxation and social protection have been exaggerated to the point where the incentives have been adversely affected. This was at least partly corrected by the Agenda 2010 of the Federal Chancellor Schröder.

As we saw in Sect. 4.5 on the issue of fairness, people tend to look at an equal distribution as fair with unearned income. However, the willingness to give up earned income is much lower. And there is a conflict of interest regarding willingness to perform. The willingness to work for income equal distribution is very low.

The level of wealth positively influenced the amount given to the public good, however.

Studies have shown that social acceptance of taxation as a norm can be crucial to tax evasion.

Thus, the possibility of making tax evasion public also generated emotional distress among subjects at the moment of evasion, such as high penalties.[75]

As seen in Sect. 4.3, identification increases the willingness to work for the group and share with the group members. This should be taken into account in taxation and redistribution within national groups. A country where citizens identify strongly with each other can redistribute more because the willingness to share with other group members is greater. Acceptance for unequal distribution differs culturally from country to country. A study examining Norwegians, Italians and Americans on their attitudes towards income redistribution showed that everyone wants redistribution but differently. Norwegians demanded a much higher redistribution in performance-related and non-performance income differentials, while Italians accepted income differentials based on benefit differences the most. The Americans interviewed were in between.[76]

Higher productivity as all as social peace arists through the building blocks of the social market economy. In general, therefore, a correlation can be drawn with the Laffer curve[77]: the productivity of an economy initially increases sharply with an increase in the social intervention of the state, but the increase lessens and then decreases from a maximum with increasing rapidity. This is a semicircular-like functional relationship (see Fig. 6.6).

---

[75]See Coricelli Giorgio; Joffily, Mateus; Montmarquette, Claude; Villeval, Marie Claire (2010), pp. 226–247.

[76]See Gianluca Grimalda, Francesco Farina, Ulrich Schmidt (2018).

[77]The Laffer curve describes the relationship between tax rates and tax revenues.

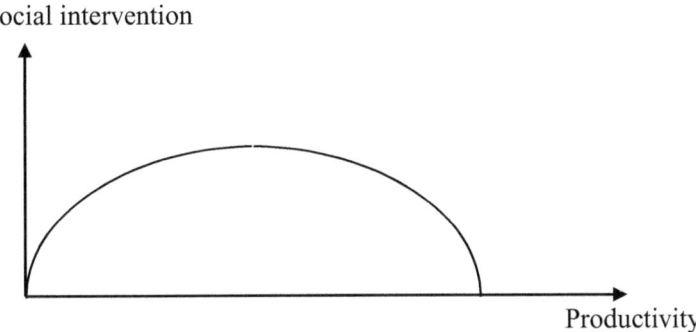

Fig. 6.6 Social intervention and productivity

Conclusion

As the example of Russia shows, the twentieth century was, among other things, the century of system competition. Various economic systems were tried, but the market economy won the system competition. At first socialism seemed to offer an answer to the many ethical problems that arose during the industrial revolution. In this context, we should mention the impoverishment of the working class or the lower poorly trained and simply poor population strata. Market and morality were perceived here as a contrast. Socialism saw the ethical basis for the unjustly perceived prosperity distribution in the central function of capital in the market economy and in the market mechanism, which was blamed for the lack of justice in needs and distribution.

The market economy is considered to be ethically superior to alternatives such as a planned economy (central administration economy) because it achieves the moral goal of adequate prosperity with a higher degree of individual freedom. The competition functions lead to an ethical result in the sense of a justice for performance. The social market economy is the ethical expansion of the market economy. It combines the productivity advantages of the market economy with ethical aspects, which can increase the productivity of a pure market economy when properly applied. However, there is a risk that overriding social interventions can severely limit competition and lead to the same problems as in the central administration economy.

Planned economy considered the abolition of private property and the central coordination of the production plans to be two tools to better meet the needs of society. But socialism, or even communism, could not unleash productive forces.

(continued)

The prosperity gap between the capitalist and socialist states became ever greater until the socialist systems collapsed. Nonetheless, the social market economy cannot eliminate all ethical weaknesses in the market economy. The greatest damage is caused by market failures, as we shall see in the next chapter.

Comprehension Questions

1. What are the advantages of the market economy as a system?
2. Name and explain the competition functions.
3. Is there a conflict between market and ethics?

References

Aristoteles. (1991). *Politik II, Werke Band 9/II*. Darmstadt.

Åslund, A. (2007). *How capitalism was built: The transformation of Central and Eastern Europe, Russia and Central Asia*. Cambridge: Cambridge University Press.

Baschek, N. (2012). *Diese Welt anerkennen - Axel Honneth geht mit seinem zweiten Hauptwerk "Das Recht der Freiheit" auf Abstand zur Kritischen Theorie*. Accessed from https://literaturkritik.de/id/16187

Böhler, T. (2004). *Der Fähigkeiten- Ansatz von Amartya Sen und die "Bevorzugte Option für die Armen" in der Befreiungstheologie -Zwei Ansätze auf dem Weg zur ethischen Begründung von Armutsforschung und Armutsreduktion*, Working Paper, facing poverty, No. 6, University of Salzburg/Austria Poverty Research Group. Accessed from https://uni-salzburg.at/fileadmin/multimedia/Zentrum_fuer_Ethik_und_Armutsforschung/documents/Working_Papers/Facing_Poverty/Böhler-FähigkeitenSenUndBefreiungstheologie.pdf

Brennan, G., & Buchanan, J. M. (1985). *The reason of rules* (p. 25). Cambridge: Cambridge University Press.

Buchanan, J. M. (1991). *The economics and ethics of constitutional order* (p. 31). Ann Arbor, MI: The University of Michigan Press.

Bundesministerium für Wirtschaft und Technologie. (2013). *Soziale Marktwirtschaft*. Accessed October 30, 2015, from http://www.bmwi.de/DE/Themen/Wirtschaft/soziale-marktwirtschaft.html

Buonanno, P., Montolio, D., & Vanin, P. (2009). Does social capital reduce crime? *Journal of Law and Economics, 52*(1), 145–170.

Büttner, S. M. (2017). Émile Durkheim: Über soziale Arbeitsteilung. In K. Kraemer & F. Brugger (Eds.), *Schlüsselwerke der Wirtschaftssoziologie* (pp. 47–54). Wiesbaden: Springer.

Conrad, C. A. (2010). *Moral und Wirtschaftskrisen*. Hamburg: dissert Verlag.

Conrad, C. A. (2018). *Business ethics - a philosophical and behavioral approach* (p. 32). Cham: Springer.

Dawkins, R. (1978a). *Das egoistische Gen* (Vol. 1978, p. 83). Heidelberg: Springer.

Dawkins, R. (1978b, 1978). *Das egoistische Gen*. Heidelberg: Springer.

Dierksmeier, C. (2013). *Ökonomische Freiheit und Verantwortung bei Amartya Sen*. Accessed from https://webcache.googleusercontent.com/search?q=cache:_Y5vVMJCrisJ:https://www.

weltethos-institut.org/uploads/media/Antrittsvorlesung_20130517.pdf+&cd=2&hl=de& ct=clnk&gl=de

Durkheim, É. (1988). *Über soziale Arbeitsteilung. Studie über die Organisation höherer Gesellschaften* (2. Aufl., Frz. Orig. v. 1893). Frankfurt: Suhrkamp.

Ebert, T. (2015). *Soziale Gerechtigkeit. Ideen • Geschichte • Kontroversen, Bundeszentrale für politische Bildung* (Schriftenreihe Band 1571, 2. erweiterte und überarbeitete Auflage). Bonn.

Feld, L. P., & Köhler, E. (2011a). Ist die Ordnungsökonomik zukunftsfähig? *Zeitschrift für Wirtschafts- und Unternehmensethik, 12*(2), 173–195. https://nbn-resolving.org/urn:nbn: de:0168-ssoar-349165, pp. 180.

Furubotn, E. G., & Richter, R. (2005). *Institutions and economic theory.* Ann Arbor: University of Michigan Press.

Gauthier, D. (1986). *Morals by agreement.* Oxford: Oxford University Press (Auflage: Revised 23 September 1999).

Giorgio, C., Joffily, M., Montmarquette, C., & Villeval, M. C. (2010). Cheating, emotions, and rationality: An experiment on tax evasion. *Experimental Economics, 13*(2010), 226–247.

Goppel, A., Mieth, C., & Neuhäuser, C. (2016). *Handbuch Gerechtigkeit.* Wiesbaden: Springer.

Grabrisch, H., & Holscher, J. (2007). *The successes and failures of economic transition: The European experience.* New York.

Grimalda, G., Farina, F., & Schmidt, U. (2018). *Preferences for redistribution in the US, Italy, Norway: An experiment study* (Kieler Discussion Papers No. 20 January 2018). Kiel Institute for the World Economy.

Habermas, J. (1992). *Faktizität und Geltung. Beiträge zur Diskurstheorie des Rechts und des demokratischen Rechtsstaates.* Frankfurt: Suhrkamp.

Heil, J. (2005). *Philosophie und soziale Gerechtigkeit: eine Ringvorlesung.* London: Turnshare Ltd.

Heuser, U. J. (2003). Die Wandlung des Jeffrey Sachs. *Die Zeit, 38*, 2003.

Hobbes, T. (1651). *Leviatan.* London, Printed for Andrew Crooke, at the Green Dragon in St. Pauls Church-yard.

Hollingshead, A. B. (1998). Group and individual training: The impact of practice on performance. *Small Group Research, 29*, 254–280.

Homann, K. (1999). *Handbuch der Wirtschaftsethik.* Band 1: Verhältnisbestimmung von Wirtschaft und Ethik, ed. W. Kor. Die Relevanz der Ökonomik für die Implementation ethischer Zielsetzungen (Gütersloher Verlagshaus, Gütersloh), pp. 322–343, pp. 335

Honneth, A. (2007). *Gerechtigkeit und kommunikative Freiheit.* Überlegungen im Anschluss an Hegel Published 17 January 2007 Original in German First published in Barbara Merker/Georg Mohr/Michael Quante (ed.): Subjektivität und Anerkennung. mentis: Paderborn 2004. Re-printed with the editors' kind permission in Critique & Humanism 22 (2006) (German and Bulgarian versions). Downloaded from eurozine.com. Accessed February 8, 2019, from https://www. eurozine.com/gerechtigkeit-und-kommunikative-freiheituberlegungen-im-anschluss-an-hegel/

Honneth, A. (2011). *Das Recht der Freiheit. Grundriß einer demokratischen Sittlichkeit.* Berlin: Suhrkamp Verlag.

Horn, A. (2018). Anerkennung und Freiheit: SubjekttheoretischeGrundlageneinerTheoriedemokratischer Sittlichkeit. *Archiv für Rechts- und Sozialphilosophie (ARSP), 104*(1), 16–40.

Hume, D. (1748). *Treatise on human nature, III. Book, Part 2, Section 1 and 2.*

Javlinskij, G. A. (1994). *Laissez-Faire versus policy-led transformation: Lessons of the economic reforms in Russia,* Moscow.

Jonas, Klaus, Stroebe, Wolfgang, Hewstone, Miles (Hrsg.), *Sozialpsychologie,* 6., vollständig überarbeitete Auflage (pp. 459). Heidelberg: Springer.

Lapidus, G. W. (1995). *The new Russia: Troubled transformation.* Boulder, CO.

Marsh, C. (2005). *Unparalleled reforms: China's rise, Russia's fall, and the interdependence of transition*. Lanham, MD.

Marx, K. (1972). *Randglossen zum Programm der deutschen Arbeiterpartei*. In MEW, Bd. 19, Dietz, Berlin 1972, 15–32. In Karl Marx/Friedrich Engels - Werke. (Karl) Dietz Verlag, Berlin. Band 19, 4. Auflage 1973, unveränderter Nachdruck der 1. Auflage 1962, Berlin/DDR. S. 13–32, S. 31. Accessed from http://www.mlwerke.de/me/me19/me19_013.htm

Maurer, A., & Schmid, M. (2010a). *Erklärende Soziologie* (1. Aufl., pp. 221). Wiesbaden: Springer

Maurer, A., & Schmid, M. (2010b). *Erklärende Soziologie* (1. Aufl., pp. 218). Wiesbaden: Springer.

Maurer, A. (2017) (Hrsg), Handbuch Wirtschaftssoziologie. (2. Aufl, p. 135). Wiesbaden: Springer 2017.

Mazouz, N. (2009). *Aspekte einer deliberativen Theorie des Guten und Gerechten*. Accessed from https://elib.uni-stuttgart.de/bitstream/11682/5348/1/veroeff_diss_2009_final.pdf

Mises, L. (1920). Die Wirtschaftsrechnung im sozialistischen Gemeinwesen. *Archiv für Sozialwissenschaft und Sozialpolitik, 47*, 86–121.

Moreland, R. L. (1999). Transactive memory: Learning who knows what in work groups and organizations. In D. M. Thompson & J. Levine (Eds.), *L* (pp. 3–31). The management of knowledge, Mahwah, NJ: Shared cognition in organizations, Erlbaum.

Müller-Armack, A. (1947). *Wirtschaftslenkung und Marktwirtschaft. Verlag für Wirtschaft und Sozialpolitik, Hamburg 1947*. München: Kastell, 1990.

Pauer-Studer, H. (2015). *Das Andere der Gerechtigkeit: Moraltheorie im Kontext der Geschlechterdifferenz*. Berlin: Walter de Gruyter.

Rawls, J. (1971). *A theory of justice*. Cambridge, MA: Harvard University Press.

Rawls, J. (1979). *Eine Theorie der Gerechtigkeit*. Frankfurt: Suhrkamp.

Rousseau, J.-J. (1755). *Diskurs über die Ungleichheit* (Hrsg. Heinrich Meier). Ditzingen: Reclam, 2017.

Rousseau, J.-J. (1762a). *Der Gesellschaftsvertrag oder Prinzipien des Staatsrechts*. Wiesbaden: Marix Verlag 2008.

Rousseau, J.-J. (1762b). *Du contracts social ou principles du droit polititiques, Livre 1, capitre 1.1.* Accessed from https://www.rousseauonline.ch/pdf/rousseauonline-0004.pdf

Rousseau, J.-J. (1988/1755). *Aufgabe der Akademie zu Dijon: Welches ist der Ursprung der Ungleichheit unter den Menschen, und ist sie durch das natürliche Gesetz gerechtfertigt? in: Jean-Jacques Rousseau, Schriften, Band 1* (p. 233). Frankfurt am Main: Fischer Taschenbuch Verlag.

Scanlon, T. M. (1998). *What we owe to each other*. Cambridge, MA: Harvard University Press.

Scanlon, T. M. (2018). *Why does inequality matter?* Oxford: Oxford University Press.

Schulte, B. (2000). Das deutsche System der sozialen Sicherheit. Ein Überblick. In J. Allmendinger & W. Ludwig-Mayerhofer (Eds.), *Soziologie des Sozialstaates* (pp. 15–38). München: Juventa.

Sen, A. (2000). *Ökonomie für den Menschen. Wege zu Gerechtigkeit und Solidarität in der Marktwirtschaft*. München: Carl Hanser Verlag.

Sen, A. (2001). Globale Gerechtigkeit Mehr als internationale Fairness, polylog. *Forum für interkulturelle Philosophie, 3*. Accessed from https://them.polylog.org/3/fsa-de.htm

Sen, A. (2003). Development as a capability expansion. In S. Fukuda-Parr, et al. *Readings in human development* (pp. 41–58). New Delhi and New York: Oxford University Press. Accessed from http://morgana.unimore.it/Picchio_Antonella/Sviluppo%20umano/svilupp%20umano/Sen%20development.pdf

Sen, A. (2009). *The idea of justice*. Belknap Press of Harvard University Press, Cambridge, MA.

Theodor, W. (1983). *May: Individuelles Entscheiden in sequentiellen Konfliktspielen*. Frankfurt am Main: Lang-Verlag.

Vanberg, V. J. (1988). 'Ordnungstheorie' as constitutional economics. The German conception of a 'social market economy'. *ORDO – Jahrbuch für die Ordnung von Wirtschaft und Gesellschaft, 39,* 17–31. p. 27.

Vanberg, V. J. (1997). Die normativen Grundlagen von Ordnungspolitik. *ORDO – Jahrbuch für die Ordnung von Wirtschaft und Gesellschaft, 48,* 707–726. pp. 713.

Vanberg, V. J. (1998). Constitutional political economy. In J. B. Davis, D. W. Hands, & U. Mäki (Eds.), *The handbook of economic methodology* (pp. 69–75). Cheltenham: Edward Elgar. p. 70.

Vanberg, V. J. (2004a). *Market and state: The perspective of constitutional political economy.* Freiburger Diskussionspapiere zur Ordnungsökonomik 10/2004. p. 4

Vanberg, V. J. (2004b). *Market and state: The perspective of constitutional political economy.* Freiburger Diskussionspapiere zur Ordnungsökonomik 10/2004. pp. 5

Vgl, Hayek, von Friedrich, A. (1971). *Die Verfassung der Freiheit,* Tübingen: J.B.C. Mohr(Paul Siebeck), p. 100-110ff, 299-310ff, 328/329, 361

von Hayek, F. A. (1975). Die Anmaßung von Wissen. *ORDO (Jahrbuch für die Ordnung von Wirtschaft und Gesellschaft), 26,* 12–21.

von Hayek, F. A. (1981). *Die Illusion der sozialen Gerechtigkeit.* Landsberg: Verlag Moderne Industrie.

Wallace, R. J. (2002). Scanlon's contractualism, symposium on T. M. Scanlon's what we owe to each other, ethics. *The University of Chicago Press Journals, 112*(3), 429–470.

Weber, M. (1980/1922). Wirtschaft und Gesellschaft. Grundriß einer verstehenden Soziologie, 5th, Tübingen: J.C.B. Mohr (Paul Siebeck)

Weber, M. (1981/1920). *Die protestantische Ethik I. Eine Aufsatzsammlung,* 6., durchgesehene Auflage, hg. von Johannes Winckelmann, München et al.: Siebenstern Taschenbuch Verlag.

Weigl, T. (2008). *Strategy, structure and performance in a transition economy: An institutional perspective on configurations in Russia.* Wiesbaden: Gabler Verlag.

Weisshaar, K. R. (2018). *Scanlon's contractualism and its critics.* New York: City University of New York (CUNY) CUNY Academic Works. Accessed from https://pdfs.semanticscholar.org/83c5/534b06ae731c71b3f9c05caa6364ceca5e89.pdf

Williamson, O. E. (1979). The economic institution of capitalism (Free Press, New York, 1985, 1979).

Williamson, O. E. (1985). Transaction cost economics: The governance of contractual relations. *Journal of Law and Economics, 12*(2), 233–261.

Yurlov, F. N. (1999). Russia: A lost decade. *World Affairs, 3*: 3. Accessed from http://www.ciaonet.org/org/olj/wa/wa_99yuf01.html

Zweynert, J. (2008). Die Soziale Marktwirtschaft als politische Integrationsformel. *Wirtschaftsdienst, 88*(5), 334–337. Heidelberg: Springer, ISSN 0043-6275.

Market Failure

7

What Follows Why?

In the first chapter we saw that the market economy, the combination of market and competition, realizes the economic-policy objective of welfare optimum. Despite the benefits of the market mechanism, it cannot be used everywhere. In the following, you will see the areas in which there is so-called market failure. Market failure is when the market does not provide allocation-efficient (socially enhancing) results.

Learning Goals

After this chapter you will be able to give examples of market failures, explain their causes and show possible solutions. The market mechanism does not provide efficient solutions for:

1. External effects
2. Public goods
3. Prisoner's dilemma
4. Lack of rationality
5. Asymmetrical information
6. High transaction costs
7. Corruption
8. Lack of transparency (benefits and costs or risks)
9. Natural monopolies
10. Available jobs
11. Disturbances in competition (e.g. market entry barriers, monopolies, etc., see extra Chap. 9 Competition policy)

© The Editor(s) (if applicable) and The Author(s), under exclusive license to Springer Fachmedien Wiesbaden GmbH, part of Springer Nature 2020
C. A. Conrad, *Political Economy*,
https://doi.org/10.1007/978-3-658-30884-1_7

7.1   Market Failure Due to External Effects

▶ **Definition** External effects are the consequences of economic action on the welfare of an uninvolved third party whose interests are not expressed in market prices, which is why they have an ethical dimension.

Negative external effects are immoral because they cause harm. If the state wants to prevent others from being harmed, it must internalize negative external effects through taxes or positive external effects through subsidies.

External effects are effects that originate from economic subjects and are not internalized by the market mechanism, which distorts the incentive system. Negative effects (negative external effects) are not sanctioned by the market and positive effects (positive external effects) are not remunerated, resulting in a suboptimal resource allocation. For example, environmentally damaging products, such as plastics, do not share the welfare costs that their disposal creates, which is a negative external effect.

Negative external effects (social costs) harm a third party. Some examples are exhaust gases, noise, waste water, damage to the environment and to the welfare of third parties. The injury is not included in the production costs and thus does not compensate the victim. Positive external effects (social benefits) favor third parties. For example, a park in a large city or the maintenance of buildings increases the value of neighboring buildings. In this case, the positive effect is measurable because it manifests itself in the appreciation of the land value.

External effects cause misallocations because not all costs or benefits are reflected in the market prices. Since the suppliers and consumers in the market only take individual advantage into account in their decisions, the market profit is not efficient from an economic point of view.

Exhaust gases, mostly CO_2, are produced during the operation of airplanes, damaging the ozone layer. Layers of the atmosphere are destroyed and the level of noise makes life near airports almost impossible. These effects are not included in the operating costs of the aircraft, which leads to a misallocation. Due to the high negative external effects, the flight prices would have to be substantially more expensive. The price does not cover the cost, which is why too many flights are in the air.

The education of the population, on the other hand, has positive external effects. In the long run, education leads to a higher productivity of the population and thus to higher tax revenues, which is why the free education system pays off for the state. Furthermore, as already shown in the social market economy, an educated population is not as vulnerable to opinion manipulation and unilateral extremist slogans, which stabilizes democracy. Overall, there is a higher welfare of the population through education.

When operating aircraft exhaust gases, such as CO_2 are produced, which damage the ozone layer. Atmospheric layers are destroyed and the high noise level makes life close to airports almost impossible. These effects are not included in the operating costs of the

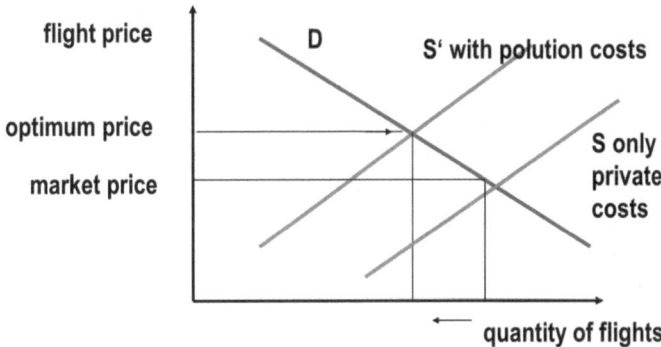

Fig. 7.1 Negative external effects during production

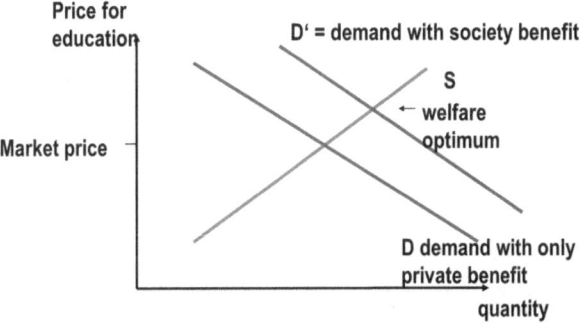

Fig. 7.2 Positive external effects from education

aircraft, which causes a misallocation. Due to the high negative externalities, the fares would actually have to be much more expensive (see S`, Fig. 7.1). The price does not cover the cost, which is why too many flights are booked.

The education of a population also causes external effects. Education (see Fig. 7.2) leads in the long term to higher productivity of the population in the economy and thus to higher tax revenues, which is why the free education system and the BAFÖG make financial sense for the state. Furthermore, as already shown in the framework of the social market economy, having an educated population stabilizes democracy because citizens are not as vulnerable to opinion manipulation and one-sided extremist slogans. Overall, the welfare of the population is increased by education.

Solutions for External Effects

Ethical Solutions

There are ethical solutions for external effects. Moral behavior requires that third parties not be harmed. Thus an ethically oriented company would either have to stop the production with negative external effects or at least compensate for the resulting damage.

However, if there is no binding regulatory framework internationally, this would mean that moral behavior is associated with major drawbacks, because it entails competitive disadvantages. This places the national governments in a prisoner's dilemma. Environmental pressures in the national market are, at the very least, short-term competitive disadvantages. The uncertainty about the behavior of the others leads to the collective worst case, insofar as no environmental requirements are implemented.

The state has developed external effect standards and sanctioned external effects such as telephoning with mobile phones on the train or smoking in restaurants. Socialization and parenting are key factors here. There are also behavioral guidelines such as "What you do not want to be done to you, do not do to others", which corresponds to the categorical imperative of Kant. It is also possible for people to take care of others, and to try to avoid negative externalities and to support positive ones.

Education and Socialization

There are private solutions for external effects. Society has developed norms for external effects and sanctions for them such as talking on cell phones in a train or smoking in restaurants. This is also where socialization and parenting show their effect.

Codes of Conduct

There are also codes of conduct such as "Do not do unto others what you would not want done to yourself" which is in keeping with Kant's categorical imperative: "Only act on maxims that you can support if they were to become a universal law."

Helpfulness, Solidarity or Compassion

People can take others into consideration and try to avoid external effects out of helpfulness, solidarity or compassion as well.

Bundling of Business Deals

Finally, business deals can be pooled to realize mutual externalities. For example, a beekeeper could team up with an apple plantation owner. The bees would pollinate the flowers as external effects and in return produce honey from the nectar to the beekeeper. Shopping malls are also based on the principle of positive externalities. The many shops side by side allow the consumer to save time. Due to these positive externalities, more customers shop in malls than in individual locations.

The Coase Theorem: Internalisation of External Effects Through Trading in Property Rights

The Coase Theorem starts with compensation for damage by allowing the injured party to sell the right to harm to the perpetrator. By commercializing the damage, the external effects are internalized. For this, the state must first assign rights of disposition to the injured party. Perpetrator and injured party negotiate allocation. The polluter must pay damages. The goal is to enter into negotiations and to achieve compensation for damages. Ronald H. Coase, received the award of the Swedish Central Bank in memory of Alfred Nobel in 1991. However, the Coase Theorem is bound by a few conditions:

1. no transaction costs when trading with property rights,
2. clear ex-ante distribution of property rights,
3. no restriction on the transfer of property rights and
4. no transaction costs on the capital.

In practice, the Coase theorem is rarely feasible, because the conditions cannot be met, since the number of participants is usually high and thus so are the negotiation costs (transaction costs). Often, the perpetrator and the injured party are unknown or the cost of the damage cannot be quantified.

It works between two neighbors, who agree that the tree of each neighbor may reach into the other's garden. Here the injured parties are known and the damage can be detected, limited and compensated.

The situation is different in the case of broad or diffuse damage. Let's say that all residents of the Rhine sell their right to claim damages from factories located there and receive some compensation. A negotiation in the spirit of the Coase Theorem is not feasible because either the injured parties are unknown or there are too many of them. How should rights be assigned? Should the residents that live within a 1 or 2 km radius of the Rhine receive damages? And what if no damages are awarded or the price is unrealistically high. How should the injured party determine the price? Is the injured party aware of the damage and can health damages be compensated in monetary terms?

In general, private solutions often fail because of

- existing prejudices on both sides,
- transaction costs too high (* negotiating with all injured parties is unrealistic),
- misjudgments of negotiating positions,
- coordination costs too high (with a large number of participants *).

For this reason, the state must intervene in the market. The aim is to get the missing costs and benefits into market prices, to internalize them (internalization).

Measures to Internalize External Effects

1. Regulation by requirements e.g. catalystic converters on cars, obligations, prohibitions, standards e.g. Requirements for desulphurisation plants for blast furnaces
2. Taxes to internalize negative externalities (Pigou tax) or subsidies for positive externalities
3. Assignment of property rights (New Institutional Economics, such as Emission Rights Trading)

The central problems remain however:

1. The damage is often not measurable.

2. The damage is not attributable to the person responsible (for example, cancer)
3. The connection between emission (exhaust) and immission (isolated effect of pollutants) is often ambiguous
4. In general, many economic transactions have both positive and negative externalities. If these concern a person, they can decide for themselves whether the positive effects outweigh the negative ones offering a net benefit. This results in distributional effects. An example of this is an expansion of the airport with the associated flight movements. The noise and the exhaust fumes from aircraft taking-off and landing cause significant health hazards when flying over densely populated areas. In addition to the health effects, there is an effect on property value, which can reach total loss.

Economic, non-external effects are higher profits for the airport, the airlines and the higher direct tax revenues of city and state. Of course, there are also positive external effects that are not included in the prices. For example, both passengers and the regional economy benefit from the improved transportation. Finally, there may be economic growth due to the lower transport costs. Companies that want to use these transportation benefits settle near the airport, which in turn brings higher tax revenues and jobs. It becomes obvious that the profiteers and the injured parties will be at odds. In terms of infrastructure measures, the state has the task of recording, assessing and balancing all effects in order to determine the social benefits. This decision-making process should be transparently documented for all concerned.

If the damage is justifiable, compensation must be paid if the damage is massive. Ideally, this would be done through a redistribution from the profit-earners to the injured parties, so that the externalities are compensated. However, in practice this will often not be feasible if e.g. the persons are unknown or the group is too big, which also means that the transaction costs are too high. Then, compensation is to be financed from tax revenue. If there are unacceptable damages, e.g. to health, which can not be compensated, the project is rejected. The decisive factor is that the state determines the **net benefit of the society** and, if necessary, ensures that negative externalities are compensated. Otherwise, there may be a reduction in societal benefits and distributional problems. Objectivity must be ensured. As a rule, the state benefits from most infrastructure projects. In addition, a minority group is often particularly affected by the negative external effects and a majority profits slightly, as in the case of airport expansion. In a democratic vote, the result could be that the project gets a political majority, although the disadvantage to the minority is greater than the majority benefit.

In such a case of imbalanced interests, politics would not be a suitably objective way to make a decision. It would be the task of the courts to review the decision of the policy makers and ensure the minority group has protection. In practice the courts are often consulted only when the building permit has already been granted and the construction is practically completed. A problem in this context also arises when the government, as in Germany, can exercise influence over the courts through the allocation of jobs and promotion.

A concept derived from the property rights approach to internalize the external effects of CO_2 emissions is emissions trading.

Emissions Trading

In general, emission trading is the trade in industrial pollution rights. This model is based on the so-called Kyoto mechanisms, which were discussed for the first time at the climate protection conference in Kyoto in December 1997.

What are the Kyoto mechanisms? The term "Kyoto mechanisms" has recently been used to summarize emissions trading (s.o.), joint implementation and the Clean Development Mechanism.[1] The background is the greenhouse gas effect, which is caused in large part by the CO_2 emissions. The objective of emissions trading is therefore to reduce CO_2 emissions in industry. For this purpose, certificates that entitle issuance are distributed to the originating companies and then reduced annually. Missing emission rights must be bought from others (incentive to reduce emissions). If you save more emissions than you need, you can sell the rights.

The approach of emissions trading has so far been largely ineffective because

1. The certificates have been issued so far for free. This means that there is no transfer of private wealth to the state to eliminate the environmental damage.
2. Nevertheless, an emission-avoidance effect would have occurred if the initial equipment with usage rights had been scarce. So far, however, too many rights have been issued, which is why the rights have only a small value.
3. The emission limits are generally too high to reverse the greenhouse gas effect. There are political reasons for this. In general, politics wants to avoid too high costs for the economy. In addition, this is not a global approach, which is why European Union policy fears competitive disadvantages.

Conclusion

The defining characteristic of external effects is that they are not included in market prices. This results in a divergence between individual and societal calculations when making market decisions. This causes market failure. The state must then intervene with measures of internalization in the market. The internalization creates costs and can only balance the external effects.

Exercises

1. Give examples of positive and negative external effects.

---

[1] See http://www.foes.de/themen/oekologische-steuerreform/lexikon/ (11.03.2013).

2. Explain what consequences these effects have on the market.
3. Which political economy measures would you recommend to internalize these effects?

7.2   Market Failure Due to Non-exclusion, Public Goods

Public goods are goods in the national economy whose benefits for society (public utility) exceed the individual, because the utility is freely available and the market participants cannot be excluded from its use. For this reason, public goods are offered in small quantities or not at all through the market mechanism. The fact that the market fails here is widely accepted. Let's take clean air. Clean air can be produced not just for one person, but everyone in the same environment also profits from it. However, using the air does not make is scarce, so there need not be rivalry to use it. Examples of other public goods from which individuals cannot be excluded would be internal and external security. There is an acknowledged market failure in all of these goods. Since no one can be excluded from their use, many would not want to participate in the cost and hope others finance its procurement. In addition, there are high transaction costs and the impossibility of an individually agreed financing, which is why the state has to provide these goods to society through compulsory contributions (taxes).

There are also public goods in the private sector, where there is the problem of free riding. Whenever several people want to purchase an item where the usage cannot be made exclusive, there is an incentive not to participate in the cost and still use the item. Let's take the acquisition of a common television in a student hostel as an example. Moral behavior would preclude such parasitic behavior and every student would honestly admit that he wants to use the television and participate in the cost.

Social morality or better ethics as practiced moral behavior is itself a public good. Everyone benefits by cooperative, considerate, and courteous behavior. Social morality is a public good. The benefit is arbitrarily divisible, thus not competitive and no one can be excluded.

The methods described in Sect.4.4. Individualism versus collectivism of public goods showed the importance of social sanctions (norms) and learning or socialization.

Only outputs for which the **exclusion principle** can be applied are able to be traded via markets, otherwise there will be a market failure because people only pay for goods that are not freely available. The exclusion principle is only applicable if it is possible to restrict access to a good until a contract exists between supplier and consumer. On the other hand, if those who don't wish to pay cannot be prevented from accessing the goods free-rider behavior will prevent the creation of a market. In 2007 Leonid Hurwicz and Eric S. Maskin, Roger B. Myerson received the economics award from the Swedish National Bank for the analysis of these relationships.

	rivality	no rivality
exclusion	privat goods	**club goods** (toll roads, pay-TV or public beach, for example)
no exclusion	**common goods** e.g. exclusion too expensive (fish stocks in the sea) or crowded streets	**pure public goods** (clean air, roads, lighthouses, dikes)

Fig. 7.3 Types of goods

The term "public good" is intended to indicate that the goods or services in question must be provided under collective or governmental administration because the market fails to deliver them. Public goods are things likesun and air.

The use of the exclusion principle for **private goods** is indisputable (see Fig. 7.3), since rivalry to secure them must exist among consumers. **Rivalry to consume** occurs when the use of a good by one consumer precludes the use of this good by others. If one person eats a candy bar, no one else can eat it. However, there is no rivalry for the protection a dyke offers against flooding because it does not diminish individual protection by allowing others to enjoy the same protection. In so-called pure public goods there is neither exclusion nor rivalry for consumption (e.g. air, lighthouses, dykes, public security). A clean environment is a pure public good. To what extent and what quality public goods are provided by the state is a political decision. The decision problem, in particular the choice of voting procedures, will be dealt with later (see Chap. 8 Political failure).

The combinations of exclusion and rivalry result in four types of property. Private and public goods have already been described. In addition, there are so-called club goods where exclusion is possible, but rivalry is not present. These goods are very interesting in the private economy, because they can be sold endlessly at no extra cost. A current example is pay-TV. For most club goods, however, rivalry eventually occurs with intensive use, which is why it then becomes a private good, such as overcrowded toll roads. If exclusion is impossible or too costly, but there is rivalry it becomes a common good. For example, pure public goods become common goods when rivalry occurs with excessive use. The fish stocks in the sea were originally a public good but due to overfishing rivalry has now occurred, so we unfortunately have to consider them common goods. They could become private goods if property rights can be attributed, like the hunting and fishing rights on shore.

How should public goods be financed? Here we can use the **Samuelson condition**. State provision of the public good is pareto-efficient if the sum of individual willingness to pay is greater than the costs of provision (marginal utility). The access costs can determine the

Need intensities	Large group (i.e.100)	Small group (i.e..5)
equal	very unlikely	Not determined
not equal	determined	very likely

Fig. 7.4 Private provision of public goods

policy, but problems occur in regards to the willingness to pay. Politicians cannot ask every citizen and often do not get an honest answer because many want to free ride.

For example, if the students of a shared flat wanted to purchase a television, they would have to vote on the funding. A TV in the common kitchen, however, is a pure public good. The utility is arbitrarily divisible (until the kitchen is full) and no one is excludable, since the kitchen is accessible to all. If you ask roommates for their opinions on whether to buy a device together, most will probably say that they do not watch TV so they would not have to contribute to the cost of purchase, but could still use the purchased tv, thus being free riders. The individual benefit increase is not transparent and thus ignored, which is why an individual gains the most advantage by downplaying their benefits and thus their contribution. The free-rider phenomenon is thus a problem in the financing of public goods.

There is no viable and unambiguous solution for optimally delivering public goods, since costs and benefits are often indeterminate. However, private provision of public goods is more likely the smaller the group (organizational costs) and the greater the benefit, since then some are willing to pay the costs to attain the good (see Fig.7.4).

Example of unequal need intensity groups: in a small group of five students looking for a t.v., it is likely that if there is an unequal distribution of needs, students with a high level of need will give in and pay for the others, otherwise they would not be able to enjoy a television.

The likelihood of those with a greater need being willing to cover the costs for something others can also use is much lower in a large group. It is not unlikely that voting on public goods and how to finance them is either impossible or too difficult in large groups. If voting is not possible, the question remains of whether the result reflects the needs of the population.

For example, in a community, the question is whether a kindergarten with a playground or a swimming pool should be built. Not all citizens of a community have children. A majority decision could lead to the construction of no playgrounds if, for example, the majority of voters have no children (see also Sect. 8.5 on voting procedures). A survey is complex and the willingness to pay difficult to determine. Even in the community there are free riders. There will hardly be enough parents willing to pay for the playground alone because the costs are too high. The pool is similar. The community needs to recognize the needs of others and implement the most useful project for the citizens. A public kindergarten with a playground will be built and the costs will be allocated to the community.

The problem of public goods can be replayed within the framework of game theoryas we saw in Chap. 4 there are dynamic behavioral adjustments in multi-round games.

Summary
There are no markets for public goods (market failure)

- due to missing exclusion technology (external security),
- due to lack of legally enforceable property rights or ownership (ozone depletion measures) or
- because the costs exclusion are too high (toll road)

⇒No exclusion
Supply is then only assured if the state takes over production, regulates distribution and finances it by compulsory levies (taxes, duty etc.). The term public goods derives from these tasks.

7.3   Market Failure Due to the Prisoner's Dilemma

Allocative problems arise when individual rational utility maximization, as in the case of the Prisoner's Dilemma (see Fig. 7.5), leads to ineffective outcomes:

Two captured criminals in custody are to be interrogated. If both confess they will go to prison for 5 years. If only one person confesses, they will be released and the other will receive a 6-year sentence. If neither of them confesses, they little evidence against them and they only have to go to prison for 1 year, which would be the best outcome for both

Fig. 7.5 Payout Matrix Prisoner's Dilemma. * Nash equilibrium represents the worst case for all. ** Best case for A. *** Worst case for A

years of prison	B con-fesses	B does not confess
A con-fesses	(5, 5)*	0, 6
A does not confess	6, 0	1, 1

together (maximum collective benefit). The dominant decision strategy however, is for each player to try and confess first. Both confessing leads to the Nash equilibrium in which no party can improve through deviating behavior. The situation of the Prisoner's Dilemma is used in the form of the Leniency Notice. Whoever confesses gets a drastic reduction in prison time, while the others are punished more severely.

The worst case for an A is if he does not confess, but B does, and the best case is if A does not confess but B does. B is in the same decision situation. The incentive for A and B is to avoid a prison sentence. Each player is under pressure to confess first. The worst-case creates a fear of sanction; because both are interrogated separately and the opponent may have already confessed, either one could get the longer imprisonment. The incentive to confess (best case) and the prison sentence as a sanction (worst case) are both known. Because of the uncertainty about the other's behavior, both must assume the worst case, in which both confess (Nash equilibrium*). Only then can both strive for the best case and avoid the worst case. This is called dominant strategy.

▶ **Definition** From the Nash equilibrium, one decision maker cannot improve with the given behavior of the other.[2]

The uncertainty surrounding the behavior of the other player is the cause of the Prisoner's Dilemma. The solution to this is binding contracts with sanction options. The sanctions must be tougher than the worst case of the dilemma situation. Thus, in the world of the mafia, confession is sanctioned with death. As a countermeasure there is the witness protection program, however.

Environmental Policy
In December 2012, a long extension of the Kyoto Protocol was discussed in Doha and the following minimum target was reached: representatives of 200 countries agreed to extend the Kyoto Protocol until 2020. However, the contract only affects 15 percent of global CO_2 emissions.[3] The balance of the previous global climate policy is worse than bad. The world is looking at a global climate crisis.

Environmental Policy Case Study
The following sentence was uttered at the Durban World Climate Summit in 2011: "Meanwhile, other important countries, such as Japan, Canada and Russia, are refusing to introduce new binding CO_2 targets for the period after 2012 unless India or China go

---

[2]In games with several rounds, the prisoner's dilemma results in special dynamic behavioral adjustments (see Chap. 4).

[3]Spiegel Online vom 8.12.2012. http://www.spiegel.de/wissenschaft/mensch/klimagipfel-in-doha-kyoto-protokoll-bis-2020-verlaengert-a-871780.html (11.10.2016).

Fig. 7.6 Decision situation of global environmental policy. ** Free rider position (free rider), as the environment is a public good, including non-exclusion

n states state A\	(1) environ- mental regulations	(2) no environ- mental regulations
(1) environ- mental regulations	(2, 2)	(- 2, 0)
(2) no environmen- tal regulations	(4, 2)**	(0, 0)*

along with it."[4] This shows the Prisoner's Dilemma in Global Environmental Policy (see Fig. 7.6).

Payoff Matrix

While all countries would benefit from global environmental regulations, it would reduce CO_2 emissions and improve the global climate for all. There would be a welfare gain of 4 in our payout matrix. There is uncertainty for each state as to how other states will behave. Every state faces n states, the rest of the world. The worst case for any state A is if it introduces environmental regulations for its economy, but the other n states do not. Then it would have to bear the costs of environmental regulations and the deterioration of the competitiveness of his industry in the amount of 2, but would get no welfare increase, because this would require almost all countries to accept environmental regulations. The best case is if all other states were to enforce environmental regulations, but A did not. A could thus save the cost of environmental regulations and still enjoy the welfare of a clean environment (free rider position). Every state finds itself in the situation of A. They will strive for the best case and want to avoid the worst case. All states behave this way, which is why no environmental regulations are implemented. One must wonder why states India and China even participate in the summits.

There should be a world government to enforce compliance. However, there is no parent state that represents the common good and the prisoner's dilemma prevents the provision of a clean environment as a public good. This problem does not exist at the national level, which is why Germany has a working environmental policy. Environmental regulations are enforced by the state. We know that mandatory prison sanctions are needed to resolve the prisoner's dilemma. The environment is a global problem and a public good. The Kyoto agreements have been non-binding self-regulating commitments of the states without

---

[4]See Schwägerl, Christian/Traufetter, Gerald (2011).

sanctions for non-compliance. Contracts should no longer be non-binding, and there should be monitoring and sanctions for non-compliance.

As we saw in Chap. 4, rational utility maximization does not necessarily mean damage to third parties. For example, in game theory multi-round games show that decision makers learn from their decisions and take into account the opponent's damaging counter-reaction, which is why they no longer maximize their advantage in the short term. According to game theory, in games over several rounds being cooperative maximizes positive results and only when the opponent is not cooperative do players counter with uncooperativeness (trigger or tit-for-tat strategy).

The trigger or tit-for-tat games describe the fundamental conflict between individual and collective rationality. Individual benefit maximization at the expense of third parties contrasts with the collective benefit of community income, such as the provision and use of public goods (such as the clean environment) in the Prisoner's Dilemma. In the 1960s', Anatol Rapoport and Albert Chammah showed experimentally that cooperation occurs in prisoner's dilemma games. On the basis of computer simulations, Robert Axelrod later analyzed the conditions for the occurrence of cooperation. The tit-for-tat strategy proposed by Rapoport proved to maximize earnings. This strategy is weak and strong at the same time. The strategy is to play fair and bnefit or at least never harm your opponent. Only if they behave uncooperatively first, then you behave likewise. This strategy always gives the opponent the opportunity to gain more by cooperating and less by behaving uncooperatively. It therefore provides incentives for cooperative behavior and sanctions for uncooperative behavior. The regulated sanctions would then be the norms of the game. Exploitative strategies harm oneself and the other, because the profits from cooperation are lacking. The individual benefit maximization at the expense of third parties in the end brings less net benefit. Rapoport also calls the principle of the strategy "In weakness is strength" and recommends it as a leitmotif in his studies on arms race and conflict prevention.[5]

Conclusion

Market failures in public goods and prisoner's dilemma market failure in public goods is mainly attributable to non-exclusion. Pure public goods also have non-rival consumption. Thus, government provision of public goods is beneficial when the costs are less than the social benefits. When provided by the state through an economic transaction, the positive externalities are realized. If there is no parent state that represents the common good, prisoner's dilemmas can make it difficult or prevent the provision of public goods.

---

[5]See Rapoport, Anatol/Chammah, Albert M. (1970); Axelrod, Robert (1987) and Schwaninger, Markus (2008).

Exercises

1. Give examples of the different goods and explain the applicable criteria on the basis of the examples.
2. According to which criteria should public goods be provided by the state?
3. Explain the Prisoner's Dilemma in Global Environmental Policy Using a Payout Matrix.

7.4 Market Failure Due to Lack of Rationality

The Homo Oeconomicus image of humanity was introduced to economics by John Stuart Mill, Utilitarianism, 1806–1873.

▶ **Definition** Homo Oeconomicus is a rationally acting individual whose only goal is its own utility maximization.

What does rational mean in this context?

▶ **Definition** Actions are rational if they maximize results by using all available information, and do not contradict one's own goals.

The model of the perfect market assumes rational behavior (Homo Oeconomicus). In reality, however, we are dealing with "limited rationality". George Akerlof, Michael Spence and Joseph Stiglitz were awarded the 2001 Nobel Prize for this concept. However, Homo Oeconomicus was originally a simplified model of thought, as shown in Sect. 3.1. Homo Oeconomicus is like the computer, which is a purely rational being. Based on a given level of information, this being always decides on the utility-maximizing action alternative and thus becomes mathematically calculable. Since almost all qualitative relationships of human complexity are not quantifiable, they usually fall through the cracks. What cannot be calculated is not suitable for an exact science and is repressed.

7.4.1 Meritorious and Demeritorious Goods

▶ **Definition** Meritorious goods are private goods whose usefulness (merits) are not properly appreciated the private economic subjects (in the view of the state).

This means that the benefits of these goods are subjectively underestimated. There is therefore no rational behavior. Since the social (state) benefit assessment is higher than the benefit assessments according to individual preferences, the state provides the meritorious goods. For example, young people often underestimate the need for care when they are older. They think they will stay young for a long time. They overvalue present needs and underestimate future needs for a old age period, in which they will not be fit for work. Therefore, there is a pension insurance obligation in Germany. Other examples include compulsory education, unemployment insurance and health insurance.

▶ **Definition** Demeritorious goods are private goods whose harmfulness (demerits) are not sufficiently appreciated by private economic subjects (in the view of the state).

This means that the harmfulness of these goods is subjectively underestimated. There is therefore no rational behavior. In the case of harmfulness the state increases purchase costs (tobacco tax, alcohol tax) or prohibits a market for dematerial goods from forming (such as drugs). Addiction is an irrational behavior, man is no longer master of his own will, he is dependent. The citizens therefore behave to their detriment when they consume such substances.

Behavioral Economics derived the so-called liberal paternalism. If a person cannot decide rationally to their advantage, the state must help them make their decision by favoring the decision alternatives that are more favorable to the citizen.

The aim is a governmental behavioral control for the benefit of the citizens, a kind of paternalism without coercion.[6]

For example, you can use the status quo bias to set the better option as the default. If the citizen wants to deviate from that, then he must actively do so. One could prescribe appointments for preventive examinations, which the citizen would then have to cancel themselves, if they do not want to accept them.

Representatives of Asymmetric Paternalism go one step further by calling for the better option to be mandatory in order to rule out irrational behavior. For example, a second doctor should be consulted prior to surgery in order to ensure the correct therapy or to avoid unnecessary surgeries. In addition, state information campaigns should prevent irrational behavior, for example by lotto in which people vividly explain the low probability to others, because otherwise they tend to overvalue small probabilities. Asymmetric paternalism proposes decision-making breaks, so-called cooling-off periods, to prevent short-term emotional and therefore not rational decisions. For example, only being allowed to commit to buying very expensive goods after a period of delay or have a right of withdrawal from the contract. Such things already exist, for example, in the consumer laws in door-to-door sales. Tobacco taxes, alcohol taxes, and entertainment taxes are also advocated for asymmetric paternalism, as time inconsistency poses short-term benefits over long-term damage. It is important that the consumer still has a choice.[7]

---

[6]See Thaler, Richard; Sunstein, Cass R. (2003).

[7]See Camerer, Collin; Issacharoff, Samuel; Loewenstein, George; O'Donoghue, Ted; Rabin, Matthew (2003); Whitman, Glen (2006) and Beck, H. (2014), pp. 372.

7.4.2   Risk-Averse or Risk-Taking Behavior

Risk-averse behavior (fear of risk) or risk-taking behavior (opportunities are rated higher than risk, opportunity-oriented) is also not rational. Rational behavior would only be given with risk neutrality. Decisions with the same expected value but varying payouts would have to be rated the same for risk neutrality. However, risk-averse decision-makers will choose alternatives with the same expected value, which have a lower probability but higher payouts. They are opportunity-oriented, which is irrational behavior. For example, playing lotto is irrational, because the expected value is much lower than the stake. However, playing lotto would become rational again if one were to value the joy of playing (tension) or even hope for the opportunity to escape from a poor life. Risk-averse decision-makers will choose alternatives with the same expected value, but with fewer losses.

7.4.3   Emotions

Fear, envy and courage are emotions. They are not always controllable and influence our actions, so rational action is not possible. This is particularly the topic of psychology and Behavioral Economics, which was discussed in Chap. 4.

7.5   Market Failures Due to Asymmetrical Information

The model of the perfect market assumes complete market transparency. Market participants have all the information relevant to their decisions.

One speaks of asymmetric information when the parties have unequal knowledge about:

(A) the properties of the product to be exchanged (Hidden Characteristics).
(B) the behavior of the partner after conclusion of the contract (Hidden Actions) and/or.
(C) the intentions of the partner in the Hidden Intentions.

The economic participants have different knowledge and one party can exploit this unethically to the detriment of the less informed. This party then has less value than expected, which leads to a non-pareto-efficient situation.

(A) Asymmetric information concerning the properties of the product to be exchanged (Hidden Characteristics)

If, prior to the conclusion of the contract, the exchange partners have different information on the objective characteristics of the goods to be exchanged (for example in the market for consumer goods), this favors the process of negative selection. For example, there is a lot of information on the goods on the used car market, which can be unethical to the advantage of the buyer.

The problem of the hidden characteristics is found particularly in anonymous markets, in which buyers and sellers do not know one another, and are not dependent on one another because they will not do business again. The seller can thus deceive the buyer because of the asymmetric information, without having to fear retaliation if the buyer has identified the fraud. One thinks of the itinerant vendors who went from village to village, and so were never accessible. In decision theory, this corresponds to the game with one round. Anonymous markets can be financial markets, but also in big cities people do not know each other and often do not see each other again after buying. This is why, as a rule, crime is higher in an anonymous city than in a village. Despite the cliché of the country bumpkin who gets rolled in the big city, he is not more naive than the city inhabitant; he has simply not had bad experiences and is therefore more trustful.

The perfect market model assumes perfect market transparency, where market participants have all the information relevant to their decisions. One speaks of asymmetrical information when the parties have different levels of knowledge in their economic transactions. This can then be used by the better-informed party, giving them an advantage over other parties. After the transacation the less-informed party has less benefit than expected, which leads to non pareto-efficient situations. The welfare optimum from Sect. 3.3. can not be reached.

Examples

1. *Medical services*

    The services of a physician correspond to a supplier-induced demand: physicians define which illnesses the consumers have and which services are as necessary. In doing so, they indirectly determine their income as well. Here, a solution is only possible through control by health insurance and the state, and patients are recommended to get several offers. However, there is an incentive problem if the patient does not have to pay for the costs, rather the health insurance. In this case, it helps to incentivize patients by applying dedictibles or controlling the medical services provided by patients and third parties.

2. *Auto Repairs*

    If you bring a car into the workshop, you often cannot exactly understand if the repair is really necessary and what was billed. Here it is advisable to obtain several offers.

3. *Food*

    When it comes to food, you can not exactly understand how the animals are kept or how the foods affect our bodies.

    In this case, the state must ensure better market transparency and prevent harmful production through controls and sanctions.

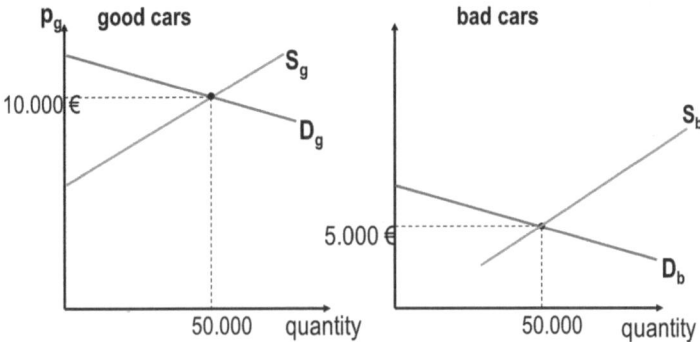

Fig. 7.7 Used car market situation 1 complete information

Case Study: Used Car Market
(G: good car, S: bad car)

1. **Situation with Complete Information (see Fig. 7.7)**

With complete information:

- Good and bad cars are sold (here: 50% each).
- With incomplete information buyers form expectations (here: "medium quality" m), buyers do not know the condition of the car, good and bad cars seem the same. The negative experiences they make after the purchase. Dealers know the condition, which is why they still try to sell good cars more expensively than bad cars.

2. **Situation of Incomplete information Part 1 (see Fig. 7.8)**

Same demand curve, but different supply curves
Contemplation of the Dm line
M: Medium quality because the quantity is uncertain
With incomplete information:

- 75% bad cars are sold and 25% good cars.
- Shoppers are downgrading their mid-range expectations, which is why they are less willing to pay for the cars and therefore buy more bad cars because dealers are willing to sell them cheaply.

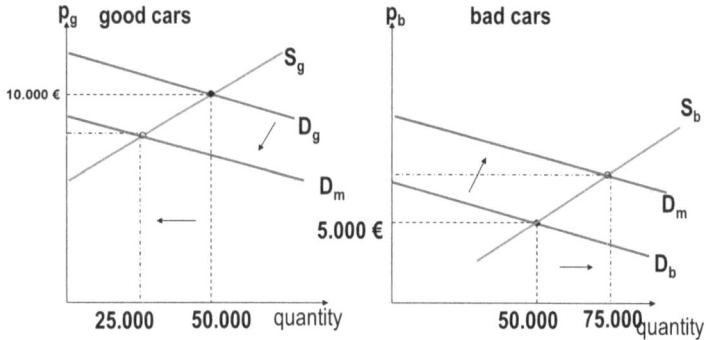

Fig. 7.8 Used car market situation 2

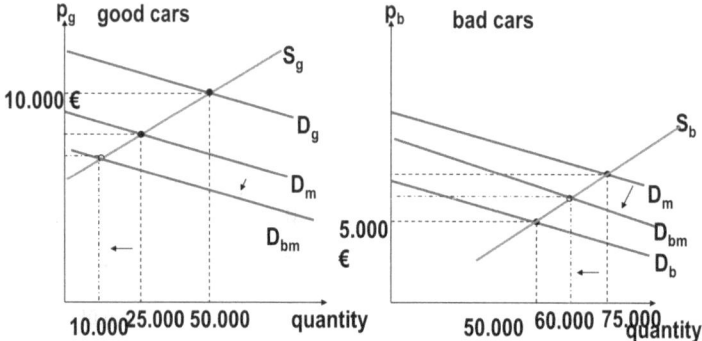

Fig. 7.9 Used car market Situation 3

3. **Situation of Incomplete information Part 2 (See Fig. 7.9)**

After renewed adjustment of expectations (see Fig. 7.10):

- Fewer cars are sold and 86% are bad and 14% are good cars.
- Buyers continue to adjust their expectations.

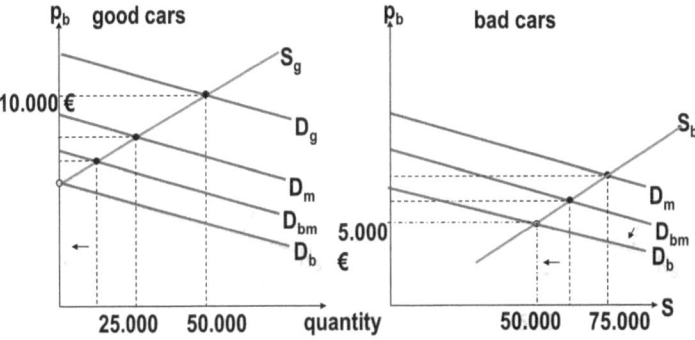

Fig. 7.10 Used car market Situation 4

Conclusion

The consequences of this process of negative selection are that poor quality supplants good quality and fewer cars are sold. Producer and consumer pensions (ie social welfare) fall.

Market failures can be countered by:

- Screening: the uninformed person improves his information level by gathering information directly or through advice from specialized third parties.
- Signaling: the better informed party provides information, for instance by offering a guarantee.[8]
- Morality: Ethical behavior in hidden characteristics would prevent the better-informed from betraying the worse-informed.
- Deannonymize markets by making the names of sellers transparent.

List simulated the behavior in markets conducted as Gift Exchange Game. He first ran the sale of baseball cards in the lab and then on an anonymous market. The sellers were expected to deliver the lowest quality for profit maximization and the buyers were expectected to maximize their gain by paying the lowest price. In the laboratory the participants could be observed, but not in the market. The result was that sellers in the lab offered better quality and customers paid more. The reputation seems to have played a role in the behavior of the buyers.

In the markets they felt unobserved and sold the customers low quality at high prices.[9]

---

[8]See Dillerup, R./Stoi, R. (2011), p. 24; Welge, M./Al-Laham, A. (2008), p. 52 and Fritsch, Michael/ Ewers, Hans-Jürgen/Wein, Thomas (2011), p. 263.

[9]See List, John A. (2006).

Another area with the problem of hidden characteristics is personnel management.[10] For example, when a new employee is hired, the quality of that person is not directly identifiable. Hidden characteristics are the qualities of the applicant, which are unknown to the employer when hiring, such as the actual degree of qualification, the integrity, the working attitude and loyalty. Hiring external employees therefore entails a high risk of failure assessment due to the hidden characteristics, associating it with high risks. It can only be recommended if no one is available internally at the time of hiring, or if external knowledge can be brought into the company that the company has no other way to access.

Ultimately, the importance of the corporate identity and, in particular, the emotional attachment of the employee to the company has decreased over the last decades. This has aggravated the principal agent problem. In the past, it could be expected that a company's management would have worked hard or at least learned about the most important value-added stages and corporate identity. This not only had the advantage that managers could better assess the impact of their decisions on the company, and they had a stronger identification with the company. Furthermore, the risk of failure due to hidden characteristics was less, because the management had to prove itself in the company for many years. However, the problems of hidden characteristics, hidden information, and hidden actions exist on every level of leadership down to the subordinate decision-making units.

In German literature, there is still the distinction between trust and experience goods. In the case of experience goods, the customer knows the characteristics of the goods after the purchase, not in the case of trust goods. The commercial audit is, for example, cited as the trust good. In the case of trust goods, self-policing is an effective solution, such as by offering a guarantee.[11]

(B) Hidden actions

Since in general the one partner does not know how the other will behave after signing the contract, this favors possible hidden actions. The contract is then not implemented to the advantage of both sides, but the one side betrays the other and the allocation optimum is not achieved.[12]

This problem of moral risk (moral hazards) is seen particularly often in the insurance industry. The behavior of the insured person may change after the conclusion of the contract at the expense of the insurer, because he will no longer be liable for his property. After completion of the insurance policy, the insured person may, under certain circumstances, influence the probability of the loss occurring without the insurance having any influence on this. For example, the owner of a fully-insured luxury car might hope that he can order a new car if he parks it in a dangerous area. Incentives such as refunds can be

---

[10]See Berthel, Jürgern/Becker, Fred G. (2013), p. 48.

[11]See Ballwieser, Wolfgang/Clemm, Hermann (1999), p. 414.

[12]See Weisser, J. (2012), p. 53 and Alparslan, A. (2006), pp. 22.

used to prevent market failures. Self selesection is a solution for health insurances if the client knows his health risks. If his health is poor he will choose health insurances rates with no co-pay.

▶ **Definition** Moral hazards are an incentive for individuals to act against or at the expense of many, society or their company.

One of the causes of the financial crisis was, for example, was paying the financial intermediaries by the volume of loans. They were not liable when a loan failed, which gave them an incentive to lend to bad borrowers. Another example is the awarding of bonuses to the managers of a company based on short-term share price increases. This creates an incentive to do everything in the short term to increase profits. This can be done by less investment. In the long term, this jeopardizes the company's success, however.

There are hidden actions with rental, since the landlord does not know how the tenant will deal with the object after the conclusion of the lease. To reduce the risk, the tenant must provide a deposit. With moral behavior this would be superfluous and he could trust the tenant.

(C) Hidden intentions.

The difference between the hidden intentions and the hidden actions is the intention. A contract partner has performed first and now depends on the other for the fulfillment of the contract. There is a one-sided dependency after conclusion of the contract.

Ignorance of the contractor's "covert intentions" can lead to the exploitation of contractual scope for interpretation by the economically stronger person to the detriment of a contract partner dependent on him (hold-up behavior).

This possible exploitation or blackmail could be attempted with a strategy of interest harmonization (incentives, such as profit sharing). Hidden intentions exist not only in leases, but also advance payment. The one-sided dependency is counteracted here with deposits and guarantees. Risks from Hidden Intentions are also present in joint ventures for market closure, where a company has the know-how. The other partner could try to build his own company as soon as he has acquired the know-how. Here, harmonization of interests can be achieved by a very high participation of the partner in the joint venture. The participation must be so high that it is no longer worthwhile for the partner to build a second company. Again, it helps if one can trust in moral behavior.[13]

Another example would be so-called "rent nomads". They never intend to make rent payments except the deposit when moving in. Years can pass until the landlord has kicked out the rent nomad. Here it is advisable to be particularly careful when choosing tenants and perhaps to obtain a landlord referral in addition to proof of income. The current landlord might have a biased view. If tenant is already resident at the property, it is often

---

[13]See Dillerup, R./Stoi, R. (2011), p. 25 and Welge, M./Al-Laham, A. (2008), p. 53.

advisable to offer the tenant a termination payment to leave rather than to enter into a drawn out legal process.

7.6   Market Failure Due to Transaction Costs

If market transactions fail because of their transaction costs, one can also speak of market failures in a broader sense.[14] Transactions can be understood as all transfers of rights to dispose of goods and services.[15] The transfer of services includes the internal sale of work through an employment contract. The transfers incur costs, such as information, negotiation, control and enforcement costs, as well as transport costs in a broader sense.

We distinguish between direct and indirect transaction costs.

1. **Direct Transaction Costs**

Over the past few decades direct transaction costs have fallen very sharply, leading to the formation of numerous new markets. Some factors in cost reduction have been the Internet, new transport techniques and English as an international business language. All together, globalization has been a key factor affecting costs. The world has become smaller because the paths have become shorter and more cost-effective. The invention of the Internet increased market transparency with reduced transaction costs. Prices and services can be compared faster and more cost-effectively. Innovation have been made in the transport techniques like container shipping, large oil tanks and reduced flight costs. The implementation of English as an international business language is comparable to the introduction of a uniform standard (e.g., metric or DIN). Translation costs are thus obsolete as people trade with other cultures, e.g. German and Chinese in a common foreign language. They have to learn only one language through the common standard in order to be able to do business.

2. **Indirect Transaction Costs**

If, as with the asymmetric information presented, the fulfillment of the contract is uncertain, there is a risk of loss. This is always the case if behavior after contract conclusion cannot be controlled absolutely. This is relevant for all forms of transactions, which include long-term contract fulfillment, thus also employment contracts. The higher the advance performance and the longer the contract duration, the higher is the risk of a lower counter-performance. This applies in particular to investments by companies in new production facilities, for example. Here, the investment is high but the return is distributed over many

---

[14]See Williamson, O. E. (1979), pp. 18 and Williamson, O. E. (1985) and Furubotn, Eirik G./Richter, Rudolf (2005), pp. 47.
[15]See Gabisch, Günter (2003), pp. 56.

periods. These indirect transaction costs can be reduced by an objective and rigorous legal system. A written Code of Law also reduces the risk and is better than a case law because case law builds on precedents. Countries that do not have a reliable law enforcement system have difficulties in attracting direct investment.[16]

The indirect transaction costs can be reduced by strong morals. Luhmann also sees trust as a means of reducing the complexity of social interactions. If the culture of a country is moral, the contracting party can trust in the implementation of its treaties.[17] There is no longer a risk of fulfillment resulting from being taken advantage of.

Transactions are completed when the indirect transaction costs are reduced, which can be considered its own business approach. Phrases like "A good name is worth its weight gold" and "My word is my bond" as well as the legal concept "good faith" stand for this approach. The reputation of a person or a company includes everything associated with its name: poor or good performance, moral or immoral behavior, etc. A reputation is formed by acts that are observed and interpreted by people, by the market. This means that every company is responsible for its own reputation.

The honor of the merchant also derives its significance from the elimination of the risk of contract settlement. This honor was institutionalized by merchant guilds. They introduced codes of ethics and sanctioned corresponding rules. Grievous violations were punished with exclusion from the guild, which was equal with the abolition of the entrepreneur's livelihood, because he lost the trust of his business partners.[18] Even in Mafia circles there is an honorary code within the criminal organization and their business partners. Thus even criminal circles need a minimum of morality to deal with their business transactions. They also need mutual trust.

Trust

After the Enron crisis confidence in the company's balance sheets was shattered, and as a result of the financial crisis (subprime crisis) no one trusted the banks, while the banks trusted themselves least of all. Confidence was lost, which almost collapsed the global economy. What role does trust play for people?

A survey of 500 employees of European companies showed the great importance of trust in ethical behavior.If employees can trust their executives, they are more ethical. Empirical behavioral experiments also confirm this.[19] The gift exchange game or trust game, which builds on the ultimatum game:

---

[16]See Steinherr, Christian/Steinmann, Horst/Olbrich, Thomas (1997), p. 1.

[17]See Luhmann, Niklas (2000).

[18]See Beschorner, Thomas/Hajduk, Thomas (2011); Albach, Horst (2003) and Lin-Hi, Nick (2014), pp. 10.

[19]See van den Akker, Lenny/Heres, Leonie/Lasthuizen, Karin/Six, Frédérique (2009).

Game 4: Gift Exchange Game or Trust Game

Two students are to split 10 pieces of chewing gum, as they did in the ultimatum game. The first (proposer) receives everything and can determine how much he gives to the second. This amount is then tripled. The second (responder) can then decide how much he will give the proposer.

The Gift Exchange Game or Trust Game is normally played with $10 instead of chewing gum. Rational behavior presupposes that the proposer should keep all money because, as a rational actor, he also assumes that the responder will give him something afterwards. After all, it is a game with one round. In the games, however, only a small proportion has chosen this strategy. Most of the proposers had confidence in the unknown responder and were rewarded because of the strong correlation between the amount of money transferred and the subsequent responses of the responder.[20]

Trust is nothing more than believing that someone will behave as expected without sanctions. Trust[21] exists in relation to good performance, moral behavior, help etc. Ethical behavior is an elementary prerequisite for human cohabitation. If one wishes to pursue common goals in a marriage for example, such as providing for each other and raising children together, the basis must be mutual trust. Without ethical, moral behavior there can be no trust between the spouses. Behaving ethically in this context, according simply to our definition, means not to damage the other party, or to be of use. Trust for companies is also important. Companies enter into transactions with new, unknown business partners because they have a good reputation. A good reputation engenders trust. As we saw in Chap. 4, if transactions occur only once, and so anonymously that damage to one's reputation is not expected, it would maximize one's advantages to fleece the business partners. The reputation of a person or company includes everything associated with them. Good or bad performance, moral or immoral behavior, etc. A reputation is made up of actions that both people and the market observe and interpret. Every company is thus responsible for its own reputation.

If the human being is descended from the monkey, similar group behaviors may also be applied to man. A solitary existence is a rare exception in the life of monkeys. They have to adapt themselves to predetermined hierarchical levels and rely on the favor of the other group members; this political behavior has even been observed in chimpanzees. The only monkey able to dominate the group must be able to unite the strongest group of supporters, a relative democratic majority. A minimum of cooperative behavior must therefore be applied to monkeys and thus also be a genetic attribute in humans. Otherwise no groups

---

[20]See Holzmann, Robert (2015), p. 129.

[21]See A hormone that promotes trust and social bonds has been discovered in the human body. Neuropeptide oxytocin caused subjects to clearly prioritize social risk over equal monetary risk. Kosfeld, M., et al. (2005).

would form, and both monkeys and man would be observable in nature only as solitary individuals.[22]

Reality shows that predetermination is by no means sufficient to ensure cooperative behavior. The incentive to behave non-cooperatively must therefore be correspondingly large. One of the reasons for this is that many decision-making situations in everyday life have a dilemma structure, such as the prisoner's dilemma presented above.[23] The dilemma is that although the overall benefit from cooperative behavior is greatest for the stakeholders, the uncertainty about the cooperative behavior of others makes non-cooperative behavior the best choice for the individual. The worst result for the individual is if he is the only cooperative player and all others uncooperative. Vice versa, the profit-gain is greatest for the individual if all others behave cooperatively. Since the insecurity in the situation is about everyone's behavior, they all opt for non-cooperative behavior, which is the worst result for everyone (ethical prisoner dilemma, see also Sect. 6.6). Here is an example from a decision-making situation on the market: The buyer buys a product which he has not yet been able to try out, or does not know. The vendor will rely on the buyer to pay for it later, after the delivery of goods. If neither one trusts the other, they will have to assume that they are going to be cheated. The consequence will be that they are also cheating, in order not to suffer from the purchase, so the business transaction is not concluded or high hedging costs arise. For example, in transactions with unknown foreign business partners, it is customary to carry out the transactions step by step with guarantees from a bank.

Dilemma and asymmetrical information are problematic, especially if the persons who are acting are not familiar with one another (on anonymous markets), cannot vote, or if they are dealing with a one-sided dependency in which uncooperative behavior can not be sanctioned later (play with one round). It is even better, then, to trust the active man directly. In the case of morality as a social basis for trust, cooperative behavior can be assumed, which is why these values are productivity-enhancing.

Citizens can trust in laws, courts and the executive branch. But as we have already mentioned, no system can control and implement the rules 100 percent, no matter what efforts are undertaken. Rules help in particular when they are clear and transparent, known by all actors, and everyone involved assumes a consistent application of the rules. Absolute control is impossible, which means that unethical behavior can pay off. Why then, do people generally behave fairly and ethically? How can we explain this "irrational" behavior? Is it deterrence or are people as social animals programmed that way? Both answers are elementary for moral behavior, but there is also the element of socialization, which teaches us how to live in our communities. Socialization as practicing behaviors and beliefs takes place mostly in childhood, but continues throughout our lives as long as people are in groups where they are at least partially in a dependent relationship. Behavior in

---

[22] See Windeler, Arnold (2014), p. 175.
[23] See Kirchgässner, Gebhard (1991), pp. 51.

conformance with the group is demanded of individuals. Sanctions are applied here as well. They can range from a refusal of recognition to exclusion from the group. People generally continue the behavior they have practiced even if the sanction is removed. Moral behavior must be practiced just like driving a car. The traffic laws provide the framework of behavior, and for interpersonal interaction there must also be rules with sanctions. The continued learning of the correct, or socially desirable, behavior begun in childhood creates a conscious value system in people as the foundation of their own goals and actions, which enters into the subconscious through constant repetition. Based on this subconscious set of values, we act as unconsciously as we drive a car, without having to reflect anew. Sanctions become superfluous. For the community this means that values must be passed on and socialization must take place in the youth. Role models are also important. They communicate beliefs that offer an explanation for behaviors. The disposition towards certain types of behavior are inherited, varied and cannot be influenced. If we want to influence people positively with business ethics, we must start with social, economic or business role models for socialization and communicating beliefs and attitudes.

Trust is an absolutely central economic factor both at the level of the individual and the whole economy. Who would want a business partner they cannot trust? How does it help a customer to be consulted by the best bank, the market leader, and have the feeling that all this intelligence and experience is working against him in order to empty his pockets, perhaps even recommending investments that will permanently damage him? The bank could recommend poor stocks still on the books from an IPO that made it a lot of money, and which the bank now wants to get rid of. Or someone could sell him life insurance with large fees hidden in small yields later on. Let's say the customer had already taken out two life insurance policies. What he cannot know is that the bank forces its consultants to sell at least five life insurance policies regardless of whether the customer needs them or not. Loyalty and confidence, or morality and ethics, are thus an important part of any service and a competitive advantage for companies on transparent markets. Once a customer's trust has been violated, if he acts rationally he will change banks, and as soon as he finds a bank he can trust he will stay there. For the bank that lost his trust he is lost forever, making the profits from the strategy with short-term success much less over the long term. The ethics campaign of Citibank, once the largest and most profitable banks, thus makes sense not just because of the imposed fines, but because the bank recognized that it went too far with its sales methods. It went so far in fact that the damage to its reputation and customer satisfaction could damage its future market position.

We have already discussed the importance of moral values for national economic development. The same applies at the microeconomic level for each company. A company that must operate in an immoral environment (such as in Russia) will have higher transaction costs. It must monitor and protect itself more. This causes inefficiency, since many economic transactions are lost to higher costs and risks. A company acts in a given social framework and recruits its employees from this society. Suppliers, customers, the legal system... everything comes from this society. The possibility for a company to influence a society is very limited, the opportunities for influence are trade associations, thus politics or advertisement. The most important thing for the company is to acquire morally suitable employees, and to hold them to moral behavior, whereby management focused on qualitative goals plays an important role, as we will show later on.

The importance of moral values for economic development has already been demonstrated. The same applies microeconomically to each individual company. An enterprise that has to operate in an immoral environment (as in Russia, for example, due to the uncertain legal situation) will have higher transaction costs. It must control more and secure more. Efficiency suffers, and many economic transactions are avoided because of higher costs and risks. A company moves in a given social context. It recruits its employees from this company. Suppliers, customers, legal order—everything comes from this company. The possibility for a company to influence society is only very limited by economic associations, such as politics or advertising. In the short term, it is also important for the company to acquire morally responsible employees and to educate employees on moral behavior, whereby a quality-oriented management plays an important role, as will be shown later.

> **Conclusion: Missing Rationality and Asymmetric Information**
> Asymmetrical information may favor the informed contractor over the uninformed and allow the uninformed contractor to benefit. Reputation, trust, morality (culture) have emerged as social solutions to this problem. In the case of irrational behavior, the state can intervene only in cases in which there are massive health impairments, since irrationality belongs to human nature. Only rarely can a restriction of human freedom be justified.

Comprehension Questions

1. Give two examples of irrational behavior from economic agents.
2. a) Give an example of both meritorial and demeritorial goods and explain the criteria to be applied on the basis of the examples.
   b) How should the state behave here?
3. a) Give an example of hidden characteristics, hidden actions and hidden intentions.
   b) What is the problem here?
   c) What do you suggest as a solution?
4. What is asymmetric information?
5. What effects can this have on business relations?
6. Give examples of the economy in which asymmetric information exists and possible tools to prevent unethical effects.

7.7   Market Failure Due to Corruption

The market economy generally has a system of rules for playing the game that must be learned and controlled. Immoral behavior in particular can damage the system in this context. The most famous example of immoral behavior and negative systemic behavior is corruption.

Case Study: Does Corruption Pay? The Example of Siemens[24]

1. Discuss the following article in the group. Why is there always corruption and why does it not pay off in the long term? Why is corruption harmful? What measures would you recommend to a company to prevent corruption?

Siemens, as one of the largest exporters of industrial equipment and train systems, maintained a widespread system of corruption. It was decentralized with the tacit approval of the group headquarters. There were a multitude of opaque transactions, insider cliques, and hundreds of accounts abroad in the many divisions and countries of the world conglomerate. The investigations of the American lawyers commissioned by the Siemens Supervisory Board, as well as the Munich public prosecutor's office, showed that between 2001 and 2006, bribe payments of at least 1.3 billion euros had flowed through those bank accounts. The recipient and the purpose of the payments are partly unknown to date.

It turned out that many orders, apparently acquired with bribes, were unprofitable. The Italian energy supplier Enel was responsible for the kick-off of Siemens, although the turbines were scarce and had to be allocated. In Argentina, the governments of Menem and de la Rúa were bribed. However, the announced, and in some cases contractually agreed, major contracts did not come about. Instead, there was blackmail on the part of the Argentinians who were involved in the distribution of orders, as they demanded money for the silence on the bribe payments. Siemens employees in Argentina reported life-threatening difficulties. Thus the seemingly lucrative business became a nightmare and a loss in business.

The US SEC initiated a corruption case against Siemens in the United States, as Siemens is listed on the US stock market. The Siemens Supervisory Board had then instructed a law firm in the US to investigate the Group and pass the findings directly to the US stock exchange supervisor. It turned out that there were far more questionable payments than the board had initially reported. In the middle of November 2006, the Munich Public Prosecutor's Office carried out a big raid at Siemens. In 2007, Siemens was threatened

---

[24]Sources: http://www.faz.net/aktuell/wirtschaft/unternehmen/bestechende-grossunternehmen-korruption-rechnet-sich-nicht-12050962.html?printPagedArticle=true#pageIndex_2;http://www.zeit.de/online/2008/51/siemens-korruption-strafe;http://www.sueddeutsche.de/wirtschaft/korruptionsaffaere-siemens-akzeptiert-millionen-dollar-strafe-1.372394;http://www.manager-magazin.de/unternehmen/industrie/siemens-zehn-jahre-nach-dem-siemens-skandal-a-1118197.html; http://www.handelsblatt.com/unternehmen/industrie/der-fall-siemens-sec-klopft-bei-staatsanwaltschaft-muenchen-an/2805400.html

with the exclusion of public contracts on the world's most important markets, huge image damage and billions in penalties. Siemens decided to make uncompromising reconnaissance and practically exchanged its entire management. At the same time, a comprehensive compliance system was set up. Siemens came away with an asset loss of an estimated 2.5 billion euros, of which were 1.2 billion euros in punitive payments. In 2008, the SEC imposed a fine of $1654 million on Siemens for the bribery of public authorities in several countries on the basis of the American Foreign Corrupt Practices Act (FCPA), of which $350 million went to the SEC, $450 million to the US Department of Justice, and $854 million went to the German prosecutor's office. The CEO of Siemens von Pierer maintained he had not known anything about the bribes. Pierer stepped down from his post. He was not prosecuted under criminal law, but had to pay damages of €5 million. A prosecution against him for neglecting the duty of supervision was suspended for a fine of €250,000. He then worked as an honorary professor and served on a supervisory board.

▶ **Definition** Private corruption is the abuse of a position in a private organization by using the position for one's own purposes and under public corruption we understand the abuse of a public office.[25]

The advantage is difficult to detect and can be hidden behind apparent powers, such as consultancy fees or excessively high prior-day auditors.[26] Personal contributions are used to influence an individual in his market decisions. Market economy as a system generally has rules, which must be learned and their implementation must be monitored. Immoral behavior can damage the system in this context, and the most well-known example for immoral and system-damaging behavior is corruption. The individual is influenced in his market decisions by personal benefit. The corrupted individual no longer makes decisions according to objective market criteria, which cancels out the market and competition functions, including the invisible hand. The person no longer optimizes in the interest of the whole system, and can thus damage the system and others.[27] If, for example, the buyer for a company were bribed by a worse and more expensive supplier he would damage the company, the market economy system and thus the entire community. The company would then have to pay out more for the same amount in preliminary production than if it had bought the objectively better product on the market, the result is production of fewer goods. As a whole the company then produces more expensive preliminary products of a poorer quality and fewer goods. This is damaging for the company, the national economy and the

---

[25]See Pritzl, Rupert F. J./Schneider, Friedrich (1999), p. 312.
[26]See Göbel, Elisabeth (2010), p. 300.
[27]See Graeff, Peter (2002), p. 295 and Homann, Karl/Blome-Drees, Franz (1992), p. 163.

community. Research in 97 countries in 1997 showed a negative statistical connection between corruption and GDP as well as between corruption and growth of the GDP.[28]

There are authors who regard corruption as a voluntary bargaining act, in which both sides win, whereby the redistribution cannot be assessed at the expense of the principal.[29] Corruption advantages are attested to by the bribe money as so-called Speed-Money. An inefficient situation created by slow bureaucracy uses the money as an incentive to get involved, thus making the situation more efficient. It is either assumed that the bureaucracy is ineffective or that efficiency is increased by corruption.[30] This implies that the bureaucratic rules are either nonsensical, inefficient, or that the officials would not apply the rules without corruption. Then the state apparatus would be an obstacle to the economy and thus better off done away with entirely. If one presupposes meaningful activity however, corruption creates an incentive to act corruptly. The decisions of the bureaucracy are at least no longer objective when corruption is involved.[31] They no longer represent the interest of the state or they give preference to companies that pay more, which leads to distortions in competition. We then have to ask who is paying the price of corruption. Bribery only pays off when it offers a greater advantage. As a rule, the damage is much greater than the benefit of bribery. Thus the damage to a bribed official who allows a drug that harms the general public is many times higher than the benefit to the pharmaceutical company.

It is in fact likely that bribery will make bureaucracy more expensive and will not make it more efficient because a corrupt official will try to get the maximum out of an administrative monopoly. A saying from China is "official and rich" and in the Philippines an official was paid up to $ 75,000 for an item that was valued at $ 10,000.[32]

Corruption is also partly classified as a voluntary contract, and therefore considered positive. However, the price and the bribe are, as shown above, at the expense of others, which is why corruption is unethical. While it is pointed out in the literature that a relationship of trust is established between the briber and the bribee of the exchange contract, this trust in the benefit, the maximization of the utility, is limited by the bribery. The briber can not usually prove that he has paid for something, and the bribery contract is not enforceable. The immorality in the abuse of trust that the bribed man commits is much easier to prove. A third party (state or company) has entrusted him to carry out a task, paid for it and yet was harmed. The fact that the payment offered was not enough cannot be used an argument, unless bribing was open to the contract between the principal and the agent.

---

[28]Corruption gross domestic product correlation coefficient: -0.80, statistically significant with a t-ratio of -13.2. Corruption gross domestic product growth correlation coefficient: -0.32, statistically significant with a t-ratio of -3.2. See Jain, Avid K. (2001), p. 90.

[29]See Homann, Karl (2003), p. 242.

[30]See Graeff, Peter (2002), p. 296.

[31]See Pritzl, Rupert F. J./Schneider, Friedrich (1999), p. 322.

[32]See Pritzl, Rupert F. J./Schneider, Friedrich (1999), p. 322.

The bribee has voluntarily entered into the contract. Corruption is, therefore, first and foremost a breach of trust, and therefore repels many people. For Kant it would be dishonesty, a defeat, and a significant weakness of personality or character. Corruption violates all three Kantian rules of reasoning (categorical and practical imperative as well as publicity rule). Someone who breaks a trust at the expense of the one who trusted him to maximize his financial advantage, can no longer be trusted.

As already described, corruption is the misuse of a position in a private or public organization for one's own purposes. This includes nepotism, the abuse of the position for relatives or friends. Using relationships for advantageous deals or even name-dropping sound familiar and unproblematic, but the effect can be the same as with financial corruption. It depends on whether the relationship provides an information advantage, a higher transparency for the principal because it gets a person or a product that is better, or whether the person or the product is worse, and can only be accepted because of the relationship. Then there is no advantage for the principal, but a disadvantage through the relationship.

The greatest negative effects of the development of corruption are found in the social impact on the society. Performance is no longer the decisive factor in improving one's own situation, but rather relations allowing nepotism and bribery in daily life, including the purchase of offices. Objective private or state decisions are made impossible by personal advantage and outside influence, which also has a long-term effect by lowering economic power. Foreign investors shy away from countries with strong corruption because they no longer have legal certainty.[33] Corrupt politicians and officials promote the uneven distribution of wealth as money leads to political power and vice versa. Money becomes the greatest factor in the system, thus displacing democratic decisions at the expense of the population who are excluded from the decision-making process. The distribution of wealth becomes more unequal.[34] In the Bible, bribery is severely condemned not only by a sense of justice, but also as a purely egoistic behavior against divine human dignity. The individual is enriched at the expense of the public.[35]

The unethical effects of corruption lead to the disintegration of the common system. If the acts are not punished, they will soon be imitated. It is always worthwhile for two parties to engage in corruption if they can benefit to the disadvantage of a third party. The incentives of corruption are quite strong and without sanction. There are plenty of arguments that play down damage to the third person and make it easier to avoid a bad conscience. This business, in which both parties profit greatly without much effort, finds imitators and, according to Kant's categorical imperative, multiply until the common system no longer works. That is, the culture is eroded as a basis for a productivity-enhancing division of labor. The damage to third parties is borne by the public through

---

[33] See Graeff, Peter (2002), p. 298 and Lambsdorff, Johann Graf (2002).

[34] See Pritzl, Rupert F. J./Schneider, Friedrich (1999), pp. 322.

[35] See Pritzl, Rupert F. J./Schneider, Friedrich (1999), pp. 324.

bribed state officials, the expense to the owners of companies as well as indirectly at the expense of all employees, insofar as the company is weakened. Overall, the company has less profit to be distributed.

Corruption is also unethical in the sense that it undermines the advantages of the market economy in the function of competition. The distribution becomes unfair because equals are given unequal reward. Performance is no longer crucial to success.

Since corruption not only affects the national economy, but also the companies themselves, Transparency International has compiled recommendations for companies on corruption prevention.[36] Transparency generally recommends companies involved in bribery to be listed in an anti-corruption register and to exclude them from the award of public contracts for several years.[37] However, this sanction would affect only a part of the companies, since not all of them participate in public contracts.

Internationally, there is a trend towards a tightening of corruption regulations. In response to the Watergate scandal, the U.S. issued the Foreign Corrupt Practices Act (FCPA) in 1977, which punished the bribery of foreign public officials by American corporations and citizens internationally. Since other countries did not follow, and Germany partly promoted the bribery of foreign companies to support exports, the FCPA initially had a negative effect on the competitiveness of American companies. In addition, all companies listed in the US are obliged to adjust their accounting to the anti-corruption rules of the FCPA.[38]

In 2008, the SEC imposed a fine of $1654 million on Siemens for the bribery of public authorities in several countries on the basis of the American Foreign Corrupt Practices Act, a settlement of which is $350 million went to the SEC and $450 million to the Ministry of Justice. $854 million went to the German government. The profit from these transactions, however, amounted to $1.1 billion for Siemens.[39]

In 1997, the OECD adopted a "Convention on Combating Bribery of Foreign Public Officials in International Business Transactions" signed by all 29 states with an obligation to incorporate the content into national law. This law, however, only regulates the bribery of foreign officials and presupposes that a breach of service duty can also be proven. This law was only ratified in Germany.[40]

The United Nations Declaration against Corruption entered into force on 16 September 2005. It is the first international treaty to fight corruption. The contracting parties undertook

---

[36]See   http://www.transparency.org/whatwedo/pub/assurance_framework_for_corporate_anti_brib ery_programmes,   http://www.transparency.de/fileadmin/pdfs/Themen/Wirtschaft/Checkliste_Self-Audits_TID.pdf (4.04.2013).

[37]See http://www.transparency.de/Stellungnahme_Entwurf-Gesetz-S.2338.0.html

[38]See Pritzl, Rupert F. J./Schneider, Friedrich (1999), p. 329 and http://www.justice.gov/criminal/fraud/fcpa/

[39]See http://www.sec.gov/news/press/2008/2008-294.htm

[40]See Elsner, Ulrike (2012); Keuchel, Jan (2002); Göbel, Elisabeth (2010), p. 300 and http://www.gesetze-im-internet.de/intbestg/BJNR232729998.html#BJNR232729998BJNG000100305

to punish various forms of corruption against officials and international cooperation. After persistent public criticism, the Bundestag passed a tightening of the rules of parliamentary deputies in 2014. A convicted deputy will be punished with up to 5 years imprisonment.[41]

Corruption is punishable for individuals, but not for companies. The introduction of criminal liability for legal persons and associations of persons failed to take hold in 1998. If a company commits a criminal offense, this is treated as an administrative offense.[42]

Bribery or attempted bribery in private business transactions is punishable for instance in Germany according to StGB §299 with imprisonment up to 3 years or with a monetary penalty. It also punishes whoever is or is trying to bribe employees or agents of a business enterprise. StGB §344 stipulates the punishment of the bribery or attempted bribery with an imprisonment of 3 months to 5 years.

Since corruption is not public, it is difficult to measure. Transparency International uses the Corruption Perceptions Index (CPI) to measure the corruption perceived in the public sector. However, this is not a direct, comprehensive measurement, but an aggregation of various studies and studies from a number of independent and well-known institutions. The countries are listed according to the degree of corruption in the public sector. According to Transparency International, the CPI is the most widespread corruption indicator in the world.[43]

Conclusion

Corruption acts as a reward for an expected risk, such as moral hazards, thus as incentives directed against the interests of the company or the community. Immoral behavior presents the greatest negative impact for top managers for stakeholders and shareholders. The company's success is jeopardized by immoral behavior. Moral, ethical behavior is therefore very important for the company. The same applies to the companies among themselves and in competition. Only a fair performance competition ensures an optimal allocation of resources and thus an efficient overall economic production. Immoral behavior harms society generally, from market processes, internal business processes and the erosion of culture.

The subprime crisis has shown that a market system without rules and controls cannot function. Although capitalism, or the market economy, is responsible for many crises with its growth and individual freedom, it remains the best of all possible economic systems. It is much more crucial that rules and controls exist to prevent damaging individual behavior. The regulatory concept of ordoliberalism has prevailed against the laissez-faire liberalism. Additionally, society has to implement moral responsibility in order to get a functioning market system.

---

[41]See http://www.transparency.de (4.04.2013) and Deutscher Bundestag Drucksache 18/476.

[42]See Bundesrechtsanwaltskammer (2013).

[43]See http://www.transparency.de (4.04.2013).

Comprehension Questions

1. What is corruption?
2. Why is corruption harmful?
3. To what extent is corruption punished?
4. Identify the forms of market failure and explain to what extent morality is necessary here.

7.8   Market Failure Due to Lack of Market Transparency

In contrast to the market failure due to asymmetric information, the information may also be incomplete or wrong. Market transactions are not carried out if there is no transparency about the services and risks or costs. If they are carried out because wrong assumptions about the contents of the transaction are the basis of the decisions, this leads to misallocations. For example, food ingredients and their effects are unknown or transparent so we cannot choose the right foods. Labeling the goods with an organic label helps to increase transparency. Stocks are the least transparent of all. The companies are so complex that not even the managers as insiders could value stocks properly. The time required to obtain the information far exceeds the expected benefits of better market transparency. For this reason, even if all the information was available, we would still have to live with a lack of market transparency.

7.9   Market Failure Due to Natural Monopolies

▶ **Definition** A natural monopoly is when an individual company can provide a given good to the whole market at a lower cost than two or more companies in a competitive situation.

This case sometimes occurs:

1. high transport costs; the so-called spatial monopolies,
2. increasing economies of scale

    And always with indivisibility of production.

7.9.1   Spatial Monopoly

▶ **Definition** Spatial monopolies give a company competitive advantages due to its location, making it the sole supplier.

Fig. 7.11 Spatial monopoly

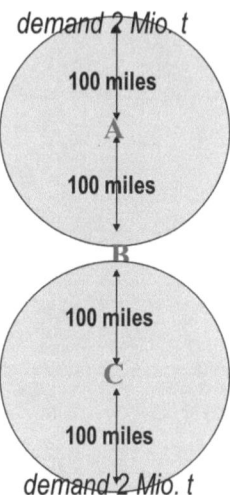

demand 2 Mio. t

100 miles

A

100 miles

B

100 miles

C

100 miles

demand 2 Mio. t

High transport costs result in price advantages for local suppliers and represent market entry barriers for third parties. The steel industry serves to illustrate a spatial monopoly. The transport costs for a ton of steel are 100 €/100 km. As a result, two markets will emerge (see Fig. 7.11). The competitor company 2 would have to be able to offer cheaper prices to penetrate the market of the other and in fact be 200 €/t cheaper to be able to supply both markets completely on the same terms as company 1. There are many spatial monopolies. Everyone knows a typical food shop in a village. But even in the refectory of a university chocolate bars can be sold more expensively, because the nearest supermarket is far away.

7.9.2   Natural Monopoly Due to Falling Unit Costs

With a high fixed cost burden (especially for large-scale plants), a significant reduction in unit costs only occurs with very large batch sizes. Examples: large-scale power generation plants, integrated steelworks, etc.

Example: Integrated steelworks.

At 80% utilization, the production costs with a 2 million ton furnace are 500 €/t. With only 50% utilization, they increase to 800 €/t (degressive unit costs). Alternatively, an oven with only a 1 million ton production capacity would also have production costs of € 800 /t. Optimum furnace size is therefore 2 million tons.

Large production plants generate high fixed costs. If only one ton of steel were produced, the cost of this ton would be the fixed costs plus the variable costs. The same applies to the capacity utilization of the 2 million t furnace. With a capacity utilization of only 50%, the allocation of fixed costs to the lower number of units results in significantly higher unit costs of € 800/t. As a result, the market in Fig. 7.12, taking into account the transport costs, is served by a company at point B with a 2 million t furnace and not by two

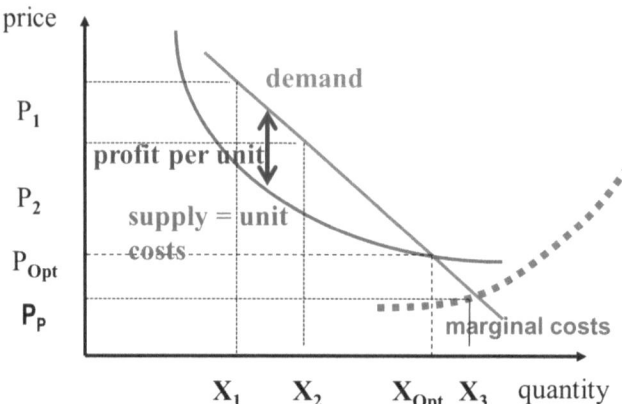

Fig. 7.12 Ruinous competition Initial situation. PP (polypol price): The competition price does not cover the unit costs, ruinous competition!! P < costs

companies with 1 million t each. It is a natural monopoly. The company that occupies this position first will prevail in the competition. In the following, we will analyze this competitive process of ruinous competition under the assumption of complete competition.

Assumption: Two companies each with 2 million tons of steel production capacity X1 and X2 can serve the entire market. U1 offers P1 and U2 P2 and thus steals some of the sales. Due to the falling unit costs U1 will follow suit. The lower price limit of this price competition is the variable cost. Everything above that brings additional marginal returns for the fixed costs (breakevenanalysis), which is why these prices are offered. This would still be within the loss range, however. In addition, the other company is offering the same product, so that the expected sales will not be reached. The production made at the low unit cost cannot be sold, resulting in overproduction, which further increases sales pressure.

That means: Falling unit or average costs lead to price undercutting and a simultaneous increase in supply. The company left standing after a ruinous price competition becomes a monopolist and the only supplier. But not X_{Opt} to P_{Opt}!

X_{Opt} and P_{Opt}

Highest welfare in the form of the consumer pension, because customers can buy at favorable but still cost-covering prices.

$X3 = PP = K'$.

The willingness to pay of the buyer is equal to the marginal cost but below the unit cost. Thus, the gain in benefits lies below the economic effort. If one were to produce and offer here, the result would be a negative welfare, a waste of resources.

The price optimum is undercut until only one supplier can survive on the market. This becomes a monopolist. The condition is that a company can supply the market more favorably than several companies in the competition. The cost advantage lies in this form of natural monopoly in production: a company produces twice that amount with decreasing

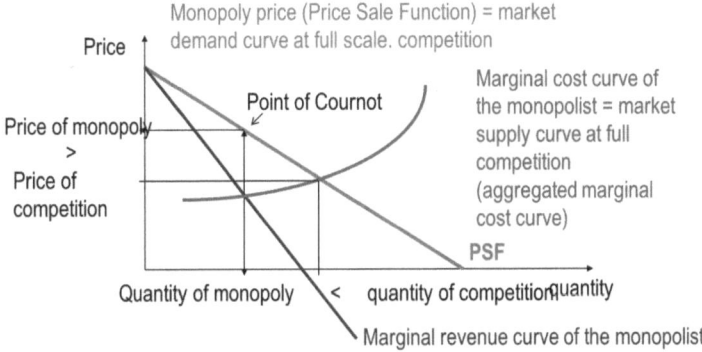

Fig. 7.13 Ruinous competition final state monopoly

unit costs. However, an economic problem arises as soon as the company has reached the monopoly position, because it can then determine the price. How will he set the price?

Pricing in Monopoly After Cournot at Normal Cost
The monopolist controls the entire market through the quantity offered only by him and can thus control the market price by the amount offered. This characterizes the behavior of a so-called Cournot monopolist. It is assumed here that the monopolist knows the course of total demand (price-sales function) (see Fig. 7.13).

Marginal cost curve of the monopolist $K' =$ market supply curve with perfect competition (aggregate marginal cost curve), price monopoly function (PAF) logo CNRS logo INIST.

Market demand curve with perfect competition.

The monopolist reaches his profit maximum in the quantity where the marginal costs correspond to the marginal revenue. He achieves the monopoly price for the monopoly quantity. Compared to the complete competition, the amount provided is too small, the price of the goods is too high. The highest welfare in the form of the consumer pension is not achieved, because customers cannot buy cheap but still cost-covering prices. This form of monopoly pricing is associated with static welfare losses.

With decreasing average costs, there is a natural monopoly which fixes the maximum output at the point where the marginal cost is equal to the marginal revenue. Natural monopolies are the opposite of the welfare optimum and are the result of price competition. This relationship is shown in Fig. 7.14.

Consider Fig. 7.14 and the quantities and prices recorded here. The monopolist makes the biggest profit in point C, but the price is too high and the amount too low. There is a market failure and thus a loss of welfare in the form of the consumer pension.

Here the price covers the unit cost, i. for the resulting costs are correspondingly high benefits of consumers. The maximum consumer surplus and thus welfare is realized. This is optimal for the economy, but suboptimal for the individual company due to the lack of profit.

Fig. 7.14 Overview of natural monopoly with declining unit costs. X_M monopoly quantity; X_M monopoly price; X_O optimum quantity; P_O optimum price

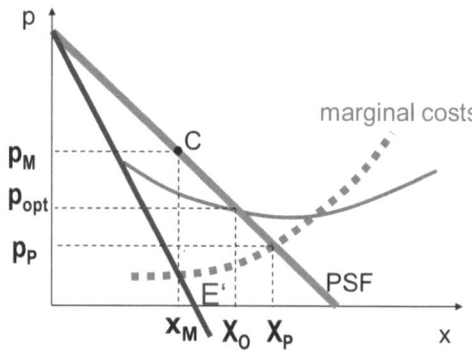

XP: Polypol Quantity,

PP: Polypol Price.

The willingness to pay of the buyer is equal to the marginal cost but below the unit cost. Thus, the gain in benefits lies below the economic effort. The costs are no longer covered by the willingness of the customers to pay. So there is no benefit to the costs of the same amount. If one were to produce and offer here, there would be a negative welfare, ie a waste of resources.

Conclusion

The company, which survived ruinous price competition, will offer the monopoly price and the monopoly price as a monopolist. This leads to welfare losses. There is a market failure because the market does not provide the socially desired results. Natural monopolies always lead to market failure. The state has to intervene in the market. There are basically two options. The state itself can offer the product, and produce and offer the optimal quantity at the optimal price or he can supervise the monopolist.

7.9.3   Natural Monopoly on Internet and Software

High development costs and low duplication costs are specific to the production of software. The high development costs represent high fixed costs, which are at the same time market entry barriers. Before software can be sold and proceeds can be realized, programming must be completed. After that, almost no variable costs arise in the production, because the software can be selectively reproduced. As a consequence, the fixed cost degression is very high. In the meantime, software can even be purchased and copied directly over the Internet. If a software application succeeds in becoming the market standard, it meets the requirements of a natural monopoly. In principle, no second software is necessary. An enterprise can supply the whole market more cheaply than two companies in a competitive situation. However, this is only static as a snapshot. Over time, the natural monopoly will have to do far less research, depending on the market entry barrier, than in a competitive situation. Constantly new products need not be associated with a benefit for the user. The monopolist can also use the standard to force users to purchase updates, if the old versions are not compatible. Software monopolies also want their programs to be incompatible with competing applications to maintain market entry barriers.

Microsoft thus has a monopoly due to its lack of compatibility with other programs and the market entry barriers resulting from high software development costs. A new word processor would have too high of development costs and must be compatible with MS-Word, otherwise no one would use it. In addition, Microsoft could undercut a new market participant at any time with the using price to push it out of the market. The same applies to the Windows operating system. Free programs such as Open-Office and Java have been developed by programmers to break the heavy dependency.

Such standard-setting also occurs on Internet platforms. The more users there are, the more interesting the platform is for other users. It is not worthwhile, for example, to offer your car on a second platform, if all those interested in buying are looking at the offers of the market leader anyway. The investment for programming is very complex, with high fixed costs and market entry barriers. For network goods and network services, the greater the number of players on the supply and demand sides, the more attractive the offer (positive network effects). Of course, this also applies to application programs that finance themselves via advertising and advertisers such as Google or Facebook.

Natural monopolies in the software and Internet sector also have a tendency to ruinous price competition. Positive feedback loops between economies of scale and positive network effects show their effects here. Price cuts attract more users, leading to further economies of scale and network effects. The more favorable cost structure due to the economies of scale and positive network effects allows the dominant supplier to win any price war. Political economy must therefore monitor the natural monopolies in the Internet and software sector for abuse of their dominant position.

7.9.4   Indivisibility of the Factors of Production

Indivisibility of the factors of production is when a single production capacity suffices to serve the entire market. A second supplier would have to build up a second production capacity. Not only is this inefficient, it would be worthless if the supplier were to withdraw from the market (irreversibility of costs). This applies, for example, to the rail network of Deutsche Bahn. Building a second rail network would be pointless as long as the capacity of the other is sufficient. New trains from another provider, would not increase competition, because there would not be an increase in train passengers; rather the rail network of Deutsche Bahn would no longer be as full.

The phenomenon of the indivisibility of the factors of production mainly affects pipeline-related supply networks, such as power lines, railways, roads, airfields or telecommunication cables, i.e. goods whose supply is linked to a specific infrastructure (electricity, gas, water, telecommunications, postal services, transport).

Of course, monopolies result in profit maximization at the expense of the consumer. The state must therefore intervene in the market to correct this failure. In principle, there are three political economy options available: nationalization, state supervision and the separation of networks.

Political Economy Concepts for Natural Monopolies
A. Nationalization = transfer of business to public ownership.

Nationalization offers many advantages. The state-owned company can produce the quantity and offer it at the price that covers the unit cost. This is how welfare optimum can be achieved. The state then maximizes welfare rather than profit. Needs can be completely met by the supply. In this way, the state can apply infrastructure policy with a state railway, thus making economically weak areas attractive as a production location through good infrastructure. It can institute social policies, for example by offering cheaper train tickets for families. Environmental policy also becomes possible by subsidizing rail travel. Environmentally damaging car trips and flights are then replaced by train journeys.

Example: Deutsche Bahn was to be privatized via an IPO. To do this, unlike a state-owned company, it had to be profitable. To achieve this, investments have been postponed and staff laid off. Delays increased as a result.

State-owned companies also have many disadvantages. State influence can lead to inefficiencies, for example by awarding posts to politicians. A bureaucratization, thus inflated administration can also be the result (see political failure).[44] A lack of work ethic and cost awareness is also attributed to state-owned enterprises due to lack of profit pressure. That is, the disadvantages of nationalization are comparable to the problems of the central administration economy. On the other hand, a private monopolist only has an interest in maximizing profits. Why should they serve better when there is no competition?

Alternative: B. Privatizationand Regulation
The second option to avoid the welfare disadvantages of a natural monopoly is state price control. Private monopolies in Germany are controlled by state regulatory authorities (BKartA, BNetzA) in their economic activities. The price control is still the prohibition of discrimination. In other words, natural monopolies must serve all consumers equally and are not allowed to use their market position to force their suppliers to lower their prices disproportionally, which is in line with the competitive approach to abuse control. We differentiate between price regulation, so-called **cost-plus regulation** and **price cap regulation**. In the cost-plus regulation unit costs must be provided by the monopolist

---

[44]Thus, the former chancellery chief Pofalla became CEO of Deutsche Bahn and then replaced the longtime chief environmental officer with his former office manager Gehlhaar.

See Spiegel Online vom 29.04.2016. http://www.spiegel.de/wirtschaft/unternehmen/deutsche-bahn-ronald-pofalla-schmeisst-einen-nach-dem-anderen-raus-a-1090019.html

and a mark-up approved. In price cap regulation, a price is set by the regulator as an upper limit. This exists currently for letter postage.

There is an information deficit with the regulator in price cap regulation. The regulatory authority does not know the cost structure of the monopolist. There is asymmetric information in favor of the monopolist that can be exploited. The control authority lacks information on production costs. Even when comparing similar markets, e.g. comparing the German electricity prices with the lower French prices there are production differences that relativize the comparison. In France there is a proportionate increase in nuclear power from outdated and thus already depleted nuclear power plants (such as Cattenom). Also, utilities can artificially raise prices, even if they include fictitious costs such as future demolition or disposal costs.

Alternative C: Separation of the Nets
The third alternative is to force monopolists to make their networks available to other providers. This is called a throughput compulsion. The monopolists have to separate their networks as their own societies (so-called unbundling) so that they can objectively determine network costs. This process, and in particular the discrimination ban on access to the network, must be monitored by a governmental agency (network agency). This is in turn linked to price regulation. For example, there is a network transmission requirement for electricity, telephone, Internet and railway networks. The implementation is supervised by the Federal Network Agency for Electricity, Gas, Telecommunications, Post and Railways.

Excursus: Competition Through Additional Providers?
Work in groups:

1. Discuss the advantages and disadvantages of competition for the national railway company from long-distance buses. Will this make the national railway company's offer cheaper and qualitatively better? Solution: Competition by private long-distance buses has since been approved. People waited for a better and cheaper offers from the national railway company due to the competition in long-distance transport. But the question is, how does competition between private companies and governments work? The national railway company will have to cut prices on long-haul routes, which is an advantage for its customers. However, taxpayers' earnings will have to offset the loss. As long as the national railway company still has the public service mission of the population as a state-owned company, and does not have to offer any profitable routes, it will not be able to cover its costs.
2. Discuss the advantages and disadvantages of competition from other railway providers on the rail network of the national railway company. The national railway company will be forced to make its rail network available to other railway service providers for a fee. The fee collection and the rail access are monitored by the state. Will this make the national railway company's offer cheaper and qualitatively better?

Again, it is questionable whether a welfare-enhancing competition will come about. For example, it is not profitable to drive a second train at only half capacity 5 min after the ICE of the national railway company has passed. In addition, connections would have to be coordinated with the national railway company to allow passengers to change trains. Will trains wait if the train of a competitor is late? Just due to the fact that regional traffic is not organized by the German Federal Railways, but the federal states, there are currently coordination problems and thus missed connections.

3. **Group work:** Discuss the advantages and disadvantages of competition through private mail services for the national post. Will this make the national post's offer cheaper and better in quality?

Solution: The admission of private postal services should also be questioned. As long as the performance is the same, nothing changes in the natural monopoly. If now two letter carriers each bring one letter, instead of one carrier with two letters nothing has been gained in efficiency. Assuming that every household receives at least two letters per day, it is more efficient for one carrier to bring the two letters instead of two letters one at a time. In the long term, therefore, only one supplier should prevail after a ruinous cutthroat competition.

Experience in Practice

What are the experiences of these approaches in practice? In the telecommunications sector, unbundling, i.e. the separation of networks, could be achieved without any major deterioration in quality. Deutsche Telekom's obligation for competitors to conduct competitions led to significantly lower prices and the same quality. Meanwhile, Telecom has separated from their networks. Negative experiences resulted in the privatization of the British railway. In Great Britain, there was a private rail operator for 8 years (railtrack, from 1994 to 2002). Before that there was the state-owned British Rail and since 2002 the infrastructure belongs to the state-owned, non-profit Network Rail. The private company railtrack had previously suffered serious accidents, which are attributed by market observers to a lack of maintenance. Energy supply was not affected by the desired price decrease as a result of competition, even though the power grids were separated from the compulsory transmission companies. To prepare for the IPO, the new railway chief Mehdorn was hired. After the plans were postponed, and there was a change in leadership, the new railway manager Grube a few years later found an investment backlog of tracks, switch points and switch towers amounting to € 30 bil.[45]

---

[45]See Handelsblatt vom 3.11.2013. http://www.handelsblatt.com/unternehmen/handel-konsumgueter/investitionsstau-im-schienennetz-bahn-chef-fordert-staatliche-milliarden-spritze/9020654.html

Conclusion

Transaction costs and lack of market transparency hamper the market mechanism. Either the transactions do not materialize or they lead to inefficient results. For natural monopolies, market failure is mainly due to the indivisibility of the factors of production, such as rails. Nationalization is usually the better alternative because the information is lacking for regulation and oversight. Technical progress in the IT sector has created new natural monopolies that must monitor competition policy.

Comprehension Questions

1. Give two examples of market transactions that cannot be achieved due to excessive transaction costs, and identify the costs.
2. Give two examples in which the market mechanism is hampered by a lack of transparency of benefits.
3. Which invention has both reduced transaction costs and increased market transparency in recent decades? Explain your assessment.
4. (a) Discuss the advantages and disadvantages of nationalization and regulation of natural monopolies.
   (b) Give an example of a natural monopoly.
   (c) Explain your assessment.
   (d) What economic measures do you propose?

7.10   Labor Market

What Follows Why?

The labor market is a central market that determines economic development and on which the welfare of the population depends. Again, there is market failure. Unemployment has far-reaching social and political consequences, which is why the state intervenes here and tries to prevent market failure.

   Learning Goals

   You should be able to explain the market failure in the labor market, how unemployment is measured and why unemployment is such a big economic and social problem.

7.10.1 Historical Development

Industrialization led to the creation of labor markets where day laborers offered their work. As a rule, they came from the countryside, meaning that they were unskilled workers who, due to the lack of transportation, were dependent on the labor demand of the local employer. Work was the only source of income for the whole family. In addition, there was strong population growth. There were many workers for only a few employers. The workers in the labor market and their families were impoverished. The pay was not enough to feed families and send children to school. In order to survive, the children also had to offer their labor under demeaning conditions. Due to the peculiarities of the labor market, market failure also occurs here. Why is this?

Neoclassical Labor Market Model
Even the neoclassical model for a macroeconomic labor market, developed under very rigid model-theoretical assumptions, proves that under certain circumstances the laws of supply and demand do not provide a stable equilibrium solution.

This is mainly due to the sometimes atypical developments of the job offer function.

Assumptions of the Neoclassical Model

1. Labor is a homogeneous factor,
2. there is complete competition in the goods and factor markets,
3. companies work with profit-based production functions,
4. employees have no other factors (no assets),
5. they cannot resort to state or equivalent income protection (no social assistance or family support) (original market – survival of the fittest), everyone is on their own and
6. They must individually negotiate the wage level with companies (no collective bargaining agreements and no trade unions → each employee must negotiate individually with the employer).

Consider Fig. 7.15. In the normal situation of neoclassicism, salary is sufficiently high. Then a rising wage leads to an increased supply of labor, because the suffering of the labor is overcompensated by the increased wage. The worker views the job as a sacrifice because it is exhausting and it costs him free time. On the other hand, the reward is added value. If the wage decreases, the employee reduces his offered labor. He is always balancing job sacrifice and compensation for wages. The loss of benefit (suffering) from 1 h of overtime is equal to the benefit from the purchase equivalent of the hourly wage.

An unstable balance is created in the labor market when wages are so low that workers cannot live off their earned income. They must take a second or even third job to survive. This increases the job supply. This is called an abnormal reaction of the work offer.

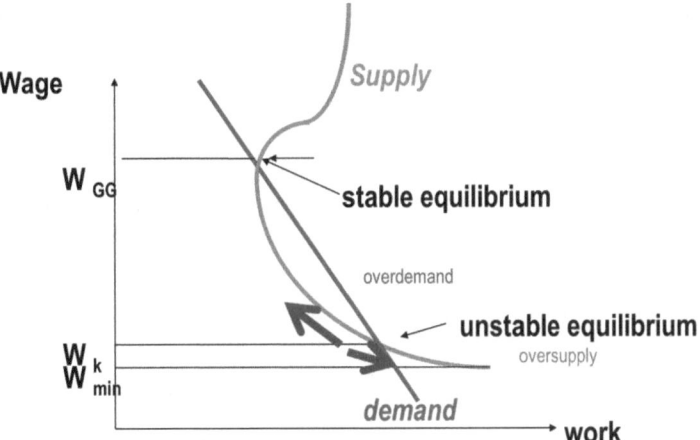

Fig. 7.15 The abnormal response of the work supply. *WGG* equilibrium; W_k critical wage; W_{min} minimum wage

As long as wages on the labor market are lower than wk., there is an oversupply of work, which means that the incomes of workers drop again and again to the minimum (W_{min}) = "iron law of wages" by Ferdinand Lassalle. Only when it is possible to raise the wage level above wk., does a wage drift set in, since the demand for labor is greater than the supply. The over-demand leads to the stable balance in W_{GG}. If the wage rises above Wk, the labor supply reduces, because the money is enough to live on, the job is too exhausting, 14 h is too long compared to 8 h, and there is no more child labor. Wages above this equilibrium wage rate cause unemployment.

One consequence of the impoverishment of industrial workers was the strengthening of socialism and communism: Marx regarded private property as the core problem. By the capitalists' ownership of the means of production, in his opinion, the "proletariat" was depended on and exploited. For this reason, in the socialist states after the forcible expropriation of the factory owners, the community property was introduced within the framework of the central administrative economy. In order to avert the exploitation and misery of workers, the state also intervened in the labor market in market-based systems, as the structural weaknesses of workers resulting from the lack of wealth could not be eliminated in the short and medium term.

The interventions of the state led

1. to legal regulations of labor law,
2. legal minimum wages
3. the constitutionally guaranteed collective bargaining autonomy. On the basis of the freedom of association guaranteed under Article 9 of the Basic Law, employees can now form unions and employers' organizations to regulate labor market conditions in the economy. The autonomy of collective bargaining enshrined here prohibits the state from

entering wage negotiations between employers and trade unions. The unions negotiate with the employers and so there is a balance of power.

Marx saw the only way to stop the misery of the workers in the expropriation of the capitalists, ie the factory owners. He did not see the emergence of trade unions as a suitable solution, in contrast to Lasalle. The job of the unions is to absorb the imbalance between labor demand and labor supply. Before unions existed, there was a monopoly of demand, and the formation of unions now provides for a bilateral monopoly. Lasalle should be right. It is not just the trade unions that have achieved a social balance between work and capital, and the market economy has been accepted by society, but also that purchasing power has been redistributed to workers, with sufficient demand for the products generated.

How is the lack of work measured? The unemployment rate is the indicator of employment. The current version of the unemployment rate covers the registered unemployed in relation to the dependent labor force, ie without the self-employed.

$$\text{Unemployment rate in}\% = \frac{\text{registered unemployed}}{\text{dependent labor force (Employed and unemployed)}} \cdot 100$$

Since unemployment is an important political campaign issue, politics not only seeks to reduce unemployment but also to influence the calculation of the unemployment rate. These include early retirement programs and job creation measures such as one-euro jobs. The consequence is that the already limited significance of the unemployment rate is impaired. There are reasons for under-recording unemployment and reasons for over-recording unemployment.

Reasons for Under-Recording Unemployment

1. Silent reserve of unrecognized unemployed persons who do not report themselves unemployed due to resignation or shame
2. Unemployed without entitlement to unemployment benefits often do not report.
3. retired workers
4. temporarily retraining or further training (job creation measures)

Reasons for Over-Recording Unemployment

1. Black market workers who register as unemployed.
2. Not willing to work, who register as unemployed.

Types and Causes of Unemployment
There are four types of unemployment: seasonal, economic, frictional and structural unemployment.

1. **Seasonal unemployment**

    Seasonal unemployment refers to varying job demand depending on the season. Since it cannot be influenced, it is not a political economy problem. It occurs at different times depending on the economic sector (for example in agriculture, tourism, construction industry).

2. **Frictional unemployment**

    This type of unemployment arises when moving from one job to the next. Being in-between jobs has become rare as workers apply for new jobs while still in their current one to avoid the risk of unwanted unemployment.

3. **Cyclical unemployment**

    As the name implies, unemployment here is due to fluctuations in general economic demand. Decline in general demand generates corresponding unemployment.

4. **Structural unemployment**

    Anything that is not cyclical, frictional or seasonal unemployment is called structural unemployment. Structural unemployment is caused by a change in the structure of the economy. Technical progress is changing production and, with it, labor demand. Further, through advances in transportation technology or market openings, the international division of labor may change. As, for example, due to the reduction of transport costs and lower labor costs abroad, production is shifted abroad, domestic labor demand is reduced. There is an imbalance between the structure of labor supply and the demand for labor such as in the steel or coal crisis.

    Workers have a very high priority because they are a factor of production (have economic value) and on the other hand also pay taxes and push the economy along. Unemployment burdens public coffers. Without work, there would be radicalization through rising dissatisfaction (political imbalance), the social environment would disintegrate, which would lead to welfare losses, etc. Germany had such experiences in the world economic crisis after 1929. With longer unemployment, knowledge is lost to production, i.e. human capital. Therefore, the goal is to ensure full employment.

Reasons for Full Employment as an Economic Policy Goal

1. Work as a value in itself (morally, man has a right to work)
2. Welfare loss, as idle factors of production and the cost of unemployment
3. Long-term unemployment means a loss of capacity as training levels are reduced
4. Unemployment can lead to political instability or radicalization

Despite all of the efforts of politics and economics to eliminate or at least reduce unemployment, a large part of unemployment will always be unaffected and must therefore be tolerated. This so-called base unemployment is due to inadequate levels of education, old age and poor health status. **Full employment** is never achievable, as there is always natural or frictional unemployment and voluntary or accepted unemployment (also seasonal unemployment, depending on the location). Approximate full employment was achieved in the 1960s. At that time wages were lower, making Germans work more competitive internationally, and there was little social security, so that people were forced to work and to take on almost any job.

Conclusion
Growth and unemployment are of political and social importance. It can be assumed that the declared unemployment is understated. On the other hand, unlike in the 1930s, there is social security at the subsistence level and, as a consequence, voluntary unemployment. Due to the compulsion to secure the subsistence minimum, an abnormal supply curve (market failure) arises in the labor market. The intervention of the state is not only welfare-promoting, but also indispensable to ensure social preservation and stability.

Comprehension Questions

1. Give reasons for under-reporting and over-reporting unemployment.
2. What types of unemployment exist?
3. Explain why there is an abnormal supply curve on the job market and what consequences it has.
4. What is the economic function of trade unions?

References

Alparslan, A. (2006). *Strukturalistische Prinzipal-Agent-Theorie*. Wiesbaden: Deutscher Universitätsverlag.

Axelrod, R. (1987). *Die evolution der Kooperation*. München: Oldenbourg.

Ballwieser, W., & Clemm, H. (1999). Wirtschaftsprüfung. In W. Korff (Ed.), *Handbuch der Wirtschaftsethik, Band 3: Ethik wirtschaftlichen Handelns* (pp. 399–416). Gütersloh: von Wilhelm Korff.

Beck, H. (2014). *Behavioral economics: Eine Einführung. 1 Aufl.* Wiesbaden: Springer.

Beschorner, T., & Hajduk, T. (2011). Der Ehrbare Kaufmann – Unternehmensverantwortung "light"? *CRS Magazine, 3,* 6–8. Accessed from http://www.alexandria.unisg.ch/export/DL/206603.pdf

Camerer, C., Issacharoff, S., Loewenstein, G., O'Donoghue, T., & Rabin, M. (2003). Regulation for conservatives: Behavioral economics and the case for "asymmetric paternalism". *University of Pennsylvania Law Review, 151,* 101–144.

Dillerup, R., & Stoi, R. (2011). *Unternehmensführung* (3rd ed.). München: Verlag Franz Vahlen.

FÖS Green Budget Germany Forum Ökologisch-Soziale Marktwirtschaft. (kein Datum). Accessed March 11, 2013, from http://www.foes.de/themen/oekologische-steuerreform/lexikon/

Fritsch, M., Ewers, H.-J., & Wein, T. (2011). *Marktversagen und Wirtschaftspolitik: Mikroökonomische Grundlagen staatlichen Handelns*. München: Verlag Franz Vahlen.

Furubotn, E. G., & Richter, R. (2005). *Institutions and economic theory*. Ann Arbor: University of Michigan Press.

Gabisch, G. (2003). Unternehmen und Haushalte. In H. Berg, D. Cassel, & K.-H. Hartwig (Eds.), *Vahlens Kompendium der Wirtschaftstheorie und Wirtschaftspolitik* (2nd ed.). München: Vahlen.

Göbel, E. (2010). *Unternehmensethik*. Stuttgart: UTB.

Graeff, P. (2002). Positive und negative ethische Aspekte von Korruption. *Sozialwissenschaften Berufspraxis 25*(3), 291–302. Accessed March 8, 2015, from http://nbn-resolving.de/urn:nbn:de:0168-ssoar-37838

Holzmann, R. (2015). *Wirtschaftsethik*. Wiesbaden: Springer Gabler.

Homann, K. (2003). Anreize und Moral. In C. Lütge (Ed.), *Unternehmensethik und Korruption* (pp. 233–267). Münster: LIT.

Homann, K., & Blome-Drees, F. (1992). *Wirtschafts- und Unternehmensethik*. Göttingen: Vandenhoeck.

Jain, A. K. (2001). *The political economy of corruption*. London: Routledge.

Kirchgässner, G. (1991). *Homo oeconomicus*. Tübingen: Mohr Siebeck.

Lin-Hi, N. (2014). Der Ehrbare Kaufmann. In Industrie und Handelskammer Nürnberg für Mittelfranken (Ed.), *Der Ehrbare Kaufmann: Tradition und Verpflichtung*. Nürnberg: IHK.

Luhmann, N. (2000). *Vertrauen: Ein Mechanismus der Reduktion sozialer Komplexität*. Stuttgart: UTB.

Pritzl, R. F. J., & Schneider, F. (1999). Handbuch der Wirtschaftsethik, Band 4: Ausgewählte Handlungsfelder. In W. Korff (Ed.), *Korruption* (pp. 310–333). Gütersloh: Gütersloher Verlagshaus.

Rapoport, A., & Chammah, A. M. (1970). *Prisoner's dilemma – A study in conflict and Cooperation* (2nd ed.). Ann Arbor: University of Michigan Press.

Schwägerl, C., & Traufetter, G. (2011). *Klinisch tot*. In DER SPIEGEL42/2011. Accessed from http://www.spiegel.de/spiegel/print/d-81015403.html

Schwaninger, M. (2008). Anatol Rapoport (May 22, 1911–January 20, 2007), pioneer of systems theory and peace research, mathematician, philosopher and pianist. *Wiley Online Library Systems Research and Behavioral Science, 24*(6), 655–658.

Steinherr, C., Steinmann, H., & Olbrich, T. (1997). *Die US-SentencingCommissionGuidelines, eine Dokumentation, Diskussionsbeitrag Nr.* 90 des Lehrstuhls für Allgemeine Betriebswirtschaftslehre und Unternehmensführung der Universität Erlangen-Nürnberg, Nürnberg.

Thaler, R., & Sunstein, C. R. (2003). Libertarian paternalism. *American Economic Review Papers and Proceedings, 92*(2), 175–179.

Weisser, J. (2012). *Pfand und Anreizsysteme* (1st ed.). Wiesbaden: Springer.

Welge, M., & Al-Laham, A. (2008). *Strategisches Management* (5th ed.). Wiesbaden: Springer.

Whitman, G. (2006, February). *Against the new paternalism. Internalities and the economics of self-control*, Cato Institute, Policy Analysis No.563.

Williamson, O. E. (1979). *The economic institution of capitalism*. New York: Free Press.

Williamson, O. E. (1985). Transaction cost economics: The governance of contractual relations. *Journal of Law and Economics, 12*(2), 233–261.

Windeler, A. (2014). *Kompetenz: Sozialtheoretische Perspektiven*. Wiesbaden: VS Verlag für Sozialwissenschaften.

Political Failure

8

What Follows Why?
Now that we have dealt with the market failure, we want to investigate the question of whether politics makes economic decisions in a pareto-efficient or socially maximizing way. The behavior of politicians and the voting procedures necessary for decisions form the political decision-making framework for economic policy. Politics manages democracy and must remedy the market failure and provide goods. To do this, it needs a bureaucracy to implement political decisions about the production of public goods. Here, too, we want to analyze the motives behind a bureaucracy and, in particular, whether it can efficiently implement political decisions.

Learning Goals
After this chapter you should be able to explain the voting procedures with their advantages and disadvantages and be able to portray the essential theories about the behavior of politicians in your own words.

8.1   The New Political Economy

An explanation for the decision-making behavior of political decision-makers is provided by the approach of the "New Political Economy".[1] According to the approach of the New Political Economy, which emerged in the early 70s, a politician does not maximize the

---

[1]The behavioral theories of Smith and Schumpeter have picked up on Downs in the USA and Herder-Dorneich in Germany, thus founding the New Political Economy.

common good, but predominantly his own benefit. Political offices provide benefits in the form of power, prestige and income. In order to achieve the desired office, the politician must collect as many electoral votes—one speaks of maximizing votes (vote-maximization hypothesis, homo politicus). This behavioral orientation is called "political rationality" (assumption utilitarianism = utility maximization).[2] There is thus a divergence between political rationality (own benefit) and social rationality (social benefit), and there may be conflicts of interest between the benefits of the policy and the social benefits,[3] but politicians should represent the social interests. For this reason, the influence of other interests on politicians must be prevented. Donations to parties and politicians as well as additional income have to be disclosed and limited.

The New Political Economy is confirmed by psychology.[4] Motivation for power, as the goal to influence or impress other people, is an act of maximizing utility and making it more difficult to act altruistically in the interests of society. Especially political offices provide power, which is why people with power motivation are attracted by them. The tendency to draw satisfaction from the physical, mental or emotional influence on others is harmful for third parties and thus also unethical. It is the tyrants who must fear democracy.

People shy away from change when they cannot assess how they are affected. The status quo is preferred over another alternative (status quo bias). Samuelson and Zeckhauser also identified an advantage of the incumbent in political elections.[5]

Fernandez and Rodrik state a status quo bias in trade liberalization reforms in developing countries. At first the population was against it, later when she realized that she benefited.[6]

Thaler showed that people discount inconsistent time because they value things that happen in the short term more than events in the future. There is a present-day preference. Experiments show that the future benefit does not decrease continuously. This is called hyperbolic discounting.[7] Politicians can take advantage of the underweighting of long-term events by making voter elections unpopular after the elections and popular pre-electoral decisions, as in the Nordhaus economic model. And they can combine underweighting of long-term events with the status quo bias by making unpopular decisions, such Establish

---

See *Starbatty, Joachim* (1985), S.40; *Schumpeter, Joseph A.* (1993), p. 427ff; *Andel, Norbert* (1990), p. 48; *Downs, Anthony* (1957) and *Herder-Dorneich, P.* (1957).

[2] An empirical verification of further parts of the New Political Economy was carried out by Meyer-Krahmer. See *Meyer-Krahmer, Frieder* (1979). See also *Franke*. See *Franke, Siegfried F.* (1996); *Downs, Anthony* (1968); *Andel, Norbert* (1990), p. 47ff; *Braybrooke, David/Lindblom, Charles, E.* (1963) and *Lindblom, Charles, E.* (1965).

[3] See also the trade-offs between economic and political objectives presented in Chap.3.

[4] See Brandstätter, Veronika/Schüler, Julia/Puca, Rosa Maria/Lozo, Ljubica (2018) and Schultheiss, O. C. (2008).

[5] See Samuelson, William; Zeckhauser, Richard (1988).

[6] See Fernandez, Raquel; Rodrik, Dani (1991), pp. 1146–1155 and Beck, H. (2014), p.165.

[7] See Thaler, Richard H. (1981); Frederick, S./Loewenstein, G./O'Donoghue, T. (2002), p. 360 and Beck, H. (2014), p. *215*.

the introduction of the euro in Germany as a jam today, but only follow the implementation in the long term. This reduces the political resistance as political costs.

Moral hazards are an incentive for individuals to act against or at the expense of many, society or their company. Politicians also have moral hazard, and politicians are not liable for the long-term damage to their policies. Only the short-term disadvantages of their policies are relevant as long as they affect reelection.

Example: It is politically rational to finance the pensions with debt, because the future generation is not entitled to vote. The funding hits the successor, so it's good for the politician. The Italian politician Berlusconi has promised tax gifts in the election campaign and funded this debt. This led Italy into the debt crisis. Berlusconi promised a tax relief for the citizens, as it brought him a large number of votes. The intergenerational contract for pensions in Germany was also paid out of the budget, and now the pension contributions are rising, but the expected pension of the next generation continues to decline. Politicians in all democracies have increased indebtedness to the detriment of future generations.

Especially in this regard, the press has the special task to point out the long-term policy consequences. The press is not allowed to be dependent on advertising or a private owner. It must analyze the work of politicians also independently and unprejudiced and explain it to the public. Freedom of expression and the press must not be impaired.

If there are hardly any altruistic (disinterested, unselfish) politicians, they need to be even more controlled. In the context of democracy, the division of powers is of particular importance in this context. The politicians must be subject to the law. In practice, political decisions by courts must be controllable. If the state is not subject to the courts, it can lead to arbitrariness and massive discrimination against minorities due to the lengthy legislative periods and the principle of a simple majority. In this context, it is also problematic if the government can exert influence on the courts via the allocation of employment and promotion. Constitutional judges, like all other judges, should be appointed from within their own ranks.

Politicians are servants of the citizens. They are instructed by you to represent your interests in government. They are similar to the principals in the principal agent theory. For this reason, an incentive (incentivization) would be conceivable as it is for managers: future pensions depend on indicators such as debt, GDP. Principal agent for politicians could be that the payout of their pension depends on a good financial management in the form of low new borrowing.

While the vote-maximization hypothesis greatly simplifies the behavioral motives of politicians,[8] it is imperative for national politicians reliant on reelection. Downs' vote-maximization model shows interesting interrelations in this respect.

---

[8] Adam Smith realized that politicians in exceptional national situations can move from a pure benefit maximizer ("man of the system") to an altruistic statesman ("man of the state") It is also conceivable that a politician on his personal authority or through generating greater political acceptance for the overriding interests of the general population. See *Smith, Adam* (1985), pp. 394.

8.2   The Vote Maximization Model from Downs

Assumptions[9]:

1. Two parties provide public goods such as social assistance, schools, etc. as electoral promises and compete for the votes of the voters for a government election.
2. Voters have different preferences and choose the politician who maximizes their utility, that is, the election program that comes closest to their wishes. Example: Socialist voters choose the politician who works for the increase in social welfare. Conservative elected voters choose the politician who works for the reduction of social welfare.
3. The political options can be arranged in a scheme from left to right (extreme: socialist to conservative). The voter distribution for these options corresponds to a normal distribution with m as median

Situation 1 (see Fig. 8.1):
Party A (left) represents option a and party B (right) point b, m stands for the median.
Situation 2 (see Fig. 8.2): If party A moves to the right, it can win all voters to the left and half the voters to their right and Party B's point of view.
Situation 3: B has to go to the left to regain votes. A must then react as well and continue to the right. This process continues until both meet at the median position. This is the dominant strategy, since any other strategy will result in losing the election if the other party behaves rationally (see Fig. 8.4).

Conclusion
The Downs model confirms the political thesis that the elections are won in the middle. This result is also called median voter theorem. Grand coalitions are more widely accepted by the public during their reign because they represent more voters in the center than middle-margins coalitions. However, the same dominant strategy also creates problems. The party programs are congruent in the middle. In the view of the voters, voting is no longer worthwhile because the electoral programs hardly differ anymore. Voter turnout declines. The members of the parties are becoming increasingly dissatisfied as the parties move away from their original positions towards the center. The edges are no longer politically covered. At some point, new parties form, covering the margins left and right again.

---

[9]See *Downs, Anthony* (1957).

Fig. 8.1 Downs model
Situation 1 and 2

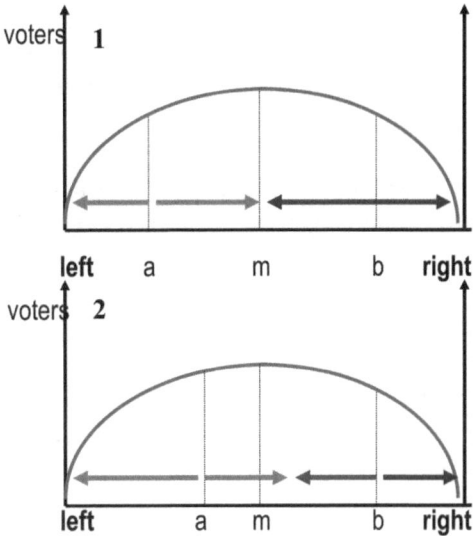

Fig. 8.2 Downs model
Situation 3 and 4

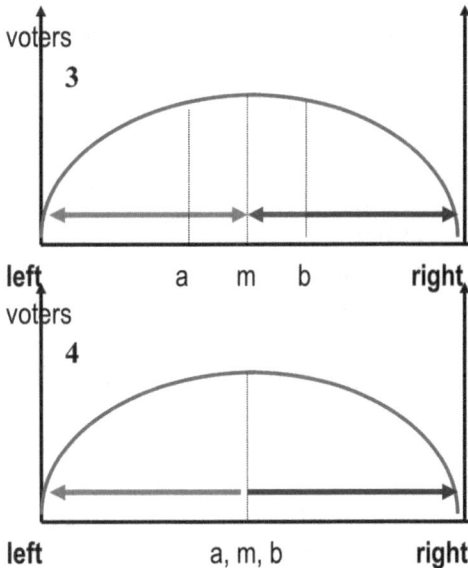

8.3 Interest Groups (Lobbying)

Lobbying, bribing and personal ties also distort the decision-making process of politicians. Through lobbyism (lobbying), companies, associations and interest groups seek to influence government and parliamentary decisions.

The groups affected by the decision of the politician can increase their political influence by organizing themselves into advocacy groups and trying to influence the politician and the public. Business associations are trying in this way to increase the profits of their member companies.

▶ **Definition** Rent-seeking is an attempt to get a government grant without reciprocating, i.e. a political payout.

Examples:

- The associations of doctors and hospitals try to receive higher compensation.
- The pharmaceutical industry is trying to meet fewer requirements for the development of medicines.

The greater the support of stakeholders by the political public, the greater their influence on the politician, who seeks to maximize electoral votes. A group's degree of organization (number of members) and the intensity of advocacy will be greater, the lower the organization costs and the higher the expected benefit for the individual.

The influence of lobbying is a particular problem of democracy. In countries without direct or representative, the will of the electorate is represented by the electorate. Representatives have the task of forming an opinion objectively to best representthe citizens. They must not consider other interests. They need to get information for forming opinions from objective sources. One sees that in a democracy lobbying is actually not permitted. The question that arises is how far political decisions are influenced by lobbying. This question is unanswerable because influence is not transparent, whichmakes lobbying so dangerous because it does not make it clear to the citizen how far a politician's decision reflects their interests or that of a lobbyist.

Lobbying is at least successful enough at influencing policymakers' decision making that it pays off for the industry to make the effort. We can thus conclude from the mere existence of a strong lobby representation that they have influence. Secondary income of politicians and election campaign sponsors are also problematic in this context. A politician and the political parties who, like civil servants, perform sovereign tasks should be financially provisioned so that they do not need additional revenue. If a member gives a speech, it must be assumed that he is doing so in the context of his official duties and therefore does not need to be paid extra. Secondary employment is also to be approved by the employer in the economy because of possible conflicts of interest both in content and time. Otherwise, lobbying will become capitalism's open door to democratic institutions. This undemocratic influence can be strengthened by the election donation dependency of the parties. The financial lobby is one of the largest campaign campaign donors. In addition, numerous public offices have been occupied by former employees, for example, by Goldman Sachs.[10]

Group task: Discuss the political influence of lobbyists. What do you suggest as a solution to the problem?

Solution One could, for example, equate the profession of representative with that of a normal employee. Then the representative would have to have their other activities approved. Or you could generally ban paid additional activities or insist that ho-norare must be donated, for example.

8.4   Economic Theory of Bureaucracy

The employees of government ministries, the so-called bureaucrats, also pursue their own interests (income, prestige, number of employees, promotion, etc.) and are therefore interested in expanding their influence and budget. Bureaucrats have no profit target and therefore no efficiency target. This fosters interventionism and leads to bureaucracy growth and more regulation.

The bureaucrats have an information advantage (asymmetry) over the politicians and the votersabout the costs and the production of public goods, which they can use to enhance their importance and budget needs. The quality of the goods provided by the bureaucracy is also difficult for politicians and citizens to assess due to the lack of comparable competitive products. Only quantity is objectively verifiable, which is why bureaucracy tends to produce quantity rather than quality. In this sense, we have the same initial problems as those already described in the bureaucracy of the central administration economy (see Sect. 6.9).

In order to increase their authority, bureaucrats depend on politicians. Politicians provide budgets (appropriation) to the bureaucrats for the production of public goods. Politicians should control the allocation of bureaucracy. However, the question arises whether the politicians have any interest in limiting the bureaucracy. Not as long as they can finance it without political voting losses. On the contrary, politicians are dependent on bureaucracy to fulfill their election promises and generally in implementing their policies. Without the bureaucracy, a politician cannot implement anything and because of the lack of specialist knowledge of the politicians, sometimes they are not even able to explain their policies and make decisions. The bureaucracy provides the public goods. Thus one can speak of a bilateral monopoly in terms of politicians and bureaucracy. Example: Greece's politicians increased the bureaucracy budget as long as it was financially viable. When

---

[10]The former Secretary of State for Finance in the Clinton administration, Rubin, as well as the Finance Minister Paulson in the Bush administration were both former employees of Goldman Sachs.

Greece ceased to receive money from the capital markets, becoming insolvent, one in four Greeks was in government service.[11]

These laws also apply to the bureaucracy at the corporate headquarters of large companies. For example, if the head of a large bank assumes more and more responsibilities, he will be promoted to divisional director due to his many responsibilities and can thus earn a higher income. The quality of his work is difficult to measure, so quantity goes before quality.

How is it possible to counteract the law of bureaucracy growth? The bureaucracy will always find reasons why they need for a higher budget. For example, a case-by-case examination and approval by Parliament hardly limits the growth of bureaucracy. Restriction can only be achieved through restrictive tax laws and debt limitations. There should be caps on indebtedness and on the tax burden of the citizens enshrined in constitutions. Exceptions to this would be very difficult to achieve, such as a two-thirds majority in parliament. Another way to limit the escalating costs of bureaucracy is to introduce competition in the provision of public goods by allowing private providers alongside public providers. Increased control of bureaucracy can also be done, for example, by external business consultants. And finally, as with managers, it is also possible to introduce performance and efficiency incentives for officials, for example, through indicators or benchmarks (in-quota).

Conclusion

If politicians do not put social benefits before their own interests they must be controlled and selected by society even more. In addition to an independent press, this requires voting procedures that aggregate the preferences of the citizens. There are also direct votes on economic policy or the provision of public goods such as referendums.

8.5   Voting Procedures

A social discourse does not automatically lead to the best result for the society. Thus we do not always get the best economic policy decisions in a democracy. We want to deal with the reasons in the following section. We already addressed one reason with the group behavior (groupthink) in Sect. 4.3.

Studies show that the group participants do not go into the discussions with an open mind, but try to form their own opinion based on their incomplete pre-information and try to enforce it in the discussion. The discussion participants do not enter the discussion to

---

[11]See   http://www.spiegel.de/wirtschaft/soziales/griechische-beamte-superstars-ausser-dienst-a-787835.html

form an opinion. More shared information is exchanged, which is also more credible in the group because it is represented by several people. If the opinions are similar on the basis of incomplete information, the preconceived opinion will prevail in the discussion regardless of whether it is correct.[12]

Schulz-Hardt et al. formed 135 three-person groups out of 405 female and male students and had discussions in various group constellations. The proportion of correct solutions increased with the diversity of opinion (dissent). Groups with the same opinion only made the right decision 7% of the time. When different but wrong opinions were presented at the beginning, at least a quarter of the groups chose the right solution and if one of the dissenting opinions preferred the right solution at the beginning, the success rate rose to 60%. Therefore, it is advantageous if there is a diversity of opinions at the beginning of the discussion. Here, the likelihood is much higher to make the right decision. It is therefore recommended to compile discussion groups with different opinions.[13]

If different opinions are important for a group to come to the right decisions through discourse, this means that marginal opinions and marginalized parties have a special significance in democracy. They should therefore not be perceived as disruptive, but enriching and included in the discussion. The problem is rather the formation of opinions in a few parties, because within the parties, the party hierarchy exerts a strong influence and thus suppresses marginal opinions.

Solomon E. Asch showed in 1955 with the Asch Conformity Experiment, that individuals can adapt to wrong group opinions if the group confidently represents them.[14]

The bigger the group, the stronger their opinion influence is if it represents the majority. Asch later showed that the pressure to conform wears off as soon as the majority opinion is confronted with a contradictory opinion. It is not the social support of the subject with his or her right mindset that is decisive, but that there are other opinions at all. For example, Asch had an assistant agreed with the false opinion, which meant that the subjects again dared to stand up to their correct opinion.[15]

Allen and Levine (1971) noted that influencing opinion also depends on the acceptance of opinion leaders in the group, and Bond and Smith (1996) found in a meta-study that collectivist cultures are more inclined to conform than individualistic cultures.[16]

---

[12]See Gigone, D., & Hastie, R. (1993); Stasser, G., & Birchmeier, Z. (2003); Mojzisch, A., Grouneva, L., & Schulz-Hardt, P. (2010); Larson, J. R., Jr., Foster-Fishman, P. G., & Keys, C. B. (1994); Dennis, A. R. (1996); Greitemeyer, T., & Schulz-Hardt, P. (2003); Mojzisch, A., Schulz-Hardt, S., Kerschreiter, R., Brodbeck, F. C., & Frey, D. (2008); Brodbeck, F. C., Kerschreiter, R., Mojzisch, A., & Schulz-Hardt, S. (2007); Mojzisch, A., & Schulz-Hardt, S. (2006); Chernyshenko, Miner, Baumann, & Sniezek, (2003) and Jonas, Klaus/Stroebe, Wolfgang/Hewstone, Miles, pp. 483.

[13]See Schulz-Hardt, S., Brodbeck, F. C., Mojzisch, A., Kerschreiter, R., & Frey, D. (2006), pp. 1080–1093.

[14]Vgl. Asch, Solomon E. (1951) and Jonas K./Stroebe, W./Hewstone M. (2007), pp. 9379.

[15]Asch, P. E. (1987), pp. 477.

[16]See Allen, V. L., & Levine, J. M. (1971); Bond, R., & Smith, P. B. (1996) and Jonas, Klaus/ Stroebe, Wolfgang/Hewstone, Miles, pp. 287.

All the influences on group decisions that hinder informative exchange, causing decisions to be made on a normative basis instead of an informational one, are called groupthink. The group members strive for conformity at the expense of a realistic assessment of alternative courses of action.[17]

How should the provision of public goods be decided? How should decisions be made in economic policy conflicts of interest? For this we need voting procedures. We are looking for a voting procedure that aggregates the preferences of citizens directly or indirectly via representatives of the people, without contradictions and pareto-efficient or use-maximizing (as long as one's own benefit increases, one can also take away something from others). Which voting procedures should be used to make economic policy decisions?

8.5.1 Unanimity Rule

At best, Pareto efficiency can be guaranteed by the unanimity rule, because everyone has to agree, and no one loses out (advantage). Decisions reached this way are satisfactory, because there is only a result if everyone agrees. It is thus the procedure with the maximum approval. But there are disadvantages:

1. The cost of decision-making is high because everyone has to agree. It therefore takes a long time to either convince everyone or find an acceptable compromise.
2. Implied right of veto, therefore often no decision is made.

Changes at the expense of everyone, but to the benefit of a decision maker cannot be corrected.

Example: EU treaty changes must be approved by all member states. This means that e.g. The Stability Pact, as a limit to the debt-equity ratio of the EU, can always be relaxed, but never tightened, because all the states concerned must agree to this treaty amendment.[18]

1. **Strategic Voting Process**

There is often a vote exchange called "**log-rolling**". This includes linking temporally successive votes, so that everyone agrees. Disadvantages, which would cause the decision makers to veto, are compensated in other votes: "I'll give my vote when I get yours" is the motto. Then there are the package deals where individual voting issues are agglomerated in a common vote, so that everyone agrees. This way if a decision maker wants to enjoy advantages, they must accept some disadvantages that are advantageous to other decision makers. A **package-deal vote**, in contrast to an

---

[17]See Levine, J. M., & Moreland, R. L. (1998) and Jonas, Klaus/Stroebe, Wolfgang/Hewstone, Miles, p. 302.

[18]See for instance https://www.welt.de/politik/ausland/article13758533/EU-Vertragsaenderung-mit-allen-27-Laendern-gescheitert.html (23.09.2016).

exchange of votes, gives decision-makers the certainty that they will get their benefits, whereas in the exchange of votes one party always has to pay in advance. The individual decisions are then no longer pareto-efficient, but the package or the sum of all votes.

2. **Loss of emergence**

The problem with undermining unanimous decisions through vote exchange and package deals is that the synergy, the emergence is lost. The whole is no bigger than the sum of its parts, because each decision maker maximizes their utility but no longer creates benefits the superordinate organization, such as the EU. One consequence may be utility maximization, but socially sub-optimal voting results (unanimity paradox).[19]

Deals can undermine important economic policy rules (institutions), such as the EU subsidy code. The EU Subsidy Code was overturned by a vote exchange on coal, steel and trade subsidies. In principle, national subsidies were prohibited under Article 4c of the ECSC Treaty. Unanimity was required under Article 95 of the ECSC Treaty for an exception by the Council of Ministers. In 1994 the United Kingdom, Denmark, the Netherlands and Portugal demanded that all subsidy applications be voted on simultaneously (keyword: package solution). The German Economic Minister REXRODT agreed with the idea, pointing out that he could only vote for subsidy applications of the Italian steel company ILVA and the Spanish company CSI if the Council of Ministers approved the application for the German EKO-STAHL. Italy, for its part, made its voting behavior clear: It would agree to the coal subsidies in the Council of Ministers only if they also approved the subsidies for ILVA (keyword: vote exchange).[20] Finally, the Council of Ministers unanimously approved all subsidy applications. By means of package solutions and the exchange of votes, some member states were thus able to circumvent the prohibition on subsidies of the ECSC Treaty or the restrictive subsidy code.[21]

Another example would be a municipal council decision, assuming unanimity. One group wants approval for a swimming pool, another a children's playground and a third group a bypass. But the community can only afford one of these three projects. How will the vote go?

Answer: All three projects are approved because otherwise there is no unanimity (maybe no majority). Each party will agree with the other in a vote exchange to get their own project approved. The damage is borne by the community.

---

[19] See Conrad, Christian, A. (2003).

[20] The main interested parties in extending the coal subsidies were Germany and Spain.

[21] See *Conrad, Christian, A.* (1997).

3. The unanimity rule does not aggregate social benefits. It is enough if a decision brings all users some benefit. If there are small disadvantages for a decision maker, they will not agree, although other people affected by the decision would very much benefit from a positive vote. A decision that could not achieve unanimity may be more useful than a unanimous decision, which can lead to socially suboptimal decisions. Conclusion: Pareto-efficient or societal benefit-maximizing voting results are unlikely.

8.5.2   Majority Rules (Absolute or Relative, Plurality Voting)

An absolute majority is reached when a decision gets at least 50% of the votes. With a relative majority the alternative with the most votes wins.

Above all, the advantage of the absolute majority decision is that the costs of the vote are lower than with the unanimity rule. Since there are only two voting points to choose from, there will almost never be stalemates. With the relative majority (plurality voting), there will be stalemates even in the case of several votes only if there is a tie. The voting procedure is simpler than the unanimity rule. According to utilitarianism, majority voting maximizes the benefits of the majority, but the preferences of the minority get lost. Under certain circumstances, the net benefit for the majority is lower than that of the minority in the vote. There are even decisions at the expense of the minority with a benefit reduction that is greater than the benefit to the majority.

Example: Imagine that in your lecture room you put the decision to the vote that all blonds should give the brunettes 100 €. If there are more brunettes than blonds, you should get the majority for this decision.

An important principle of democratic voting is therefore that all parties involved in the decision must be involved in the vote, otherwise decisions are made at the expense of third parties (for example, the financing of government expenditure with debt at the expense of future generations). To include the future generations more intensively, one could discuss that parents have a separate right to vote on behalf of their children. Even if it would only count as half a vote and parents do not always know what their children want, at least the interests of future generations could be included in the vote.

Another Example German Gorleben was chosen for the question of nuclear waste disposal. The residents cannot win a vote against the rest of Germany, which is glad that the nuclear waste is not stored in their vicinity.

In a democratic vote, the result could be that the project receives a political majority, although the loss of value for the minority is greater than the benefit of the majority. Especially in this case, politics would not be a suitably objective decision-maker. Here it would be up to the courts to review the decision of the politicians and to ensure minority protection (see above). In practice, however, the courts are only consulted when the building permit has already been granted and the construction is practically completed.

In this context, it is also problematic if the government can exert influence on the courts via the allocation of employment and promotion.

Condorcet or Arrow Paradox
There is still a problem of cyclical majorities in paired majority voting: If there are more than two alternatives for more than two voters and if the preferences are not unimodal, the order of voting is crucial to the outcome. There is no transitivity. Condorcet paradox was discovered by MARQUIS DE CONDORCET, French philosopher and mathematician, and occurs in pairwise voting at multi-modal preferences.

Example
Decision makers 1, 2 and 3 are to vote on alternatives A, B and C. The result is the following payoff matrix and preference matrix (Figs. 8.3 and 8.4).

The preference matrix shows that the preferences of decision maker 2 are multi-pronged.

Fig. 8.3 Payout matrix

decision maker\alternative	1	2	3
A	0	60	40
B	50	0	50
C	55	45	0

Fig. 8.4 Preference matrix

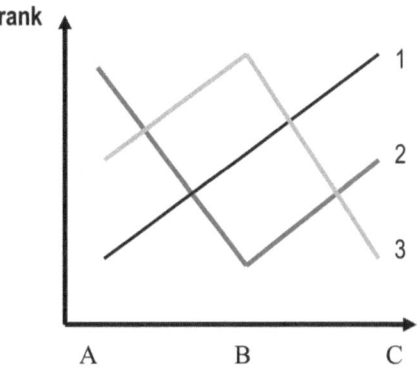

Cyclic majorities

$$\left.\begin{array}{l} \textbf{1. vote: A} \Leftrightarrow \textbf{B: 1:2} \Rightarrow \textbf{B} > \textbf{A} \\ \textbf{2. vote: B} \Leftrightarrow \textbf{C: 1:2} \Rightarrow \textbf{C} > \textbf{B} \\ \textbf{3. vote: C} \Leftrightarrow \textbf{A: 1:2} \Rightarrow \textbf{A} > \textbf{C} \end{array}\right\} \quad \begin{array}{l} \textbf{C} > \textbf{B} > \textbf{A} \\ \Rightarrow \textbf{C} > \textbf{A} \end{array}$$

↑   ↑
Control vote   └──────── **contradiction!**

The order is decisive in the vote C > B > A or A > C, so there is no consistent aggregation of individual preferences and no correct solution.

8.5.3   Borda Rule

The Borda Rule is a ruling rule that was named after the French mathematician J.C. Borda. In the Borda rule, the intensity of the preferences is weighted, e.g. for three alternatives each decision maker can give 1, 2 and 3 points. The alternative with the most points wins. The weighting makes the social benefits transparent and thus also the willingness to pay for the financing of public goods. Example: The Eurovision Song Contest. Each country can give each song from 1 to 12 points. By the distribution of the points one can weight something more, because 12 points are worth 12 times more than 1 point.

Problem

– If an alternative fails, the order of evaluation of the remaining alternatives changes. You have to re-vote.
– With so many alternatives, the process is too time-consuming, because the decision-maker has to be aware of the relative benefits of all alternatives: how much is this decision-making alternative better than the other.

Exercise Voting Rules
The economist Leininger reconstructed the vote on the German capitol in the Bundestag after the reunification.[22] Here he also took into account various proposals to estimate the preferences of MEPs (see Fig. 8.5). There was a difference in the number of Members' votes in the different ballots, as well as abstentions, which is why the figures do not always add up to 657. We wonder if the result of the vote would always have been Berlin, irrespective of the voting procedure. It is your turn: what is the result of the ballot when using the

1. majority rule,
2. relative majority rule and
3. the Borda rule

---

[22]See Leininger, W. (1993).

	1. preference	2. preference	3. preference
A:Bonn & Berlin	146	222	289
B: Berlin	222	265	170
C: Bonn	289	170	198

Fig. 8.5 Preferences of the 657 Members

Historical Result

At the suggestion of the Council of Elders and after the approval of the Bundestag, the then President of the Bundestag, Süssmuth, had her first vote on the Bonn and Berlin compromise proposals. As a result, only MPs who had Alternative A as their first preferences chose A. Other MPs still hoped to have their first preference confirmed at the next vote. A was rejected by 489 votes to 147. Ballot B versus C then gave 338 for B and 320 for C, so Berlin became the capitol. This was because Berlin had more first and second preferences.

Conclusion

- Voting results depend on the choice of voting procedures.
- Aggregation of preferences can only be guaranteed through the Borda procedure. (social benefit maximum)
- The unanimity criterion guarantees Pareto efficiency in the individual vote, but not in several decisions (due to vote exchange and package deals).
  - If politicians and bureaucracy pursue their own interests, and not those of the general public, the economic constitution must be immunized against the influence of the politicians, so the institutions should be designed so that they place the interests of society above the interests of the politicians,
  - "How can we organize political institutions in such a way that it is impossible for bad or incompetent rulers to inflict too much damage."[23] Elements of direct democracy are recommended here. They would also counteract the strong influence of lobbying and accommodate the argument of the constitutional economists that citizens should be given legitimacy in shaping the institutions.[24]

---

[23]Popper, K. R. (1957), p. 157.
[24]See Feld, L. P., & Köhler, E. (2011), p. 179.

8.6   Political Manipulations

Group Discussion

Framing can be used as a political instrument. As long as one persuades people with horrible pictures of sick people not to smoke or get a check-up, the purpose may justify the means, but where are the limits to such manipulation of free will? Discuss!

For example, as a politician one can take advantage of citizens' loss anxiety and represent a different taxation of citizens by emphasizing the lower taxation of a group as a benefit (benefit) rather than mentioning the taxation of the other group as a loss. This also leads to illusion of money: An increase of 5% in wages with an inflation rate of 12% is more likely to be accepted than an equivalent real wage reduction of 7%.[25]

Another possibility for manipulation is the so-called shaming. Shaming is the attempt to provoke feelings of guilt in people in order to prevent them from doing certain things.[26] Shaming identifies emotions that are triggered in the individual in relation to the group. This does not necessarily have to be negative. On the contrary, they act as regulation in order to enforce collective behavior towards self-oriented utility maximization. One feels guilty about breaking the norms of the group and is proud to be fulfilled. So a group can also promote the productivity of their members.[27] Political manipulation has natural limits, however. Shaming is voluntary insofar as it only works when the individual enters shaming and allows guilt to be generated. However, this happens predominantly in the area of the subconscious, which can be controlled by the individual only to a very limited extent consciously. Furthermore, shaming can lead to sanctions in the group (e.g., exclusion) and is associated with discomfort, so that it would only be ethically justifiable for a democratic open discurs to transparently legitimize shaming. The reasons must be known and understandable for those affected. This kind of manipulation is part of the political discourse, such as the so-called "political correctness",[28] which is why it is cited here, not least in order to create a sensitivity in dealing with morals as a political instrument. However, for a democratic discourse to be successful, it is also important to allow minor opinions and not to suppress them through shaming.

Schulz-Hardt et al. made up of 405 female and male students, 135 three-person groups were formed and discussions were held in various group constellations.

The proportion of correct solutions increased with the diversity of opinion (dissent). Groups with the same opinion only made the right decision 7% of the time. If different but

---

[25]See Kahneman, Daniel; Tversky, Amos (1986).

[26]See Gopalan, Sandeep (2007).

[27]See Lindbeck, Assar; Nyberg, Sten (2006) and Beck, H. (2014), p. 290.

[28]Political correctness is understood here in a politically neutral way as an opinion stipulated by the group that dominates public opinion. Those who think differently are sanctioned by extreme moral exclusion from this group when they express their opinion. This is not a new phenomenon. The zeitgeist, i.e. the opinion of the group, and the dominant group change.

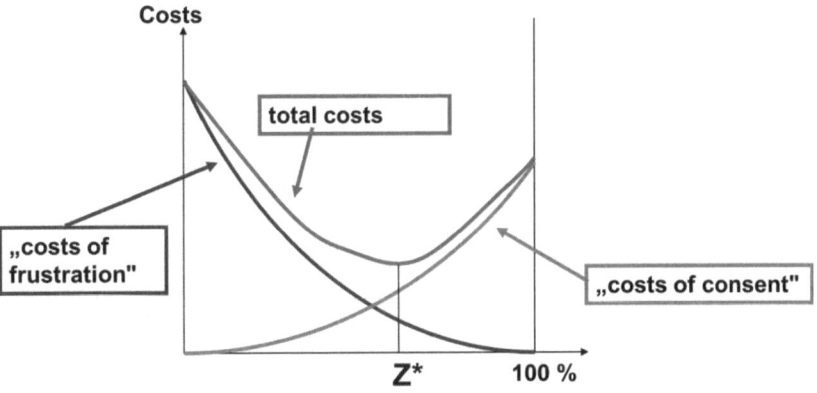

Fig. 8.6 Optimal approval requirement Z *

wrong opinions were represented at the beginning, at least a quarter of the groups chose the right solution.

And if one of the dissenting opinions preferred the correct solution in the beginning, the success rate rose to 60%. It is therefore advantageous if there is a variety of opinions at the beginning of the discussion. The probability of making the right decision is significantly higher here. It is therefore recommended to set up discussion groups with different opinions.[29]

"You can fool all the people some of the time and some of the people all the time, but you cannot fool all the people all the time."[30]

Conclusion
Politicians, bureaucrats and citizens, according to the New Political Economy, like Homo Oeconomicus, maximize their own benefit first, not that of society. Politicians must therefore be controlled by independent bodies (Federal Constitutional Court) and by institutional guidelines as well as by the press. Each voting procedure has advantages and disadvantages. In addition, as the voting procedures influence the results, it is important to weigh carefully what procedure is chosen. Although the borda method best expresses the social benefits by taking preferences into account, it is surprisingly rarely used in practice. Aggregation of preferences can only be guaranteed by the BORDA criterion. Figure 8.6 shows the relationship between the costs arising from the consideration of all interests in a vote and the "frustration costs" of the voters because they are not sufficiently considered in the vote.

---

[29]See Schulz-Hardt, S., Brodbeck, F. C., Mojzisch, A., Kerschreiter, R., & Frey, D. (2006), pp. 1080–1093.

[30]Abraham Lincoln on September 2, 1858, speaking in Clinton, Illinois, during the famous Lincoln-Douglas debates. https://historynewsnetwork.org/article/161924 (8.05.2019).

Conprehension Questions

1. Weigh the pros and cons of the voting procedures against each other. Which would you prefer and why?
2. What is meant by the Condorcet paradox?
3. (a) What is meant by package deals and the exchange of votes?
   (b) Explain the pros and cons.
4. Give an example from politics where political benefits and social benefits diverge. Justify your choice. What do you suggest to encourage the politician to pursue more of the social benefits?
5. Are you aware of examples where politicians have decided against their own benefit in order to pursue the social benefits? Explain your assessment. Is this the refutation of the New Political Economy?
6. What does the vote-maximization model of Downs show?

References

Allen, V. L., & Levine, J. M. (1971). Social support and conformity: The role of independent assessment of reality. *Journal of Experimental Social Psychology, 7*, 48–58.

Andel, N. (1990). *Finanzwissenschaft* (3rd ed.). Tübingen: Mohr.

Asch, P. E. (1987). *Social psychology* (p. 477). New York: Oxford University Press.

Bond, R., & Smith, P. B. (1996). Culture and conformity: A meta-analysis of studies using Asch's (1952b, 1956) line judgment task. *Psychological Bulletin, 119*, 111–137.

Brandstätter, V., Schüler, J., Puca, R. M., & Lozo, L. (2018). *Motivation und emotion*. Wiesbaden: Springer.

Braybrooke, D., & Lindblom, C. E. (1963). *A strategy of decision*. New York: Free Press.

Brodbeck, F. C., Kerschreiter, R., Mojzisch, A., & Schulz-Hardt, S. (2007). Group decision making under conditions of distributed knowledge: The information asymmetries model. *Academy of Management Review, 32*, 459–479.

Conrad, C. A. (1997). *Europäische Stahlpolitik zwischen politischen Zielen und ökonomischen Zwängen*. Baden-Baden: Nomos.

Conrad, C. A. (2003). The dysfunctions of unanimity: Lessons from the EU steel crisis. *Journal of Common Market Studies, 41*(1), 157–169.

Dennis, A. R. (1996). Information exchange and use in small group decision making. *Small Group Research, 27*, 532–550.

Downs, A. (1957). *An economic theory of democracy* (New York 1957 (deutsch 1968), Ökonomische Theorie der Demokratie). Tübingen: Mohr.

Fernandez, R., & Rodrik, D. (1991). Resistance to reform: Status quo bias in the presence of individual-specific uncertainty. *American Economic Review., 81*(5), 1146–1155.

Franke, S. F. (1996). *(Ir) rationale Politik?* Marburg: Metropolis.

Frederick, S., Loewenstein, G., & O'Donoghue, T. (2002). *Time discounting and time*.

Gigone, D., & Hastie, R. (1993). The common knowledge effect: Information sharing and group judgment. *Journal of Personality and Social Psychology, 65*, 959–574.

Gopalan, S. (2007). Shame sanctions and excessive CEO pay. *Delaware Journal of Corporate law, 32*, 757–797.

Greitemeyer, T., & Schulz-Hardt, P. (2003). Preference-consistent evaluation of information in the hidden profile paradigm: Beyond group-level explanations for the dominance of shared information in group decisions. *Journal of Personality and Social Psychology, 84*, 322–339.

Herder-Dorneich, P. (1957). *Theorie der Bestimmungsfaktoren finanzwissenschaftlicher Staatstätigkeit, wirtschaftswissenschaftliche Dissertation*, Freiburg.

Larson, J. R., Jr., Foster-Fishman, P. G., & Keys, C. B. (1994). Discussion of shared and unshared information in decision-making groups. *Journal of Personality and Social Psychology, 67*, 446–461.

Leininger, W. (1993). The fatal vote: Berlin versus Bonn. *Finanz Archiv, 50*(1), 1–20.

Levine, J. M., & Moreland, R. L. (1998). Small groups. In D. T. Gilbert, P. T. Fiske, & G. Lindzey (Eds.), *Handbook of social psychology* (Vol. 1, 4th ed., pp. 415–469). Boston, MA: McGraw-Hill.

Lindbeck, A., & Nyberg, S. (2006). Raising children to work hard: Altruism, work norms, and social insurance. *Quarterly Journal of Economics, 121*(4), 1473–1503.

Lindblom, C. E. (1965). *The intelligence of democracy*. New York: Free Press.

Meyer-Krahmer, F. (1979). *Politische Entscheidungsprozesse und Ökonomische Theorie der Politik*. Frankfurt: Campus Verlag.

Mojzisch, A., & Schulz-Hardt, S. (2006). Information sampling in group decision making. In K. Fiedler & P. Juslin (Eds.), *Sampling and adaptive cognition* (pp. 299–326). Cambridge, MA: Cambridge University Press.

Mojzisch, A., Schulz-Hardt, S., Kerschreiter, R., Brodbeck, F. C., & Frey, D. (2008). Social validation in group decision-making: Differential effects on the decisional impact of preference-consistent and preference-inconsistent information. *Journal of Experimental Social Psychology, 44*, 1477–1490.

Mojzisch, A., Grouneva, L., & Schulz-Hardt, P. (2010). Biased evaluation of information during discussion: Disentangling the effects of preference consistency, social validation, and ownership of information. *European Journal of Social Psychology, 40*, 946–956.

Popper, K. R. (1957). *Die offene Gesellschaft und ihre Feinde*, Bd. 1, Der Zauber Platons, Francke, Bern; 7. Auflage, Tübingen: Mohr Siebeck 1992, p. 157.

Samuelson, W., & Zeckhauser, R. (1988). Status quo bias in decision making. *Journal of Risk and Uncertainty, 1*, 7–59.

Schultheiss, O. C. (2008). Implicit motives. In O. P. John, R. W. Robins, & L. A. Pervin (Eds.), *Handbook of personality: Theory and research* (3rd ed., pp. 603–633). New York: Guilford.

Schulz-Hardt, S., Brodbeck, F. C., Mojzisch, A., Kerschreiter, R., & Frey, D. (2006). Group decision making in hidden profile situations: Dissent as a facilitator for decision quality. *Journal of Personality and Social Psychology, 91*, 1080–1093.

Schumpeter, J. A. (1993). *Kapitalismus, Sozialismus und Demokratie* (7th ed.). Tübingen: Francke.

Smith, A. (1985). *Theorie der ethischen Gefühle* (2. unv. Nachdruck der ersten Auflage von 1926). Hamburg.

Starbatty, J. (1985). *Die englischen Klassiker der Nationalökonomie*. Darmstadt: Wissenschaftliche Buchgesellschaft.

Stasser, G., & Birchmeier, Z. (2003). Group creativity and collective choice. In P. B. Paulus & B. A. Nijstad (Eds.), *Group creativity* (pp. 85–109). New York: Oxford University Press.

Thaler, R. H. (1981). Some empirical evidence on dynamic inconsistency. *Economic Letters, 8*, 201–207.

Competition Policy

9

What Follows Why?
The chapter on competition policy is designed to give you, as a future manager, an insight into German and European competition policy. Later, you can use this insight both to boost your company's profits by averting unfair competition from your competitors and to avoid fines for competition violations.

Learning goals
The aim is that you explain the main issues of competition policy in your own words.

▶ **Definition of competition policy:** All state measures to promote competition.

Definition of market power: ability to influence the market price. Both from the supply and the demand side.

The main themes of competition policy are impaired competition, such as

1. Building market power through horizontal (cartels) and vertical agreements
2. Building market power through mergers
3. Abuse of existing market power
4. Unfair competition

There are different competition conceptions that propose different competition policies to achieve the competition objectives.

9.1   The Theory of Competition Policy: An International Synthesis

There is no universally accepted definition of competition because of the many forms it can take.[1] The basic character of competition in a market economy can be understood as the contention between at least two participants on the supply side and those on the demand side.

The requirements of an international system of competition rules are different from those for national rules in one main way. Private companies compete with each other at the national level whereas sovereign states compete for their share of the international value creation. Just as individuals try to maximize their advantage in a national system, so do governments at the international level. As international actors they represent the collective interests of their companies and try to maximize the welfare and growth of their country by way of nation economic policies, and to this end they have economic policy instruments at their command.

> The central purpose of competition law is to benefit society as a whole by ensuring that markets operate efficiently, as free as possible from conduct that distorts competition.[2]

We addressed the advantages and workings of the market and competition in the preceding chapter. The question that begs to be asked however, is how the framework of a competition policy order that optimises market and competition should look. Various conceptions of competition try to answer just this question. Competition systems are based on functional goal-means conceptions. Assuming a certain theoretical basis they advise us which competition policy instruments to use in order to achieve our desired goal. There are also many approaches to the construction of a competition system, which is why the most important[3] will be analysed in the chapters that follow in view of their applicability.

Discussions on guidelines for competition policy have taken place at the international level especially in Germany and the USA. The German concept of Ordoliberalism (Freiburg School) will be presented, compared and evaluated in part one. Part two addresses the American Workability Concept of Industrial Organization and the German concept of feasible competition. The German concept of free competition, the Austrian School the American Chicago School and the theory of Contestable Markets will all be addressed in part three. Part four is the evaluations of the presented concepts. Part five describes the newer competition concepts: the Neo-Austrian School, the Post-Chicago School and the European School. In part six we will then attempt to create a general, ideal

---

[1] See *Herdzina, Klaus* (1999), p. 9.

[2] OECD (2001), p. 103. See also *Vautier, Kerrin M.* (2000), p. 93.

[3] Scientific and political Discussions on the creation of such a competition system have taken place almost exclusively in the USA and Germany See *Kantzenbach, Erhard/Krüger, Reinhard* (1994), p. 196.

picture of an international competition policy as synthesis bringing the concepts herein examined together.

9.1.1   The Ordoliberalist Concept from Walter Eucken

Ordoliberalism, also known as the Freiburg School, can be considered historically to be the most comprehensive system theory. The system of the social market economy in Germany was a product of this theory, as were the competition laws and policies of the European Union. Up to the present time there have been many empirical studies that reaffirm Ordoliberalism, and none of the theses contained therein have yet to be falsified.[4] Walter Eucken was the main founding father of Ordoliberalism. He agreed with Adam Smith and other classical theorists that the market form of completely free competition would create the best market results, and that the neo-classical microeconomic models were out of touch with reality. Complete competition[5] exists, according to Eucken, when the market participants accept market prices as fact and (are forced to) compete according to ability. In this case market strategies and obstructive competition would then be neutralized.[6] Those who follow Ordoliberalism don't share the optimism that the market would develop perfect competition without state intervention, however, since it might be in the interest of companies to rid themselves of irksome competition, such as price agreements, mergers, vertical restraints etc., and secure profits through a monopoly.[7] The individual freedom in the market is a competition policy goal for ordoliberalism inasmuch as the assumption holds that companies will try to abuse their freedom at the cost of others within competition processes.[8] Thus a strong state is necessary to channel the behaviour of market participants through laws and prevent or remove restrictions to competition through intervention.

The concept of Ordoliberalism was the first to distinguish between the system of competition and competition policy.[9] The system of competition represents the framework that the state provides economic actors for their activities. It determines the long-term rules of the game, which themselves are generally laid down as laws. The institutional framework is meant to guarantee economic freedom for the individual. Competition policy in contrast, can be understood as the active engagement of the state, with the goal of preserving or enhancing competition.[10] The state's constant surveillance of the market

---

[4]See *Mantzavinos, Chrysostomos* (1994), pp. 160.

[5]Eucken's perfect competition doesn't match the price theory form of perfect competition. See *Mantzavinos, Chrysostomos* (1994), pp. 76.

[6]See *Lenel, Hans Otto* (1989), p. 308.

[7]See Starbatty, *Joachim*, pp. 570.

[8]See *Starbatty, Joachim* (1983), p. 569 and *Hildebrand, Doris* (2002a), p. 160.

[9]*Eucken* does not explicity use this term himself.

[10]See *Görgens, E.* (1988) and *Brendel, Herwig* (1997), p. 98.

for possible restrictions on competition and intervention in the market if competition is threatened belong to competition policy. The system has to capable of limiting interventions to exceptional cases. Euken developed two types of principles to address this capability; one type constitutes a competition system and the other a regulation of the market developments. According to the regulation principles, markets unsuitable for complete competition should be directed, or damages and imperfections eliminated, which can be expected even in perfect competition.[11] The Freiburg School has been criticized for its missing analytical basis, and the resulting lack of useful suggestions and test criteria for competition policy. Some authors have also found the efficiency and welfare goals of competition to have received too little attention.[12] Last but not least it was accused of being normative; a biased scientific approach.[13] Institutions do matter, however.

The question is rather how to research institutions. Empirical observations don't make the cut because they would have to compare countries with different institutions or would have to capture the impact of institutions over time. However, there are too many influencing factors here to isolate and capture the institutional influences.

Empirical observation therefore remains only a logical derivation of the interdependencies and an extremely crude examination of the developments of countries according to their institutional design. Does institutional economics differ from other orientations of economics? Economics abandoned the theory of order in the late 1990s and devoted itself entirely to econometric research. It was assumed that the statistical coverage of the economy and the calculation in models would be more accurate and that qualitative institutional economics could be dispensed with. However, this hypothesis has questioned at least since the financial crisis.

The classical liberalist conception of perfect competition, such as the model of Adam Smith, and the concept of competition as purported by Walter Eucken mostly assume a static competition. Static competition is primarily of importance for short-term price setting, however. The decisive long-term competition process as a constant string of advancing and following moves of a dynamic competition remains mostly ignored with these theories.[14] Other concepts of competition policy provide a valuable complement.

---

[11] See *Starbatty, Joachim* (1983), p. 569 and *Lenel, Hans Otto* (1989), p. 309. The seven *constitutive principles* of a competition system are: (1) The creation of a functional price system for perfect competition (2) Stabilization of the monetary value (3) Keeping the markets open for new participants (4) Private property (5) Contractual freedom (6) Full responsibility of companies for their decisions and (7) Consistency in competition policy. The four *regulating principles* of competition policy are: (1) The creation of a state monopoly authority (2) Correction of the economic calculations by integrating external effects (3) Including anomalies in supply relations, such as on the labour market and (4) Redistribution to achieve social equality. See *Eucken, Walter* (1952).

[12] See *Hawk, Barry E.* (1995), p. 978 and *Hildebrand, Doris* (2002a), p. 162.

[13] See Feld, L. P., & Köhler, E. (2011), 173–195. https://nbn-resolving.org/urn:nbn:de:0168-ssoar-349165, p. 176.

[14] See *Lenel, Hans Otto* (1989), p. 309.

9.1.2   The Workability Concept of Industrial Organization and the German Conception of Functional Competition: The Pessimists

The Workability Concept is based on the thinking of Clark.[15] Based on the realization of the Industrial Organization research founded in 1939 by E. S. Mason,[16] Clark considered the model of perfect competition to be a worthy goal, but not realizable due to the market imperfections found in reality. He considered the model to be a "first-best solution". Clark saw a causal relationship between market structure and market behaviour in the Industrial Organization conclusions however, and drew conclusions on market results from it. It is assumed that a certain market structure creates a certain competitive behaviour, which in turn leads to a specific market result. This cause-and-effect relationship is why Clark argues that influencing market structures could increase economic welfare, and thus hopes to reach the "second-best conclusion" of workable competition. Competition is considered to be workable if it leads to the results desired by competition policy. In later works Clark even goes so far as to suggest making markets more efficient by having the state create new market imperfections, an example being the reduction of market transparency in an oligopoly, which would make cartel agreements and coordinated behaviour more difficult.[17]

Clark's theory has been developed further by several authors into the Workability Concept, otherwise known as the structuralist school.[18] In the USA the main proponents are Scherer, Bain, Markham and Philips, and Kantzenbach in Germany.[19] To differentiate the Workability Concept from the later Chicago School, it became known as the Harvard School.[20] The Workability Concept shaped international competition policy in a lasting way, and currently dominates the policies of most national competition regimes. The dilemma theory from the Industrial Organization as regards economic efficiency and competitive freedom is a characteristic example. Only large, market capable companies can make use of the economies of large scale, take on the necessary costs of research and development and implement innovations in the market. On the other hand, large companies restrict the potential numbers of market participants, which of course provides fertile

---

[15]See *Mason, Edward* (1939), pp. 61–74.

[16]See *Clark, J. M.* (1940), pp. 241–256 and *Aberle, Gerd* (1992), pp. 30.

[17]See *Mason, Edwards* (1939).

[18]Different definitions for "Workability Competition" can be found in *Markham, Jesse W.* (1950), pp. 348–361; *Poeche, Jürgen* (1970), pp. 9–32 and a good summary in *Sosnick, Stephan H.* (1958), pp. 380–423.

[19]See *Kantzenbach, Erhard* (1967). For a theoretical conception of functional competition see also *Kantzenbach, Erhard/Kallfass, Hermann H.* (1981); *Mantzavinos, Chrysostomos* (1994), pp. 23; *Poesche, Jürgen* (1970) and *Berg, Hartmut* (1999), pp. 299–362.

[20]The two main representatives of this school of thought are Mason und Bain, and work at Harvard University.

ground for restrictions on competition. Behaviourist representatives of the Workability Concept, such as Scherer, have expanded the connection between market structure and market results identified by Clark in an attempt to more fully address the aspect of market behaviour. The original thrust of the pure structuralists, such as Bain, still exists in a parallel strand of thinking. Both strands work out criteria by which to test practical competition policy[21] for workability on the markets to be controlled. In other words, they test whether or not competition in effective. If not, it is the responsibility of competition policy to restore functionality to competition through a change in the market structure.[22]

Market structure criteria provide the market form that it worth striving towards as a morn, such the number of customers and suppliers, and market access barriers. Market behaviour criteria determine the desired competition policy actions and reactions of the market participants. Price setting behaviour of suppliers, product strategies, or research and innovation activities are all examples. The criteria for market results then determine the desired economic market outcomes, such as the efficiency or productivity and the technological progress according the cause-and-effect change as determined by the Workability Concept. Not only are norms and criteria isolated, but they are also applied in all imaginable combinations.[23] In American law, as an example, a two-tiered market test within the framework of the Rule of Reason (weighing advantages against disadvantages[24]) is used as a control on mergers. A market situation test is first and foremost a necessary tool to determine whether or not a workable competition exists at all. A sufficient requirement for a competition policy intervention is the failure to pass a second criterion, namely the market result test, which would mean that the results were intolerably deviated from the norm. The EU Commission acts similarly within the framework of its Extended Structure Conduct Performance Concept.[25]

The Industrial Organization has been extended in the last twenty years to a sustainable theoretical basis of the Workability Concept by way of the Game Theory and the further development of empirical tests. The absolute connection between market structure and market result has been rejected. The typical feedback in a dynamic competition process between structural behaviours and result variables has been taken into account. Market

---

[21] In addition, the Workability-interpretation from Markham should be mentioned, which springs from the idea that optimal competition cannot be achieved, and that competition policy should only intervene until no further improvement in market results can be achieved. Bartling sees the danger in this concept that an uncontrollable, counter-productive intervention will occur. See *Bartling, H.* (1988), p. 767.

[22] See *Bartling, H.* (1988), p. 767; *Schüller, Alfred* (1987), p. 58; *Viscusi, W. Kip./Vernon, Joseph E./ Harrington, Joseph Emmett* (2000), p. 62 and *Berg, Hartmut* (1999).

[23] Structure → Behaviour → Result; Structure → Behaviour; Behaviour → Result and Structure → Result.

[24] On the Rule of Reason see *Schmidt, Ingo* (1981), pp. 282–284.

[25] See *Hildebrand, Doris* (2002b), pp. 6.

behaviour can also lead to changes in the market structure. Excessively high prices are not exclusively the result of the market structure, contrary to the traditional conception of Bains, but rather they are also due to exclusionary practices that aim to create market entry barriers. It is still assumed that the market structure can provoke competition-restricting behaviour, but the strict structural determinism is no longer accepted. Structure is understood within Game Theory as the external determining factors that are relevant for businesses in decision-making. The models have also meanwhile been given a new dynamism. Despite further academic development however, there will always be a structural factor that cannot be calculated either because it is not quantifiable (such as the level of market entrance barriers) or because it is only partially calculable (such as the limits of fixed and variable costs). [26]

Despite numerous attempts to make the Workability Concept more precise and easier to implement there are still many problems in differentiation and clarity in both the norms and the characteristics. Specifying the relevant market is especially problematic. The market results themselves aren't of much practical use, since comparable results would be necessary to make an evaluation. Comparative markets have to be used as a measure, since the optimal performance of a market remains an unknown quantity, but no two markets have the same conditions. Because of this the Workability Concept is preferable with its generality that includes subjective value judgments as norms.[27]

The central thesis of the Workability Concept, namely that there is a fundamental connection between market structure, behaviour and result, is not always true.[28] Market results for example, can also be brought about by faulty management behaviour or in general from irrational human behaviour. In addition, the requirements placed upon competition policy are different in each branch, and can change quickly due to technological progress, which would limit market tests to a specific point in time if they were to have any credibility.

Despite this critique of the Workability Concept, there can be no question as to its success in developing recommendations for competition policy based on micro-economic price theory, which would allow the policies to increase general welfare. [29] Since the Workability Concept is mostly criticized for its limited applicability and general credibility, the criticism is in fact for the subject to be studied, the competition itself. Competition is an open process that cannot be so easily quantified. The Austrian School is the best instance of this concept.

---

[26]See *Kowalski, Angelika* (1997) and *Hildebrand, Doris* (2002a), pp. 130.

[27]See *Mantzavinos, Chrysostomos* (1994), p. 30.

[28]See *Mantzavinos, Chrysostomos* (1994), pp. 38.

[29]See *Oberender, Peter/Vath, Andreas* (1989), p. 12 and *Mantzavinos, Chrysostomos* (1994), pp. 40.

9.1.3   The Austrian School

The Austrian School has its roots in Carl Menger's book "Grundzüge der Volkswirtschaft" published in 1871. His ideas were taken up and developed further first by Eugen von Böhm-Bawerk and Friedrich von Wieser and then later by Gottfried Haberler, Oskar Morgenstern, Fritz Machlup and Friedrich August von Hayek.[30] Hayek was the first economist to include the dynamic character of competition in economics, which he did in 1949.[31] He considers competition to be evolutionary, and sees it as a method for the discovery of facts that would never be discovered or at least remain unexploited if not for competition. It could also be called a search. No one can predict innovations in products and processes to any exact degree. The Austrian School thus contradicts the neo-liberal theory of balance. In a dynamic process a balance can be striven towards but never reached. The innovations are constantly changing the market conditions and thus the balance point.[32] The task for enterprises is to seek out and realize innovations, and their incentive to do so is the reward for pioneering companies from the market. This is how technical progress is realized. Enterprises must be free to embark upon their search for innovative ideas. This puts the onus on state competition policy to assure that the discovery process is allowed to take place without hindrance. It has only the job of providing a framework in the form of contract and civil law, and intellectual property rights. Hayek rejects any state intervention that alters or distorts competition processes.[33]

9.1.4   The German Concept of Free Competition

The German concept of free competition takes up the dynamic, open, undeterminable character of competition as purported by the Austrian School, and along with the Chicago School, considers the dynamic aspects with the most intensity. It has also been called the Concept of Competition Freedom, and goes back to Erich Hoppmann.[34] Since the process of competition is determined by the actions of competitors, especially dynamic companies, concrete results from competition structures or state intervention cannot be predicted. The clear correlation between market structures and results, as assumed by the proponents of the Workability Concept, is not considered realistic by supporters of the Concept of Free

---

[30]See *Hildebrand, Doris* (2002a), p. 154.

[31]See *Hayek, Friedrich August von* (1949). See *Hayek, Friedrich August von* (1978), p. 180; *Hayek, Friedrich August von* (1969), p. 249 and *Hayek, Friedrich A. von* (1975), p. 15.

[32]See *Mantzavinos, Chrysostomos* (2001), pp. 212.

[33]Even the German Commission of Monopolies was rejected by Hayek because of its discretionary power. See *Mantzavinos, Chrysostomos* (1994), pp. 119 und 121; *Mantzavinos, Chrysostomos* (2001), pp. 212 and *Hildebrand, Doris* (2002a), pp. 154.

[34]On the concept of free competition see *Hoppmann, Erich* (1977) and *Mantzavinos, Chrysostomos* (1994), pp. 158.

Competition. This position is supported by the results of empirical research, which has falsified the assumption of a compelling, systematic dependency of market results upon market structures.

Because competition is a process that cannot be determined, there can be no market results for competition policy to aspire to. In the best case scenario pattern predictions may be accurate. Hoppmann uses the idea of free competition from classical theorists, relying a great deal on the fundamental works of J. A. Schumpeter on the dynamic competition of innovation and creative destruction,[35] and on F. A. von Hayek on freedom and competition.[36] Competition is equated with freedom and thus represents an independent goal of competitive freedom. The freedom of decision for market participants is also seen as a fundamental requirement in order for competition to be able to increase welfare. The dilemma theory of the Workability Concept is therefore not rejected, but seen rather a harmony between freedom of competition and increasing economic efficiency (the non-dilemma theory). The Concept of Competitive Freedom rejects all state interventions that aim to achieve a certain competition situation by influencing the market structure. Just like the Austrian School, it accepts only state interventions in the competition process aimed to preserve competition and competitive freedom. According to this concept competition policy should guarantee open and flexible markets, and prevent agreements and behaviours that limit competition.[37]

Intervention would be necessary however, if artificial restrictions to competition resulting from enterprise or state actions occur. Behaviours that restrict competition are then to be dealt with, when they are based upon an inappropriate use of power in the market. If they occur within the framework of normal competition processes, then they are to be considered necessary. Desirable and undesirable limitations must be defined for competition policy in the form of regulations. The Concept of Competitive Freedom uses market tests in order to determine both competitive freedom and market power. Cross price elasticity of the products on offer or the flexibility of production are used for the tests. In the case of natural limitations on competition, understood to include market failures and natural monopolies, regulation regarding competition-establishing exceptions such as state price controls would be necessary.

---

[35] See *Schumpeter, Joseph A.* (1961) and *Schumpeter, Joseph A.* (1993), pp. 318.

[36] According to *von Hayek*, competition is characterized as an experience to discover facts that would remain hidden without its existence or at least not used. See *Hayek, Friedrich August von* (1969), p. 249 and *Hayek, Friedrich August von* (1975). For Hayek is competition evolutionary.

[37] See *Schüller, Alfred* (1987), p. 58; *Aberle, Gerd* (1992), pp. 40 and *Schmidt, Ingo/Rittaler, Jan B.* (1986), pp. 767.

9.1.5 The Chicago School of Antitrust Analysis

The Chicago School of Antitrust Analysis also denies any connection between market structure and competitive behaviour.[38] In the USA the Chicago School represents the antithesis of the Workability Concept, or Harvard School. It is characterized by a market and competition optimism, and thus sees no role for an interventionist state in either market structure or competition policy. The ideas of Aron Director form the base of the Chicago School, and the main proponents of the concept are Posner, Bork, Stigler and Demsetz. They have enjoyed a good deal of influence on the American antitrust policies and laws since the early 1980s.

The Chicago School applies Darwin's Natural Theory to the phenomena market and competition. Since spontaneous trial-and-error processes create optimal market structures, products and forms of production, an optimal welfare in the form of maximum consumer welfare is automatically created by the survival of the fittest. It considers ruinous competition, such as dumping to achieve a monopoly position, to be unrealistic since the costs of squeezing out their competitor would be too high for such an unreliable result. Competition can be restricted by way of cartels however (horizontal restrictions), which from this viewpoint should be the focus of competition policy controls. The Chicago School sees vertical restrictions to competition as beneficial to efficiency. The welfare-reducing effects that may result from restrictions on competition are not denied, yet the welfare-increasing benefits based on theoretical analyses of mergers take such a central position that the negative side is neglected. Mergers increase productivity by way of assumed scale effects, transactional and organizational advantages, learning processes and the betterment of management qualities. Possible restrictions on consumer profits from market power derived from the potential competition from new suppliers (allocative efficiency) are neglected, however.[39] This explains the Chicago School's positive take on company mergers. The most efficient and therefore optimal company size is automatically brought about by competition. This line of reasoning explains why the Chicago School views the connection between company concentration and profit discovered by the Harvard School as an expression of a high efficiency level, rather than a restriction on competition that reduces consumer profits.

Williams offers a competition policy compromise in that estimated profits be weighed against welfare losses caused by reduced competition intensity when examining mergers—a process that has meanwhile become standard. He himself admits that not all mergers increase efficiency. Both Schools seem to have found a common denominator, seeing as

---

[38]See *Shepherd, William G.* (1990) and *Posner, Richard A.* (1979), pp. 951–952.

[39]See *Posner, Richard A.* (1979), pp. 927 and pp. 937. "The Chicago school does not deny that concentration is a factor that facilitates collusion of a sort difficult to detect, although it attaches less significance to concentration per se than do the oligopoly theories" op sit., p. 945. Comprehensive literature on intervention criteria in the case of mergers can be found in *Stigler, George J.* (1968), pp. 296.

how representatives of the Harvard School suggest weighing the advantages and disadvantages, and do not condemn all monopolies as welfare reducing per se:

> These costs of monopoly may possible be offset, in part or whole, by benefits from scale economies or an increase in innovation.[40]

A fundamental difference between the Harvard School and Ordoliberalism (Freiburg School) on the one hand and the Chicago School on the other rests in the evaluation of vertical price assurances (vertical relationships). According to the competition policy envisioned by Ordoliberalism, vertical restrictions are a hindrance to competition. They contradict two of the constituting principles from Eucken, namely a functional system of free prices and perfect competition, and the principle of open markets for new participants. A prohibition per se would be the consequence. Should unavoidable vertical restrictions occur, they would be placed under the supervision of a monopoly commission that would set as-if competition prices according to the regulating criteria.[41] Whereas the Harvard School and Ordoliberalism see restrictions on competition that reduce welfare in vertical price setting, the Chicago School perceives a welfare increase. The latter argues that the consideration of efficiency must prevail in suppliers' efforts at vertical concentration, since demand for their own product would be reduced by a price increase for both sales and service.[42] The producers, so the argument goes, use price-setting as a means to prevent traders from free-riding by shirking their share of welfare-increasing costs of advertisement, warehousing, and guarantees on service and all-inclusive pricing. The Chicago School considers advertisements as providing information, and thus in principle beneficial to efficiency.[43]

The Theory of Contestable Markets[44] complements the concept of free competition and the Chicago School. It focuses on the direction of potential competition. The goal American group based around Baumol was to develop a theoretically founded application for competition policy based on the reference model of perfect competition.[45] Perfect competition as a market situation is artificially created here with the absence of market entrance and exit barriers. If a monopolist tries to raise their prices clearly above the average costs of production for example, it becomes worthwhile for other suppliers to offer that product.

---

[40] *Shepherd, William G.* (1985), p. 2. See also *Hildebrand, Doris* (2002a), pp. 136.

[41] See also *Glasow, Bernhard* (1999), pp. 5 and *Hildebrand, Doris* (2002a), pp. 159 and *Dieckheuer, Gustav* (2002).

[42] This argument can only come true with a price elastic demand.

[43] See *Posner, Richard A.* (1979), pp. 926.

[44] The theory of contestable market should not be put on the same level as the Harvard and Chicago School. It is an academic attempt but never has worked in competition practice yet. But the pointed ideas are suitable for the understanding of the different viewpoints on competition.

[45] See *Baumol, Willia J.m/Panzar, John C./Willig, Robert D.* (1988) and *Mantzavinos, Chrysostomos* (1994), pp. 56.

Should the monopolist then reduce their prices because of the new competition, the new suppliers would be able to then leave the market with temporary profits—or so it is said. This market situation of "as though competition" can influence market behaviour just as perfect competition can. According to this concept the market entrance barriers must be kept low and vertical or horizontal barriers such as cartels and dominant market positions restricting newcomers must be prevented.[46] The Contestable Markets theory recommends that state competition policy be to reduce market exit barriers, which in turn leads to an extensive deregulation and the removal of exit costs such as social plans.[47]

Although Baumols intended to create a viable approach for competition policy based on price theory, the concept of Contestable Markets is not much more than an ideal and an intellectual approach. The fact that potential competition and actual competition can influence market behaviour is disputed neither academically nor in practice, and was recognized by national economists in the eighteenth century.[48] The assumption that barriers to market entrance can be neglected is unrealistic, however. Adjusting manufacturing to a new product always entails costs. The concept of Contestable Markets has weaknesses as an intellectual approach as well, especially in the assumptions about market behaviour. Game theory predicts that potential competitors will anticipate a defensive strategy from the established monopolist or at least an immediate decrease in price, and will thus rethink the venture if they would not gain any competitive advantage.

> **Conclusion**
> The attempts of the Free Competition Concept and the Chicago School to grasp the dynamic and open nature are commendable, as is the classification of "freedom of competition" as a value in and of itself. There may be an overstatement within these efforts however, as is also the case with the Austrian School. Not all possible behaviours in competition are socially desirable or beneficial for welfare. For example, a company might finance dumping with cross subsidies, squeezing more competitive producers from the market, which would reduce welfare. Even freedom can be abused. Hoppmann has seen this possibility and thus insists on rules of play. These rules would have to be controlled and implemented by a market supervisory authority. Problems of putting the rules and establishing criteria for intervention into practice still have to solved, however. It would be folly to think that all possible restrictions to free competition could be covered. The actions of all market participants evade clear categorization as restrictive or non-restrictive for competition, clearly illustrated with the example of publicized price lists. Determining areas
>
> (continued)

---

[46]See *Shepherd, William G.* (1990), p. 14.

[47]See *Aberle, Gerd* (1992), pp. 40.

[48]See *Bartling, Hartwig* (1997), p. 21.

of competition policy for exemption is also problematic. For one thing the areas are not easily determined and isolated, which opens the way for lobbyist influence. Another problem is that the prerequisites for a market failure over time disappear with technical progress (or sometimes new ones are created), yet the exemption rules remain in place.

The general applicability of the assumptions made by the Chicago School is questionable. The assumption of negligible market entrance barriers doesn't hold for most branches[49]; these barriers can be generally defined as the costs or resistance that a new producer has to come up with in order to be able to offer a comparable product. Market exit barriers are the costs or resistance faced by a producer wanting to withdraw their product, in effect leave the market. Entrance barriers are differentiated into absolute, individual cost advantages for the companies already in production, high fixed costs especially in economies of large scale, and product differentiation such as the software standard from Microsoft. The indivisibility of production factors and high fixed costs (including high research costs such as is found in the pharmaceutical industry) are the main causes of market entrance barriers. Besides high fixed costs there are also networks and production know-how that play an increasing role as barriers.[50] The entrance barriers can also become exit barriers, such as the expenditure for production facilities that are usually lost upon exit (sunk costs).

The discrepancy between the analysis instrument of the statistical neo-classicists and their dynamic orientation is another point of critique on the Chicago School. The clear orientation towards the model of perfect competition and the monopoly as the extreme opposite creates distortions in the statements from economic policy and makes the theory immune to attempts at falsification.[51] The same is true for Hoppmann's conception of freedom of competition.[52] The one-dimensional theory of contestable markets is explainable by way of its historical background. The main motivations behind the formulation of the Theory of Contestable Markets from Baumol were the many market interventions of the American government, which created artificial market entrance and exit barriers.[53] The Harvard and Chicago

(continued)

---

[49] See *Pratten, C. F.* (1971); *Silberston, A.* (1992), p. 369–391; *Grichting, Alois* (1976), and *Frohn, J./Krengel, R./Kuhbier, P./Oppenländer, K.H./Uhlmann, L.* (1973).

[50] A comprehensive list of market entrance barriers can be found in Boner and Krueger. See *Boner, Alan Roger/Krueger, Reinald* (1991), p. 6.

[51] See *Mantzavinos, Chrysostomos* (1994), pp. 52.

[52] See *Mantzavinos, Chrysostomos* (1994), p. 168.

[53] "Thus we must reject as perverse the propensity of regulators to resist the closing down of unprofitable lines of activity. This has gone even so far as a Congressional proposal (apparently

Schools were created because of changing economic conditions. The academic origins for these concepts—computation of markets using the newly available computer technology by the Harvard School in the 50'ties, and changes in the political environment for the Chicago School—have had significantly influenced outcomes.

Both the Harvard and the Chicago School have had a large influence on American competition policy and regulations. The Chicago School was increasingly able to take over the prominent position of the Harvard School in the 1980s under President Ronald Reagan.[54] Neither of the concepts had a particularly strong representation in the regulations at that time, rather a case-by-case judgment of the economic effects of a restriction on competition was the norm (rule of reason). Neither of the concepts was able to claim complete authority because of the complexity of competition.[55] The different conclusions on competition policy were due to differing analytical tools. The Harvard School was based upon competition behaviour and market results within the framework of studies based on individual markets. Competition policy norms were formed from inductive analysis based on the Industrial Organization Theory. The Chicago School in comparison, reaches its conclusions on competitive behaviour and market results through deductive analysis based on price theory.[56] The policy conclusions of the Industrial Organization Theory (Harvard School) have been confirmed by the findings of modern price theory, however. If one leaves the framework of the idealized traditional price theory and includes search, transaction and control costs as well as insecure decision-making circumstances, market entrance and exit barriers, spatial monopolies and a clear reduction in company efficiency advantages result.[57]

There is a definite correlation between market structure or market power and market behaviours in the goals of an enterprise wanting to optimise its profits. A monopolist must behave differently than a polypolist if they want to maximize their profits, although the two forms represent the two extremes. Seen in this light the Structure-Conduct-Performance-Theory certainly has its justification, but a

(continued)

---

supported by Ralph Nader) to require any plant with yearly sales exceeding $250.000 to provide fifty-two weeks of severance pay and to pay three years of taxes, before it will be permitted to close, and that only after giving two years notice!" *Baumol, William J.* (1982), p. 14.

[54]"In the early 1980s, as part of a plan to free business from excessive government regulation, antitrust was re-engineered from policy that favoured open markets and entrepreneurial opportunity to law narrowly focused on output-limiting conduct that provably raises prices to U.S. consumers." *Fox, Eleanor M.* (1997), p. 10.

[55]See *Schmidt, Ingo/Binder, Steffen* (1996), pp. 131 and *Reder, Melvin W.* (1982), pp. 1–38, pp. 15.

[56]See *Posner, Richard A.* (1979), pp. 930.

[57]See *Nelson, Richard R.* (1979), pp. 951.

monopoly and a polopoly are still extreme cases. Most markets can be classified somewhere in-between the two.[58] The market constellations are unlimited, which means that the competition policy case in practice must weigh the advantages and disadvantages. Market entrance barriers can also not be ignored; depending on the branch they can even be several times the yearly production costs. Human relations, and thus competitive behaviour, cannot be pre-determined. Companies are led by people that do not always act rationally, in fact rationality is not even necessarily a natural quality of humans. Our environment rewards us for certain behaviours when we act rationally, or optimally in relation to the given circumstances. In Hayek's words, rational behaviour is the result of competition, or the market process, and not vice versa.[59] Because of this, practical competition policy must weigh the advantages and disadvantages according to each case. The existence of market barriers is also indisputable, and can represent many times the annual costs of production, depending on the branch. It is also an indisputable fact that human behaviour, and thus competitive behaviour, cannot be principally determined. Not every company behaves rationally; rationality is not a natural and inevitable phenomenon enjoyed by everyone. Our environment rewards us when we act rationally, in other words optimally in relation to the given framework. As von Hayek would say, rational behaviour is a result of competitive and market processes, and not of human behaviour.[60] As Hayek shows, competition is an open and unspecific process of discovery. Market situations will never be identical because of the large number of influential factors, making prognostications near impossible. Competition theory will never be able to deliver competition policy makers exact directives for making a decision in a specific situation. The politics must therefore be limited to guaranteeing the rules of the game, playing the role of referee for competition.[61] This is in fact an essential role for a market-based economic system.

(continued)

---

[58]Möschel points out that with seven structural market parameters (market share, market entrance barriers, market transparency, cost function, product variation, price elasticity and income elasticity,) and three values for them (small, middle and large) allows for 116,280 possible combinations. See *Möschel*, Wernhard (1991), p. 18.

[59]See *Matzavinos, Chrysostomos* (1994), p. 137.

[60]See *Matzavinos, Chrysostomos* (1994), p. 137.

[61]"In my view, the ignorance from which we suffer is unavoidable. Economists cannot fill the gap in our knowledge with analytic methods now available to them, and probably will not be able to do so in the future either. ... In fact, the great danger in antitrust today is not that there will be too little economic analysis, but that there may soon be too much. Just as qualification may create the illusion of certainty, econometric sophistication may provide the illusion of a scientific method." *Glinsburg*, Douglas H. (1991), p. 28.

The concept of free competition has to be rejected inasmuch as it demands the removal of all restrictions on competition. An example of this would be patents, which give the pioneering enterprise an advantage on their innovation for a limited time. They are necessary in order to make investment in research and development worthwhile. It must also be possible for a pioneering enterprise to break into existing markets with their new product. The openness of national markets is thus a prerequisite for the functionality of dynamic competition and needs to be solidly incorporated into an international system of competition regulations. Openness of markets is also necessary that the imitators of the pioneering enterprise also have access to markets, since the monopoly created from the competitive advantage wouldn't be broken up after an appropriate length of time. Open market support competition, since the companies represented on the market can count on new competitors if there is a good potential for profit, and remain under constant pressure similar to that of competition. There is a danger that competition will decrease with market participants either exiting or merging that results from blocked market entrance. This could lead to the market form of a monopoly or a friendly oligopoly.[62]

Uncontrolled competitive freedom can also lead to a monopoly and be thus self-defeating. It is therefore important on the international level to insure that subsequent competition is not restricted. As purported by the Theory of Contestable Markets, artificial market entrance and exit barriers must be identified and removed. The importance of potential competition needs to be tested for individual cases for the point in time that they occur. General bans on restrictions to competition are alone not enough. Market structures themselves can lead to a failure in competitive behaviour, such as collective action or failing to offer a better price—a common occurrence in tight oligopolies. Controls on competitive behaviour are clearly indispensable. Conceptual development continued apace however, bringing ever more ideas into the field.

9.1.6   The Neo-Austrian School

The Austrian School has made a comeback since the 70'ties in the form of the Neo-Austrian School. Representatives of this school include Murray N. Rothbard, Israel Kirzner, Gerals P. O'Driscoll, Mario J. Rizzo and Roger W. Garrison. Despite its name, the Neo-Austrian School is located mostly in the USA and represents an opposition to the dominant mathematical econometric theory of balance. Competition is for them an evolutionary, creative and thus incalculable trial-and-error process of discovery, just as it

---

[62]See *Berg, Hartmut* (1999).

was for Hayek.[63] Markets never reach a balance according to this school of thought.[64] The market forces strive for an equilibrium, but competition processes are constantly affected by new conditions within the dynamic, evolutionary system. Microeconomic models of balance, such as those used by the Chicago School, are thus rejected by the Neo-Austrian School. State intervention in the market process is also rejected, since the market price used as an orientation for the market participants seeking competition gets distorted and the process of discovery is drawn out as the market forces seek a new balance.[65] Just as in the Austrian School, the state should be restricted to establishing a system framework, giving market forces the most freedom possible to develop. The individual freedom of an enterprise is the means and the end of competition policy. Efficiency is an automatic result of the evolutionary, dynamic competition process—in contrast to the Chicago School—and not a criterion one could use to evaluate mergers, for example.[66] The free market should provide for new competitors to guarantee enough competition to force market participants into the desired dynamic, evolutionary process. Competition policy must make sure that markets remain open. Enterprises that have already established themselves in a market must not be protected from competition through direct or indirect interventions, as it would make market entrance all the more difficult for new competitors. Thus we see an overlap with the Theory of Contestable Markets.[67]

Just how boundless the optimism of the Neo-Austrian School regarding competition is, can be seen clearly with the example of a monopoly on resources. Any advantage enjoyed from the monopoly will be short-lived once competition is attracted that uses a different production technique.[68] According to the Neo-Austrian School, should competition policy redistribute monopoly earnings to consumers by way of a market intervention, the interests of enterprises in creating a monopoly would abate, which could mean an untapped synergistic effect and thus losses in welfare.[69] Even if the market entrance barriers created by the state are ignored, there are still many others, as shown in the critique of the Theory of Contestable Markets and the Chicago School.[70] Every market entrance comes with costs and the risk of a poor investment. There are technological advantages, in that some

---

[63]See *Hildebrand, Doris* (2002a), p. 156; *Kirzner, Israel M.* (1992), pp. 6 and *Maks, J. A. H.* (1995), pp. 197.

[64]"The equilibrium is hypothetical, it will never be reached." *Maks, J. A. H.* (1995), p. 198.

[65]See *Hildebrand, Doris* (2002a), pp. 156, p. 2.

[66]See *Hildebrand, Doris* (2002a), p. 156; *Kantzenbach, Erhard* (1990), p. 203.

[67]See *Hildebrand, Doris* (2002a), p. 156 and *Mantzavinos, Chrysostomos* (1994), p. 129.

[68]See *Maks, J. A. H.* (1995), p. 198.

[69]See *Maks, J. A. H.* (1995), p. 198 and *Mantzavinos, Chrysostomos* (1994), p. 130.

[70]Boner und Krueger offer an extensive listing of market entrance barriers. See *Boner, Alan Roger/ Krueger, Reinald* (1991), p. 6.

products are simply cannot be duplicated, and some spatial monopolies exist because of prohibitive transportation costs. Neither the Austrian, nor the Neo-Austrian Schools offer solutions to the issue of market power.

9.1.7 The European School in EC Competition Law

The German ordoliberal ideas have influenced the EC competition rules from the beginning. The problem has been that the Ordoliberal School is not an empirically oriented model with analytic tools for competition policy. The EC Commission has just started to develop a new approach to competition based on the ordoliberal ideas, itself based on dynamic Industrial Organization theory and New Industrial Economics. The Commission has adopted several guidelines from the EC Court's case-law over the past few the years, and has written several of its own guidelines for competition policy.[71] Nearly all competition theories were thus drawn upon, as well as the latest economic insights. While the Chicago School remained too general in outlook with its deductive approach using microeconomic models, and the Harvard School (Workability-School) inappropriate because of considerable theoretical weaknesses, the New Industrial Economics enabled a more realistic, case-orientated approach. With the help of game theory and more sophisticated microeconomic models, New Industrial Economics tries to deduce the most likely strategic behaviour from companies in oligopolistic situations. The result has been the revival of the Structure-Conduct-Performance approach and the creation of an empirical case-orientated analysis. A new European School of Competition has since become a name.[72] In contrast to the originally stark rejection of vertical agreements from Ordoliberalism and the Harvard School, the European School prefers to weigh the advantages and disadvantages on a case-by-case basis (Rule of Reason).[73] It can generally be assumed that a restriction on competition by way of vertical restraints is only acceptable if sufficient intra-brand competition does not exist.[74]

9.1.8 The Post-Chicago School

A synthesis of different competition theories also took place in the US in the form of the Post-Chicago School. As with the European School, it grew out of the demands from

---

[71] For instance: *EU-Commission* (2001); *EU-Commission* (1997), para. 24.

[72] *Hildebrand, Doris* (2002b), pp. 3–23, pp. 4.

[73] The following factors would be analysed by the EC Commission under Art. 81 (1) EC treaty investigation: 1. Market position of the supplier, of the competitor and of the buyer; 2. Entry barriers; 3. Maturity of the market; 4. Level of trade; 5. Nature of the product and other factors, depending on the case.

[74] See *Hildebrand, Doris* (2002b), pp. 16.

administrative justice and recommended action for competition policy. The findings of the New Industrial Economics, new and modern Industrial Organization Theory and Game Theory all influenced this school. The result was in an international adaptation of competition concepts and thus the European/American competition policies. The term "Post-Chicago" School must be understood historically, not theoretically or methodologically. This school developed out of the critique in the 1980s of the Chicago School dominant in the US at that time.[75] It was expressed in 1992 for the first time in the judgment of the U.S. Supreme Court on the case Eastman Kodak Company vs. Image Technical Service, Inc.[76] From a theoretical perspective it could be called the Contra-Chicago School.

The methodological critique of the Post-Chicago School on the Chicago School is that the constantly efficient microeconomic market model is too abstract and theoretical to be used for the complex market conditions that exist in reality. An additional critique is the short-term perspective taken by the models of the Chicago School. Those who follow the Post-Chicago School prefer models that are dynamic and tailored to specific individual markets, with the capability of taking market imperfections, external factors of influence and strategic behaviour into account. Empirical evidence and analysis are added as well.[77] They can also be considered competition optimists, as opposed to followers of the Chicago School. They believe neither that markets are efficient per se (due to incomplete information and market entrance barriers, for example), nor that dominant market positions are automatically dismantled over time, nor that the market itself will always sanction inefficient economic behaviour. According to the Post-Chicago School, market participants that are not dominant are also capable of distorting competition to their advantage over the long-term, by unfair competitive behaviour such as dumping. If the market is made up of a few large companies, they don't necessarily act as competitors, and technological cooperation can meld into competition hindrances.[78] Differences between the two "Chicago" Schools are also evident in the judgment of mergers. The Post-Chicago School criticizes its predecessor for the almost exclusive inclusion of static allocated effects and increased production efficiency, while failing to address dynamic losses in efficiency that can come about over time with a restriction on competition—such as lost innovation. It also sees that vertical mergers can be a danger in that competitors are denied access to primary products

[75]The Chicago-School had a large influence on the "Vertical Restraint Guidelines" from 1985, which were subsequently removed by the Clinton Administration in 1993. See *Hildebrand, Doris* (2002a), p. 152.

[76]See *Hildebrand, Doris* (2002a), pp. 156 and *Schleicher, Tara* (1997), p. 310.

[77]See *Royal, Sean M.* (1995), pp. 445–454, p. 445, *Hovenkamp, Herbert* (1985), p. 256; *Hovenkamp, Herbert* (1994); *Hildebrand, Doris* (2002a), p. 151 and *Langlois, Richard N.* (2001), pp. 200.

[78]See *Kattan, Joseph* (1993), p. 1–21; *Krattenmaker, Thomas G./Salop, Steven C.* (1986), pp. 254, *Hovenkamp, Herbert* (1994); *Price, Tony Curzon* (1997), pp. 219–254; *Schleicher, Tara* (1997), p. 311 and 315; *Hildebrand, Doris* (2002a), p. 152f and *Langlois, Richard N.* (2001), p. 201.

and emphasizes the danger of producers taking advantage of consumer dependence.[79] According to Lande, a representative of the Post-Chicago School, competition law—thus competition policy—must provide for the lowest price for consumers, a price close to production costs.[80] Market interventions would then be unavoidable.

In summary, it is important to keep in mind that none of the competition concepts introduced in this paper is alone qualified to provide an optimally functioning competition. The critique offered here are also reasons why competition policy has moved towards a comprehensive concept for competition, coming away from the individual restrictions on competition.[81] Thus a general ideal for an international system of regulation for competition will be proposed in the following section. It brings the findings of all of the concepts previously addressed together and can be used as a model for Doha, even though political acceptance of ideals is often quite low.

9.1.9   A Concept of a New Neo-Ordoliberalism as an Economic Ideal for an International System of Competition Regulations

What should the goal of an international system for the regulation of competition be? The options presented by the competition concepts introduced here are freedom, protection of enterprises from restrictions on competition, efficient allocation, innovative progress and the welfare of consumers.

In this context the broadly accepted view that American and European competition policies have different goals is important. It is said that the USA concentrates more on the goal of allocation efficiency and consumer welfare, while Europe is more focused on protecting competition as a goal in and of itself.[82] We will therefore look into whether or not a conceptual opposition is possible. It became clear in our explanation of the functions and concepts behind competition that it has an intrinsic value by providing the individual with options in how they want to act. Individual freedom is not an appropriate goal given the current differences in political and cultural opinion at the international level. It is quite another matter however, if freedom is seen as a medium with which to increase national welfare. This concept of freedom as a goal belongs to every market economy-oriented state already.[83] The means of reaching this end would be the further efficient allocation,

---

[79] See *Hovenkamp, Herbert* (1985), pp. 249; *Ordover, Janusz A./Willig, Robert* (1985), p. 311; *Hildebrand, Doris* (2002a), pp. 152; *Langlois, Richard N.* (2001), pp. 202 and *Schleicher, Tara* (1997), pp. 315.

[80] See *Lande, Robert H.* (1989), p. 632. and *Schleicher, Tara* (1997), pp. 315.

[81] See *Schmidt, Ingo/Binder, Steffen* (1996), pp. 13 and *Reder, Melvin W.* (1982), pp. 15.

[82] See *Möschel, Wernhard* (1991), p. 11.

[83] Although the concept of the "Economic Freedom Index" is contested and the results of the studies have varied, the most recent calculations have shown a positive connection between freedom rights and per capita income. See *Voigt, Stefan* (2002), pp. 147.

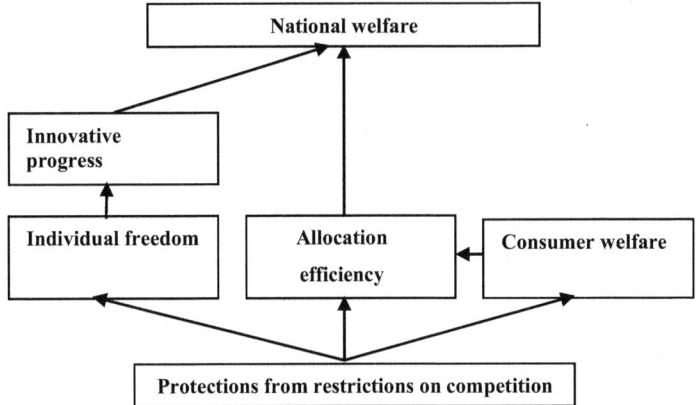

Fig. 9.1 Interdependence of competition policy goals

protection of companies from restrictions and a dynamic innovative competition as the prerequisite for innovative progress. Consumer welfare is also a means by which to increase national welfare, since a demand that can choose from several offers compels an efficient selection from which to choose as well as an efficient production. The consumer profits thus remain for the consumers and a monopoly profit rendered impossible. Competition between suppliers for demand falls under "protection from restrictions to competition", which guarantees individual freedom and not allocation efficiency and consumer welfare. The individual freedom makes the creative process of discovery possible, which then brings innovative progress with it.

It is our goal then, to frame a system of competition that guarantees protection against restrictions to competition, in other words the rules of the game that will allow competition to develop fully. The protection of competition as an end of itself, as the Europeans see it, is the prerequisite for consumer welfare and allocation efficiency, and thus the wider base from which to reach our common goals (see Fig. 9.1).

Consequently we have to conceive regulations for competition that guarantee competition freedom as a protection of enterprises from restrictions on competition for an efficient allocation of resources and a dynamic competition process to promote innovative progress in order to maximize consumer and nations welfare. The conditions that are required can be found for the most part in Eucken's constituting principles: private property and contractual freedom, market openness, and full enterprise liability. A legal system that makes it possible to do business is the basic condition for competition. Private property guarantees an entrepreneur that they will profit from any success their efforts have, whereas contractual freedom makes it possible to start an enterprise. Liability is a logical extension of the competitive system of incentives. If an entrepreneur is to use their resources efficiently, they must be forced to calculate risk into their plans. They will only do so if they can count on success with profits as well as failure with profits.[84] All competition concepts agree on these constituting principles for a system.

Competition is interdependent and dynamic, as stressed by the Austrian and Chicago Schools and the concept of competitive freedom. It must be assured on the international level that subsequent competition is not hindered. Artificial market entrance and exit barriers must be identified and dismantled, according to the Theory of Contestable Markets, the Austrian and Neo-Austrian Schools. The function of competition to sanction assumes that non-efficient marginal suppliers fall out of the market. Direct subsidies of any kind would work contrary to this goal and protect companies from new competition, thus sealing off the markets. Liability for decisions and entrepreneurial risk must lie exclusively with the enterprises themselves; a system that risks and opportunities must also confront. Interpreted narrowly, all majority participation from states in companies must cease, which also applies to the innovation function. Innovations are encouraged when the profits from them are high and calculable for companies. The interests of international consumers in contrast, are to eradicate monopoly profits that result from innovation. Both goals must be weighed against one another.

That competition regulations provide an opportunity for competition between national markets is a further condition for maximizing wealth through optimal international resource allocation. The demand of Ordoliberalism for openness in national markets is an important condition in this sense for the functionality of a dynamic, evolutionary competition based on innovation as stressed by the Austrian School, and must therefore be well-established in an international system of competition. It must be possible for a pioneering business to bring new products or production experience into markets that already exist. Open markets are also necessary to guarantee that the imitations of the pioneering company retain market access; otherwise the monopoly created by a competitive advantage won't be dismantled within an appropriate time frame.

Open markets are also beneficial to competition from the perspective of the Theory of Contestable Markets, the Austrian and the Neo-Austrian Schools. The companies represented in an open market can count on competition if they have a high potential for profits, which places them under a similar competitive pressure. If market access is blocked there is a danger that competition will peter out by companies either leaving the market or merging, which in turn would create the market form of a monopoly or congenial oligopoly.[85] Criteria and a legal platform for interventions to preserve market access must therefore be incorporated into regulations on competition. The principle of keeping markets open is universally applicable, and thus open foreign trade also counts as a principle of any competition system.

---

[84] See *Sachverständigenrat zur Begutachtung der gesamtwirtschaftlichen Entwicklung* (1985), No. 309.

[85] See *Berg, Hartmut* (1988), p. 236.

As became clear in the evaluation of competition concepts, a control mechanism for competition that includes market intervention in certain cases cannot be done without. Control is necessary to counteract or at least restrict the negative impact of cartel agreements, predetermined behaviours, price setting, exclusionary contracts and any other competition hindering or discriminating behaviour. Despite all the optimism, an incentive to limit competition is inherent in the market system. The findings of the modern Industrial Organization and New Industrial Economics make this abundantly clear. As a general statement all concepts of competition besides the New Austrian School would be in agreement. Persistent divergence in opinion is to be found over the controls on mergers and vertical agreements. A competition policy compromise might be to weigh the assumed efficiency gained by a merger with the welfare losses from the reduced intensity of competition; a policy that has become the standard. The same applies to vertical agreements.

The international community should set the framework for entrepreneurial activity. The first priority are the laws that regulate market structures, such as cartel and merger laws, and thus serve as a basis for national policy for the regulation of competition. This point is the most contested between the concepts we have looked at, as well as in theories and national governments. On the other hand, the concept that currently dominate the discourse, the European and Post-Chicago Schools, are generally agreed that enterprises and consumers must be protected from practices that hinder competition. The Workability Concept (the Harvard School) is especially applicable on this point. There must be laws that protect from deception, fraud and breaches of common decency, so that competitive advantages are not gained that are not based on achievement.[86] In order to solve inter-state conflicts however, it is sufficient if such laws exist at the national level and the contractual partners have agreed on a place of jurisdiction.

Fundamental, thus a constituting principle according to Eucken, is a feasible price system. Prices must reflect the relative cost structure exactly in order for enterprises to be able to recognize affordable primary products. All conceptions and theories of competition are in agreement on this point. An international economic system that maximizes welfare must ensure that the relative international cost and price structures do not become distorted. Subsidies should be prohibited in principle because of the distorting effect they have on competition. In fact price rigidities should be dismantled in order to adjust the entrance of primary products as quickly as possible in the case of changes in the relative cost structure, which would allow international division of labour and resource allocation to be optimised and general welfare increased. Discrepancies on a common competition law codex exist even in the case of the United States and Europe however. This is due to the different economies but also to the different economic concepts applied (in the US antitrust policy is a goal of economic law whereas in the European Community competition law is embedded in other legal objectives such as market integration, social policy, etc.). A worldwide

---

[86]See *Heuß, Ernst* (1980), p. 693.

competition law/policy concept is even more difficult to achieve because of the differences between countries. Currently, the common understanding is that what is achievable based on Doha is a minimum consensus of antitrust principles.

Limiting influence to making and enforcing rules for competition is fundamental to the expanded Ordoliberal concept. Generally accepted economic policy decisions that are directly applicable to particular cases are impossible to achieve due to the various market situations and the dynamic, changing character of competition. Economic theory can offer only partial analyses for specific cases based on restrictive assumptions, which means that an economic policy oriented towards specific cases (Rule of Reason) is adequate. It is the goal of an expanded Ordoliberal economic policy to allow for the full development of competition functions. The instruments to guarantee this would be everything from market interventions to the breaking up of monopolies, yet the method used must be appropriate for the restriction on welfare or infringement on competition. The main goal is the engagement of all forces of competition to maximize welfare. According to the Kaldor-Hicks criterion the benefit of the individual may be compromised for the sake of increased general economic benefit that clearly compensates the effect on the individual. Compensation is an alternative. Intervention in the chances of an individual to fully develop themselves must generally be weighed against the restrictions to competition and the market economy system, since the freedom of creative economic development is the basis of all welfare.

The goal of an international competition system must therefore be to see that the advantage-seeking of private companies and the government leads to maximum global welfare, in other words that the "invisible hand" of international competition can fully develop. We may call this concept Neo-ordoliberalism.

Conclusion
In summary, it should be noted that none of the presented competition concepts is in itself suitable for optimally guaranteeing all competition functions. The above-mentioned criticisms are also the reason why competition policy has begun to consider the individual restrictions of competition detached from a comprehensive competition concept. However, it can be considered as certain that there is a connection between market structure or market power and market behavior in the company's goal of optimizing success. A monopolist must behave rationally differently than a polypolist if he wants to maximize his profits. Nevertheless, mono-pol and polypol are borderline cases. The vast majority of markets are in between. The market constellations are unlimited. For this reason competition policy has to weigh case-by-case between the advantages and disadvantages of restrictions of competition.

9.2   Cartels

9.2.1   Basics

Competition is not self-sustaining, but can be restricted by law (merger) or de facto (without contract). Collusion as restrictive business strategies that serve to build market power are of particular importance to regulatory policy. Market power restricts formal freedom of action and material freedom of resolution to the advantage of powerful third parties. Market power makes it possible to restrict pensions by restricting competition, i.e. revenue without return. Competitive agreements between legally independent companies restrict competition and thus create market power. Within the framework of the negotiating strategies, horizontal agreements (cartels: companies at the same level of production) and vertical agreements for the development of market power can be distinguished.

▶ **Definition** In the case of **cartels**, competition between several companies at the same stage of production is limited by collusion on important competition-relevant action parameters, whereby it is characteristic that the independence of the companies involved is maintained.

Agreements between market competitors with the same level of added value that restrict competition, so-called horizontal agreements such as cartels, are addressed by all national competition authorities, but treated differently. The Prohibition Principle (Rule of Law) and the Abuse Principle are possible instruments for competition policy. The advantage of a prohibition on principle is its transparency, or legal security, and the policy-relevant prevention of the welfare-reducing effect from cartels. Cartels are sometimes credited with partially positive market (and thus welfare) effects however, which is why exceptional cases are a part of many national competition policies. In the EU for example, stemming from a general prohibition from the General Direction III, cartels are approved after checking out and weighing the effects of individual and group releases.[87] Exceptions to the general prohibition on cartels cannot be explained with competition theory.

Most states try to prevent monopolies and cartels domestically for reasons of competition policy, but they are encouraged if they seem to help increase export competitiveness.[88] This is also why domestic cartels are prohibited in many national competition regulations,

---

[87]See *Boner, Roger Alan/Krueger, Reinald* (1991), pp. 50 and *Wins, Henning* (2000), pp. 27. The EU Commission wants new regulations for the cartel prohibition in article 81 of the EU treaty. In the future the obligation for cartels to register themselves should be replaced by the legal exception, according to which companies no longer have to report their agreements to the Commission. The cartels would then be valid until the prohibition of the commission. This would of cause make a control of cartels more difficult for the commission. See *Without Author* (2002).

[88]See *Scherer, F. M.* (1997), p. 13.

but export cartels are allowed.[89] Export cartels aim to create monopoly profits at the expense of the foreign countries, and thus represent not only welfare-reducing restrictions on competition, but disadvantages for international distribution and free-rider behaviour in respect to the public good of free trade. A reform of the international system of competition regulations must therefore have a per-se prohibition on export cartels. The "Voluntary Export Restraints (VERs)" are not included in the GATT effectively mean export cartels, and are thus also to be done away with.[90]

International consensus has been reached on the prohibition of hard-core cartels, at least.[91] Most reform strategies that have been suggested in the current reform debate are based on this assumption.[92] The majority of national competition systems allow certain forms of cartels. An international prohibition on cartels per se that did not provide for exceptions would thus be politically very difficult to implement. An exception for specific cases is also economically reasonable if a restriction on competition due to little market power on the part of the company involved can be ruled out.[93] The Rule of Reason—weighing the possible efficiency advantages against welfare disadvantages in the face of a restriction to competition—is internationally used for all non-cartel forms of horizontal cooperation, such as in research.[94] A strategic solution would be to allow exceptions to a per se prohibition, which would be subjected to individual scrutiny from an international competition authority. Such an institution could then weigh the arguments offered by the applicants against the expected effects on competition and welfare according to the Rule of Reason (weighing the advantages and disadvantages of an amalgamation[95]), which corresponds to the Neo-ordoliberal concept that has been developed here. The exception would have a set duration, so that the hurdle of getting approval would have to be repeatedly overcome. The effects of the exception would also be better judged over time. If the expected efficiency gains are not realized, or the negative effects on competition increase and it leads to complaints from consumers, a renewed exception would be very difficult to achieve.[96]

---

[89] See *Gröner, Helmut* (1987), p. 364 and *Victor, Paul A.* (1992), pp. 572.

[90] The Federation of German Industries (BDI) was successful in getting a law based on the formulation in the strategy from *Ludwig Erhard* and *Alfred Müller-Armack* against competition restrictions quite watered down, with support from the once Federal Chancellor *Konrad Adenauer*. See *Drude, Michael* (1991), p. 7 and *Lenel, Hans Otto* (1989), p. 311.

[91] See *Immenga, Ulrich* (1996a), p. 602.

[92] See *Conrad, Christian* (2003).

[93] See for instance the EU-treaty. See *Hildebrand, Doris* (2002b), p. 18 and *Nagy, Anke* (2002), pp. 118.

[94] See *World Bank/OECD* (1999), p. 29 and *Morici, Peter* (2000), pp. 29.

[95] On the Rule of Reason see *Schmidt, Ingo* (1981).

[96] See *Wins, Henning* (2000), p. 149.

9.2.2 Types of Cartels

Cartels according to the form of the agreement:

1. Tacit collusion

   Tacit agreements to restrict competition are also prohibited.
2. Informal cartel

   Formally arranged cartels (gentlemen's agreements)

   These are verbally agreed behaviors, without contract
3. Contractual cartels (= cartels in the legal sense)

   Here, the cartel agreements are recorded in writing between the participants.

   More complex cartels often have to be fixed in writing, otherwise there would be misunderstandings between the cartel members. Even if cartels are concluded over many years between many cartel members, a written regulation is required. It may also be necessary to regulate the distribution of cartel contracts among each other if the market advantages and antitrust tasks are not evenly distributed. The disadvantage is obvious. There is evidence that can be seized during searches or seizures and used against the cartel members.

Cartels according to the purpose of the agreement:

1. Submission cartels: Agreements in public tenders

   Example: A community says that a road needs to be rebuilt. The prices of the offers are very high, only one of them is cheaper. This behavior was previously agreed among the companies. The favorable offer gets the order. At the next tender, another road builder will get the job through a low-cost offer. In order to regulate this compensation in the long term, there is a written antitrust agreement.
2. Export cartels: breakdown of foreign markets, quantity or price agreements

   Example: German companies in mechanical engineering divide the countries. Company A gets Brazil and company B Chile.
3. Import cartels: Example: bundling of purchasing power to compensate for foreign market power

Cartels according to the content of the agreement

1. Price cartels
   - Discount cartels: standardization of the rebate system

     Example: At 100 kg purchase, 10% discount
   - Calculation cartels: Unification of cost accounting, overheads in price calculation— Freight based cartels: standardization of the transport cost calculation (also for the study of cartel outsiders). Places are agreed upon from where the transport costs are calculated to keep competitors away from overseas.

Price cartels can arrange factory prices or home delivery prices. These prices may be provided either as list prices or as prices set for the individual offer. The cartel may agree to these prices as fixed prices, minimum prices or maximum prices (demand cartel).

2. Quantity cartels
   - Quota cartels (agreement on the production or sales quantity)
   - Customer protection and territorial agreements (division of customers or territories with the competitors). The customer then gets so-called defense offers from the provider, so he does not notice that there is a cartel agreement.

3. Production cartels
   regulate the production over ...
   - Standard and type cartels
     Standardization of product and packaging sizes
   - rationalization cartels,
     e.g. joint procurement or sales).
   - Specialization cartels
     Pruduction distribution according to customer

The prices agreed in the price cartel do not have to be the same. Different prices can occur because: the cartel members need time to adjust their price strategy (it would also be too noticeable if all competitors increase their prices at the same time), the products offered by the cartel members are heterogeneous (quality differences), there is a submissions cartel or a cartel member is fighting an outsider. What options are there to enforce antitrust discipline? The cartel can undercut the outsider (price dumping). If a cartel of 4 companies had an 80% market share and the outsider only 20%, any cost undercutting would hit the outsider 100%, while in the cartel it would spread across the four companies. For example, if a cartel member is given the role of an outsider, for example, because of the locally lower transport costs, it must be compensated by the other cartel members.

There is then the disadvantage that this also damages the cartel. However, the cartel can also turn to the upstream suppliers, who depend on the cartel for a market share of 80%. The upstream suppliers may also expect the formation of a cartel to be more advantageous, in the form of less competitive pressure in the sector concerned and perhaps also a higher margin. The cartel may ask the subcontractors to sanction the outside party, for example by providing poor quality or a delayed delivery.

9.2.3 Cartels as Prisoner's Dilemma

The cartel situation corresponds to the Prisoners' Dilemma with the dominant strategy of antitrust deviations (Nash equilibrium *): the worst case for a company is if it adheres to the cartel agreement, but not the other company and the best case is if it is does not comply with

Fig. 9.2 Cartel situation

company A\B	deviate	adhere
deviate	(2, 2)*	5, 1
adhere	1, 5	4, 4

the cartel agreement, but the other company does. Therefore, the combination occurs in which neither company adheres to the cartel agreement as a dominant strategy. Cartels must be unstable by nature because it is profit-maximizing to deviate and take sales from the other and prevents competition from getting ahead (Fig. 9.2).

Nevertheless, there are many cartels in practice. Why is that?

Cartels are stable when vendors can control and sanction each other.

The following conditions facilitate the capacity to create cartels on markets:

1. Low number of vendors: Fewer vendors make it easier to sign agreements, better monitoring and control
2. Homogeneity of the product: A better comparison is possible, you can equate the prices better
3. Symmetric production cost conditions: production costs must be similar, so the same basis for the calculation is available, which facilitates an agreement.
4. High entry barriers: If outside companies could simply undercut prices, the cartel would not be sustainable.
5. Low direct price elasticity of demand: Only if sales remain nearly constant with rising prices can the profit be increased. This is the case for products that cannot be substituted or only substituted poorly.
6. High supply elasticity: The price goes down, the supply goes up. If there is a risk of ruinous price competition, the willingness to conclude binding cartel agreements will increase. For example, in a situation of overcapacity, steel producers often try to return to profitability through higher production volumes with decreasing unit costs.
7. High market transparency: Good overview of the markets makes it possible to detect infringements by the companies against the cartel agreement.
8. Internal and external cartel enforcement: Agree on sanctions if the cartel is not complied with, such as price dumping or penalties. Outsiders: The cartel outsiders force themselves to join the cartel through price dumping or putting pressure on upstream suppliers (buying power) by ordering them to increase prices when non-cartel members request a quote or blackmailing them to allow time for delivery.

9. Low threat of punishment: no punishment, so low fines increase the profitability of
   cartels

Cartel Susceptible Products Cement, concrete, steel, bricks, cables, street signs,
firecrackers, elevators, de-icing salts, vitamins, LPG, paper, toothpaste . . .

Cement has many characteristics that facilitate cartel building including the homogeneity of the product and the same cost of production. There is little direct price elasticity as cement is irreplaceable and there are a small number of suppliers. There are also high market entry barriers, as the cement plants are large and therefore expensive production facilities.

9.3   Vertical Agreements

Vertical agreements (also referred to as "bonds") are understood to mean restrictive agreements between producers or producers and traders of different production stages (see Fig. 9.3).

This means that there is a restriction of competition between legally and economically independent companies with regard to one or more action parameters through so-called exchange contracts, in which one of the contracting parties is limited in freedom of contract formation with third parties, with whom he is bound in direct buyer-seller relationships. This includes z. B. Price Bindings (Content Bindings) and Sales Restrictions and Exclusivity Bindings.

Vertical relationships are understood to be agreements between producers or between producers and retailers at different production levels. Examples would be price assurances (content assurances) and production restrictions, exclusivity assurances and linking agreements (business assurances).[97] This type of market access restriction has become well-known through the Japanese "Keiretsu" system. Many markets are protected with exclusivity assurances in Japan. Retailers and producers are dependent on one another. These relationships are partially assured by familial connections. Competition exists only between the Keiretsus.[98]

Vertical agreements of any kind are a hindrance to both domestic and international competition, yet they may also represent an advantage in the form of efficiency. Any advantages in efficiency are rarely passed on to consumers, however.

---

[97] See *Herdzina, Klaus* (1999), pp. 157 and *Goldfarb, Lewis, H.* (1995), p. 126.
[98] See *Matshushita, Mitsuo* (1995), p. 129 and *Sadao, Nagaoka/Goto, Akira* (1997), p. 23.

Fig. 9.3 Structure of vertical agreements

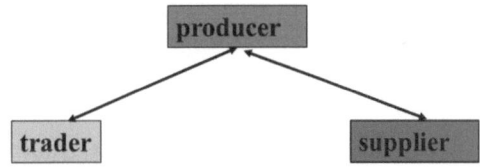

Case Study: Vertical Agreements at the Dealer Network of Automobile Manufacturers

Many dealer networks in Germany include price fixing, exclusivity agreements and distribution restrictions. Discuss whether they should be allowed.

1. Price maintenance (mainly for producers without dealer network) = Final sale price is determined.

    Example: List prices of cars

    This results in an advantage for the producer, since the intra-brand competition is turned off, because the VW dealer X is not cheaper than VW dealer Y. (In contrast: interbrand competition = competition between brands such as VW and BMW)

2. Exclusivity

    The VW dealer may only sell cars that are produced by the VW Group. This prevents VW from creating competition in the distribution network.

3. Sales restrictions, territorial protection

    Sales restriction e.g. every VW dealer gets assigned to a specific area. No other VW dealer may move in or advertise.

As an aid to the discussion, the common arguments for vertical agreements are attached: There are many authors who see vertical relationships as a necessary evil, and even attribute positive effects to them:

1. An argument of the Chicago School claims that if exclusivity assurances between producers and retailers were to disappear, both would have to set a profit margin, which in turn would mean a higher price for the consumer than the exclusive price set by the producer.[99]

2. The most relevant argument for the positive net welfare effects of vertical relationships is that the creation of monopolies in a certain field make it possible to finance an extensive service and business network.

3. A third and final argument is that the retailers would not be able to afford the market development costs, such as marketing expenses, without an exclusive market agreement. They would otherwise have to fear being squeezed out of the market by another retailer who could undercut their prices by being a free-rider and avoiding the market

---

[99]See *Tirole, J.* (1988), Chapter 4.

development costs.[100] Vertical agreement could therefore strengthen competition against other producers in some cases.[101]

Solution

The first argument is easy to disprove. If one assumes that producers operate according to profit maximization, the monopolist producer will set prices on the foreign market dependent upon the demand elasticity to be found there, and offer the retailer a share of the item profits. In free international competition the prices cannot be differentiated, since the arbitrage, as exports would otherwise go from the low to high-priced country. This is the reason for exclusivity resale price maintenance. The final sale price would be lower without them. The argument of the Chicago School, that efficiency consideration must take precedence in the producer's attempts at vertical concentrations, since a price increase in production and service automatically reduces the demand for the product, only applies for a price elastic demand. That would support competition policy judgment of vertical price assurances through the competition authorities based on the individual cases, in order to be able to differentiate according to the relative price elasticity.[102]

The second argument is valid based on the interviews with car dealers conducted by the author. Exclusivity assurances are standard in the auto industry. The dealers commit themselves to a market, train their employees in the corresponding auto types, and stock their replacement parts. They attempt to establish their brand regionally on the market and create a customer loyalty. In this case vertical exclusivity assurances lead to a reduction in transaction, information, and repair costs for dealers through specialization, which in turn can be passed on to the customer as long as competition is prevalent. In return they demand regional protection, so that no other supplier can undercut them in cost without the service obligations. For the dealer it is decisively important that the supply of the producer is so comprehensive that the desires of the customer can be met. This means that the producer must have a broad enough pallet of products and the necessary logistics in order to break into a foreign market. The biggest market entrance barrier is these fixed costs.[103]

The manufacturer can use the brand monopoly to implement their own price and market policy. The intra-brand price competition is expressly prohibited. If the manufacturer is successful in differentiating their product from others in this way, they have attained a nearly perfect monopoly, with which they can maximize their profits through market divisions and price differentiation at the cost of the consumer.[104] Exactly because vertical

---

[100]See *Motta, Massimo/Onida, Fabrizio* (1997), p. 604 and *Kühn, Kai-Uwe/Seabright, Paul/Smith, Alasdair* (1992), p. 14.

[101]This is above all the view of the Chicago-School. See *Posner, Richard A.* (1979), pp. 927.

[102]See *Viscusi, W. Kip./Vernon, John, E./Harrington, Joseph Emmett* (2000), p. 236.

[103]See also *Boner, Roger Alan/Krueger, Reinald* (1991), pp. 57 and *Kühn, Kai-Uwe/Seabright, Paul/Smith, Alasdair* (1992), pp. 14.

[104]See *Viscusi, W. Kip./Vernon, John, E./Harrington, Joseph Emmett* (2000), pp. 236.

relationships often lead to the sealing off of national markets and thus go against the EU-domestic market principle, the EU prohibition principle applies to vertical restrictions on competition as well as horizontal. (Art. 81 EC-Treaty).[105]

However, this argument does not take into account the fact that price control manufacturers also exclude repair competition and try to make it more difficult for contractually non-commited workshops to repair them by means of design peculiarities.

The third argument needs to be differentiated. The argument only applies for high market development costs that don't automatically lead to a consumer relationship with the retailer. A time limit on the exclusivity agreements based on the example of patent protection would contribute more to overall welfare than an unlimited brand monopoly. It is all the better that there is meanwhile broad international consensus to prohibit at least the fixing of resale prices, even if they don't seem capable of prohibiting exclusivity agreements.[106]

Conclusion

Vertical agreements remain dangerous. Vertical agreements hinder domestic and foreign competition equally. First and foremost, the vertical sales and distribution channels, value-added or pre-production chains and thus market access for third parties are blocked. Competition parameters such as the price will be equal and the wholesale competition and/or competition between the sales units (intra-brand competition)

The vertical agreements allow powerful competitors to emerge across multiple markets that are far in excess of "simple" dominant market positions. The exclusivity commitments may prevent third parties from entering the market. Without a dealer and service network, a car manufacturer abroad cannot sell cars.

Abuse of this market power, for example through price dumping, financed by vertical subsidization, in order to force competitors out of the market at individual value creation stages or to prevent them from entering the market, becomes possible. For example, an automotive group can only prevent a foreign competitor from entering the market by undercutting sales if it can force dealers to pass on the agreed price to customers without increasing their own profit margin, like equal market behavior or horizontal agreements between the then few, vertically organized market participants.

(continued)

---

[105]See *Fox, Eleanor M./Ordover, Janusz A.* (1995), p. 24; *Nicolaides, Phedon* (1994), p. 21; *Wins, Henning* (2000), p. 29; *Boner, Roger Alan/Krueger, Reinald* (1991), p. 57 and *Carlton, Dennis W.* (1994), p. 544 und 845. For a complete analysis of the EU competition policy on vertical relationships, see *Duijm, Bernhard* (1997).

[106]See *Immenga, Ulrich* (1996a), p. 604.

In summary, whether vertical business relationships lead to restrictions on competition depends on whether or not competition with another substitutable product exists (inter-brand competition), and whether or not manufacturers use exclusivity agreements to create price differentiation. These variables could be investigated on an individual case basis. This is why vertical business relationships should be dealt with on the international level using the 'rules of reason,' in other words weighing the advantages and disadvantages for each case independently with the use of a regulating competition institution. [107] The approved vertical business relationships should then be placed under the supervision of an abuse supervisory authority.

Summary

Horizontal and vertical agreements restrict competition and thereby cause a reduction in economic efficiency and the consumer pension. The competitive features are impaired, resulting in limited market failure. In exceptional cases, this can lead to efficiency and consumer benefits. Both forms of agreements are banned at both national and European level, with companies themselves having to check in advance whether their agreement is subject to legal exemption.

Comprehension Questions

1. Define horizontal and vertical agreements.
2. What facilitates the formation of cartels?
3. Name three types of cartels.
4. What do you, as a manager, have to pay attention to when making agreements with their competitors? What is the regulation of the legal exception?
5. What is your opinion: when should horizontal and vertical agreements be allowed?

---

[107]The EU Commission has also chosen to consider possible competition hindrances with the Rule of Reason, which might include advantages resulting from vertical agreements in the form of efficiency gains. They consider the following aspects under article 81 (1) of the EC treaty: 1. The market position of the supplier, competitors and consumers; 2. Market entry barriers; 3. The maturity of the market; 4. The extent of trade; 5. The type of product, and other factors depending on the case. See *Hildebrand, Doris* (2002b), pp. 16. See *Hoekman, Bernhard* (1997), p. 396; *Petersmann, Ernst-Ulrich* (1996), p. 10 and *Brinker, Ingo* (1999), p. 62 and 64. The EU Commission stresses that a vertical restriction can only come about if there is a lack of inter-brand competition or the agreements have a market share of more than 20%. See *Brinker, Ingo* (1999), p. 64 and *Morici, Peter* (2000), p. 31. See *Duijm, Bernhard* (1997) and *Hildebrand, Doris* (2002b), pp. 16 for the way the EC-Commission has deal with vertical restrictions on competition.

9.4   Abuse Supervisory Authority

The European Court of Justice defines market dominance based on article 82 of the EC treaty as follows:

> ... a position of economic strength ... which enables [a firm] to prevent effective competition being maintained on the relevant market by affording it the power to behave to an appreciable extent independently of its competitors, customers and ultimately of its consumers.[108]

In most national competition systems a dominant market position is defined by "exploitive behaviour", so that the market position makes fixed prices above the market level under normal circumstances possible.[109] The so-called abuse supervisory authority has the goal of protecting competitors on economic levels both above and below that of the cartel from obstructions unrelated to performance and from exploitation in competition. Abuse controls are an international standard. Placing a company under the supervision of a supervisory authority is assumes proof of a market-controlling position on the relevant market in all national competition laws. The requirements for this, besides the demarcation of the relevant market, are determining the market share and investigating the competition situation in that market. Monitoring a market-controlling position requires control over the competitive behaviour of the controlling company.

Possible sanctions for an established abuse in national competition laws are omission decrees, monetary penalties, break-ups, or even jail sentences. Originally the USA was the main country to force the break-up of cartels. However now American competition courts establish market-dominating positions relatively seldom in comparison with the EU and Germany. There are still certain differences in international interpretations.[110] The shares that the EU uses as the lowest parameter for a market dominating position vary according to markets between 45 and 70%.[111] The markets in the USA tend to be more widely demarcated and most courts consider a dominant position to begin with a 70% market share, which is why such a market dominating position is more rarely established. The large variances in the market share to be considered market-dominating show that generally accepted and clear guidelines are not yet possible. A meeting in the middle between the European and American competition authorities in recent times can be established, however, as long as the initial conditions are similar.[112]

---

[108] Quoted from *OECD* (2001), p. 82.

[109] See *OECD* (2001), p. 82.

[110] See *Fox, Eleanor M./Ordover, Janusz A.* (1995), p. 26; *Wins, Henning* (2000), pp. 30 and *Bridgemann, John* (2002), p. 62. For the abuse control of the EU see *Decker, Eric* (2002).

[111] See *Nicolaides, Phedon* (1994), p. 22; *FIW* (1990), p. 18f and *OECD* (2001), pp. 86.

[112] See *Holmes, Peter* (2002), p. 155.

The abuse of a dominant market position can be dealt with as a criminal act in the USA,[113] whereas the EU Commission can only impose fines. Bridgeman reads from this that the USA can afford to be more lenient[114] on mergers than the EU[115] because of their tougher sanctions in the case of an abuse. The USA uses a two-level market test within the framework of the so-called Rule of Reason for merger controls, for example. A market situation test should clarify as a necessary condition whether or not a functional competition exists. In order for the conditions to call for competition policy intervention, the second test criterion must come out negative. In other words the market results do not diverge within a reasonable limit from the norm. The EU commission acts similarly within the framework of its Extended Structure-Conduct-Performance Theory.[116]

The abuse authority can also be used for cartels tolerated by states. In Germany, Canada and the Netherlands the abuse principle also applies to cartels exempt from the per-se prohibition. In Great Britain, Denmark, Norway and Switzerland it is even applied to hard-core cartels, such as price, quota, submission and market distribution cartels.[117] The abuse authority is bound to proven abuses of sufficient market power, however.

9.4.1 Criteria for a Competitive Abuse of Power

Market tests, in addition to determining the market share, are conducted in order to determine whether a market-dominating position exists. Different criteria are determined according to the Harvard School; market structure, market behaviour, and market performance tests. Criteria for the market structure tests, used in order to estimate whether or not sufficient competition takes place, include the number and size of competitors, the possi-

---

[113]Under the Sherman Act abuses can be sentenced to a maximum of tree years. See *Morici, Peter* (2000), p. 42.

[114]The ECJ recently removed various prohibitions on mergers from the Commission (1990: Airtours/First Choice, 2001: Schneider/Legrand, 2001: Tetra Caval/Sidel). The ECJ has explained this decision with mistakes in the calculation of market share. The market share of the merged companies were overestimated, and the competition underestimated. In the future the EU Commission should take possible advantages for consumers from a merger. See *Without Author* (2001) p. 1 and *Morici, Peter* (2000), pp. 31. This is why the USA claims that there is a current trend in European competition policy away from the ordo-liberal theory, which aims above all to protect competing companies, towards the model of the USA which aims to increase consumer welfare through efficiency increases from mergers. See *Gifford, Daniel J./Kudrle, Robert T.* (2002), p. 233.

[115]See *Bridgemann, John* (2002), p. 62.

[116]See UNCTAD (1997), p. 291; *FIW* (1990), p. 18; *Trebilcock, Michael J.* (1996), p. 98; *Hildebrand, Doris* (2002b), p. 6ff; *Wins, Henning* (2000), p. 32 and *Bridgemann, John* (2002), p. 60; *Nagy, Anke* (2002), pp. 122 and *Boner, Roger Alan/Krueger, Reinald* (1991), pp. 69.

[117]See *OECD* (1996), p. 18; *Hay, Donald* (1993), pp. 9 and *Wins, Henning* (2000), p. 28.

bility of market entrance from a third party,[118] and the degree of market transparency. These criteria are applied differently internationally, mostly due to their number and inexactness. The same applies for the market behaviour test, although the criteria could be the same pricing behaviour of market competitors and the absence of price-setting behaviour of the consumers. Whether the quality and amount of goods is in relation to their price, thus whether of not the market situation reflects that of competition and whether the prices develop as they would under the patterns attributed to normal market and competition conditions, is the goal of market performance tests. Market situation and market behaviour tests that build the basis for controls on abuse of an established market-dominating position. These instruments are unfortunately very subjectively interpretable and applicable. This is particularly clear in relation to the market situation test with an analysis of the use of national anti-dumping measures.[119] It is virtually impossible to find an objective measure for the costs and thus the price calculations of a company. Neither can we establish applicable market situations using the comparative market concept, due to the differences in markets and companies.[120] There aren't even standardized criteria to determine the market position of companies on the national level since the relevant markets can be narrowly or broadly defined with the flexibility of interpretation. There haven't been any objective standards up to now with which to measure the degree of a market access restriction for example, or the intensity of involvement between companies.

If a dominant market position can be determined despite the above-mentioned difficulties, the abuse of this position must also be determined. Abuse can take the form of discrimination, obstructions or exploitation. Exploitation in this context is the discrimination against market competition through price setting, in other words maximizing the monopoly or cartel profits. The exploitation abuse, in contrast to the obstruction abuse, is mostly effective against suppliers and buyers.[121] It is imperative to draw on parameters of

---

[118]Borrowing from the more fully developed behaviourist Workability Conception, the EU Commission uses a dynamic market structure-behaviour-performance theory. Effects that boomerang are taken into consideration, such as the effects of the profitability of a branch (performance) on market structures over time. The higher the profits, the more likely is the entrance of another company. See *Hildebrand, Doris* (2002b), pp. 6.

[119]See *Conrad, Christian A.* (2002).

[120]See *Knorr, Andreas* (1999), p. 419; *Herdzina, Klaus* (1999), pp. 46, pp. 52 and pp. 62; *Gröner, Helmut* (1987), p. 373; *Berg, Hartmut* (1999), pp. 309 and 350; *OECD* (1994a), p. 12 and *Wins, Henning* (2000), p. 38.

[121]In the USA the Clayton Act prohibits a monopolistic price differentiation. Such differentiations are only allowed if they correspond to differences in the manufacturing, sales, or delivery costs. The market position of the supplier is not of importance in this case. The accused company can exculpate itself if a reasonable price adjustment to the competitors prices can be proven. In contrast to the German Act Against Restraints on Competition (ARC), in which only cartels, market-dominating and price-setting companies are prohibited from price-discrimination in §26 Paragraph 2. See *Posner, Richard A.* (1979), pp. 926; *Petersmann, Ernst-Ulrich* (1996), p. 30; *Niels, Gunnar/Kate, Adriaanten* (1997), p. 36 and *Gifford, Daniel J./Matsushita, Mitsuo* (1996), pp. 294.

action from markets with exploitation-free competition as a measure of comparison in order to determine exploitation. This is problematic however, since market situations are never identical. The latitude of an administration in measuring is thus increased, and with it arbitrary interventions. It is on the other hand just as necessary to ensure that competition laws don't lose their effectiveness because of inactivity on the part of the authorities.

There is an extra-territorial problem on the international level especially for exploitation abuses, since the country of the monopolist has very little incentive to stop the exploitation of foreign consumers,[122] but according to the new foreign trade theory more probably sees it as a chance to maximize its own welfare through rent-seeking at the cost of the other country.

The maximization of the market position profits in the case of obstruction abuses occur only indirectly by of a reduction in competition, for example to market entrance through exclusion agreements, linking agreements and discount practices. Besides defining the market, the formulation of criteria for intervention poses a problem. The motives of a company can't be determined from outside, and the criteria for the obstruction of competition are only determinable under consideration of competition behavioural norms in the sense of a law against dishonest competition. Thus Germany for example, puts a stop to the effects of the abuse in case of a proven restriction to competition. The Act Against Restraints on Competition (ARC) therefore considers it an abuse when "a market dominating company... impedes the competitive potential of other companies as regards their competition on the market without a factually justified reason" (§ 19 Abs. 4 No. 1 ARC).

9.4.2 Dumping as an Abuse of a Market Dominating Position

According to the above definition for abuse, dumping—understood to be the assumed sale of goods below cost—represents an obstruction to competition without a factually justified reason. The sale of goods on another (foreign) market at a lower price than one's own domestic market would be an obstruction abuse as well. In both cases however, a market-dominating position on the part of the dumping company would have to be proven, in order for it to be censured as an abuse. Anti-dumping measures would thus be reduced to curbing the specific hindrance to competition and all dumping cases would fall through the cracks except market position dumping, price differentiation and aggressive dumping.[123] Aggressive dumping aims to create a monopolistic position in the foreign country by selling below production costs. An international market-dominating position would necessarily be present in this form of international obstruction abuse through price dumping, since other foreign suppliers would otherwise take the place of the displaced domestic supplier. The

---

[122]See *Duijm, Bernhard/Winter, Helen* (1994), p. 230 and *Wins, Henning* (2000), p. 150.

[123]See *Conrad, Christian A.* (2002).

American definition of abuse reflects this focus as well, and prohibits behaviours that "substantially lessen competition, or tend to create a monopoly".[124]

In order to determine the market position of the exporter in the market of the importing country, competition policy has to cross borders. Not only the domestic suppliers and the exporter must be taken into account, but other actual and potential suppliers as well. The cooperation of the competition authorities in the exporting country is essential, in addition to the importing country. The goal of the dumping, namely the crowding-out of competitors on the domestic market could be looked into more effectively with the support of the competition authorities in the exporting country and thus better determined as it would be from the authorities in the importing country, since the relevant internal documents from the company would be accessible. Cross-subsidies, the financing of dumping by way of other company branches or products would also be able to be determined.

Market position dumping and price differentiating are actually representing an advantage for the importing country, but are still considered dumping from the national anti-dumping procedures.[125] The deciding cause for the distortion in competition, the monopoly or cartel on the market of the exporting country, creating a disadvantage to the exporting country through different price-setting, is not included however. An abuse supervisory authority able to cross borders would make this possible. The competition authorities of the exporting county would have to break up, or at least control the monopoly or cartel in the case of a market position dumping and price differentiation.

Seen from a competition policy perspective, replacing national anti-dumping procedures with an international abuse supervisory authority would be the best solution. This would probably encounter considerable resistance from national industries however, since the dumping cases that would then no longer be considered, getting rid of over-production at below-cost prices in a foreign country for example, would run counter to their interests. According a study conducted by the OECD, only 28 of 282 US anti-dumping procedures between 1979 and 1989 met the criterion of a market-dominating position.[126] In addition, an important protectionist instrument would disappear with the national anti-dumping procedures.

---

[124]Clayton Act, quoted in *Bruns, Joseph W.* (1969), p. 7.

[125]See *Conrad, Christian A.* (2002).

[126]See *Niels, Gunnar/Kate, Adriaan ten* (1997), p. 38. Under the condition of a market-dominating position most anti-dumping duties in the 1980s could not have been imposed. See *Knorr, Andreas* (1999), p. 426.

9.4.3   Abuse Supervisory Authority at the International Level

The abuse supervisory authority is a very inexact competition policy instrument due to the difficulties in determining the relevant market and the position of the company in this market, but we cannot do without it for lack of better options. The analytic difficulties in ascertaining the market and the relative position are surmountable even with the two imprecise variables,[127] but it may be assumed even more difficult on the international level to set the criteria for an abuse of a market-dominating position due to culture differences and the expected lobbying influence. One task of an international system of competition regulations would thus be to prevent the abuse of market-dominating positions on the international level and another would be to create legal clarity with a unified framework for the abuse supervisory authority and to prevent the abuse of these instruments as a protectionist device.

There is a very great need for harmonization, since markets are internationally very different in more ways than their distinctive geographical features alone, and their use of the abuse controls vary greatly. A decentralized application of the abuse principle should therefore be carried out through national competition authorities. The international coordination of the abuse controls would have to make sure that the markets are defined and controlled across boundaries. An after-the-fact harmonization within the given competition policy framework could be undertaken by an international reference authority, which would establish the unified interpretation of an international abuse supervisory authority without a real loss of sovereignty. This does not apply to the necessary after-the-fact coordination of competition policies against international abuses from the national authorities. An intrusion upon national sovereignty from an international competition authority is in this case unavoidable. This task cannot be fulfilled by a court, since a court is not a permanent institution and therefore unable to consistently coordinate or direct the international competition policy procedures of several national competition authorities.

9.5   Merger Controls

In terms of competition policy, mergers are business combinations in which at least one competitive unit gives up its independence. Also in the form of so-called corporations or trusts, in which self-employed companies have a unified management via a majority share capital. By means of the eligibility criteria for German merger control, the legislator seeks to cover all cases in which a company is subject to the potentially controlling influence of one or more other companies.

The goal of merger controls is to prevent a market-dominating position from being either created or strengthened from which welfare-reducing restrictions on competition

---

[127]See *Immenga, Ulrich* (1996a), p. 605.

could be implemented. The potential reduction in welfare from such restrictions stands opposite the welfare gains that are to be had from size advantages such as economies of large scale or efficiency gains from saving on such institutions as staff-departments or research departments. Merger controls thus have to look at each case individually and weigh the expected welfare gains and losses. This is why an individual consideration based on the so-called 'rule of reason' takes place in all national merger control measures regardless of whether they are undertaken by competition authorities or courts.[128]

Globalization is having an impact on mergers, with a focus on strengthening the market position. While 46.5% of mergers targeted the use of synergy effects and rationalization potential in the years 1985–1986, in 1991–1992 they were only 16.2%. Conversely, the motivations for expansion and/or strengthening of the market position developed. Only 27.7% of mergers had this goal in 1985–1986, compared to 76.8% in 1991–1992. It can therefore be stated that, market-conquest or defense strategies are behind the mergers, whereas research projects are mostly pursued by means of the less complex and less profound strategic alliances or cooperations. In this context, the question arises as to whether national competition authorities are always objective and uninfluenced by the alleged interests of their own country, assessing the mergers of their domestic companies, i.e. weighing the reduction of competition in foreign markets against the efficiency gains from the merger. For example, the merger between Boeing and McDonnell-Douglas was approved by the US Federal Trade Commission (FTC) despite a global market share of 70% (Airbus 30%), whereas the EU Commission almost prohibited the merger. On the other hand, the European Commission approved the merger of Mannesmann-Vallourec/ Ilva despite a market share of 70% due to an unspecified potential competition of Japanese companies.

The great importance attached to market conquest and market defense is in line with the globalization trend and is of particular importance for competition policy due to the associated reduction of providers and, as a consequence, the intensity of competition. While it is likely that intensified international footing activities are largely a consequence of increased competition due to globalization, strategic alliances are primarily aimed at increasing research efficiency. However, international price cartels or monopolies cannot be ruled out.

Mergers, to the extent that they bundle the market interests of different actors, pose a threat to competition and thus to international market access. Concentrating market power through business combinations prevents competition not only through concentration of power, such as the misuse of power, for example through monopolistic pricing but also weakens dynamic competition by reducing the number of participants in the search and discovery process. Strategic alliances are mostly viewed favorably in industrial economics literature due to synergistic effects, especially in research, the pooling of resources and the

---

[128]See *Wins, Henning* (2000), p. 31.

expected positive spillover effects on other industrial sectors. However, the reduction of the participants is generally the same thing as a reduction in the number of research directions.

Whereas a possible restriction on competition through power concentration is placed in the foreground for horizontal mergers, vertical mergers can restrict market access by way of easily coordinated behaviour and denying the competition access to materials.[129]

Although merger controls are not internationally taken for granted as a part of national competition regulatory systems, 40 countries implemented merger controls in 1998.[130] There are criteria for almost all national merger controls that determine the approval reservations for mergers. Notification is dealt with in various ways, however. In Canada, Ireland, New Zealand, USA and Germany only mergers that meet certain criteria have be registered ahead of time. In Japan all mergers have to be registered, yet in France it is completely voluntary. There are also general differences internationally in the application. Merger controls are less important in the USA than in the EU for example, since the American courts currently weight the efficiency gains from mergers heavier due to the influence of the Chicago School.[131]

The implementation of merger prohibition is faced with several problems in its practical application. The insufficiencies of the criteria for intervention in the market-dominating position on the part of the abuse supervisory authority are also found in merger controls, since these criteria are also a requirement for intervention. The size criterion seems arbitrary since the relevant market is so difficult to determine with any definitiveness. The fact that structural changes and branch specificities cannot be taken into consideration just adds to this factor. Since it is difficult to prove a market domination, as was already explained, courts tend to decide in favour of mergers in case of doubt.[132] The EU had prevented only 8 mergers up to February 1998.[133] The effects of merger controls cannot be underestimated however, since the approval reservations have already prevented many companies from competition-restricting mergers.

Unlike the German merger control, which takes non-competition policy aspects into account only in the context of a ministerial approval examination, the European Commission weighs all advantages and disadvantages of the merger as part of a merger decision (Rule of Reason) against each other. Market dominance by large companies reduces competition and thus the welfare that results for consumers. Conversely, large companies can realize cost savings from economies of scale or economies of scope, which also translates into welfare gains. However, if market power is too large, companies will not

---

[129]See *World Bank/OECD* (1999), p. 44.

[130]See *Wins, Henning* (2000), p. 31.

[131]See *FIW* (1990), p. 18; *Trebilcock, Michael J.* (1996), p. 98 and *Wins, Henning* (2000), p. 32. Boner provides a description of the national merger control mechanisms. See *Boner, Roger Alan/ Krueger, Reinald* (1991), pp. 69.

[132]See *Schüller, Alfred* (1987), pp. 58.

[133]See *Wins, Henning* (2000), p. 32.

pass on these efficiencies (productive efficiency) to consumers. The EU Commission thus decides the so-called Williamson trade-off as the conflict of objectives between productive and allocative efficiency. The EU Commission guidelines include "the general consideration of efficiency advantages and the evolution of technical and economic progress" through the merger.

Added to this is the consideration of welfare redirections through the creation of global players or global champions. According to the New Foreign Trade Theory by creating large internationally competitive companies, it is possible to achieve a so-called Rent Shifting, which is a welfare transfer from abroad to the domestic one. The EU Commission considers the EU single market to be at a disadvantage compared to the US, because it was founded much later. Due to the historical fragmentation of the European markets, the EU also has smaller and therefore less internationally competitive companies relative to the USA. If a fusion of, say, a French company with a German company succeeds in creating such a global group, it can sell products abroad, divert profits to Europe and create jobs.

The blueprint of a global player is the company Airbus that politically as equals the monopoly of Boeing in the market for passenger aircraft. France, Great Britain and Germany created a joint venture for the production of passenger aircraft from national companies. Subsidies were paid to overcome market entry barriers.[134]

The state could thus increase national welfare by promoting the emergence of such large companies in the industries concerned. It could initiate mergers, support growth through financial grants, or even artificially create large new state-owned enterprises. Overcoming barriers to market entry could be facilitated by government grants, encouraging business activity in areas that would otherwise occupy foreign companies. According to the "New Foreign Trade Theory", subsidies and, in particular, state funding for research can overcome market entry barriers or create new barriers for foreign companies and hence create competitive advantages for domestic industry. If such a governmental activity succeeds in redirecting international demand to domestic companies, the economies of scale—as an efficiency bonus, so to speak—also increase at the expense of foreign producers. In the terminology of the "New Foreign Trade Theory" this means "rent-shifting".[135]

The New foreign trade theory can be called the theoretical basis of the "new protectionism". For the classical foreign trade theory free trade guarantees the optimal division of labor and resource allocation. According to Ricardo, even unilateral liberalization of foreign trade would benefit the importing country.[136] According to Eucken's demand for markets open internally and externally, free trade complements the internal through external competition and guarantees the most efficient production through continuous adjustment pressure. Foreign trade policy and competition policy are complementary. By

---

[134]See Kösters, Wim (1992), p. 49–56.

[135]See *Siebert,* Horst/*Rauscher,* Michael (1991); *Siebert,* Horst (1988) and Van *Bergeijk,* Peter A.G./ *Kabel,* Dick L. (1993).

[136]See *Conrad,* Christian A. (2003a).

contrast, the New Foreign Trade Theory states a conflict of objectives between trade and competition policy. Based on the production characteristics of individual sectors, it uses microeconomics to derive the state task of increasing national welfare through targeted industrial and foreign trade policy interventions.[137] The resulting economic policy is called strategic trade policy.[138]

Recent research confirms the hypotheses of the New Foreign Trade Theory. However, these are partial models based on very specific assumptions. For example, a reaction of the country disadvantaged by rent-shifting is not included. One problem is the lack of empirical foundation of the New Foreign Trade Theory. The empirical cost trends of most industries are unknown. Furthermore, the New Foreign Trade Theory assumes a static comparison. In the dynamic analysis, other influences affect the efficiency of the industries concerned.[139] As a result of the concentration associated with mergers, additional macroeconomic costs arise as a result of competitive constraints, which are offset by efficiency gains from declining average costs. Furthermore, as the size of an enterprise increases, efficiency losses occur which are caused by higher organization costs, increasing bureaucratization, and increasing distance of decision makers to the market.[140] In the case of free competition, the overall economically optimal size of the enterprise automatically emerges internally and externally. If a takeover is too small, the high average costs relative to larger companies due to the lack of economies of large scale either force it to expand the company size or exit the market. If a company is too large, the costs of size inefficiencies and the cost of underutilized capacity in competition also force it to exit the market or at least to reduce production or to abandon unprofitable production areas. Last but not least, the efficiency gains from economies of large scale only become effective in macroeconomic terms if there is sufficient competition that compels companies to pass on the cost advantages in the form of price reductions. The last, most lasting criticism is that a behavioral adjustment inevitably leads to a protection race according to the policy recommendations of the "new foreign trade theory".[141]

---

[137]See *Helpman*, Elhanan/*Krugman*, Paul R. (1989), *p. 2* and *Molsberger*, Josef (1994), p. 428f.

[138]See *Bletschacher*, Georg (1992), *Siebert*, Horst (1988); *Bletschacher*, Georg/*Klodt*, Henning (1992); *Welzel*, Peter (1991); *Holzkämper*, Hilko (1995), p. 139ff; Szettele, Dieter (2000), p. 61ff and *Christl*, Claudius (2001), p. 64.

[139]See *Siebert*, Horst/*Rauscher*, Michael (1991), p. 505f; *Bergeijk*, Peter A.G./*Kabel*, Dick L. (1993), p. 185; *Szettele*, Dieter (2000), p. 306; *Krüger*, Malte (1998), p. 222 and *Christl*, Claudius (2001), p. 39.

[140]A negative empirical relationship between the size of research departments and the market share of companies was found. See *Bruke*, Terry (1991), p. 221.

[141]See *Weizsäcker*, C. Christian von/*Waldenberger*, Franz (1992), p. 404 and *Bergeijk*, Peter A.G./ *Kabel*, Dick L. (1993), p. 175.

If the states follow the guidelines of the new foreign trade theory, it would be the task of an international competition order to avoid a "beggar-thy-neighbor policy" to increase international welfare.See *Christl*, Claudius (2001), p. 47.

In summary, the many points of agreement in all important competition policy instruments—as shown by Subramanian—is to be considered very positive.[142] This realization contradicts the common assumption that national competition systems are too fundamentally different that an international standardization is impossible.[143] It's true that an internationally recognized theory of competition doesn't yet exist, and thus exact, detailed common guidelines, yet trends are visible. International agreement exists for example on the damage caused by horizontal restrictions on competition, such as supply and price cartels, and subventions for exports. An international prohibition on such competition restrictions ought to meet therefore with very little resistance.[144]

Conclusion

In practice, the enforcement of merger bans faces some problems. The inadequacy of the intervention criterion of the dominant or market-dominant position continues in merger control, since this criterion is also an intervention requirement. The size criteria also seem arbitrary in the light of the non-deductibility of the relevant market. In addition, structural changes and sector specificities cannot be taken into account. Since—as already stated—the proof of market dominance is difficult, the courts decide rather in favor of the mergers in cases of doubt. Nevertheless, the effect of merger control should not be underestimated, since the approval requirement is likely to discourage many companies from restrictive mergers.

Summary

Merger control should prevent the emergence of dominant positions, whereas abuse control should prevent a restriction of competition by an existing dominant position. In both cases, the competition authority must distinguish the relevant market, measure concentration and assess the competitive situation by means of market tests. Abuse control also includes evidence of abuse.

---

[142]See *Subramanian,* Arvind (1994) and *Boner,* Roger Alan/*Krueger,* Reinald (1991). Also the EU comes to this result: "However, it should be noted that the diversity of national competition laws—while important—is not to be exaggerated. There is a core of commonality regarding a number of the key elements of competition law and policy. If one analyses the nearly 100 existing competition law regimes, a high degree of convergence can be detected regarding the following main characteristics of competition law and policy despite differences on substantive provisions and institutional structures: ....." See *Working Group on the Interaction between Trade and Competition Policy* (2002b), p. 1.

[143]See also *Hauser, Heinz/Schoene, Rainer E.* (1994); *Plompen, Peter M. A. L.* (2001), p. 31f and *Noland, Marcus* (1999).

[144]See *Immenga, Ulrich* (1996a), pp. 602.

Comprehension Questions

1. Why is it necessary for the state to control competition?
2. Define cartels. What is a vertical agreement?
3. What conditions must be fulfilled in order to punish the abuse of a dominant position?
4. What criteria are used in merger control?

9.6   International Competition Policy

9.6.1   International Merger Controls

International mergers and take-overs have increased dramatically in the last few decades. The transaction volume of the global mergers and take-overs reached US$2.5 billion in 1998, five times that of the early nineties.[145] There still aren't any coordinated international controls on mergers. Purely foreign mergers can be reported to national competition authorities according to the Effects Doctrine if they have an effect on domestic competition, however.[146] According to the so-called Effects Doctrine, the national competition law can be used against all restrictions on competition both domestically and against foreign companies. [147]

The fusion controls applied by the national competition authorities is costly, time-consuming, and not calculable for international groups of companies, since they have to apply for approval in each country in which they show economic activity, and thus have to deal with the different legal systems.

In the case of international trade the above-mentioned practice leads to multiple investigations of the same market position from different national competition authorities, since the market power on foreign markets is always taken into consideration.[148] The Canadian aluminium producer ALSAN, the Swiss ALGROUP, and the French company

---

[145] See *Klodt, Henning* (2000), p. 53 and *Hagedoorn, J.* (1995).

[146] The Effects Doctrine was used in the USA for the first time in 1945. In the so-called Alcoa Case under the Sherman Acts the U.p. Supreme Court forbid a quote cartel of foreign aluminium producers that had determined the quotas for the US market in Switzerland. See *Klodt, Henning* (2003), pp. 46 Klodt put together the most important application of the Effects Doctrine. The overview can be found in the Annex in Table 5.

[147] Here we are dealing with a legal basis used especially by the USA and is internationally hotly disputed. See *Rishikesh, Deepa* (1991), pp. 34; *Immenga, Ulrich* (1996b), pp. 156; *Immenga, Ulrich* (1996a), p. 596 and *Pengilley, Warren* (1997), pp. 22.

[148] See *Motta, Massimo/Omida, Fabrizio* (1997), p. 83.

PECHINEY would have had to have registered their merger in 40 countries, for example. They did so in 16.[149] Exaggerated merger requirements can arise when different national competition authorities demand the sale of various branches or subsidiaries even though a single sale would have brought about the desired reduction in market power.[150]

From the academics of economics there is also a demand to internationally coordinate at least the merger controls. The purported strategy is similar to the subsidiary principle. The greater the international external effects of the merger, and the smaller the difference in the national competition policy concepts, the more internationally the merger controls ought to be placed.[151] The Merger Task Force of the EU has been suggested as an example in this regard, as it is only used for mergers that cross borders and leaves all other merger controls to the national competition authorities of the member states.[152]

A decentralized use of the international merger controls through the national competition authorities, as was the case with the abuse advisory authority, is advisable to overcome the difficulties in its application. They can define the markets more exactly due to their closeness to the markets themselves, and thus better determine the market position. Because ever more mergers are taking place across borders however, a decentralized merger control would have to be internationally coordinated with uniform criteria. Adopting a unified framework of action through the international community of states is a viable solution. In order not to complicate such an agreement any more than necessary, the criteria for action or intervention should remain as general as possible. There aren't any reasonable, binding, internationally valid criteria due to the highly variable market constellation. Specification would take place in the decentralized application according to each case by way of the national competition authorities.

An appeal authority could assure the coordinated application of the competition policy framework for mergers, similar to the abuse supervisory authority, but it would be unable to bring about the necessary cooperation across borders for the national competition authorities. The Rule of Reason seems a feasible competition policy solution especially for international merger controls, in order to be able to weigh the positive externalities in the form of synergy effects against the negative welfare effects from the restriction on competition case for case, which corresponds to the Neo-ordoliberal concept that has been developed here[153] An international authority is absolutely necessary, however. This is the one weakness of the current system of competition regulations, if one ignores the distortions to competition caused by national economic politics, which cannot be eliminated except with an intrusion upon national sovereignty. A regulation at the international level is absolutely necessary for the international coordination of the merger controls

---

[149]See *O.V.* (2000), p. 12.

[150]See *Van Miert, Karel* (1996), pp. 3.

[151]See *Neven, Damien/Siotis, Georges* (1993), pp. 89.

[152]See *Motta, Massimo/Onida, Fabrizio* (1997), p. 89.

[153]See also *Kühn, Kai-Uwe/Seabright, Paul/Smith, Alasdair* (1992), p. 28.

and abuse supervisory authority.[154] The intrusion upon national sovereignty can be kept to the minimum necessary for competition policy coordination, which would be the competence and assignment of the national competition authorities.

> **Conclusion**
> We note that there are two main problems of an international competition policy: there is a lot of room for national decision-making. There is no international competition authority for effective and objective competition oversight.

9.6.2 The Requirements for an International Competition Authority

There are several reservations to an international institution for competition. First, an obligatory system of competition regulations would go against the foreign trade interests and definitions of sovereignty for several countries.[155] Second, some warn against transferring competition policy competence to a single supranational institution. They fear that this institution could become an uncontrollable, dictatorial central authority far removed from reality, which could make faulty decisions for a competition conception based on unclear competition theory guidelines.[156] Third, a uniform international codex of competition would prevent the most efficient system of competition between states.[157]

The first critique is of a principle nature, and could also be used against the WTO as a super-ordinate supranational authority in its field. Despite deserved scepticism, the progress towards trade liberalization within the GATT reached up this point should not be discounted, and that fact that in 1947 with the ITO an international competition authority was almost created, failing only due to the USA.[158] Who would have expected that the Uruguay Round would change the dispute settlement from unanimous acceptance of the panel proposals to a unanimous rejection? National competition laws are already being brought into line with each other in a liberal direction and intensified competition controls.[159] It is also an explicitly stated goal of the new world trade rounds in Doha to set international rules for competition in 2003. At the national level there seems to be

---

[154]See esp. *Campbell, Neil/Trebilcock, Michael J.* (1997) for more on the difficulties of a border-crossing merger.

[155]"But such reforms, even though they would enhance national welfare and due process of law, are unlikely to come about through unilateral reforms or through negotiations between the representatives of the antidumping bureaucracies." *Petersmann, Ernst-Ulrich* (1993), p. 63.

[156]See *Hauser, Heinz/Schoene, Rainer E.* (1994).

[157]See *Freytag, Andreas/Zimmermann, Ralf* (1998), pp. 49.

[158]A constant stream of states join the WTO. The GATT had 85 signatories in 1980, and in 1999 134 states had joined the WTO. See *World Bank* (2000), p. 7.

[159]*Scherer* provides many examples. See *Scherer, F. M.* (1997), pp. 5.

increasing acceptance of the inherent necessity for state controls on competition. The USA and the EU see themselves forced to bring their merger control mechanisms into line with one another, due to the cross-border merger and take-over designs of their companies. The increased importance of the EU in world trade and its growing extraterritorial legal stance[160] demonstrates to the USA the advantage of an internationally harmonized merger authority. Since the USA can't force their interests in the face of resistance from the EU, it will probably give up its stubborn position at least on the point of an international merger control.

The second critique should be taken seriously, but a dictatorial exercise of power can be prevented with appropriate controls on the international institution. The third point of critique can be contradicted with the competition policy problems in international trade that have been explained in this article. For one thing, competition between nations, and their companies, takes place within competition policy anarchy, due to the prisoner's dilemma at the cost of international welfare. The market mechanism thus fails at the international level. For another, there are inefficiencies above all in the international merger controls—as has been shown—due to a lack of regulations. Arguments against the creation of an effective international system of competition regulations are far from convincing when seen in the light of competition-distortions in international trade. Critics of such an international system generally agree on this point:

> Maybe the setting up of an international antitrust policy is the price for abolishing these anti-competitive and trade distorting trade policy instruments. If the focus was on eliminating these trade policy instruments, and if the implementation of an international antitrust policy was the complement to abolishing these measures, our evaluation would clearly be more positive.[161]

9.6.3 Subsidies and Anti-subsidy Measures

▶ **Definition of subsidies:** State services (transfers) to companies without receiving something in return.

Here is everything that characterizes subsidies:

1. A transfer, a state monetary and non-monetary benefit (income without output) and
2. a political selection of the beneficiary companies.
   They are called transfers when made to private households.

---

[160]The EU commission refrained from an extra-territorial application of their law in the case of the foreseen merger between Boing-McDonnell Douglas (under the pretence of a concession) despite the negative comity of nations not least of all due to the threat of trade policy sanctions from the USA. The merger between General Electric and Honeywell was prevented by the EU however, despite bitter resistance from the USA. See *Wins, Henning* (2000), p. 82 and 88 and *O.V.* (2001a), p. 13.

[161]See *Hauser, Heinz/Schoene, Rainer, E.* (1994), p. 219.

Reasons for Subsidies Political goals are pursued with subsidies. For example, pursuing government goals means maintaining jobs or promoting exports, research, or companies at risk of bankruptcy.

At European level, subsidies are prohibited if they "affect trade between Member States" (Article 107 of the EUA). Competitiveness would be improved in favor of the subsidized company, resulting in distortions of competition. However, there are a number of exceptions (for example sectoral aid, research aid, regional aid, aid to small and medium-sized enterprises, environmental aid and restructuring aid). All subsidies must be reported to the EU Commission (notification).

Function of anti-subsidy measures: They should compensate for this distortion of competition in international trade and prevent damage to the non-subsidized economy of the importing country.

The effects of subsidized imports on the exporting and importing countries cannot be clearly classified as positive or negative. The long-term importation of subsidized goods at prices below production costs corresponds to a transfer of resources from abroad to the domestic market, thus a gain in domestic wealth. This is offset by the injurious effects of subsidized imports on domestic industry and its jobs. If the goods are only subsidized by the exporting country over a short period of time, such as bridging subsidies, the negative effects are not offset by sufficiently positive welfare effects, thus damaging the importing country as a whole. Subsidies generally have negative effects on international resource allocation and the market system because they are financed by the taxpayers' money of the exporting country and thus price undercutting does not reflect a competitive advantage generated by the market in the market.

The "General Agreement on Tariffs and Trade" (GATT) are—as the name suggests—the currently valid international trade rules. The GATT regulates the compensatory measures which States may take against dumped or subsidized imports. In order to be able to continue trade in spite of the distortions of competition and to prevent industrial injury to the importing country, the objective of the anti-dumping and anti-subsidy duties on import duties is to offset precisely the price advantage which the dumping or subsidization gave rise to thereby injuring the importing country.

The Agreement on Subsidies and Countervailing Measures and the GATT 1994 Agreement of Article VI are among the most significant parts of the GATT.

Since the signing of GATT in 1947 by 23 Member States, 7 multi-lateral GATT rounds of negotiations have been conducted with the aim of facilitating the exchange of comparative cost advantages through the removal of trade barriers and thereby increasing world welfare. This concept was successful. Over the past fifty years, the average tariff burden on commercial and industrial goods has fallen to negligible levels. Meanwhile, GATT as a contract became part of the newly created WTO (World Trade Organization).

GATT allows countervailing duties on subsidized and dumped imports if dumping leads to significant injury to an already existing industry or significantly delays the establishment of an industry.

The new Subsidies Code from the Uruguay Round of the GATT incorporates several improvements.[162] Various forms of subsidies have been classified for the first time, and respective allowable retaliation measures have been defined. The breakthrough was made possible by the organization of the different forms of subventions into three categories: (1) "red light category" forbidden export subsidies; (2) "yellow light category" actionable subsidies and (3) "green light category" non-actionable subsidies:

1. Prohibited subsidies for exports (red light category) are subsidies that are linked to the export performance of the company or its performance in competition with imports.
2. Traceable subsidies (yellow light category): if imports of the subsidized goods caused damage, threatened or hampered the construction of a domestic industry, which is the main reason for anti-subsidy measures, or if they caused a significant disadvantage to the trade interests of other countries. Damage is caused by import to domestic companies.
3. Non-traceable subsidies (green light category) Non-traceable subsidies are those that are accessible to all companies, in other words not aimed at strengthening the competitiveness of a particular company. Examples are research and development grants, regional aid, environmental aid.

The GATT anti-subsidy procedure
Steps:

1. Application for anti-subsidy proceedings
2. Preliminary subsidy analysis
3. Preliminary injury analysis
    ⇨ preliminary anti-subsidy duty
5. Final subsidy analysis
6. Final injury analysis
    ⇨ Final anti-subsidy duty

The defenses against subsidized exports consist of a provisional and a definitive anti-subsidy duty. Both tariffs are determined through a national procedure governed by the GATT Anti-Subsidy Code. The anti-subsidy procedures are divided into two sections:

The domestic industry and its lawyers request that an anti-subvention procedure be initiated by the competent national authority (in the EU). In exceptional cases, where domestic producers are not organized, the national authority may also initiate proceedings on its own initiative. The authority then examines whether the subsidy evidence submitted by the applicants is sufficient to initiate a procedure. If that is the case, it calculates, in the case of an anti-subsidy proceeding, the subsidy share of the export price of the products concerned (subsidy analysis). The defendant exporters are given the opportunity to

---

[162]See Conrad, Christian, A. (1996), pp. 187–198.

comment. In order to be able to react as quickly as possible to subsidized imports, the actual investigation is preceded by a provisional determination of subsidies and damages, with a provisional anti-subsidy duty being levied if the outcome of the proceedings is positive. The subsequent injury analysis examines whether imports were damaged, threatened or impeding the construction of a domestic industry.

In a second stage of the procedure, the final subsidy investigation and the final injury analysis are then carried out, which, if they are positive, result in a definitive anti-subsidy duty to be paid by the importer or exporter upon crossing the border.

Anti-subsidy procedures are used far less frequently than anti-dumping measures because:

1. Subsidizing governments creates a conflict for the investigating national authority not just with one company, but with another government.
2. all governments subsidize, so there is enough retaliatory potential.
3. Anti-dumping procedure, as will be shown, offers more scope to the investigating national authority to set countervailing duties.

9.6.4 Dumping and Antidumping Measures

▶ **Definition** Dumping is the sale of a product on a foreign market below the price on the domestic market, usually assuming a sale below production cost. Dumping as a sale below cost price is prohibited in some countries, such as in Germany. Within the EU, however, there is no ban on dumping except as a misuse of a dominant market position. Internationally, within GATT, there is a code that regulates anti-dumping measures.

The role of anti-dumping measures: they should compensate for this distortion of competition in international trade and prevent damage to the economy of the importing country.

After having lowered the general import duties in the various GATT rounds however, anti-dumping measures became one of the most important import restrictions in global trade. Anti-dumping duties are on average 10–20 times higher than the existing import duties and can be as high as 100 times the import duties.[163] Dumping is defined in international economics according to two criteria: the sale of goods on an importing market at a price lower than that charged on the domestic market, or the sale on a foreign market at a price lower than the cost of production. Art. VI of the GATT (General Agreement on Tariffs and Trade) prohibits dumping in the international rules of fair trade if it causes or threatens to cause material injury to an existing industrial branch or greatly hinders the development of

---

[163] See *Prusa, Thomas J.* (2001), p. 593.

a new branch (Art. 4 GATT). Antidumping measures should create and maintain a state of fair competition, taking on the role of a competition organization, which is still lacking on an international level. Antidumping duties are supposed to compensate the distortion in the competition, since the costs would be raised to those of the exporter's domestic prices or the production costs. The following chapter analyses the reasons for the strong increase of antidumping measures, which is described. It deals with the effects of the constructed normal value application on the outcome of the antidumping procedures. Further we will search for biases in the injury investigation. More protectionist biases of antidumping-complaints are finally analysed.

9.6.4.1 The Procedure for Antidumping Measures

The USA implemented its first anti-dumping regulation in 1916, the purpose of which was to act against the "predatory pricing" of foreign cartels, as opposed to providing compensation for the damage done to the domestic industry. The reforms of 1974 added damage and cost criteria, and in 1979 the Ministry of Trade took over the competence of conducting antidumping proceedings from the US Finance Ministry. The number of antidumping proceedings in the 1980s increased tremendously because of these two changes. Half of the proceedings can be directly or indirectly traced to considerations based on the cost criterion.[164] The assumption behind the creation of a set of rules governing competition is that cost would be the most expedient criterion to encourage efficient international production. It is only logical that the international company with the most reasonable costs produces the most efficiently. But the question is how costs can be utilized as a criterion.

The GATT anti-dumping procedure
Steps:

1. Application for anti-dumping proceedings
2. Preliminary dumping analysis
3. Preliminary damage analysis
   ⇨ preliminary anti-dumping duty
4. Final dumping analysis
5. Final damage analysis
   ⇨ final anti-dumping duty

Defensive measures against dumped imports that conform to GATT regulations include a preliminary and a final antidumping duty. In its dumping analysis, the investigating national authority compares the export price with the modified price in the domestic market of the exporting country. Transport costs and total costs attributed to the export of the product are added to the price of the product in the exporting country (see Fig. 9.4). The resulting sum is the so-called normal value. If a product isn't sufficiently purchased in the home country, or if a normal market situation isn't present in the home country, such as in

---

[164]See *Petersmann, Ernst-Ulrich* (1993), p. 62.

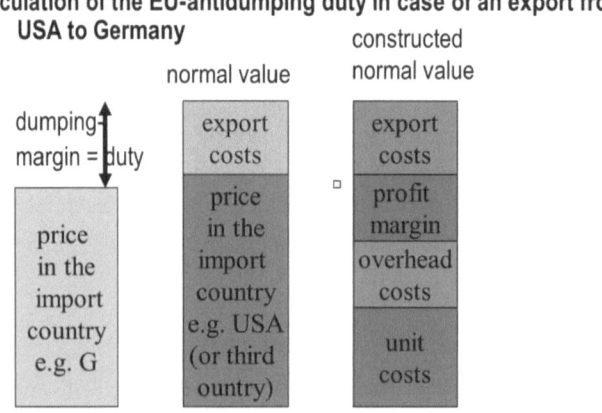

Fig. 9.4 Calculation of the antidumping duty

planned economies, one can fall back on the selling price in a third country. If this strategy doesn't prove effective in establishing a normal value, it can also be calculated out, which is usually the case in practice.[165]

The mathematically determined normal value for the so-called cost criterion represents the sum of material and production costs, with proportional overhead costs and a minimum profit margin added on (calculated normal value). The difference between normal value and export price equals the dumping margin. After a dumping analysis has determined whether the foreign exporters are offering their products on the import market at prices lower than those on their home market or under their production costs, the injury analysis should determine whether or not this incorrect competitive behaviour has caused lasting damage to the importing country's industry. If injury is expected in the first phase of the process, a preliminary antidumping duty will be collected with a maximal sum of the dumping margin, in order to be able to react quickly to the dumped imports and thus avoid damage. Anti-dumping duties in this context are supposed to compensate the distortion in the competition caused by the dumping of the foreign exporters, since the costs of the export would be raised by the antidumping duty to those of the exporter's domestic prices or the production costs. A second phase in the process looks into the possible effects of a permanent antidumping duty.

The national authority has significant latitude in the antidumping-investigation. The calculation of the constructed normal value is probably the biggest discretionary cost-calculation issue. The costs involved in the production of a certain product are very difficult to determine. In the exceptional case that National competition authorities taking action against domestic dumping is an extreme rarity, but when it does take place the variable of

---

[165]More that two thirds of the EU antidumping procedures between 1980 and 1985 were based on the calculated normal value. See *Messerlin, Patrick A.* (1995), p. 43.

cost as the measure of the lowest price level (Areeda Turner Rule)[166] is applied. The term "variable costs" is also slippery to define due to the need for exactness in determining what comprises the general costs. Even something as straight forward as the purchase of a machine evades exact calculation since the depreciation generally diverges from the time of usage. Despite the most complete and balanced methods of calculations, an objective value simply isn't to be found for the determination a fair comparative price within an anti-dumping proceeding.

In the antidumping proceedings one would have to assume that the investigating national authorities consider the interests of the foreign industry and the interests of domestic industry to be equally important, an assumption which is not especially plausible. Additionally, due to the fact that the interpretation guidelines for this regulation in the appendix of the current GATT contain numerous exceptions and ambiguous rules, the investigating authority has significant latitude in its investigations. Here are three examples:

1. How the profit margin should be calculated is not included in the regulations stipulated in the current antidumping agreement, which creates an artificial dumping situation. This allows the investigating national authority to consider only above-cost sales, increasing the constructed normal value and thus the dumping margin.[167]
2. Strategically singling out selling prices in the exporting country causes a similar discretionary issue. According to current GATT regulations,[168] if sales below production costs comprise more than 20% of total sales in the exporting country, the investigating authority is not required to take account of all sales prices from the exporting country when determining the normal value. This gives the authority the choice between two options: to use the calculated normal value, comprised of cost-estimations, or only those prices in the normal value calculation that exceed production costs, a so-called "twisted price criterion". The United States is particularly fond of this second option. Applying this method causes a distortion in the dumping investigation, putting the foreign producer at a disadvantage.[169] The need for the cost calculation regulations to be standardized with clear specifications can be clearly seen as illustrated with these examples.
3. Art. 2.2.1.1 requires that all costs documented in the exporters' accounts be part of the calculations for the normal value. National authorities are not obliged to consider these costs if they are not directly associated with the production and sale of the product,

---

[166]See *Messerlin, Patrick, A.* (1995), p. 42 and *Areeda, R./Turner, D.* (1975).

[167]See for the EC-regulation *Vander Schueren, Paulette* (1996), p. 279 and for the US-regulation *Blonigen, Bruce A.* (2003), pp. 5.

[168]See Agreement on Implementation of Article VI of the General Agreement on Tariffs and Trade 1994 (in the following abbreviated as AIA) VI, Art. 2, Par. 2.2.1, footnote 5.

[169]See *Kawahito, Kiyoshi* (1982), p. 161 and *Blonigen, Bruce A.* (2003), p. 8.

however. General costs not directly related to the production of the product involved is habitually disregard when calculating the normal value (i.e., research and development or depreciation). The normal value resulting from the calculations can thus still be underestimated, resulting in an inflated dumping margin.[170]

Another discretionary cost-calculation issue is the choice of information when the constructed normal value is calculated. US policy requires exporters accused of dumping to turn over any information that the American ITA (International Trade Administration) requests for its calculation of the constructed normal value within a rather short period of time. The amount of information requested and its substance have become ever more extensive; to the extent in fact, that exporters find themselves overburdened and unable to provide the required information. When this happens ITA uses the information available (best information available), which in practice means the biased view of the domestic complainants.[171] This approach throws the burden of proof onto the foreign exporters—to their disadvantage. A new provision to come out of the Uruguay-round was the obligation on investigating authorities to examine whether the exporter was capable of supplying the information required of them within the antidumping process. If the exporter seems to have been cooperative, all available information must be considered in the investigation.[172] If the authority establishes uncooperativeness, it may reject information provided in the questionnaires and may consider the information from the biased domestic complaint documents as it has historically done. This gives the investigating authority free rein to decide which information it takes into consideration for an investigation.

The attractiveness of the cost criterion can thus be explained by the tendency to put foreign exporters at a disadvantage when using the cost criterion within national antidumping measures, in other words to be protectionist. The cost criterion made it into the GATT antidumping codex due to a gentlemen's agreement between the main instigators of antidumping procedures (USA, EU, Canada, Australia) as part of the Tokyo Round, which is hardly surprising when one takes the shown protectionist effects into account.[173]

9.6.4.2 Biases of the Injury Analysis

The purpose of antidumping duties is to rectify the distortion in competition that dumping from foreign exporters causes, achieved by raising the costs of the export with an anti-dumping duty to match the costs either on the exporter's domestic market or of production. National authorities' injury analyses are not normally meant to determine whether dumped

---

[170]*Vander Schueren* sees this discretionary-problem in the new Anti-Dumping-Regulation of the EC. See *Vander Schueren, Paulette* (1996), p. 280.

[171]See *Blonigen, Bruce A.* (2003), pp. 6.

[172]AIA VI, Art. 2, Par. 6.8 as well as Appendix II. This interpretation is also in compliance with the decision of the GATT Panel in the case of imports of steel containing iron and bismuth from the EU. INSIDE TRADE, October 21, 1994, p. 9.

[173]See *Knorr, Andreas* (1999), p. 416.

imports have injured the domestic industry at the time of their import. Moreover, the potential to help the domestic industry by way of an antidumping duty is a main consideration of authority investigates.[174] It is clear from this perspective that import competitors are indeed in a position to hurt a poorly competitive domestic industry.

As of Tokyo Round of the GATT, regulations stipulate that the imports under consideration in the injury analysis do not have to be a notable cause of injury, let alone a major cause.[175] It is sufficient for the imports to be *a* cause of injury to domestic industry—among others—for damage to be ascertained. Domestic competition may be the main contributor to injury, or perhaps structural change, recession or even mismanagement; all of which do not affect the ascertainment of injury. In fact, the injury to domestic consumers as a byproduct of an antidumping duty may be worse than the injury to domestic producers caused by the imports. National authorities fail to consider this aspect in injury investigation's.[176]

Art. 9.1 of the current Antidumping Code prohibits antidumping duties from being levied at a leer higher than that necessary to compensate injury. There is no clear method in the agreement for determining the margin of injury. Maximum protection will still be the rule however, as duties will be levied to the level of the full dumping margin.[177]

We have shown here that in spite of several improvements, the current international Antidumping Code leaves the national authorities more than enough possibilities for discrimination against foreign producers. Both the dumping and the injury analyses go beyond a defensive protection against competition violations from foreign producers. The protectionist effect of the antidumping laws is thus undiminished, even after the Uruguay Round.[178]

9.6.4.3 Additional Advantages of Antidumping-Complaints

Prusa looked into the effects of the antidumping duties imposed by the USA between 1980 and 1994. On an average the import volume was reduced by around 50% in the following three years after the duties were levied. The duties affected the import amount doubly as much as it did the prices. On average, a duty of 10% causes a reduction in the import volumes of 1.9% in the first year. This 10% also caused a redirection of trade, so that the import of the same goods, just not those in the antidumping complaint, increased by 6% in the first year. Where self-restriction agreements or voluntary price commitments were

---

[174]See *Kulms, Rainer* (1988), p. 207.

[175]See *Kulms, Rainer* (1988), pp. 78 and 204.

[176]In the EU Antidumping Law it is laid down, that the EU-Commission is required to consider general public interests, among which are the consumer interests, in its final dumping decision. However, in not one of the 903 antidumping procedures in the 1980s was an antidumping complaint rejected because of the damaging effects to domestic consumers brought about by the introduction of an antidumping duty. See *Schuknecht, Ludger et al* (1992), p. 137.

[177]See *Vander Schueren, Paulette* (1996), pp. 289.

[178]See *Conrad, Christian A.* (1999).

closed, the import volume sank by 60%.[179] Alternatively, Messerlin calculated an import reduction of 40% for products affected by the EU antidumping measures taken from 1980 to 1985.[180]

Domestic industry finds anti-dumping complaints to be quite advantageous. They lay open the competition's production costs which provides the information necessary to create a supply cartel within the framework of the foreign (exporting country's) self-restraint agreements.[181] The domestic industry will most likely decline the offer of self-restraint if it isn't interested in a cartel, or wishes to withhold the advantages of cartel returns from its foreign competitors. The US American steel industry acted along this line of reasoning in the mid-1990s.[182] The average legal costs of approximately $400,000 per complaint are much less than the expected returns for the domestic producers even if the complaint is rejected.[183] Domestic producers benefit on two fronts: one, foreign producers are deprived of their competitiveness on the U.S. market by preliminary antidumping duties, losing their market position. The other benefit is that price levels rise when foreign supply drops off, providing American producers with windfall profits. This explains the findings of Prusa that show an average reduction in imports by 20% between 1980 and 1984 even for the American antidumping complaints that were rejected.[184] If we consider the US integrated steel producers' annual output of approximately 40 million tons in 1993, an average price increase of just $1 per ton would mean an increase in profit of $40 million. Experts estimate a price increase of $20 per ton as a result of the US-anti-dumping and anti-subsidy-actions in 1992 and that the American steel producers' legal costs amounted to $40 million, creating a net increase in profit of US$760 million.

The importer is the one responsible for paying the preliminary antidumping duty, which works like a security deposit; this up-front money is then lost to the importer if a final duty is in fact levied. Should things go well for the importer, they will only be out the opportunity costs. On the other hand, the preliminary duty becomes a financial risk should the importer not be so confident that the complaint is groundless. A shrewd importer will then decline to pursue the business relationship with that particular exporter. Domestic producers are of course aware of this, and have been known to threaten foreign exporters with antidumping complaints as a way of forcing an agreement on unofficial export restrictions.

---

[179]See *Prusa, Thomas J.* (2001), pp. 602.

[180]See *Messerlin, Patrick A.* (1989), p. 586.

[181]According to Staiger, Wolak and Messerlin anti-dumping complaints play a significant role in enforcing price collusions in international cartells. See *Nicolaides, Phedon* (1990), p. 126; *Staiger, R./ Wolak, F.* (1989) and *Messerlin, P.* (1989), pp. 563–587.

[182]See *Conrad, Christian A.* (1995) and *Theuringer, Martin* (2003), pp. 60.

[183]THE ECONOMIST, May 5, 1992 and METAL BULLETIN, February 1, 1993, p. 3.

[184]See *Prusa, Thomas J.* (2001), p. 603. Other empirical studies reaffirm that the preliminary antidumping duties already have a protectionist effect. See *Staiger, R. W./Wolak, F. A.* (1994).

Antidumping measures thus increase the risk associated with export business, and create legal costs by way of antidumping complaints not only for the protection-seeking domestic industry, but the exporter as well. The expenses for the Japanese companies alone for their legal support in the antidumping complaints of the USA against Japanese steel importers in the 1990s was around US$10 million.[185] With this in mind, it is hardly surprising that foreign exporters agree to voluntary price commitments. The domestic producers can use the antidumping complaints to force unofficial price commitments, a phenomenon that seems to hold especially true for the USA. Sometimes the mere threat of an antidumping complaint is enough. The protectionist dimension of voluntary price commitments is seen in how widely spread it is practiced. In the 1980s the exporters agreed to such a commitment in almost half of the proceedings in order to avoid an anti-dumping duty. There were also parallel price increases from the domestic and foreign producers. The protective effect therefore begins even before the antidumping procedures are set in motion.[186]

The alternative to voluntary price commitments is the self-restraint agreement. The concept of convincing a third country to sign up to a self-restraint agreement was first developed by American steel producers and later adopted by the EU.[187] The EU Commission for example, reopened the antidumping process against Spain the minute Spain failed to renew its self-restraint agreement at the end of 1978.[188] The EU Commission offers countries an additional incentive to enter into self-restraint agreements, namely that it promises its exporters the right to adjust their prices to those of non-agreement countries.[189]

Contrary to common assumption, highly concentrated sectors that are weak competitively profit a great deal from anti-dumping measures. The criteria for determining both dumping and damage are central factors. Sectors with numerous national suppliers tend to have intense competition, causing prices to be generally lower than in highly concentrated sectors. Anti-dumping complaints against foreign competitors are then superfluous. Price underbidding from exporters automatically damages sectors incapable of keeping a competitive edge, however. A case for "damage to an industry branch" can be made with more ease in concentrated industries, by overlooking damage from domestic competition.[190]

Anti-dumping complaints arc cspccially promising for company branchcs with high fixed costs, such as the steel industry. This is due to the fact that the foreign producers' export prices are automatically dumping prices resulting from the increased costs of producing under capacity.[191] The production costs for branches with a high level of fixed

---

[185] See Metal Bulletin from 14 March 1994, p. 3.

[186] See *Petersmann, Ernst-Ulrich* (1993), p. 63; *Freytag, Andreas/Zimmermann, Ralf* (1998), p. 44; *Levonsohn, James A.* (1994), p. 12 and *Wins, Henning* (2000), p. 99.

[187] See *Bohnert, Walter/Reising, Susanne* (1990), pp. 30.

[188] See *Bael, I.v./Bellis, J.F.* (1985), p. 136.

[189] See *Kulms, Rainer* (1988), p. 192.

[190] See *Langer, Stefan* (1995), p. 367.

[191] See *Conrad, Christian A.* (1995).

costs vary with the capacity usage. Dumping can also be a result of a below-average degree of capacity usage, as seen in the steel industry. Capacity employment is contingent upon the business cycle in the steel industry. Many steel products are intermediate products for the investment goods industry, causing this interdependence. Should a recessionary phase cause a decline in capacity usage, the steel industry would be forced to raise sales prices to cover fix costs. Increasing prices is illusionary if demand is already low. The only option open to companies is to sell below production costs as long as the recession lasts, in other words to "dump". When calculating a representative normal value for the industry, and ascertaining the production costs for the dumping analysis, the basis must be an entire business cycle,[192] otherwise an 85% capacity usage would have to be assumed. This explains the fact that 65% of antidumping processes in the USA and 53% in the EU between 1979 and 1989 were in the metal branch and chemical industry.[193]

The transaction costs theory of the new institutional economy offers another explanation for the dominance of concentrated sectors as plaintiffs[194]: There are fewer transaction costs involved in the coordination of anti-dumping complaints with fewer producers. The interests of the steel using manufacturers contradict a protectionist policy, since it would increase their consume expenditures and restrict their product choice, but the high transaction and organizational costs of the many steel-using manufacturers and product consumers for steel prohibit the creation of a lobby interest group. The organizational costs for the producers are conversely much less. There are few producers and many consumers, which is why the profits of protectionism get distributed between few producers and the costs of protectionism distributed across many consumers.[195] The expenditure side of protectionism is difficult for the individual consumers to determine due to the number of products that are differently affected.[196] This explains why the integrated steel producers of the USA, being concentrated and competitively weak, turned in a record number of anti-dumping complaints.[197]

Countries seeking to protect their national industries from foreign competition need to be aware that antidumping duties are not a particularly effective instrument. The high level of administration required by antidumping procedures and the minimal protection gained from the duty are clearly disadvantageous factors. Although antidumping duties are ill qualified to isolate an entire market, they can most certainly be used as a weapon turned against foreign producers to keep them out of a market or to coerce them into an agreement on price controls or voluntary export restraint treaties. The resulting protection effect of antidumping procedures is often underestimated by overlooking these factors.[198] The fact

---

[192] See *Kulms, Rainer* (1988), pp. 135.

[193] See *Messerlin, Patrick A./Reed, Geoffrey* (1995), p. 1567.

[194] See *Arrow, K. J.* (1969), p. 48.

[195] See *Glismann, H.H.* (1986), p. 138 and *Frey, B.S.* (1984), p. 25.

[196] See *Frey, B.S.* (1984), p. 25 and 30.

[197] See *Conrad, Christian A.* (1995).

[198] See *Conrad, Christian A.* (1995).

that they are not openly protectionist—as is the case with self-restraint treaties—works to their advantage; with cards well played it may even seem that domestic industry needs to be protected against the unfair dumping practices of foreign companies.[199] Another factor is that reductions of foreign duties have rendered protection provided by traditional import duties negligible. Product-specific safeguard duties have their own problems, since the exporting country is allowed to retaliate with its own measures should it find the safeguard duty unacceptable. Safeguard duties can lead to demands for compensation from the enacting country.[200] This leaves antidumping and anti-subsidy duties as the only really suitable protection instruments.

Anti-dumping and anti-subsidy proceedings would therefore seem to be lucrative, particularly for companies in large markets, because the "return" increases with the size of the market, whereas legal costs remain roughly constant.[201] The same applies for the necessary expenses to keep up an antidumping authority. It is therefore rather plausible that protection against foreign competition increases with the size of a market. Antidumping measures as a protectionist instrument are thus mostly applicable for industries larger than states or free-trade zones.

If one uses the concept of the "new political economy"[202] to explain the behaviour of politicians, and assumes that politicians want to maximize their own profit above that of the general good, and that the votes necessary to achieve reelection have top priority, one comes to the conclusion that free trade as a means to an end is clearly inadequate. It can in fact have negative consequences. The national anti-dumping measures, used by states with the intention of smoothing out competition distortions in international trade, can end up having a protectionist effect.[203] Not taking advantage of such a competitive advantage in international trade would probably mean short-term unemployment and thus higher social costs for the state, business closures and perhaps a short-term decrease in the GDP. This would likely lead to a loss of votes and perhaps threaten the reelection chances of the politician, since at the time of the vote only the costs of fair competition would be seen, and not the profits to be reaped only over the long-term.[204] According to the New Political Economy, only directly accreditable and short-term causal relationships are relevant for

---

[199]"Vigorous administration of existing antidumping laws is not procedural protectionism, in my view. Rather, the trade administrators are the real champions of free trade" *Ecker, Alfred E.*, p. 34. Alfred Ecker was a commissioner on the U.S. International Trade Commission from 1981 until 1990, and in that time chairman from June 1982 until June 1984.

[200]See *United States—General Accounting Office* (1994), p. 79.

[201]See *Conrad, Christian A.* (1995).

[202]The behavioral hypotheses from *Smith* und *Schumpeter* took up *Downs* in the USA and *Herder-Dorneich* in Germany and thus founded the New Political Economy. See *Starbatty, Joachim* (1985), p. 40; *Schumpeter, Joseph A.* (1993), pp. 427; *Andel, Norbert* (1990), p. 48; *Downs, Anthony* (1957) and *Herder-Dorneich* (1957).

[203]See *Conrad, Christian A.* (1999) and *Conrad, Christian A.* (2002).

[204]See *Frey, B.p.* (1984), p. 20.

politicians. Uncertain long-term welfare gains of unknown proportions, as in the case of free trade, have a lower present utility for voters of the current election period.[205] The problem is therefore political: it is politically significant whether the competition that squeezes out jobs is domestic or foreign. Politicians tend to favour domestic considerations over foreign in their own interest, despite knowing better than to reject free trade and free market access as fair and equal competition.[206]

Dumping is generally understood as the sale of goods on a foreign market at a price lower than the domestic price or below production costs.[207] Anti-dumping duties are supposed to compensate this distortion in the competition, since the costs would be raised to those of the exporter's domestic prices or the production costs. The following chapter analyses the effects of dumping and anti-dumping measures on international competition and resource allocation and questions the appropriateness of the measures as an instrument of international competition politics. Finally alternatives and improvements will be suggested.

9.6.4.4 The Effects of Dumping

Dumping can only take place if foreign and domestic markets (market segmentation) are separated, which prevents arbitrage from eliminating price differentials—the competition is imperfect. The reasons for market segmentation are a lack of transparency and transactions costs, which might be caused by transportation costs, different currencies, languages, laws and both tariff and non-tariff trade barriers in general.

The effects of dumping are difficult to determine and thus controversial. Dumping generally has negative effects on the international resource allocation and competition if financed through profits from other branches of the company, subsidies, or monopoly rents, because in this case the price under-bidding does not reflect the company's performance on the market. One argument for the necessity of anti-dumping proceedings is the detrimental effect on the domestic industry and jobs caused by short-term dumping. The importing country would experience welfare losses greater than the gains from the cheap imports. Long-term dumping on the other hand represents a transfer of resources from the exporting country to the importing, and thus a net welfare benefit. Safeguard measures, such as anti-dumping duties, prevent the exploitation of the welfare gains to be had as a result of the low price and the consequent harm to the importing country. To be able to determine the effects of dumping, we have to know how long the dumping takes place. This question can only be answered if we know the motivations of the companies to offer their goods on a foreign market at a price below their own market's or even their production costs. There can be different reasons for exporting companies to decide on dumping as a viable practice:

---

[205] See *Downs, Anthony* (1968) and *Herder-Dorneich, Phillip* (1957).

[206] See *Zohlnhöfer, Werner* (1984), pp. 114–115.

[207] See *United States—General Accounting Office* (1994), pp. 68.

Selling Below Production Costs

1. The company can try to increase its share of the foreign market (*aggressive dumping*), or see itself forced into sinking its price by a dumping pricing advance from a competitor (*defensive dumping*[208]). In both cases, the exporting companies must finance their sales below average prices with profits from other markets or other products and will raise their prices as soon as the motivating competition disappears, which makes it a short-term dumping and thus damaging to the importing country. Aggressive dumping is the classic case of Viners[209] predatory pricing. The first US-antidumping-act of 1916 addressed only this case.[210] The damaging effect comes from the exporter establishing himself as a monopolist by destroying the competition through dumping and subsequently raising his prices. Aggressive dumping occurs rather seldom.[211] In the second case the exporting company fights for its market shares in the importing country by defensive dumping because it expects that the future earnings will compensate for the losses. Apart from that, a retreat would change the previous foreign investments into sunk costs. In both cases we have short-term dumping in which the importing country suffers, which justifies anti-dumping measures.

2. As production is planned in advance and fixed costs are either unchangeable or capacities may be too costly to adjust, another motivation for price dumping is to compensate a temporary reduction of demand on the domestic market by increasing exports (*demand compensation dumping*). In the presence of fluctuations in demand it would make no sense to adjust the capacities. This is also a short-term dumping in which the importing country suffers, and thus justifies anti-dumping measures.[212]

3. A similar motivation is the compensation of a reduction in sales caused by protectionist trade measures on the part of the importing country (*detour of trade dumping*).[213] The time frame of the dumping plays an important role, since the dumping could be long-term if the restrictive measures are as well, and thus have a positive net effect. The assumption that a profit-seeking company would continue to offer its product below cost is faulty however.[214] The company would seek other markets where it could ask a

---

[208]For reciprocal dumping see *Brander, James/Krugman, Paul* (1983).

[209]See *Nicolaides, Phedon* (1990), p. 116 and 123; *Viner, J.* (1923); *Küng, Emil* (1975), p. 516 and *Van Bael, Ivo* (1990), p. 23.

[210]The institutions had to intervene if the selling price was substantially less than the actual market value and there was the intent of injuring or destroying an industry. See *Scherer, Frederic* (1994), p. 83.

[211]The OECD analysed 1051 cases of antidumping investigations from September 1988 to December 1991. Only in 63 cases the intent of destroying and replacing the industry of the importing country was even thinkable. See *OECD* (1996), p. 17.

[212]See *Nicolaides, Phedon* (1990), p. 121; *Bernhart, D.* (1984), pp. 349–370; *Ethier, W.* (1982), pp. 487–506 and *Hillman, A./Katz, E.* (1986), pp. 403–416.

[213]See *Conrad, Christian A.* (1998).

[214]Price policies with the use of contribution margin calculation represent an exception.

higher price or increase production, and thus we again have a damaging short-term dumping for which anti-dumping measures are legitimate.

4. The company can gain additional contribution margins, especially by decreasing unit costs (*contribution margin dumping*). This can take place long or short-term, depending on whether it is a tactical, short-term or strategic long-term decision (*strategic dumping*[215]). If it plans to transfer part of its production over the long-term, it is beneficial for the importing country and an overall welfare gain, but if it is just to increase capacity, the effects are the same as those for a shift in demand. Since the plans of the exporter can't be determined from an external observer, preventative anti-dumping measures are justified.

5. In order to avoid a loss in sales on the foreign market the exporter can keep the sales price in the foreign currency despite a revaluation his own currency, even though he would have had to raise his prices (*exchange rate compensation dumping*[216]). Such a price policy blocks the function of the exchange rate to equalize trade imbalances and disparate level of competitiveness. The revaluation then holds, which distorts international real exchange relations of goods as well as international resource allocation. The company has to finance this type of dumping as well, since it makes fewer profits from the exports in its own currency. If the changes in the exchange rate were caused by a longer-lasting trend, the company will increase its export prices sooner or later. If the changes are short-term, the firm will keep its prices steady in order not to risk its market position; all of which makes this a short-term dumping and anti-dumping measures reasonable.

Selling Below the Price on the Home Market

1. If the company has a monopoly on both the domestic and foreign markets, and the price elasticity of demand is greater on the foreign market, it will fix the price on the foreign market below that of the domestic (*price differentiation dumping*). A monopolist sets the price (p) equal to the marginal costs. The marginal returns (MR) are negatively dependent on the elasticity of the demand (η). The profit maximum is reached if the marginal return equals the marginal costs on all markets. This is expressed in the following equation:

$$MR_1 = MR_2 = \ldots = MR_n = MR$$

With reference to the Amoriso-Robinson Relation of price elasticity of demand:

---

[215]See *Messerlin, Patrick A./Reed, Geoffrey* (1995), p. 1568.

[216]See *Feinberg, Robert M.* (1989).

$$p_1 \left(1 + 1/\eta_1\right) = p_2 \left(1 + 1/\eta_2\right) = \ldots = p_n \left(1 + 1/\eta_n\right)$$

For two markets, i and k, the following applies:

$$p_i / p_k = [(1 + 1/\eta_k)/(1 + 1/\eta_i)]$$

Consequently, the monopolist sets equal prices on the different markets given equal price elasticity of demand.[217] If the price elasticity is higher, meaning the consumers will react more sensitively to increasing prices, the monopolist will set the price lower than it is domestically and thus dumps. One can assume that the price elasticity of demand remains relatively stable over the long-term, which means that this type of dumping represents welfare benefits for the importing country.[218] In this case anti-dumping measures would be disadvantageous.

2. In general, if demand sinks in a market of perfect competition, a supplier has to lower their price. If the demand in the export market is not stable and experiences a downturn and the exporter expects a normalization of the demand in the future, they will try to remain in the market and charge a lower price than on their home market (*demand fluctuation dumping*). This is also true in the case of price differentiation as described above with equal elasticities of demand.[219] This is a short-term dumping in which the importing country suffers, and thus justifies antidumping measures.

3. If the supplier has a monopoly in his own country, but not on the foreign market, he must accept the price level and adjust his prices accordingly (*trade position dumping*). Since trade positions tend to remain in place over the longer-term, the dumping does as well. This makes anti-dumping measures disadvantageous for the importing country. This shows that dumping is not per se "unfair competition," and does not necessarily have a detrimental effect on the importing country. However, even if it has one, the negative effects of the antidumping-measures on the importing country can be higher than the detrimental effect of the dumping, as will be shown in the following.

Can Anti-Dumping Duties Balance Out Distortions in Competition?
Several basic weaknesses can be determined when the GATT anti-dumping code is judged according to its role in creating rules of competition designed to minimize distortions in competition.

---

[217]See *Corden, W. M.* (1978); *Caves, R.E./Jones R.W.* (1981) and *Stobbe, Alfred* (1989), p. 200. For the question if sale taxes lead to price differences on the exporting and importing market, which can be regarded as dumping see *Pohmer, Dieter* (1979).

[218]See *Nicolaides, Phedon* (1990), p. 118.

[219]See *Nicolaides, Phedon* (1990), pp. 118 and 121.

The Criterion of Cost as the Measure of Judgment for Dumping

Assuming that the task of a set of rules for competition is to encourage the most efficient international production, cost would be the best criterion. The international company with the most reasonable costs produces logically the most efficiently. The first anti-dumping regulation of the USA in 1916 wasn't meant to compensate the damage done to the domestic industry, but rather was directed against the "predatory pricing" of foreign cartels. The USA introduced damage and cost criteria in their reforms of 1974, and in 1979 the competence to handle anti-dumping proceedings was transferred from the US Finance Ministry to the Ministry of Trade. Both of these changes caused the huge increase in anti-dumping proceedings in the 1980s, the half of which were based directly or indirectly on the cost criterion.[220]

Advantages in competition or cost for foreign producers generally plays a role in anti-dumping laws only then when a calculation of the normal value of a product based on the production costs is required. The production costs aren't determined objectively, however. The investigating national authorities currently determine the costs, and the defendants have only a restricted possibility to give a counter argument.[221] Due to the fact that the guidelines on interpreting this regulation in the appendix of the current GATT contain numerous exceptions and ambiguous rules, the investigating authority is more or less free to decide which information it includes in its proceedings. If the national authority decides that the exporter did not behave cooperatively, it has the option of refusing to use the information provided in the questionnaires, and may restrict itself to the subjective information provided in the complaints of the domestic industry.

Furthermore, it is by no means certain that the interpretation of the information will be applied objectively. One might assume that the investigating national authorities would weight the interests of the foreign industry and the interests of domestic industry, an assumption which is not especially plausible. The discretionary power of the national authorities is significant due to the lack of exactness in the cost criterion. The result is that in many cases the dumping analysis determines dumping offences where no dumping has occurred.[222] In these cases the effects of anti-dumping duties are similar to those of protectionist duties, which is one reason for the international increase in anti-dumping proceedings. Since both the investigating national authority and the domestic and foreign producers are biased by their interests, the cost inquiry should be conducted—if at all—by an independent international authority.

In addition to other variables, the production costs by product are very difficult to measure. In the exceptional case that national competition authorities take action against domestic dumping, they use the variable of cost as the measure of the lowest price level

---

[220]See *Petersmann, Ernst-Ulrich* (1993), p. 62.

[221]See *Conrad, Christian A.* (1999).

[222]See *Conrad, Christian A.* (1999).

(Areeda Turner Rule).[223] The term "variable costs" doesn't lend itself to an exact definition because of the difficulty in what exactly comprises the general costs. Even the purchase of a machine doesn't lend itself to an exact calculation since the depreciation generally diverges from the time of usage. It is clear that despite the most complete and balanced methods of calculations, there is no way to determine an objective value as a fair comparative price within the anti-dumping proceeding.

Antidumping measures are meant to create and maintain a state of fair competition. Surprisingly enough, the national competition regulations do not contain sanction mechanisms against dumping in the case of offences by domestic companies. Price discrimination and price differentiation are interpreted here as being the result of market competition, as long as they are not seen to signal the misuse of a dominant market position. To what extent imports can be classified as positive or negative is in reality a political question: the difference between domestic industries losing jobs and profits due to competition with one another, or due to competition with foreign companies, is politically relevant.

Damage Analysis

National authorities' injury analyses are usually not interpreted as procedures for determining whether or not dumped imports have caused injury to domestic industry at the time of their import. Rather the authority investigates whether or not the critical situation of the domestic industry can be improved by introducing an antidumping duty.[224] Using this interpretation, it is not difficult to prove that import competitors represent a source of injury for a domestic industry with a weak competitive position.

According to GATT regulations, even more so since the Tokyo Round of the GATT, the imports under consideration in the injury analysis don't even have to be a notable cause of injury, let alone a major cause.[225] It is therefore sufficient that the imports are proven to be *one* cause of injury to domestic industry—among other causes—in order for injury to be ascertained. For example, the main cause of the determined injury may be domestic

---

[223] See *Messerlin, Patrick, A.* (1995), p. 42 and *Areeda, R./Turner, D.* (1975).

[224] See *Kulms, Rainer* (1988), p. 207.

[225] See *Kulms, Rainer* (1988), pp. 78 and 204. In the Uruguay Round the lower limit for possible damaging imports was set at a minimum import share of 3% as a threshold. However in the Dunkel Text, the basis for calculating the negligible share of imports was originally the market and not the import share. This was changed due to the insistence of the United States. The odd result is that the more effectively an industry is protected, the larger the relative import share is as a proportion of the total import share and, therefore, determining imports to be non-negligible becomes easier. Furthermore, there is a regulation which allows for an exception: even if the individual import shares of the imports are each less than 3%, an accumulation of imports is permittable if the combined import share of the imports is greater than 7%. This strengthens the tendency towards filing bundled antidumping complaints (Agreement on Implementation of Article VI of the General Agreement on Tariffs and Trade, Art. 5, Par. 5.8.). See *Horlick, Gary N.* (1993), p. 14; *Horlick, Gary N./Shea, Elenor C.* (1995), pp. 27 and *Conrad, Christian A.* (1999), p. 124.

competition, structural change, recession or even mismanagement, but this does not affect the determination of injury. On the contrary, the injury to domestic consumers brought about by the introduction of an anti-dumping duty may turn out to be greater than the injury to domestic producers caused by the imports. This aspect is not taken into consideration in the injury investigation of national authorities.[226]

With all of the inaccuracies and huge expenditures involved, it is not surprising that national authorities hesitate to interfere in domestic dumping cases, and begs the question as to the appropriateness of such proceedings. This problem exists in other forms of abuse control that set a certain market price. Such procedures are quite protracted and laborious, thus the better option for competition policies is the guarantee of market structures that make abuse more difficult due to more evenly distributed market power. Such a constellation would be the task of an international monopoly authority, which as yet doesn't exist. In addition, the effect of competition remains neglected within the anti-dumping proceedings.

9.6.4.5 Consideration of the Effect of Competition Within the Anti-dumping Proceedings

Aggressive dumping should be prevented by antidumping duties. The main contention on this point however, is that the exporter can only be sure that he will remain the only supplier either if the importing market is protected, or there are no other foreign suppliers who could compete with them in the market.[227] Unfortunately this aspect is not addressed in the antidumping investigations.

In the case of demand-fluctuations dumping, a situation in which both foreign and domestic producer have the same cost structure is possible. If the price falls in both markets to the same level below the minimum average costs and both adjust their offers, the exporting firm can be accused of dumping in the importing country though both companies have the same price, market conditions and cost structure.[228] Both foreign and domestic suppliers will have to sell below their production costs. The injury to the domestic industry would be less without the supply of the foreign producer on the market, but anti-dumping measures would be disadvantageous since they could lead to a domestic monopoly or at least impede competition on the domestic market long-term if the foreign supplier retreats. This aspect is also neglected in the anti-dumping investigations.

The effects of competition can be distinguished, as an example, as to whether dumping as a price differentiation is based on a monopoly or exporting cartel in the exporting country. There are two cases here to be distinguished. If the exporter sells below the price

---

[226]The EU Antidumping Law established that the EU Commission is required to consider general public interests, among which are the consumer interests, in its final decision on dumping. However, in not one of the 903 anti-dumping procedures in the 1980s was an antidumping complaint rejected because of the damaging effects on domestic consumers brought about by the introduction of an anti-dumping duty. See *Schuknecht, Ludger* et al (1992), p. 137.

[227]See *Nicolaides, Phedon* (1990), pp. 121 and 123.

[228]See *Nicolaides, Phedon* (1990), pp. 118 and 121.

of the importing country because he's a polypolist in that country, but above cost, the anti-dumping authorities in the importing country will impose an anti-dumping duty. In this case the duties don't compensate the distortion in competition, rather it just transfers the distortion from the monopolistic position in the exporting to the importing country. The desired effect from the authorities, namely to make the exporter no longer competitive, is not a fore-gone conclusion. It would be successful only when the producers in the importing country can produce at a lower cost than the exporter.

In the second case of price differentiation the exporter sells below his own costs but above his variable costs.[229] In this case the exporting monopolist would already have financed his fixed costs through domestic sales; either through sales above cost or his monopoly rent. An anti-dumping duty would take care of this distortion. Long-term dumping can't be assumed in this case since the price calculation and competitive position could change. If the dumping had created a monopolistic position for the exporter in the importing country, the consequent increase in price as well as the elimination of competing industries would limit the welfare benefits. Anti-dumping duties would be justified here as well.

Another possible situation in that a monopoly or cartel exists in both the exporting and importing countries, which isn't taken into consideration in anti-dumping proceedings. The exporter would be forced to raise his price after duties being imposed, whereas the anti-dumping code would have prevented the competition between the two producers. According to welfare theory this situation is not desirable either internationally or in the importing country. An international competition authority could consider this aspect, since it could observe the import as well as the export market.

Last but not least, a short-term dumping in the form of sales on a foreign market under production costs can be necessary in a limited time frame in order to overcome market accessibility barriers and make competition under the same conditions possible. Seen in this light, even short-term dumping with a negative effect on the market can stimulate cost economisation and thus increase the welfare benefits. As long as dumping isn't used to completely force competitors out of the market, or create monopolies or oligopolies, it can support an international resource allocation through a comparative cost advantage, which is not taken into consideration in anti-dumping proceedings. In this case as well an international competition authority would be more qualified than a national anti-dumping authority since it could observe and influence the over-arching market structures and behaviours.

9.6.4.6 Anti-dumping Measures as Violations of Competition

The international anti-dumping law can in fact increase a distortion in competition if the exporter is forced into committing to a price within the framework of an anti-dumping proceeding. If the exporter isn't a monopolist in his own country he'll have to join an

---

[229]Sales under variable costs can only occur in exceptional cases, with the exemption of subventions, when surplus is to be cleared.

export cartel in order to be able to adhere to the price. Once the export cartels exist, the transaction costs for the extension of the price agreements to other markets in minimal. If the dumping isn't from sales below cost, but rather a trade position dumping for example, the commitment to certain prices prevent the international exchange of comparative cost advantage.

The protectionist dimension of voluntary price commitments is seen in how widely spread it is practiced. In the 1980s the exporters agreed to such a commitment in almost half of the proceedings in order to avoid an anti-dumping duty.[230] The legal character of the current international regulation on competition is clear. A voluntary commitment to a price corresponds to a settlement out of court in which neither the degree of the distortion to competition nor the cause is determined; only the individual economic damages to the plaintiff in the importing country are dealt with.

Anti-dumping complaints are quite advantageous for the domestic industry. They reveal the competition's production costs and offer a basis for a supply cartel within the framework of the foreign (exporting country's) self-restriction agreements.[231] If the domestic industry isn't interested in building a cartel, or wants to prevent its foreign competitors from enjoying cartel returns, it will turn down the offer of self-restriction. Such was the case in the US American steel industry in the mid-1990s.[232] Furthermore, even in the event that the complaint is rejected, the expected benefit for the domestic producers is notably higher than the average legal costs of approximately $400,000 per complaint.[233] The benefit for domestic producers consists of two components: one, foreign producers on the U.S. market are rendered unable to compete because of the preliminary antidumping duties, and the other is the reduction of foreign supply causing the price level to rise, resulting in windfall profits for American producers.

Anti-dumping complaints promise to be especially successful for company branches with a high level of fixed costs, the steel industry for example, since the foreign producers' export prices immediately become dumping prices as a direct result of the increased costs of producing under capacity.[234] Amazingly enough, highly concentrated sectors weak in competition profit from anti-dumping measures. The criteria for dumping and damage are determining factors in this case. There is intense competition in sectors with many national suppliers, which causes prices to be generally lower than in highly concentrated sectors. This makes anti-dumping complaints against foreign competitors superfluous. Foreign price underbidding leads automatically to damage in sectors that aren't capable of

---

[230] See *Petersmann, Ernst-Ulrich* (1993), p. 63.

[231] According to Staiger, Wolak and Messerlin anti-dumping complaints play a significant role in enforcing price collusions in international cartells. See *Nicolaides, Phedon* (1990), p. 126; *Staiger, R./ Wolak, F.* (1989) and *Messerlin, P.* (1989), pp. 563–587.

[232] See *Conrad, Christian A.* (1995).

[233] THE ECONOMIST, May 5, 1992 and METAL BULLETIN, February 1, 1993, p. 3.

[234] See *Conrad, Christian A.* (1995).

competing, however. Proving "damage to an industry branch" is also easier in concentrated industries, since damage from domestic competition can be overlooked.[235] There are also fewer transaction costs involved in the coordination of anti-dumping complaints with fewer producers. This explains why the integrated steel producers of the USA, being concentrated and competitively weak, turned in a record number of anti-dumping complaints.[236]

The separation of competition from anti-dumping proceeding can lead to negative results. The dyopolitically structured[237] European soda ash industry was protected by the general direction I (GDI) of the EU commission (foreign policy) in the form of anti-dumping duties on the foreign industry. The very same industry was hit with a punishment for taking advantage of a dominant market position and price agreements from the general direction IV (competition), however. The GDI even put an anti-dumping duty on the imports from the US subsidiary of both European companies.[238] In 62% of the cartel proceedings directed against EU companies and 10% of those to determine whether a market-controlling position were exploited domestically conducted in the 1980s, the EU commission simultaneously carried out an anti-dumping proceeding against foreign producers.

To summarize, it is by no means the goal of anti-dumping duties to eliminate the cause of competition distortions in the exporting country, rather simply to alleviate the symptom in the form of damage to the domestic industry. Dumping can be founded, as in the case of a monopoly on the export market. The anti-dumping duties are directed against the dumping, but the welfare-reducing effect of the exporter's monopoly remains untouched.

Conclusion

The goal of this chapter is to show that within the framework of the current GATT rules of competition, the welfare benefits that one ought to expect from national antidumping proceedings with the ultimate aim being an optimal international resource allocation, just aren't a reality. The recurrence of protectionist effects is made clear through an analysis of the current antidumping code, in specific its execution through national authorities.[239]

The many inaccuracies and huge expenditures involved are a good explanation as to why national authorities are quite slow to interfere in domestic dumping cases, which then leads us to ask whether such proceedings are in fact appropriate. There

(continued)

---

[235] See *Langer, Stefan* (1995), p. 367.

[236] See *Conrad, Christian A.* (1995).

[237] SOLVAY held 70% of the market share in central Europe in 1990, whereby ICI in Great Britain has nearly a monopoly.

[238] See *Motta, Massimo/Onida, Fabrizio* (1997), pp. 76.

[239] See *Conrad, Christian A.* (1999).

are no sanction mechanisms for dumping perpetrated by domestic companies within national competition regulations, however. As long as price discrimination and differentiation are not established as a misuse of a dominant market position, they will be interpreted as the result of market competition; a problem found for other abuse controls that set a certain market price as well. The procedures to deal with such as abuse are both protracted and taxing, making market structures inauspicious for abuse the better option for competition policies with the resulting increase in evenly distributed market power. An international monopoly authority, which as yet doesn't exist, would have the task of creating and maintaining such a situation. The effect of competition still remains to be dealt with within anti-dumping proceedings, as well.[240]

The proven tendency of states to misuse antidumping procedures as protectionist instruments, and the fact that dumping within the WTO states isn't explicitly forbidden as long as it doesn't involve the abuse of a market-dominating position, make a case for an international antidumping codex in national competition law under the supervision of national authorities according to a neutral competition authority. The national antidumping measures developed historically out of competition law. The American Wilson Tariff Act extended the controls on predatory price undercutting in the Sherman Antitrust Acts ("predatory pricing") into the first law on international trade from and in the USA.[241]

An international competition authority would take the interests of both the domestic industry and the import competition into account with the goal of an optimal resource allocation. It would have privileged access to company figures from both sides, not least of all because no partiality or indiscretion would be feared, as may be the case with national anti-dumping authorities. It could also take action against destructive effects of international duping in the country from which the exports originated, by controlling or even breaking up monopolies and cartels for example. This would begin to cure the cause, and not just the symptoms, as is currently the case.

If an international competition authority should prove to be politically unfeasible, at the least the antidumping procedures would be limited to the cases in which a market competitor breaks the rules of competition to the point that it reduces international welfare. Short-term dumping, and dumping based on a monopoly in the exporting country would be exactly such cases. One sees here again the pressing need for international controls on competition. Reforming national antidumping

(continued)

---

[240]See *Conrad, Christian A.* (2002).

[241]See *Knorr, Andreas* (1999), p. 417 and *Cass, Roland A./Boltuck, Richard D.* (1996), p. 361.

procedural rules so that the real damage to the importing country could be assessed would be highly desirable, whereby one must distinguish between suspected long-term and short-term duping as well as keep the consumer interests always in view.[242] Antidumping duties and the costs of a procedure must of course never exceed the actual damages inflicted upon the importing country.

We must keep in mind that the number of countries that have used antidumping measures has increased tremendously, and the countries that were once those affected by the measures now actively use them themselves.[243] This will lead to more countries using antidumping duties not only and protectionist instruments for their industries, but will notice the restrictions on their own exports as well. They will have to defend the interests not only of their domestic producers, but also of their exporters within the GATT negotiations, perhaps resulting in a more balanced antidumping codex. The increasing articulation of import demand consumers' interests is a positive development in this context, as seen in the steel consumers in the USA.[244] Hope remains that others in other countries will follow suit.[245]

We have shown that with the current rules of competition in the GATT, national anti-dumping proceedings don't bring about the welfare benefits that an optimal international resource allocation ought. The analysis of the current anti-dumping code, especially its execution through national authorities, shows how the protectionist effect tends to reoccur.[246] A fair international competition based on performance is not guaranteed. Unwanted welfare benefit-reducing effects of competition are caused by neglecting to consider the potential of these effects within the anti-dumping proceedings.

Messerlin suggests for example, connecting anti-dumping proceedings with an automatic market control proceeding through the domestic competition authorities. He hopes to see a deterrent effect on domestic industries looking to protect themselves from imports.[247] Other authors would like to expand objective competition criteria in the GATT anti-dumping code, which would then have to be incorporated into the national anti-dumping proceedings.[248] Yet others call for the abolition of both the GATT anti-dumping code and the proceedings, suggesting instead that the

(continued)

---

[242] See *Conrad, Christian A.* (2002).

[243] See *Prusa, Thomas* (2001), p. 596 and *Messerlin, Patrick A.* (2000), pp. 159.

[244] Coalition of Steel Using Manufacturers (CASUM) und Coalition of American Businesses for Stable Steel Supplies (CABSSS).

[245] See *Conrad, Christian A.* (1995).

[246] See *Conrad, Christian A.* (1999).

[247] See *Messerlin, Patrick, A.* (1995), pp. 48 and 50.

[248] See *Hauser, Heinz/Schoene, Rainer E.* (1994), pp. 214.

dumping of both foreign and domestic producers be investigated by national competition authorities. This would necessarily have to include defining the relevant markets, determining the market share and evaluating the price politics from a competition policy perspective.[249]

Dumping within WTO countries is only prohibited in the case that someone wants to take advantage of a market-dominating position.[250] This fact would support the transfer of the international anti-dumping code to national competition regulations under the supervision of an institution, or at least amenable to controls through the WTO arbitration committee. If the damaging effects of international dumping were addressed in the exporter's country of origin, breaking up monopolies and cartels for example, the causes and not just the symptoms would be cured.

This suggestion of transferring the anti-dumping code to the national level is by no means unrealistic, as we will show in the next chapter.[251] There are also many examples of trade agreements in which national anti-dumping laws were substituted by a common competition policy. The best example is the EU, followed by trade agreements between New Zealand and Australia and between Chile and Canada.[252] However, the international application would probably be nearly as difficult as creating an international competition authority with sanctions capabilities to be used against individual states.

The next chapter uses current national competition policies to formulate the guidelines necessary to synthesize them into an international competition policy. The first part addresses the most important restrictions on competition, points out the international similarities and differences in national competition policies, and combines this information with competition theory as a synthesis to produce a suitable strategy for competition policy on the international level. The second part discusses the advantages and disadvantages of an international institution for competition based on the current academic discussion. In closing, we will derive the necessary institutions for the international system of competition regulations in the third part.

---

[249]See *Gifford, Daniel J./Matsushita, Mitsuo* (1996) and *Gröner, Helmut/Knorr, Andreas* (1996), p. 586.

[250]In the US the plaintiff has to prove a significant probability to the court that the defendant accused of dumping is capable of earning the losses caused by the dumping by raising the prices after he has obtained a monopolistic position, which makes it almost impossible (or at least very difficult) for a legal argument on predation to prevail. See *Petersmann, Ernst-Ulrich* (1996), p. 30; *Niels, Gunnar/Kate, Adriaan ten* (1997), p. 36 and *Gifford, Daniel J./Matsushita, Mitsuo* (1996), pp. 294.

[251]One obstacle will of course be the fact that a lot of WTO-members still have lack a domestic competition law. More and more countries are introducing their own competition laws however, and it would be sufficient if the group of WTO-members with their own competition laws and authorities start.

[252]See *Hoekman, Bernhard* (1997), p. 400.

Comprehension Questions and Exercises

1. Define "subsidies".
2. What is the procedure for anti-subsidy and anti-dumping proceedings?
3. Calculate the EU anti-dumping duty on the basis of:
    (a) The price of shoes brand Ching in China is €10. In the EU they are sold for €5. The export costs are €1 per pair of shoes.
    (b) The unit costs for the production of one kg of screws amount to €15 in China. In the EU they are sold for €12. The export costs are €2. The profit margin is estimated at 5% of the total cost of ownership (including pro rata overheads) and the proportional overhead costs at 10% of the unit cost.
4. Why can anti-dumping measures be used as a protectionist instrument?

References

Aberle, G. (1992). *Wettbewerbstheorie und Wettbewerbspolitik*. Stuttgart: W. Kohlhammer.

Bartling, H. (1988). Wettbewerbstheorie. In A. Woll (Ed.), *Wirtschaftslexikon* (3rd ed.). München: Humboldt-Taschenbuchverl.

Baumol, W. J. (1982). Contestable markets: An uprising in the theory of industry structure. *American Economic Review, 72*(1), 1–5.

Baumol, W., Panzar, J. C., & Willig, R. D. (1988). *Contestable markets and the theory of industry*. San Diego: Harcourt Brace Jovanovich.

Berg, H. (1999). Wettbewerbspolitik. In D. U. A. Bender (Ed.), *Vahlens Kompendium der Wirtschaftstheorie und Wirtschaftspolitik* (Vol. 2, 7th ed., pp. 299–362). München: F. Vahlen.

Bletschacher, G. (1992). *Strategische Handels- und Industriepolitik*. Tübingen: Mohr.

Bletschacher, G., & Klodt, H. (1992). Strategische Handels und Industriepolitik: theoretische Grundlagen, Branchenanalysen und wettbewerbspolitische Implikationen. *Kieler Studien, 244*, Tübingen: Mohr, ISBN 3161459628.

Boner, A. R., & Krueger, R. (1991). *The basis of antitrust policy: a review of ten nations and the European communities*. The world bank technical paper no. 160, Washington, DC.

Brendel, H. (1997). Wettbewerbspolitische Konzeptionen, Positive Theorie in normativer Einbindung. In K. von Delhaes & U. Fehl (Eds.), *Dimensionen des Wettbewerbs, Schriften zu Ordnungsfragen der Wirtschaft* (Vol. 52, pp. 79–101). Stuttgart: Lucius und Lucius.

Bridgemann, J. (2002). International mergers and acquisitions. *European Business Journal, 14*(2), 58–62.

Bruke, T. (1991). *Competition in theory and practice*. London: Croom Helm.

Caves, R. E., & Jones, R. W. (1981). *World trade and payments – an introduction*. Boston: Little, Brown.

Christl, C. (2001). *Wettbewerb und internationaler Handel, Eine Analyse ihrer Interdependenzen und institutionellen Voraussetzungen im Rahmen einer internationalen Wettbewerbsordnung, Walter Eucken Institut Untersuchungen zur Ordnungstheorie und Ordnungspolitik, Band 42, 2000.* Tübingen: Verlag Mohr Siebeck.

Clark, J. M. (1940). Towards a concept of workable competition. *The American Economic Review, XXX*(2), 241–256.

Conrad, C. A. (1996). Der neue GATT-Subventionskodex. *Zeitschrift für Wirtschaftspolitik, 45*(2), 187–198.

Conrad, C. A. (1998). Antidumping nach der uruguay-runde. *List Forum, 24*(3), 261–278.

Conrad, C. A. (2002, June). Dumping and antidumping measures from a competition and allocation perspective. *Journal of World Trade, 36*, 563–575.

Conrad, C. A. (2003). Außenwirtschaftliche Marktmechanismen zur Integration der Weltwirtschaft. *WiSt (Wirtschaftswissenschaftliches Studium), 32*(6), 345–350.

Corden, W. M. (1978). *Trade policy and economic welfare*. Oxford: Clarendon Press.

Dieckheuer, G. (2002). Competition, environment and trade in the globalized economy. In T. Koehler, & S. Kooths (Eds.), *Preparing a world antitrust framework: An ordoliberal approach*, Frankfurt.

Eucken, W. (1952). *Grundsätze der Wirtschaftspolitik* (4 unveränderte Auflage). Tübingen: Mohr.

Feinberg, R. M. (1989). Exchange rates and "Unfair trade". *The Review of Economics and Statistics, 71*(4), 704–707.

Feld, L. P., & Köhler, E. (2011b). Ist die Ordnungsökonomik zukunftsfähig? *Zeitschrift für Wirtschafts- und Unternehmensethik, 12*(2), 173–195. https://nbn-resolving.org/urn:nbn:de:0168-ssoar-349165. p. 176.

Forschungsinstitut für Wirtschaftsverfassung und Wettbewerb (Ed.). (1990). *Internationale Zusammenschlüsse und Wettbewerbspolitik, FIW-Dokumentation* (Vol. 13). Köln: Heymann.

Fox, E. M. (1997). Toward world antitrust and market access. *The American Journal of International Law, 91*(1), 1–25.

Glasow, B. (1999). *Vertikale Preisbindung, Wettbewerbstheorie und Wettbewerbsrecht in den USA, Deutschland und Europa*. Frankfurt: P. Lang, Cop.

Görgens, E. (1988). Wettbewerbspolitik. In A. Woll (Ed.), *Wirtschaftslexikon* (3rd ed.). München: Humboldt-Taschenbuchverl.

Groenveld, K., Maks, J. A. H., & Muysken, J. (Eds.). (1990). *Economic policy and the market process-austrian and mainstream economics*. Amsterdam: North-Holland.

Gröner, H. (1987). Internationale Wettbewerbspolitik. In M. Borchert, U. Fehl, & P. Oberender (Eds.), *Markt und Wettbewerb, Festschrift für Ernst Heuß zum 65* (pp. 359–377). Stuttgart: Geburtstag.

Hagedoorn, J. (1995). The economics of cooperation among high-tech firms. In H. Albach, G. Koopmann, & H.-E. Scharrer (Eds.), *The economic of high technology competition and cooperation in global markets*. Baden-Baden: Nomos Verlagsgesellschaft.

Hawk, B. E. (1995). System failure: Vertical restraints and EC competition law. *Common Market Law Review, 32*, 973–989.

Helpman, E., & Krugman, P. R. (1989). *Market structure and foreign trade*. Cambridge, MA: The MIT Press.

Hildebrand, D. (2002a). *The role of economic analysis in the EC competition rules*. New York: The Hague (Kluwer Law International).

Hildebrand, D. (2002b). The European school in EC competition law. *World Competition, 25*(1), 3–23.

Hoekman, B. (1997). Competition policy and the global trading system. *The World Economy, 20*(4), 383–406.

Holzkämper, H. (1995). *Forschungs- und Technologiepolitik Europas, Japans und der USA: eine ordnungstheoretische und empirische Analyse*. Bayreuth: Verl. PCO.

Horlick, G. N. (1993). How the GATT became protectionistic – an analysis of the uruguay round draft final antidumping Code. *Journal of World Trade, 27*(5), 5–17.

Hovenkamp, H. (1985). Antitrust policy after chicago. *Michigan Law Review, 84*(213), 213–284.

Hovenkamp, H. (1994). *Federal antitrust policy: the law of competition and its practice*. St. Paul, MN: Place West.

Immenga, U. (1996a). Rechtsregeln für eine internationale Wettbewerbsordnung. In U. Immenga, W. Möschel, & D. Reuter (Eds.), *Festschrift für Ernst Joachim Mestmäcker* (pp. 593–609). Baden-Baden: Nomos.

Immenga, U. (1996b). Wirkungsgrenzen bilateraler Verträge für eine internationale Wettbewerbsordnung. In J. Kruse & O. G. Mayer (Eds.), *Aktuelle Probleme der Wettbewerbs- und Wirtschaftspolitik, Erhard Kantzenbach zum 65* (pp. 155–165). Geburtstag, Baden-Baden: Nomos.

Kantzenbach, E. (1967). *Die Funktionsfähigkeit des Wettbewerbs* (2 durchgesehene ed.). Göttingen: Vandenhoeck & Rupprecht.

Kantzenbach, E. (1990). Competition policy in West Germany: A comparison with the antitrust policy of the United States. In A. Jacquemin (Ed.), *Competition policy in Europe and North America: Economic issues and institutions*. Chur: Harwood Academic Publisher.

Kantzenbach, E., & Kallfass, H. H. (1981). Das Konzept des funktionsfähigen Wettbewerbs. Workable Competition. In H. Cox, U. Jens, & K. Markert (Eds.), *Handbuch des Wettbewerbs*. München: Wettbewerbstheorie, Wettbewerbspolitik, Wettbewerbsrecht.

Kattan, J. (1993). Market power in the presence of an installed base. *Antitrust Law Journal, 62*(1), 1–21.

Kirzner, I. M. (1992). *The meaning of market process: Essays in the development of modern austrian economics*. London: Routledge.

Klodt, H. (2000). *Freihandel braucht Wettbewerbsregeln*. Handelsblatt, 4.04.2000, p. 53.

Kösters, W. (1992). Freihandel versus Industriepolitik. In *Wirtschaftsdienst* (Vol. 72(1), pp. 49–56). Hamburg: Verlag Weltarchiv, . issn 0043-6275

Kowalski, A. (1997). *Die Marktprozeßanalyse der Harvard School und neuere Systemtheorie*. Hamburg: S + W Steuer- und Wirtschaftsverlag.

Krattenmaker, T. G., & Salop, S. C. (1986). Anticompetitive exclusion: Raising rivals's cost to achieve power over price. *Yale Law Journal, 96*(2), 209–293.

Krüger, M. (1998). Kann Industriepolitik die Wettbewerbsfähigkeit verbessern? In J. B. Donges & A. Freytag (Eds.), *Die Rolle des Staates in einer globalisierten Wirtschaft, Schriften zur Wirtschaftspolitik, N.F* (Vol. 6, pp. 217–235). Stuttgart: Lucius & Lucius.

Kulms, R. (1988). *Das Antidumpingrecht im amerikanischen und europäischen Recht*. Baden-Baden: Nomos.

Küng, E. (1975). Dumping und Dumpingabwehr. *Wirtschafts Studium, 4*(11), 513–519

Lande, R. H. (1989). Chicago's false foundation: Wealth transfers (not just efficiency) should guide antitrust. *Antitrust Law Journal, 58*(2), 631–644.

Langer, S. (1995). Kritik und Neukonzeption des internationalen Antidumpingrechts. *Zeitschrift für vergleichende Rechtswissenschaft, 96*(1995), 353–383.

Lenel, H. O. (1989). Walter Eucken. In J. Starbatty (Ed.), *Klassiker des ökonomischen Denkens* (Vol. 2, pp. 292–311). München: Von Karl Marx bis John Maynard Keynes.

Maks, J. A. H. (1995). Economic theory and competition policy in the Netherlands. In G. Meijer (Ed.), *New perpectives on Austrian economics*. London: Routledge.

Mantzavinos, C. (1994). *Wettbewerbstheorie: Eine kritische Auseinandersetzung*. Berlin: Duncker & Humblot.

Mantzavinos, C. (2001). *Individuals, institutions, and markets*. Cambridge: Cambridge University Press.

Markham, J. W. (1950). An alternative approach to the concepts of workable competition. *The American Economic Review, XL*, 348–361.

Mason, E. S. (1939). Price and production policies od large-scale enterprises. *The American Economic Review, XXIX*(1), 61–74.

Messerlin, P. A. (1995). Should antidumping rules be replaced by national or interna-tional competition rules? (Aussenwirtschaft, September 1994, reprinted). *World Competition, 18*(3), 37–54.

Messerlin, P. A. (2000). Antidumping and safeguards. In J. J. Schott (Ed.), *The WTO after seattle* (pp. 159–183). Washington D.C: Institute for International Economics.

Messerlin, P. A., & Reed, G. (1995). Antidumping policies in the United States and the European communities. *The Economic Journal, 105*(433), 1565–1575.

Möschel, W. (1991). The goals of antitrust revisited. *Journal od Institutional an Theoretical Economics (JITE), 147*(1991), 7–23.

Motta, M., & Onida, F. (1997). Trade policy and competition policy. *Giornale degli Economisti e Annali di Economia, 56*(1–2), 67–97.

Nelson, R. R. (1979). Comment on Posner, Richard A. (1979), the chicago school of antitrust analysis. *University of Pennsylvania Law Review, 127*, 951–952.

Nicolaides, P. (1990). The competition effects of dumping. *Journal of World Trade, 24*(5), 115–131.

Nicolaides, P. (1994). Towards multilateral rules on competition – the problems in mutual recognition of national rules. *World Competition, 17*(3), 5–48.

O. V. (2000). Rufe nach transatlantischer Fusionskontrolle. *Handelsblatt*, 16.08.2000, p. 12.

Oberender, P., & Vath, A. (1989). Von der Industrieökonomie zur Marktökonomie. In P. Oberender (Ed.), *Marktökonomie* (pp. 3–27). München: F. Vahlen.

OECD. (1996). *Trade and competition: Frictions after the uruguay round, economic department working papers, no. 165*. Paris: OECD.

OECD. (2001). *Trade and competition policies – options for a greater coherence*. OECD, Paris.

Ordover, J. A., & Willig, R. (1985). Antus for high-technology industries: Assessing research joint ventures and mergers. *Journal of Law & Economics, 28*, 311–333.

Pengilley, W. (1997). The extraterritorial impact of U.S. trade laws – is it not time for "ET" to "Go home"? *World Competition, 20*(3), 17–55.

Petersmann, E.-U. (1993). International competition rules for the GATT-WTO world trade and legal system. *Journal of World Trade, 27*(6), 35–83.

Poeche, J. (1970). Workable Competition als wettbewerbspolitisches Leitbild. In J. Poeche (Ed.), *Das Konzept der "Workable Competition" in der angelsächsischen Literatur, Cologne* (pp. 9–32). Köln: Heymanns.

Posner, R. A. (1979). The chicago school of antitrust analysis. *University of Pennsylvania Law Review, 127*, 951–952.

Pratten, C. F. (1971). *Economies of scale in manufacturing industries, department of applied economic occasional papers, no. 28*. Cambridge: Cambridge University Press.

Price, T. C. (1997). Using co-evolutionary programming to simulate strategic behaviour in markets. *Journal of Evolutionary Economics, 7*(3), 219–254.

Prusa, T. J. (2001). On the spread and impact of anti-dumping. *Canadian Journal of Economics, 34* (3), 591–611.

Reder, M. W. (1982, March). Chicago economics: Permanence and change. *Journal of Economic Literature, XX*, 1–38.

Rishikesh, D. (1991). Extraterritoriality versus souveraignty in international antitrust jurisdiction. *World Competition, 14*(3), 33–66.

Royal, S. M. (1995). Symposium: Post-chicago economics – editor's note. *Antitrust Law Journal, 63* (2), 445–454.

Scherer, F. M. (1994). *Competition policies for an integrated world economy*. Brookings Institution: Washington DC.

Scherer, F. M. (1997). Competition policy convergence: Where next? *Empirica, 24*(1), 5–19.

Schleicher, T. J. (1997). The U.S. supreme court's use of post-chicago antitrust theory in Eastman Kodak v. image technical services: Implications for marketing practice. *Journal of Public Policy & Marketing, 16*(2), 310–318.

Schmidt, I. (1981). Per se Rule oder Rule of Reason. *Wirtschaftswissenschaftliches Studium, 10*(6), 282–284.

Schmidt, I., & Binder, S. (1996). *Wettbewerbspolitik im internationalen Vergleich: die Erfassung wettbewerbsbeschränkender Strategien in Deutschland, England, Frankreich, den USA und der EG,* Heidelberg

Schmidt, I., & Rittaler, J. B. (1986). *Die chicago school of antitrust analysis.* Baden-Baden: Nomos-Verlagsgesellschaft.

Schüller, A. (1987). Grundlagen der Wettbewerbspolitik. In *Unterrichtung der Bundesregierung, Materialien zum Bericht zur Lage der Nation im geteilten Deutschland 1987,* BT-D 11/11, 18.02.1987.

Schumpeter, J. A. (1961). *Konjunkturzyklen. Eine theoretische, historische und statistische Analyse des kapitalistischen Prozesses* (Vol. 1). Göttingen: Vandenhoeck & Ruprecht.

Schumpeter, J. A. (1993). *Kapitalismus, Sozialismus und Demokratie* (7th ed.). Tübingen: Stuttgart UTB Narr Francke Attempto.

Shepherd, W. G. (1985). *The economics of industrial organization* (2nd ed.). New Jersey: Prentice-Hall.

Shepherd, W. G. (1990). *The economics of industrial organization* (3rd ed.). Englewood Cliffs, NJ: Prentice Hall.

Siebert, H. (1988). Strategische Handelspolitik. Theoretische Ansätze und wirtschaftspolitische Empfehlungen. *Aussenwirtschaft, 43*(IV), 549–584.

Siebert, H., & Rauscher, M. (1991). Neuere Entwicklungen in der Außenhandelstheorie. *Wirtschaftswissenschaftliches Studium, 20*(10), 503–509.

Sosnick, S. H. (1958). A critique of concepts of workable competition. *The Quarterly Journal of Economics, LXXII,* 380–423.

Staiger, R. W., & Wolak, F. A. (1989, June). *Strategic use of antidumping law to enforce tacit international collusion.* National bureau of economic research working paper no. 3016, Cambridge, MA.

Starbatty, J. (1983). Ordoliberalismus. *Wirtschaftswissenschaftliches Studium, 12,* 570.

Stigler, G. J. (1968). *The organization of industry.* Oxford: Oxford University Press.

Szettele, D. (2000). *Auswirkungen der Industriepolitik in der EU auf die internationale Wettbewerbsfähigkeit der europäischen Wirtschaft.* Freiburg im Breisgau: Haufe.

Theuringer, M. (2003). *Antidumping und wettbewerbsbeschränkendes Verhalten.* Köln: Inst. für Wirtschaftspoltik.

Van Bael, I. (1990). EEC-dumping law and procedure revisited. *Journal of World Trade, 24*(2), 5–23.

Van Bergeijk, P. A. G., & Kabel, D. L. (1993). Strategic trade theories and trade policy. *Jounal of World Trade, 27*(6), 175–187.

Van Miert, K. (1996). Transatlantic relations and competition policy, in: EU-Commission (Hrsg.). *Competition Newsletter, 2*(3):1–5.

Victor, A. P. (1992). Export cartels: An idea whose time has passed. *Antitrust Law Journal, 60*(2), 571–581.

Viner, J. D. (1923). *A problem in international trade.* Chicago: University of Chicago Press.

Viscusi, W. K., Vernon, J. E., & Harrington, J. E. (2000). *Economics of regulation and antitrust.* Cambridge: MIT Press.

Voigt, S. (2002). *Institutionenökonomik.* München: Fink Verlag.

von Hayek, F. A. (1949). *The meaning of competition in individualism and economic order.* London: Routledge.

von Hayek, F. A. (1969). Der Wettbewerb als Entdeckungsverfahren. In F. A. von Hayek (Ed.), *Freiburger Studien*. Tübingen: Mohr.

von Hayek, F. A. (1975). Die Anmaßung von Wissen. *ORDO (Jahrbuch für die Ordnung von Wirtschaft und Gesellschaft)*, 26, 12–21.

von Hayek, F. A. (1978). Competiton as a discovery procedure. In *New studies in philosophy, politics, economics and the history of ideas*. Chicago: University of Chicago Press. (first printed as a lecture 1968).

von Weizsäcker, C. C., & Waldenberger, F. (1992). Wettbewerb und strategische Handelspolitik. *Wirtschaftsdienst: Zeitschrift für Wirtschaftspolitik, 72*(8), 403–409.

Welzel, P. (1991). *Strategische Handelspolitik: nationale Anreize und internationale Koordinationsaufgaben*. Heidelberg: Physica Verlag.

Wins, H. (2000). *Eine internationale Wettbewerbsordnung als Ergänzung zum GATT*. Baden-Baden: Nomos.

Industrial Policy

10

What Follows Why?
Industrial policy is the agglomeration of all state measures to influence the structure and development of the economy. Industrial policy is above all the attempt of politicians to strengthen their own economy through government grants, subsidies, or to delay an inevitable structural change and thereby to mitigate it socially. Although this policy is highly controversial, it is currently a significant resource with a high financial volume.

Learning Goals
After this lecture chapter, you should be able to delineate the essential forms of industrial policy and present them with their economic advantages and disadvantages.

10.1 Active Shaping Industrial Policy: Above All Research and Technology Subsidies

▶ **Definition** In the active shaping industrial policy, the state does not wait for economic development, but tries to make the economic structure welfare enhancing.

This takes place within the framework of financial research funding. It has to be distinguished whether it is the promotion of basic research or application-oriented research.

▶ **Definition**   Basic research differs from applied research in that no marketable products can be derived from it.

A direct exploitation of the research results is not possible. For companies, there is no added value because the company can not derive any innovation from it, in order to achieve pioneering profits in the market, therefore it comes to market failure: the economic outlay is greater than the benefit. But application-oriented research builds on basic research. We have positive externalities, because the benefits go far beyond the costs and not rival consumption, because the knowledge is arbitrarily divisible. All researchers can use the results of basic research and derive applications as product or process innovations. Most basic research is done by universities.

Basic research is the basis for the competition as a discovery process according to Hayek, in which entrepreneurs, based on the results of basic research, try to realize process and product innovations. Basic research is thus an important prerequisite for technical progress. State subsidies should compensate for the incentive distortion.

Example: BASF materials are based on the periodic table. But the periodic table can also be used by any other company.

Conclusion
State funding of basic research is welfare-enhancing, so it can be justified in terms of competition policy.

It can therefore be stated that research funding can only be justified economically in cases where the market's research performance is insufficient. This applies to the cases of Market failure, external effects and non-rival consumption in basic research, so not insofar as it is economically viable research In the case of economically viable applied research funding for research and technology always constitutes a subsidy to normal corporate expenses and thus leads to distortions of competition in foreign trade. Research and technology subsidies in these cases correspond to a protectionist instrument, as research funding artificially increases competition-relevant production know-how as a comparative cost advantage. In the following, the example of the EU will be used to investigate whether the research subsidies are limited to the promotion of basic research or whether application-oriented research is also subsidized, creating distortions to competition.

10.2   The Awarding of Research and Technology Subsidies

The recession in the early 1980s and Europe's declining competitiveness led European politicians to seek solutions to problems. There was a need for action. Japan and the USA had a clear competitive advantage. For this very reason, the nascent EU considered

Japanese and American research and technology policy and the US domestic market as a copiable concepts of success. The superiority of American companies in competition also curtailed European politicians, which is why cross-border mergers were called for in order to pool European resources.[1] This view is not an isolated case. Most states are trying to prevent, and yet encourage, monopolies and cartels on the ground of their domestic welfare-reducing effects, if welfare reduction, with a strong focus on exports, mainly affects foreign countries and leads to an avoidable increase in export competitiveness.[2]

While the EU presents its research and technology policy in response to third-party attacks and breaches of competition, and sees itself more as a victim rather than a perpetrator, the other countries adopt the same line of argumentation. The US is forced to take countermeasures by the EU's and Japan's unfair competition practices, and in Japan it feels like it's being squeezed by western industrialized countries and emerging economies.,[3] Microelectronics has been chosen by governments as a key industry for international competitiveness. It is an elementary component of almost all high-tech products and has a high development potential. In the US, research in this industry is subsidized under the SEMATECH program. The Japanese government is promoting micro-group research collaborations, and in Europe this industry is being promoted both nationally and at EU level through the EUREKA and JESSI programs.[4] There are now new areas of technology that are being promoted, such as Nano- and biotechnology.

The establishment of the EU single market promised, on the one hand, a better use of the comparative cost advantages and thus a more efficient allocation of resources and, on the other hand, the realization of economies of scale. Similar things seemed to apply to European research: for many projects, it seemed that the necessary company size was not achieved or inefficient duplicate research. Targeted promotion of research in the future key industries should allow for catching up on research and competition.[5]

---

[1]"The first problem of an industrial policy for Europe consists in choosing 50 to 100 firms which, once they are large enough, would be the most likely to become world leaders of modern technology in their fields. At the moment we are simply letting European industry be gradually destroyed by the superior power of American corporations. Counterattacks requires a strategy based on the systematic reinforcement of those firms best able to strike back. Only a deliberate policy of reinforcing our strong points—what demagogues condemn under the vague term of "monopolies"—will allow us to escape relative underemployment" *Servan-Schreiber,* Jean-Jaques (1968), p. 159.

[2]See *Scherer,* F. M. (1997), p. 13.

[3]See *Thurow,* L. C. (1992); *Tyson,* L. D'Andrea (1992); *Nakamura,* T. (1994) and *Morici,* Peter (2000), pp. 58.

[4]See *Grundlach,* Erich/*Klodt,* Henning/*Langhammer,* Rolf J./*Soltwedel,* Rüdiger (1995), p. 14; *Krüger,* Malte (1998), pp. 218f; *Greloh,* Philipp M. (2000); *Gurbaxani,* Indira (2000) and *Szettle,* Dieter (2000), pp. 101 und 103.

[5]See *Starbatty,* Joachim/*Vetterlein,* Uwe (1995), p. 6 and *Szettle,* Dieter (2000), p. 307.

With the adoption of the Single European Act in 1986, the European research and technology policy was adopted as an explicit contractual objective, first in the EEC Treaty and finally in the Treaty of Nice) (Article 157 of the EC Treaty, now 173 TFEU[6]).

1. The Union and the Member States shall ensure that the necessary conditions for the competitiveness of the Union industry are provided. To this end, its activity is geared to the following, according to a system of open and competitive markets:—facilitate the adaptation of industry to structural changes;—encouraging a favorable environment for the initiative and development of enterprises throughout the Union, especially small and medium-sized enterprises;—promoting an environment conducive to cooperation between enterprises;—Promoting better use of industrial potential in innovation, research and technological development.

Research funding mainly takes the form of grants for research projects that are applied for by all companies but also by research institutes. To this end, the EU sets up so-called research framework programs. In addition, the research cooperation is promoted above all.[7] The implementation of the framework programs takes the form of more detailed sub-programs, also called actions. The EU makes a distinction: Direct actions serve to realize the positive external effects of basic research. Research areas such as the environment or the safe use of atomic energy have the character of public goods that override European importance, since environmental pollution and atomic radiation (negative externalities) cannot be stopped by national borders and their benefits to all are indefinitely beneficial (positive external effects). In addition, the EU wants to pre-empt double research with the help of direct actions.

Indirect actions are the actual strategic research funding. Research projects proposed by industry are subsidized in selected key technologies to half the cost. The indirect actions in particular are based on the apparently successful research programs of the USA and Japan. The selection of the projects to be supported is based on the anticipated innovation progress, i.e. the contribution to the increase of the European competitiveness and on the extent of the included research cooperation. Once approved, the Commission has no direct influence on the research project and assumes no responsibility, which is why it chose the term indirect action.

Concerted actions should bundle European research and thus prevent duplication of research. These programs therefore finance only the research co-ordination carried out by the Commission. It usually brings together government research institutions, advises them and coordinates the division of labor and research contracts. Each Contracting Party bears

---

[6]The Treaty establishing the European Community (EC Treaty) was renamed "Treaty on the Functioning of the European Union" (TFEU) with the entry into force of the Lisbon Treaty on 1.12.2009.

[7]See *Starbatty*, Joachim (1987), p. 160; *Starbatty*, Joachim/*Vetterlein,* Uwe (1995), p. 9 and *Szettle,* Dieter (2000), p. 113.

its own research costs. The research results are available to all parties involved. Nevertheless, individual Member States and also the Commission as a contracting party may participate in the research costs.[8]

Horizontal actions should ensure the necessary research infrastructure and efficient research funding. These programs will finance the networking of European research institutes or research files, congresses and, in general, the exchange of research, but also, for example, the evaluation of research actions, forecasts and the exploitation and dissemination of research results. The funds from these programs, together with Structural Funds, will also be used to support research projects in or involving a limited number of technologically advanced Member States.[9] With the sixth Framework Program, the EU defined seven thematic research priorities.[10] The new funding instruments were the Networks of Excellence and the Integrated Projects. Integrated projects should bundle research in the seven priority areas in projects that, on the one hand, have important socio-economic objectives and, on the other hand, strengthen European competitiveness. The networks of excellence aim at coordinating the scientific and technological competencies and activities of the participating research partners in the seven priority areas. The eighth EU Research Framework Program"Horizon 2020" will provide a total of approx. 87 billion euros to support research and innovation projects.[11]

The EU Commission takes the view that its programs are in the area of basic research and only promote innovation in the pre-competitive area. However, the analysis of EU research programs has shown that this is not the case for indirect actions. The focus of funding and business demand is on programs that are close to the market. On the other hand, as part of its research cooperation, is the Commission promoting competition between researchers by, for example, promoting research transparency and knowledge sharing. Increased by European research institutes and databases in the context of direct, horizontal or concerted actions, this will increase efficiency without distorting competition.[12]

We note the following regarding the direction of EU research funding:
Targets[13].

---

[8]See *Starbatty,* Joachim/*Vetterlein*, Uwe (1995), p. 9.

[9]See *Starbatty,* Joachim (1987), p. 160.

[10]1. Genomics and biotechnology for health (€ 2.255 billion); 2. Information society technologies (€ 3.625 billion); 3. Nanotechnologies and nanosciences, knowledge-based multifunctional materials and new production processes and equipment (€ 1.300 billion); 4. Aerospace (€ 1.075 billion); 5. Food quality and safety (€ 0.685 billion); 6. Sustainable development, global change and ecosystems (€ 2.120 billion) and 7. citizens and government in science (€ 0.255 billion).
Büro für internationale Forschungs- und Technologiekooperation (2003).

[11]Büro für internationale Forschungs- und Technologiekooperation (2003).

[12]See *Starbatty,* Joachim/*Vetterlein,* Uwe (1995), p. 13, 15f und 16; *Szettle,* Dieter (2000), p. 307 and *Stehn,* Jürgen (2001), p. 206.

[13]See Conrad, Christian A. (2005), pp. 68.

1. Promoting the competitiveness of national or European industry
2. Avoidance of duplicate research. The research program Horizon 2020, for example, stipulates that the applicants come from three different EU countries. This should generate a European added value. By coordinating research, the aim of the Commission is to prevent companies from wasting research funding because they are all exploring the same thing.
3. Through research coordination and research funding, the EU Commission also wants to overcome market entry barriers. Alone, the companies could not finance the extensive research. This leads to rent shifting: overcoming market entry barriers through subsidies (Airbus, New Foreign Trade Theory: International Demand and thus also Gains, Jobs, Welfare are redirected to the domestic market at the expense of foreign competitors, see Sect. 6.8),

Characteristics:

– Funded research areas are determined by politics.
– Applications must be submitted with an average processing time of 294 days.[14]
– The research is coordinated between the companies.

Assessment
Is it basic research or applied research?

10.3   Are Research and Technology Subsidies of National Advantage?

The European Commission developed European research and technology policy in response to US research funding on the defense budget, justifying its exit from the international code of conduct on competition: "As the laws of the marketplace are replaced by ambitions of political power, so too does a liberal-trade rule system for world trade—as the GATT should be—lose a substantial part of its business base. The growing tendencies towards the bilateralization and politicization of trade relations, especially in the area of so-called cutting-edge technology, are a sign of this."[15]

This quotation shows the dynamic erosion of international competition. Since competition violations are not punished, one rule violation invites the next one. The EU Commission asserts that the United States is promoting competition through the defense budget of American industry and, in addition, restricts subsequent competition by restricting the dissemination of such research results. International competition is distorted to the detriment of foreign countries.[16] Therefore, to test the validity of this argument, the effect of

---

[14]See duz, Unabhänige Deutsche Universitätszeitung, Europa kompakt, Nr. 2, vom 13.03.209, p. 4.
[15]*Narjes,* Karl Heinz (1986), p. 11.
[16]See *Narjes,* Karl Heinz (1986), p. 12f.

resource redirection by the US government must be considered for the entire American industry and not for the individual benefiting company.[17]

The Commission's argument that the secrecy of research results hinders subsequent competition is objectively correct. However, American companies are not allowed to use commercially exploitable military research results. These conditions imposed by the US Department of Defense consequently hinder not only subsequent competition but also future competition. Although these requirements make American research funding seem unattractive to US companies, they are widely used. Consequently, in addition to the not always secure military production contracts, another benefit of this money is likely to be its use as a contribution to financing the research infrastructure of enterprises. The military-funded research institutes would then also conduct private research.

Gegen die Effizienz der amerikanischen Forschungsförderung durch das Pentagon sprechen die politisch orientierte Vergabe und die verschwenderische Abrechnungspraxis. Die Fördermittel werden teilweise vergeben, um Wahlkreise zu gewinnen oder verdiente Politiker zu unterstützen. Die Pentagon-Forschungsaufträge werden zu Selbstkosten plus einer 8% Gewinnmarge abgerechnet, was einen Disincentive für eine effiziente Mittelvergabe darstellt.[18]

The politically oriented allocation and wasteful accounting practice speak against the efficiency of the American research funding by the Pentagon. The funds are partly awarded to win constituencies or to support deserving politicians. The Pentagon research contracts are calculated at cost plus an 8% profit margin, which is a disincentive to efficient allocation of funds.[19]

In general, it is doubtful whether research and technology subsidies are of national advantage. For example, the cost of processing the application alone amounts to approximately 10% of the funding to be distributed by the EU. In other words, the processing costs would exceed the funding from an acceptance/rejection ratio of 1:10 applications. The disproportionate amount of work involved in the allocation of funds was also reflected in the report commissioned by the German Federal Ministry of Research by the Cologne-based consulting firm Scientific Consulting Dr. Ing. Schulte Hillen criticizes.[20] The European Court of Auditors also criticized the lack of targeted and efficient allocation of research funds.[21]

EU technology policy should also increase competitiveness as a purposeful research funding model based on the Japanese model. The Commission considers that research funding and research coordination makes cost-intensive projects possible in the first place. Furthermore, technology policy has often prevented duplication of research.[22] However,

---

[17]See *Starbatty,* Joachim (1987), p. 167.

[18]See *Starbatty,* Joachim (1987), p. 168.

[19]See *Starbatty,* Joachim (1987), p. 168.

[20]See *Starbatty*, Joachim/*Vetterlein,* Uwe (1995), p. 17.

[21]See *Krüger*, Malte (1998), p. 227f.

[22]See *EU-Kommission* (1992), p. 1 and *Szettle,* Dieter (2000), p. 307.

the Commission is replacing the resource allocation of the market by its own with targeted research and technology funding in certain future sectors. According to Friedrich August von Hayek, competition is a process of discovering knowledge that would otherwise remain unknown or unused. The market rewards product innovation with pioneering results if it meets the needs of demand, and process innovation if it leads ceteris paribus to cost reductions. These profits can be realized by high-risk companies in the so-called (innovative) competition in which they implement the innovations, which is equivalent to technical progress. Subsequent competition erodes those winnings by imitation. Ultimately, because of process innovations, the economy is producing the same amount of goods more efficiently, using fewer resources, and could use the saved resources to meet new product innovation needs. The competitive process makes the knowledge of each usable for all, it is nationalized.[23] Following this approach, the Commission, through its research steering and coordination, eliminates research competition and market evaluation. It must therefore be able to identify the most efficient future industries and research projects better than the market.

Breakthrough products or process innovations, however, are one-offs. Apart from the fact that research success often depends on chance, research forecasts cannot be based on trend analysis because research is not a deterministic process.[24] The uniqueness of pioneering research results most aptly describes the call "eureka" of the Greek Archimedes in discovering the hydrostatic basic law. In addition, there must be market demand for the success of the innovations, and this, too, would have to be forecast by the Commission.[25] Schumpeter sees in an innovation, according to the meaning of the word, something fundamentally new and not the improvement of something known.[26] It is just a break in the trend. The more successful an innovation is, the bigger must be the new, the trend breaker. Research results can therefore be hoped for, but not reliably predicted, unless it is maturation research of an already well-known production process or product. Hayek calls this kind of research guidance presumption of knowledge.[27]

Researchers need to forecast their research outcomes when submitting their application, so that the Commission can assess which research project is most promising. The Commission must be able to judge, when choosing, whether the researchers' predictions about the results of the research are correct. Who can know which still unknown research results are researchable? When it comes to unknown research results, this cannot be predicted. At best, this could be a creator god who has built this world and knows the blueprint, so knows what kind of natural laws apply, what kind of radiations exist and how matter is composed. A person cannot know this, he can only discover.

---

[23] See *Starbatty,* Joachim/*Vetterlein,* Uwe (1995), p. 14.

[24] See *Hamm,* Walter (1979), p. 430f and *Starbatty,* Joachim (1987), p. 166.

[25] See *Staudt,* Erich (1986), p. 89 and *Starbatty,* Joachim (1987), p. 166.

[26] See *Schumpeter,* Joseph A. (1949), p. 150.

[27] See *Hayek, Friedrich August von* (1975) and *Starbatty,* Joachim/*Vetterlein,* Uwe (1995), p. 14.

Conversely, one can ask what would happen if marketable innovations were generally predictable and thus could be planned for. All companies have the same level of information. If the forecasts are positive, then there are two possible developments:

1. All companies invest in capacity expansion, then there are overfull markets and no company profit or
2. No companies invest because they expect overfull markets as a result of the above decision combination. The so-called Morgenstern paradox emerges as an infinite chain of mutually presumed reactions and counterreactions, which can never be interrupted by an act of knowledge, but only by an arbitrary act.[28]

Thus, by setting a research focus, the Commission reduces the breadth of research. This increases the probability of error. Consequently, the EU Commission's research steering and pooling prevents a diversified research focus and thus indirectly reduces the chances of success.[29]

In addition, the likelihood of error is compounded by the fact that the Commission is off the market as a central political entity in Brussels. According to the decision theory, the likelihood of error decreases with the level of information. The best information about the research projects is provided by the investigating companies and researchers. The companies are closer to the market and the researchers are closer to the current state of knowledge. Accordingly, both have an information advantage over the Commission, which they can use to their advantage in the application. However, if the Commission ultimately decides to accept research projects with a higher probability of error, the likelihood of resource mislocation increases. Added to this are the welfare losses due to the restriction of competition itself. In extreme cases, all competitors are involved in one research project. The sanctioning mechanism of the market and thus also the research pressure are eliminated. Success in the market is going from relative to absolute. It is no longer vital for a company to realize the innovation ahead of its competitors, because there is no competition. On the contrary, it can be hoped that the research cartel organized by the Commission will also become a price cartel after the product has been realized, which will allow it additional market position profits.[30]

In summary, research funding can only be justified economically in cases where the research performance of the market is achieved insufficiently or not at all.This applies to the cases of cross-border external effects already mentioned. For example, in basic research or for the production of public goods (harmonization of standards, creation of a European transport infrastructure, environmental area).[31] In all other cases, research funding is either

---

[28]See *Morgenstern,* Oskar (1966), p. 258.

[29]Zu dem gleichen Ergebnis kommt *Szettle.*See *Szettle,* Dieter (2000), p. 309.

[30]See *Starbatty,* Joachim (1987), p. 176 and *Starbatty,* Joachim/*Vetterlein,* Uwe (1995), p. 16. The Commission's policy in the European steel sector can serve in this context as an example. See *Conrad,* Christian A. (1997), p. 157.

[31]See *Starbatty,* Joachim (1987), p. 177.

inefficient, to the detriment of the sponsoring country, or it directly transfers economic benefits to the beneficiary companies, thus creating distortions in international competition coupled with corresponding welfare reductions. While application-based research subsidies can artificially increase the competitiveness of individual companies, the inefficiencies and competitive constraints associated with the award of research weakens the national economy much more, so that the net benefit is negative. Ultimately, neither the United States, nor Japan, nor France, nor, ultimately, the European Union, can achieve sustainable industrial policy successes.[32]

Summary of the Assessment of Applied Research
We can note the following disadvantages of application-oriented research: Benefits exist only in the promotion of basic research, as there are market failures, positive externalities and non-rival consumption. In application-oriented research, only disadvantages could be identified.

1. Distortion of competition to the detriment of non-subsidized companies
2. Restricted competition: (a) Commission organizes research cartel of several companies, which could also become a price cartel after realization of the product (b) At least the pressure for research lapses as research competition is lacking as the companies coordinate their research and know how advanced their competitors are.
3. Wealth redirection to the detriment of taxpayers
4. High processing costs (about 10% of the delivery volume)
5. The Pro-Argument Avoidance of Double Research
   (a) Information problem: state needs to know the successful direction of research. How should the EU Commission know this? Companies always have an information advantage. Really relevant topics are Top Secret! Because companies do not want to share these research results and lose their competitive advantage.
   (b) The research competition is made irrelevant. According to Friedrich August von Hayek, competition is a method of discovering knowledge that would otherwise remain unknown or unused. But research is not a deterministic process: the result often depends on chance. Example Meisner porcelain: Johann Heinrich Böttgen wanted to manufacture gold but created porcelain in the attempt.

(continued)

---

[32]See *Laussel,* Didier/*Montet,* Christian (1995), p. 58; *Winter,* Helen (1994), p. 218 and *Szettle,* Dieter (2000), p. 305.

(c) If marketable innovations were foreseeable, either all companies would invest, which would lead to overcapacities or none because they fear the same insoluble Morgenstern paradox.

(d) According to the decision theory, the likelihood of error decreases with the level of information. The Commission has limited knowledge, both scientifically and with regard to the probability of market success. *Asymmetric information* to the detriment of the EU Commission (State), as the candidate companies are closer to the market and the researchers are closer to the current state of knowledge. This has mainly deadweight effects. Due to the long processing time of the research applications, it is more worthwhile to implement top research immediately than to apply for research funding. You get the research funds only after 1–2 years. In the meantime, it would have been possible to earn more on the market with the researched product and not jeopardize the competitive advantage by waiting. Furthermore, in the context of research coordination, the danger of industrial espionage is put to the test, as one must communicate his research with the competitors. It is therefore natural not to apply for research funding for the best projects. The laboratories funded by research funds can then also be used for secret research, with which one can realize the pioneer profits.

Conclusion

Consequently, the EU Commission prevents with its research steering and bundling a diversified research orientation and thus indirectly reduces the chances of success. An alternative to a research grant is for instance the German Renewable Energy Act. It created a market through a declining 20-year guaranteed feed-in tariff for renewable energies. Apart from the solar sector, this law can be described as successful. For example wind energy was not competitive when comparing costs with nuclear power generation. Therefore, there was no market for wind energy and therefore none for wind turbines. The price increase and planning reliability of the feed-in tariff for wind energy enabled wind parks to be financed, which also allowed the wind turbines to be funded. However, competition among companies was not eliminated as there was no direct support to companies, quite the opposite. Since companies were aware that the feed-in tariff fell each year, they had to offset this with cost savings. The research pressure was thereby increased. The German wind turbine manufacturers are therefore among the technologically leading companies worldwide.

10.4   Reactive Industrial policy with the Help of Maintenance Subsidies

Are maintenance subsidies such as in the coal and steel industries of national advantage? Subsidies create artificial competitive advantages that are not based on companies' performance in the marketplace. In international trade, this means that governments can get by at the expense of foreign employment at the expense of foreign employment through subsidies if they succeed, with the help of subsidies, in strengthening their companies in such a way that they are more competitive than the foreign companies are. The reduction in employment will be passed on to foreign countries as in the case of import restrictions. This is why one speaks of a "beggar-thy-neighbor-policy" or of internal protection. The subsidies are used in this case to cover lost sales below production costs or for investments in more productive production facilities.

However, subsidies are dynamically not market-consistent because they impede subsequent competition. New entrants and dynamic entrepreneurs anticipate this and seek out other markets for their investments and innovations. What remains is a market in which the success of a company is primarily determined by the political criteria of state subcontracting and no longer by its existence in the performance competition. The profitability of private capital declines. The consequence is that the non-subsidized companies withdraw their capital from the economic sector and steer them into areas with better profitability. The dynamic employees are also looking for more profitable economic sectors for their innovations.

In the form of subsidies, companies have a second source of income, which is not regulated by competition on the market, but rather by lobbying, which is much more lucrative than the production of goods, which is called rentseeking.[33] A company will thus increase lobbying until its marginal cost equals its marginal revenue. Once a government has decided to make a regulatory exception and to keep the companies and their jobs in the market by means of subsidies, ending the granting of subsidies is almost impossible due to internal political resistance. The government has broken the regulative subsidy taboo and therefore can no longer call upon it.

The new lucrative source of income will therefore also be claimed by the non-subsidized companies and other sectors of the economy, where they can invoke the subsidies already granted. The subsidy recipients thus develop the practice of customary law. Companies are getting used to subsidizing and anticipate future subsidies on their financial plans. The resistance of the benefiting stakeholders will therefore be significantly greater if the granting of subsidies is withdrawn than if the subsidies were denied from the outset. The actual entrepreneurial performance is no longer worthwhile in this sector and is behind the Rentseeking for the entrepreneur. As a result, entrepreneurial performance will decline and competition as a discovery process will wither away. Overall, this leads to a decrease in

---

[33]The term "rent-seeking" goes back to Anne O. Krueger. See *Voigt*, Stefan (2002), p. 122.

technical progress. The affected economic sector shrinks and falls behind in international competitiveness.

Import restrictions and subsidies of any kind create artificial competitive advantages that are not based on the performance of companies in the market. The artificial competitive advantage restores the balance of competitiveness with foreign countries. However, this balance can only be maintained for a temporary period, as the backlog of pressure on imports due to import restrictions or subsidies usually does not diminish the gap with foreign trade but increases it. The protective country is unleashing its industry out of international dynamic competition and risks being lost forever. If it wants to maintain its jobs, it must continually tighten import restrictions or increase subsidies. A long-term realization of the goal of increasing competitiveness cannot be achieved in this way. On the contrary, subsidization, as a resource diversion into a sub-optimal use, weakens the economy as a whole.[34]

Conclusion
Maintenance subsidies can only be justified to cushion a structural change socially. However, from the outset they must be limited in time and decline in order to limit the negative effects of the market intervention. Unemployment that inevitably occurs in the context of structural change can best be counteracted by a negative income tax. It does not intervene in the market mechanism but low wages as a result of low labor demand in areas affected by structural change will be increased by a governmental overpayment for a limited period of time to allow the worker to enjoy a higher standard of living despite low market wages. Due to the low market wage, the location remains attractive for investment.

Summary: Advantages and Disadvantages of Reactive Industrial Policy
Advantages
Temporal extension and thus social cushioning of structural change, the structural change is delayed but not stopped (eg coal and steel), but Disadvantage:—international "beggar-thy-neighbor-policy", as efficient jobs are lost there.—Distortions of competition.

(continued)

---

[34]The EU Commission also fears that the European level of subsidies will remain high and that the EU's international competitiveness will be weakened due to the distorted allocation of resources. See *Borries*, Raimer von (1999), p. 101.

1. static market conformity: The allocation function, the incentive function * and the sanctioning function of the competition are eliminated (= companies would be leaving the market in the normal way).
2. dynamic market conformity: The dynamic adjustment function is switched off. Not more performance, but rent-seeking (pursuit of political pension) is rewarded. Businesses become accustomed to subsidizing and anticipate future subsidies (as well as unions) in their financial planning.

Old structures are kept alive artificially. The efficiency of companies is lost because there is no more pressure.* There is no longer any incentive, because without profits, companies receive subsidies, but if they generate profits, they no longer receive any subsidies.

Examples: coal, steel

The subsidies hinder the non-subsidized subsequent competition. Innovations are no longer worthwhile. New entrants and dynamic entrepreneurs anticipate this and seek out other markets for their investments and innovations.

→ Competition stunted as a discovery process.
→ Decline of technical progress (innovation function).
→ Economic sector is shrinking and falling behind in international competitiveness.
→ Result:

Welfare losses and system damage. If the social support is needed, due to less allocation and incentive distortions it is better to support direcly the individuals (negative income tax) and not te companies.

10.5   Explanations for Subsidies

As noted, the high subsidy allocation in the EU cannot be justified economically. The negative effects exceed the positive many times over. In the following, we will look for the reasons for this development in order to be able to take into account possible implementation obstacles in the drafting of our competitive order.

10.5.1 The Behavior of Policy Makers

In the EU, economically inopportune decisions have repeatedly been made, such as the granting of subsidies or the granting of protection. Even with a broader notion of utility, for example involving employment as a benefit, the decisions taken remain sub-optimal in the long term, as the subsidy and protection costs for maintaining competitiveness are matched by the increasing competitiveness of competing firms over time foreign industries is rising. As has been shown, the political voting procedures distort the decision results. The question arises as to whether political decision-makers also follow their own laws in their decisions. An explanation for the decision-making behavior of political decision-makers is provided by the approach of the "New Political Economy". According to the New Political Economy approach, a politician does not maximize the common good, but predominantly his own benefit (see also Sect. 8.1). Political offices grant this benefit in the form of power, prestige and income. In order to achieve the desired offices, the politician must collect as many electoral votes—one speaks of maximizing votes. This behavioral orientation can be described as political expediency or as "political rationality".

While the voice maximization hypothesis greatly simplifies the behavioral motives of politicians, it is imperative for national politicians reliant on reelection. This behavioral hypothesis provides a further explanation of the inadequate EU subsidy decisions to maximize overall welfare. The preservation of subsidies is advantageous for the politician because the gain of votes in the persons dependent on the company (workers, traders, etc.) is greater than the loss of votes in the group of taxpayers charged with the financing of the subsidies. The group of taxpayers is large and diffuse, so their organizational costs are high. The different size of the group also has the effect that the loss of benefit for the individual through the tax increases is smaller than the individual gain in utility for those who profit from the subsidies. This explains why taxpayers' political level of organization is lower than that of companies benefiting from the subsidies.

The vote-maximizing decision is to finance subsidies through public borrowing—as is also the case in practice—because the burden on the electorate is unclear here and in some circumstances even the next generation may pay for the subsidies. However, this is a group that has not yet participated politically in the decision-making process. In addition, avoiding subsidies increases short-term unemployment and thus increases the social costs of the state. However, the welfare gains resulting from unhindered competition will only materialize in the long term and cannot be directly attributed. Therefore, these profits cannot be used by a politician as a political success. Consequently, according to the approach of the New Political Economy, it is only logical for the politician to prefer interventionism and protectionism to free trade, although these are the decisions that are worse in terms of overall welfare. Political rationality thus doubles economic rationality.

10.5.2 A Subsidy-Free Market as a Public Good

"Each Member State naturally tends to protect its domestic businesses or industries without regard to the consequences for the other Member States or the Community. However, the same Member State with the same self-image demands strict control of state aid in the neighboring countries."[35]

The tendency in the subsidy race for one state in the EU or internationally to outdo the other with subsidies can be explained with the help of game theory. A subsidy-free market is a public good. The good is the welfare gains resulting from the non-subsidized resource allocation in free trade. There is non-rival consumption and non-excludability. How could one make these welfare gains of the competition understandable and tangible? Most likely, by referring to the economic development of the FRG in the last 40 years before reunification and comparing this with the economic development of the GDR. Here a competition system there in the east a subsidy system without competition.

The economic and political costs incurred by the governments of the EU Member States, if they decide to subsidize their own industry or, in the other case, not to subsidize, should be converted into a pay-out matrix (see Fig. 10.1). Here, only a distinction is made between the government of a single state A and the 14 other governments of the EU Member States, N. Welfare income, which arises in a sub-income-free market through the more efficient allocation of resources for each state, is set at 4 and the amount of subsidy payments at 2. The social costs, such as unemployment benefits and the internal political costs incurred by the government in avoiding the subsidization of its own industry by the reactions of the affected interest groups (trade unions, voters) to the then necessary job losses, are estimated at 2, Also, the political gain, which occurs in the form of subsidization, or more precisely in the preservation of jobs in the form of increased political acceptance, is estimated at 2 (Fig. 10.1).

There are four combinations:

- If only a does not choose to subsidize, while the other governments subsidize, a bears the social and political costs of refusing subsidies without any benefit in the form of a welfare benefit (combination 1–2).
- For a to receive the maximum payout, a has to subsidize, but all other governments will have subsidies. In this case, a can avoid his political social costs, since he succeeds in strengthening the competitiveness of his industry beyond that of foreign countries within the framework of the "beggar-thy-neighbor-policy". Added to this is the welfare gain of the state through imports that have become cheaper abroad within the non-subsidized market. The state thus takes part in the public good without contributing anything (free-rider behavior; combination 2–1).

If a and all n governments decide not to subsidize, then for all governments, after deducting social and political costs, the increase in wealth caused by the optimal allocation of resources results in the payment of 2 (Comp. 1–1). However, no

[35] *Wettbewerbskommissar Monti* quoted from *Noll*, Bernd (2002), p. 19. The theoretical background and economic implications of this behavior under the unanimity rule in the Council of Ministers. See *Conrad*, Christian A. (2003).

a\n	not subsidize [1]	subsidize [2]
not subsidize [1]	2, 2	(− 2), 0
subsidize [2]	4, 2	0, 0

Fig. 10.1 Decision situation of the subsidy race

government will be willing to subsidize its industry without being certain that all other governments will do so.

- All will therefore tend to "beggar-thy-neighbor-policy", ie to take the free-rider position, which automatically leads to the suboptimal combination 2–2 (dominant strategy), where no non-subsidy market as a public good comes. It is thus the game-theoretical situation of a prisoner's dilemma.[36]

However, the Government has certainty that all other governments will refrain from subsidies if it receives binding commitments in the form of contracts with the other governments or through an enforceable third party. The two alternative approaches to international subsidy control are therefore either binding, enforceable contracts or an international competition authority with its own sanctioning instruments. Crucially, a code of conduct and sanctions that exclude free-rider behavior are to be instructed.

Summary

Why are there subsidies I?

New Political Economy: Maximizing the votes of politicians in organized unions at the expense of poorly organized taxpayers (burden of taxes is smaller than organizational costs and not directly attributable). Even better to subsidize subsidies through loans, since the future generation is not represented (Decisions at the expense of third parties), unemployment burdened the state funds. Subsidy or subsidy programs can be marketed as political activities. Welfare gains from unrestricted competition are diffuse and only set in the long term. Political rationality thus dominates economic rationality. Subsidies are negative in the long run. Research

(continued)

---

[36]On the background of the situation of a prisoner's dilemma in game theorysee *Holler* M. J./*Illing*, G. (1993), pp. 8f and *Voigt,* Stefan (2002), pp. 48.

funding sounds good, but see disadvantages. Intervention in competition reduces welfare!

Why are there subsidies II?

Subsidy-free market as a public good, prisoner's dilemma leads to the subsidy race: Solution: Binding commitments in the form of contracts with other governments (Subvention Code) or by an enforceable third party (International Competitions Authority). The active, formative industrial policy tries to strengthen the national economy through targeted research funding, whereas the reactive industrial policy aims to delay the structural change with the help of subsidies. Neither active nor reactive industrial policy are welfare-promoting. Rather, they intervene in a functioning market mechanism and thus reduce welfare. Only the financing of basic research is welfare promoting.

Comprehension Questions

1. Weigh the pros and cons of:
   (a) active shaping of industrial policy through research funding?
   (b) reactive industrial policy with the help of maintenance subsidies?
2. Why are subsidies so widespread despite their disadvantages?

   Graph the decision-making situation: A subsidy-free market is a public good. The good is the increase in wealth that results from the non-subsidized resource allocation of free trade. There is non-rival consumption and non-excludability. It only distinguishes between the government of a single state a and the other governments of the EU Member States, n. The welfare gain that arises in a non-subsidy-free market (in n-countries) through the more efficient allocation of resources for each state, especially through cheap imports, is 4. The social costs, such as unemployment benefits and the domestic political costs contributed by the government, renouncement of subsidization of the proprietary industry by the reactions of the involved interest groups (unions, voters) on the then necessary job losses, are numbered with 2.

References

Büro für internationale Forschungs- und Technologiekooperation. (2003). *Das 6. Rahmenprogramm für Forschung, technologische Entwicklung und Demonstration*, Internetabfrage vom 16.11.03. Accessed from www.bit.ac.at/FP6.hmt

Conrad, C. A. (1997). *Europäische Stahlpolitik zwischen politischen Zielen und ökonomischen Zwängen*. Baden-Baden: Nomos.

Conrad, C. A. (2003). The dysfunctions of unanimity: Lessons from the EU steel crisis. *Journal of Common Market Studies, 41*(1), 157–169.

Conrad, C. A. (2005). Taking stock: The history of European steel crisis policy. *The Journal of European Economic History, 34*(1), 283–306.

EU-Kommission. (1992). *EGKS-Stahl, 10 Jahre Forschung und Entwicklung 1981-1990*, Brüssel.

Hamm, W. (1979). Staatsaufsicht über wettbewerbspolitische Ausnahmebereiche als Ursache ökonomischer Fehlentwicklungen. *ORDO (Jahrbuch für die Ordnung von Wirtschaft und Gesellschaft), 29*, 156–172.

Holler, M. J., & Illing, G. (1993). *Einführung in die Spieltheorie*. Berlin: Springer.

Krüger, M. (1998). Kann Industriepolitik die Wettbewerbsfähigkeit verbessern? In J. B. Donges & A. Freytag (Eds.), *Die Rolle des Staates in einer globalisierten Wirtschaft, Schriften zur Wirtschaftspolitik* (Vol. 6, pp. 217–235). Stuttgart: Lucius & Lucius.

Laussel, D., & Montet, C. (1995). Discussion. In P. Buigues, A. Jacquemin, & A. Saphir (Eds.), *European policies on competition, trade and industry* (pp. 49–64). Aldershot: Edward Elgar.

Morgenstern, O. (1966). Vollkommene Voraussicht und wirtschaftliches Gleichgewicht. In H. Albert (Ed.), *Theorie und Realität*. Mohr Siebeck: Tübingen.

Narjes, K. H. (1986). Europas Antwort auf die technologische Herausforderung. *ifo-Schnelldienst, 23*, 9–27.

Noll, B. (2002). *Wirtschafts- und Unternehmensethik in der Marktwirtschaft*. Stuttgart: Kohlhammer.

Schumpeter, J. A. (1949). The creative response in economic history. *The Journal of Economic History, VII*, 149–159.

Starbatty, J. (1987). Die ordnungspolitische Dimension der EU-Technologiepolitik. *ORDO (Jahrbuch für die Ordnung von Wirtschaft und Gesellschaft), 38*, 155–180.

Starbatty, J., & Vetterlein, U. (1995). *Die Technologiepolitik der Europäischen Gemeinschaft, Entstehung, Praxis und ordnungspolitische Konformität*. Baden-Baden: Nomos.

Staudt, E. (1986). Forschungs- und Technologiepolitik – unverzichtbares Element moderner Staatsführung? In N. Walter (Ed.), *Was würde Erhard heute tun?* Stuttgart: Poller.

Stehn, J. (2001). Wettbewerbs- und Industriepolitik. In W. Weidenfeld & W. Wessels (Eds.), *Jahrbuch der europäischen Integration 2000/2001*. Berlin: Duncker & Humblot.

Szettle, D. (2000). *Auswirkungen der Industriepolitik der EU auf die internationale Wettbewerbsfähigkeit der europäischen Wirtschaft*. Freiburg: Haufe.

Voigt, S. (2002). *Institutionenökonomik*. UTB: München.

von Borries, R. (1999). Statement: Grundsätzliche Aspekte des europäischen Beihilfenrechts. In J. Schwarze (Ed.), *Neue Entwicklungen auf dem Gebiet des europäischen Wettbewerbsrechts*. Baden-Baden: Nomos.

von Hayek, F. A. (1975). Die Anmaßung von Wissen. *ORDO (Jahrbuch für die Ordnung von Wirtschaft und Gesellschaft), 26*, 12–21.

Winter, H. (1994). *Interdependenzen zwischen Industriepolitik und Handelspolitik der Europäischen Gemeinschaft*. Baden-Baden: Nomos.

Monetary Policy and the European Central Bank

11

What Follows Why?

Since you have gotten to know the first fundamental monetary theory relationships and also the subject of inflation in neoclassical terms, we will now deal with the monetary policy of the European Central Bank (ECB), whose primary objective is price stability. The knowledge gained here will allow you to form your own opinion about the development of money market interest rates.

In order to be able to correctly assess the goal of maintaining price stability, we first need to understand what inflation means.

Learning Goals

You should be able to

– explain in your own words how inflation is calculated and
– describe the economic effects.

The goal is finally that you can explain

– which instruments the ECB
– uses to track what goals
– how it uses them and
– what effect they have on the money market.

© The Editor(s) (if applicable) and The Author(s), under exclusive license to Springer
Fachmedien Wiesbaden GmbH, part of Springer Nature 2020
C. A. Conrad, *Political Economy*,
https://doi.org/10.1007/978-3-658-30884-1_11

11.1   Inflation

▶ **Definition Inflation (Deflation)** Continuing increase (decline) in the general price level.

11.1.1 What Is Inflation?

It is important to note that this definition refers to the general price level and a sustained increase. This means that an average of many prices must rise and that this increase is permanent so does not regress. The idea is to prevent the constant fluctuations of individual prices.

Perceived inflation is when households notice inflation more than they are affected by it, due to their distorted perception. If the prices of everyday commodities increase more than the prices of the commodities one buys less often, more inflation can be "felt" than usual.

> Lenin is said to have declared that the best way to destroy the Capitalist System was to debauch the currency. By a continuing process of inflation, governments can confiscate, secretly and unobserved, an important part of the wealth of their citizens.[1]—John Maynard Keynes

Discuss What does Lenin mean by that and why is he quoted by Keynes?

First, he says that inflation is a means to destroy the capitalist system. He points to the harmfulness of inflation or, conversely, to the importance of price stability for the market economy system. He also shows us the central effect of inflation on wealth and income distribution. For example, in many wars the currency of the enemy was reprinted and distributed in order to damage the economic system of the enemy.[2] The second part of the quote describes the possibility that the state finances its expenditures by printing money. The new money displaces the old in the bidding process for the same amount of goods. As a result of the increase in the price of money, citizens can no longer buy the same amount of goods as before.

Measuring Inflation

To calculate the persistent changes in the general price level, you need a representative shopping cart. The consumer price index (inflation rate) is intended to reflect the consumption structure of an average German household. It is a Las Peyres price index with a fixed

---

[1]Keynes, John Maynard (1929), p. 219–220.

[2]See Handelsblatt vom 17.02.2012, http://www.handelsblatt.com/panorama/aus-aller-welt/zweiter-weltkrieg-nazis-wollten-mit-gefaelschten-pfundscheinen-den-briten-schaden/6225748.html

base year. H. the index values refer to the consumption structures of the year (volumes 2005: 5chocolate bars and 2 pieces of chewing gum), which is set as base year.

$$Lp(x, y)_{0,1} = \frac{px_1 \cdot qx_0 + py_1 \cdot qy_0}{px_0 \cdot qx_0 + py_0 \cdot qy_0}$$

(p: Preise, q: Mengen, mit den Perioden 0 und 1)

Example

$$Price\ Index\ (Laspeyres) = \frac{(5 \times current\ chocolate\ bar\ price) + (2 \times current\ chewing\ gum\ price)}{(5 \times chocolate\ bar\ price2010) + (2 \times chewing\ gum\ price2010)}$$

What Does the Reported Inflation Rate Tell Us?

If you look at the weighting scheme, you should ask yourself if you buy the same goods in this structure throughout the year. Only if that is the case does the declared inflation apply to you. For example, not all people will spend about 3.8% of their annual expenditures on alcohol and tobacco.

Often one sees overviews over the historical development of the inflation rate. However, one has to keep in mind that inflation rates are hardly comparable as there were substantial changes in information gathering. From 2002, quality improvements will be excluded from the prices in Germany, and from 2004 the hedonic price inflator will be used, which will exclude capacity improvements. If a computer calculates twice as fast, it will only be included in the shopping cart at half the price. Unfortunately, the influence this has on price development cannot be estimated. Unfortunately, the Federal Statistical Office does not provide statistics according to the old calculation.[3] However, if one imagines that since then it is trying to grasp everything that represents a quality improvement, then the influence becomes more tangible. For example, the computing power of computers increases and the standard equipment add-ons for cars are excluded from the price. The impact of quality adjustments will be limited to those goods where quality improvements are possible, ie technical products. But this approach is unilateral, quality deteriorations are not considered.

We must wonder what the advantage of such a method can be from the point of view of consumers. Statistically, it may be correct if the Office tries to make the products comparable in order to capture the price effect. But this is not known to the consumers. And even if it were known to them, the influence on their expenses could not be assessed. On the contrary, the consumer assumes that the quality improvements will benefit him fully from his income. However, he will not be able to explain that he can no longer buy the same

---

[3]See Statistisches Bundesamt, Qualitätsbereinigung in der
  Verbraucherpreisstatistik, Juli 2006/Themenkasten der Preisstatistik Nr. 35.

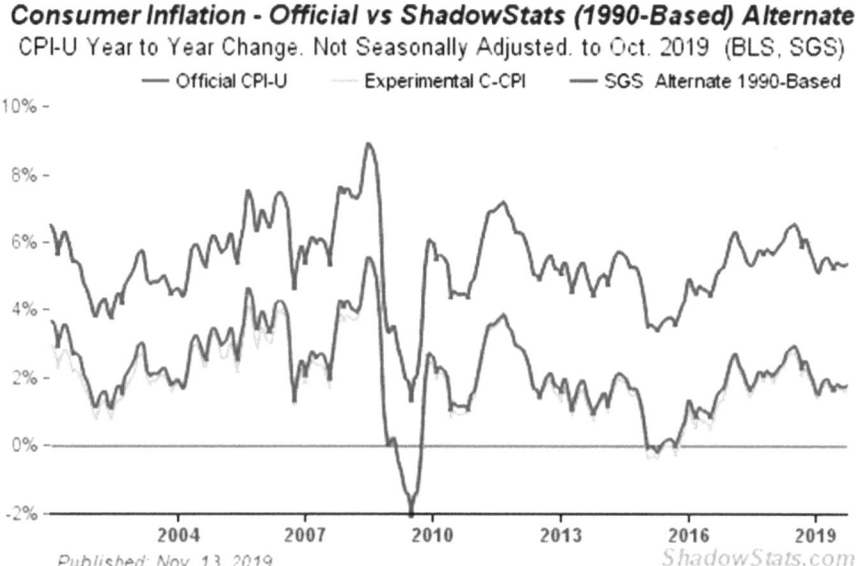

Fig. 11.1 Consumer price index according to old (90s) and new calculation in the USA. Source: Shadowstats, http://www.shadowstats.com/alternate_data/inflation-charts (18.11.2019)

goods as in previous years with zero inflation at constant income. He will not realize that this is due to quality improvements. It is also questionable whether the consumer, for example, would still see a Commodore64 as a PC today and thus consider it as equivalent. The structure of the shopping basket also influences the rate of inflation. Thus, the change of the basket of goods has reduced the inflation rates from 2010 to 2012.

For the US, the Internet site Shadowstats calculated an annual inflation rate of approx. 5% on the basis of the 1990 method compared to a reported one of approx. 1.1% (see Fig. 11.1).[4]

11.1.2 Disadvantages of Inflation

1. **The price relations are distorted**

   Inflation is a staggered process of price increases. Not all companies raise prices at the same time. As a result, some prices rise while others remain the same. Relative price increases can occur at the high absolute levels. If all prices rise, price increases are no longer distinguishable from inflation increases due to higher demand or higher costs. Allocating production to the more cost-effective or demand-driven direction then

---

[4]See On the basis of the calculation method of 1980 Shadowstats even comes to approx. 8%. http://www.shadowstats.com/alternate_data/inflation-charts (Abfrage vom 11.06.2016).

becomes difficult. In addition, it can lead to misallocations. For example, if the price of plastic increases faster than steel, companies could shift the production of technical equipment to higher steel shares. This is associated with costs. Finally, when the price of steel rises, the reorganization of production turns out to be a misallocation.

2. **The function of money as a store of value is lost**

   The loss of value of money will cause investors to switch to more stable money or to invest it in real assets. It comes to capital flight.

3. **Asset loss**

   If money loses its value, this is equivalent to the expropriation of wealth owners with far-reaching consequences. People who have worked all their lives are cheated of the proceeds of their labor. So it was a mistake to save, to work more than you need for a living, thus losing the most important performance incentive of the market economy, property.

   Assuming that the inflation rate is 2.5% (ECB inflation target: below but close to 2%), then the purchasing power of capital would be halved after 30 years. If a sum of €50,000 increases to €100,000 in the same period, then this growth covers just the purchasing power reduction by the inflation.[5] Taxation would reduce the purchasing power of capital. A flat deduction of the inflation rate in the tax base or at least higher tax exemptions would be urgently needed here because only real interest rates represent an increase in efficiency. In addition, the taxation of nominal interest rates prefers investment forms without capital consumption through inflation, such as rentable real estate, for which reason the capital allocation is distorted.

4. **Redistributions**

   Even a small, creeping inflation leads to sustainable redistribution. For example an inltation rate of 2,5% leads to a 50% reduction of purchasing power in 30 years. All persons who are entitled to fixed payments are disadvantaged, whereas the debtors, or better the ones who must pay, profit.

   Creditor-Debtor Hypothesis: Debtors have to repay less in purchasing power than they have borrowed. Crucial here is the question of whether the lending rate sufficiently compensates for the loss of value.

   Treasury hypothesis: The state is usually the largest debtor. It benefits because its tax revenues increase with inflation. The VAT increases proportionally and the income tax is delayed. Here the state benefits from the cold progression, i.e. the increase in tax rates due to inflation-related income increases. Finally, the state profits from the nominal interest tax. The inflation compensation contained in the interest is also taxed. Companies, too, benefit from inflation because they buy their inputs earlier and thus cheaper than they sell the produced goods. Retirees and fixed income recipients are at a

---

[5]See Manager Magazin vom 27.06.2007 http://www.manager-magazin.de/finanzen/geldanlage/0,2828,490041,00.html and http://www.0711-aktienclub.de/download_gratis_Inflation.htm (Abfrage am 3.05.2011).

disadvantage because their salaries are only adjusted, if at all, to inflation (pensioner hypothesis, wage-lag hypothesis).

5. **Risk premium on interest**

In the short term, households are subject to so-called money illusion. They are surprised by the inflation. The real interest rate falls, because timely inflation is not demanded. The investor bears the interest rate risk of rising interest rates. In this case, a later investment would have been more advantageous for him. Though he could improve, but because of the uncertainty he wants to get paid with a risk premium. Added to this is the risk of inflation. In the long term, however, savers not only demand an inflation equalization, but due to the uncertainty of how inflation develops, there is also a risk premium on interest rates. That means the real interest rate is rising, which reduces the economic growth.

6. **Employment effects**

Real wages also fall because workers do not promptly seek inflation compensation because of illiquidity. As real wages fall, employment increases, which is why the context of the Phillips curve is valid in the short term (see Fig. 11.2). In the long term, however, the expectations are adjusted to why the wage-price wage spiral can come about (see Fig. 11.3). Like savers, workers demand a risk premium on wages to hedge against inflation. Real wages increase, causing unemployment. Here's a quote from Abraham Lincoln: " You can fool some of the people all of the time, and you can fool all of the people some of the time, but you can not fool all of the people all of the time."

Politicians in particular are tempted to aim for inflation because the population rates unemployment more negatively than inflation.

The welfare losses from inflation of ten percent are estimated at between 0.3% and 0.45% of the national product. The impact coefficient of an inflation increase on life satisfaction is -1.2 and that of unemployment is 2.

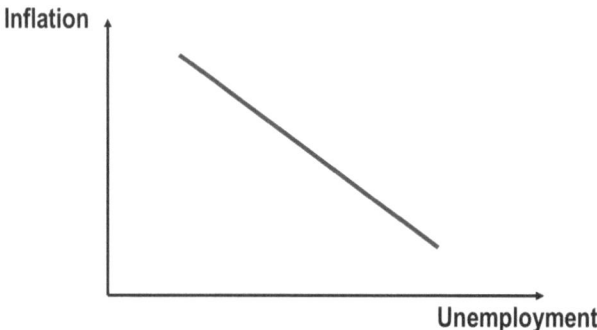

Fig. 11.2 Short-term Phillips curve (The original Phillips curve of 1958, based on UK data from 1861 to 1957, showed the relationship between average nominal wage increases and the unemployment rate)

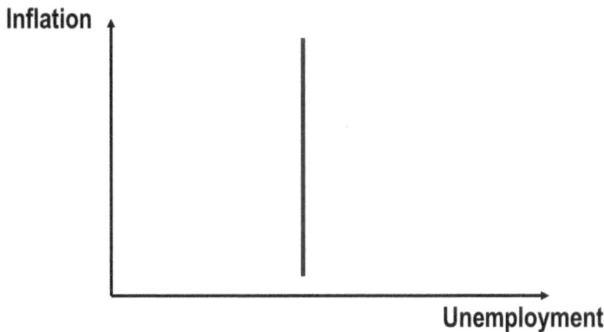

Fig. 11.3 Long-term Phillips curve

The welfare losses from unemployment (0.028 points) are estimated to be higher than those from inflation (0.012 points), so it seems understandable if, according to Di Tella et al., people were willing to increase the inflation rate by 1.66% if the unemployment rate increases by 1%.[6]

Disadvantages of Deflation
Deflation is the reverse process of inflation. The key issue is that companies spend less than they spend on inputs, because they buy their inputs earlier and thus more expensively than they sell the goods they produce. This results in losses, which can lead to bankruptcies. If prices fall very heavily, there may also be a shift in purchases because one hopes for an even cheaper purchase. For this, however, substantial price reductions may be required. One can observe in sales that the prices must be lowered by 30% and more in order to reach a purchase incentive.

This has a negative effect on the sales of the companies. However, as we will see later, the real problem is the cause of deflation, the massive decline in demand. Deflation then occurs together with depression.

▶ **Definition** Hyperinflation is when the monthly inflation rate is over 50%.

This implies a more than a hundredfold price increase in 1 year (13,000%). Hyperinflation occurs when the state finances large budget deficits through the money printing press. The profits of the state, which come to him through the monopoly of money production, are called seniorage. The rapid destruction of value and value change leads to the money losing its function as a store of value, arithmetic unit and medium of exchange. The money is then

---

[6]See DiTella, Rafael; MacCulloch, Robert J.; Oswald, Andrew J. (2001), pp. 335–341.

rejected by people as a means of payment. The monetary functions then go to unofficial currencies, such as US dollars or cigarettes as in the German hyperinflation of 1923 shows.

Conclusion
Inflation has a system-destroying effect, because central functions (price signals) and incentives (property) of the market-based system are impaired just as much as the functions of money as a store of value, arithmetic unit and medium of exchange. The measurement concepts can only partially capture inflation.

Comprehension Questions

1. Define inflation.
2. Why are inflation and deflation harmful?

Exercises
1. In an economy, only cell phones and caravans are manufactured. Using the data in the table, calculate the rate of price increase for the sample quantities car and bread analogous to the price index of the standard of living (Laspeyres).

Year	2010	2020
Caravan Price	60.000€	70.000€
Cell phones	10€	15€
Number of caravans	1.100	1.200
Number of cell phones	900.000	300.000

11.2 Advantages of a Single European Currency Area

There are many reasons for the creation of a European Monetary Union.

1. **Exchange rate fluctuations omitted**
   This is especially beneficial for the economy. The prices for imports and exports can be planned. Hedging and conversion fees are waived. For private individuals this eliminates the annoying exchange of currencies on the border. Prices are shown in one currency in EMU, which increases market transparency. The buyers can compare the prices better, which is why competition increases. It is produced locally and the inputs purchased where it is cheapest. As a result, the European division of labor increases. European markets grow together. However, the merger of many different countries also gives rise to distributional effects resulting from the common currency. If

you take e.g. Germany, Germany traditionally shows a high export surplus, which caused a strong currency with a steady appreciation trend against other currencies whose countries tended to import more than they exported. If all these countries are in a single currency area, there are upward and downward tendencies. This means that the currency will become weaker from a German point of view and stronger from a southern European point of view. For the German economy, this means an increase in their competitiveness and, as a result, more jobs. For German households, however, this will increase the price of their imports or foreign travel. The same applies vice versa for the southern European countries.

2. The vulnerability to disruptions in the foreign exchange markets is lower. For example, speculators need much more capital to move the euro in some direction than they would have with one of the previous currencies.

3. Larger currency areas enable more developed capital markets, more products and lower costs (economies of large scale)

4. Greater seniority profits arise as the single currency becomes more attractive as a reserve, transaction and clearing currency. A large currency becomes the reserve currency and is used as the transaction currency. Consequently, a higher demand arises. The respective central bank prints the money and gets an equivalent for it. If the foreign exchange is invested abroad, interest can be earned.

5. Common European currency strengthens European citizens' identification with Europe, integration and political cohesion.

11.3   The Founding of the European Central Bank

On 9/10 in December 1991, the EC Heads of State and Government agreed on a European Union, which would initially have three pillars: a common foreign and security policy, cooperation in domestic and legal affairs, and finally Economic and Monetary Union (EMU). These were important historical steps on the way to a political unification of Europe, unprecedented in this form. The preamble to the EU Treaty states: "Determined to take the process of European integration launched by the founding of the European Union to a new level". In terms of European policy, the founding of the European Monetary Union was a success. All EU Member States except Great Britain, Denmark and Sweden opted for EMU accession over time. The start of EMU can also be described as successful in relation to the organizational and institutional tasks to be solved. Without delay, all the steps in the Maastricht Treaty for the establishment of the European Central Bank have so far been implemented. In addition, EMU already fulfilled many tasks and expectations with the introduction of the euro as the single European currency: the transaction or exchange costs of the European currencies fell away. The EU internal market got the lack of price transparency through a single European transaction and accounting unit and the European political integration as an incentive at least once in advance a democratically decisive European monetary policy. With the euro, companies have a consistent and therefore predictable accounting unit for their intra-European exports and imports, and the size of the currency area of the euro offers protection against the dreaded currency attacks by speculators. With the introduction of the euro, the second largest capital market in the world was created and the euro area has become more independent of foreign trade.

The right way to politically integrate Europe has long been argued. The current European Monetary Union is in line with the idea of monetarists of creating a political and economic integration through a single currency rather than the economists' approach that the single European currency should be the culmination of political and economic integration (coronation thesis). Political and economic integration now needs to be implemented. There is still much to do. Finally, the euro sums up countries with different economic and political backgrounds without a single government in a single currency area. The following chapter gives an overview of the numerous unsolved problems of the European Monetary Union. It gives the impression that European politicians and the ECB have rapidly failed in their efforts to comply with the pre-EMU objectives.

11.4   The National Budget Policy

A key problem is the European coordination of national budgetary policies. It remains difficult to understand that European interest rate policy could not be influenced by barely inflated public interest charges or that the ECB and its Member States would accept the insolvency of one of its members. In principle, the rules of EMU were clearly and restrictively defined. Article 123 of the Treaty on the Functioning of the European Union (TFEU) prohibits the ECB and national central banks from financing public deficits. Here there is a legal interpretation that the ECB allows government bonds to be bought on the secondary market because this is not a direct state financing. On the other hand, if this provision is based on economic considerations, this is a state financing not covered by the Treaty. Economically, it makes no difference whether the ECB buys the bond directly from the states or indirectly from third parties. If the ECB buys government bonds on the secondary market, it creates demand for these bonds. The interest and thus the cost of the national debt will fall and possibly create a demand if there was no private demand. If market participants know that and when the ECB buys government bonds, they can buy them before the ECB gets them and use the bid and asked discrepancy at its expense (frontrun strategy).

Article 125 TFEU: 'The Community is not liable for the liabilities of central governments. . . . ("No-bail-out clause"). Art. 126 TFEU: "Member States avoid excessive government deficits." It is true that neither the EU nor its member states are liable for the debts of individual EU countries. However, Article 103a (2) TFEU does not provide for financial assistance if a Member State is experiencing difficulties or is threatened by serious difficulties. Although the ECB is independent in its decisions and lending to governments is contractually forbidden, European monetary policy does not take place in a vacuum and is also decided by central bankers from countries with different economic cycles, economic interests and cultures of stability. Uncoordinated budgetary policy is therefore also referred to as the open flank of EMU. This has then been confirmed in the case of Greece.

Following strong fiscal consolidation coupled with some accounting policies, a large number of countries have largely met the convergence criteria. Italy and Belgium, however, exceeded the predetermined debt ratio of 121.6% and 122.2% of their gross domestic product in 1997, and were nevertheless allowed entry. So far, the convergence criteria and the inexplicable exit of EMU from stability-oriented countries during the transition phase have led to a disciplining of these countries. From 1 January 2001, however, according to the prevailing opinion, only the Stability Pact can prevent excessive budgetary policy at the expense of the EMU community. At the insistence of Germany, which was considered a model for stability policy, in 1997 the EU member states adopted the so-called Stability Pact in the form of two Council ordinances and a resolution of the European Council. It envisages fines by a decision of ECOFIN, the Council of Ministers for Economic and Financial Affairs, with a qualified majority if the government deficits of 3% of GDP continue to be exceeded after several interim steps. Exceptions are only possible on a temporary basis in the event of a serious economic situation, which must also be determined by ECOFIN by a qualified majority. In addition, non-binding annual stability and convergence programs to be submitted annually by the EMU countries will ensure a balanced medium-term budget. Background of the Stability Pact is the fiscal-political prisoners' dilemma of a monetary union of states with autonomous national financial policy. The domestic benefits of sovereign debt benefit the respective government alone, while the disadvantages of a deterioration in the creditworthiness of the EMU as a community of all countries are in the form of increased long-term interest rates (free-rider problem).

The Stability and Growth Pact therefore seeks to achieve an almost balanced budget or a budget surplus as a medium-term objective.

All the more dangerous was the decision of the EU Council of Ministers, in June 1999, to approve a transgression of the upper limit for Italy's new indebtedness under the Stability Pact, due to a much lower than expected growth rate of the gross domestic product. The decision by the European Commission to reject Greece's entry into the EMU on 01.01.2001 despite the clear lack of convergence criteria and the ECB's doubts regarding the consolidation of the European Central Bank, as the debt ratio stood at 104.4% in 1999 State finances, must be criticized in this context.[7]

While still in their 1998 stability and convergence programs, countries planned to further reduce the budget deficit (Belgium, Austria, Portugal, Greece, Germany, Spain, France, Italy and the Netherlands) or to further increase their budget surplus (Luxembourg, Ireland, Finland and Sweden as well as Great Britain and Denmark). The average deficit in the euro area should therefore decrease from 2.3% of its gross domestic product to 0.8% in

---

[7]See Conrad, Christian A. (2002), p. 97–100.

2002. However, some influential factors were not taken into account in this superficial perspective even at that time, which is why both the European Monetary Institute and the Deutsche Bundesbank saw in the convergence programs of the countries for the reference year 1997 not only significant shortcomings in the field of public finances, but the need for urgent action. Meanwhile, it is clear that the postulated goals of the countries are achieved by almost no one.

Already in meeting the convergence criteria when entering the EMU, the countries retouched their accounts to reach the deficit targets. Debt obligations were postponed, shifted to non-budgetary positions, or quiet reserves liquidated (state assets privatized) to generate extraordinary income. In addition, governments increased taxes and duties. Government spending was reduced—but above all in government investment rather than state consumption. The government investment ratio of the EU fell from 3% in 1991 to 2.2% in 1997. This development was understandable against the background of the convergence criteria to be met, but even then it was questionable whether it made sense and whether it should be permanent. It must not be forgotten that the reduction in budget deficits was achieved thanks to a positive economic trend and thus also high tax revenues and historically low interest rates. The EU Commission has therefore calculated so-called deficit benchmarks for individual countries, taking into account their respective sensitivity to the economy. Germany, Greece, France, Italy and Austria had a deficit of a maximum of approx. 1%, Belgium, Denmark, Spain, Ireland, Luxembourg, the Netherlands, Portugal and the United Kingdom have a deficit of between 0% and 1%, and Sweden and Finland even show a surplus in order to maintain the targeted 3% deficit even if the economy slows down in order to reach that goal. The target projections of the Stability Programs and Convergence Programs were too ambitious: under the 1997 economic conditions, Italy and Belgium would need 15 years and Greece 10 years to achieve the 60% debt-to-GDP ratio. From this point of view, even then there was a certain likelihood that the cyclical exception of the Stability and Growth Pact would be claimed. It should also not be forgotten that even holding the debt ratio at 60% with a deficit ratio of 3% is based on the assumption of nominal economic growth of 5%. A significant interest rate and thus also budgetary risk was seen in the high debt levels of Belgium, Italy and Greece.

In 1999, the ECB was already criticizing the planned deficit ratios as too high to be able to compensate for cyclical tax reductions.[8] Unfortunately, a qualified majority in the Council of Ministers was too quick to accept a blue letter, which would have been very inconvenient for the Schröder government in the Bundestag campaign year. This political decision, also referred to as the "decision of the crows",[9] has discredited the European Monetary Union. Finally, since all the sanctions of the Stability Pact must be adopted by a qualified majority, its importance is called into question. A loss of confidence was certainly

---

[8] See EZB (1999), p. 63.
[9] See Hort, Peter (2002).

also the result of Germany being the former model of stability policy and the initiator of the Stability Pact, which for the first time politically erased the mechanism of the Stability Pact.

11.5   Problems of a Uniform Interest Rate Policy

Monetary policy is overwhelmed by such different economic situations in the individual euro states. A uniform euro interest rate is always based on the average development of all euro states. As a result, the rate of interest rates for Germany was relatively high at the beginning of the monetary union, and too low for the southern European countries and Ireland due to differences in economic conditions, which led to a sharp rise in consumer and property prices in these countries.[10]

The first rate cut on 9.12.1998 to a uniform level of 3% means only an interest reduction of 0.3% for Germany, whereas for Spain a reduction of interest rates of at least 1.75%, for Portugal of 2.10% and for Ireland even of 3.35%.[11] The consequence was significant deviations in the rates of price increase between the countries. In most countries with traditionally high inflation rates, the 2% were already exceeded in 1998 and 1999 (Spain: 1999, Portugal and Ireland: 1998 and 1999).

How difficult the transition to a common currency is when countries show different economic trends and also pursue diverging fiscal policies was demonstrated by the sovereign debt crisis following the financial crisis. Countries such as Ireland, Spain, Greece and Portugal had pursued an expansionary fiscal policy or, as in the case of Ireland and Spain, a credit and real estate bubble. Both led to high demand-related growth rates combined with corresponding wage and price increases. From a monetary policy perspective, key interest rates in these countries would have had to increase and the money supply would have had to be reduced, which was not possible due to the divergent economic development of the euro area (see Figs. 11.4 and 11.5). After the financial crisis, strong domestic demand was missing. The states were over indebted and no longer competitive due to wage and price increases.

Lacking their own currency, they were no longer able to regain their competitiveness through currency devaluation.

---

[10]See Schrader, Klaus/Laaser, Claus-Friedrich (2010); Sachverständigenrat für die gesamtwirtschaftliche Entwicklung (2011) and FAZ vom 14.09.2011, http://www.faz.net/aktuell/wirtschaft/eurokrise/beamte-in-griechenland-die-ueberfluessigen-11167253.html

[11]See Starbatty; Joachim (2001), p. 375.

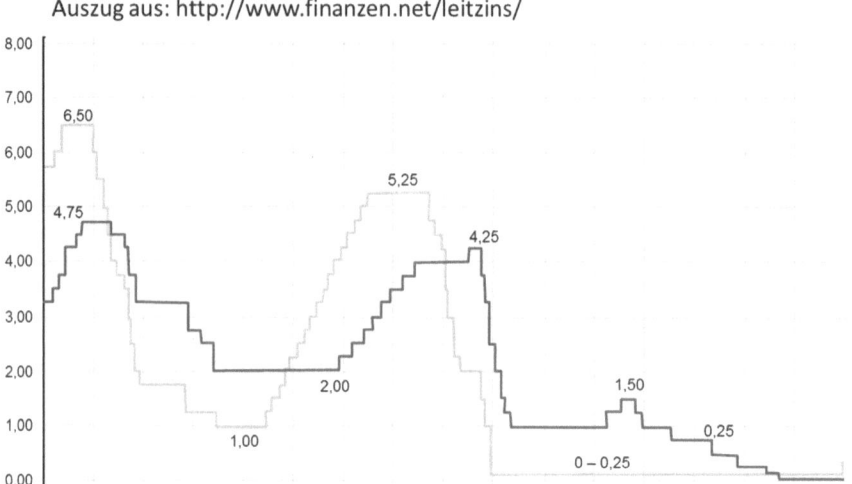

Fig. 11.4 Development of the ECB interest rate in comparison to the US interest rate 2000–2015 (Imprint by courtesy of finanzen.net GmbH. http://www.finanzen.net/leitzins/)

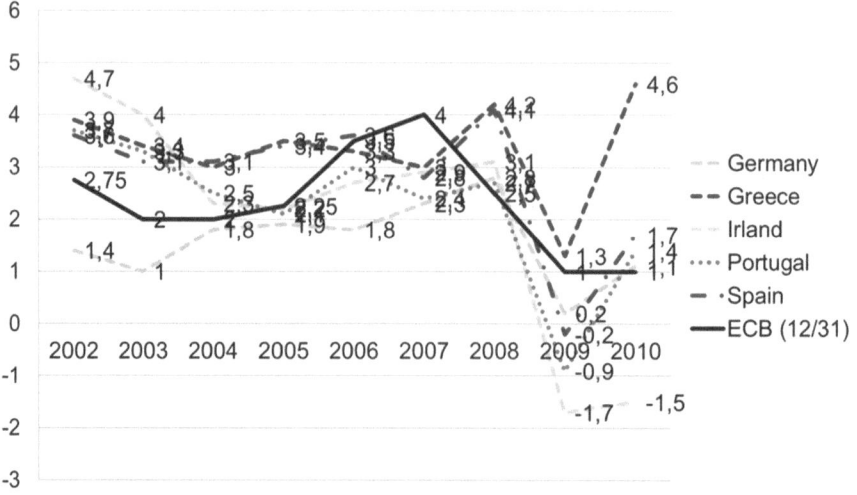

Fig. 11.5 Interest rates and euro area inflation rates. Source: EU-Commission, OECD, EUROSTAT, WKO

11.6   The Lack of Political and Economic Unification of Europe

The ECB also sees sustainable reforms in the labor and goods markets as essential for increasing European growth potential. The strongly segmented or nationally structured bond and equity markets cause ten times higher transaction costs in the euro area than in the US. There are also different supervisory regulations and accounting regulations. A politically unified approach by governments is also lacking in the eurozone as opposed to the US. An inconsistent policy paralyzes. The effects of opposing policies counteract each other. This applies not only to financial and economic policy, but also to foreign policy. Although significant progress on integration was achieved in Amsterdam in 1997 with regard to domestic and legal policy and foreign and security policy, competencies remained with the Member States and there is no Community law. A common military action by the EU still requires unanimity and the use of national armed forces. A political agreement wins not least after the decline of the USSR in foreign policy importance. It lacks a balancing second political global player beside the USA. A one-sided dominance of the USA in world politics would not find international acceptance in the long term. At present, European politicians still owe the unfinished political and economic integration to the euro.

In light of what has been said so far, it is clear how important it is for idealists and politically independent institutions and individuals to pursue the overall objective of a stable currency and the political unification of Europe. European integration has reached a critical point. The move to monetary union has been taken. Many Member States benefited from this. Last but not least, the reduction in long-term interest rates was a major reason for the traditionally less stable EMU countries to join, in order to benefit from the reputation of traditionally stability-oriented countries. The long-term interest rates of the traditionally stabilized countries were in some cases 6.5% lower than those of the less stability-oriented countries before the introduction of the euro.[12]

In the case of state interest payments, formerly less stability-oriented countries were thus able to save billions. Now it is the overriding European interest as a public good to enforce the state's individual interests and the interests of other groups. A levy of national sovereignty is inevitable. The public good Europe is everywhere, in a stability-oriented budgetary policy, domestic and legal policy, the common foreign and security policy or in subsidy-free intra-European competition. What is decisive is that the free-rider behavior of individual states is prevented, in which one state can secure a greater benefit through non-compliant behavior at the expense of others and thus the community solution with the higher benefit for all can no longer be realized. The findings of the New Political Economy are opposed to this. According to the New Political Economy approach, politicians usually do not maximize the common good, but mostly their own benefit. Political offices grant this benefit in the form of power, prestige and income. In order to achieve the desired offices,

---

[12]Annual yields of 10-year government bonds or similar financial instruments, here Italy to Germany in 1985. See Zahlen, Köln (2001), p. 133.

the politician must collect as many electoral votes—one speaks of maximizing votes. This behavioral orientation can be described as political expediency or as "political rationality".[13] The separate national interests of the Member States are therefore of primary importance to the politician. European interest is only important for him if it serves the national interest as long as he is not elected by Europe.

Conclusion

A prerequisite for the realization of the advantages of the European Monetary Union is that the currency is stable, and thus accepted long-term, predictable, and without risk premiums. Furthermore, the economic, wage and fiscal policies of the countries must be stable and not very divergent, because excessive cost increases (different competitiveness) or cyclical differences can no longer be offset by exchange rate changes. However, as emerged after the introduction of the euro, many southern European countries did not follow this rule. More favorable interest rates after the introduction of the euro were used, as in the case of Greece, to widen the level of debt. The borrowed money went into consumption. Almost one in four Greek employees worked in the civil service. Greece consumed more than GDP. The missing goods were imported from abroad and increased foreign debt. The money was not invested, which was one reason why there was a lack of productivity in the following years to service the debt. Due to the high credit-financed government demand, prices and wages rose. In the euro, this competitive disadvantage could no longer be offset by a currency devaluation.[14]

11.7   Organs of the ECB

The Governing Council of the ECB

The Council is responsible for the monetary policy of the ECB. The Governing Council is the supreme governing body of the European Central Bank. It consists of the six members of the Executive Board and the Governors of the national central banks of the 19 Member States of the European Union. As a rule, the Governing Council meets twice a month at the ECB's headquarters in Frankfurt am Main. It evaluates economic and monetary developments as part of the two-pillar strategy and takes its monetary policy decisions every 6 weeks. All national bank governors have a vote in the ECB Governing Council. The accession of Lithuania to the euro area on 1 January 2015 led to an organizational

---

[13]A comprehensive theoretical analysis of political rationality can be found in Frey, Bruno P. (1981).

[14]Sachverständigenrat zur Begutachtung der gesamtwirtschaftlichen Entwicklung (2011); Schrader, Klaus/Laaser, Claus-Friedrich (2010) and faz.net vom 14.09.2011, http://www.faz.net/aktuell/wirtschaft/eurokrise/beamte-in-griechenland-die-ueberfluessigen-11167253.html

reform to limit the number of members. Thus, a rotating system was introduced for the voting rights of the Governors of the national central banks in the Governing Council of the ECB.

The Board of Directors
The Board of Directors is composed of the Presidents, the Vice-Presidents and four other members. Its members are elected by the European Council by qualified majority. The Executive Board is the permanent executive body of the ECB. In this sense, it prepares the Governing Council meetings and sets monetary policy in accordance with the decisions of the Governing Council, and can hereby issue instructions to the national central banks.

Supervisory Board
The Supervisory Board consists of:

- the Chairman (appointed for a non-renewable term of 5 years)
- the Vice-Chairman (chosen from among the members of the ECB's Directorate)
- four representatives of the ECB as well as
- representatives of the national supervisory authorities.

If the national supervisory authority designated by a Member State is not a national central bank (NCB), a representative of the relevant NCB may attend the meetings in addition to the representative of the competent authority concerned.

Conclusion to the Euro Introduction
The performance of the euro up to this point is mixed, as expected. Despite many advantages, the long-term problems of a non-optimal currency area without a single fiscal policy have accumulated lately. In principle, the euro has many advantages, as shown at the beginning, but there are also disadvantages from two of the advantages.

1. The exchange rate fluctuations are eliminated.
    This is especially beneficial for the economy. The prices for imports and exports can be planned. Hedging and conversion fees are waived. For private individuals this eliminates the annoying exchange of currencies on the border. The prices are shown in one currency in the EMU. This increases market transparency. The buyers can compare the prices better, which is why the competition is increasing. It is produced there and the inputs purchased where it is cheapest. As a result, the European division of labor increases. European markets are growing together. However, the currency combination of many different countries also results in distributional effects. If you take e.g. Germany, as Germany traditionally shows a high export surplus. This was followed by a strong currency with a steady appreciation tendency to other currencies whose countries tended to import more than to export. If all of these countries are in a single currency area, there are signs of upward and downward trends. This means that the

currency will become weaker from a German point of view and stronger, for example from a southern European point of view. For the German economy, this means an increase in their competitiveness and, as a result, more jobs. For German households, however, this will increase the price of their imported goods or travel abroad. The same applies vice versa for the southern European countries.

2. A common European currency strengthens European citizens' identification with Europe, integration and political cohesion.

However, as we said earlier, the prerequisite for the realization of these benefits is that the currency is stable, and therefore accepted in the long term, predictable, ie without any risk premiums. Furthermore, the economic, wage and fiscal policies of the countries must be stable and not very different, because excessive cost increases (different levels of competitiveness) or cyclical differences can no longer be offset by changes in exchange rates.

However, as emerged after the introduction of the euro, many southern European countries did not follow this rule. In particular, the more favorable interest rates after the introduction of the euro were used, as in the case of Greece, for an expansion of debt. The borrowed money went into consumption. Almost one in four Greek employees worked in the state. Greece consumed more than it produced when Greek GDP was higher. The missing goods were imported from abroad and increased foreign debt. The money was not invested, which was one reason why there was a lack of productivity in the following years to service the debt. Due to high credit-financed government demand, prices and wages rose. In the euro, this competitive disadvantage could no longer be offset by a currency devaluation.

Monetary policy is overwhelmed by such different economic situations in the individual euro states. A uniform euro interest rate is always based on the average development of all euro states. As a result, the interest rates for Germany were relatively high at the beginning of the monetary union, and too low for the southern European countries and Ireland due to differences in economic conditions, resulting in a sharp rise in consumer and property prices in these countries.

This may be one reason why the ECB's asset study[15] found such distortions between German and Southern European private wealth. Ultimately, however, it cannot be ruled out that the wealth differences can also be attributed to a higher level of tax evasion, also as a consequence of weaker financial management in these countries. How else should a higher fortune have been created with a lower GDP over years? At least it remains out of a sense of justice to demand that these private assets be used for the debt service of the over-indebted countries. Why should German taxpayers pay for the rich Greeks? Last but not least, the German consumer also bears some of the burdens of the introduction of the euro with the weaker buying power of the euro. Of course, this is offset by a higher level of export

---

[15] See Nienhaus, Lisa (2013).

competitiveness. However, unless the wages increase proportionally, this advantage benefits above all the German company owners.

The euro is a historical experiment that combines not only economically, but also culturally different states into one currency area. Heavy adjustment processes were to be expected. This adjustment requirement is currently affecting the southern European countries. Since they can no longer depreciate their currency vis-à-vis the German one in order to become competitive, they must lower wages and prices, which had previously been increased too much, relative to the northern states. Unfortunately, there is no alternative to such a painful adaptation. Especially the higher competitive pressure that results for the southern European countries from the common currency with Germany, must not lead to a European fiscal equalization. This would be unfair for the northern states.

11.8   Fundamentals of the Monetary Policy of the European Central Bank

11.8.1 Political Independence

The history of hyperinflation teaches us that governments are often tempted to finance their expenditures through the central banks if they control them. The result would be hyperinflation. For this reason, many central banks today are politically independent. The independence of the ECB is defined in the institutional framework for the single monetary policy (the Treaty on the Functioning of the European Union, Article 130 TFEU, and the ESCB Statute). Neither the ECB's institutions nor a national central bank nor any member of its decision-making bodies may seek or obtain instructions from EU institutions or bodies, governments of EU Member States or other entities. The European Union (EU) and the governments of the Member States undertake to comply with Article 130 of the FEU Treaty to observe that principle and not to seek to influence the members of the ECB's decision-making bodies.

The ECB has its own budget. Its capital was paid in by the national central banks of the euro area in accordance with the agreed shares.

There is the distinction between the European System of Central Banks (ESCB) and the Eurosystem. The ESCB, on the other hand, comprises the ECB and the NCBs of all EU Member States (Article 282 (1) of the FEU Treaty). The Eurosystem, on the other hand, consists of the ECB and the national central banks of the EU Member States, which have already adopted the euro. The Eurosystem was conceived as a temporary solution, since the formulation of the TFEU assumed that all EU Member States would sooner or later adopt the euro. The distinction between the Eurosystem and the ESCB remains necessary as long as there are EU Member States whose currency is not the euro.

11.8.2 Goals of the ECB

The primary objective of the Eurosystem is to ensure price stability in accordance with Article 127 (1) of the FEU Treaty. It also has a subordinate objective: 'Where possible without prejudice to the objective of price stability, the ESCB shall support the general economic policies of the Union in order to contribute to the achievement of the Union's objectives set out in Article 3 of the Treaty on European Union.' Article 3 of the Treaty on European Union sets out a number of objectives, including sustainable European development based on balanced economic growth and price stability, and a highly competitive social market economy aimed at full employment and social progress. Price stability is thus the primary objective of the ECB's monetary policy. Once this has been achieved, it does everything it can to ensure a favorable economic environment and a high level of employment.

In order to support the economic development of the euro area, the ECB wants to weaken the economic cycles, which is why monetary policy is implemented as counter-cyclical monetary policy. In recession, when aggregate demand is weak, an expansionary monetary policy should stimulate investment the money supply is increased and interest rates are reduced. As a result, commercial banks will be able to spend more on loans and finance investments more cheaply:

$$M \uparrow, i \downarrow \Rightarrow (p \uparrow) \Rightarrow i \downarrow \Rightarrow I(i) \uparrow$$

In the economic boom, when aggregate demand is greater than supply, the ECB takes the opposite measures. Restrictive monetary policy is designed to reduce demand to prevent misallocation and price increases. The money supply is reduced and the interest increased. Banks get less liquidity from the ECB and need to raise interest rates on loans: $M \downarrow, i \uparrow \Rightarrow p \downarrow \Rightarrow i \uparrow \Rightarrow I(i) \downarrow)$.

The Governing Council pursues the objective of price stability by seeking to keep the inflation rate below, but close to, 2% over the medium term. The basis of ECB monetary policy is its two-pillar strategy, which consists of an.

1. Analysis of economic development and comparison with
2. The analysis of monetary development exists.

The background is that the price level defined according to the equation of quantity about the development of the quantity of goods in relation to the money supply, taking into account the speed of money circulation:

$$M \cdot v = Y \cdot p$$

Quantity equation in growth rates: $Y + P = M + V$.

The reference value for money growth would be 4.5% in normal times. The ECB has as a target price level growth below but close to 2%, e.g. 1.8%. Assuming 2.5% real GDP growth and a slight decline in the circulation speed -0.2%, the growth rate is calculated using the equation of quantity:

$$M = Y + P - V, \text{ie } 2.5\% + 1.8\% - (-0.2) = 4.5\%.$$

How can the ECB control the money supply?

11.8.3 The Money Creation Process

The Features of Modern Money (Computer Age)
Today money is no longer just coins and banknotes, but mostly bits and bytes. We can call it virtual money. This computer money can be transported via fiber optic cable in seconds around the world. The electronic money can be increased arbitrarily (almost without costs) and very fast. The electronic money is account money, exact sight deposits or sight deposits. These are the credit balances that you see in your checking account (bankroll), which correspond to claims on the credit institutions or banks.

The central bank has a monetary monopoly. But the banks can multiply the monetary base of the central bank by the money creation process. Only the central bank can increase its liquidity by creating additional money. Only it has received the sovereign monopoly on money and may produce money. Apart from the cash flow from the issue of banknotes and coins, there is still money-laundering through the lending of the commercial banks. Although the central bank has the monopoly on money, banks can multiply the money base of the central bank by the money creation process: Banks do not keep the money of their customers credited to checking or savings accounts in their vaults, but use it to lend credit to other customers. Lending by banks on customers' deposits is one of their key business strategies and economic functions. The loan contribution is made available to the debtor in an account so that it can be used e.g. to buy a car. In each step, new money is created as a sight credit and thus increases the circulating money supply. However, these are not money in the strict sense, as the banks have lent the money, the liquidity, so no longer have it. Only one demand was created and no liquidity as money in the narrower sense. Clients who have deposited their money with the bank are given sight deposits, entitling them to withdraw liquidity at any time, even though the liquidity was already passed on as a loan. If the customer withdraws their sight deposits or uses them to buy goods, the bank must provide it with liquidity again. The banks statistically calculate how much liquidity they have to keep as a reserve based on average customer behavior. This is why every bank becomes illiquid if the customers all simultaneously withdraw the deposited money. This is called a banking run. Customers' sight deposits are considered money because they can be used to buy goods at any time, just like cash in the cash register. From

Fig. 11.6 Balance at 100%
reserve

A	Balance Bank A	P
(2) Reserves **1.000€**		**(1) Deposits** **1.000€**

this point of view, it does not matter that the bank first has to provide liquidity for the purchases.

Since the customer can always pay with the sight deposits, the ECB sees the sight credits as money.

How does the creation of sight deposits by commercial banks work?

Example of Money Creation

1. **Case bank system with 100% reserve hold**

   H. Anton deposits € 1000 at the bank. The bank has 100% reserve in case H. Anton withdraws his money. Since no money is lent here, there are no sight deposits. There is no money creation (see Fig. 11.6).

2. **Case Bank system with proportional reserve**

   H. Anton does not withdraw his money immediately (see Fig. 11.7), which is why the bank lends 80% to H. Bose (which means the amount of money is €1800). H. Bose paid with the money H. Cantor deposited the money at Bank B. Bank B again holds 20% (€160) in reserve and lends €640 to H. Dahmen (making the amount of money €2440), etc. (the process of financial intermediation is a task of the banks). In the process of repeated bank credit, a multiple of the €1000 is spent. But since a part is always kept as a reserve, the process stops when the €1000 have been completely put into reserve. Nevertheless, the economist Friedrich August von Hayek called this the perverse elasticity of the supply of credit. On the other hand, the demand for income generation would be missing if the bank did not re-lend the €1000 from H. Anton. H. Anton worked in a company for €1000 added value so created production. The difference is the profit earned by the company owner.

   The production of his €1000, however, is not in demand if he saves it, rather than consuming anything, but the bank does not lend it and therefore can not turn it into an investment.

In reality, there is a statutory minimum reserve that has to be deposited pro rata with the ECB for each deposit. The minimum reserve reduces the bank multiplier: The banks have to

Fig. 11.7 Money creation and bank balance sheets (Figure based on Mankiw, N. Gregory (2000), p. 539)

Bank A balance

Assets		Liabilities	
Reserves	€ 200	Deposits	€ 1000
Credit	€ 800		

Bank B balance

Assets		Liabilities	
Reserves	€ 160	Deposits	€ 800
Credit	€ 640		

Bank C balance

Assets		Liabilities	
Reserves	€ 128	Deposits	€ 640
Credit	€ 512		

Fig. 11.8 Money cycle with a proportionate reserve of 20%

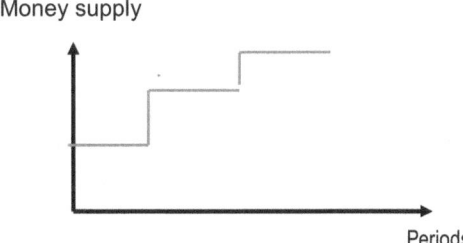

Money supply

Periods

pay 1% to the central bank as a reserve deposit on the banks' short-term liabilities (above all deposits from customers). In addition, depending on the risk, each loan granted must average approx. 8% equity backed by the banks. This means that they can loan approximately 12.5 times their equity as credit. This slows down the money creation process even more.

Money is brought to the bank. There are sight deposits (bank deposits or deposits) Assumption: The money is borrowed from the bank in the same quarter with 20% reserve, again, which is why the money supply increases by 80%. This happens in each period, which is why the money supply increases in each case by 80% of the previous bank deposit. The money supply is as shown in Figs. 11.7 and 11.8 by the repeated lending a multiple of 1000 € (money base B).

The process of creating money can also be described as an infinite geometric series. With a reserve deposit ratio (R/D) of 0.2 the result is:

(with C: cash, R: reserve, D: demand deposits, B: monetary base (C + R), LZ: maturity)

$$\text{Money supply} = [1 + (1 - 0,2) + (1 - 0,2)\,2 + \cdots]\,1.000\;€$$

$$= \frac{1}{0.2}\,1.000\;€ = 5.000\;€ \text{ (infinite geometric series)}$$

Money supply multiplier:

M1	C^P	D^1	Cash + sight deposits = actual money supply
M2	$C^P + D^1$	$+ D^2$	Savings with legal cancellation period (3 months) + long term time deposits up to 2 years
M3	$C^P + D^1 + D^2$	$+ D^3$	Money market fund shares, **repo transactions**, long term bank bonds up to 2 years

Fig. 11.9 ECB monetary terms

$$\Delta M = \frac{1}{R/D} \; \Delta B$$

A multiplier indicates the relationship between a triggering resizing (e.g., change in investment) and the resulting multiple change in dependent variables. The change of Y is examined, if a different size changes permanently. The monetary multiplier indicates how much the money stock has increased at the given reserve/deposit ratio at the end of the money-making process of the commercial banks.

In its monetary policy, the ECB distinguishes M1, M2 and M3 as so-called monetary aggregates (see Fig. 11.9). These are the well-known monetary assets, such as cash and sight deposits (M1), which are being extended by further forms of investment. Outside of the banking sector, this includes circulating liquid cash and overnight deposits from non-banks. These daily deposits can be converted into cash at short notice. M1 is the money that can be used at any time (purchasing power).

The further the money supply is extended to other forms of investment, the lower the likelihood that the money will be used to buy goods and thus affect the price. One criterion here is the duration of the assets. For example, savings accounts have a notice period of 3 months and form with term deposits of up to 2 years maturity M2. This money supply therefore includes M1 plus savings deposits and term deposits with a term of up to 2 years. Term deposits are funds that are invested at the banks for a fixed interest and for a specific term. That is why there are also term deposits. During this term, these funds cannot be disbursed, unless for a fee. At the end of the term, these time deposits are converted back into sight deposits. Savings deposits, on the other hand, are deposits that are usually indefinite and can only be claimed back after the statutory notice period of 3 months. In contrast to sight deposits, time deposits and savings deposits cannot always be used for payments. The interest rates for these changes with the general trend in interest rates.

The aggregate M3 contains M2 and other short-term investments. These include short-term bank bonds (original maturity of up to 2 years), money market fund shares issued by money market funds and so-called repurchase agreements. Bank bonds are securities in which the issuing bank undertakes to repay the nominal value of the bonds after the end of the term. Besides, the buyer gets interest on his invested capital. A repo transaction is a transaction with a repurchase agreement. It serves for short-term fund raising for the bank. (Eg: the bank sells a security to another bank (or central bank) against payment of a sum of money with the obligation to buy back the security after a certain period of time.) The term is usually not more than a year, Often only a few days or one night, this is primarily the financing of commercial banks at the ECB via open market operations. With open market operations, the ECB provides liquidity to commercial banks against the sale or provision of collateral. The transaction will then be redeemed after 7 days and M3 is an important indicator of Eurosystem monetary policy.

Schematically represented as follows:

Money supply: M1 = C + D = short-term purchasing power
Monetary base: B = R + C (liabilities side of the central bank)
C: Cash
R: Reserve
D: Sight deposits

11.8.4 Process of Financial Intermediation by Commercial Banks

How does our financial system work and what is the role of commercial banks in providing money and credit to the economy? The commercial banks are provided with liquidity by the ECB through open market operations (see Fig. 11.10). For this they pay the ECB an

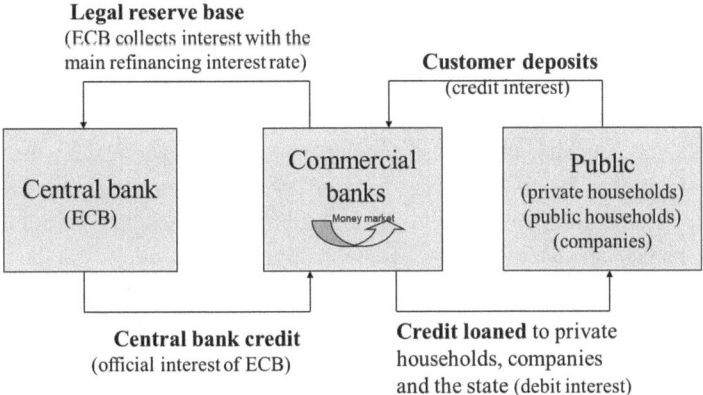

Fig. 11.10 Process of financial intermediation

interest rate. At the same time they receive liquidity through the deposits of the public. These include households, businesses and the state. The commercial banks usually pay an interest (credit interest) for this purpose. For deposits, they must deposit the minimum reserve with the ECB. Conversely, they lend to the public and take a higher borrowing rate.

At the same time, commercial banks can still provide liquidity through the money market.

This shows the central importance of commercial banks for the economic system. The bankruptcy of a commercial bank affects the economy in many ways. The claims of customers to the commercial bank may be lost depending on the deposit insurance. If the bank had provided credit lines to companies, these are no longer available. Both may result in bankruptcies. If necessary, other banks are affected who either have claims on the commercial bank or on companies that are insolvent due to the shortfall in deposits or the lack of credit facilities. If several commercial banks are affected, a financial crisis can occur. For example, during the recent financial crisis, due to the lack of transparency of US real estate derivatives it was enough to collapse the inter-bank market if banks were unable to rule out the default of other banks. The banks did not trust each other and no longer borrowed money. At the height of the crisis even remittances were held back. If you want to get an idea of the effects that the write-downs on US real estate derivatives entailed, you need only imagine in Fig. 11.7 that banks A, B and C would have to write off their loans. The resulting deficit on the asset side is then offset against the equity of the banks.

The above-described process of financial intermediation by the commercial banks (see also Fig. 11.10 above) should also be presented below in the balance sheets of the actors involved: central bank, commercial bank and public.

The commercial banks are provided with liquidity by the ECB through open market operations. This corresponds to a loan from the ECB to the commercial banks. This loan is reflected as a receivable in the ECB balance sheet and as a liability in the balance sheet of the commercial banks (see Fig. 11.11). The commercial banks also get liquidity through the deposits of the public. This results in a demand from the public to the commercial banks, the deposits or sight deposits, and a liability of the commercial banks to the public. The commercial banks usually pay an interest (credit interest) for this purpose. For deposits, they must deposit the reserve reserve with the ECB. This creates a liability for the ECB and a claim on the ECB from the commercial banks. Conversely, commercial banks lend to the public. This creates a demand of the commercial banks against the public and a liability of the public to the commercial banks. The public still holds the cash. In a broad sense, this constitutes a claim on the ECB because it has spent the cash. At the ECB, cash is a liability in the balance sheet (see also Fig. 11.11).

Central bank

Assets (Claims)	Liability (Obligations)

- Currency reserves (Foreign currency purchase = money creation)
 - Credit to the state (bonds as securities)
 - Credit to credit institutes (refinancing)
	- Cash
	
	 - Reserve holdings of credit institute R
	   a) voluntary reserve
	   b) minimum reserve

Credit institute

Assets (Claims)	Liabilities (Obligations)
- Credit to non-banks - R (minimum reserve, reserves at the central bank)	- Deposits (Claims from non-bank deposits) - Refinancing credits from central bank

Non-banks

Assets (Claims)	Liabilities (Obligations)
- Cash C - Claims on banks D (sight deposits) Determining money supply (purchasing power) $M = C + D$	- Credit

Fig. 11.11 Process of financial intermediation in balance sheet form

11.8.5 The Monetary Policy Instruments of the ECB

For monetary policy instruments, a distinction is made between open market operations, constant credit conditions and minimum reserves.

1. **Open market operations**

   Open market operations are monetary policy operations carried out at the initiative of the Central Bank. Their aim is to provide or withdraw liquidity from the banks. There are four categories of open market operations that differ in terms of objective, maturity, frequency and execution: main refinancing operations, longer-term refinancing operations (90-day maturity), fine-tuning and structural operations (no repurchase obligation, 7 days). The main refinancing operations are, as the name implies, the main control instrument of the ECB and make up approx. 70% of the bank refinancing. They correspond to a short loan from the central bank to the commercial banks for 7 days with repurchase obligation, against securities (WP) as collateral. This is also called "repo operations" or "repurchase agreements". The provision of collateral takes place via a temporary transfer of the securities, with a repurchase agreement or as a pledge credit, or securitization of securities, which is for example the current practice of financing German banks through the Deutsche Bundesbank as the executive body of the ECB. The security quality of eligible securities is specified by the ECB. For example, government bonds and commercial loans are an option here.

This loan must be paid by the commercial banks with a main refinancing rate, also known as interest rates.

With the open market transactions, the ECB directly controls the money stock M3 (repurchase or repo transactions). There are two ways in which the ECB can pass on liquidity to the commercial banks, the interest rate and the volume tender. In the case of the floating rate tender, the ECB sets the level of interest and the commercial banks ask for the desired amount of money. The distribution repartition is proportional. In the case of interest rate tenders, banks must state both the desired amount and the interest rate at which they want to lend money (currently in use with a minimum bid rate). The interest rate and volume tenders will be described in more detail by means of an example on the following pages.

The ECB also carries out longer-term open market operations with a maturity of 3 months. They make approx. 20% of the refinancing of commercial banks. In addition, there are hourly quick tenders for fine-tuning as well as definitive structural open market transactions.

2. **Standing facilities**

The standing facilities are among the monetary policy instruments that banks can use on a daily basis on their own initiative. The standing facilities serve commercial banks to provide or absorb unplanned liquidity shortfalls or short-term liquidity overnight as well. A distinction is made between two standing facilities: deposit facility and credit facility. The interest rates for this form an interest rate corridor within which the overnight money rate moves in the money market.

Marginal lending facility

The marginal lending facility corresponds to a giro overdraft facility for banks. It is available in the short term and in unlimited quantities in the event of liquidity bottlenecks at commercial banks. Again, the banks get the liquidity only against the deposit of collateral.

3. **Deposit facility**

This facility serves banks as a short-term investment option. The money is safe at the ECB. In normal times, the ECB pays a credit interest on these liquidity surpluses of commercial banks. The credit facility interest rate and the deposit facility interest rate together form an interest rate corridor for the market interest rate. All banks with collateral can refinance with the ECB at the credit facility interest rate and at least put up their money at the deposit facility interest rate.

4. **Minimum reserve**

   The minimum reserve creates a need for central bank money, because some of the deposits must always be deposited with the ECB as a reserve, before the rest can be lent and new sight deposits can be created (money creation brake). Changing the minimum reserve requirement can help steer long-term money supply in general.The minimum reserve is discounted at the main refinancing interest rate (prime rate).

Quantity Tender

Here, the interest rate is set by the ECB. The participating commercial banks tell the ECB the amount of money they want to receive at the predetermined interest rate. The allocation (repartition) is proportional. In the case of an over-demand, the allocation will be proportional to the amount of money demanded. The advantage of the fixed rate tender is that the ECB can set the interest rate. The question that arises for commercial banks is how their bids position themselves. If they demand too much, they have to invest the surplus amount again at a loss on the money market. If they demand too little, they have to borrow money at a higher interest rate. Example: In Fig. 11.12 the ECB wants to allocate € 80 billion to banks at 2%. 5 banks make bids.

You can also calculate the allotement rate directly (here 0.4) and apply it to the bids of the banks to determine the allocation: $50 \times 0.4 = 20$, $25 \times 0.4 = 10$, $25 \times 0.4 = 10$, $50 \times 0.4 = 20$, $50 \times 0.4 = 20$

Interst Rate Tender

This is an auction process (American procedure). The commercial banks must tell the participating commercial banks the desired amount of money and the interest rate at which they want to receive the money offered. The ECB sets a minimum bid rate. The bids of the banks are ranked according to the amount of the interest offered. The allocation is made according to the amount of the interest bids until the money has been allocated. If the last amount of money is spread over several banks, the money is distributed proportionately according to the requested amount of money (repartitioned). The last interest rate used is

Banks	Requested amount	Shares in%	Allotment	Allocated amount	Interest rate
A	50	25	25% x 80	20	2%
B	25	12,5	12,5% x 80	10	2%
C	25	12,5	12,5% x 80	10	2%
D	50	25	25% x 80	20	2%
E	50	25	25% x 80	20	2%
	200	100	A-rate: 0,4		2%

Fig. 11.12 Quantity tender

Banks	Requested amount	Interest rate bided	Allotement	Allocated amount	Weighted interest rate
B	40	2,3%		40	(40 x 2,3%
A	20	2,2%		20	+ 20 x 2,2%
E	20	2,1%	50% x 20	10	+ 10 x 2,1%
C	20	2,1%	50% x 20	10	+ 10 x 2,1%)
D	50	2,0%		0	: 80 = 2,2%

Fig. 11.13 Interest rate tender

called the marginal interest rate. To find out how the market interest rate was affected by the amount of money allocated, the ECB calculates the average weighted interest rate. The advantage of this procedure is that the ECB does not influence market interest rates by its target. The commercial banks do not receive an allocation if they offer too low of an interest rate.

Example: In Fig. 11.13 the ECB wants to allocate € 80 billion with a minimum bid rate of 2%.

Conclusion
The main objective of the ECB is price stability. For money supply control, there are open market operations, the credit facility, the deposit facility and the minimum reserve. The money creation process is limited by the capital adequacy requirements and the minimum reserve.

Comprehension Questions

1. Explain how interest rate and volume tenders work.
2. Describe the money creation process.
3. Why is the ECB's independence so important to the ECB's objective of price stability?

Exercises
1. The ECB wants to achieve a price increase of 1.8%. GDP growth is expected to reach 2% next year. The money circulation speed remains constant. How much does it have to raise M3?
2. The Governing Council of the ECB decides to transfer to the money market € 25 billion through a main refinancing operation by means of a variable rate tender and, some time later, € 30 billion by means of a volume tender with an interest rate of 3.06%. Five banks (A to E) make the following bids in € billion (see Fig. 11.14):

Bank	Interest rate tender	Requested amount	Quantity tender	Requested amount
A	3,07	10	3,06	15
B	3,06	10	3,06	5
C	3,05	10	3,06	10
D	3,05	10	3,06	15
E	3,03	5	3,06	15

Fig. 11.14 Task interest rate and quantity tender

Determine:

(a) the distribution of bank liquidity as well as for the tenders
(b) the marginal allotment rate
(c) the weighted average interest rate

11.8.6 Quantitative Easing, the New Monetary Policy on the Capital Market

▶ **Definition** Quantitative easing (QE) is a monetary policy of the central bank of increasing the money supply massively by purchasing government bonds on the capital market.

There are three goals that are pursued with QE.

– The increase of the money supply should firstly have an inflationary effect, i.e. fight deflation.
– Secondly, liquidity provision should also reduce long-term interest rates on the capital market and thus increase the willingness of companies to invest. If commercial banks hold the bonds, they would have to reinvest excess liquidity after selling the bonds.
– Thirdly, this should support banks' lending to companies.

In January 2015, the ECB approved a government bond purchase program. The main reason for this was the ECB's low inflation rates. Securities totaling EUR 60 billion per month were purchased, with 80% of purchases being made by the national central banks.

So the risk of loss should remain with the nation states, so not be redistributed. The total volume adds up to 2.6 trillion euros by end 2018. The negative deposit rate was raised from 0.3% to 0.4%. In addition, the ECB issued TLTROs (Targeted Longer-Term Refinancing Operations) with a term of up to 4 years.[16]

Conclusion

The ECB has chosen the 2% inflation target itself. The figure of 2% is arbitrary and under price-level stability, many people would understand something different. Article 123 TFEU prohibits the financing of public deficits. If the ECB buys government bonds on the capital market, this will have the same effect as if it directly gave the states the money. Expecting ECB to buy everything, states get money that would otherwise have gotten nothing from private investors. It is clearly a circumvention. Consolidation pressure on states is declining, even if they are committed to the restructuring program. Are there any effects and if so which ones? Ultimately, quantitative easing extends the ECB's zero interest rate policy and monetary expansion from the money market to the capital market. The losers from a zero interest rate policy are savers and commercial banks. There is a redistribution from creditors to savers. Creditors are mainly companies, homeowners and the state. Business banks need to reduce their credit and investment margins in the face of very low credit and debit interest rates. In addition, there is a risk of misallocation and speculation bubbles.

The effects are difficult to determine ex post. In the case of the USA, the low interest rate policy of the then central bank governor is parltly made responsible for the US mortgage credit crisis. Japan's economy has not recovered to its previous level despite decades of QE. Instead, public debt has risen exorbitantly. The same applies to the USA. Finally, one must historically refer to the negative experiences that came with the financing of government loans by the central bank. Although the ECB, unlike the historical examples of central banks, is politically independent, it nevertheless becomes dependent on the more government bonds it buys. The euro states are becoming ever more dependent on the central bank for financing, so that the ECB can no longer withdraw the money from them, cannot cut it loose (too big to fail). Conversely, a policy shift to higher interest rates is becoming more and more expensive for the ECB as more government bonds have been bought at a low interest rate level. The rise in interest rates would cause the prices of these bonds to fall. The central question remains whether artificial investment can be generated through an

(continued)

---

[16]See   http://www.welt.de/wirtschaft/article136673946/Tag-des-Triumphs-fuer-EZB-Chef-Mario-Draghi.html;http://www.finance-magazin.de/maerkte-wirtschaft/kapitalmarkt/ezb-kauft-jetzt-auch-unternehmensanleihen-1375781/;   http://www.n-tv.de/wirtschaft/EZB-Geldmaschine-ist-voll-im-Einsatz-article14686981.html   and   https://www.wiwo.de/finanzen/geldanlage/analyse-der-ezb-ratssitzung-bei-2-6-billionen-euro-ist-schluss-oder-doch-nicht/23758802.html

expansive monetary policy and extremely low interest rates close to zero. Companies will invest when the return minus the risk premium is higher than the market rate. This means that investments depend not only on the cost of debt, but also on the return on investment. And that is supply-side, thus neoclassically determined. In Greece, nobody will invest in hotels if the same product, Mediterranean holiday, is offered much cheaper in Turkey.

Rather, an expansive monetary policy carries extreme risks, as will later be presented in the analysis of monetary policy theories.

Targeted monetary expansion combined with a zero interest rate policy corresponds to a capital subsidy. The difference is that subsidies burden the budget of the state and expansive monetary policy burdens the citizens as money holders. The central bank can draw money indefinitely at almost no cost. The purchasing power of the new money, however, supplants that of the existing one, which sooner or later leads to inflation. The purchase of corporate bonds is a contradiction to the principle of a two-tier banking system in which the central bank pursues the public mission of monetary stability and therefore operates as a public organization for profit and the private commercial banks, which are to be held liable with their equity capital allocation and therefore have to work for profit. Apart from the fact that corporate financing by the central bank leads to competitive distortions, it can also be assumed that the central bank will make more mistakes in this area of business, i.e. lose capital, because it has less expertise and is not liable with private equity but with taxpayers' money. The system is increasingly approaching the central administration industry.

Overall, the ECB's policies have moved far from the Maastricht Treaty, so it is highly questionable whether it not only broadens its mandate, but also transgresses it legally, and it is already doing so economically.[17] Another problem is that these ECB decisions were taken in the context of the ECB votes, in which the major countries

(continued)

---

[17]With its ruling of May 5, 2020, the Federal Constitutional Court of Germany ruled that the judgement of the European Constitutional Court that the PSPP (Public Sector Purchase Program), under which the ECB had already bought 2.6 trillion € in government bonds by the end of 2018, was in line with the Maastricht agreements, is not comprehensible and therefore not binding and the purchase program is partially unconstitutional. Furthermore, the Federal Constitutional Court of Germany prohibited the German Central Bank (Bundesbank) from participating in the ECB purchase program after a transitional period of no more than three months, unless the ECB Bundestag and Federal Government can prove the proportionality of the purchase program. The Bundestag has now confirmed the proportionality on the basis of ECB documents. See https://www.bundestag.de/dokumente/textarchiv/2020/kw27-de-anleihekaeufe-703660; https://www.handelsblatt.com/finanzen/geldpolitik/bundesverfassungsgericht-rechtsstreit-um-ezb-anleihekaeufe-bringt-bundesbank-in-schwierige-lage/25799360.html?ticket=ST-7611479-MsCxvohzEC2xrkwCdkIh-ap6

such as France and Germany, although with ECB losses, are more liable than the smaller countries that had the same voting rights.

Also, the problem of Target II balances has not yet been resolved. There are balances from the cross-border movement of goods and capital that will not be compensated. The claims of the Bundesbank from TARGET2 against the other national euro central banks amount to € 942.319.065.584,45 (as of 30th june, 2019).[18]

These balances stem mainly from external trade deficits, which indicate increasing differences in competitiveness between the northern and southern Eurasian states. German goods are ordered from southern Europe, but the Bundesbank pays the bill for German exporters because the importer's money is only passed on to its national central bank.

Thus, the southern European countries have no choice but to lower prices and wages and reduce government spending. At present, however, it does not look as if the politicians want to go that way, and as long as the southern European countries have the majority in ECB votes, ECB policy will not change. However, this would result in a further increase in Target2 balances. Here the German government is called upon to negotiate. And the Bundesbank should define a maximum amount for the Target2 balances that it is willing to contribute. It is still committed to the interests of the Germans and must insist on covering the receivables if it is foreseeable that they will not be compensated. The question of what happens to these claims when a state leaves the euro is still unclear. Opportunities exist, such as an exchange of Target2 claims into national government bonds at market value. Bonds, unlike the Target2 balances, are due for repayment, generate interest and are tradable on the market. The long-term hopefully avoidable alternative would be an at least temporary exit of Germany from the euro while retaining the clearing system with the ECB. This would have the advantage that the claims of the Bundesbank to the southern European central banks or the ECB are denominated in euros and could therefore be more easily repaid by the states than the exit of the less competitive southern states. After the euro had depreciated against the new German currency, the products of the southern states would become competitive.

There would be current account surpluses, which would result in the repatriation of Target2 balances.

---

and https://www.deutschlandfunk.de/urteil-des-bundesverfassungsgerichts-was-sie-ueber-den-kauf. 2897.de.html?dram:article_id=472136.

[18]See https://www.bundesbank.de/de/aufgaben/unbarer-zahlungsverkehr/target2/target2-saldo/target2-saldo-603478

References

Conrad, C. A. (2002). Die Geldpolitik und die Akzeptanz des Euros. *WiSt (Wirtschaftswissenschaftliches Studium), 31*(2), 97–100.

DiTella, R., MacCulloch, R. J., & Oswald, A. J. (2001). Preferences over inflation and unemployment: Evidence from surveys of happiness. *American Economic Review, 91*(1), 335–341.

EZB. (1999). Die Umsetzung des Stabilitäts- und Wachstumspaktes. In *EZB – Monatsbericht Mai* (pp. 49–68). Frankfurt: EZB.

Frey, B. S. (1981). *Theorie demokratischer Wirtschaftspolitik*. München: Vahlen.

Hort, P. (2002, February 13). *Koalition der Krähen*. F.A.Z.

Keynes, J. M. (1929). *The economic consequences of the peace* (London, 1920).

Nienhaus, L. (2013). *Wenig Vermögen Wo ist das Geld der Deutschen hin?* In F.A.Z. vom April 21, 2013. Abfrage vom May 18, 2016, from http://www.faz.net/aktuell/wirtschaft/wenig-vermoegen-wo-ist-das-geld-der-deutschen-hin-12156406.html

Sachverständigenrat zur Begutachtung der gesamtwirtschaftlichen Entwicklung. (2011). *Chancen für einen stabilen Aufschwung– Jahresgutachten 2010/2011*. Paderborn: Bonifatius GmbH Buch-Druck-Verlag. Accessed from http://www.sachverstaendigenrat-wirtschaft.de/fileadmin/x_ga_2010_11/ga10_ges.pdf

Schrader, K., & Laaser, C.-F. (2010). Den Anschluss nie gefunden: Die Ursachen der griechischen Tragödie. *Wirtschaftsdienst, 90*(8), 540–537.

Starbatty, J. (2001). Die EZB muss sich das Vertrauen der Märkte erst noch erwerben. *Wirtschaftsdienst, 81*(VII), 374.

Zahlen, K. (2001). Institut der deutschen Wirtschaft, Deutschland. p. 133.

Business Cycles Policy

What Follows Why?

Economic fluctuations, above all as fluctuations in demand, are a major problem for people and businesses and can only be influenced to a very limited extent by economic policy. In the following lecture section, we will analyze the economic phenomenon and the effects on the economy and show the reasons for cyclical fluctuations.

12.1 The Business Cycles Phenomenon

Real-world non-seasonal fluctuations in aggregate demand are referred to as business cycles. They express themselves in an increasing and decreasing degree of utilization of production potential. We can therefore define economic cycles as follows.

Economic cycles are fluctuations in the degree of utilization of production potential. They express themselves in cyclical fluctuations of the gross domestic product (measure of the annual output of an economy) by the level required for normal utilization of the productive potential of an economy.

The economy and growth tend to be mutually dependent. The net investment demand becomes growth of the production potential and income for the consumer demand in the following periods. In the narrower sense, therefore, the distinction between economy and growth is artificial. The empirical time series of the national product always contain both

C. A. Conrad, *Political Economy*,
https://doi.org/10.1007/978-3-658-30884-1_12

growth and economic components.[1] Business cycles differ greatly simplified in terms of their qualities, amplitude and temporal cycle length as the distance between two maxima. The actual trends in the gross domestic product show irregular developments, from which a variety of other fluctuations can be filtered out in addition to the stylized sinusoidal cycles.[2]

The fluctuations in the degree of utilization of the production potential entail high welfare-economic costs. In the under-utilization phase, part of the value creation potential is fallow. People are without employment and thus without income and a socially integrating task. Inflation threatens particularly in the boom phase, which is difficult to get under control due to their interdependencies and time-lags and causes severe allocation and distribution distortions.[3] An estimate of the economic cost of fluctuations by the National Bureau of Eco-nomic Research showed a 2% decline in growth over a 35-year period.[4]

In view of the economic phenomenon, two questions arise from a theoretical point of view: firstly, why are there any changes in the overall economic utilization of production potential and secondly, how can the tendency of sinusoidal development, that is to say, the existence of turning points, be explained. A business cycle theory thus has the task of explaining the causes and relationships of cyclical fluctuations. However, in order to minimize the welfare-economic cost of fluctuations, it should also be able to forecast the development of the national product and derive instruments for smoothing out fluctuations in economic policy from the explanatory notes.

The empirically observed "stylized facts" compiled by SCHEBECK and TICHY[5] 1984 adequately describe the economic phenomenon. Characteristic of the economic cycle are, in particular, the pro-cyclical development of the investment ratio, the nominal wages, the profit share, prices and short-term interest rates, the real wage and the counter-cyclical development of the adjusted wage share.[6] These "stylized facts" should serve in this chapter as a yardstick for assessing the illustrated economic theories: on the one hand, a realistic theory should at least not contradict these facts and on the other hand, a theory that claims to be universally valid should be able to explain many of these facts.

Economic cycles are expressed in cyclical fluctuations in gross domestic product (the measure of the annual output of an economy) around the level required for the normal utilization of the productive potential of an economy (see Fig. 12.1).

After a first upturn (1. phase: expansion, recovery or upswing), there is a boom-like overstrain of existing supply capacities (second phase: boom or peak) as a result of aggregate demand. The providers respond with it

---

[1]Developments in which the net investments are zero are also conceivable. The production potential would remain unchanged. Fluctuations in the utilization of production potential would be a pure economic phenomenon.

[2]See *Albers, Willi u.a.* (Hrsg.) (1976), p. 479.

[3]See auch *Zarnowitz, Victor* (1997), p. 1f. and 25f.

[4]See *Ramey, Garey Ramey, Valerie A.* (1991).

[5]See *Schebeck, Fritz/Tichy, Günther* (1984).

[6]See *Schebeck, Fritz/Tichy, Günther* (1984).

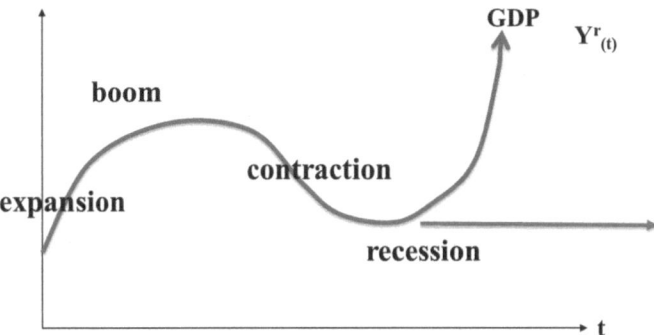

Fig. 12.1 The stylized business cycle

1. Increased use of factors,
2. Reduction of inventories or increase in order backlog and/or
3. Inflationary price increases.
4. Capacity expansion, new hires

And after a downturn (3. phase: downturn or contraction), there is underutilization of supply capacities due to the cyclical decline in demand.

This is called a recession (fourth phase: recession or throgh).

▶ **Definition** The most common definition of recession is at least two consecutive quarters with negative growth, ie falling GDP.

In this economic phase, numerous insolvencies, mass unemployment and short-time work occur, economic unemployment and usually only small inflationary price level increases.

The heightening of the recession is depression as a persistent stagnation (underutilization of productive capacity) with deflationary tendencies.

Economic Indicators
Leading Indicators: Investment in fixed assets and purchasing managers' index are, for example, a leading indicator relative to GDP, whereas consumption is a lagging indicator (lagging indicator).

12.2   Reasons for Economic Fluctuations from the Economic Theory and Political Economy Conclusions

12.2.1 Dynamic Keynesian Approaches: The Hicks's Super-multiplier

According to Keynes, fluctuations in autonomous investment, as well as multiplier effects (continued effects of increasing demand) and accelerator effects (increased demand for capacity utilization causes investment), can lead to cyclical fluctuations, as shown below by Hicks's super-multiplier (1950).

Fig. 12.2 Growth cycles of the
Hicks model

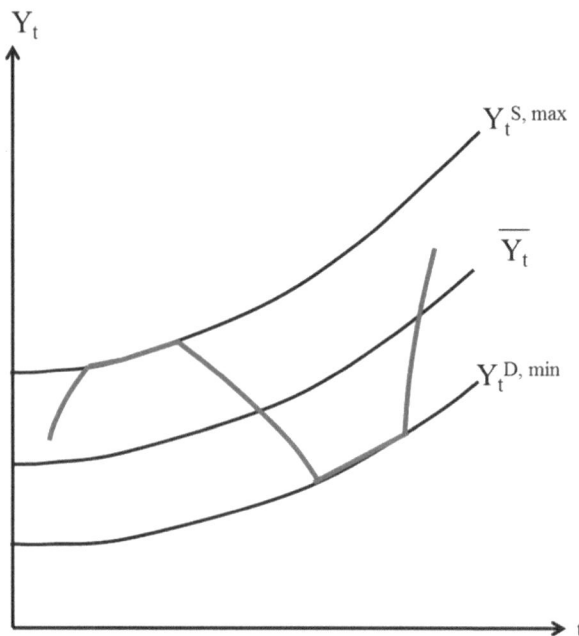

SAMUELSON[7] was the first in 1939 to combine the Keynesian Demand Multiplier and Investment Accelerator into a demand-side investment function model, generating regular fluctuations in aggregate demand. However, the drawback of Samuelson's economic model is that the fluctuating gross domestic product does not follow a growth trend, but moves according to the parameter constellation around or to a constant value or moves away from it in explosive fluctuations. HICKS[8] finally succeeded in 1950 in clarifying the fluctuations in the utilization of a constantly growing production potential by taking into account induced and autonomous investments.[9] HICKS (1950) combines a simple consumption function and an accelerator into a dynamic Keynesian approach. The system is in dynamic equilibrium when gross domestic product is growing at the same constant rate as autonomous investment (see Fig. 12.2). Hicks[10] uses the consumption function $C_t = c\, Y_{t-1}$ and the acceleration factor I ind$t = \beta * (Y_{t-1} - Y_{t-2})$. By taking into account induced and autonomous investments I aut$t = A_0 * (1 + w)\, t$ [A_0: initial value, w: constant growth rate

---

[7]See *Samuelson, P.A.* (1939).

[8]For the Hicks's super-multiplier See *Hicks, J.R.* (1950); *Tichy, G.* (1995), p. 11; *Assenmacher, Walter* (1998); *Teichmann, U.* (1997), p. 11.; *Wagner, A.* (1990), p. 222 and *Ott, A.* (1963), p. 196.

[9]i.e. all investments that are not caused by a change in demand, ie long-term investments such as public infrastructure investments and innovations.

[10]See Hicks, J.R. (1950); Tichy, G. (1995), p. 11; Assenmacher, W. (1991); Wagner, A. (1990), pp. 222 and Ott, A. (1963), p. 196.

of autonomous investment] HICKs succeeds in explaining fluctuations in the utilization of a constantly growing production potential.

$$Y_t = C_t + I^{ind}_{t+} I^{aut}_t = c\ Y_{t-1} + \beta \cdot (Y_{t-1} - Y_{t-2}) + A_0 \cdot (1+w)^t \Leftrightarrow$$

$$Y_t = \frac{I^{aut}_t}{1 - \frac{c+\beta}{(1+w)} + \frac{\beta}{(1+w)^2}}$$

Figure 12.2 shows the autonomous capital expenditures and other development components of the national product, which would develop in the absence of cyclical fluctuations and external disturbances according to the Yt line, ie the long-term equilibrium path. This is the imaginary equilibrium path, the real national product, which grows at the same constant rate as the autonomous investments. The induced investments have no capacity effect. $Y_t^{S,\ max}$ represents the capacity limit (full employment) and $Y_t^{D,\ min}$ of the disinvestment floor. Capacity limit and disinvestment floor are the upper and lower bounds of a tunnel in which growing gross domestic product moves. On the disinvestment basis, investment demand corresponds to the steadily growing autonomous investment.

The actual development of the gross domestic product is an oscillation[11] around the long-term growth path of the gross domestic product. If the gross domestic product in the initial equilibrium at time t_0 is in a cyclical upturn due to a positive exogenous post-crisis shock, it reaches t_1 highest value for the time being, which is limited by the growth of production potential (path A). Due to the accelerator context I indt $= \beta * (Yt-1 - Yt-2)$, a constant growth rate is a prerequisite for a constant demand. The mere decline in the growth of demand can thus already initiate a downward process. The lower limit of this contractionary process is reached when investment has fallen to the level of failed reinvestment. Induced investment has shrunk to zero as a result of the decline in demand, and gross domestic product growth is determined solely by autonomous investment and pro rata consumption. The upward process is initiated by investment demand induced by the growth of autonomous investment. As soon as Yt + 1 > Yt again, investments are induced.

The biggest shortcoming of this model is the neglect of the monetary side (the investments are not interest-dependent). Price level changes are excluded as an economic determinant. An over-demand has no negative consequences. Furthermore, demand-induced investments have no capacity effect. HICKS, however, highlights the dynamic importance of changes in demand. This makes it possible to explain the sinusoidal fluctuations that can be observed in reality by an increasing gross domestic product growth path. On the other hand, HICKS provides no explanation as to how the growth rate of

---

[11]Due to the choice of: $1 < \beta < (1 + \sqrt{s})^2$.
these are explosive oscillation.

autonomous investment assumed by him comes about.[12] But he himself admits that the growth rate of autonomous investments does not have to be constant and can even be greatly reduced:

> One of the most dangerous things that can happen (and on one occasion, at least surely has happened) is that autonomous investment itself is severely checked by financial breakdown.[13]

Starting from the model of HICKS there were numerous further developments. CHENERY has designed an investment function that depends on both demand and capacity utilization, taking into account the capacity effect of past investments.[14] GOODWIN develops an overall model in which consumer demand consists of an autonomous and an income-dependent part. From the model of GOODWIN arise economic cycles with very realistic properties, with each cycle initiating the following. The cycles do not expire, nor do any explosive oscillations occur—unlike the HICKS model—that would require the introduction of Ceilings. Moreover, the type of oscillation does not depend on the initial conditions or the model coefficients. The missing endogenisation of the money market was provided by PHILLIPS and the labor market BERGSTROM. PHILLIPS succeeds in using its model to show the cyclically stabilizing influence of utilization-dependent price changes triggered by wage responses.[15] Based on the PHILLIPS model, BERGSTROM endogenizes the labor market by means of a production function. Corresponding to the profit maximization conditions under perfect competition, the marginal productivity of capital determines the demand for capital, and the marginal productivity of labor determines the demand for labor, which also fixes interest and wage levels. Increases in wages cause ceteris paribus an increase in labor supply, but also a decline in labor demand and thus a decline in gross domestic product. The income decline affects the multiplier.[16]

Conclusion
The policy conclusions that can be drawn from this model are similar to those of the advanced theory of Keynes. The state must compensate for the Nachfra fluctuations by autonomous demand impulses. Therefore discretionary countercyclical fiscal policy is necessary:

(continued)

---

[12]"Public investment, investment which occurs in direct responce to inventions, and much of the 'long-range' investments (as Mr. Harrod calls it) which is only expected to pay for itself over a long period, all of these can be regarded as Autonomous Investment for our purpose." Hicks J. R. (1950), p. 59.

[13]Hicks J. R. (1950), p. 129.

[14]See *Chenery, H.* (1952) and *Assenmacher, Walter* (1998), pp. 186.

[15]See *Goodwin, R. M.* (1951) and *Assenmacher, Walter* (1998), pp. 120.

[16]See *Bergstrom, A.* (1962); *Teichmann, Ulrich* (1997), p. 17 and *Assenmacher, Walter* (1998), p. 18.

Recession: debt-financed increase in government spending, tax relief
Boom: Government spending cuts, tax hikes

However, HICKS also reveals in its model the sensitivity with which the economy reacts to changes in demand in a dynamic process. Taking into account the now well-known practical recognition and implementation problems of state follow-up taxation, a warning against discretionary political economy can be deduced from this. A one-off (one-period) increase in demand by the state would correspond in the following period (c.p.) to an overall economic decline in demand and thus initiate a downward process. At the same time, the model thus highlights the dangers of discretionary cyclical policy management.

12.2.2   Neoliberal Versus Keynesian: A Synthesis

The counter-cyclical fiscal policy approach was practiced around the world in the 1960s through the mid-1970s. It was included in the Stability and Growth Act of 1967, which is no longer used. In the government of former Federal Chancellor Schmidt, this policy was also practiced. However, there were significant implementation issues. First of all, there was the problem of correctly interpreting the economic fluctuations. The question of when there was a recession that required an increase in government spending was not clear, as the cycles are not schematic. It then usually took too long for the cyclical measures to be implemented, so that it was often the case that the government's increase in demand did not materialize until the economy was back on the upswing.

However, the crucial problem was the one-sided implementation of the concept of anticyclical fiscal policy. The expansion of public spending in the recession was easy for politicians, but not saving in the boom. In the boom, the ministers want to increase their budgets, as they have "gone without" for years. Politically, cutting spending was not popular in the boom. The politicians feared electoral losses if they cut public spending on their citizens. The consequence of this was that borrowing in the recession was increased by the expansionary fiscal policy, but was not reduced again in the boom. Ultimately, the wide-ranging interpretation of Keynesian depression theory was responsible for the sharp increase in government debt in the 1960s and 1970s.

Monetarism or "Neoliberals" (Supply-Oriented Policy)

As a countermovement to discretionary demand management in the 1960s and 1970s, monetarism, with its main representative Milton Friedman, and Neo-liberalism in general, formed an extremely market-oriented economic orientation.

They argued that due to the numerous implementation problems (detection, planning, implementation and impact) and the difficulty of clearly defining the cause responsible for the current economic development, fiscal policy should be used in the short term rather than discretionarily,

Neoclassicism, and in particular quantity theory (M • v = Y • P) again became the dominant doctrine. Above all, monetary policy must serve to ensure price stability and may only help cushion external shocks in exceptional circumstances. Real gross domestic product growth cannot be artificially created by an expansionary monetary policy.

The neo-liberals start from the "policy inefficiency hypothesis". Consequently, the influence of politics on the economy must be kept as low as possible. The future environmental conditions are unknown. The market participants therefore make decisions under uncertainty. The state must not further increase this uncertainty by a "non-constancy" of political economy. Rather, what is needed is a binding rule in the form of clear, long-term policy programs, based on a comprehensible system-conforming conception, ie a regulatory instead of process policy.

Only in a depression, that is, in a continuing underutilization of production potential for lack of demand, should the state intervene, because otherwise there will be no recovery for the foreseeable future. Clear rules and framework conditions must be created.

The rule-based countercyclical monetary policy remains: In the long term, for example, the ECB orients on production potential, but in the short term also on its utilization or GDP. So in the Recession it lowers the key interest rates and increases the money supply in order to give the economy an expansionary impetus and in the

Boom interest rates rise and tightening liquidity to prevent overheating of the economy as well as price increases above its inflation target.

Recession: expansionary monetary policy: $M\uparrow$, $i\downarrow \Rightarrow (p \uparrow)$, $\Rightarrow i\downarrow \Rightarrow I(i)\uparrow$ and

Boom: restrictive monetary policy: $M\downarrow$, $i\uparrow \Rightarrow p\downarrow$, $\Rightarrow i\uparrow \Rightarrow I(i)\downarrow$

With the neo-liberal orientation, demand-oriented economic policy was replaced by supply-side economic policy. Profit and/or yield expectations of the enterprises returned to the fore, because the creation of jobs over investments should be again supply-oriented and not demand-oriented. The goal of supply-oriented economic policy is therefore to improve investment conditions and increase profit expectations:

1. Increase competition: (a) Reduction of bureaucracy and deregulation, (b) Privatization of public enterprises, (c) Degradation of subsidies, (d) Reduction of public debt
2. Reduction of non-wage labor costs
3. Reduction of social benefits to a minimum, job offers ↑
4. Simple control system with low rates
5. Monetary stability: Orientation of the money supply to the GDP, otherwise inflation results

Political applications (in part): USA Reaganomics, GB Thatcherismus, reforms of German Chancellor Schröder "Agenda 2010"

Figure 12.3 presents the differences between the Keynesian and neo-liberal economists.

Neoliberal	Keynsian
Markets tend to balance; they are stable and efficient (market optimists)	Markets and their balances are unstable and inefficient (market pessimists)
Therefore, markets are to deregulate	Therefore, markets have to be regulated
Policy inefficiency hypothesis, rule-binding policy	State must correct market, policy efficiency
Supply conditions for companies are crucial	Demand on the goods markets is crucial
Labor market is largely autonomous	Labor market is derived from the goods markets
Economic framework is crucial, regulatory policy	State intervention is crucial, process politics
Long-term oriented	Short-term oriented

Fig. 12.3 Comparison of Neoliberal and Keynesian

12.2.3 Technical Progress: The Schumpeter Business Cycle

Characteristic of the starting point of almost all major stock market bubbles is a fundamental real-world economic spark, which establishes a long growth trend. These are product or process innovations that are not a spin off of well-known technologies, but represent exceptional technical advances that result in a sustainable increase in productivity. Often one speaks then of a "new era". Schumpeter (Joseph Alois Schumpeter 1883–1950) speaks of a "creative destruction". The old production processes will be replaced by new, better ones and the economy as a whole raised to a higher level of productivity. The profits of companies using the new technology or producing new products are increasing. A new wave of growth as a discrete business cycle, a sustainable boom of real growth, is emerging. Due to the length of these cycles, they would most likely correspond to the so-called Kondratieff waves. Schumpeter developed his business cycle theory from the two central dynamic competitive functions.

Innovation Function

For the growth process of an economy, the dynamic nature of the competition is of particular importance. Dynamic competition, according to Friedrich August von Hayek, is a search and discovery process.[17] Hayek characterizes competition as a process of discovering facts that would either remain unknown or at least be unused without their existence. For Hayek, competition is above all evolutionary. This applies both to process innovations and to product innovations, whereby an innovation is generally understood to mean the economic realization of an invention, also called invention. In the expectation of

---

[17]See Hayek, Friedrich August von (1969).

an above-average market reward, the entrepreneur is constantly looking for cheaper production processes and new products for which there is potential market demand. To this end, he conducts research at his own risk or evaluates foreign research results economically. The market, and ultimately the consumer or processing producer, decides on the success of a process.

Imitation Function

According to Joseph Schumpeter, competition is a process of innovation and subsequent imitation.[18] The pioneer entrepreneur's successful innovation gives him a competitive advantage in the marketplace over the companies that have retained their old production structure. This competitive advantage results in an above-average profit, which then incites other entrepreneurs to imitate the innovation, or at least forces it to do so if they do not want to be forced out of the market. This leads to a proliferation of new, resource-saving production processes and thus to a comprehensive enforcement of technical progress and, with it, to a growth in production. Innovation and sanctions thus support each other in dynamic competition.

From the innovation function and the imitation function Schumpeter derives his dynamic business theory[19]:

1. **Phase: state of equilibrium**

    The prerequisites for a recovery are new productive combinations, with which a far above average profit can be achieved. These productive combinations are so fundamental that they affect the whole economy. This allows:

- Above all, product and process innovations (such as the Internet), fundamental innovations such as the assembly line
- New sources of supply or intermediate consumption
- Development of new markets, e.g. due to the abolition of the "Iron Curtain"
- Organizational corporate reforms (stock corporation etc.)

    A dynamic entrepreneur (or inventor) implements this profit potential with the support of a dynamic, risk-taking banker. Both together realize the gain from technical progress (innovation function). By being the first to implement the more productive combinations, they have a temporary monopoly on the market and can reap the pioneering benefits that will lead to Phase 2.

---

[18]See Schumpeter, Joseph Alois (1911).

[19]See Schumpeter, Peter (1939).

2. **Phase: imitation (upswing and boom)**

The pioneer profits attract many entrepreneurs to imitation (imitation function). They mimic the more productive combinations. For this they have to invest. As there are many who invest, aggregate demand increases. It creates an economic euphoria. The upswing begins. Higher demand will increase the prices and profits of companies, not just in the area of new production combinations. Further investments are encouraged.

$\Rightarrow$investments (I) st in the area of $\Rightarrow$ prices (P)) st in the area $\Rightarrow$investments (I) $\uparrow$

3. **Phase: erosion process of pioneer business profits (downturn)**

The high demand leads to rising prices for the precursors. Wages and interest rates, the cost of capital, are also rising, which is why profit margins are falling. After the maturity of the investment, the new offer of imitators comes on the market. The competition and the new offer cause prices to fall. Investments are significantly reduced, which reduces demand and initiates the downturn.

1. Competition of imitators $\Rightarrow$ prices (P) $\downarrow$, profits (G) $\downarrow$
2. Rising costs of primary products, labor and capital (interest) $\Rightarrow$profits (G) ca $\Rightarrow$ investments (I) al (interest^D) $\downarrow$ prices (P) $\downarrow$

4. **Phase: Creative destruction (recession)**

In the recession demand is greater than supply. Production cuts and unemployment are the result. The gross domestic product is falling. The oversupply of new production combinations is pushing companies out of the market with the old non-competitive production processes or products. The companies that have not imitated must apply for bankruptcy. This is how technical progress is enforced. This is a necessary process. Schumpeter speaks of the "elixir of life of capitalism". There is no need for economic policy. On the contrary, a credit-financed fiscal policy would artificially keep uncompetitive companies in the market, which is undesirable.

Schumpeter explains the long cycles caused by fundamental economic changes. A Schumpeterian business cycle would be the boom that occurred in the late 1990s with the Internet boom and the new market that was created, which was followed by a similar downturn, but also left a new economic structure above all in the service area.

The creative product and process innovations, in addition to the positive effect of increasing productivity, still have a negative connotation. On the one hand, as Schumpeter points out, they destroy the old, no longer efficient economic structures, but this also implies structural unemployment.

12.2.4 Overinvestment Theories

Overinvestment can also be a cause of economic fluctuations. The key problem for companies is that when making their investment decisions, they do not know how stable the increase in demand is and to what extent competitors are expanding their capacities. As a company, they have to agree on how much each company invests and how much the capacity should be extended. Since such coordination does not exist, companies must approach demand with their production plans. It always comes back to overcapacity and undercapacity. In the upswing, demand is rising ($Y^D \uparrow$). As a result, prices and profits rise (p $\uparrow$, gains $\uparrow$). It is invested (I $\uparrow$). There is overcapacity as markets must first coordinate all business plans. Capacities must be reduced again in the adaptation process. Here, too, there are exaggerations, since the capacity reduction as well as the capacity was not coordinated. A similar process in microeconomics is also called pork cycle or cobweb theorem. An example is the overinvestment theory of Karl Marx, which builds on technical progress as a stimulus to the economy.

The overinvestment theory with technical progress by Karl Marx[20] (1818–1883) or the law of the tendency of the rate of profit

Technical progress needs capital for implementation. Marx divides capitalists into owners of the means of production and workers who make a living from their labor. Labor-saving technical progress allows the capitalists higher productivity and thus a higher rate of profit. They invest (accumulation of capital), the demand increases, it comes to the upswing. The higher productivity leads to increased competition and thus to a fall in prices and thus also the rate of profit. Labor forces are released by technical progress (impoverishment of the proletariat, formation of an industrial reserve army). As a result, in addition to oversupply, demand is also falling. The dismissed workers can no longer consume anything. It comes to a downturn. The capitalists eliminate each other due to high oversupply in the ruinous competition (recession). The supplier concentration increases (concentration of capital). The rate of profit rises again (upswing) and the process starts from scratch until the collapse of the capitalist system (dictatorship of the proletariat and planned economy) comes.

However, Marx's fears did not materialize in Germany. Through the formation of the unions, the unilateral became a bilateral monopoly on the labor market, the workers no longer competed with each other driving pay down. Strikes were possible. Due to the now balanced distribution of power, the unions can enforce wage increases. Demand increased and there was no sales problem. In addition, product innovation led to a new demand for labor that could be paid for productivity-related wage increases. Existing purchasing power and the re-employed previously released work thus led to an ever higher level of prosperity.

---

[20]See Marx, Karl (1864) and Stavenhagen, Gerhard (1969), pp. 157.

12.2.5 Distribution Struggles to Explain Economic Fluctuations: The GOODWIN Model

The question that has not been answered despite the extension of the HICKS model by BERGSTROM is the question of factors influencing wage developments. This shows a basic problem of the business cycle theory. If a factor influencing the economy is endogenized, new factors to be explained arise. However, in order to maintain the clarity of the model and thus its explanatory value, it is advisable to consider the influencing factors in isolation and to use a new model. The explanation of wage development is dedicated to another model of GOODWIN.

Goodwin developed a model of interdependent, nonlinear differential equations in 1967. In his model, he succeeds in simultaneously explaining the economy, growth and distribution.[21] From his model equations, two sinusoidal oscillations of the wage share (q, hunter population[22]) and the employment rate (b, prey population) result, which are offset by one phase. A complete business cycle can be modeled (see Fig. 12.4), which also reflects the empirically observed anti-cyclical development of the adjusted wage share and the pro-cyclical development of the profit and investment ratio. According to GOODWIN, his model confirms the instability of capitalist economies identified by MARX. High profits cause entrepreneurs to accumulate capital. Due to the additional demand for work, however, they are worsening their bargaining position, which is why they can no longer maintain the given functional income distribution. The investment increase sinks and the downward process is initiated. Economic stability and full employment can never be realized.

Conclusion
The Goodwin model explains the empirically observed anti-cyclical development of the adjusted wage share and the pro-cyclical development of the profit and investment ratio. According to GOODWIN, his model confirms the instability of capitalist economic systems indicated by MARX. High profits cause entrepreneurs to accumulate capital. Due to the additional demand for work, however, they worsen their bargaining position, which is why they can no longer maintain the given functional income distribution. The investment increase sinks and the down process is initiated. Economic stability and full employment can thus never be realized. Moreover, GOODWIN's model explains the relatively constant rate of profit observed with increasing real wages, contrary to the forecasts of MARX and RICARDO.

---

[21]Zum GOODWIN-Modell See *Goodwin, R. M.* (1967), pp. 54; *Heubes, J.* (1986), pp. 86; *Kurz, Rudi* (1986); *Teichmann, Ulrich* (1997), pp. 18 and *Wagner, A.* (1992), pp. 225.

[22]The hunter population (wage share) develops with a time lag of one phase, depending on the prey population (employment rate). The term hunter and prey populations comes from the biology that found a similar correlation for predators (e.g., lynxes) and prey (e.g., rabbits) (so-called LOTKA-VOLTERRA equations).

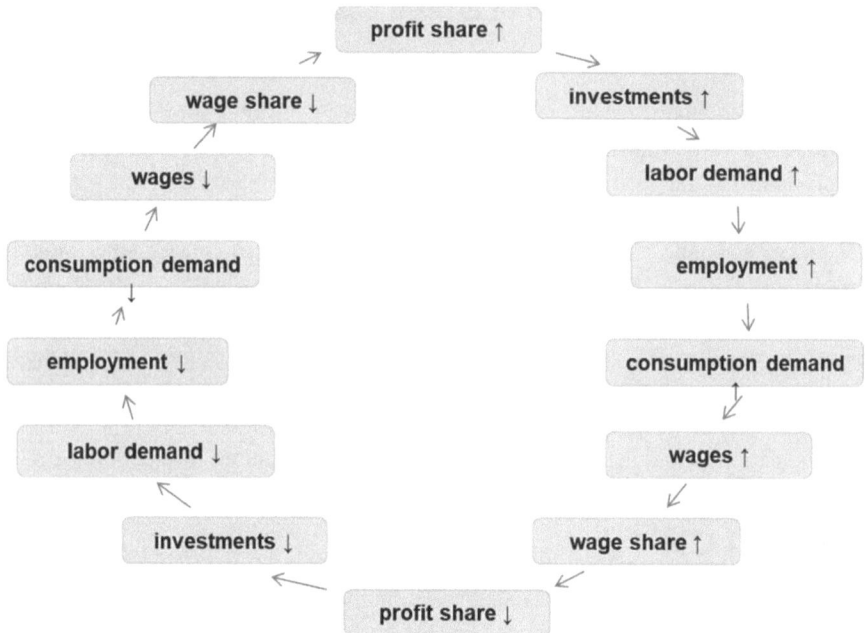

Fig. 12.4 The Goodwin distribution cycle

However, GOODWIN's economic statement is one-sidedly geared towards distribution struggles. Exogenous demand shocks, expectations, price developments and monetary and fiscal policy are not taken into account. The investments are not interest-dependent. Also, the assumption of an extremely classic economy function is unrealistic. The model is designed exclusively for the capacity effect of investments. The investments do not develop a demand effect on the goods market. Fluctuations in workers' demand for labor have no impact, as capacity is assumed to be always full. Given these constellations, the model is far from reality. The model explains endogenously, ie without the aid of exogenous influencing factors, growth, employment and distribution fluctuations. However, it cannot explain the fluctuations in the degree of utilization of the production potential observed in reality: since it is assumed that I = S, there is neither under nor overdemand. Goodwin economies are therefore pure growth and employment fluctuations. Employment and wage rates are constant over the long term. On the other hand, all absolute sizes grow.

Since, as with HICKS, the state was not included in this model, no direct economic policy conclusions can be derived. In GOODWIN's model, however, the state cannot even be indirectly integrated into the model by exogenously influencing demand. GOODWIN's economic fluctuations are distribution-determined. However, governmental redistribution policy would only slow down economic recovery in this model, due to the reduction in profits and thus in investment. The same applies to the crowding-out of credit-financed expenditure policy, as WOLFSTETTER shows in his model.[23] What is needed are automatisms to mitigate the vibration fluctuations. A pro-gressive taxation of profit would be cyclically damaging. The state is also in demand as a mediator of distribution fights, for example in the form of a concerted action. Due to the assumption of the extremely classic investment function, however, any redirection from profit to labor income slows down the growth process and, at the same time, the economic upturn. Nonetheless, a continuation of the positive growth and employment trends could be achieved if, as a result of the lower employment growth rate, the unions increased their wages less or used the tax revenues on an investment basis. Pure redistribution taxation always reduces growth and employment, unless the workers also save and thus compensate for the reduction in investment of the recipients.

12.2.6 Political Economic Cycles: The Political Economic Model of Nordhaus

The Nordhaus approach goes back to the "New Political Economy". According to the New Political Economy approach, a politician does not maximize the common good, but maximizes their own benefit. Political offices grant this benefit in the form of power, prestige and income. In order to achieve the desired offices, the politician must collect as many electoral votes—one speaks of voice maximization. Positive economic indicators can be used as a political track record and secure voter approval. If the politician starts from the controllability of the economy, he will try to use the instruments at his disposal in such a way that at the time of the election the economic indicators are the best. Already from this behavioral hypothesis can be concluded on the existence of politically induced economic cycles. However, until Nordhaus's economic model was published, the New Political Economy approach lacked the mathematical behavioral model that allowed economic cycles to be endogenously deduced and explained politically initiated business cycles.[24]

The economic indicators used by Nordhaus are inflation and unemployment. Every voter is directly affected by inflation in his role as a goods buyer. Unemployment affects him directly if he loses his job. He may also be indirectly affected if he feels threatened by unemployment, expecting that he could lose his job in the future. Nordhaus cites various reasons for a trade-off between inflation and unemployment. First, low unemployment creates higher aggregate demand, which also affects the price level. Secondly, higher overall demand implies higher strike costs than opportunity costs of lost sales due to lack of production. These cause the employer to accept the wage demands of the workers. In addition, Nordhaus justifies a short-term trade-off with the adaptive reactions of the workers to unemployment and inflation and the consequences on the price level. With

---

[23]See *Wolfstetter, E.* (1982) and *Assenmacher, Walter* (1998), pp. 229.

[24]See Frey, B.S./and Lau, L.J. (1968).

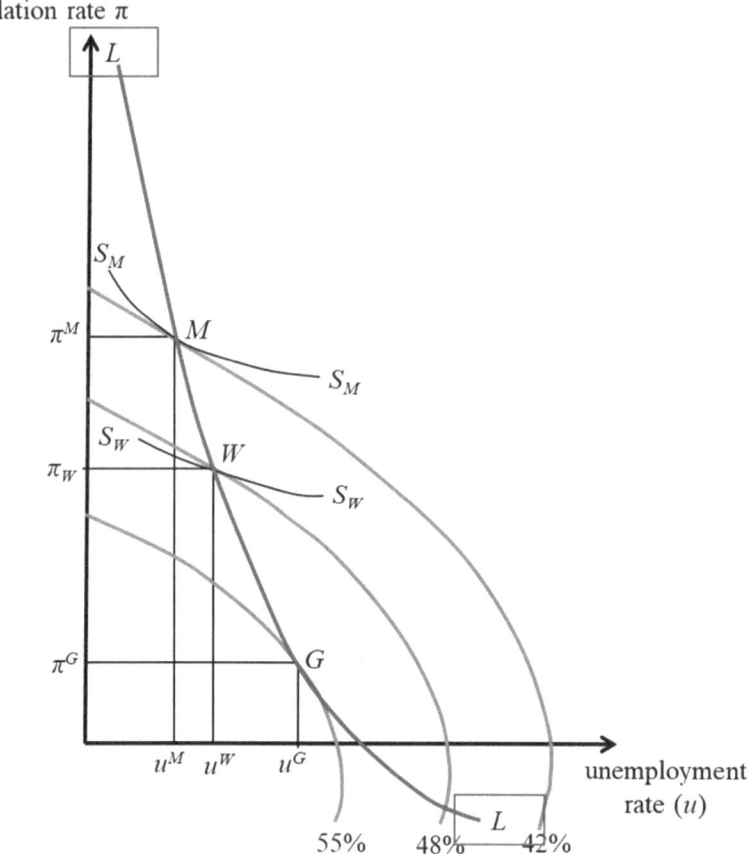

Fig. 12.5 Long-term policy strategies

high unemployment, they reduce their wage demands. The reduction of production costs leads to a price reduction and, in turn, to a reduction in wage demands. When inflation occurs, the workers realize the real wage reduction late and therefore adjust their wage demands late. The long-term "Phillips curve" L is thus steeper than the short-term "Phillips curve" S (see Figs. 12.5 and 12.6).

As part of the "Phillips curve," the politician can select combinations of inflation and unemployment. However, this only works as long as the money illusion persists. Once the economic subjects have adjusted their expectations, the short-term Phillips curve shifts upward. The politician chooses the maximum vote combination. Citizens 'decisions to re-elect the government are made in response to meeting citizens' expectations: improvements in economic indicators are rewarded with electoral votes. Longer-term improvements and deterioration in the legislature are less significant than recent developments. Consequently, it is maximizing for the ruling party to implement restrictive measures at the beginning of the parliamentary term and expansive measures at the end of

inflation rate
π

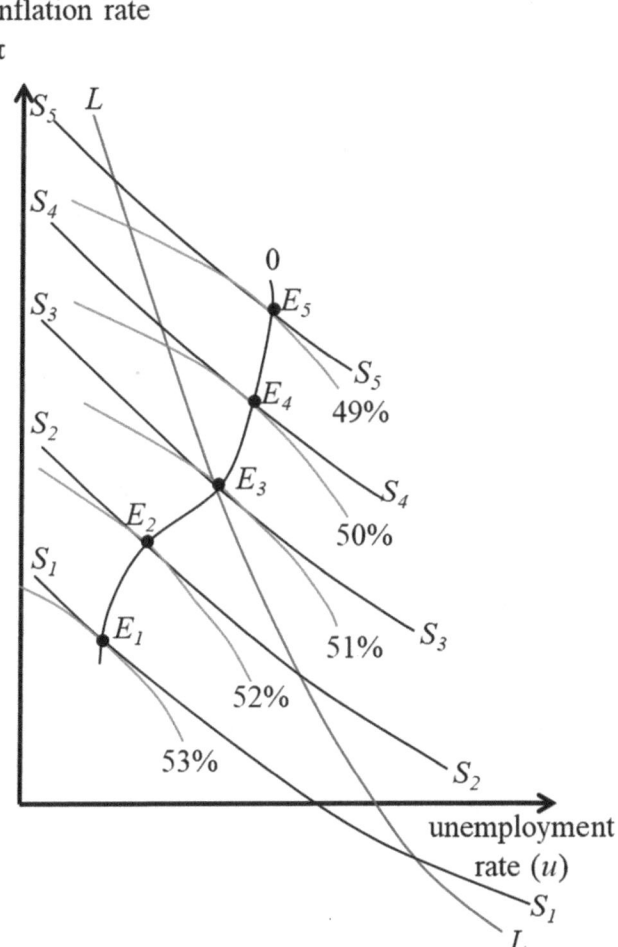

Fig. 12.6 Short-term election result. Source: Nordhaus, William D. (1975), p. 177 and 179

the election period. After expansive measures, the short-term Phillips curve shifts from bottom to top. If the government does not pursue a restrictive policy after the election, then before its next re-election, it must increase the inflation rate more than in the first term to reduce unemployment despite higher inflation expectations. The new, worse combination of unemployment and inflation is rated by the electorate with less agreement (measured in electoral votes), which is why the governing party cannot sustain this policy for long. In point E3, the system is in the long-term equilibrium: both expansionary and restrictive pre-election policies would deprive the government of its majority (see Fig. 12.6). After re-election, the government must try to reach the original Phillips curve with the old inflation expectations through a restrictive policy. The discretionary, politically motivated interventions generate business cycles.

NORDHAUS attributes to its political economic model the well-known Phillips curve. As part of the Phillips curve, the politician can select combinations of inflation and unemployment. The politician can deceive the workers in the short term in terms of the inflation rate, which is why they adjust the nominal wages of the inflation rate only delayed and the real wage decreases. As a result, entrepreneurs expand labor demand and thus production. In the short term, the real national product (asymmetric time delay/wage-lag hypothesis) increases.[25] However, this only works as long as the money illusion persists. Once the economic subjects have adjusted their expectations, the short-term Phillips curve shifts upward. The politician chooses the maximum vote combination. Citizens' decisions to re-elect the government are made on the basis of meeting citizens' expectations: improvements in economic indicators are rewarded with electoral votes. Longer-term improvements and deterioration in the legislature are less significant than recent developments. Consequently, it is maximizing for the ruling party to implement restrictive measures at the beginning of the parliamentary term and expansive measures at the end of the parliamentary term. After expansive measures, the short-term Phillips curve shifts from bottom to top. If the government does not pursue a restrictive policy after the election, then before its next re-election, it must raise the inflation rate more than in the first term to reduce unemployment despite higher inflation expectations. The new, worse combination of unemployment and inflation is rated by the electorate with less agreement (measured in electoral terms), which is why the ruling party cannot hold this policy long. On one point, the system is in a long-term equilibrium: the government would lose its majority, both through expansive and restrictive pre-election policies. After re-election, the government must try to reach the original Phillips curve with the old inflation expectations through a restrictive policy. The discretionary, politically motivated interventions generate business cycles according to the election cycles.

In democracies, as a result of the present overemphasis, the average unemployment rate is lower and the average inflation rate above the general welfare optimum (W, see Fig. 12.5) for the present and future generations. Furthermore, the time preference of voters in government politicians suggests a tendency to rate today's positive economic developments higher than future ones. Nordhaus concludes that politicians tend to maximize current prosperity at the expense of wealth for future generations. Nordhaus business cycles also occur in centrally planned economies. Since these are usually one-party systems governing through dictatorship, however, the cycles will only emerge at times when the

---

[25]NORDHAUS gives different reasons for the trade-off between inflation and unemployment: 1. That a low unemployment rate means that the demand for labor is relatively high, hence the price of labor, the wage that acts as a cost on the general price level. 2. There would be asymmetrical delays (lags) in the effect of changes in the unemployment rate on the general price level because, on the one hand, wage demands are lower in the case of high unemployment and, on the other hand, because an increased inflation rate increases inflation expectations and so that the wage demands of the employees to keep the real wage constant. NORDHAUS concludes that the long-term Phillips curve is steeper than the short-term one. See *Nordhaus, William D.* (1974), p. 169f.

government needs short-term popular support. For the governing party to maximize voting, to implement restrictive measures at the beginning of the parliamentary term and expansive measures at the end of the parliamentary term (Nordhaus model).

NORDHAUS assumptions and conclusions are mostly plausible. The model endogenously explains the emergence of political business cycles and thus highlights the dangers of political influence on the economic process. NORDHAUS has confirmed his theories for Germany, New Zealand and the USA. He identified low political cycles for France and Sweden, whereas the likelihood of political influence on the business cycle was low in the other cases he examined.[26] However, NORDHAUS model requires a controllability of the economic indicators unemployment and inflation. The macroeconomic fluctuations are not the result of a miscalculation, but of political manipulation. However, this only marginally diminishes the significance of the model since politically induced fluctuations in disorder would only occur more irregularly.

In his fundamental essay NORDHAUS addresses several alternatives that could reduce political fluctuations in the economy. The simplest thing would be to shorten the electoral period to account for the forgetfulness of voters. However, there was a danger that the government would no longer be sufficient for a long-term, strategically oriented policy, and that therefore the policy would only be geared to a short-term perspective. In addition, inefficiencies in the administration would come from the frequent change of government. To refresh the level of information of the voters over and over again, seems to be an unrealistic alternative, given the lack of interest among people in past events (present-day preference). Of particular interest is the fact that the demand for the political independence of central banks and even finance ministries (in the area of short-term spending decisions) can be derived from this model. However, NORDHAUS sees it as a disadvantage that monetary and fiscal policy is lost as a political instrument to be able to implement the wishes of voters. This statement contains a certain contradiction to the model-immanent critique of politically induced business cycles. Political and economic rationality (utility) are rarely identical. Another alternative would be to reduce the tendency of the Phillips curve, ie the short-term trade-off between unemployment and inflation, for example through price and wage freezes or through automatic induction or inflation compensation. Apart from the inflation adjustment, these measures are incompatible with a market-based economic system. They would be market and thus system destroying. Automatic wage inflation or indirect inflation compensation, as with Italian Scala Mobile, would lead to less resistance to inflation and, ultimately, inflation acceleration. For his part, NORDHAUS tends to prevent voter manipulation by exploiting their short-term memory through greater transparency and broader participation in the political decision-making process.

---

[26] Australia, Canada, Japan, Great Britain Australia, Canada, Japan, United Kingdom.

Fig. 12.7 Upswing due to
non-reaction of the central bank

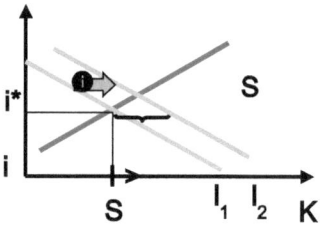

12.2.7 Monetary Policy as a Reason for Business Cycles

12.2.7.1 The Interest Rate Theorem of Knut Wicksell

Wicksell (1851–1926) attributes cyclical fluctuations to the wrong decisions of monetary policymakers, i.e. the central banks (at that time still commercial banks) in controlling interest rates.[27] The profitability of investments, the marginal productivity of capital (or internal rate of return), increases due to external factors (due to technical progress).

1. The central bank does not react or reacts too late (see Fig. 12.7), which is why the internal rate of return (profitability of an investment) is higher than the monetary interest rate. The interest rate of the central bank (i) is therefore lower than the profitability of investments and below the equilibrium interest rate (i *), which would offset supply and demand. There is therefore an over-demand for capital. The result is more investment than savings. The demand shortfall caused by saving is smaller than the additional demand from the companies' investments. Due to the over-demand, it is booming. The central bank does not raise the interest rate, which is why the equilibrium interest rate i * is not reached.

2. Due to excess demand, the cost of inputs (labor and pre-products) increases, which is why the internal rate of return falls.
3. Since the aggregate demand is greater than the supply, the price level rises (see Fig. 12.8). As a result of the price increase, the central bank reacts and raises interest rates, which is why the internal rate of interest is now below the interest rate ($\Rightarrow$ equilibrium interest rate i * < i), which is why investment is now smaller than savings. That the central bank again reacts wrongly and thus triggers the downturn ($\Rightarrow$ I <S $\Rightarrow$ downturn). The intervention of the central bank in the market thus causes cyclical fluctuations, because the market mechanism is disrupted

---

[27]See Grossekettler, Heinz (1989), pp. 203; Wicksell, Knut (1898), pp. 109 and Wicksell, Knut (1922), p. 231.

Fig. 12.8 Downturn due to belated reaction of the central bank

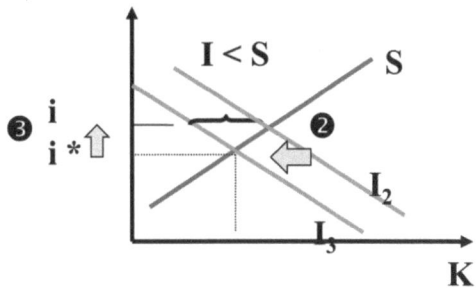

12.2.7.2 The Perverse Elasticity of Credit Supply of Hayek

In contrast, Friedrich August von Hayek (pupil of Wicksell) blames the cyclical overheating for the perverse elasticity of the credit supply, i.e. the uncontrolled development of money supply, in its economic theory.[28] Due to the uncontrolled money creation process there is too much money supply. In the banks' money creation process, these companies pass on the sight deposits of their customers (deposits) to third parties, which creates new sight deposits (see the chapter on monetary policy above). The money will be returned to the bank and can be borrowed again. Hayek calls this unlimited credit a perverse elasticity of the credit supply. Money creation by the banks does not increase interest rates, even though capital demand has increased. Investments are thus greater than savings, which is why the demand on the goods market is greater than the supply ($\Rightarrow I > S$). It creates an upswing. There is an uncontrollable upswing as more money is spent than is saved.

Due to excess demand, the cost of inputs (labor and pre-products) increases, which is why the internal rate of return falls and prices generally rise. Now, lenders are raising interest rates to get inflation compensation, which is why the internal rate of return is now below interest rates and many investments are no longer profitable. There are investment failures and depreciation. The investment demand drops because of saving as a demand failure on the part of the households. The additional demand from companies for investments is not enough to compensate for the drop in demand for savings ($I < S \Rightarrow$ downturn).

> **Conclusion**
> Wicksell and Hayek highlight the dangers of central bank intervention. The central banks prevent the natural market mechanism of the money market from balancing out surplus and short supply. This criticism speaks in favor of rule-based monetary policy, which is geared towards the growth of production potential. Only in
>
> (continued)

---

[28]See Hayek, F. v. (1967 [1935]).

exceptional cases does the intervention of the central bank in the money market appear justified. If the central bank intervenes, it bears a responsibility for the economic development. The central bank must monitor lending and the speed of money circulation.[29]

12.2.7.3 The Effects on Investment Behavior of Zero Interest Rate Policy, Evidence from a Roulette Experiment

The Federal Reserve implemented an extreme expansionary monetary policy (Quantitative Easing) and turned to unconventional monetary policy tools such as forward guidance and large-scale asset purchases. The ECB and the central banks of Switzerland, Sweden and Japan went one step further and set their target rates below zero (zero interest rate policy). This monetary policy is controversial and its effects barely researchable, because the influence of monetary policy on the economy cannot be isolated. There are too many additional factors (Nishad Nishad 2018). The development of growth rates in Japan also raises doubts as to whether there will be positive effects if the zero interest rate policy is applied over a longer period of time. Rather, this policy of cheap money is made responsible for exaggerations on stock markets (Conrad and Stahl 2002) even including the financial crisis. The allegation is that money is wasted and used for risk-taking if it costs nothing.

Historically, the question is very controversial as to how a central bank can generate real growth through monetary policy instruments. According to monetarism, real gross domestic product growth cannot be artificially generated by an expansionary monetary policy. Friedman and Schwartz used historical time sequences and economic analyses to argue that changes in the money supply had unintended adverse effects, and that sound monetary policy is necessary for economic stability. Hayek and Wicksell even blamed the central bank for boom and bust cycles (Wicksell 1898, 1922; Hayek 1935; Friedman and Schwartz 1969).

Against such a background this chapter examines the effects of interest rate cuts on investment behavior using an experiment. Human behavior is examined in this context. The methodology is to simulate investment decision making under different capital costs. How does the borrower with the borrowed money act in relation to the price of the borrowed capital? They may be bank or non-bank investors. The business banks borrow the money from the central bank and then invest it by lending it to private borrowers just as private investors borrow the money from the banks to invest it, for example, in their own companies, real estate or equities.

---

[29] See Conrad, Christian, A./Stahl, Markus (2003), pp. 685–693.

The existing literature and studies are presented and compared to the experiment presented here. Next the experimental design of the study is explained. Finally, the results are presented and the conclusions drawn.[30]

Related Literature

"The more money there is the better it is for the economy", is the conclusion of most studies about quantitative easing (Gagnon 2016) and "the lower the better" is their conclusion for the interest rate. For a long time it was common sense that nominal interest rates cannot fall below zero. This barrier was called the "lower boundary." Scientists have been discussing how to break the Lower Boundary to achieve more economic stimuli since the financial crisis. The arguments for and against a zero-percent policy can be found at Tymoigne (2018).

There have been numerous studies about zero interest rate policy, or negative interest rate policy. For example, Cúrdia estimates that in the US, the decline in GDP during the recession would have decreased by half a percentage point if the Fed had lowered the federal funds rate to -0.75% (Cúrdia 2019). The question arises as to what other consequences follow from subsidizing credits by the central bank. If money is cheap it may be wasted like every other product.

So others argue that low interest rate policy could lead to a buildup of leverage, or asset bubbles by encouraging excessive risk taking by financial market participants (Conrad and Stahl 2002; Caruana 2013; Feldstein 2013; Stiglitz 2016). Confronted with low interest rates bank and non-bank investors may switch to excessive risk in order to compensate the smaller interest income (Hannoun 2015).

The mechanism is called "search for yield". If financial institutions have long-term commitments (such as pension funds and insurance companies) they come under pressure to earn the yield they promised on their liabilities. If they obtain only a low interest return on their assets they might be forced to go in risk (Rajan 2005; De Nicolò et al. 2010). Unilaterally constructed bonus-based compensation schemes encourage excessive risk-taking and were one reason for the financial crisis (Conrad 2015).

Empirical studies show (e.g., for Spain, Maddaloni and Peydró 2010; Ongena et al. 2009) that credit standards tend to loosen when policy rates decline. Maddaloni et al. (2009) show that if overnight rates are lowered credit standards are loosened.

De Nicolò and others (2010) found a negative relationship between the monetary policy rate and ex ante risk taking in a study about US banking policy. The average internal risk rating by banks and the spread over the federal funds rate decline as monetary policy rate increases. They also test the relation between interest rate to the ratio of the bank's risk-weighted assets to total assets of U.S. commercial banks and bank holding companies using their quarterly financial statements (Call Report filings). They find a strong negative

---

[30]See Conrad, Christian A. (2019), pp. 18–27.

relationship between real interest rates and the riskiness of banks' assets. The relationship is weaker when bank capital is low.

Expansive monetary policies and low interest rates, especially long lasting ones, have been made responsible for credit booms and excessive risk taking. The context is as follows. Lower interest rates lead to higher asset prices and borrower's fortune, in turn allow higher and cheaper lending. Analytical models (Stiglitz and Weiss 1981), show more risk-taking when interest rates decline and vice versa a reallocation to more quality and safe investments when interest rates rise. The withdrawal leads to less availability of external financing.

Easy and cheap money access encourages greater risk-taking, which leads to asset bubbles. Later crashes of such bubbles could be damaging for the real economy. If they take place in the housing market they may affect balances of credit institutes and thus lead to credit crunches, which affect the real economy severely (Conrad and Stahl 2002; Claessens et al. 2012; Mian et al. 2015). The cheap central bank money is seen as a reason for the US housing market bubble. The relatively low interest rates in the U.S. during 2001–2004 resulted in a rapid increases in house prices and household leverage (Lansing 2008; Hirata et al. 2012).

Accommodative monetary policy is blamed as one reason for the global financial crisis. Persistently low real interest rates and excess liquidity fueled a bubble as a boom in asset prices and securitized credit and seduced financial institutions into take on increased risk and leverage. Had central banks raised the interest rates earlier and more aggressively and preempted this buildup of risk, the consequences of the burst would have been much less severe (Borio and Zhu 2008; De Nicolò et al. 2010). Claessens and Kose state that whether and how monetary policy affects risk taking, and thereby asset prices and leverage, remains a subject for further research (Claessens and Kose 2013).

This paper details a simple incentive-based experiment regarding investment behavior in relation to borrowing cost based on roulette. There have been several experiments with roulette but with the objective to scrutinize the gambling behavior (Rubio, Hernández, and Santacreu) and guessing tendencies (Rubio et al. 2010). In 2015 there was a roulette experiment, that simulated most common short-term bonus compensation schemes without accountability (Conrad 2015).

Roulette Experimental Design

The purpose of this paper is to test the hypothesis that decreasing the interest rate to zero encourages excessive risk-taking in the financial system. The methodology is to simulate investment decision making under different capital costs. Therefore an experimental environment similar to the investment conditions had to be constructed. Roulette has the advantage of clearly demonstrating the probabilities for gains and losses. In the original game (apart from zero) the probability of losses is compensated with higher payouts. A higher risk has an equivalent higher payout.

The experiment was conducted with 107 students from different Business Bachelor courses at the University of Applied Science HTW at Saarbrücken. The students played

3 rounds of Roulette (A, B and C), each with three games. They could bet on red or black, on one of the three thirds of the 36 numbers or on one number. The winning number and color was determined by the roulette wheel. If it was zero, the game was repeated and not registered. The payouts were distributed according to the probability of winning ($\times 2$, $\times 3$, $\times 36$).

The task was to invest borrowed capital like a manager of a company. The participants were asked to maximize the profit as it is the obligation of a manager as agent for a principal (company owner resp. shareholder). Maximal profit in the group resulted in 10€ real money as variable compensation. In order to reduce change in behavior due to learning effects the game consisted of three rounds each with three games. Learning effects should therefore arise early with small influence.

In order to simulate investment behavior with different interest rates thus capital costs, decision-makers were be exposed to three different investment situations. In round A they were allowed to borrow up to 10,000€ (maximum) at 10% interest, in round B at 5% and in round C at 0%. Losses and gains were credited at 100%. The payouts could be reinvested and were accumulated in each round and afterwards the borrowed capital deducted. The results of the rounds A, B and C were added and the player with the highest result was rewarded with €10 real money. The rules were explained to the students before starting the experiment. The students were asked to check each other's calculations after each game. This simple experiment shows clear results.

Results
The sum of the average borrowed capital rose from €5,439.93 in round A to €9,931.78 in round C, thus by 81.03%. The sum of theaverage capital setrose from €7,211.05 in round A to €14,244.15 in round C, thus by 97.53% (see Figs. 12.9 and 12.10).

How was the risk behavior? The highest possible profit (calculated as the product of the set capital and the possible payout multiple) in all three games rose continuously from €37,483.12 in round A to €98,754.77 in round C, by 163.46% (see Fig. 12.11). The significantly higher standard deviation in round C shows that some players were more willing to take risks than the average (see Fig. 12.12).

If you set the maximum possible gain in relation to set capital as a risk measurement indicator, the willingness to take risks increased by 33.27% from 5.20 in round A to 6.89 in round C (see Fig. 12.13). The same development shows the risk measurement indicator maximal possible gain in relation to the borrowed capital as a risk measurement indicator. The willingness to take risks increased by 46.67% from 6.90 in round A to 10.04 in round C (see Fig. 12.14).

How were the results? How successfully did the investors set their capital? The average gains of round A and B with 10% and 5% interest rate stayed pretty much the same (A: €51.68 and B: €63.60€) whereas in round C the students realized an average loss of €297.66 (see Fig. 12.15).

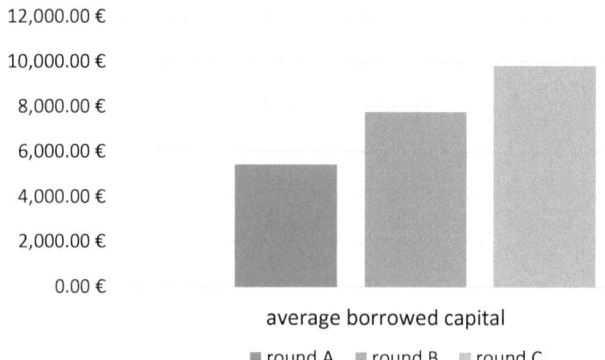

Fig. 12.9 Average borrowed capital

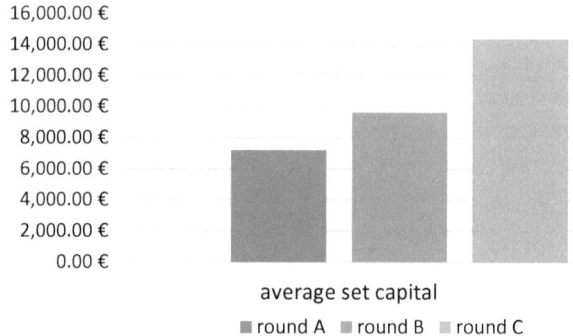

Fig. 12.10 Average set capital

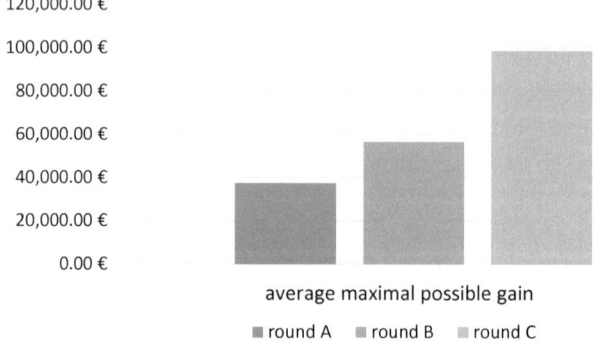

Fig. 12.11 Average maximal possible gain

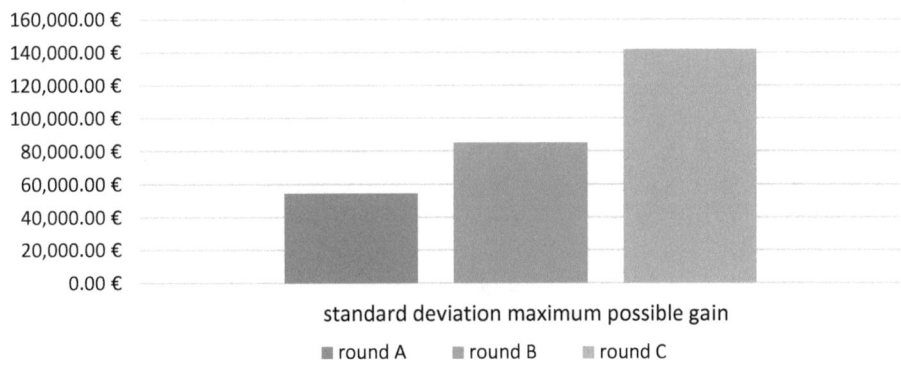

Fig. 12.12 Standard deviation maximum possible gain

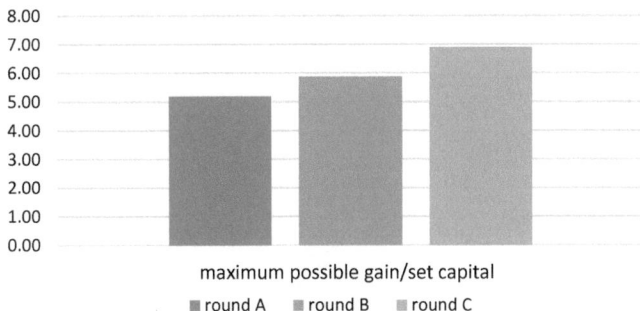

Fig. 12.13 Maximum possible gain in relation to set capital

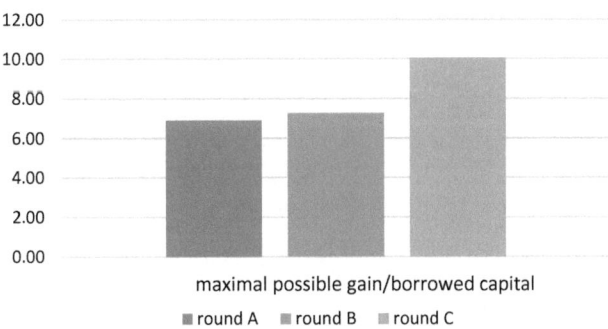

Fig. 12.14 Maximum possible gainin relationtoborrowed capital

Interestingly, with the decreased interest rate as borrowing costs, the risk taking increases continuously, which means that there are proportional effects of the borrowing costs to the risk behavior (see Fig. 12.16). But the strongest reaction was detected at zero interest rate, where there were no capital costs.

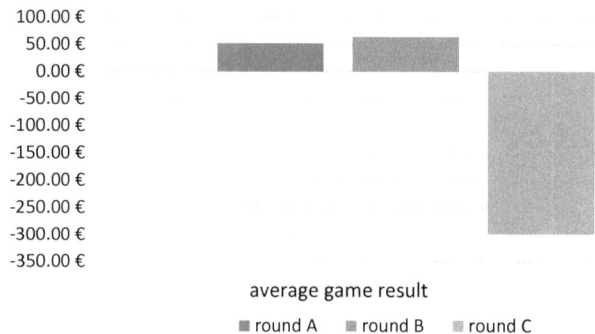

average game result

■ round A   ■ round B   ■ round C

Fig. 12.15 Average game result

	Round A	Round B	Round C
Average borrowed capital	€5,430.93	€7,759.81	€9,831.78
Average set capital	€7,211.05	€9,617.37	€14,244.15
Average maximum possible gain	€37,483.12	€56,466.74	€98,754.77
Standard deviation average maximum possible gain	€54,490.10	€85,157.77	€141,764.15
Risk as max. possible gain/set capital	5.2	5.87	6.93
Risk as max. possible gain/borrowed capital	6.90	7.28	10.04
Average game result, +gain, -loss	€51.68	€63.60	- €297.66

Fig. 12.16 Statistical data

Conclusion

The experiment showed that decreasing interest rates encourage risk-taking. With the decreased interest rate as borrowing costs the risk taking increased weakly but continuously. The risk taking increased strongly when the interest rate reached zero. The experiment showed excessive risk-taking when there were no capital costs. With no capital costs the average result of the game was a net loss, whereas before there was a small profit. It seems that if money is free, human beings react less rationally. This finding supports the hypothesis that extreme expansive monetary policy with low, zero or negative interest rates encourage financial bubbles and overinvestments or wrong investments in the real economy. Bank and non-bank

(continued)

investors are less prudent and rational the less the capital costs are and extremely irrational and incautious if there are no costs at all.

Decreasing the interest rate to zero encourages excess risk-taking in the financial system. Low interest rate policy could lead to a buildup of leverage, or asset bubbles by encouraging excessive risk taking by financial market participants. Bank and non-bank investors may be encouraged by low interest rates to take excessive risk in their search for profit, which can create asset bubbles on the stock market and housing market. If they are financed by credit, credit crunches and strong economic downturns may follow, which caused the 1929 financial crisis (stock market crash), followed by the great depression and the financial crisis of 2008 (housing credit crisis).

Moreover, it has been demonstrated (Conrad 2015) that unilaterally constructed incentive schemes encourage excess risk-taking. This would indicate that common bonus-based compensation schemes enhance risk because of the asymmetries in the treatment of gains and losses. Unilaterally constructed compensation schemes were one reason for the financial crisis.

After the financial crisis many central banks turned to quantitative easing (QE) to support economic growth. In order to reduce long-term borrowing costs they purchased massive and unprecedented amounts of long-term bonds, which created liquidity and decreased the long term borrowing costs. Some central banks even pushed short-term interest rates slightly below zero to stimulate the economy. But the slow recovery, especially in Europe, has raised questions about the benefits of QE bond purchases versus their detriments and whether their effectiveness has reached a limit.

The example of Japan should give pause. Japan is a pioneer of zero interest rate policy and quantitative easing. In 2001 and 2013, the Bank of Japan implemented zero interest rates alongside quantitative easing. Neither managed to stimulate the economy sustainably or to increase inflation (Drozd 2018). Often when pursuing an inflation target, we forget that we are in a long phase of globalization with falling import prices. In particular, the goods made in China are pushing down prices for many consumer goods.

The question remains as to why the long period of low interest rates in Japan has not led to a second bubble. For a bubble, a constant inflow of liquidity is required, which is financed by loans. After the real estate and equity crash in Japan in the 1980s, Japanese banks still had a lot of bad credit on the books after huge write-offs. They were not recapitalized, so even if they wanted to make the same mistake again, they lacked the equity to real estate and equity loans. Rather, one spoke at that time of a credit crunch, since the Japanese banks and the real economy barely forgave loans for lack of equity, which is why the economy stagnated at a low level. Dell'Ariccia

(continued)

et al. (2013) showed that the extent of bank capitalization appears to be an important factor for recovery. They found out that facing a lower interest rate, a well-capitalized bank is willing to give more credit, it decreases its monitoring and takes more risk, while a highly levered, a low capitalized bank does the opposite (Dell'Ariccia et al. 2010; Claessens and Kose 2013).

There are a lot of market distortions due to the market intervention of the central bank apart from the shift to investments with higher yields. If the interest rate is below the inflation rate, there are redistributive effects from creditors to debtors. Insurance companies and pension funds do not have enough earnings to meet their obligations. Money market funds might not earn enough to cover their costs of running. The pension of the population becomes a problem, as the interest income is missing. The effects of a prolonged zero interest rate phase on the financial system has not yet been handled in depth. Banks lack the float profits from loaning their deposits, as well as the margin between investment and lending rate. Negative investment rates are usually not enforceable on the market and neither is a high credit margin if the refinancing rate is zero (Arteta et al. 2016). Lowering the interest rates thus means narrowing net interest margins—the gap between commercial banks' lending and deposit rates. Several studies found a positive relationship between short-term interest rates and net interest margins. A low interest rate environment has the adverse effect on banks' profitability (Claessens et al. 2016; Borio et al. 2015).

The Bank Lending Survey of April 2016 already noted a collapse in European bank profit as a result of low interest rate policy and quantitative easing (Arteta et al. 2016). If the banks lack income, equity is also lacking to lend and to survive new crises. The zero interest rate policy is thus counterproductive. In addition, if the central bank buys corporate and government bonds, it shuts the commercial banks out of this market, especially since it lacks the expertise to manage corporate risk. The financing of enterprises by state organizations is not market-compliant, but characteristic of central administration economies.

All studies assume an interest rate responsiveness to investments. As we know from the Great Depression of 1929, this does not have to be the case. If the expectations of return on investments are negative, interest rates would have to be so negative that they more than offset losses on the investment. But then it would be less risky for companies if they did not invest the money but let it go and take the central bank's negative interest rates as a safe return.

The expectations of the return on investments must not only be negative due to poor economic expectations, they can also be due to a lack of competitiveness. For example, in spite of zero interest rates, nobody would invest in Greek hotels if the

(continued)

comparable Mediterranean holiday in Portugal is much cheaper due to lower labor costs.

Falling interest rates, on the other hand, always affect equity and real estate prices. For one thing, they are the alternative form of investment to bonds and, on the other hand, they can be financed by loans. If the cost of credit decreases, the present value of real estate and equities increases. The demand for shares and real estate and thus also the price will rise. The profits of companies increase due to lower borrowing costs, which also increases the demand for shares and thus the price.

In conclusion, one can say that the side effects of an extremely expansionary monetary policy such as zero interest rate policy, negative interest rate policy or quantitative easing are so great that such an intervention in the markets is only justified in a Keynesian depression situation (Great Depression) as in 1929 and 2008 and only for a limited time. One can only warn against recent suggestions, such as de-bundling cash from electronic currency and making cash depreciate relative to electronic currency, to further reduce key interest rates to negative territory (Assenmacher and Krogstrup 2018), because the negative effects of these options are not predictable.

12.2.7.4 Case Study: The US Monetary Policy in the Field of Tension of the Stock Market Development

The ECB has pursued an expansive monetary policy since its central bank president Draghi took office. Following the interventions in the context of the financial crisis and the sovereign debt crisis, Draghi tried with an expansionary monetary policy to combat deflation and stimulate economic growth. His program for buying government bonds also served this purpose. Thus, in addition to money being pumped into the market, the banks are forced to lend to companies because of the absence of government bonds as an investment possibility. Furthermore, the purchase of government bonds on the capital market should also reduce the lending rate. The US has also pursued an expansive monetary policy since the crash of the financial crisis but also before (see Fig. 12.17).

The following chapter uses the example of the USA to examine the extent to which an expansionary monetary policy can cause speculative bubbles and thus economic fluctuations.

Exercise

Read and discuss the following case study on US monetary policy. To what extent can the monetary policy of a central bank affect assets (asset prices)? Does the central bank have a responsibility here?

The Federal Reserve has been providing ample liquidity with the US economy since 1994 amid the productivity gains of the economic epoch of the time called the "New

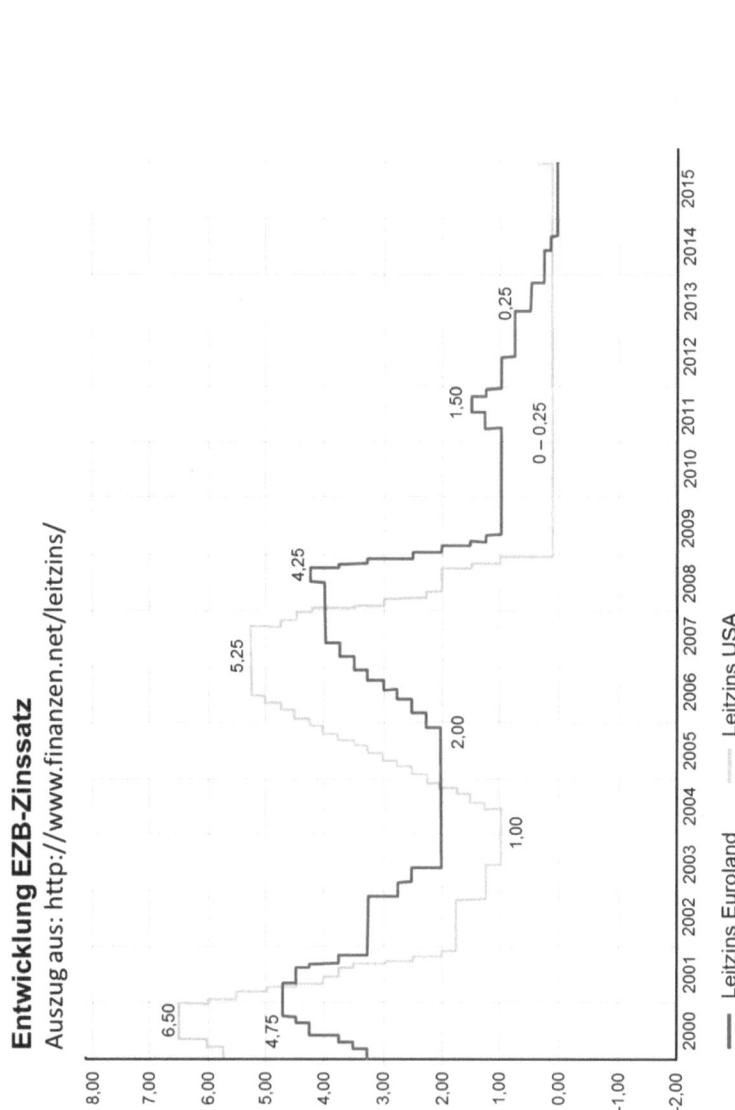

Fig. 12.17 Development of the ECB and US interest rates 2000–2015 (Imprint with friendly permission of finanzen.net GmbH. http://www.finanzen.net/leitzins/)

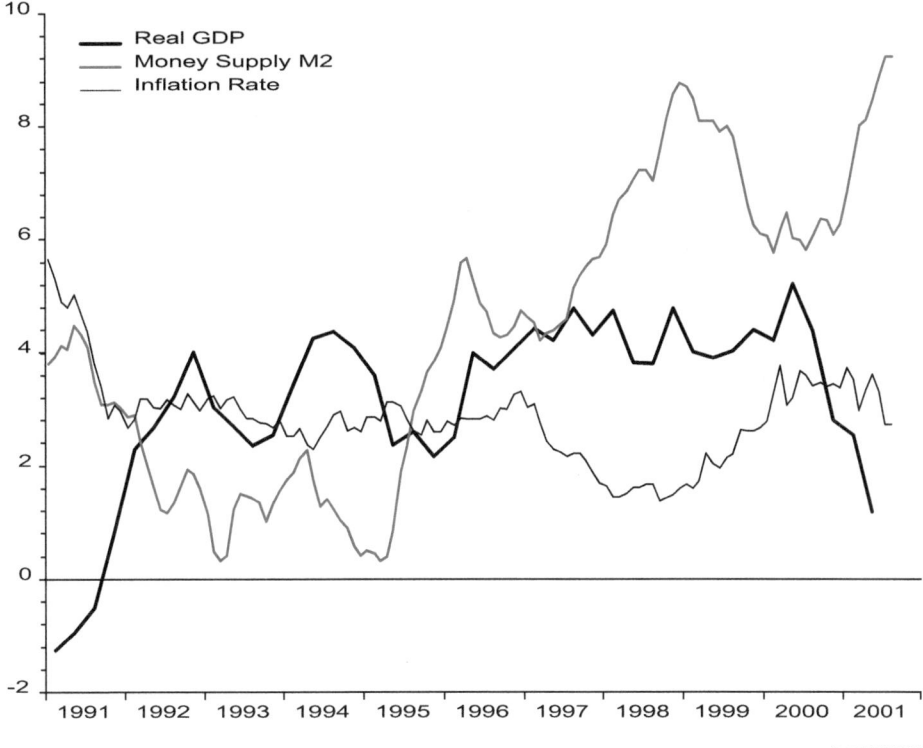

Fig. 12.18 Real growth (bottom right), inflation rate (center right) and money stock M2 (top right)

Economy". The over-proportional growth in money supply in relation to real GDP in recent years (see Fig. 12.18) not only supported the productivity forces of the US economy, but also inflated share prices to an unprecedented degree. From September 1994 to March 2000, the S&P500 gained more than 250%, giving an annual return of around 25%. The Russian crisis and the subsequent bankruptcy of the hedge fund LTCM[31] in the fall of 1998 proved to be only short-term shifts. Already in the aftermath of the October 1987 crash, Greenspan saved the US stock market with his pragmatic interest rate cuts. In 1998, he managed this for a second time by organizing a rescue operation for the LTCM hedge fund. In addition, he saved the world financial system from a serious crisis. However, the verbal statements and actions of the US Federal Reserve fell wide apart in 1997 and 1998. Already in 1996, Greenspan warned of an "irrational exuberance" when the Dow Jones 30 Industrial Average stood at 6600 points. Just as the development trends of the time of US growth and inflation rates suggested a more restrictive policy, the Fed opted for three cuts in interest rates in the fall of 1998 given the sharp fall in the US stock market. From September 28 to

---

[31]See Markus Stahl/Christian Conrad (2000), pp. 415–422.

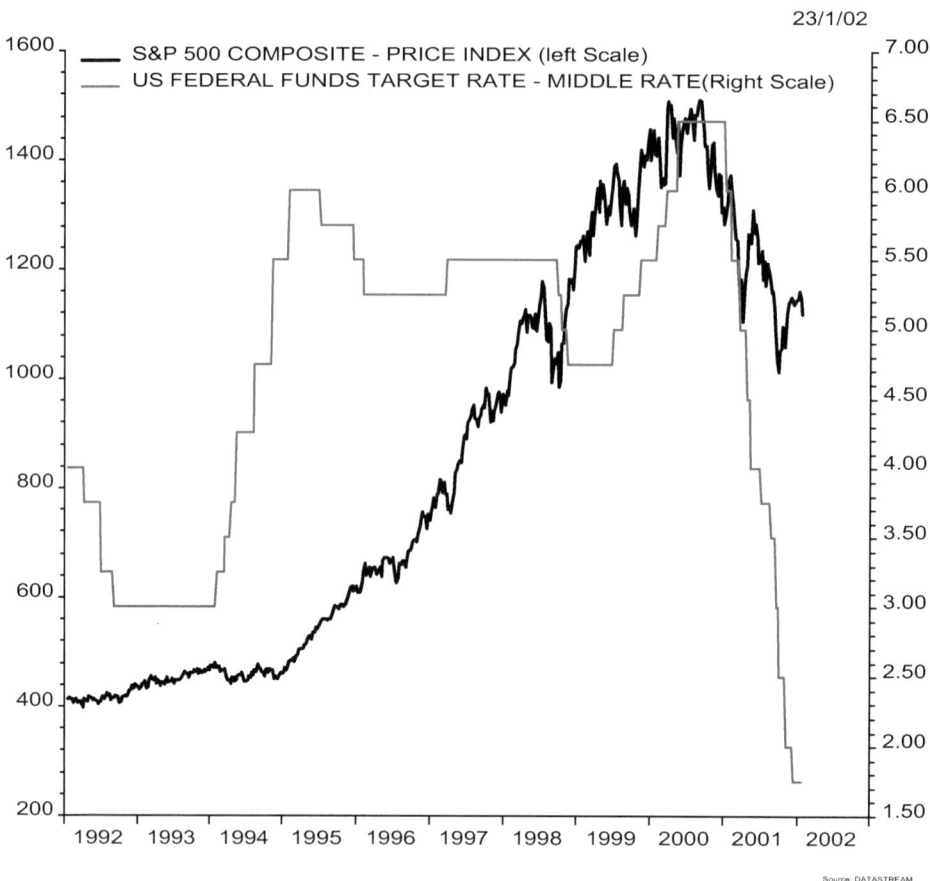

23/1/02

Fig. 12.19 S & P 500 stock index (left scale) and Fed Funds Rate (right scale). *A* fundamental reasons; *B* technical reasons; *C* psychological reasons

November 17, 1998, the federal funds target rate was reduced by a quarter percent from 5.5% to 4.75% (Fig. 12.19).

It was only these interest rate cuts by the US Federal Reserve Bank that were able to halt the downward process on the stock markets. What could have caused Greenspan to cut interest rates?

We remember the US Federal Reserve's monetary policy in the run-up to the stock market crash of 1929, which was followed by a long-lasting global economic crisis. To what extent American monetary policy contributed to the speculative excess in the twenties and the current stock market upswing, economists divided then as now. It is undisputed that the initial phase of both boom movements was accompanied by an expansionary monetary policy. After 1921, the last year of restrictive monetary policy introduced to combat post-war inflation, the central bank lowered the discount rate from 6% in 1921 to 3.5% by mid-1927. For a more restrictive line, there was no reason behind the traditional concept of inflation. The rates of increase in goods prices were consistently below the critical tolerance thresholds. The growth of the money stock M1 developed largely parallel to the real gross domestic product, so that the danger of a pent-up money overhang, which could be steered in the short term on the goods consumption comparatively small. The actual inflation and credit creation, however, took place in the securities sector. Then in 1929 the broker loans reached about 10% of the market capitalizationwith about 8.5 billion US dollars. When some members of the US monetary system sensed the danger emanating from the securities loans, it was already too late to stop the speculative carousel. When the central bank finally decided to intervene, the three discount rate hikes were no longer enough to slow the speculative movement by a total of 1.5% to the level of 5% in the summer of 1928. This is hardly surprising, given the partially over 10% interest paid on the broker loans, which were mainly fed by industrial companies and foreign banks. Also, Fed Chairman Roy Young's warning that central bank money should not be misused for credit-financed speculation, but is only available for productive purposes, went unheeded, with the US Federal Reserve finally setting the discount rate on 9 August 1929 once more from 5% to 6%.[32] The decisive blow, as it turned out only two months later.[33]

In the light of the global economic crisis of 1929, Greenspan's interest rate cuts are understandable. The interest rate cut signal, however, not only stopped the stock market downtrend, but also stimulated investors' willingness to speculate.[34] With the first rate cut being made outside of the regular session round, Fed Chairman Alan Greenspan has earned the—questionable—reputation of savior, because he would not allow future capital markets to fall dramatically below their current levels. This implicit bailout guarantee really encouraged investors to quadruple technology stocks between the autumn of 1998 and the first quarter of 2000. After that, however, the Federal Reserve (Fed) was in a dilemma comparable to 1929. The unleashing of speculative forces and the furious development of Internet stocks in the winter of 1999/2000 could not be stopped by the interim transition to a more restrictive monetary policy. Only the increase of the federal funds target rate to 6.5% showed effects on the US stock exchanges in April 2000. However, the S&P500 was already at approx. 1500.

As in the 1920s, as part of this interest rate hike, the stock price bubble in the technology stocks also finally broke in March 2000. The US technology exchange Nasdaq lost more than 60% of its high at 5050 points since March 10, 2000. The downswing also included the classic default values. After the previous exaggerations in the consumer sector, the US economy could also threaten a recession. In contrast to 1929, the US Federal Reserve reacted immediately and drastically. During the course of 2001, the Fed downgraded the key rate in eleven steps to 1.75%. From a dynamic point of view, the interest rate reduction

---

[32]See Clarke, Stephen (1967), Library of Congress Catalog No. 67-17650.

[33]The monetary circumstances of the crash of 1929 examined in particular Temin, Peter (1976), und Friedman, Milton/Schwartz, Jacobson (1965).

[34]Conrad, Christian, A./Schoett, Harry (2000), pp. 151–159.

trend exceeded the key interest rate cuts in the run-up to the global economic crisis of 1930–1933.[35]

The Fed justifies its very expansionary monetary policy with the growing economic weakness during the course of 2001. It pointed to the decline in consumer confidence and the reluctance of many companies to invest. Added to this was the further deterioration in sentiment related to the terrorist attacks on September 11, 2001. The Fed also openly discussed the weakness of the US stock market and the extent to which investor asset losses could negatively impact their demand. Such comments on monetary policy and the reaction patterns of interest rate policy impressively prove that the stock market development was a key factor in the monetary policy of the US Fed. In contrast to other central banks, the American Fed's goals are not only the price stability, but—among other objectives—the objective of adequate economic growth. The way in which these goals are filled in and weighted according to the respective economic situation is up to the Fed.

In Japan as well, in the mid-1980s, monetary aggregates grew much faster than GDP. With plans for tightening monetary policy already in place, following the global stock crash in October 1987, the Bank of Japan was forced to make its contribution to stabilizing world financial markets by maintaining monetary expansion. While Wall Street and the stock markets in Europe needed more time to digest the price setbacks, the Japanese Nikkei 225 stock index swiftly rose to new highs. From October 1987 to December 1989 it was able to grow again by 80%. At the beginning of 1990, the bubble burst. The Nikkei Index lost almost 70% of the December 1990 level in the following years.[36]

After discussing the influence of monetary policy on assets such as equities in the context of the case study, we will now examine this relationship in more detail.

12.2.7.5 Review of Monetary Policy Objectives

In many cases, as the crisis unfolds, the central bank is forced to mitigate emerging problems in the financial system and the real economy through the printing press and devaluations. The history of money is replete with examples where an inappropriately accommodative monetary policy provided the financial basis for inflation in capital market prices (asset inflation) without rapidly rising commodity prices. The culmination of serious crises in the financial system, the undermining of the external and domestic value of the currency and excessive demands on public finances. Already in England in the eighteenth century, a speculative stock price bubble shook the financial markets.[37] Under the leadership of John Blunt, the South Sea Company was mandated to convert government debt and annuity payments into treasury shares with fixed dividend payments.

Although the exact conversion plan was not announced, a run on shares of the South Sea Company began in the spring of 1720. From January to June of 1720, the stock price rose

---

[35] See Christian A. Conrad/Markus Stahl (2000), pp. 25.

[36] See Daxhammer, Rolf/Schmied-Wörle, Tatjana (2000), pp. 45-58.

[37] Or the South Sea Bubble See Chancellor, Edward (1999), pp. 58-95.

from £ 128 to £ 1050. The entire English stock market was carried away by the speculative fever. The speculative mania was driven by the money creation of the banks, which spent more and more collateral on new securities loans. In France, it was the John Law-based Banque Generale, a forerunner of today's Central Bank, which offered similar services to the French Crown as did the South Sea Company. When Louis XIV died in 1715 he left an extremely high debt of 2.4 billion livre for his successor Louis XV. John Law relieved the royal finances by issuing shares of the Banque Generale and the Mississippi Company against the deposit of government bonds. Speculation in these acts degenerated into a veritable popular movement in the autumn of 1719. Bank John Laws, now renamed Banque Royal, financed speculative excesses by issuing paper notes that were no longer covered by the bank's gold holdings.[38] In the end, the wealth of stock and paper money owners in England and France had been largely destroyed by the uncontrolled cash of the then still private central banks.[39]

The inflation measures used by central banks mainly include consumer goods prices and producer prices. Price developments in the financial sector and asset prices (asset prices) are thus systematically hidden by the measurement method.[40] So it is possible that excessive money production is reflected not in rising prices for consumer goods, but in asset price volatility. If only consumer goods prices are considered, this can lead to unpredictable inflation. However, price distortions in the financial sector are just as damaging to long-term steady and balanced economic growth as unchecked commodity price inflation. Price distortions in the asset markets can lead to serious misallocations in the real economy and ultimately jeopardize the functioning of the financial system as the central payer and transmission belt of monetary policy.

A stock market boom is supported by an excessive supply of money by the central banks. The parlor game "Monopoly" can serve as a simple example here. After an initially very slow start-up phase with rather low prices for street trains during negotiations between the players, incredibly high amounts for roads are scored in the final phase of the game. The background to this phenomenon is neither the special strategy achievement of the few players who have become rich, nor the luck or misfortune of throwing the dice. The key to the explanation is the universally popular lot-playing field. Passing go gets you 4000 monetary extra units.

The blessings bestowed by "Go" do not mean that the amount of money per player per round is increased by 4000 monetary units. With 5 players and 15 rounds, the money supply increases by 300,000 monetary units. The initial cash amount is 30,000 monetary units per player; so for 5 players a total of 150,000 monetary units. After 15 rounds, the

---

[38]For the financial scandal of Law see Kiehling, Hartmut (2000), pp. 19-29

[39]Gold investments could be successful in such a scenario.
   See Mezger, Markus/Stahl, Markus (2001a), pp. 372–378 and Conrad, Christian, A./Stahl, Markus (2002).

[40]See Mezger, Markus/Stahl, Markus (2001b), pp. 15–22.

lottery money source now provides more than three times the money supply (150,000 + 300,000 = 450,000). Therefore, one should not be surprised if in bilateral price negotiations between the players on individual streets ever increasing amounts are offered and achieved in the course of the game. The asset price bubble, limited in the original game to the real estate sector, begins to inflate further and further.

The relationship between money supply development and asset prices has been examined in several empirical studies. They show, for example, that in the second half of the 1980s, in addition to increased productivity of the Japanese economy and increased demand for real estate in Tokyo, the sharp rise in prices for Japanese equities, art and real estate in Japan spurred an expansionary monetary policy. Above all, it expressed itself in increased bank lending.[41]

However, the scientific content of the predominantly Granger-based econometric studies has to be questioned. We have fundamental method problems here. Because of the risk of false results, the Granger test is discouraged if the variables under study are extremely volatile.[42] For highly volatile variables such as stock prices, a lack of covariance stationarity was found, which does not provide a condition for the regression of time series.[43] Due to innumerable influencing factors on supply and demand, we have a strong multi-causality here in which the individual influencing factors cannot be filtered out precisely. If causal variables are not extracted, Granger tests can show correlations that are not present (spurious regression). The same applies to purely random correlations, which may arise in particular in the case of short observation periods or incorrect time intervals.[44]

Different analyses[45] show a positive correlation between the variables, which can be interpreted differently:

1. For example, the productivity of companies could have increased and thus the profits of listed companies and, subsequently, the stock prices. In this case, the central bank would only have expanded the money supply in line with the increase in real production.
2. If the central bank increases the money supply or directly lowers the key interest rate, this may result in a reduction of the long-term interest rate as a discounting factor for the

---

[41] See Ito, Takatoshi/Iwaisako, Tokuo (1995).

[42] See Irwin, Scott H./Sanders, Dwight R. (2012), pp. 258.

[43] See Pagan, A./Schwert, C. (1990), p. 165–170.; Phillips, P./Loretan, M. (1990); Frenk, David U. A., (2011), (p. 43-49), p. 45 and http://www.matthias-schlecker.de/kointegrationsanalyse-stationaritaet-und-augmented-dickey-fuller-test (4.04.2014).

[44] See Frenk, David u.a. (2011), a.a.O. pp. 47.

[45] See International Monetary Fund (2000) and *Baks, Klaas/Kramer, Charles* (1999).

expected corporate profits, which corresponds to a higher present value. As a result, stock prices rise. This connection can easily be illustrated. Apart from the retained profits, the return of a share for a period (r_k) as the yielt on the capital gains in percent plus the dividends in percent be represented as follows[46]:

$$r_k = \frac{p_{t+1} - p_t}{p_t} + \frac{D_{t+1}}{p_t} \tag{12.1}$$

$$= \frac{p_{t+1} + D_{t+1} - p_t}{p_t} \tag{12.2}$$

[where p is the price of the stock (price) and D is the dividend. t stands for the period]

In the allocation equilibrium, the stock return must correspond to the alternative investments, including the yield on government securities. It can therefore be regarded as a minimum return. Equation (12.2) can be solved for p_t, i.e. the stock price. You get:

$$p_t = \frac{p_{t+1} + D_{t+1}}{1 + r_k} \tag{12.3}$$

To increase the informative value of Eq. (12.3), we make two simplifying assumptions. On the one hand, dividends are growing at a constant rate g and on the other hand, the price gains are also constant. As a growth rate of D then g can also be subtracted from the discount factor r_k.

$$p_t = \frac{D}{r_k - g} \tag{12.4}$$

Consider the constellation $r_k = 10\%$ (0.1), $g = 0.05$ and $D = \$2$, we get for pt $= \$2/(0.1 - 0.05) = \$40$. With this equation, the effect of a rate cut on the price is derived, as well as the interest rate elasticity. We leave all other numbers unchanged and reduce the interest rate r_k by 40% from 10% to 6%. As a result, the price increases $160 (400%) to $200. The interest rate elasticity of the share price is thus 10, an effect that would certainly not have been expected to that extent.

3. Lower interest rates mean lower financing costs for companies, thus increasing their profits, which also leads to a price increase. Assuming that the financing structure of companies consists of 70% debt and 30% equity, an interest rate cut from 5% to 1% as a result of an expansionary monetary policy, assuming an return on equity of

---

[46]See Braley, R. (1983), An Introduction to Risk and Return, 2nd ed., Oxford 1983

Actually, all future periods must be included. However, due to the limited real-time forecast horizon, this is not the case here.

10% would increase the corporate profit by 93.33% (70 × 4% = 2.8, return on equity: 3 + 2.8 = 5.8, calculated with 30 parts of equity capital to 70 parts of debt).

The valuation indicators for equities would have to be adjusted for the refinancing costs. Even a smooth price-earnings ratio like that of Shiller (CAPE, Cycle-Adjusted Price Earnings Ratio) could be distorted by a prolonged period of low interest rates.

4. Real estate is predominantly financed with debts. A fall in interest rates has a direct effect on the refinancing rates and thus on direct purchasing power. The following applies to a bullet loan:

$$\text{Interest cost} = \text{debt} \times (1 + i/100)^{n-} \text{debt}$$

Example: If a house cost € 100,000 and the lending rate were 5%, the interest cost would be $100.000 \times (1 + 5/100)^{10}$, or € 162,900. If the central bank now lowers the interest rate to 1%, the interest costs amount to $100.000 \times (1 + 1/100)^{10}$ 110.500 €, which corresponds to a reduction of 30%. The home buyer can thus afford a 30% more expensive house. Conversely, the 30% can also be seen as a return potential if you finance an externally leased property with constant rental income.

5. If the money supply is greatly increased, the portfolio of investors shifts in favor of the cash position. Investors want to restore their desired portfolio relation between money and equity investments and therefore demand more shares. The price of shares then rises as well as the price of other goods. This is an expression of inflation as the real productivity of the stock market has remained the same.

We can thus record the following. If the yield on bonds as a competitive investment has a significant impact on stock prices, this also applies indirectly to monetary policy as a determinant of interest. In his business cycle theory, Friedrich August von Hayek[47] has blamed the perverse elasticity of the banking system, that is, the uncontrolled development of money, for the economic overheating. On the other hand, Knut Wicksell[48] attributes them to the wrong decisions of monetary policy makers in controlling interest rates. A fixed interest rate below the equilibrium interest rate on supply and demand on the capital market causes an inflation of the money supply, more precisely a shift of the goods-money exchange relationship in favor of the money. Due to the low interest rate, demand for credit is rising. Increased lending creates new sight deposits. The speed of money and thus also the money supply are rising. As the cash holdings of the investor have risen relative to the securities holdings, portfolio diversification has occurred. The new money flows into the stock markets and drives up the prices. Due to the function of interest rates as the benchmark return and discount factor,

---

[47] See Hayek, Friedrich August von (1929), pp. 81.
[48] See Wicksell, Knut (1928), p. 231ff; Wicksell, Knut (1898), p. 101ff, and Grossekettler, Heinz (1989), p. 203f.

an artificial interest rate cut not only causes a rise in stock prices, but also an excessive allocation of resources to stock prices, which can lead to overheating.[49]

In addition, there are self-reinforcement effects: Increased stock prices (and/or real estate prices) signal profit potential and provide collateral for the banks, with which they can operate the credit and thus indirectly the money creation. It comes to a self-reinforcing upward process on the stock market. Refinancing pledges (lender of last resort bailouts) in the event of liquidity squeezes such as those of the International Monetary Fund or the central banks increase the security of speculation and thus support such a development (moral hazard problem). In addition, the low level of interest rates promotes credit-financed equity purchases. However, the bubble can not expand indefinitely, as the price spiral and the rising stock market turnover tie up more and more of the available liquidity. By the time the total money stock is absorbed by the stock market, the market capitalisations of the stocks begin to fall below their own weight. Falling prices trigger further compulsory liquidation in a kind of chain reaction. The crash happens.[50] The same applies to the real estate market.

The Consequences of Asset Bubbles
If high stock prices do not reflect future corporate profits, but rather the exaggerated expectations of a majority of market participants, there may be misallocation of economic resources if companies put out new stocks or bonds at excessive rates and make unprofitable investments. For example, up until March 2000 the bubble on the technology exchanges led to a general over-dimensioning of real investment in this sector.[51] This is where the theories of Hayek and Wicksell take effect. Too much liquidity and a lowering of the interest rate below the equilibrium interest rate encourage speculative bubbles. Overinvestments, which subsequently had to be written off, were also characteristic of the real estate bubble in the USA, Spain and Ireland before the financial crisis. Free money increases your appetite for risk. In addition, investors are taking higher risks in their search for returns due to the lack of alternatives. This was another reason for the financial crisis.

National resources would have been partially misdirected. Investors and lenders would then be faced with significant losses. If the banking system were affected by this industry through high levels of stock ownership or extensive credit exposure to defaults it could lead to crisis developments in the banking industry. Since the credit-forgiveness of the banking system is a direct function of equity, write-offs on equity could lead to growing restrictions on lending. The economy could then suffer from a crippling credit crunch in the banking sector. This situation, for example, was countered by the collapsed stock market bubble in the Japanese economy. At a time when the Bank of Japan forgave money virtually for free,

---

[49]See *Conrad, Christian A.* (2000), p. 135–146.
[50]See Conrad, Christian A./Stahl, Markus (2000), pp. 24–32.
[51]See Stahl, Markus (2000a, b).

Japanese companies had difficulty obtaining bank loans. There was also a credit crunch as a result of the financial crisis.

The contagion of the real economy through a bursting stock market bubble is—besides going through the banking system (credit crunch)—also via the wealth effect of consumption. If the breezy stock market profits dissipate, only a fiction should be lost. But like all fictions, stock market fictions can also deeply intervene in real economic life. Consumers who have not the slightest fear to spend their budgets months ahead during the bull market in the expectation that they will be able to settle the installments due through stock market profits, have a hard time meeting their obligations after a crash. New acquisitions are unthinkable. On the basis of their securities ownership and the increasing value of their own shares and holdings, entrepreneurs and their companies increasingly borrow on additional investments during the stock market upswing. Overnight they become dubious debtors to whom the bank terminates the loans. It can lead to a vicious cycle of consumer restraint, investment stop, production restrictions, wage losses, mood deterioration and renewed consumer and investment restrictions.

The strength of the wealth effect is shown in the following example: we calculate the consequences of a correction of stock prices by ten percent, assuming a wealth effect of five percent. Market capitalization of US $16 trillion (US $12.8 trillion, NASDAQ index: US $3.2 trillion) at end of April 2001 such a 10% correction represents a $1.6 trillion asset destruction. Consequently, due to the wealth effect of 5% decline in consumption by $80 billion. Total US private consumption in 2000 was approximately $6,800 billion. The wealth effect thus implies a decline in private consumption of about 1.1%. Since consumption in 2000 grew by nominally about 7.8%, this is a very serious order of magnitude. However, the uncertainty band of this estimate is large, since empirical studies put the wealth effect at 2% to 10% of consumption. For a 10% decline in the stock market, the decline in consumption could thus amount to 0.47% (2% wealth effect) or 2.3% (10% wealth effect). Regardless of the exact size of the wealth effect, however, it remains clear that a drastic stock market crash, e.g. 30% is likely to exert a very sustained cyclical effect. Here, the decline in consumption would at best be around 1.5%, but in the pessimistic case almost 7%.[52]

The resource misallocation as a result of an expansionary monetary policy after the bursting of the bubble caused massive loss of assets and economic slumps. In addition to resource misallocation, massive allocative redistributive effects can be identified. They add to the speculative effects of the expansionary monetary policy that monetary policy creates by artificially low interest rates. Even without a negative real rate of return due to inflation, there are massive distributional effects in favor of the debtors to the detriment of the creditors, e.g. savers who can jeopardize the pensions of the population over a longer period of time.

---

[52]See Conrad, Christian, A./Stahl, Markus (2002).

Conclusion

The current objective is that central banks guarantee price stability. In that sense, they would also have to control inflationary risks resulting from the upgrading of equity and a corresponding increase in household consumption. With regard to the recording of the potential for inflation, therefore, consideration should at least be given to measurement that which include a more comprehensive spectrum of prices than the current price trend of the basket of goods. In the case of an intertemporal interpretation of the concept of inflation, in addition to current consumer prices, future price developments—derived from asset price changes—could also be taken into account. Estimates based on the correlation between equity market capitalization and aggregate consumption can be used for this purpose. The central banks would therefore consider a price indicator when considering their monetary policy target, which includes not only current consumer prices but also price developments on the asset markets. As a result, asset price developments would become part of monetary policy governance.

So far, the price development on the stock and real estate markets has not been included in the monetary policy objective. There are reasons for this. Monetary policy, if it wants to remain predictable, can only be based on measurable indicators. However, in contrast to consumer price indices, there are neither empirically recognized values on the overall economic impact of asset price distortions, nor are there any ratios that could indicate any deviation or imbalance. A stock market bubble isn't predictable through empirical-methods because share prices always include expectations about the uncertain, unpredictable future. Ultimately, the central banks cannot determine the fundamentally correct price level of the shares better than the large number of market participants who determine the price level in the markets every day through their buying and selling decisions.

The central bank could also come under pressure if it were accused of destroying equity or real estate assets with its policy, or excessively curtailing the money supply of the real economy and thus slowing down the economy, only to counteract an undetectable stock market bubble. However, the opposite accusation that the central banks represent the interests of the stock exchange investors that see themselves beholden to the US Fed which is damaging to the reputation of a central bank.

In principle, a bubble cannot be determined exactly, but it can be suspected. The central bank should first check whether there is a fundamental reason for the exorbitant price growth, which will usually be the case. If the stock exchange in question is an

(continued)

economically representative one, the central bank should, on the one hand, compare the growth rates of the stock market indices with the historical values and, on the other hand, with the current growth of the gross domestic product. If it finds a sustainable historical or relative increase, then the assumption of a bubble is obvious.[53]

Finally, we can record the following recommendations for monetary policy:

1. Potential-oriented, rule-based monetary policy

    As asset prices are mainly driven by expectations and at the same time expectations about future monetary policy play a central role, the most constant, potential-oriented monetary policy is recommended. It contributes significantly to the stabilization of expectations. Orienting the money supply at the development of the gross domestic product and the production potential prevents money overhang, which in turn makes a stock market bubble no longer possible.

2. Inclusion of asset prices as further indicators of monetary policy governance

    Asset prices should be integrated into the models of the central banks as an "early inflation indicator", so that a rule-based countermeasure is possible. This includes informing the public about the development of the indicators. Investors would anticipate the countermeasures of the central bank in a departure of the indicators and no longer speculate on an increase in prices. This would additionally counteract a bubble.

3. No bail-outs

    The rule-binding of monetary policy also includes the consistent enforcement of the basic principle of liability and thus a waiver of explicit or implicit bail-out promises. If investors can no longer pass speculative risk onto the central bank, this will counteract self-reinforcing speculation. On the other hand, it must be ensured beforehand by the described rule-bound automatisms that there will be no system-endangering asset bubble, which would make a bail-out necessary.

4. Flanking monetary policy through measures taken by the banking and stock exchange regulators:

    (a) Reducing the lending rate for equity loans (i.e. the percentage of crediting of shares as collateral for lending) could reduce stock demand in the event of a presumed stock market overheating.

    (b) A prudential increase in safety clearing margins would reduce the leverage effect of derivatives on equity demand.

---

[53]See *Shleifer, Andrei* (2000b), p. 21 and *Stahl, Markus/Conrad, Christian A.* (2000), a.a.O., pp. 415–422.

(c) Including hitherto unregulated financial market participants, such as hedge funds and offshore banks in financial market supervision and capital adequacy principles would prevent the spread of financial market crises.

Bubbles cannot be prevented with these measures, but they can be counteracted earlier.[54]

12.2.8 Speculative Bubbles as a Business Cycle Trigger

Speculative bubbles can trigger economic fluctuations through wealth effects and high profits. Corporate interests are valued more by the companies at fair value measurement under ISFR or US GAAP, which increases profits. Household equity assets are also rising and encouraging households to increase their consumption expenditure (wealth effect). Banks are prone to higher lending due to high assets. Here, credit bubbles can arise through credit-financed securities purchases, such as in the world economic crisis of 1929 or credit-financed real estate purchases, as in the case of the US sub-prime financial crisis of 2007. If this development is accompanied by a lax monetary policy, mostly share price and real estate bubbles are created in parallel (as for example with the Japan bubble in the late 1980s). The downturn is triggered by the impairment of loans in the banking system, with only a sufficient inflow of liquidity for the price increase sufficient for the trend break.[55]

Speculative Bubbles is a colloquial phrase commonly used to characterize a strong overvaluation in prices.

▶ **Definition** A speculative bubble can be define as a deviation in the price of an asset from the price consistent with the fundamentals.[56]

In the literature, depending on the alleged cause, various names for speculative bubbles like rational and irrational bubbles as well as agency-oriented bubbles, intrinsic bubbles and stochastic bubbles.[57] The distinction between rational and irrational bubbles is artificial, since deviating prices from fundamental data is always irrational. However, according to a broad definition of rationality, all decisions that are confirmed over time are considered rational. With a dynamically growing bubble, however, the yield expectations are always confirmed by rising prices, so that each bubble can be described as rational. Conversely,

---

[54]See Markus Stahl/Christian A. Conrad (2000), pp. 383–385 and Conrad, Christian, A./Stahl, Markus (2002).

[55]*Stahl, Markus/Conrad, Christian, A.* (2000), pp. 415–422.

[56]See *Santoni, Gary J./Dwyer, Gerald P. Jr.*(1990), p. 190 and *Diba, Behzad T./Grossman, Herschel I.* (1988), p. 520.

[57]See *Bruns, Christoph* (1994), pp. 23.

every bubble—rational in its broadest definition—becomes an irrational bubble after it bursts.

Intrinsic Bubble is when a change in the fundamental sizes is overvalued by the market once and for this reason it does not come to an inflation of the bubble.[58] Agency-oriented bubbles are the result of distorted information processing by investors. This explanatory approach is currently being buoyed by New Behavioral Finance, which will be discussed later. Last but not least, one speaks of stochastic bubbles when there is an auto-accumulating, thus self-reinforcing, psychological overvaluation development. The original price increase may well be fundamentally justified. The past price increases, however, are forecast by investors as an expectation into the future and overreaching, so that psychological backgrounds dominate the investment decision (social dynamics). These exaggerated expectations are repeatedly confirmed by higher prices as a result of the purchases (self-fulfilling prophecies or self-fulfilling expectations) until the bubble bursts.[59]

Bubble expresses the opinion that the overvaluation will not last long—a bubble bursts. In the narrower sense, there can be no overvaluation of a good, since the market price is determined by supply and demand and is always an equilibrium price. The overvaluation must therefore relate to the permanence of the market price.

A dynamic, growing bubble can only arise if the current market price is positively dependent on its expected rise.[60] The goods must not be subject to a temporal decline in value that is greater than the possible increase. They must not spoil or cause excessive storage costs. As a result, equity investments are particularly vulnerable to the formation of speculative bubbles, as their retention costs are low and potential future increases in profit are very high.[61]

12.2.8.1 The Efficient Market Hypothesis

Until the mid-1980s, the efficient market hypothesis in financial market theory had an undisputed sole representation claim. The Efficient Market Hypothesis was significantly influenced by Milton Friedman of the University of Chicago. This hypothesis assumes that all accessible price-relevant information of the past, present and future are included. If there were a fundamental price imbalance, arbitrageurs would use this source of income immediately and restore the fundamental price through counter-transactions. So-called "smart money" of funds and in the hands of professional arbitrageurs, supported by researchers who examine in which direction the fundamental market trend moves 24 h a day, guarantee the efficiency of the market. Since, in principle, rational investor behavior is assumed, irrational investor behavior or wrong decisions are not influencing the price.

---

[58] See *Aschinger, Gerhard* (1991), p. 271.

[59] See *Bruns, Christoph* (1994), p. 25 and *Aschinger, Gerhard* (1991), pp. 270.

[60] See *Flood, Robert P./Garber, Peter M.* (1980), p. 746.

[61] See *Ito, Takatoshi/Iwaisako, Tokuo* (1995), p. 1.

Non-fundamentally justified investment decisions are punished by the market immediately. Investors who behave irrationally lose money and have to withdraw from the market. Stock market prices therefore reflect the latest and best information. Course changes can only be caused by new information. Also, purchases and sales must not have any impact on prices, since the smart money is always ready to form the other side, so to buy or sell up to the fundamental price. According to the Efficient Market Hypothesis, investors can therefore not outperform the market by increasing their level of individual information.[62]

For a long time, the explanation of stock market bubbles was dominated by a clarification approach that assumed rational behavior among market participants. Representatives of this theory include Flood, Garber, Blanchard and Watson.[63] After this explanatory approach, investors know well that the prices are speculatively exaggerated and thus unrealistic. While the likelihood of a crash is greater than that of further bubble growth, the expected gains overcompensate for the likelihood of a crash, so that the expectation of a further rise in price is greater than that of a crash. Every investor assumes that he can get out in time, that is, before the others. This may apply to the individual but not to the whole of the investors. In that sense one could speak of rational errors. The bubble bursts when the price increases necessary to compensate for the crash probability are no longer expected for some reason. But do these explanatory approaches correspond to the course patterns of stock market bubbles that can be observed in practice?

12.2.8.2 Review of the Efficient Market Hypothesis

In the known crashes of 1929 and 1987, parallels can be observed in the price development. First, there is a steep upward process, the growth rate then decreases a few weeks before the crash. In this short phase before the crash, stronger price drops and strong growth in turnover can be observed relative to the upswing.[64] The stock market upswing takes several years. The downturn or price collapse usually takes place within a few days.[65] The sales and the subsequently falling prices induced new sales and price falls:[66]

> As **the 19th** wore on, investors witnessed symptoms of market failure and were frightened by rumors that the NYSE would close. They also worried that other investors had come to believe the market was overvalued. Fear fed upon fear as investors en masse rushed to sell their stocks.[67]

---

[62]See *Sloan, A./Stern, R.L.* (1988), p. 55-59; Shleifer, Andrei (2000), pp. 1.
   and Mankhoff, Likas/Röckemann, Christian (1994), p. 278.

[63]See *Flood, Robert P./Garber, Peter M.* (1980), p. 746 ff and *Blanchard O.J./Watson, M.W.* (1982), and *Jüttner, Johannes* (1989), p. 474.

[64]*See Rasch, Steffen* (1993), p. 300.

[65]The stock price display was several hours late in 1987, which is why the NYSE expanded the computer-based automatic trading systems to a sales volume of 1 billion shares per session. *See Rasch, Steffen* (1993), pp. 282.

[66]Vgl.*The Presidental Task Force* (1988), p. V.

[67]*Leland, Hayne/Rubinstein, Mark* (1988), p. 46.

Here, psychology is one of the most important influencing factors of stock market development. An old stock market saying goes: "The stock market consists of 50% facts and 50% psychology." However, models based on the theory of rational behavior proved unsuitable for explaining or depicting the performance of the '87 crash, which is why economists were called upon to create new models:

> We need to build models of financial equilibrium which are more sensitive to real life trading mechanisms, which account more realistically for the information of expectations, and which recognize that, at any one time, there is a limited pool of investors available with the ability to evaluate stocks and take appropriate action in the market.[68]

Opinion polls on the causes of the crash were carried out after the 1987 crash. The most significant was performed by the Brady Group and gave the following picture:

Respondents in percent

Noticeable in Fig. 12.20 is the increased influence of psychological factors at the time of the crash. An old stock market saying goes: "50% of the stock market consists of facts and 50% of psychology." However, the models built on the theory of rational behavior proved unsuitable for explaining or reflecting the price development of the 87 crash. Why economists demanded new models:

> We need to build models of financial equilibrium which are more sensitive to real life trading mechanism, which account more realistically for the information of expectations, and which recognize that, at any one time, there is a limited pool of investors available with the ability to evaluate stocks and take appropriate action in the market.[69]

For example, Shiller pointed out that the historical evolution of stock market prices cannot be explained solely by expectations of future profits and dividends. He calls this phenomenon "excess volatility".[70] Meanwhile, the assumption of rational investor behavior has been falsified. Investors generally behave irrationally and have similar patterns of behavior.[71] Where does the strong influence of psychological factors on the development of stock prices come from and how does it affect itself?

12.2.8.3 Noise Trading Approaches

In return for Efficient Market Hypothesis, a series of psychologically-oriented explanatory approaches emerged called noise trading approaches, where "noise" stands for a disturbance (noise) that causes prices to deviate from the fundamental data, In their models, some noise trading approaches explicitly work with groups of investors who make their decisions

---

[68]*Leland, Hayne/Rubinstein, Mark* (1988), p. 50.

[69]*Leland, Hayne/Rubinstein, Mark* (1988), p. 50.

[70]See *Shiller, Robert J.* (2000), pp. 180.

[71]See *Shleifer, Andrei* (2000), S., pp. 10.

Respondents in percent

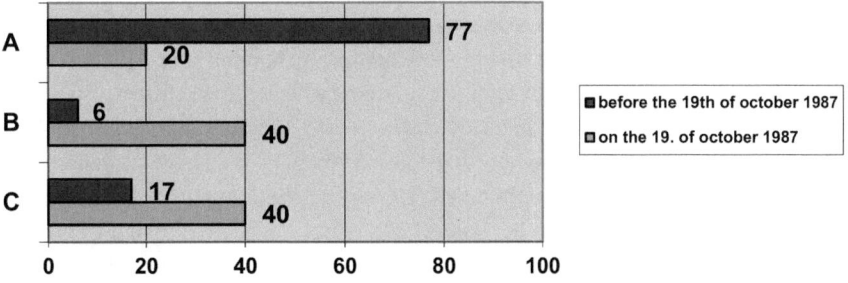

A: fundamental reasons, B: technical reasons, C: psychological reasons

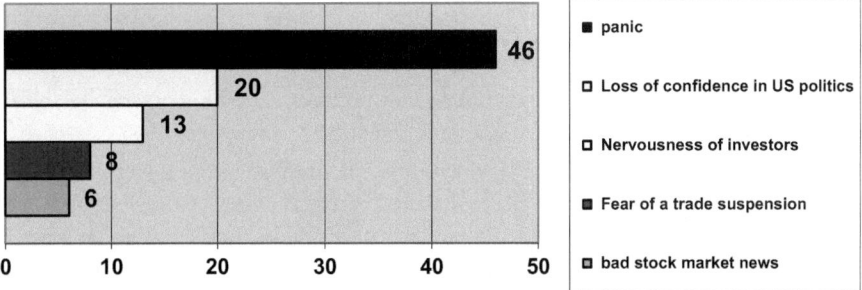

Fig. 12.20 The most important reasons for the price decline on the US stock exchange in 1987 (470 (top graph) and 231 market participation (bottom graph) were surveyed)

on the basis of distorted probability distributions, thus unconsciously behaving irrationally.[72] For example, Shiller models an emotionally charged cyclical stock market demand, with speculative bubbles forming.[73] Bubbles can also be triggered by positive moods of the market participants (price euphoria), which are amplified by feedback (positive feedbacks) and can lead to a rectified mass behavior (so-called herd mentality).[74] An example of Shiller's "information cascade" illustrates the herd behavior (herding).[75] Two restaurants, A and B, are one-on-one identical to one another through a shop window. At first they are empty. Then comes a hungry guest and has to decide for one of the two restaurants. There is another hungry man coming. He has no additional information on the quality of the

---

[72] See *Blume, L./Easley, D.* (1992), pp. 9–40.

[73] See *Shiller, R.J.* (1984), pp. 457–498.

[74] See *Froot, Kenneth A./Scharfstein, David S./Stein, Jeremy C.* (1992), pp. 1461.

[75] See *Shiller, Robert J.* (2000), p. 152.

restaurants, but only sees that no one is eating in one restaurant and in the other restaurant A at least the first guest has arrived. He will probably trust the choice of the first guest and also choose restaurant A. The decision-making situation continues with other hungry guests until Restaurant A is overcrowded as the most popular restaurant, even though it is one hundred percent identical to B. Although this behavior leads to a distorted result, it is rational when considered from the point of view of the individual guests, and could have been quite successful if the assumption that those already dining have a higher level of information were correct. In general, human behavior is oriented towards learning through copying. First a person learns from his parents and trusts them blindly, and in his further development he gets his information from other people. This information often cannot be reviewed due to its complexity and limited decision making time. Man has to create simplifying behavioral schemas. If people are fleeing, he will join them, though he does not know what they are fleeing from. In the stone age this behavior seems to have ensured survival, as the people who waited for the pursuing predator were killed.

It has also proven worthwhile when enjoying berries to copy those that have eaten the same kind of berries and survived.

With herd mentality the sociological group orientation of man comes to the fore. In the typical stock market situation of uncertainty, the investor orients themself by the other market participants, which the stock exchange rewards with increasing prices—at least in the short term. In the approach of Shefrin and Statman bubbles build, then burst, when the irrational Noise Traders again adjust their distorted expectations of the rational market participants.[76] The expectations of the market participants influence each other. For example, empirical studies show that the estimation of market developments by analysts and investors is influenced by previous valuations from other analysts.[77] Extrapolative expectation and technical analysis strategies also lead to share sales when prices rise. Herd behavior is intensified by the short-term speculative horizon. A crash seems less likely. This is especially true for professional investment managers who are subjected to a one-year performance evaluation.[78]

Individual market participants cannot oppose the development of herd behavior, even if they notice deviation from the fundamental price factors. If they speculate against such a strong market trend, they will lose as long as the bubble does not burst. On the contrary, in the upward process, there are self-reinforcing distribution effects that aid the creation of a bubble.[79] For example, suppose that in a given uncertain situation on the stock market there are investors with two risk positions, and that they have the same purchasing power. The optimists (bulls) expect the same level of information to lead to higher price or corporate profits than the risk-averse pessimists (bears). If new positive information is added that

---

[76]Zitiert nach Quotes after *Menkhoff, Lukas/Röckmann, Christian* (1994), pp. 284.

[77]See De Bondt, Werner F. M./Forbes, William P. (1999).

[78]See *Shleifer, Andrei/Vishny, Robert W.* (1990), pp. 148–153.

[79]See *Treynor, Jack* (1998), pp. 69–74.

leads to a price increase, the long-term buyers (long position) have more purchasing power than the sellers (short position) that did not invest in the stock, but rather liquidity or a short position due to the previous price gains, and thus incurred losses.[80] The unequal purchasing power causes a demand surplus and thus favors the upward process. Since the bulls can bring about their own success in the form of higher prices due to the surplus, the upward process is self-reinforcing. On the other hand, the bears lose even more purchasing power because it is a zero-sum game. These effects are reinforced by the change in refinancing options. If the stock portfolio of the bulls wins, so do their credit lines with the banks. The same applies vice versa for the bears. The mirror image downward trend occurs when the new information is negative.

In addition, there is a psychological effect that unilaterally strengthens the stock market's upwards movement. The investor feels richer because of his increased equity portfolio, which will increase his purchasing position (wealth effect). Man adapts his behavior to his environment, more precisely to his experiences. If new price increases occur over a longer period of time, he will adjust his risk assessment. His own price gains reinforce this and make it rational to reinvest in equities. As a rule, capital investment will be greater in the second investment because the investor expects to repeat his successful initial investment.

12.2.8.4 The New Behavioral Finance

Overconfidence is the human tendency to overestimate one's self that has been demonstrated in numerous experiments as early as the 1970s. Here one can establish a subjective, positive self-judgment. Subjects regularly overestimate their own knowledge, their control options, their abilities as well as their achievements.[81]

Recent studies of the behavioral research direction New Behavioral Finance confirm the psychologically oriented, non-deterministic explanatory approach. It turned out that investors perceive and evaluate the information available to them in a very subjective way and in their decisions—contrary to the neo-classical model world do not always maximize the expected benefits. The investor is more upset about losses than he is pleased about profits and behaves more risk-averse with losses than with profits, which is why he tends to let shares in the profit range go rather than in the loss range (disposition effect). He is upset about his "poor decision" and hopes to recover later on—a phenomenon that could usually be observed even in oneself. For example, investment decisions are also influenced by the presentation of the information (framing effect). If the historical yield development of a paper is shown, this leads to an undervaluation of future price volatility. The so-called splitting effect, on the other hand, causes security types with more investment options (for example, German and foreign shares) to be valued equally with better alternatives (for

---

[80]A person who tends to be a seller (bear) does not have to be passive on the market by holding liquidity, but can also buy short positions (long-short futures or long-put options).

[81]See Metcalfe, Janet (1998) and Beck, H. (2014), p. 62.

example, bonds). It can also be observed that investors tend to overestimate their level of information and skills. This is called overconfidence. Overconfidence causes an overestimation of the probability of success of one's own decisions. Behavioral finance researchers, for example, attribute the frequent, yield-reducing buying and selling of stocks to overconfidence, which would be comparable to the constant change of lane in a traffic jam. Investors tend to overvalue the information that they first hear over any later info. Conversely, older information is relegated to the background when people receive new information. The same can be observed with regard to information complexity. Investors are paying more attention to reports of takeovers, sales slumps and IPOs than information that they cannot classify or need to process, such as the release of balance sheet ratios. New information is processed and converted with a delay. This causes an overreaction on the exchanges in both directions (overreaction).[82]

DeBondt and Thaler (1985) showed overreaction on the US stock market on the basis of the 35 best and worst stocks. The worst stocks outperformed the overall market as much as the best 35 stocks underperformed it. It is obvious that the market has processed the information late. The bad stocks were not that bad and the good ones were not that good.[83]

Overvaluation and undervaluation happen because information contradicting the trend is taken into consideration too late in the decision-making process. Lastly, the value of the source of information is not properly ranked. The investor hardly considers the information coming from an investment adviser or a designated expert, but rather how determined they present themselves.[84]

Since the psychologically oriented approaches are not deterministic, their drawback is the lack of a uniform universal model conception and the possibility of verification independent of the situation. However, in view of the weaknesses of the classical theory based exclusively on rational behavior, they have considerably enriched financial market theory. The psychologically oriented approaches blame the over-interpretation of the assumption of rational behavior, which is always valid in reality, on the original abstract model approach of neoclassicism, which adopted the rational homo economicus merely to simplify the complexity of human behavior.[85] However, if human behavior is not determinable and predictable because it is not rational, then the applicability of exact mathematical models is limited, as well as the universality of economic knowledge as a whole.

---

[82] See *Behavioral Finance Group* (2000), p. 29. See auch Menkhoff, Lukas/Röckmann, Christian (1994), a.a.o., pp. 287 and *Shleifer, Andrei* (2000a).

[83] See De Bondt, Werner F. M.; Thaler, Richard (1985), Beck, H. (2014), p. 363.

[84] See *Behavioral Finance Group* (2000), p. 29. The study was conducted by the Chair of Banking at the University of Mannheim, Prof. Martin Weber and Andreas Laschke. See also Menkhoff, Lukas/ Röckmann, Christian (1994), pp. 287 and *Shleifer, Andrei* (2000).

[85] See *Behavioral Finance Group* (2000) and Conrad, Christian A. (2016).

This is best shown by the failure of the hedge fund LTCM co-founded by Nobel laureates Robert Merton and Myron Scholes. Merton and Scholes had been awarded the Nobel Prize for discovering a method of calculating the price of options. Based on this calculation approach, the LTCM fund operated primarily in the market-neutral bond arbitrage. However, the method of calculation is based primarily on historical volatilities and does not take into account irrational human behavior, such as panic, as was to some extent due to the Russian crisis. In the fall of 1998, the LTCM fund was finally close to bankruptcy. His open positions and loan commitments threatened the international financial system to such an extent that Alan Greenspan was forced to organize a rescue operation.

> **Conclusion and Summary of the Psychological Economic Determinants**
>
> Man is not Homo Oeconomicus, but—as was presented in Chap. 4.—an irrational and often unsuccessful happiness maximizer, who tries to implement his complex need structure within groups. Stock market fluctuations can be transferred to cyclical fluctuations. However, psychological factors can also have a direct impact on corporate decisions, triggering or intensifying cycles. How do psychological factors affect cyclical fluctuations?

New Behavioral Finance Theory

1. It can be observed that investors tend to overestimate their level of information and skills. This is called **overconfidence**. Overconfidence causes an overestimation of the probability of success of one's own decisions. People tend to overestimate their own abilities after a series of successes and then take excessive risks. This human weakness underlies the business approach of shell or cone game. The inexperienced player is initially skeptical, so the game master lets the player win first to lull him into a feeling of safety. Then, when the player thinks he knows how to master the game and the success, the game master tricks, plays faster than before, and thus takes his money away from the player. This human weakness is also effective in a boom when, due to high demand, almost all business decisions and investments are successful. The managers then tend to high self-esteem and invest too much. As a result, the boom will be further increased and the upcoming supply overhang will be even greater if the investments have been realized and the supply comes onto the market.

2. New information is processed and implemented with a delay. This causes an overreaction in the boom and in the recession, thus in both directions (**overreaction**). There are exaggerations and understatements in the investments, because the information that contradicts the trend is taken seriously too late in the decisions of the corporate drivers. In the boom, the managers realize too late that now the cost of primary products and wages have increased, other companies have invested or demand has already weakened. They invest too much in expanding their capacities. Conversely, in the downturn, they

realize too late that costs have fallen again, demand has stopped falling or suppliers have left the market. They invest too late. The downturn therefore lasts too long.

Noise Trading Approaches

3. Shiller, for example, modeled an **emotion**-driven cyclical stock market demand, with speculation bubbles forming. Imagine that even entrepreneurs are plagued by envy, greed and fear. In the upswing, the entrepreneurs have earned well, now they want more and more and expand too much. The boom is intensified and the downturn afterwards as well. Envy of the success of other entrepreneurs would have the same effect. Conversely, anxiety causes entrepreneurs to not invest in the recession, although the highest profits would be possible here because investment costs, wages and input costs are low.
4. Bubbles can also be triggered by positive moods of the market participants (price euphoria), which are amplified by feedback (positive feedbacks) and can lead to a rectified mass behavior (so-called **herding**).

The herd approach can be transferred to the business cycle theory. Even unorthodox, rectified human behavior can trigger business cycles. Fear and panic trigger a downturn, while overconfidence causes an exaggeration, an overshoot in the boom.

The Confirmation Bias describes how people process facts in such a way that they confirm their own opinions.[86] Contradictory facts are not taken into account or are subordinated to the held opinion. Added to this is the illusion of control as an overestimation of one's influence on processes. People shy away from change when they can not assess how they are affected. The status quo is preferred over another alternative (status quo bias). The status quo bias is strengthened by the omission bias. People rate negative results from actions they actively participated in higher than negative results from non-action, ie omission.

Managers react too late to the economic indicators. You can also find a status quo in spending behavior. Samuelson and Zeckhauser examined the spending behavior with fictitious companies with test persons. The test subjects were provided with changing business forecasts. With good forecasts, they increased their expenditure, but did not reduce it with poor forecasts.[87]

If all market participants behave in the same way with their investment and purchasing decisions, economic cycles emerge. Boni systems can reinforce this by supporting rectified risk-taking behavior.[88] If the actors are only involved in the opportunities and not in the risks, ie are not liable for losses but are involved in the profits, this destabilizes the system. Risk-taking overinvestments drive the upswing, while depreciation in the financial system causes the crash and downturn.

---

[86]See Wason, Peter C. (1960); Nickerson, Raymond p. (1998).

[87]See Samuelson, William; Zeckhauser, Richard (1988), pp. 22 and Beck, H. (2014).

[88]See Conrad, Christian A. (2015).

For the business cycles, the managers are pessimistic and depressed in the downturn and recession. The opportunities are undervalued and the risks are overstated. The negative emotions are transmitted. Conversely, in the boom the managers are euphoric. Everything succeeds, they sell and earn more than expected. You hear about start-ups, expansion investments and acquisitions. This positive mood is on. Upswing and boom are strengthened.

12.2.9   Shocks and Price Rigidities in the New Keynesian Macroeconomics

Classical theory assumes that prices react quickly and quantities are delayed. However, since an auctioneer who finds an equilibrium price ex ante in a tonneau process does not exist, a simultaneous market equilibrium at equilibrium prices is rather the exception than the rule. Empirically, it can be observed that real wages do not fluctuate countercyclically in the course of the economy, as one would expect. Likewise, in periods of economic underutilization, companies maintain wage levels despite needing less labor. In goods, labor and other markets, prices react only very slowly—in extreme cases in the short term—to supply and demand surpluses.[89] Two major criticisms of the older Keynesian approaches are the incomplete logic of the decision-making and the neglect of the repercussions of quantity rationing on other markets. The New Keynesian Macroeconomics[90] therefore picks up on the Keynesian assumption of fixed prices and wages and takes into account the points of criticism mentioned in the model concept. In the New Keynesian Macroeconomics, neither prices nor wages respond in the short to medium term. Exogenous demand or supply shocks disturb market equilibrium and cause rationing of the opposite supply or demand side, without prices or wages immediately compensating.

The original static model of Malinvaud mislead to the conclusion that only an underdose of public demand has negative macroeconomic implications but not an overdose. After all, at least in the short term, there are no demand and supply-determined price changes. Not least because of this, Malinvaud has made his static approach more dynamic in a second model, endogenizing some variables and giving up on fixed prices and wages. The following conditions apply: The job supply is constant. Consumption depends positively on consumption in the previous period and negatively on the unemployment rate. The production function is linearly limitational and is determined by the factors labor (constant, first bottleneck), labor productivity, and production capacity as the second bottleneck and rationing variable. Aggregate demand is composed of consumer demand and investment demand, which is positively affected by a period lagged by both labor returns (labor

---

[89]See *Gerfin, H./Möller, J.* (1980b), p. 201.

[90]See *Malinvaud, E.* (1977), *Barro, R.J./Grossmann, H.I.* (1976); *Gerfin, H./Möller, J.* (1980a); *Gerfin, H./Möller, J.* (1980b); *Barro, Robert J.* (1971); *Clower, R.W.* (1965); *Heubes, Jürgen* (1991), pp. 65 and *Rothschild, Kurt, W.* (1981).

productivity—real wages) and by capacity utilization. Depending on the real wage and production capacity, four temporary balances emerge, in which the development of real wages depends on the respective regime.

In classical unemployment, real wages fall with the rise in unemployment; with suppressed inflation it rises due to surplus demand in the labor market. Because of the oversupply of Keynesian unemployment, both the nominal wage due to unemployment and oversupply drop the price level, leaving real wages constant. In Walrasian equilibrium, neither nominal wage nor price level change, as no market side is rationed. In the medium term, there are only two stable equilibria in which real wages do not change: the Keynesian regime and the Walrasian equilibrium. In Walrasian equilibrium stability is maintained by balancing a positive labor return effect and a negative capacity under-utilization effect on investment demand. However, an eventual disruption of this balance automatically initiates development into one of the three regimes, which is why the Walrasian equilibrium can not be considered stable, thus leading all combinations to the Keynesian regime in the long term.

For the Keynesian regime, the further development of the GDP depends on the combination of the nominal wage rate and the adjustment parameter of the capital stock. There are two possible developments. In the first case a monotonous approach to a stable equilibrium and in the second more probable case a much longer approach to the stable Keynesian equilibrium with subdued oscillations of the social product around the equilibrium social product, i.e. to cyclical fluctuations until the Keynesian equilibrium is reached. From this point no economic fluctuations can occur or be explained endogenously, which also occurs in the New Keynesian macroeconomics as in the still-to-be analyzed New Classic macroeconomics, namely the persistence problem of how to explain the continuity of cyclical fluctuations, since exogenous shocks must be a part of the explanation. It cannot explain a complete business cycle, which is why both theories in the narrower sense are not among the economic cycle theories.[91]

The pro-cyclical investment and profit rates observed in reality emerge in the model of the New Keynesian macroeconomics as an automatic consequence of changes in the cost-income relations. Prices, wages and interest rates will also behave pro-cyclically, but with a time lag. Although positive shocks can be simulated with the New Keynesian Macroeconomics, it is again a one-time departure from equilibrium followed by a tendency towards a new static equilibrium.

The New Keynesian Macroeconomics result in a new distribution of roles in collective bargaining. According to the New Keynesian Macroeconomics, the responsibility for full employment cannot be attributed either to the collective bargaining parties (entrepreneurs and trade unions) or to the state. The wage bargaining parties must pay attention to wage

---

[91]Nevertheless, these models explain variations in the utilization of production potential, which is why they are listed along with the other economic theories.See *Mankiw Greory M. (1998)* and *Assenmacher, Walter* (1998).

policies that do not create the situation of classical unemployment, whereas in the situation of Keynesian unemployment the state is obliged to stabilize its policy in the form of an autonomous increase in demand. The flexibility of wages downwards is to be restored by deregulating the labor market (for example by opening clauses). While the New Keynesian macro-economics approach provides further justification for the need for discretionary government demand-side management, it does not solve the recognition and implementation problems associated with practical economic policy. On the contrary, abrupt exogenous demand shocks require an even faster economic policy recognition and reaction than a permanent underemployment situation.

12.2.10 Price Adjustment Costs and Information Asymmetries in the New Keynesian Macroeconomics

A number of recent approaches have been developed with the aim of establishing the Keynesian assumption of price rigidity in a microeconomic way. Representing this direction, this chapter presents two causes, price adjustment costs and information asymmetries. If one does not assume imperfect competition, but supply monopolies at least in submarkets, MANKIW and BALL[92] show that price adjustment delays happen when the price adjustment costs are higher than the increased raw material prices due to an expansionary monetary policy. The companies calculate their prices from the outset in such a way that they have enough room for small changes in the inflation rate, in order to avoid a costly price adjustment, be it in advertising leaflets or with excellent goods. Changes in money supply, under this assumption and even rational behavior, can cause a change in the relative price structure, leading to real employment effects. There is also a twofold asymmetry in price adjustments. On the one hand, price adjustments only take place in the case of large changes in the amount of money or changes in inflation, and on the other hand, companies only adjust prices if pricing is worsened as a result of monetary policy because it is expansionary. As a result, the real impact on employment and the social product is greatest if the price reductions of the primary products do not have to be passed on by the companies, that is, if the monetary policy is highly restrictive.

Furthermore, they are expansive and thus have an expansive effect against the drop in investment demand due to the increased level of interest rates.

One criticism of this approach is that the price adjustment costs, but not the adjustment costs of production and employment, are taken into account. In addition, the positive employment effect of the restrictive change in money supply is likely to be more than offset by the negative effect of lower investment demand. Consequently, the value of these

---

[92]See *Mankiw, G.N.* (1985) and *Ball, L./Mankiw, N.G.* (1994).

models lies above all in the economic justification of the old Keynesian hypothesis that prices are rigid downwards and flexible upwards.[93]

The second central New Keynesian research direction[94] examines the effect of asymmetric information distribution between companies as borrowers and lenders (banks in particular), assuming that companies ration their equity because they cannot find equity investors due to the information asymmetry and consequent higher risk. For employment and production expansion they therefore have to borrow. Since the lenders want to secure their capital on time, so as to withdraw from the company, per this theory they cause bankruptcies earlier than equity investors. The risk of capital loss increases during the recession, which is why credit rationing takes place in this economic phase. This approach explains the empirical pro-cyclical evolution of the pay gap: while labor productivity increases in the recession due to the release of inefficient production factors, there is still an over-supply in the labor market as companies rally due to credit rationing and cannot expand their employment. Restrictive monetary policy may exacerbate the recession because of negative repercussions on lending. On the other hand, an expansionary monetary policy cannot change the long-term equilibrium, since marginal productivity, in turn, determines real wages, with an asymmetry in the effects of restrictive and expansive monetary policy.

Due to the partial non-neutrality of monetary policy, these newer approaches at first sight call for a discretionary economic policy, in particular for an expansive monetary policy in the recession. But they also indirectly show the dangers of mismanagement. Assuming—as the monetarists—unknown or changing time delays in the mechanisms of action, the interventions can increase the economic destabilization due to the asymmetry of effect: An expansionary monetary policy, which will only take effect when the economy is no longer in recession, but in the upswing phase or in the boom causes above all inflation and practically no positive real effects. A subsequent disinflationary policy would be all the more restrictive to social product and employment.[95]

The inclusion of mathematical chaos equations in equilibrium systems (Chaos theory) emphasizes this conclusion. It turned out that, depending on the initial parameter constellation, cyclical as well as chaotic solutions are possible as they move away from equilibrium. However, if in practical economic policy neither the parameter constellation in the initial situation can be determined exactly, nor can the economic policy instruments be precisely dosed, the risk of a malfunction is all the greater.[96]

---

[93] See *Kugler, Peter* (1998), p. 32 and *Homburg, Stefan* (1996), pp. 60.

[94] See *Stiglitz, S.E./Weiss A.* (1992) and *DeLong, B.D./Summers, L.* (1988) and *Homburg, Stefan* (1996), p. 64.

[95] See *Kugler, Peter* (1998), p. 32.

[96] However, the use of nonlinear behavioral functions based on the mathematical chaos theory in neoclassical growth models leads only in exceptional cases to stable solutions, which is why the empirical explanatory content is assessed as very low.

See *Teichmann, Ulrich* (1997), p. 24.

In the following, the theories are presented and analyzed for their economic policy statements, which, contrary to the Keynesian, non-Walrasian oriented theories, proceed from an inherent market stability or an automatic market balance mechanism. Here, essentially, the monetarist theories and the New Classical Macroeconomics are to be ascribed to their further developments.[97]

12.2.11 Adaptive Expectation in Monetarist Theories

The monetarist economic theories are in the narrow sense no economic theories, since they explain only nominal fluctuations in social product, and not real fluctuations in the degree of utilization of the production potential. The two best-known monetarist approaches are those of FRIEDMANN[98] and LAIDLER.[99] FRIEDMANN reinterprets the quantum theory of money by assuming the interest rate as negligible for money demand on the basis of empirical studies. Thus, the nominal income above the money circulation rate is proportional to the monetary development and the circulation rate is a stable function of the inflation rate. The economic agents have a given asset portfolio structure with a real estate income dependent transaction cash demand. The balance is disturbed by an increase in the amount of money that is not perceived immediately by the economic agents, but only late (adaptive expectation). The increase in the monetary balance causes an increase in the cash position of the economic subjects above the desired level. The difference turns directly into consumer demand or first to capital offer and then to investment demand. Given production, only the nominal income increases as a result of the price level increase. The economic agents correct their inflation expectations upwards and react with a shorter cash duration (higher circulation speed), which leads to a renewed increase in the nominal income (overshooting). Over time, inflation expectations converge to the actual rate of inflation, with fluctuations in nominal income decreasing. Thus, this is a market clearing model or shock reaction model with which no complete business cycle can be simulated. FRIEDMANN seeks to circumvent this limitation by accepting regular monetary shocks. However, FRIEDMANN does not present the real effects of the shocks.

LAIDLER fills this gap by connecting the monetary and real sectors via the Phillips curve. The real income results from the degree of utilization of the labor force potential. The money supply is given exogenously; money demand depends positively on real income and price levels. As with FRIEDMANN, the Phillips curve is based on the assumption of adaptive inflation expectation formation and thus a delayed wage reaction. In the long term, changes in money supply have no effect on the real sector. The old equilibrium with a constant natural unemployment and inflation rate, resulting from the

---

[97]Conrad, Christian (1999), pp. 188–220 and Stavenhagen, Gerhard (1969).

[98]See *Friedman, M.* (1970); *Heubes, Jürgen* (1991), pp. 84 and *Teichmann, Ulrich* (1997), p. 20.

[99]See Laidler, D. (1976a, b); *Heubes, Jürgen* (1991), pp. 87 and *Teichmann, Ulrich* (1997), p. 21.

difference between the rate of monetary growth and the growth rate of income, keeps coming up. Short-term, unexpected increases in the money supply cause an increase in the employment level through the wage bill as a result of the illiquidity of the employees. As with FRIEDMANN, the monetary shocks must occur regularly to represent a business cycle. The real sector then responds to expansion or contraction depending on the prevailing expectations.

12.2.12 Exogenous Change of Political Variables: The New Classical Macroeconomics

The New Classical Macroeconomics has been developed in numerous publications and goes back to LUCAS (1975), MCCALLUM (1980) and BARRO (1981).[100] The approaches are a response to LUCAS's 1976 criticism of the assumption of constant coefficients within structural econometric models. In view of the systematic change in exogenous political variables that occurs in reality, this is far from reality (LUCAS criticism).[101] In the New Classic Macroeconomics, therefore, the exogenous change in policy variables is a major economic determinant. The New Classical Macroeconomics can be divided into exogenous and endogenous approaches. The exogenous approaches again differentiate between monetary theories according to the nature of the external economic cause, where the money supply is the exogenous cause, and the real business cycle theories, which regard real shocks as determinative of the economy. The endogenous theories exhibit a nonlinear internal dynamics (intrinsic dynamics, chaos theory) or explain the cycles by means of a modified theory of rational expectations (Sunspot theories).[102]

Demand fluctuations due to wrong adaptation reactions:

The basic assumptions are the existence of a state of equilibrium that always occurs in the long term as well as rational expectations in the sense of a subjective formality. The last point is the difference to the monetarist models, which in principle assume adaptive expectations. The economic agents have a consistent target system and optimize their decisions on the basis of their subjective information about the economic conditions. They use all the information available to them. However, the information is incomplete (asymmetrically distributed), so that an uncertainty prevails. The economic subjects are informed about the fundamental economic connections, d. H. they do not make any systematic mistakes.

---

[100]Zur Neuen Klassischen Makroökonomik To the New Classical Macroeconomics See *Assenmacher, Walter* (1998), S.302.; *Ramser, H. J.* (1988), pp. 96; *Lucas, R.E.* (1975); *McCallum* (1980); *Barro, R.J.* (1981); *Tichy G.* (1995), G., p. 185ff; *Minford, Patrick/Peel, David* (1983) and *Fischer, S.* (1980).

[101]See *Lucas, R.E. Jr.* (1976) and *McCallum, B.T.* (1980).

[102]See *Heubes, Jürgen* (1991), pp. 83 and *Assenmacher, Walter* (1998), pp. 301.

Due to the incomplete information about the economic conditions the economic actors are subject to wrong judgments. There are two types of upset: permanent-transitory confusion and absolute-relative confusion. In the case of permanent-transitory confusion, economic agents cannot distinguish whether a change in monetary indicators is permanent or only temporary. On the other hand, if the economic agents cannot see whether relative prices or the entire price level is rising, it is called an absolute-relative confusion. Uncertainty is exacerbated by the assumption of a randomly variable state demand on the submarkets. It follows that only unexpected monetary changes can influence the real variables. Politically initiated changes in the money market give the economic agents complete information. They are therefore anticipated and are ineffective (policy inefficiency hypothesis). Only unsystematic changes in the money supply can cause misperceptions and thus real adjustments.

It is also assumed that market equilibrium always automatically occurs in the long term. Economic fluctuations can therefore only be caused by exogenous factors. Exogenous, staggered, unexpected monetary shocks (e.g. fiscal mismatches, imported inflation at fixed exchange rates, short-term monetary constraints due to international collusion (G7, EMS), etc.) lead to a change in monetary indicators (prices, interest rates). The data changes are misinterpreted by the business entities. The real adaptation reactions of the economic subjects thus triggered differ depending on the underlying type of confusion. An absolute-relative confusion, for example, causes economic agents to increase production $[X = X (p)]$, whereas a permanent-transitory confusion can lead to an expansion of investment due to the lower interest rate. There is a self-reinforcing (cumulative) upward process. After a while, in the case of absolute relative confusion, economic agents recognize that all prices—including those of their primary products—are on the rise, and not just those of their own sales products. They then revise their expansive production decision. In the case of permanent transitive confusion, a correction of the data changes made by the political decision-makers takes place in the medium term. The monetary expansion or interest rate cut is reversed, whereupon the economic agents also correct their decisions. The correction of the decisions triggers contractive effects that initiate a cumulative contracting process.

The New Classical Macroeconomics thus offers a transmission mechanism between the monetary and the real sector and thus also an explanation for the empirically established positive correlation between money supply and real social product. However, the general assumption of the New Classic Macroeconomics of a complete market clearing is critical to question. The wage and price mechanism always works. There is consequently no involuntary unemployment. This hypothesis is in contrast to the empirical short-term wage and price rigidities. Furthermore, in the New Classic Macroeconomics, upset can immediately increase production. That is, either sub-utilization or a time-lag of zero must always be assumed, both of which are unrealistic. Also, the assumption of isolated market behavior in terms of absolute-relative confusion seems remote with today's generally available information, especially as economic agents generally operate in several markets at the same time.[103] In general, all pro-cyclical "stylized facts" can be explained with the New Classic Macroeconomics. They occur as a result of confusion in the cumulative upward process. However, using New Classic Macroeconomics, it is not possible to explain economic cycles, but only short-term deviations from equilibrium, which are corrected again (persistence problem). The economic fluctuations as a result of the adjustment reactions lead back to the pareto optimal balance. Another neglected but compelling issue of New Classic Macroeconomics is whether the behavior of economic subjects will not change once they become subject to confusion and thereby suffer monetary losses. It is likely that they will either stop responding or transfer their assets to investments that are not affected by monetary shocks, such as property, plant and equipment.

All in all, however, it can be said that the difficulty of economic theory, whether and to what extent monetary shocks are transferred to the real sector, supports the hypothesis that monetary causes generally have less of an economic impact than real ones.[104]

There are three further unconnected directions, which are classified as neoclassical, Walrasian, the Real Business Cycles models, the Sunspot theories, and the nonlinear models of chaos theory. First, we will analyze the real business cycle approaches that have emerged as a consequence of the criticism of the transmission mechanism from the monetary to the real sector. They reverse causality and see the money supply as a function of real exogenous shocks.[105]

Disturbance of market balance by real exogenous shocks: The Real Business Cycles theories

According to the Real Business Cycles approaches, real positive shocks, such as technical progress, longer working hours and foreign direct investment as well as government demand, are the cause of fluctuations in the degree of utilization of production potential. The monetary adjustment to the new real social product is prompted by money-making institutions, such as the central bank and the banking system: the real shocks act, whereas the money supply only reacts. Representing the real business cycle

---

[103]See *Assenmacher Walter* (1998), p. 309.

[104]In addition, the assessment of the New Classic Macroeconomics on credit-financed fiscal policy should be mentioned. According to the Ricardian equivalence theorem, borrowers are already anticipating the future tax increases necessary for debt service, which is why they do not feel wealthier and therefore no longer consume by issuing government securities. There remains only the demand effect of government spending, which is offset by the future reduction in consumption due to the tax increase. Since the economic subjects also anticipate this and preventively increase their savings rate, this effect is also eliminated. See *Felderer, Bernhard/Homburg, Stefan* (1989), pp. 275. This view is critically questioned. Above all, it is argued that economic subjects will distinguish between the taxes levied during their lifetime and the taxes which the next generation must pay. To discuss the financing effects of government demand increase See *Musgrave R.A./Musgrave P.B./ Kullmer L.* (1987), pp. 120.

[105]For the Real Business Cycles theory see *Kydland, F. E./Prescott, E. C.* (1982); *Long, John B./ Plosser, Charles I.* (1983); *Azariadis, C./Guesnerie, R.* (1986); *Ramser, H. J.* (1988); *Tichy, G.* (1995), pp. 191; *Stadler, George W.* (1994) and *Komphardt, Jürgen* (1989), p. 213.

approaches, the economically relevant parts of the model of KYDLAND and PRESCOTT[106] will be presented here.

The central component of the model is a stochastic progress function. Technical progress, along with labor and capital, is a factor in a neoclassical production function with constant economies of scale. In maximizing profits, the demand for capital and labor depends on their marginal productivity, to which technical progress has the same effect. For technical progress (λ_{t+1}) is true: $\lambda_{t+1} = p\lambda_t + E_t$; with $0 \leq p \leq 1$ as a coefficient for the effect on the social product. Et, the technology shock variable, is stochastic and autocorrelated according to a first-order Markov process. Et is exclusively random, independent and identically distributed. At $p = 1$ the shocks are transmitted unchecked over time to the social product, at $p = 0$ the shock affects only the period of its onset to the social product. The investment function is positively dependent on technical progress and a stochastic differential equation of first order, which is why, due to the autocorrelation of technical progress, cyclical oscillations can occur which are exacerbated by the investments due to the assumed time lag.

The Real Business Cycles Theory has introduced a new empirical methodology into macroeconomics. Since these models are not suitable as an economic forecasting model due to the exogeneity of their economic causes (persistence problem), we examine whether it is possible to simulate observable economic developments using realistic input variables in reality. This succeeds in an amazing number of cases.[107] However, KYDLAND and PRESCOTT's own empirical examination of the model criticizes stochastic modeling as being adapted to the real social product trajectories until the desired agreement has been reached. Whether the real shocks occurring in reality, apart from exceptions, are sufficiently strong to produce cyclical fluctuations remains open. In the Real Business Cycles approaches, probability distributions, in this case innovations (ie technical progress), explain the course of the business cycle. Again, there is the persistence problem: only with the help of the assumption of repeated, independent, strong, exogenous technology shocks can cyclical fluctuations in employment and demand become apparent. Unfortunately, without a well-founded empirical review, Real Business Cycles theories will remain abstract mathematical models.

In addition, in many approaches **psychological variables** were included as random variables in the New Classical Macroeconomics. So-called "sun-spot variables" are psychological factors that influence expectations of model-related variables, without, however, affecting preferences, technologies or original equipment. It does not matter if these factors have a real impact on economic development. The key is that the economic agents accept this and carry out real transactions. In this way, "sunspots" (sunspots) can cause cyclical fluctuations.

---

[106]See *Kydland, Finn E./Prescott, Edward C.* (1982) and *Assenmacher Walter* (1998), pp. 310.
[107]See *Kugler, Peter* (1998) p. 33.

In the approaches of the New Classic Macroeconomics and the Real Business Cycles as well as in the psychological approaches, the short-term negative real economic effects of misjudgements, expectations and psychological factors are demonstrated with the help of mathematical modeling. They evoke fluctuations in supply and demand, i.e. instability. The monetarist approaches, as well as those of the New Classic Macroeconomics, show that a discretionary monetary policy has no long-term impact on employment, on the contrary. Consequently, for political economy, it can be concluded that the institutional framework (such as that of the financial markets) must be designed so as to minimize the upset and misjudgment of private economic agents.[108] A rule-bound monetary policy must guarantee a constant relation between the quantity of goods and money. EUCKEN's demand for the constancy of economic policy[109] takes on particular significance as a result of these approaches, since the state can also act as a disconcerting factor through discretionary interventions. The New Classic Macroeconomics suggests a stabilization of money and interest rates. On the other hand, the state can deliberately use the mistakes of economic subjects such as the permanent transitory confusion and counteraction in shock situations where overreaction of the economic subjects is to be expected. One example of such a response is the expansive monetary policy that has been implemented in many countries in response to the 1987 stock market crisis. The lower interest rates caused a positive, expansive confusion, which could later be corrected again. The New Classical Macroeconomics emphasizes the importance of "moralsuasion": politicians and other persons with public influence must be aware of the economic impact of their statements. If they spread rumors that give rise to a misjudgment of the economic policy indicators, economic fluctuations will ensue. However, if they explain their policies and pursue them consistently, they can prevent cyclical fluctuations.

12.2.13 Determinants of Growth as Economic Factors: The New Growth Theory

The term "New Growth Theory" summarizes various recent theories that seek to endogenize growth-determining factors, thus dissolving the traditional distinction between economic and growth theory.[110] It can be seen—also empirically—that the economic trend influences the growth trend. Based on the efficiency-enhancing effect of Schumpeter's creative destruction, for example, it follows from the approach of AGHION and PAUL[111]

---

[108]See *Ramser, H. J.* (1988), pp. 98.

[109]For the necessity of the constancy of economic policy See *Eucken, Walter* (1952), pp. 285.

[110]See *Ramey, G./Ramey, V. A.* (1995). Business-cycle theory and growth theory have traditionally been treated as "unrelated areas of macroeconomics", which is why it is often assumed that"growth and business-cycle volatility are unrelated." Ramey, G./Ramey, V. A. (1995), p. 1138. See auch *Franz, Wolfgang u.a.* (1999).

[111]See *Aghion, P./Saint-Paul, G.* (1993).

that under certain assumptions with the recession's strength and frequency, the growth rate of the social product also increases.

The approaches of the New Growth Theory are concerned with the endogenisation of the determinants of innovation waves, fluctuations in the level of technical and organizational knowledge or changes in the capital stock, but not with their effects on economic development as a fluctuation in the degree of utilization of production potential. Based on these approaches, conclusions about political economy can only be drawn indirectly. For example, the approach of SHLEIFER is a warning against restrictive stabilization policy in boom phases, since in this approach companies only realize their investments in times of high demand because, due to the higher contribution margins on the liquidity to implement the invention feature. While a stabilizing restrictive policy would compensate for this pro-cyclical effect, at the same time as reducing aggregate demand, it would reduce innovation, technical progress and hence economic growth.[112]

Also in the model of STIGLITZ (1994), the boom phases have positive feedback on innovation activity. STIGLITZ justifies this with learning effects with high capacity utilization, which stimulate inventions and with the fact that a company will increasingly invest in research and development if it is based on high demand. Moreover, he also supports SHLEIFER's argument that, except for capital market imperfections, companies only have the liquidity needed for research and innovation in boom phases.[113]

The contribution of the New Growth Theory to cyclical policy has so far been low. However, this research direction can be expected to provide significant new insights, especially with regard to the financing effects of discretionary stabilization policy. The state capital demand for deficit spending and alternative tax financing, through their repercussions on companies' innovation activities, directly intervene in the intergenerational distribution between present and future consumption. Given that firms' innovation activity is positively dependent on profit expectations in a secure environment, a redistributive policy at the expense of corporate profits and an incalculable discretionary economic policy that creates an uncertainty environment should have a negative impact on innovation activity and hence growth.

12.3   Conclusion Determinants of the Business Cycle

If we try to work out an economic-political trend statement of the presented business cycle the following can be stated:[114]

---

[112]See *Shleifer, A.* (1986) and *Ramser, Hans Jürgen* (1997), p. 200.

[113]See *Stiglitz, J.E.* (1994) and *Ramser, Hans Jürgen* (1997), p. 221f.

[114]This is the basic tenor in almost all summaries of the business cycle theory of the last 50 years. See insbesondere *Kugler, Peter* (1998), p. 34f.

- Long-term national product development is determined by the growth determinants of physical and human capital, including technical progress.
- There is no long-term positive relationship between inflation and employment. On the contrary, the price distortions and the uncertainty of the planning economic agents lead to a reduction of long-term economic growth.
- For the effects of monetary and fiscal policy, the expectations of economic agents are crucial.
- Due to the numerous implementation problems (recognition, planning, implementation and impact) and the difficulty of clearly defining the cause responsible for the respective economic development, fiscal policy should be used on a long-term rather than discretionary basis in the short term.
- Monetary policy must primarily serve to ensure price stability and may only help to cushion external shocks in exceptional circumstances. Real national product growth cannot be artificially generated by an expansionary monetary policy.

The economic-theoretical approaches developed after Keynes complement each other to a much more comprehensive and balanced understanding of the business cycle. They extend the previous models by new economic determinants or a consideration over several periods (dynamization). The most important gain in knowledge that Keynes's economic theory produced is the theoretical proof that fluctuations in the degree of utilization of production potential do not have to be exclusively due to demand, but that supply shocks can also be the cause. This is the merit of the New Keynesian Macroeconomics and New Classical Macroeconomics with its advancements. The shortcoming of these approaches is that they cannot endogenously explain a complete business cycle. They all suffer from the persistence problem and are dependent on exogenous stochastic shocks to simulate cyclical fluctuations. The cyclically acting influences, i.e. the trend component of the time series, are not deterministic here, thus explained, but stochastic, which is less convincing. The explanatory value and thus also the value for the economic education is lower than with the deterministic models. In addition, due to undeterminedness, these models are unsuitable for economic forecasting.

Since many models assume a closed economy, the international economic context is often forgotten in the economic policy debate. This is incompatible with the current framework conditions, as the current globalization discussion shows. With a large share of imports in domestic demand, the effects of a government increase in demand are greatly reduced. The interest-rate sensitivity of investment is also lower in an open economy, since investment in international free capital and goods flows is made where the highest expectations of profitability exist.[115]

The development of the business cycle theory according to KEYNES has above all pointed out the limits of the theory of economics. If the German Stability and Growth Act

---

[115]See Jaeger, Klaus (1999), p. 31 and Hesse, Helmut (1999), p. 39.

still testified in 1967 to a belief in the controllability of the economy, then this view is hardly represented today. This applies above all to discretionary demand management. If we want to explain this change of mind, we must search for the causes of the variance in the applied economic theory. What is available to economic researchers as short-term indicators is the statistically aggregated impact of billions of decentralized individual decisions by economic agents coordinated across many different markets. From this sentence, the four unsolvable problems of the applied business cycle theory can be deduced:

1. The multi-causality due to the billions of individual decisions. Only a high abstraction can filter out dominant determinants.
2. Aggregation addresses the structural problems of sectors or anomalies of individual markets, for example due to distortions of competition.
3. The Overlay and Lag Problem: The effects of the many different economic determinants appear superimposed and time delayed.
4. The nondeterminable behavior of human decision makers. This is especially true if you assume unrational behavior. However, KYDLAND and PRESCOTT showed that even with rational behavior, optimal economic governance becomes impossible due to the unpredictable responses of economic agents as a result of the adaptive expectations they have built on previous economic policies.[116]

Most of the newer approaches are based on the "policy inefficiency hypothesis". Consequently, the influence of politics on the economy must be kept as low as possible. The future environmental conditions are unknown. The market participants therefore make decisions under uncertainty. The state must not increase this insecurity by a "non-constancy" of economic policy in addition. Rather, what is needed is a redefinition in the form of clear, long-term policy programs based on a comprehensible, orderly conception, that is, regulatory rather than process policymaking. KYDLAND and PRESCOTT therefore recommend—as does LUCAS—the institutional involvement of politicians in firm codes of conduct, which were chosen by economic theory as being the most appropriate in advance, depending on the economic situation.[117] Politicians are then encouraged within this institutional involvement to explain their goals and instruments to the economic agents, and then to implement them rigorously. Discretionary intervention is acceptable only in those cases where upset already exists and the policy can prevent possible overfunctioning or malfunctioning. Moralsuasion is a suitable instrument in this context. However, in order not to affect the credibility and thus the effectiveness of this instrument, it is restrained in use. The political influence on the economic process must be limited to the minimum (minimum policy). This gain of knowledge should not be underestimated in its contribution to the recent economic theories of political economy.

---

[116]See *Kydland, Finn, E./Prescott, Edward C.* (1977).

[117]See *Kydland, Finn, E./Prescott, Edward C.* (1977) and *Lucas, R.E. Jr.* (1976).

The new economic theoretical approaches make a significant contribution to a better understanding of economic developments.[118] They extend the previous models by new economic determinants or a consideration over several periods (dynamisation). It turns out that the causes of cyclical fluctuations are much more complex than many Keynesian economists assumed in the 1970s. Although Hicks and the New Keynesian Macroeconomics succeeded in providing a new theoretical foundation for the need for state countercyclical demand management, these models call for a state even more omniscient than Keynesian Demand Management. The new Keynesian-oriented models take into account more influencing factors and developmental interdependencies over a longer period of time. The state must therefore pursue more influencing factors by means of suitable indicators, and detect maldevelopments even more quickly in order to prevent negative dynamic demand processes, which can initiate a cyclical downward trend. The recognition and implementation problems were, however, already on the basis of the "old" Keynesian theory in the economic policy practice not solvable.[119] The demand of the state in its structure never corresponds to the loss of demand, which severely restricts the effect of government demand increases and, in addition, leads to a crowding out of private demand, which at the same time causes a partial increase in prices. The likelihood of economic policy action seems even greater than under the "old" theories.

All in all, the newer approaches represent the business cycle as a dynamic process that is influenced by many factors. The factors taken up by the theories, with their variety and diversity, point out the complexity of the business cycle and thus also the dangers of influencing economic policy. As a result, economic cycles are no longer controllable, but can be influenced at best.

For practical political economy, therefore, the value of the new economic theories lies above all in pointing out the dangers of discretionary government demand management. The theoretical finding is that economic developments are not controllable due to the unavoidable multicausality and the unpredictable temporal interdependencies. Therefore, automatisms are required that weaken individual procyclical determinants, such as progressive taxation. For economic policy, it follows that the state has to shape the economic framework in such a way that intransparency causes the least possible misjudgment of the economic subjects. Moreover, the state must abstain from intervention so as not to increase the irrationalities. This understanding is mainly due to the New Political Economy and NORDHAUS. The New Classical Macroeconomics also assumes a "Policy Inefficiency Hypothesis". Consequently, the impact of policy influence on the economy is as small as possible. The actions of market participants, especially investors, are future-oriented. The future environmental conditions are unknown. The market participants therefore make decisions under uncertainty. The state must not increase this insecurity by "inconsistency" of economic policy. Rather, what is needed is a binding rule in the form of clear, long-term

---

[118]See also *Conrad, Christian, A.* (1999).

[119]See Berg, Hartmut; Cassel Dieter 1992, pp. 163–238.

policy programs that are based on a comprehensible, regulatory-compliant concept. Politicians are required to explain their goals and instruments to economic agents and then implement them consistently. Discretionary intervention is justifiable only in cases where upset already exists and the policy can prevent possible overfunctioning or malfunctioning. Moralsuasion is a suitable instrument in this context. However, in order not to affect the credibility and thus the effectiveness of this instrument, it is restrained in its use.

The financing effects of the government's increase in demand have not been integrated into the new economic models. All models are based on a closed economy. Foreign influences are exogenous factors. This is incompatible with the current framework conditions, as the current globalization discussion shows. With a high share of imports in domestic demand, the effects of a governmental increase in demand are greatly reduced. Also, the interest rate responsiveness of investment is lower in an open economy, since investments are made where the highest profitability expectations exist for internationally free capital and goods traffic. Overall, it should be noted that all models directly or indirectly show the dangers of political economic influence. The political influence on the economic process must be limited to the minimum (minimum policy). This is the contribution of the New Economic Theories to Economic Policy. Conjuncture cycles are part of economic development.

Summary: Determinants of the Business Cycle

In the following, we want to summarize the main factors influencing economic development (see Fig. 12.1):

1. Market adjustment, marginal vendors are eliminated, profit margin is also increasing due to restructurings, initial recovery
2. Pro-cyclical banks (lending only for positive corporate figures), strengthening the upswing and downswing. The credit policy of banks is pro-cyclical. Companies only get credit for presenting good balance sheets and good economic conditions.[120]
3. Psychology (good and bad mood due to expectations about the future economic development are self-reinforcing, overconfidence)
4. Interdependencies (multipliers and accelerators), reinforcing ups and downs. Keynes: Demand leads to more demand
5. If demand is greater than supply, this will cause investment, which will increase over-subscribers. As the companies cannot assess the demand and also the capacity expansions of the competitors, overinvestments can occur. The reverse

(continued)

---

[120]See also on the credit behavior of banks Rottmann, Horst/Wollmershäuser, Timo (2010).

process takes place in a downturn when demand is less than supply. $Y^D > Y^S \to I > S$ and $Y^D < Y^S \to I < S$.

6. Ripening time of investments, initiating downswing (Schumpeter, overinvestment theory).
7. Pro-cyclical profit margin, strengthening ups and downs. Godwin Model -> High profits lead to high investment, low profit leads to few investments
8. Valuations of Assets and Equity Investments, (wealth effect: not only more consumption with more income, but also more wealth -> if the economic agents feel richer, they also spend more), reinforcing ups and downs. Fair value measurement approaches such as IFRS and US GAAP also increase the cycles of valuation fluctuations (mark-to-market and fair value measurement).
9. Downstream wage and price adjustments, introducing turning point.

Exercises

1. Which economic phases are there?
2. What types of business cycles exist, differentiated by length?
3. Name a leading and a lagging economic indicator.
4. What are three main reasons for economic fluctuations?
5. To what extent can economic fluctuations be caused by monetary policy?
6. Describe the phases of the Schumpeter business cycle.
7. To what extent does psychology play a role in business cycles? Which theories can be used for this?

References

Aghion, P., & Saint-Paul, G. (1993). *Uncovering some causal relationship between productivity, growth and the structure of economic fluctuations: A tentative survey* (Working Paper No. 4603). Cambridge: National Bureau of Economic Research.

Albers, W., et al. (Eds.). (1976). *Handwörterbuch der Wirtschaftswissenschaften* (Vol. 4). Göttingen: Vandenhoeck und Ruprecht.

Arteta, C., Kose, M. A., Stocker, M., & Taskin, T. (2016). Negative interest rate policies sources and implications. *Worldbank Policy Research Working Papers, 7791.* Accessed August 2016, from http://econ.worldbank.org

Aschinger, G. (1991). Theorie der spekulativen Blasen. *Wirtschaftsstudium, 20*(6), 270–274.

Assenmacher, W. (1998). *Konjunkturtheorie* (8th ed.). München: Oldenbourg.

Assenmacher, K., & Krogstrup, S. (2018). Monetary policy with negative interest Rates: Decoupling cash from electronic money, *IMF Working Paper*, 18/191. Accessed from https://www.imf.org/en/Publications/WP/Issues/2018/08/27/Monetary-Policy-with-Negative-Interest-Rates-Decoupling-Cash-from-Electronic-Money-46076

Azariadis, C., & Guesnerie, R. (1986). Sunsports and cycles. *Review of Economic Studies, 53*, 725–738.

Baks, K., & Kramer, C. (1999). *Global liquidity and asset prices: Measurements, implications and spillovers* (IMF Working Paper No. 99/168). Washigton: International Monetary Fund.

Ball, L., & Mankiw, N. G. (1994). Asymetric price adjustment and economic fluctuations. *The Economic Journal, 30*, 247–261.

Barro, R. J. (1971). A general disequilibrium model of income and employment. *American Economic Review, 61*, 82–93.

Barro, R. J. (1981). *Money, expectations and business cycles.* New York: Academic Press.

Barro, R. J., & Grossmann, H. I. (1976). *Employment, and inflation.* Cambridge: Harvard University Press.

Beck, H. (2014). *Behavioral economics: Eine Einführung. 1 Aufl.* Wiesbaden: Springer.

Behavioral Finance Group. (2000). Behavioral Finance – Idee und Überblick. *Finanz Betrieb, 5*, 311–318.

Berg, H., & Cassel, D. (1992). Theorie der Wirtschaftspolitik. In *Vahlens Kompendium der Wirtschaftstheorie und Wirtschaftspolitik* (Vol. 2, 5th ed., pp. 163–238). München: Vahlen.

Bergstrom, A. (1962). A model of technical progress, the production function and cyclical growth. *Economica, New Series, 29*(116), 357–370.

Blanchard, O. J., & Watson, M. W. (1982). Bubbles, rational expectations, and financial markets. In P. Wachtel (Ed.), *Crises in the economic and financial structure.* Lexington Books: Lexington.

Blume, L., & Easley, D. (1992). Evolution and market behavior. *Journal of Economic Theory, 58*, 9–40.

Borio, C., & Zhu, H. (2008). Capital regulation, risk-taking and monetary policy: A missing link in the transmission mechanism? *BIS Working paper*, 268.

Borio, C., Gombacorta, L., & Hofmann, B. (2015). *The influence of monetary policy on bank profitability.* Bank for International Settlements, Working Paper, 514.

Boxall, P., Adamowicz, W. L., & Moon, A. (2009). Complexity in choice experiments: Choice of the status quo alternative and implications for welfare measurement. *The Australian Journal of Agricultural and Resource Economics, 53*, 503–519.

Braley, R. (1983). *An introduction to risk and return* (2nd ed.). London: Oxford University Press.

Bruns, C. (1994). *Bubbles und Excess Volatility auf dem deutschen Aktienmarkt.* Wiesbaden: Betriebswirtschaftlicher Verlag Dr. Th. Gabler GmbH.

Caruana, J. (2013). *Hitting the limits of "outside the box" thinking? Monetary policy in the crisis and beyond*, Official Monetary and Financial Institutions Forum lecture (Golden Series Lecture), London. Accessed from https://www.bis.org/speeches/sp130516.htm

Chancellor, E. (1999). *Devil take the hindmost. A history of financial speculation.* New York: Plume.

Chenery, H. B. (1952). Overcapacity and the acceleration principle. *Econometrica, 20*, 1–28.

Claessens, S. & Kose, M. A. (2013). Financial crises: Explanations, types, and implications, *IMF Working Paper*, 13/28. Accessed from https://www.imf.org/external/pubs/ft/wp/2013/wp1328.pdf

Claessens, S., Kose, M. A., & Terrones, M. E. (2012). How do business and financial cycles interact? *Journal of International Economics, 87*(1), 178–190.

Claessens, S., Coleman, N., & Donnelly, M. (2016, April 11). *Low-for-long interest rates and net interest margins of banks in advanced foreign economies.* Federal Reserve Board, IFDP Notes.

Clarke, S. (1967). *Central Bank Cooperation: 1924–31.* Federal Reserve Bank of New York.

Clower, R. W. (1965). The Keynesian counter-revolution: A theoretical appraisal. In F. H. Hahn & F. Brechling (Eds.), *The theory of interest rates* (pp. 103–125). London: Macmillan.

Conrad, C. (1999). Entwicklungen der Konjunkturtheorie seit Keynes und ihr Beitrag zur Konjunkturpolitik – eine vergleichende kritische Bewertung. *Konjunkturpolitik, 45*(3), 188–220.

Conrad, C. A. (2000). Theorie und Praxis der "speculative Bubbles". In C. A. Conrad & M. Stahl (Eds.), *Risikomanagement an den internationalen Finanzmärkten* (pp. 135–146). Stuttgart: Schäffer-Poeschel.

Conrad, C. A. (2015). Incentives, risk and compensation schemes: Experimental evidence on the importance of risk adequate compensation. *Applied Economics and Finance, 2*(2), 50–55.

Conrad, C. A. (2016). The image of man in the economic sciences in light of the financial crisis and recent research results. *Applied Economics and Finance, 3*(1), 95–103.

Conrad, C. A. (2018). Weaknesses of financial market regulation. *Applied Economics and Finance, 5* (s), 32.

Conrad, C. A. (2019). The effects on investment behavior of zero interest rate policy, evidence from a roulette experiment. *Applied Economics and Finance, 6*(4), 18–27.

Conrad, C. A., & Schoett, H. (2000). Das Börsenjahr 1998 – nur knapp vorbei am Crash? In C. A. Conrad & M. Stahl (Eds.), *Risikomanagement an den internationalen Finanzmärkten* (pp. 151–159). Stuttgart: Schäffer-Poeschel.

Conrad, C. A., & Stahl, M. (2000). Wirtschaft, Börsenfieber und Geldpolitik in den USA. *Orientierungen zur Wirtschafts- und Gesellschaftspolitik der Ludwig-Erhard-Stiftung, 85*, 24–32.

Conrad, C. A., & Stahl, M. (2002). Asset-Preise als geldpolitische Zielgröße - das Beispiel der USA. *Wirtschaftsdienst, 82*(8), 486–493.

Conrad, C. A., & Stahl, M. (2003). Geldpolitik und Spekulationsblasen – Das Beispiel der USA. *Österreichisches Bankarchiv, Zeitschrift für das gesamte Bank- und Börsenwesen, 51*, 685–693.

Cúrdia, V. (2019, February 4). How much could negative rates have helped the recovery? *FRBSF Economic Letter*, 2019-04, Research from the Federal Reserve Bank of San Francisco. Accessed from https://www.frbsf.org/economic-research/publications/economic-letter/2019/february/how-much-could-negative-rates-have-helped-recovery/

Daxhammer, R., & Schmied-Wörle, T. (2000). Japan seit 1990: Das schmerzhaft lange Platzen einer Bubble. In C. Conrad & M. Stahl (Eds.), *Risikomanagement an den internationalen Finanzmärkten* (pp. 45–58). Stuttgart: Schäffer-Poeschel.

De Bondt, Werner, F. M., & Thaler, R. (1985). Does the stock market overreact? *The Journal of Finance, 40*(3). Papers and Proceedings of the Forty-Third Annual Meeting American Finance Association, Dallas, Texas, December 28–30, 1984 (Jul., 1985), pp. 793–805. Beck 363.

De Bondt, W. F. M., & Forbes, W. P. (1999). Herding in analyst earnings forecasts: Evidence from the United Kingdom. *European Financial Management, 5*(2), 143–163.

De Long, B. D., & Summers, L. (1988). How does macroeconomic policy affect output? *Brookings Paper on Economic Activity, 2*, 433–480.

De Nicolò, G., Dell'Ariccia, G., Laeven, L., & Valencia, F. (2010). Monetary policy and bank risk-taking. *IMF Staff Position Note*, SDN/10/09. Accessed from https://www.imf.org/external/pubs/ft/spn/2010/spn1009.pdf

Dell'Ariccia, G., Laeven, L., & Marquez, R. (2010). Monetary policy, leverage, and bank risk-taking, *IMF Working Papers*, 10/276, International Monetary Fund. Accessed from https://www.imf.org/external/pubs/ft/wp/2010/wp10276.pdf

Dell'Ariccia, G., Igan, D., Laeven, L. & Tong, H. (2013). Policies for macrofinancial stability: Dealing with credit booms and busts. In S. Claessens, M. A. Kose, L. Laeven, & F. Valencia (Eds.), *Financial crises, consequences, and policy responses*. IMF. Accessed from https://www.elibrary.imf.org/view/IMF071/20264-9781475543407/20264-9781475543407/20264-9781475543407.xml?redirect=true

Diba, B. T., & Grossman, H. I. (1988). Explosive rational bubbles in stock prices? *The American Economic Review, 78*(3), 520–530.

Drozd, L. (2018). *The policy perils of low interest rates*, Federal Reserve Bank of Philadelphia, Discussion Paper, Q1. Accessed from https://philadelphiafed.org/-/media/research-and-data/publications/economic-insights/2018/q1/eiq118-policy_perils.pdf?la=en

Eucken, W. (1952). *Grundsätze der Wirtschaftspolitik* (4th ed.). Tübingen: J.C.B. Mohr.

Felderer, B., & Homburg, S. (1989). *Makroökonomik und neue Makroökonomik*. Berlin: Springer.

Feldstein, M. (2013, September 30). *The taper chase*. Project Syndicate. Accessed from https://www.project-syndicate.org/commentary/why-the-fed-postponed-the-qe-taper-by-martin-feldstein?barrier=accesspaylog

Fischer, S. (1980). *Expectations and economic policy*. Chicago: University of Chicago Press.

Flood, R. P., & Garber, P. M. (1980). Market fundamentals versus price-level bubbles: The first tests. *Journal of Political Economy, 88*, 745–770.

Franz, W. (Ed.). (1999). *Trend und Zyklus, Wirtschaftswissenschaftliches Seminar Ottobeuren* (Vol. 28). Tübingen: Mohr.

Frenk, David U.A., (2011). *Review of Irwin and Sanders 2010 OECD Report*. In: Institute for Agriculture and Trade Policy (Hrsg.), Excessive Speculation in Agriculture Commodities, Selected writings from 2008–2012, http://www.iadb.org/intal/intalcdi/PE/2011/08247.pdf (26.03.2013), (p. 43-49), p. 45 and http://www.matthias-schlecker.de/kointegrationsanalysestationaritaet-und-augmented-dickey-fuller-test (4.04.2014)

Frey, B. S., & Lau, L. J. (1968). Towards a mathematical model of government behaviour. *Zeitschrift für Nationalökonomie, 28*, 355–380.

Friedman, M., & Schwartz, A. J. (1965). *The great contraction 1929–1933*. Princeton, NJ: Princeton University Press.

Friedman, M., & Schwartz, A. (1969). *A monetary history of the United States*. Princeton, NJ: Princeton University Press.

Froot, K. A., Scharfstein, D. S., & Stein, J. C. (1992). Herd on the street: Informational Inefficiencies in a Market with Short-Term Speculation. *The Journal of Finance, XLVII*(4), 1461.

Gagnon, J. E. (2016, April). Quantitative easing: An underappeciated success, Peterson Institute for International Economics. *Policy Brief*, PB16-4. Accessed from https://piie.com/system/files/documents/pb16-4.pdf

Gerfin, H., & Möller, J. (1980a). Neue Makroökonomie. *Wirtschaftswissenschaftliches Studium, 9*, 201–206.

Gerfin, H., & Möller, J. (1980b). Neue Makroökonomische Theorie. *Wirtschaftswissenschaftliches Studium, 4*, 153–160.

Goodwin, R. M. (1951). The nonlinear accelerator and the persistence of business cycles. *Econometrica, 19*, 1–17.

Goodwin, R. M. (1967). A growth cycle. In C. H. Feldstein (Ed.), *Socialism, capitalism and economic growth, essays presented to maurice dobb* (pp. 54–58). Cambridge, MA: Cambridge University Press.

Grossekettler, H. (1989). Johan Gustav Knut Wicksell (1851–1926). In J. Starbatty (Ed.), *Klassiker des ökonomischen Denkens* (pp. 191–210). München: Beck.

Hannoun, H. (2015, April 22). *Ultra-low or negative interest rates: What they mean for financial stability and growth*. Speech at the Eurofi High-Level Seminar, Riga. Accessed from https://www.bis.org/speeches/sp150424.pdf

Hesse, H. (1999). Korreferat zum Referat K Jaeger, Der Beitrag der traditionellen Theorie zur Erklärung von Trend und Zyklus. In W. Franz et al. (Eds.), *Trend und Zyklus, Wirtschaftswissenschaftliches Seminar Ottobeuren* (Vol. 28, pp. 1–34). Tübingen: Mohr.

Heubes, J. (1986). *Grundzüge der Konjunkturtheorie*. München: Vahlen.

Heubes, J. (1991). *Konjunktur und Wachstum*. München: Vahlen.

Hicks, J. R. (1950). *A contribution to the theorie of the trade cycle*. Oxford: Clarendon Press.

Hirata, H., Kose, M. A., Otrok, C., & Terrones, M. E. (2012). *Global house price fluctuations: Synchronization and determinants.* NBER International Seminar on Macroeconomics 2012, National Bureau of Economic Research, Working Paper No. Accessed from https://www.nber.org/papers/w18362

Homburg, S. (1996). Makroökonomik. In A. Börsch-Supan, J. von Hagen, & P. J. J. Welfens (Eds.), *Springers Handbuch der Volkswirtschaftslehre.* Berlin: Springer.

International Monetary Fund. (2000). *World economic outlook.* Washington: International Monetary Fund.

Irwin, S. H., & Sanders, D. R. (2012). Testing the masters hypothesis in commodity futures markets. *Energy Economics, 34,* 256–269. pp. 258.

Ito, T., & Iwaisako, T. (1995). *Explaining Asset Bubbles in Japan* (Working Paper No. 5358). National Bureau of Economic Research.

Jaeger, K. (1999). Der Beitrag der traditionellen Theorie zur Erklärung von Trend und Zyklus. In W. Franz et al. (Eds.), *Trend und Zyklus, Wirtschaftswissenschaftlichses Seminar Ottobeuren* (Vol. 28, pp. 1–34). Tübingen: Mohr.

Jüttner, J. (1989). Fundamentals, bubbles, trading strategies: Are they the causes of black monday? *Kredit und Kapital, 22*(4), 470–486.

Kahneman, D., & Tversky, A. (1981, January 30). The framing of decisions and the psychology of choice. *Science, 211,* 453–457.

Kahneman, D., & Tversky, A. (1982). The psychology of preferences. *Scientific American, 146,* 160–173.

Kahneman, D., & Tversky, A. (1984). Choices, values and frames. *American Pschologist, 39*(4), 342–350.

Kahneman, D., & Tversky, A. (1986). Rational choice and the framing of decisions. *Journal of Business, 59*(4), 5251–5278.

Kahneman, D., Knetsch, J., & Thaler, R. (1991). Anomalies: The endowment effect, loss aversion and status quo bias. *The Journal of Economic Perspectives, 5*(1), 193–206.

Khan, A. (2018a). *A behavioral approach to financial supervision, regulation, and central banking.* IMF working paper, No. WP/18/178.

Khan, A. (2018b). *A behavioral approach to financial supervision, regulation, and central banking* (p. 46). IMF working paper, No. WP/18/178.

Kiehling, H. (2000). *Kursstürze am Aktienmarkt* (2nd ed.). München: Dtv Deutscher Taschenbuch.

Komphardt, J. (1989). Konjunkturtheorie heute: Ein Überblick. *Zeitschrift für Wirtschafts- und Sozialwissenschaften, 109,* 173–231.

Kugler, P. (1998). Neuere Entwicklungen in der Konjunkturtheorie. *Allgemeines Statistisches Archiv, 82,* 25–36.

Kurz, R. (1986). Zyklische Wachstum und Verteilung: Das Goodwin-Modell. *WiSu, 86*(6), 305–310.

Kydland, F. E., & Prescott, E. C. (1977). Rules rather than discretion: The inconsistency of optimal plans. *Journal of Political Economy, 85*(3), 473–491.

Kydland, F. E., & Prescott, E. C. (1982). Time to build and aggregate fluctuations. *Econometrica, 50,* 1345–1370.

Laidler, D. (1976a). Inflation in Britain – A monetarist perspective. *American Economic Review, 66,* 467–484.

Laidler, D. (1976b). Inflation – Alternative explanations and policies: Tests on data drawn from six countries. *Journal of Monetary Economics, 4,* 251–306.

Lansing, K. J. (2008). *Speculative growth and overreaction to technology shocks,* Working Paper Series, 2008-08, Federal Reserve Bank of San Francisco.

Leland, H., & Rubinstein, M. (1988). Comments on the market crash: Six months after. *Journal of Economic Perspectives, 2*(3), 45–50.

Long, J. B., & Plosser, C. I. (1983). Real business cycles. *Journal of Political Economy, 91*(1), 29–69.

Lucas, R. E. (1975). An equilibrium model of the business cycle. *Journal of Political Economy, 83* (1975), 1113–1144.

Lucas, R. E. (1976). Econometric policy evaluation: A critique. *Carnegie Rochester Conference Series on Public Policy, 1*(1), 19–46.

Maddaloni, A. & Peydró, J.-L. (2010). *bank risk-taking, securitization, supervision and low interest rates: Evidence from the Euro Area and the U.S. Lending Standards.* Working Paper Series, 1248, European Central Bank. Accessed from https://www.ecb.europa.eu/pub/pdf/scpwps/ecbwp1248. pdf

Maddaloni, A., Peydró-Alcalde, J. L. & Scope, S. (2009). *Does Monetary Policy affect bank credit standards? Evidence from the Euro Area Bank Lending Survey.* Accessed from https://www. researchgate.net/publication/256000197_Does_Monetary_Policy_Affect_Bank_Credit_ Standards_Evidence_from_the_Euro_Area_Bank_Lending_Survey

Malinvaud, E. (1977). *The theory of unemployment reconsidered.* Oxford: Basil Blackwell.

Mankiw, G. N. (1985). Small menu costs and large business cycles. *Quarterly Journal of Economics, 100*, 529–539.

Mankiw, G. N. (1998). *Makroökonomik* (3rd ed.). Stuttgart: Schäffer-Poeschel.

Marx, K. (1864). *Das Kapital: Kritik der politischen Ökonomie. Der Gesamtprozeß der kapitalistischen Produktion* (Vol. 3, 3rd edn, Kap. 1–3). Berlin: Dietz.

Masciandaro, D., & Favaretto F. (2014). *Behavioral economics and monetary policy.* Baffi Carefin Centre Research Paper Series, No. 2015–1.

McCallum, B. T. (1980). Rational expectations and macroeconomic stabilization policy. *Journal of Money, Credit and Banking, 18*, 716–746.

Menkhoff, L., & Röckemann, C. (1994). Noise trading auf Aktienmärkten. *Zeitschrift für Betriebswirtschaftslehre, 64*(3), 277–295.

Metcalfe, J. (1998a). Cognitive optimism: Self-deception or memory-based processing heuristic? *Personality and Social Psychology Review, 2*(2), 100–110.

Mezger, M., & Stahl, M. (2001a). Gold – Stabilitätspfeiler in Krisenzeiten. *Die Bank, 5*, 372–378.

Mezger, M., & Stahl, M. (2001b). Neue Erkenntnisse über Inflation und Finanzkrisen. *Orientierungen zur Wirtschafts- und Gesellschaftspolitik der Ludwig-Erhard-Stiftung, 87*, 15–22.

Mian, A. R., Sufi, A., & Verner, E. (2015). Household debt and business cycles Worldwide, *NBER Working Paper, 21581*. Accessed from https://www.nber.org/papers/w21581.pdf

Minford, P., & Peel, D. (1983). *Rational expectations and the new macroeconomics.* Oxford: Martin Robertson.

Musgrave, R. A., Musgrave, P. B., & Kullmer, L. (1987). *Die öffentlichen Finanzen in Theorie und Praxis* (Vol. 3). Stuttgart: UTB.

Nickerson, R. S. (1998). Confirmation bias: an ubiquitous phenomen in many guises. *Review of general Psychology 1998, 2*(2), 175–220.

Nishad Nishad, P. (2018). Effectiveness of Japan's zero and negative interest rate policy, *MPRA Paper*, No. 89442. Accessed from https://mpra.ub.uni-muenchen.de/89442/. MPRA Paper No. 89442

Nordhaus, W. D. (1975). The political business cycle. *Review of Economic Studies, 42*, 169–190.

Ongena, S., Vasso, I. & Peydró, J. L. (2009). *Monetary policy, risk-taking and pricing: Evidence from a quasi-natural experiment.* Discussion Paper 2009-31, Tilburg University, Center for Economic Research.

Ott, A. (1963). *Einführung in die dynamische Wirtschaftstheorie.* Göttingen: Vandenhoeck & Ruprecht.

Pagan, A., & Schwert, C. (1990). Testing for covariance stationarity in stock market data. *Economics Letters, 33*(2), 165–170.

Phillips, P. & Loretan, M. (1990). *Testing covariance stationarity under moment condition failure with an application to common stock returns* (Discussion Paper No. 947). Cowles Foundation for Economic Research at Yale University, New Haven, CT.

Rajan, R. G. (2005). *Has financial development made the world riskier?* NBER Working Paper No. 11728. Accessed from https://www.nber.org/papers/w11728

Ramey, G., & Ramey, V. A. (1991). *Technology commitment and the cost of economic fluctuations* (Working Paper No. 3755). National Bureau of Economic Research.

Ramey, G., & Ramey, V. A. (1995). Cross-country evidence on the link between volatility and growth. *The American Economic Review, 85*(5), 1138–1151.

Ramser, H. J. (1988). Neuere Beiträge zur Konjunkturpolitik: ein Überblick. *IFO-Studien, 34*, 95–115.

Ramser, H. J. (1997). Konjunktur und Wachstum: Der Beitrag der Neuen Wachstumstheorie. *ifoStudien, 43*(2), 211–223.

Rasch, S. (1993). Crashs-Naturkatastrophen an den Finanzmärkten? *ZEW-Wirtschaftsanalysen, 1*(3), 269–305.

Ritov, I., & Baron, J. (1992). Status-quo bias and omission-bias. *Journal of Risk and Uncertainty, 5*, 49–61.

Rothschild, K. W. (1981). *Einführung in die Ungleichgewichtstheorie*. Berlin: Springer.

Rottmann, H., & Wollmershäuser, T. (2010). *A micro data approach to the identification of credit crunches* (Working Paper No. 3159: Monetary Policy and International Finance). CESifo.

Rubio, V. J., Hernández, J. M., Zaldívar, F., Márquez, O., & Santacreu, J. (2010). Can we predict risk-taking behavior? Two behavioral tests for predicting guessing tendencies in a multiple-choice test. *European Journal of Psychological Assessment, 26*(2), 87–94. http://www.uam.es/proyectosinv/psimasd/risktaking.pdf.

Rubio, V. J., Hernández, J. M., & Santacreu, J. *The objective assessment of risk tendency as a personality dimension*. University Autónoma of Madrid. Accessed from www.uam.es/proyectosinv/psimasd/assessrisk.pdf

Samuelson, P. A. (1939). Interactions between the multiplier analysis and the principle of acceleration. *Review of Economics and Statistics, 21*, 235–241.

Samuelson, W., & Zeckhauser, R. (1988). Status quo bias in decision making. *Journal of Risk and Uncertainty, 1*, 7–59.

Santoni, G. J., & Dwyer, G. P., Jr. (1990). Bubbles or fundamentals: New evidence from the great bull markets. In E. N. White (Ed.), *Crashes and panics: The lessons from history*. New York: Wiley.

Schebeck, F., & Tichy, G. (1984). Die "Stylized Facts" in der modernen Konjunkturdiskussion. In G. Bombach, B. Gahlen, & A. E. Ott (Eds.), *Perspektiven der Konjunkturforschung* (pp. 207–224). Tübingen: JCB Mohr.

Schumpeter, P. (1939). *Business cycles*. New York: McGraw-Hill.

Shiller, R. J. (1984). Stock prices and social dynamics. *Brookings Papers on Economic Activity, 2*, 457–498.

Shiller, R. J. (2000). *Irrational exuberance*. Princeton, NJ: Princeton University Press.

Shleifer, A. (1986). Implementation cycles. *Journal of Political Economy, 94*, 1169–1190.

Shleifer, A. (2000a). *Inefficient markets, an introduction to behavioral finance*. Oxford: Oxford University Press.

Shleifer, A. (2000b). Stock prices and social dynamics. *Brookings Papers on Economic Activity, 2*, 457–498.

Shleifer, A., & Vishny, R. W. (1990). Equilibrium short horizons of investors and firms. *American Economic Review, 80*(2), 148–153.

Sloan, A., & Stern, R. L. (1988). How Vo=VgN(d1) – E/ert N(d2) led to black monday. *Forbes, 25*(1), 55–59.

Stadler, G. W. (1994). Real business cycles. *Journal of Economic Literature, 32*, 1750–1783.

Stahl, M. (2000a, June 6). *Die Goldenen Zwanziger im Lichte der Internet Revolution, Chancen und Risiken der Neuen Ökonomie, Die Wirtschafts- und Börsenentwicklung in den USA heute weist große Ähnlichkeit auf mit der Lage vor dem Schwarzen Freitag 1929.* Süddeutsche Zeitung, 129.

Stahl, M. (2000b). Die Lektionen des Jahres 1929. In C. Christian & M. Stahl (Eds.), *Risikomanagement an internationalen Finanzmärkten* (pp. 3–20). Stuttgart: Schäffer-Poeschel.

Stahl, M., & Conrad, C. A. (2000). Die Finanzmärkte im Spannungsfeld der New Economy. *Wirtschaftsdienst, 80*(7), 415.

Stavenhagen, G. (1969). *Geschichte der Wirtschaftstheorie.* Göttingen: Vandenhoeck.

Stiglitz, S. E. (1994). Endogenous growth and cycles. In Y. Shinoya & M. Perlmon (Eds.), *Innovation in technology, industries and institutions, studies in schumpeterian perspective* (pp. 121–156). Ann Arbor: The University of Michigan Press.

Stiglitz, J. (2016). *What's wrong with negative rates?* Project Syndicate, April 13. Accessed from https://www.project-syndicate.org/commentary/negative-rates-flawed-economic-model-by-joseph-e%2D%2Dstiglitz-2016-04?barrier=accesspaylog

Stiglitz, J., & Weiss, A. (1981). Credit rationing in markets with imperfect information. *American Economic Review, 71*(3), 393–410.

Stiglitz, S. E., & Weiss, A. (1992). Asymmetric information in credit markets and its implications for macroeconomics. *Oxford Economic Papers, 44*(4), 694–724.

Teichmann, U. (1997). *Grundriss der Konjunkturpolitik* (5th ed.). München: Vahlen.

Temin, P. (1976). *Did monetary forces cause the great depression?* New York: Norton.

The Presidental Task Force. (1988). *Report of the presidental task force on market mechanisms (Brady-Report).* New York: US Government Printing Office.

Tichy, G. (1995). *Konjunkturpolitik* (3rd ed.). Berlin: Springer.

Treynor, J. (1998). Bulls, beers and market bubbles. *Financial Analysts Journal, 54*(2), 69–74.

Tymoigne, E. (2018). *On the optimality of a permanent zero central-bank rate: Why were central banks created?* Paper presented at 12th Conference of the Research Network Macroeconomics and Macroeconomic Policies, October 2008. Accessed from https://www.boeckler.de/pdf/v_2008_10_31_tymoigne.pdf

von Hayek, F. A. (1929). *Geldtheorie und Konjunkturtheorie (Nachdruck der ersten Auflage von 1929, S. 81 ff).* Salzburg: Wolfgang Neugebauer.

von Hayek, F. A. (1935). Prices and production (2nd ed.). Clifton: Kelley (reprint in The Ludwig von Mises Institute (Eds.). *Prices & production and other works. F. A. Hayek on money, the business cycle, and the gold standard.* Auburn 2008. Accessed from https://mises.org/library/prices-and-production

von Hayek, F. A. (Ed.). (1969). *Der Wettbewerb als Entdeckungsverfahren.* Tübingen: Freiburger Studien.

Wagner, A. (1990). *Makroökonomik* (2nd ed.). Stuttgart: UTB.

Wicksell, K. (1898). *Geldzins und Güterpreise. Eine Studie über den Tauschwert des Geldes bestimmenden Ursachen (Berichtigter Neudruck der Ausgabe Jena 1898).* Aalen: Scienta Verlag.

Wicksell, K. (1922). *Vorlesungen über Nationalökonomie auf Grundlage des Marginalprinzipes* (Vol. 2) Geld und Kredit (schwedische Erstveröffentlichung Stockholm 1906, Jena 1922). Aalen: Scienta Verlag.

Wicksell, K. (1928). *Vorlesungen über Nationalökonomie, Theoretischer Teil, zweiter Band.* Jena: Gustav Fischer.

Wolfstetter, E. (1982). Fiscal policy and the classical growth cycle. *Zeitschrift für Nationalökonomie, 42*, 375–393.

Zarnowitz, V. (1997). *Business cycles observed and assessed: Why and how they matter* (Working Paper No. 6230). National Bureau of Economic Research.

International Financial Markets

What Follows Why?

The financial crisis led to the worst depression since 1929. Only by massive economic programs could worse be prevented. Here Keynesian theory came into play. Only through globally agreed massive credit-financed government spending increases could depression be prevented. The banks had to be saved with tax money, as many banks had invested in the government bonds of weak European countries whose solvency was called into question. The sovereign debt crisis has emerged from the financial crisis. Against this background, the question arises of state regulations that limit the risk of banks. Such regulation of the financial markets has been urged by politicians and economists since the onset of the 2007 financial crisis. What has happened in the meantime? Were the right reforms implemented or could there be another financial crisis? After analyzing the causes of the crisis, the main reforms are examined below.

Learning Goals

You should be able to explain the reasons for the financial crisis and the attempts to counteract it.

© The Editor(s) (if applicable) and The Author(s), under exclusive license to Springer Fachmedien Wiesbaden GmbH, part of Springer Nature 2020
C. A. Conrad, *Political Economy*,
https://doi.org/10.1007/978-3-658-30884-1_13

13.1   The Financial Crisis and the Reforms to Stabilize the Financial Markets

13.1.1 The Subprime Crisis, the Biggest Financial Crisis After 1929

In 2003, Warren Buffet said of the credit derivatives market that they were "financial weapons of mass destruction, carrying dangers that, while now latent are potentially lethal." Others also warned that credit based derivatives coupled with a lack of transparency were leading to a significant concentration of risk. Unfortunately, they were right.

Derivative products such as CDOs (Collateralized Debt Obligations) can be directly traced as being one of the major factors leading to the subprime crisis and the greatest financial crisis since the Wall Street crash of 1929. CDOs are structured financial products comprised of a variety of loans, bonds, mortgages and credit derivatives such as Credit Default Swaps or CDSs. For the most part, CDOs were put together using home mortgages and then resold as investment products by the major Wall Street investment banks. These CDOs were structured to meet the requirements of the major US rating agencies which based their risk calculations on complicated economic models and statistical analysis. Two apparently ingenious combinations of factors made it possible to create an innovative financial product with a combined calculated risk in the portfolio lesser than the sum of the individual risk associated with each element in the portfolio.

The basis for the evaluation of risk associated with these financial products as calculated by the rating agencies was based upon the historical default rate of US mortgages. As this data was not always available, it was necessary to draw upon estimates that fit within established portfolio theories and expectations and which would produce the desired reduction of risk between two comparative portfolios. Part of this process was to investigate the relationships and correlations between the individual elements of these portfolios to determine the probability that both or more elements could be eliminated from risk calculations. The complex statistical financial models used by the rating agencies were not always understood or even available to those in the market place as investors. This situation was not considered to be an issue at the time, as the capital markets had a great deal of trust and confidence in the ratings provided by the rating agencies. For decades, the ratings provided by the rating agencies concerning potential risk had been used to determine the terms for credit and loans to borrowers in the capital markets. As a consequence of the subprime crisis, the objectivity of these ratings agencies has now been called into question, most notably due to their previous relationships with the investment banks for which they provided the CDO ratings.

The second situation by which a portfolio rating could be improved was through the use and subordination of various "risk tranches". In the event of a default or failure of one of the elements or "tranches" in the portfolio, the most subordinated tranche (junior note) would be affected. This process would continue on up the scale to the tranches with AA to BB ratings, (mezzanine notes) and in the extreme case on up to the most senior tranches with AAA ratings.

For decades, the value of American real estate has steadily increased. After all, the USA has been a country of considerable growth both in terms of population and economic expansion. This growth has also been the basis for a historically low level of home mortgage defaults. For the most part, home values have been sufficient to cover outstanding mortgage balances in the event of a default. As a consequence, lenders were encouraged to offer ever-increasing mortgage loans based on the projected future value of homes in an ever-expanding market. As home values rose, lenders would offer homeowners access to their equity through refinancing or home equity lines of credit which would support even further consumption. Much of the mortgage financing made available to borrowers by Freddie Mac and Fannie Mae was also supported by political incentives to encourage home ownership among socially and economically disadvantaged minority groups. This initiative originated in the mid-1990s with the Clinton administration as lending criteria were relaxed[1] and continued under the Bush administration. In 2003, Congressman Ron Paul warned that this relaxed lending policy would eventually lead to individuals borrowing to buy homes that they could ill-afford and eventually require financial intervention on the part of government. In 1994, the market for subprime mortgages made up only 5% of the total mortgage market and amounted to $35 billion dollars, and by 2006 it had increased to become 20% of the mortgage market for a total of approximately $600 billion dollars. This increase in lending volume was only made possible by ever more relaxed lending standards. Borrowers were able to obtain mortgage loans without showing any proof of income or employment or assets, the so-called "ninja loans" meaning "No Income, No Job, and No Assets". This situation was further encouraged by ever-falling interest rates as initiated by the Federal Reserve under the leadership of Alan Greenspan, with short-term rates reaching a low of 1% in 2004. Subprime borrowers were also offered ARMs, or Adjustable Rate Mortgages with low, interest-only payments required, as well as "teaser loans" with initial interest rates well below market rates that would dramatically increase or reset at a later date. Also available were payment option loans which made it possible for borrowers to set their own repayment schedule and thereby postpone repayment for as long as possible. Altogether, US mortgage borrowing rose from $680 billion in 1974 to $14 trillion in 2001. From a total of 8.8 million homeowners with mortgages, about 10.8% had no actual equity in their property or, in fact, owed more than their home was worth.

---

[1]". . . the Fannie Mae Corporation is easing the credit requirements on loans . . . The action . . . will encourage those banks to extend home mortgages to individuals whose credit is generally not good enough. . . Fannie Mae. . . has been under increasing pressure from the Clinton Administration to expand mortgage loans among low and moderate income people and felt pressure from stock holders to maintain its phenomenal growth in profits. In addition, banks, thrift institutions and mortgage companies have been pressing Fannie Mae to help them make more loans to so-called subprime borrowers whose incomes, credit ratings and savings are not good enough for conventional loans. . . Fannie Mae is taking on significantly more risk. . . the government subsidized corporation may run into trouble. . . prompting a government rescue. . . the move is intended in part to increase the number of. . . home owners who tend to have worse credit ratings. . ." September 30, 1999 New York Times.

Average home values in the USA increased 126% from 1997 to 2006, while the relationship between home values and annual income changed from a ratio of 2.9 in 2001 to 4.6 in 2006. This dramatic change in home values, as compared with annual income, was not considered a problem as long as borrowers were able to service their debt and maintain their mortgage payments. The crisis only came about as a consequence of changing interest rates and the payment structures built into these loans.

Banks can, but in a limited manner, restructure loan intervals as needed to meet business requirements but if they require refinancing at a later date, then it will be necessary for them to draw upon their own liquidity. Therefore every banking student is taught the golden rule of lending, which is to restructure loans through refinancing at appropriate coverage intervals.

When restructuring loans, the risks associated with changing interest rates and refinancing are to be carried and collateralized by the banks themselves. These fundamental rules of finance were unfortunately ignored when it came to the issuance of CDOs by investment banks, which finally amounted to a market value of over $2 trillion dollars. Long-term mortgages were repackaged and sold by the investment banks as special purpose vehicles (conduits) and collateralized at fairly low capital ratios through the use of short-term commercial paper (CPs). In this way, the CDOs could be refinanced at lower interest rates which created more profitable margins for the banks. The CDOs in these "special purpose entities" did not surface on the bank's balance sheet. As was the case with Enron, these obligations were not listed as consolidated third party liabilities and therefore not readily apparent at first glance. On bank balance sheets these obligations were simply listed as possible liabilities in the comments section and often escaped notice. In the unlikely event that banks were unable to sell these securities on the market, they would be required to provide adequate liquidity to cover these obligations. High leveraging of stock purchases was also a reason for the financial crisis in 1929.

Deregulation further encouraged the direct and indirect use of leverage by investment banks. For example, in 2004 the SEC allowed investment banks to expand their use of leverage by lowering their capital margin requirement from 8% to 6%. By 2007, the five largest US investment banks had increased their borrowing for investment purposes to $4.1 trillion dollars, which equalled approximately 30% of the US gross domestic product. What motivated the investment banks to take on this level of risk? This was the era of the "shareholder value concept", of short-term gain and exceptional bonuses. The simplest way to increase shareholder value and therefore also stock value was to use leverage to boost returns on investment. Finally, in order for a bank to receive a rating of "excellent" from the rating agencies, they were required to show a 25% return on investment of capital and therefore a favourable rating for future refinancing. An attractive aspect of CDOs was that it was not required that they be rated as loans, but could be rated as a security product. This classification allowed the investment banks to realize additional profits by selling them on to other investors and not hold bank funds in reserve as collateral.

Using CDOs, investment banks were therefore able to boost their profitability on invested capital as well as their internal rate of return. Loans would be classified as CDO securities and therefore positively influence the banks balance sheet. As securities, these CDOs would appear to be without risk. In addition, the rating agencies would assign them AAA status, indicating that these "securities" were without risk. As securities, the CDOs were not subject to the strict federal regulations required for debt products nor would they have to be evaluated as debt obligations on the books of the already highly leveraged banks. Free from complying with external financial requirements and internal lending limits, investment bankers were able to secure profitable sources of revenue and therefore substantial bonuses as well. By repackaging US mortgages as investment products, bankers were able to realize approximately $23.9 billion dollars in bonus payments in 2006. In 2007, Swiss bank UBS paid out $10 billion Swiss Francs in bonus payments alone. The availability and easy access to credit for home mortgages encouraged not only dealers but also lenders who provided loans to ever less qualified borrowers. In the end, these lenders were selling these loans on to other investors and therefore did not have to contend with the risk. The relationship between the lenders issuance of credit and mortgages and the associated risk of default were distinctly separated from one another, which lead to a fundamental violation of the market (order) principles of accountability and transparency. The exceptionally complex structure of the CDOs also contributed to this lack of transparency. It only became clear later that it was all but impossible to separate the various problem loans within the CDOs from the total in the portfolio, and impossible to trace them back to the original borrowers. Also, the system of bonus payments made to bankers selling the CDOs appears to be in contradiction to principles of accountability, as their bonuses were based on short-term profitability while the potential long-term negative consequences of their actions were ignored.

The bubble in the US housing market burst in 2006. A contributing factor was the dramatic rise in short-term interest rates which made it impossible for many mortgage borrowers to maintain their payments. This rise in interest rates lead to ever greater defaults and bank repossessions and home prices fell. The consequences for the financial sector first became apparent in February 2007 as HSBC was compelled to write off loans repackaged as CDOs valued $10.5 billion dollars. While serious, the crisis seemed to be limited to the banking sector and did not pose a threat to the real economy. In November 2007, the volume of subprime mortgages was valued at $148 billion dollars. At this point, the extreme difficulty in placing an accurate value on the CDOs became all too apparent. The lack of transparency associated with the CDOs and the high level of risk they carried due to the subprime mortgages they contained made them all but impossible to sell or accurately value. The market for CDOs collapsed entirely, leading to a crisis of capital liquidity for those banks carrying them on their books. This issue lead to an unexpected reduction of liquidity at the banks. In December, the amount of subprime debt was corrected from $200 billion to $300 billion, and then finally in March 2008 from $350 billion to $600 billion dollars.

A rating of AAA was now considered worthless and all trust in the rating agencies had been lost. Without accurate and reliable ratings from the agencies, the capital markets were crippled. It soon became obvious that the crisis was not limited to just the US. As CDOs had been sold on the international market, the risk that they carried was now also an international problem. Swiss banks such as UBS, and German banks IKB and Sachsen Landes Bank had built up considerable portfolios filled with CDOs and as a consequence experienced severe liquidity problems. In addition, these banks required ever increasing amounts of fresh capital to cover the write-offs associated with CDOs and to support lines of liquidity. The banks which had invested too much of their client's capital were in danger of going bankrupt. US investment banks and larger banks such as UBS were able to raise additional capital on their own, while banks such as Germany's IKB and Sachsen Landes Bank had to be rescued by the German federal government. British mortgage lender Northern Rock experienced a run on the bank and had to be nationalized.

The crisis continued to expand. Two basic issues became apparent: increasing suspicion and mistrust between banks and ever further write-offs due to CDOs, which served to accelerate the crisis of liquidity and available capital. Banks felt that they could no longer trust one another and therefore stopped lending to each other. Without transparency and trust between banks, no one could be sure which banks were solvent and how much remaining debt had to be written off. Ratings given to the banks by the ratings agencies could no longer be relied upon. The inter-banking market collapsed. Banks without branch offices and therefore without access to investors found themselves short of liquidity. Central banks were compelled to provide infusions of capital into the marketplace and to lower interest rates. The quarterly reports by banks concerning their ever-increasing CDO related write-offs only served to further depress the already discouraged mood in the marketplace. As European banks primarily followed US-GAAP for accounting purposes as well as the internationally accepted IFRS standards, this lead to an even greater difficulty in accurately assigning a value to the CDOs. Following US accounting standards which tend to favour shareholder interests, securities and other financial products such as the CDOs must be "mark to market" to assign a current market value. In contrast to European accounting standards, the costs of acquisition are not included if a reduction in value is only temporary. Although home mortgages continued to operate for the most part unchanged, the market for CDOs had collapsed and banks were compelled to write down the market value of their CDOs by as much as 70%. This development culminated in the partial illiquidity of US investment bank Bear Stearns in March of 2008. The head of Germany's Deutsche Bank Josef Ackermann was quoted at this time as saying that "he no longer believed in the ability of the markets to self-correct and heal themselves".

Bankers called on the government to help them out of the situation. JP Morgan purchased Bear Stearns for $1.2 billion dollars after receiving a bail-out loan of $29 billion from the US Federal Reserve. After this action by the Federal Reserve the financial markets seemed to settle down. The danger of collapse of further large financial institutions seemed to be over. At the beginning of 2007, market participants started to believe that perhaps the worst of the subprime crisis was over, only to have the crisis flare up again. But the worst of the crisis was yet to come. The crisis would continue as the banks CDOs increasingly lost value and were written down to comply with accounting regulations. Prices for homes on the US real estate market and the almost non-existent CDO market continued to fall ever further. A shortage of liquidity compelled the banks to sell additional securities which lead to a vicious cycle of price declines. The mistrust of ratings assigned by the ratings agencies and the general uncertainty in the market lead to investors selling all forms of securities and to seek refuge in government bonds and treasuries.

In September 2008 the entire financial system came close to collapse. Only through a massive intervention by national governments up to and including the nationalization of many banks could the financial crisis be contained. Many newspapers compared the current financial crisis to that of the Wall Street crash of 1929. The US mortgage lender Silver State bank and many other smaller real estate lenders had to be closed and both major mortgage lenders Fannie Mae and Freddie Mac were nationalized. The growing crisis lead to the bankruptcy of Lehman Brothers, the 4th largest investment bank in the US. The CEO of a major German bank was quoted as saying "Lehman was the downfall that lead the financial crisis to a mass panic."

US Treasury secretary Paulson wanted to make an example of Lehman Brothers. Wall Street needed to realize that things could not continue as before, with the government prepared to bail out every bank facing insolvency,... as if in keeping with the motto "Privatization of profit and nationalization of loss." This concerned the concept of "moral hazard" as versus the adage "too big to fail". The majority of Americans were against the idea of using taxpayer money to bail out bankers on Wall Street. Paulson had drastically miscalculated the situation. Mohamed El-Erian, co-manager of the market's largest bond fund PIMCO made the case that, after the fall of Lehman Brothers all sense of trust and confidence was lost in the ability of financial institutions to be extricated from the crisis in an orderly fashion. In actuality, the collapse of Wall Street's 4th largest investment bank was an event beyond comprehension. All the major players in the financial markets had expected that the adage "too big to fail" certainly applied to Lehman Brothers, and that after the rescue of Bear Stearns by the federal government that Lehman Brothers could expect the same treatment.

That Paulson allowed the collapse of Lehman Brothers shook the financial world to its core. Nothing more seemed to be certain, and there was no longer any relying on a bail out. The danger for the financial system was that Lehman Brothers was one of the largest traders of derivatives and so its collapse would have profound consequences. The sword of Damocles, as wielded by George Soros in the form of billions of dollars of derivatives contracts, fell. After the bursting of the internet bubble banks discovered derivatives as the next major source of almost unlimited revenue potential. Derivatives are a form of obligation with their value tied to the occurrence of specific events in the financial markets. Options, for example, give the investor or speculator the right to buy or sell a specific security at specific price during a pre-determined period of time. Options, however, do not belong to the classic form of derivative. A derivative is normally used to cover an exposure to risk as a hedge. For example, the owner of a share of stock would use a sell option (Put-option) to sell his shares at a pre-determined price, or for speculation. The attraction of options derivatives is that with relatively little money an investor can speculate on the movement of a stock price with greater leverage, and also greater risk, than if he had to actually buy and own the underlying stock. Especially risky were a fairly new form of financial innovation known as Credit Default Swaps or CDSs. They also were developed in the US at the start of the 1990s as a form of hedge against loan risk. If a bank, for example, desires to reduce the risk of default for a loan that it has with a borrower, it can hedge the risk of default by buying a CDS from a third party. With a CDS it was possible for banks to increase their rates of return on capital while avoiding the use of their own capital to cover loans. In contrast, those providing the risk coverage were not bound by any specific regulations. They were not required to put up any capital of their own, so the actual risk of default was not covered. Investment banks and highly leveraged hedge funds[2] were also partly involved in these transactions as contrarian speculators. In 2001, the nominal value of outstanding CDS contracts reached approximately $1 trillion dollars, and in 2005 it amounted to $10 trillion dollars. For the most part, this increase in CDS volume was due to speculation on the part of contrarian investors and not from actual transactions to hedge loan risk. The bankruptcy of auto parts supplier Delphi stands as a good case in point, whereby $5.2 billion dollars in loans and bonds were hedged by $28 billion dollars in CDS contracts. In 2008, the total value of all outstanding CDS contracts was approximately $62 trillion dollars. The degree of counter-party risk had become impossible to ignore.

After the collapse of Lehman Brothers complete panic broke out. The domino effect was enormous. It was not only that the banks no longer trusted each other or their level of solvency, but rather the entire financial system was called into question leading to worst case scenario. The capital markets collapsed. The banks could no longer refinance or restructure the portfolios effectively. In addition, subprime securities such as corporate bonds were no longer marketable, or could only be sold at greatly reduced value. The consequences for the real economy were immediately apparent.

Lehman Brothers certificates had been sold to investors around the world. Now they were worthless. The media took advantage of the negative publicity by running dramatic headlines leading to widespread fear and uncertainty. In this way they helped to spread the panic. Everyone became convinced of a pending catastrophe and recession, and so reduced their investment and consumption. This became a self-fulfilling prophesy. People became fearful of potentially losing their jobs and stopped spending. As a consequence of reduced liquidity and a shortage of available capital, banks stopped making loans. The "credit crunch" had arrived. The greater economy became fearful of declining sales and liquidity problems and stopped investing. Due to the negative sentiments it came to the classical Keynesian case of underinvestment together with the liquidity-trap. Savers lost faith in banks and withdrew their deposits, which further exacerbated liquidity problems at the banks. In order to generate liquidity, the banks sold shares. Falling market prices lead to even further price declines as risk limits triggered computerized trading and stock sales at

---

[2]In 2000, warnings were issued as to the threat posed to the financial system due to the lack of regulation on Hedge Funds as counter-parties to derivative transactions. See Conrad, Christian/Stahl, Markus (2000).

many hedge funds. Investment bank Merrill Lynch was taken over by the Bank of America. The US government set up a special fund of $700 billion dollars to buy up the bank's portfolios of non-performing loans. In a form of reverse auction process, banks were permitted to sell their portfolios of non-performing securities to federal funds offering the highest percentage of face value for the securities. The two remaining US investment banks, Goldman Sachs and Morgan Stanley had to give up their previous business model so as to be considered as universal banks and gain access to refinancing funds from the US Federal Reserve. Further access to capital was given to suffering banks by the federal authorities. The world's largest insurer AIG was in-part nationalized through this process. AIG had been speculating as a counter-party to billions of dollars in obligations using CDSs and CDOs following a trading strategy based on the mathematical-statistical model of Yale Professor Gary Gordon. The probability of default as calculated by Gordon proved to be mistaken, however. Further banks were forced into bankruptcy or taken over. Hypo Real Estate in Germany was saved by a combination of private banks and the German federal government. Banks in England and elsewhere had to be nationalized to prevent the collapse of the financial system. Governments came to the rescue of banks through the use of bail-out funds from taxpayers. By this time the world's stock markets had fallen from a peak in August 2007 by more than 50% and set the world on the path to recession. Between March 1st and June 18th 2008, the FBI arrested 406 individuals for loan and mortgage fraud, ranging from small mortgage brokers to bank presidents who were later charged with having deceived investors as to the risks of the subprime market.[3]

As with Enron, Merrill Lynch was insolvent. With approximately $9 billion dollars in losses, Merrill's CEO O'Neal was responsible for the worst financial results at the bank in its 93 year history. And in 2008, there were an additional $15 billion dollars in write-offs. Similar to Skillings at Enron, O'Neal was also possessed of an unusually overbearing management style and obsession with profit results. The consequences would soon become all too apparent. By taking on more risk, O'Neal could produce better profit results while the top management at Merrill cashed in on huge bonuses. At Citigroup, CEO Prince was also facing more than $20 billion dollars in write-offs. Here as well, in 2008 it was necessary to write off huge sums. Both Prince and O'Neal were not only responsible for billions in write-offs, but as senior management received exceptionally handsome compensation packages (Prince received $26 million dollars and O'Neal $48 million dollars in 2006), and a severance package in the $100 million range. O'Neal received about $160 million in cash and stock options while Prince received approximately $100 million.[4] The losses would be assumed by others, namely the shareholders who lost a portion of their

---

[3]See Mayr, Brigitte (2007); Handelsblatt 23.10.08 and 10.1.08, p. 30; Süddeutsche Zeitung 17.11.08, p. 22, Neue Zuricher Zeitung 7.02.08; Zeit Online, 26/2008, p. 24, Der Spiegel, No. 47 (2008), p. 46–79 and Conrad, Christian A. (2010), p. 21.
[4]This income was exceeded by Goldman Sachs CEO Henry Paulson, who earned a bonus of $18.7 million along with realizing proceeds from the sale of $480 million in stock by exercising options issued prior to his becoming US secretary of the treasury. See Der Spiegel No. 8 (2009), p. 62.

investment in the banks while many employees lost their jobs. In other words, not only did the agents of disaster gamble away their investor's money but they were well-rewarded for it. With this disconnect between risk and compensation it's easy to understand why so many bankers took on such huge risks which lead us to today's subprime crisis.[5]

* * *

And when the financial markets had just stabilized somewhat, the sovereign debt crisis began in 2010. Many banks had invested in the government bonds of weak European countries, whose solvency was called into question.[6]

With the crises described above, the general question arises as to what went wrong? What economic dysfunctions are responsible for this huge resource destruction?

13.1.2 Some Causes of the Financial Crisis

13.1.2.1 Technical Mistakes

The first serious debate as to the infallibility of the capitalistic economic system arose in 2000 within the framework of the Enron crisis. By 2007, it was obvious that the world economy was in a fundamental crisis with the emergence of the subprime crisis. The subprime crisis was seen as the epitome of the ethical failure of our modern economy. Everything came together and many saw in the crisis the final act of "turbo capitalism",[7] the limitless enrichment of the few at the expense of society, which almost lead to a total collapse of the financial system. The lack of regulation and belief in the self-correcting power of the market was used by a few to take advantage of the situation. Considered historically, financial crises have increased significantly in recent years. This is not the result of simple coincidence, but rather much more an indication of a massive weakness in the present economic system. The market economy has always placed the individual at the forefront for the economic creation of value, which provided him with an ever-growing range of opportunity. Through the pursuit of individual interests, it was believed that this motivation would also create the most beneficial results for society and the greater good. This appears to not be the case. The absence of rules and the belief in the self-healing forces of the markets were exploited by individuals to their advantage.

Could the worst financial crisis since 1929 have been prevented? Naturally, in hindsight it would be easy to answer the question with a "yes", given what we know now about the causes and course of the crisis. Above all, the crisis can be traced back to a violation of market order principles through political intervention. Let's start with the inappropriate

---

[5]See also Shiller, Robert (2007); Gold, Gerry/Feldmann, Paul (2007); Muolo, Paul/Padilla, Matthew (2008) and Woods, Thomas E. (2009).

[6]See Shiller, Robert (2007); Gold, Gerry/Feldmann, Paul (2007); Muolo, Paul/Padilla, Matthew (2008); Woods, Thomas E. (2009); Financial Crisis Inquiry Commission (2010), and Conrad, Christian A. (2010).

[7]See Dahrendorf, Ralf, (2009).

involvement of the US government in the financial markets. The crisis started in the early 1990s as a consequence of a misguided social program on the part of politicians. In 1995, Fannie Mae and Freddie Mack received a mandate from the office of Housing and Urban Development (HUD) to lend to subprime borrowers using funds to be provided by HUD at below market interest rates. These funds were to provide mortgages to subprime borrowers in what were considered to be economically disadvantaged social groups, so that they could buy homes that they normally could not afford. The volume of loans and the regulations concerning the classification of subprime loans were increasingly expanded. These cheap loans made it possible for both Fannie Mae and Freddie Mac to boost their profit margins. Executives at Freddie Mac reciprocated with illegal campaign contributions while mortgage lender Connie Wide offered low-interest loans to influential politicians in Washington. One could say the basis for the subprime bubble can be traced back to the US government. It's also worth mentioning that the low interest rate policies of Alan Greenspan played an important role. By making cheap money readily available and supporting deregulation, the Fed created fertile ground for the bubble to grow.[8] One can also blame the US government for an exceptional lack of financial oversight. US financial regulators were aware of the growing problem but chose not to act, so as not to influence competition in the markets.

Rather than acting to regulate and control the mortgage markets, they put their faith in the ability of the market to correct itself and deregulated. Without regulators, it was possible for companies to hide the risk inherent in these loans from appearing on their balance sheets. Greenspan refused to act to control these new and innovative financial products. Despite the LTCM crisis,[9] Greenspan and the US government remained unconvinced that unregulated speculation by the hedge funds posed as serious threat to the financial system. Many governments, including the German government had been pushing for more regulation. Belief in the markets and the influence of financial lobbyists was more powerful, however. At no point during this phase of the crisis did financial regulators seem to be aware of the combined risk posed by CDOs and how it was spread among the banks.[10] With their complex mathematical models and AAA ratings, these deceptively secure financial innovations and the risk that they posed were able to escape the attention of over-worked federal regulators.

---

[8]See the film "Inside Job" of 2010 by Charles Ferguson (Sony Pictures) and Conrad, Christian, A./ Stahl, Markus (2002).

[9]In 1998 this hedge fund named Long Term Capital Management (LTCM) then lost the investors around 90% of the $4 billion invested, which threatened to trigger a chain reaction on the international finance markets. The issue here is not just the credit taken by LTCM, but also the derivative positions of LTCM as contracting party, with which other finance market actors had protected themselves. Only when the then US central bank president Alan Greenspan intervened personally and pulled together an emergency package of billions from several large banks could the capital market crisis be averted. See Conrad, Christian A. (2005).

[10]"What we have found over the years in the marketplace is that derivatives have been an extraordinarily useful vehicle to transfer risk from those who shouldn't be taking it to those who are willing to and are capable of doing so." "We think that it would be a mistake" to more regulate the contracts. Greenspan in front of the Banking Committee in 2003. New York Times, 20.10.2008.

National regulators, in the case of those in the US were divided and under-manned. At the federal level in the USA there were four uncoordinated regulating authorities and at the state level additional independent authorities. The most powerful authority, the SEC was considerably weakened and unable to deal with the problem due to massive reductions in personnel in their department for risk control and regulation.[11] These cuts in personnel occurred during a time in which a former head of Goldman Sachs acted as the head of the Office for Management and Budget, and while Henry Paulson, the future head of the Treasury department was CEO at Goldman Sachs. Later, the head of the German banking regulatory authority admitted that his office was unable to come to terms with and regulate the rapid developments of these new financial products. Although they were aware of the problems posed by these unregulated financial products, they chose to not intervene. The banks had complete independence of action. Motivated by short-term profits and handsome bonuses, banking managers took on ever greater levels of risk using ever greater amounts of leverage. Many wanted to just get rich quick and gave little thought to the consequences of their actions. This actions lead as well to criminal activity. The most dangerous risk was kept off the balance sheets or allocated to unregulated, hidden off-shore accounts. Also, the level of risk to counter-parties through the use of these innovative financial products seemed to be unknown to the regulating authorities. Due to the excessive use of leverage, many of the hedge funds had also taken on considerable risk. Nonetheless, the hedge funds remained unsupervised.

Paulson seemed to be unaware that the collapse of Lehman Brothers would lead to an unstoppable chain reaction. With the bankruptcy of Lehman, US policy regarding the issue became unpredictable. For the financial markets, it seemed that the Fed was willing to allow for the collapse of some banks, and that an intervention to save those in crisis should not be expected. Market participants completely lost their trust and confidence. Permitting the collapse of Lehman was one of two major mistakes made by Paulson. The other was the failure to change financial accounting requirements for the balance sheet in a timely manner. The mark-to-market regulations concerning CDOs as securities was the main reason for the ongoing write-offs, along with continuous reductions in the value of CDOs due to an almost non-existent market for them. On-going earnings warnings and loss reports strained not only the existing capital of the bank, but also awakened in the mind of the public the perception that a huge, uncontrollable and uncontainable financial catastrophe was occurring. Unfortunately, we will never know how many mortgage loans could have been saved from default by quick government intervention, as the opportunity was missed to act quickly to prevent the financial crisis from spreading to the real economy. At least it's certain that if the banks had been permitted to balance the value of their CDO portfolios, taking into account the portion of the securities not affected

---

[11]The chief controller of the SEC later spoke at a conference when questioned about "the systematic elimination of personnel from the regulatory office, so that became impossible for the office to perform any regulation whatsoever." Der Spiegel, No. 47 (2008), p. 78.

by bad mortgage loans, the write offs could have been greatly reduced. In consideration of this remaining base value, the banks could apply to the Fed as a "lender of last resort" for refinancing with the CDOs acting as collateral. This funding conversion and extension of debt servicing could have been implemented at the beginning of the crisis, already in the middle of 2007 and not at the end of 2008. The banks and the US administration must have had great interest in keeping mortgage borrowers facing foreclosure in their homes. This could have kept the pressure off of the housing market and home prices. As this did not happen, many borrowers lost their homes and some even ended up living on the streets as the homeless, which raises the question of moral and economic responsibility. Many vacant houses were neglected and others were vandalized.

The banks' trading departments responsible for internal and external credit supervision withdrew their risky long-term loans and refinanced them as short-term securities. Any bank would realize that this was a violation of the golden rule of lending and would have significant consequences. This lack of control, the failure to implement responsible business practices and immoral behaviour deserves critical review. It is beyond comprehension how bankers could be so misled by their statistical and mathematical models, as well as how many could have such unlimited trust in the rating agencies and their recommendations. Despite the ratings assigned by the rating agencies, we can expect senior management planning an investment of billions of dollars to perform at least some degree of due diligence to gain an understanding of the rating agency's procedures. To rely so completely on the judgement of what may be a biased third party is completely irresponsible. In the USA, the dramatic increase in home prices had become impossible to ignore and the easy access to subprime loans was often criticized. Warnings were sounded as to the impending bursting of the real estate and derivatives bubble.

The central problem of derivatives is that the leverage of the invested capital distorts the risk distribution between the speculator and the financial system. If the speculator is wrong he will lose only a portion of what is at stake for the system. The loan derivatives CDS did not have to be funded with equity, so banks earned much more than was appropriate on a risk adjusted basis in the good years. When the bad years came there was no capital to cover the losses so society had to bail out the speculators because they were too big to fail. Bonus payments had been made in the good years and there were no repayments in the bad years, when the bill was presented.

Speculators normally do not speculate against each other, but with each other. A slogan says "the trend is your friend". Only a stable trend facilitates speculation with nearly no risk. The biggest danger of derivatives is the leverage. If futures are used for speculative purposes for instance, the leverage multiplies artificially the effects of the derivatives on prices (via arbitrage and expectations)[12] and does not reflect an underlying real demand or supply. Therefore derivatives can distort the fundamental market functions. As a

---

[12]Empirical studies show that the spot prices follow the future prices. See Deutsche Bundesbank (2006), pp. 59.

consequence, the price develops differently as it would normally to cover the needs of demand and supply. The price signals become distorted, which leads to wrong resource allocation. For instance, if prices of commodities like oil become too high because from derivative speculation, it increases the costs for the producing economy and for the consumers. Because of the high commodity prices the commodity sector invests to increase its capacities. The missing demand causes the speculation bubble to burst sooner or later. The new capacities are overcapacities and the commodity sector is in trouble.[13]

The economy worked well without derivatives. Either the risks of derivatives can be controlled or the use of derivatives should be restricted to a mere hedge against risks, their original purpose. An underlying transaction should be compulsory. At least the leverage of the derivatives should be reduced significantly and credit derivatives should be treated like credits so they have to be funded with equity. Otherwise the next financial crisis might be too big for the governments to bail out. The argument that regulations on financial markets cannot be implemented because the world is too divided might be true. Also, the incentive not to regulate is strong, since the free rider position is the most profitable.[14] But also the losses of a possible crisis are too big for each single state. An unregulated financial market is a risk for all other countries. This loss risk has to be paid for to avoid distortion. A tax on financial deals of individual states with unregulated institutions would be the right solution to avoid a free-rider behaviour and it could be implemented by each state individually.

At least the current reforms on banking regulation go in the wrong direction as they increase the equity requirements to cover the systemic risk instead of decreasing the risks of derivatives. We will discuss that below.[15]

13.1.2.2 Exaggerated Belief in Figures

During her visit of the London School of Economics in November 2008 the British Queen asked: "Why did no one see it coming?"[16]

---

[13]For the discussion of the effects of food and commodity speculation see *Conrad, Christian A.* (2014).

[14]Governments find themselves internationally in a dilemma, since the best outcome for a single state is if all other sates regulate their financial market and it is therefore with its unregulated market the most attractive location for financial institutions (Free-rider position). The worst result for the individual state is if it regulates its financial market while the others do not. Since everyone is subject to this situation of insecurity, everyone decides to behave uncooperatively, which provides the worst results for everyone, national and international not regulated financial markets. Such a dilemma is called in the Public Choice Theory "prisoner's dilemma". For the expression "prisoner's dilemma" see *Brennan, G./Buchanan, James* (1985), p. 3.

[15]See *Conrad, Christian A.* (2014).

[16]See The Financial Times, November 25th 2008. https://www.ft.com/content/50007754-ca35-11dd-93e5-000077b07658

Krugman responded: "As I see it, the economics profession went astray because economists, as a group, mistook beauty, clad in impressive-looking mathematics, for truth."[17]

As the Classic-Neoclassic theory after the Great Depression of 1929, today's economic theory has explanation and justification problems. Neither of the statistical models foresaw the crisis nor are they now able to explain it. Moreover, the econometric models based on historical figures pretended there was a safety where there wasn't one, which was itself one reason for the crisis. Nassim Nicholas Taleb wrote about the delusions of control and reliability held by Wall Street and many other businesses. He pointed at the dangers of trusting the "bell-curve" models used by many financial institutions to mitigate risks. He questions the reliance on past historical information and brings the example of the black swan, that nobody expected until its discovery in Australia, or the example of the turkey who spends a thousand days being well-fed before being killed on the thousand-and-first day.[18] Justin Fox also criticises the belief in models and especially the belief in efficient markets—a belief that was qualified by Robert Shiller as the "most remarkable error in the history of economic theory."[19]

Derivative products such as Collateralized Debt Obligations (CDOs) can be directly traced as being one of the major factors leading to today's subprime crisis and the greatest financial crisis since the Wall Street crash of 1929. The calculation of risk and value or price for derivatives on the basis of historical time periods was celebrated as a major breakthrough. This advance in financial mathematics was only made possible through the use of the ever more powerful calculating capacity of computers. This made it possible to create many new financial products. It later became apparent that these calculations were in error, and that it was only due to the confidence people had in the ability to calculate them that made these products possible. For example, it was determined that the risk and therefore the price for credit derivatives (Credit Default Swaps) as calculated by Yale Professor Gary Gorton was inaccurate. The confidence and faith in his calculations almost cost AIG its existence and the US government several billion dollars, as it was bailed out to save the financial system in October 2008 and in-part nationalized. Gordon blamed the problem on the use of non-conforming data from the current marketplace and unprecedented developments which deviated from his forecasts based on historical data. But the future is never like the past.

It is difficult to understand why such an over-confidence in these calculations endured for so long, finally resulting in the subprime crisis, although the LTCM crisis had already illustrated the dangers and weaknesses of these financial calculations. In 2005 there were

---

[17]Krugman, Paul (2009).

[18]See Taleb, Nassim Nicholas (2007) and Taleb, Nassim Nicholas (2001).

[19]See Fox, Justin (2009) und Conrad, Christian A. (2010), p. 56.

already warnings against using models for financial calculations based on historical figures.[20] The best example for the incalculability of the economy are the formulas for option prices (Black & Schools-Formel) which were responsible for the LTCM-crisis. Robert Merton, Myron Scholes and Fischer Black received the Nobel Prize in 1997 for groundbreaking work in Option Pricing Theory. Based on the volatilities of the past, the formulas were developed to calculate prices for rights to sell or buy assets in the future (options). This is apparently an instrument to calculate the future. A hedge fund named Long Term Capital Management (LTCM) wanted to use for speculation, and he hired Robert Merton as a consultant. In 1998 LTCM then lost the investors around 90% of the $4 billion invested, which threatened to trigger a chain reaction on the international finance markets. The issue here is not just the credit taken by LTCM, but also the derivative positions of LTCM as contracting party, with which other finance market actors had protected themselves. Only when the then US central bank president Alan Greenspan intervened personally and pulled together an emergency package of billions from several large banks could the capital market crisis be averted. The second of the hedge funds Merton consulted, named IFC Continuum, closed in 2006. The future was in fact not predictable.[21]

The flaw in the option price theory or risk values such as "value of risk" which were determined on the basis of historical volatility was that future relationships between demand and supply could not fundamentally be accurately depicted. This is how in 2008 Porsche could raise its stake in VW to 74% through the purchase of VW call options, at a much reduced price than if it had bought the shares on the open market. The option price for VW shares did not reflect the actual shortage of shares, which had been calculated on the basis of past price volatility. This miscalculation lead to the share prices being set much too low. The excessive demand for VW shares eventually lead to a short squeeze.

The use of the same seemingly correct risk models led also to a similar investing behavior of the market participants. If the models were wrong all investors came to the same wrong risk assessment, what worsened the subprime crisis. Also the rating agencies used the wrong models to calculate their CDO-ratings. Based on these wrong ratings the investors underestimated the risks substantially and decided all to invest. Therefore the risk models increased the systemic risk and did not decrease it.

Abstract and isolated models of thought are fine in principle. They make it possible to take the complex economy apart into separate connections and thus to allow discoveries about economic processes. Econometrics is thus a valuable ancillary science for economics. There is also nothing to be said against using mathematics, as long as the effort remains proportional to the usefulness of knowledge gained. The models have unfortunately become so complex however, that they are no longer useful for teaching purposes. The

---

[20]"The method of calculation is based upon historic volatility and does not take into account irrational human behaviour, such as panic,. . . ." Conrad, Christian A. (2005), p. 398.

[21]See Conrad, Christian (2005) and Welt-Kompakt dated 08/22/06, p. 15.

effort required to learn them is greater than the knowledge gained. It is problematic when econometrics, thus the statistics applied to the economy with economic mathematics, are taught as exclusive representation of the only true economics. Without order theory and order politics of order there can be no understanding of the state and economics.

Derivatives as the so called Collateral Dept Obligations were the trigger and the main reason for the subprime crisis. They are based on complex economic modelling and statistics. Basically we can say that the image of the economy is distorted when only determinist models are applied. More thinking and less calculating would have been much more appropriate. So can the subprime crisis can also be traced back to developments in the economic sciences.

Be that as it may, econometrics, statistics and mathematics have contributed significantly to the continued development of economic science. They deserve recognition, no doubt, but this is no reason for economic science to consist solely of these subjects. At the end of the scientific chain there must be somebody to explain the science of practice and weigh the various theories and approaches against one another on the basis of practical considerations in order to make statements relevant to practices in a comprehensive economic overview. To make statements relevant for practical application the theories and models must be related to the respective practical situation. Only then is it possible to decide what parts of the respective models of thought can be applied. In this highest of disciplines, the relation exists both in theory and in practice, at least within economic science. This requires an analytic, combining intelligence. The considerations must be logically deductive and verbal, since there is no calculability of the economy as a whole. In economic science as a social science mathematic abilities are less important, and the creative approaches to explanation gain importance.

13.1.2.3 Missing Moral Values

The enrichment of managers at the expense of their company and the society was criticized long before the subprime crisis. A scandal is really nothing more than immoral conduct in the eyes of society. Whether we look at top managers just trying to get the most out of the company they have been entrusted with, or manipulating the balance sheets to get rich with stock options or bonus payments at the expense of clueless stockholders, or employees lower down in the hierarchy who try to cheat their colleagues or the market, we are looking at proof that across the globe the economy has to wrest with massive ethical problems. It is worth noting that even model companies, such as Enron, are affected by moral lapses. There are many US companies, as well as internationally known investment banks such as Merrill Lynch, Morgan Stanley and Credit Swiss First Boston in the USA and Goldman Sachs, Morgan Stanley and Deutsche Bank in Germany, who have all been accused of stock analyses advocating sales.[22]

---

[22]See Chediak, Felipe/Escudero, Silvio (2004), p. 79 and Ogger, Günther (2001), pp. 103.

The largest bank in the world and the American branch leader Citigroup seems to have had ethical problems as well. The Citygroup head Charles Price addressed his employees with these words: "No one may damage our long-term interests for short-term advantages." He said he would check into "unnecessary risks and unethical behavior" personally if necessary.[23] He prescribed ethics seminars for his employees and had a behavioral code drawn up, and established a department where the employees could anonymously inform the company of unethical behavior. What happened? His predecessor Sandy Weill had set the employees a growth rate target of 15% and seems to have implemented it absolutely. The pressure was apparently so great that the employees, voluntarily or involuntarily, turned to illegal methods to reach the targets. The bank was then only able to avoid lawsuits and the subsequent damage to its image by agreeing to pay out settlements, connected with damage compensation. In.2002 it paid $400 million because Citi analysts portrayed stocks too positively, which Citi investment banking wanted to sell. In 2004 the Citigroup paid $2.65 billion for Worldcom and $70 million to the US Federal Reserve after being accused of lending usury credit and giving credit only in connection with the sale of superfluous insurance. Another accusation was that the bank did not pass on rebates to the customers of their investment funds. In 2004 Citygroup lost their license for private banking in Japan because of abuses of the law against money laundering and market manipulation. In 2005 the US bank supervision forbid Citigroup from any new takeovers until internal rules of ethics had been implemented. In 2005 there were also settlements paid for involvement in the bankruptcies of Global Crossing ($75 million) and Enron ($2 billion). There was also a 4 million British Pound settlement and returned profits of 9.96 million British Pounds for manipulated prices on the London bond market. These are of course just the ethical missteps that were brought to light.[24]

It seems conspicuous that those firms which for years seemed to be among the most financially stable would wind up in a state of collapse. This is valid for Enron and other firms as well as for Citigroup and the investment banks involved in the subprime crisis. But with an unethical business policy they were only successful in the short term. Long term these firms had financial problems.

The subprime crisis can be considered the epitome of the ethical failure of our modern economy. Everything came together, and many saw in the crisis the final act of our "turbo capitalism", the limitless enrichment of the few at the expense of society, which almost lead to a total collapse of the financial system.[25] The lack of regulation and belief in the self-correcting power of the market was used by a few to take advantage of the situation. The victims were, above all, the socially and economically disadvantaged who were convinced by predatory lenders to buy homes that they could ill-afford and which would lead them to personal bankruptcy, or at worst, homelessness and a life on the streets. This was truly the

---

[23] Quoted from Capital, 18/2005, p. 54.

[24] See Wirtschaftswoche dated September, 01, 2005, p. 52–58 and Capital, No. 18, 2005, p. 54–56.

[25] See Dahrendorf, Ralf, (2009).

creation of social misery. Mortgage lenders had to be aware of this, as they were directly involved in working with the subprime borrowers most at risk of default, which should be considered the height of moral irresponsibility. These lenders only gave thought to their personal profit without any consideration for the fate of borrowers. In the end, they were rewarded on the basis of their success in issuing loans. The difficulties that these borrowers would have in repaying these loans were of no consequence to them. For the most part, these borrowers did not have the education or the capacity to understand the nuances of how their mortgages were structured, and lacked the protection of appropriate consumer agencies or law enforcement. All those who knowingly took part in this deception and intentionally inflicted this suffering on unsuspecting borrowers are morally culpable. The Clinton and Bush administrations who encouraged lending to subprime borrowers through Fannie Mae and Freddie Mac as part of an ill-conceived social program are also in-part responsible. Also culpable are those who knowingly encouraged this process and profited from the housing and mortgage bubble while helping to finance the ensuing social misery. Noteworthy here are also those bank managers who knowingly gambled with the long-term viability of their banks and the financial system so that they could maximize their profits and bonuses over the short-term. The moral responsibility lies with the financial regulating authorities who tolerated the creation and growth of the real estate bubble and the spread of subprime mortgage products that made it possible. They permitted the creation of a new, unregulated credit market without intervening. In the USA, there were wide-spread and timely warnings concerning the dangers of a bubble in the real estate, the subprime mortgages and financial innovations that made it all possible.

It is no wonder that societal recognition for managers has dropped to the current low, which the manager's guild should be taking to heart. In a Wall Street Journal survey in 2003, 64% of those questioned said that they do not trust managers. This result was only trumped by one other profession. Only 16% of those questioned trusted politicians, and 84% expressed distrust.[26] Other studies determined that managers in the USA and Germany to have a very utilitarian attitude on ethical and moral questions, in particularly among young managers and American economic students. Typical statements included "One has to look after one's own interests," "Morality is just a matter of feelings," or "Sometimes small injustices are necessary in order to reach greater goals."[27] According to a survey among Swiss managers, 75% assume that the market forces automatically provide for an ethically and morally justifiable behavior.[28] It is interesting to note that many managers do not seem to feel comfortable with immoral, unethical conditions. Studies have shown that meanwhile the majority of managers go to work with more or less consciously felt fear.[29]

---

[26] See Ergenzinger, Rudolf/Krulis-Randa, Jan S. (2004), p. 4.

[27] See Noll, Bernd (2002), p. 168.

[28] See Ulrich, Peter (1993), pp. 1173.

[29] See Noll, Bernd (2002), p. 168.

It is interesting that many managers in immoral unethical conditions do not seem to be able to lie. Studies show that the majority of executives now have more or less consciously felt anxiety at work. The fear of job loss, the fear of making mistakes and the fear of misinformation are dominant here.[30] Fear at the workplace, exaggerated performance pressure and interpersonal competition pressure play an important role in mental illness.[31]

The behavior of bankers did not change significantly after the financial crisis. In 2013, only 36% of Wall Street employees surveyed believed their industry had changed for the better. On the other hand, 52% were convinced that the competition was involved in "illegal or unethical" actions. This information was answered by nearly a quarter of respondents in the "own house experienced" or "first hand" experienced. However, 29% considered unethical or illegal tricks "to be successful," an increase of 17% over 2012 when the study was first conducted. Particularly in the case of younger employees, an ethical attitude seems to be lacking. 36% of young bankers with less than ten years of experience advocated windy tricks, versus 18% of Wall Street veterans with more than 20 professional years. A quarter would be ready for insider trading "if they could earn at least ten million dollars." In the case of the younger colleague, this share even rises to 38%. 17% are convinced "that their bosses look away if they suspect a top performer of insider trading." This is justified by the fact that the income is too low: 26% think that the remuneration plans or bonus structures of their companies are an incentive to betray ethical norms or break the law. This is the case for the younger 31% and the older 21%.[32]

The managers are thus not fulfilling their role model function. The internal company contract for the distribution of work, stress and income is turned upside down, which is rightly felt to be unfair, thus has negative effects on the other employees.

13.1.2.4 The Importance of Risk Adequate Compensation

Since the Enron, Worldcom and the financial crisis, compensation for bank managers and managers in other public companies have come under intense scrutiny. Compensation has been held responsible for encouraging excess risk-taking, particularly within the financial system. It has been asserted that bonus compensation schemes have caused asymmetries in the treatment of gains and losses, which can lead to excessively risky behavior. The purpose of this chapter is to test this hypothesis.[33] Do unilaterally constructed incentive schemes encourage undue risk-taking? This question is examined with a behavioral experiment using the game roulette. It is used to analyze how unilateral compensation affects risk behavior.

---

[30]See Volk, Hartmut (2000), p. 57.

[31]See Volk, Hartmut (2006).

[32]See Sucharow, Labaton (2013).

[33]See Conrad, Christian A. (2015).

Related Literature

According to principal agent theory (Ross 1973; Jensen and Meckling 1976) correlating a manager's compensation with either their performance or that of the firm promotes better incentive alignment and leads to higher motivation and thus stronger company values. However, there is an asymmetric imbalance between the term, magnitude and probability of gains and losses in common compensation schemes. Short-term results are rewarded even when these results are later reversed. This encourages risk taking by the employees—agents—at the cost of the company—the principal. The agents undertake actions that generate a high probability of gains in the short-term, while the risk of a larger loss in the longer-term is not taken into consideration, causing the principle to bear all of the long-term risk. A substantial body of literature has emerged to test the relationship between manager compensation and manager behavior and performance.

Figures of the Office of the New York State Comptroller show that bonuses in Wall Street financial institutions continued to register large positive numbers in 2007 and 2008, even while the banks suffered large losses (Sharma 2012). Surveys by the Financial Stability Forum (2009) showed that over 80% of financial market participants and experts believe that compensation practices played a role in promoting the accumulation of risks that led to the financial crisis. Cuomo (2009) shows that bonuses and overall compensation did not vary significantly even though profits diminished during the financial crisis. Cai et al. (2010) studied the pay structures of banking executives before the financial crisis. They found some problematic practices (such as too much bonus and stock-related compensation). These practices might have encouraged "short-termism" and excessive risk-taking.

Agarwal and Ben-David (2011) results show that the explosion in mortgage volume during the crisis and the deterioration of underwriting standards can be partly attributed to the incentives of loan officers. They studied a controlled experiment conducted by a large bank. The compensation scheme of loan officers was changed from fixed salary to commission-based compensation. Loan officers were 19% more likely to accept loan applications, approved loan amounts larger by 23%, and the loans were 28% more likely to default. The increase in default occurred primarily within the population of loans that would not have been accepted in the absence of commission-based compensation.

However, Gregg et al. (2012) found that the cash-plus-bonus pay-performance sensitivity of financial firms is not significantly higher than in other sectors and concluded that it is unlikely that incentive structures could be held responsible for inducing bank executives to focus on short-term profits. This would mean that we are facing a general compensation problem.

Cooper et al. (2014) found evidence that industry and size-adjusted CEO pay is negatively related to future shareholder wealth changes for periods up to five years after payment. Sun reviewed the early executive compensation studies, bonus plan maximization hypotheses and equity-based compensation. Use of opportunistic management incentives encourage earnings management based on executive compensation for contracts is promoted when earnings management is driven by opportunistic management incentives.

He shows that firms pay a price and its negative impact on shareholders is economically significant (Sun 2012).

Schotter and Weigelt (1992) use four different compensation schemes to demonstrate that a compensation scheme that induces behavior consistent with lower discount rates is a necessary condition for reconciling divergent time preferences between principals and agents, and that subjects become more myopic in their investment decisions if compensation contracts are incorrectly structured.

Colesa et al. (2006) found that higher sensitivity of CEO wealth to stock volatility encourages riskier policy choices, including relatively more investment in R&D, less investment in PPE, more focus, and higher leverage. They also provide empirical evidence of a strong causal relation between managerial compensation and investment policy, debt policy, and firm risk. Cheating is also influenced by compensation schemes. Gilla et al. (2013) show that exposing workers to a compensation scheme based on random bonuses makes them cheat more but has no effect on their productivity.

Andersson et al. (2013) studied risk-taking on behalf of others in an experiment. The decision makers were facing high-powered incentives to increase the risk on behalf of others through hedged compensation contracts or with tournament incentives. The decision-makers responded strongly to incentives that result in an increased risk-exposure for others. There have also been experimental studies concerning the binary choice task and the study concerning the binary double gamble to explore the predictive validity of dispositional traits and affective states in decision making under risk and uncertainty (Papaeconomou 2012).

This chapter provides a simple incentive-based experiment regarding unilateral bonus compensation schemes based on the game roulette which can be easily repeated with the students. There have been several experiments with roulette but with the objective to scrutinize the gambling behavior (Rubio, Hernández and Santacreu) and guessing tendencies (Rubio et al. 2010). The following experiment simulates most common short-term bonus compensation schemes without accountability. They were also the dominating compensation schemes before and during the financial crisis.

Experimental Design Roulette
The purpose of this chapter is to test the hypothesis that unilaterally constructed incentive schemes encourage excess risk-taking. The methodology is to simulate decision- making under asymmetric incentive structures. Therefore an experimental environment similar to the compensation schemes had to be constructed. Roulette has the advantage of clearly demonstrating the probabilities for gains and losses. In the game Roulette the probability of losses is compensated with higher payouts (apart from zero). A higher risk has an equivalent higher payout. In order to simulate behavior with different incentive and risk structures, decision-makers have to be exposed to different remuneration schemes, which is why there were game rounds with different considerations of gains and losses.

Game 5: Roulette

The experiment is started with symmetrical incentive structures. Round A and B have identical incentive structures. Round A serves as a control round for B. Finally in round C a unilateral consideration of the profits takes place and the changes in the betting behavior are recorded. An indicator for higher risk-taking would be a higher capital set even though the winning probability stayed the same.

In round A, the students are able to play Roulette with an initial play capital of €1000. Losses and gains are credited with 100%. The students are asked to check each other's calculations after each game.

In the round B the gambling losses and gains are counted each with 50% and are added to the initial capital of €1000. Thus there were still no conflicting interests and no asymmetries in the treatment of gains and losses. Round B therefore has identical incentive structures as round A. So A is able to serve as a control group for B.

In round C a unilateral consideration of the profits takes place. The set capital is not deducted, if the roulette bet is wrong. Conversely, the payout is credited with 50%, and added to the €1000 of initial capital. The results of the rounds B and C are added, starting from an initial capital of €1000 each and the player with the highest result is rewarded with €10 real money. For this game we chose real money to have a stronger link to compensation in real life. The rules are explained to the students before starting the experiment.

Round C thus corresponds to the unilateral performance-based remuneration of the common bonus-based compensation schemes. Loss and profit incentives are not equally distributed. Losses are borne by the companies and profits are rewarded with bonuses. This simple experiment shows clear results.

Results

The experiment was conducted with 69 students from different Business Bachelor and Master courses at the University of Applied Science HTW at Saarbrücken.[34] The students played 3 rounds Roulette (A, B and C), each with three games. They could bet on red or black, on one of the three thirds of the 36 numbers or on one number. The winning number and color was determined by the roulette wheel. If it was zero, the game was repeated and not registered. The payouts were distributed according to the probability of winning ($\times 2$, $\times 3$, $\times 36$) and accumulated in each round.

In round C, the sum of the average capital set rose from €1361.88 in round B to € 3899.28, by 186%. The highest possible profit (calculated as the product of the set capital and the possible payout) in all three games rose to €30,000.72 (see Figs. 13.1 and 13.2).

---

[34]See Conrad, Christian A. (2015).

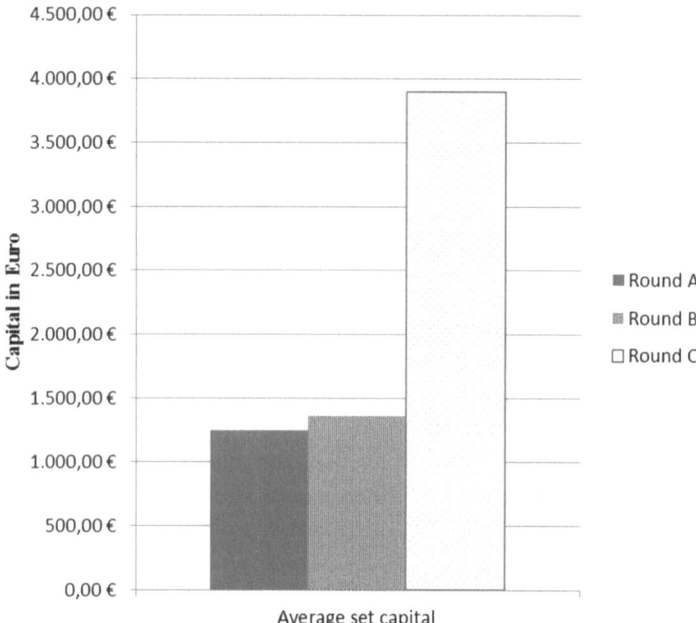

Fig. 13.1 Set capital

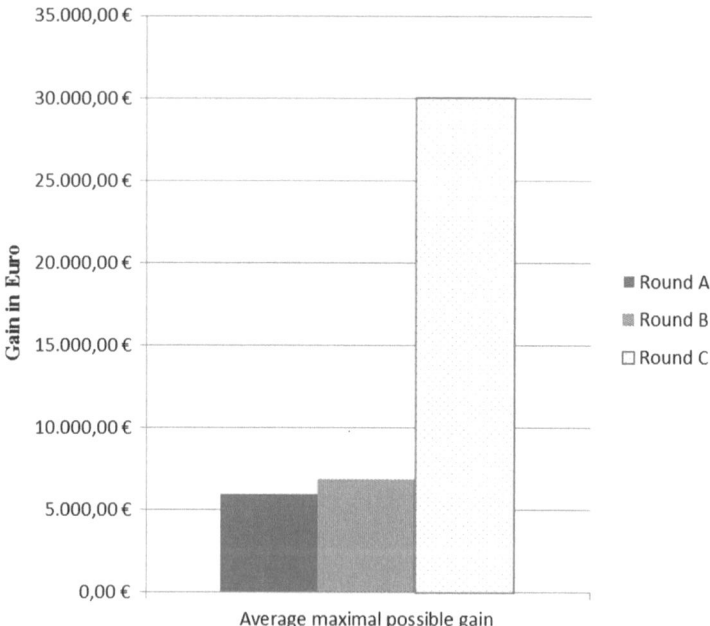

Fig. 13.2 Maximum possible gain

	Round A	Round B	Round C
Average set capital	€1,252.63	€1,361.88	€3,899.28
Average maximal possible gain	€5,946.83	€6,874.49	€30,000.72
Risk as max. possible gain/set capital	4.75	5.05	7.69
Standard deviation average set capital	€779.65	€650.32	€2,408.89
Standard deviation maximal possible gain	€634.21	€9,687.06	€31,585.46

Fig. 13.3 Statistical data

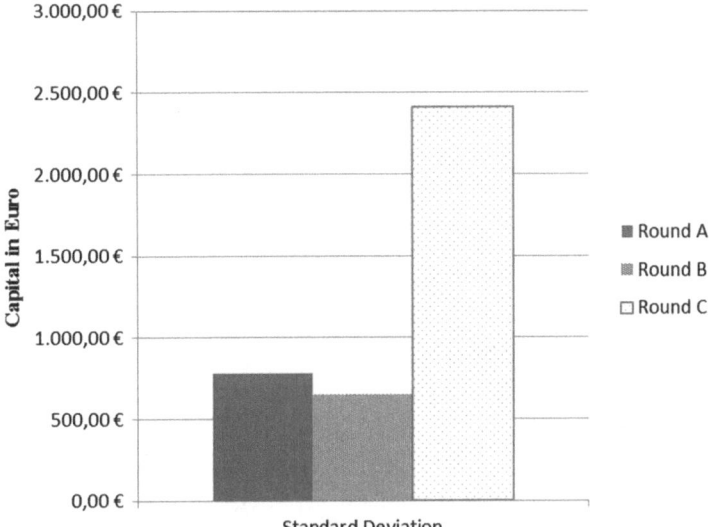

Fig. 13.4 Standard deviation set capital

If you set the maximal possible gain in relation to set capital as a risk measurement indicator, the willingness to take risks increased from 5.05 to 7.69 (see Fig. 13.3). The significantly higher standard deviation in round C shows that some players were more willing to take risks than the average (see Figs. 13.4 and 13.5).

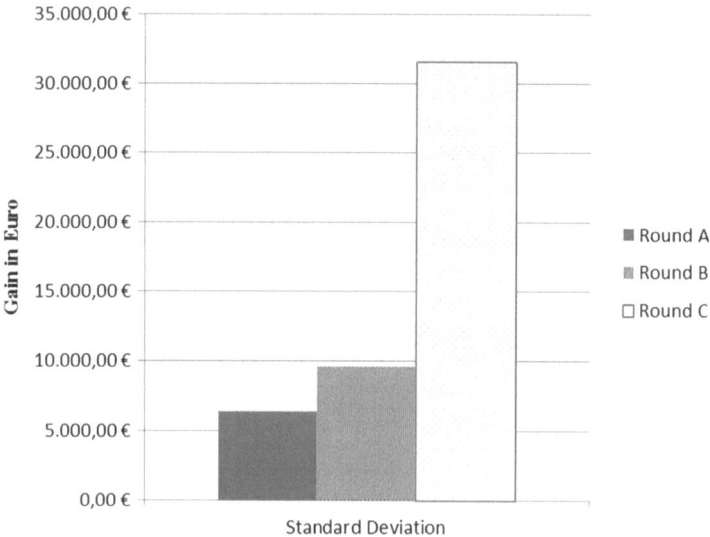

Fig. 13.5 Standard deviation maximum possible gain

Conclusion

The experiment showed that unilaterally constructed incentive schemes encourage excess risk-taking. This would indicate that common bonus-based compensation schemes are not a good idea and in face enhance risk because of the asymmetries in the treatment of gains and losses. In most cases compensation can only decrease down to the base salary while gains from bonuses can be limitless. Short-term results are rewarded even when these results are subsequently reversed. This encourages risk-taking by the employees (agents) at the cost of the company (the principal). They undertake actions that generate a high probability of gains in the short-term while the risk of a larger loss in the longer-term is not taken into consideration, thus becoming a liability to the principal. This does not align with the basic idea of principal-agent theory. Of course a connection between a manager's compensation and a firm or manager's performance will promote better incentive alignment and lead to higher motivation, which increases firm value, but only if losses and profits are remunerated symmetrically.

The existing asymmetries of bonus compensation schemes have led to a divergence of interests between employees on the one hand and the health of financial institutions and other companies at large on the other hand. Compensation packages for CEO's and other managers have gotten out of control. Remuneration and bonuses depend on short-term profitability, which increases share prices in the short-term, but

(continued)

not the long-term health of the company. In the financial system, investment managers increased the risks for their employer by buying highly profitable but risky assets and were rewarded with high bonuses which led to the financial crisis in the long term. In addition, the review of research literature showed that cheating is promoted by high and unilateral variable compensations. CEOs have incentives to manipulate earnings if executive compensation is strongly linked to performance. Opportunistic earnings management behavior has been detected.

Risk adequate compensation is therefore an important prerequisite for good performance in all risk-handling professions. Without accountability variable compensation schemes become unilateral bonus maximation schemes with negative effects for the company and the principal. It means risking other people's money which will generally be abused (moral hazards) (Andersson et al. 2013).

Summary

As we have seen unmoral aspiration for enrichment of managers was common in all crisis. People are influenced in their behavior by their view of the world. Ideas and attitudes, or moral values, must be shown by example and included in education.

Bad examples can ruin common decency as much as it can be dangerous to continually preach thinking in models and maximizing benefit as the only reasonable, rational behavior. The consequence will be that people orient themselves on these behavioral maxims and repress their positive human characteristics such as sympathy, helpfulness, general willingness to sacrifice and selflessness. Management education in particular must ask itself if it did not indirectly create monster managers; business ethics receives too little attention.

Comprehension Questions

1. Name some causes of the Enron crisis.
2. Name some causes of the financial crisis.
3. What are the common moral causes of economic crisis?
4. Can you imagine some reasons for the unethical attitude of the managers?

13.1.3 The Reforms of the International Financial Market Order

After the financial crisis several studies analyzed the risks management practices and came to the conclusion that the investors have underestimated the risks due to products complexity and over-reliance on quantitative analysis (studies by the Financial Stability Forum, the Working Group on Risk Assessment and Capital, the Senior Supervisors Group, the Basel Committee on Bank Supervisions, the International Institute of Finance and the International Monetary Financial Committee) (Voinea and Anton 2009).

New financial instruments such as derivatives showed their risk potential in the financial crisis. There were also new market participants, whose market influence has grown. By using a qualitative research approach we examine in this chapter the extent to which these two developments affect the economic processes of the market and put financial markets at risk. We also analyze the extent to which the new financial market regulations Basel III and the American Dodd Frank Act are sufficient to limit the systemic risk they cause.

13.1.3.1 Risk and Non-transparency in Derivatives

One central problem in the financial crisis were the bilateral over-the-counter derivatives (OTCs), which are not traded on the stock exchange and therefore not registered. The supervisory authorities still do not know the exact amount and distribution of the derivatives, which means they cannot know the systemic risk (e.g. the CDS to Greece in the European debt crisis) and cannot intervene. In the financial crisis, the counterparty risks were not properly priced, for example through a reasonable capital securitization. The default of a counterparty or credit could lead to a system risk as a result of contagion, as in the case of Lehman.

Basel III and the Dodd Frank Act provide a framework for trading via central clearing houses (stock exchanges) as well as standards for a collateral deposit of the CDS seller and a capital backing which the CDS buyer must take to hedge the counterparty risk. The equity requirements of derivatives is determined by comprehensive models; the rating-related bond equivalence approach and the internal Advanced CVA (Credit Value Adjustment) approach, which is based on market data, specifically spreads, have been developed for this purpose (Hofman 2011; Deutsche Bundesbank 2011; Peirce and Soliman 2016; Giancarlo 2016). For the remaining OTC derivatives, higher equity requirements apply to counterparty risk, which makes them unattractive to banks. The volume of OTC derivatives is already decreasing (Gaumert et al. 2011; Conrad 2013). However, the collateral provided and the equity capital for the counterparty risk are insufficient to cover the systemic risk of derivatives. The financial crisis has shown very clearly how fast market data can change. If the spreads of the CVA and ratings of the bond equivalence approach change, banks must collateralize the difference.[35]

13.1.3.2 Weaknesses of Risk Indicators and Pricing Methods
Ratings

Uniform ratings are dangerous because all market players are subject to this assessment. If securities such as AAA-rated CDOs prove to be worthless in the financial crisis, asset bubbles can occur, followed by asset crashes. The financial innovations created a false

---

[35] See Conrad, Christian A. (2018), pp. 32–40.

sense of security with their complex mathematical models and AAA ratings. One of the main causes of the subprime crisis was that investors relied on the credit judgements of the rating agencies. The ratings were too good, which meant that the credits were understated with insufficient capital and that during the crisis the valuation adjustments put the creditors at risk.

The Dodd Frank Act decouples the acceptable amount of capital securitization from external ratings. In general, the regulatory and supervisory authorities should remove all references to external ratings and rating agencies from the regulations (Dullien 2012). In addition, the Dodd Frank Act subordinates the rating agencies to the SEC. The SEC will regularly monitor the ratings and methods of the agencies and impose fines in the event of infringements, which may include the revocation of licenses. In the financial crisis, rating agencies were not responsible for their valuations. According to the Dodd Frank Act, the rating agencies can be sued for damages by the investors in case of grossly negligent rating errors (*US-Senate*).

The German Council of Experts still sees a risk in wrong or matching external ratings. In the Liquidity Coverage Ratio (LCR) of Basel III, government bonds are equated with cash and, in principle, the government bonds are weighted lower in the net-stable funding ratio (NSFR). All OECD government bonds and loans are weighted at zero capital, which is what the EU Commission has assumed for the EU Member States. As a result, government bonds are preferred by the supervisory regulations, which is why it is assumed that the banks will continue to invest disproportionately in government bonds.

While this preference is desirable for governments, it raises the systemic risk substantially, which does not make sense in view of the present state debt crisis. This preference for government bonds is currently being discussed and has also prompted the Advisory Council to point to the risk of lump risks associated with government bonds. He also proposed foregoing a risk weighting of the claims and advocated large credit limits on government bonds (especially those of one's own state) (Sachverständigenrat 2011). In the case of bonuses based on equity returns, the zero risk weighting causes moral hazards and discriminates against other loans, such as companies (Schäfer 2011). In general, risk weighting is an incentive to manipulate ratings.

Value at Risk and Option Pricing Models

The problem with a distorting basis of past values is that it results in other capital market approaches, such as the value at risk (VaR) (Taleb 2001, 2007), a risk indicator for securities, mainly derivatives, which is based on the historical value changes (volatilities) or assumed distributions of future influencing factors (Conrad 2005). VaR failed as risk indicator in the financial crisis (Stulz 2009). VaR models assume that prices correspond to a normal distribution. The occurrence of the financial crisis was incompatible with the assumption of a normal distribution. There are such "fat tail" phenomenon every 5–10 years (Crotty 2009). Actually, the term "value at risk" promises too much and encourages a false sense of security, because the risk is the maximum possible loss and this is usually the capital employed. In order to circumvent the historical limitations of environmental conditions, Basel III prescribes fictitious stress scenarios for the VAR models (Deutsche Bundesbank 2011). This is a significant improvement, but it should be a general understanding that the future remains unpredictable, and the rating is a very imprecise estimate (Stahl and Conrad 2000a, b).

The best example of the non-calculability of the economy is the option price formulas (Black & Schools formula). Robert Merton, Myron Scholes and Fischer Black received the Nobel Prize for Breaking Breakthroughs in War Warfare. Building on the volatilities of the past, they developed formulas for the price of buying or selling rights to values that can be exercised in the future (options). It is therefore apparently an instrument with which one can calculate the future, which is why they are also suitable for speculation. A hedge fund hired Robert Merton as a consultant. In 1998, this hedge fund, with the name Long Term Capital Management (LTCM), lost 90% of the $ 4 billion invested and threatened to trigger a chain reaction on the international financial markets.

This was not only about the loans taken by the LTCM, but also by the derivative positions drawn up by the LTCM as a counterparty, which had secured other financial market participants. It was not until the then Federal Reserve president Alan Greenspan personally intervened and created a several billion dollar rescue package that the capital market crisis could be averted (Single and Stahl 2000a, b). In 2006, the second Merton advisory hedge fund with the lofty name IFC Continuum closed. So the future could not be calculated.

The weakness of the option price theories or risk indices such as value at risk, which are based on historical volatilities, is that they do not represent the future supply and demand ratios. For example, Porsche was able to buy the majority of VW stock by buying call options more favorably than on the stock market and increased its VW share secretly to 74%. The option prices did not reflect the scarcity of VW shares, as they had been calculated on the basis of past price fluctuations. They were much too low. The demand overhang then led to a short squeeze.

Is Risk Calculable?

Just like the Classic-Neoclassic theory after the Great Depression in 1929, today's economic theory has explanation and justification problems. The statistical models neither foresaw the crisis nor are they now able to explain it. Moreover, the econometric models based on historical figures presumed a safety where there was none, which was in itself one reason for the crisis (Stulz 2009).

Ratings are estimates of future developments based on past figures. Strictly speaking, the risk of default cannot be calculated because the possible environmental conditions and the probability of their occurrence are not known. Unlike the static experiment of throwing a coin, the basic conditions of random events change constantly. The financial crisis has once again shown how quickly ratings can turn out to be wrong or fall behind events. The risk models thus led to an increase in the systemic risk rather than to a reduction. Nassim Nicholas Taleb wrote about the delusions of control and reliability under which much of Wall Street and many other businesses function. He pointed at the dangers of trusting the "bell-curve" models used by many financial institutions to mitigate risks. He questions the reliance on past historical information and uses the example of the black swan, which nobody expected until its discovery in Australia or the example of the turkey who spends a thousand days being well fed before being killed on the thousand-and-first day (Taleb 2001, 2007). Justin Fox also criticises the belief in models and especially the belief in efficient markets—a belief which was qualified by Robert Shiller as the "most remarkable error in the history of economic theory." (Fox 2009; Malkiel 2014).

We acknowledge that due to the countless and constantly changing environmental influences and the unpredictable factor of man, only trend forecasts for economic development can be made. This was already recognized by Hayek. There can be only so-called "pattern predictions" (Hayek 1974).

Even after the financial crisis, the principle still applies that the worse the rating the more equity capital needs to be put aside in order to cover the default risk. Oddly, Basel III and the Dodd Frank Act massively increased the capital requirements for banks (Kern 2010). The proposals of the Basel Committee on Banking Supervision (BCBS), as well as those of the Swiss and British expert groups, called for even higher capital requirements on investors (Sachverständigenrat 2011). On the other hand, no one can predict how the ratings will change in a crisis and thus also how high the capital requirements will be in order to prevent the insolvency of a system-relevant institution. For example, according to the Basel II criteria, the Swiss UBS had a constant risk-weighted equity ratio of 10%, while the unweighted equity ratio had already fallen to 2% (Sachverständigenrat 2011).

Basel III tries to solve this problem by a 2.5% additional anticyclical capital buffer (Gaumert et al. 2011). This is a good approach but arbitrary and inconsistent. No one can guarantee that this buffer is sufficient. If credit or default risks are still weighted with ratings, any accuracy that does not correspond to reality is just made up. The financial crisis has shown that ratings are too uncertain as a future prognosis in order to build up the stability of the financial system. The apparent predictability under Basel II led to a dangerous feeling of security. It would therefore be more consistent and risk-averse to forego a risk weighting (Miller 2016). As in Basel I, the rating should not be decisive for capital adequacy, but all loans should be subject to a flat rate of 8%. Different creditworthiness could then be reflected, as in the periods of Basel I, in the banks' internal risk assessments, and thus in the loan interest rates. A global deterioration of the creditworthiness or an increase in the risks would not, as in the financial crisis, force a higher capital requirement in the short term, which would intensify the crisis. Then, government bonds should also be subject to equity, which seems urgent in view of the current international debt crisis.

13.1.3.3 Introduction of a Separation System

Debt write-offs for banks came mainly from investment banking, both in the financial crises and in the latest state debt crisis. There were also huge bonuses, which were paid out after short-term targets were reached. There should not be long-term credit risks here, which is why this bank is not subject to the credit rules. Bank-internal risk control and monitoring is much lower than in the credit sector. If, therefore, business with credit derivatives and bonds is to be continued in proprietary trading, the credit and default risks from investment banking should be subject to the same internal and external supervision and control. In particular, the rules on equity capital and the treatment of cluster risks must also apply to trading positions. Basel III stipulates that, the banks carry out their own model-based internal risk assessment in the purchase of bonds (securitization positions) and base the price risk in the account books on the basis of the investment portfolio with more equity. However, equity underwriting in the account books is still lower than in the investment portfolios, despite the fact that in the classic corporate and real estate lending businesses there were relatively minor failures in the financial crisis. In addition, the short-term trading positions, unlike corporate loans, are not included in the liquidity indices, which means they do not have to be refinanced. This is difficult to understand in light of the experience gained during the financial crisis when the markets for many trading positions disappeared. After the bankruptcy of Lehman many derivatives could no longer be sold. The failure of Lehman as a major derivative counterparty triggered the system crash. Lehman was too big to fail (Deutsche Bundesbank 2011; Götzl 2012).

After the financial crisis fewer and bigger thus even more systemic relevant banks were left in de market (Miller 2016). The designation of "too big to fail" was introduced in 1998 with the rescue of LTCM by the US Federal Reserve president Greenspan and has been considered irrefutable since then. Here, too, there is a breach of the market-based principle of private liability. This led to negative incentives, so-called moral hazard problems (Conrad and Stahl 2002, 2003). The profits from high risk investments in the financial markets are only limited by a corresponding loss potential. For this, there is only one solution approach: system-relevant banks must be dismantled. Banks must also be able to go bankrupt in order for market incentives to work. Otherwise, a system change takes place moving toward a central administration economy, that is, to socialism. A break-up of the large corporations would also strengthen competition between the banks again.

An alternative approach would be the reintroduction of the separate banking system, i.e. the separation of investment and lending business. This would take account of the different business concepts of investment banking and commercial banking, and would give the financial institutions a non-contradictory objective function. An important argument for a separate bank system is greater risk transparency because processes and risks are handled through markets and are not visible only internally in a universal bank. The supporters of the universal system are opposed to the advantages of combining, scaling and information. However, the extremely high systemic costs of the financial crisis, which had to be borne mainly by taxpayers, are opposed to this (Blum 2012).

The Glass Steagall Act and thus the separation system was abolished in 1999 by US President Clinton and his Finance Minister Rubin. It was originally introduced as a result of the financial crisis in 1929, which was mainly caused by a credit-financed stock bubble. Against the background of the experience in the financial crisis, the reintroduction in the USA or the international introduction of the separation banking system would only be consistent to prevent the transfer of risks from investment banking to credit banks and thus a systemic domino effect of outstanding claims and the transfer to the real economy. Investment banks would no longer be too big to fail and would no longer have to be saved by the state. According to the English Vickers report, the risky investment businesses are no longer allowed for retail banks internally shielded and demarcated within the framework of a ring-fence approach. By 2019, Britain's banks must have ringfenced their retail banking operations from their parent companies (Sachverständigenrat 2011; Jenkins 2017). Like the corresponding American Volcker rule in the Dodd Frank Act, these approaches are not as broad as the Glass Steagall Act (Conrad 2013; Krahnen and Schüwer 2017).

The introduction of a separation system would only prevent the risks of investment banking from bleeding into to the retail area of banks, while the debtor and counterparty risk of the investment banking and the accompanying systemic risk would continue. A ban on retail banks financing hedge funds by offering credit—as the Vickers report demands—is a complementary conditio sine qua non. A possible total write-off must be considered when banks invest in investment houses, which is why we need a ban on the participation of retail banks in financial institutions with investment risks or at least giving up the value of these holdings. In the Dodd Frank Act the upper limit for investments in investment institutions was set at 3%. These American and English approaches are structurally complementary to Basel III and should therefore be adopted by European governments. The Volcker rule served as a model for the German Separation Act, which came into force on 14 January 2014 (Kern 2010; Sachverständigenrat 2011; Conrad 2013).

If the pure investment banks only had receivables and liabilities in a separate banking system, all the institutions could theoretically fail without the deposits and loans of the commercial bank system being affected. However, it is precisely the CDS that creates a risk division between all market players, which also entails a risk transfer from the investment banks to the commercial banks. In order to ensure the functioning of a separation system, it would therefore be important to exclude trade of CDSs between these two types of institutes.

13.1.3.4 The Trade-Off Between Yield and Risk and Unilaterally Constructed Incentive Schemes

The high credit risks associated with too little reserve equity also explain the relatively high returns in the financial sector. Between 2002 and 2003, the profits of the financial sector accounted for 40% of domestic corporate profits, and between 2009 and 2011 still 25% (Dullien 2012). The credit risk of the CDS was not covered by equity as it is with comparable loans, which is why the banks have shown much higher profits in recent years than would have been permissible. When then the bad years came in the form of the subprime crisis, no capital was available to bear the losses. Many speculators had to be bailed out because their failure threatened the financial system. On the other hand, the bonuses were paid in the good years and did not have to be repaid as it turned out that the reported earnings were not sustainable. The financial crisis thus also revealed weaknesses in corporate governance. The bonuses of the companies violated the principle of liability, because only the short-term goal was rewarded. Long-term negative developments were not considered.

An experiment showed that unilaterally constructed incentive schemes encourage excess risk-taking. This would indicate that common bonus-based compensation schemes are not a good idea and in fact enhance risk because of the asymmetries in the treatment of gains and losses (See Sect. 13.1.2.4 and Conrad 2015). In most cases compensation can only decrease down to the base salary while gains from bonuses can be limitless. Short-term results are rewarded even when these results are subsequently reversed. This encourages risk-taking by the employees (agents) at the cost of the company (the principal). They undertake actions that generate a high probability of gains in the short-term while the risk of a larger loss in the longer-term is not taken into consideration, thus becoming a liability to the principal. This does not align with the basic idea of principal-agent theory. Of course a connection between a manager's compensation and a firm or manager's performance will promote better incentive alignment and lead to higher motivation, which increases firm value, but only if losses and profits are remunerated symmetrically.

The existing asymmetries of bonus compensation schemes have led to a divergence of interests between employees on the one hand and the health of financial institutions and other companies at large on the other hand. Compensation packages for CEOs and other managers have gotten out of control. Remuneration and bonuses depend on short-term profitability, which increases share prices in the short-term, but not the long-term health of the company. In the financial system, investment managers increased the risks for their employer by buying highly profitable but risky assets and were rewarded with high bonuses, which led to the financial crisis in the long term. In addition, the review of research literature showed that cheating is promoted by high and unilateral variable compensations. CEOs have incentives to manipulate earnings if executive compensation is strongly linked to performance. Opportunistic earnings management behavior has been detected.

Risk adequate compensation is therefore an important prerequisite for good performance in all risk-handling professions. Without accountability, variable compensation schemes become unilateral bonus maximization schemes with negative effects for the company and the principal. It means risking other people's money which will generally be abused (moral hazards) (Andersson et al. 2013).

In view of the principal agent problem and the resulting lack of shareholder control, a state intervention seems unavoidable to prevent moral hazard. The Dodd Frank Act offers at least a legal basis to demand that overly generous bonuses be repaid, in the event of a balance sheet correction (Kern 2010). In addition, many bank managers seem to lack the professional qualification to correctly assess the risks from subprime loans. This also reveals weaknesses in corporate governance, particularly in the case of staff recruitments. Here, the national financial supervisory authorities are called upon to review in particular the experience of the board members in the lending business.

13.1.3.5 Fair Value Loan Valuation

Bank loans are not impaired until they are no longer serviced or permanent deteriorations in the creditworthiness of the borrower exist, which jeopardize the repayment of the loan. One problem, however, is the balance sheet valuation of tradable loans, so-called securitizations, at fair value, i.e. at market value. This was reflected in the financial crisis when the markets for the CDOs had fallen away and the values plummeted. In other words, the fair values were meaningless because of exaggerated values, and they devolved into understated values because of lack of demand and transparency.

The fair value problem reappeared again during the European debt crisis. As the prices of government bonds declined, many European banks needed fresh equity because the price losses resulted in write-offs. US-GAAP and IFRS are aligned to the shareholder's informational needs, which reflect the level of the fair value. A long-term evaluation based on creditor protection and caution would be more appropriate, as it avoids excessive volatility in both revaluations and devaluations (Ballwieser et al. 2009). Market values are determined by supply and demand. This can lead to imbalances that have nothing to do with creditworthiness, or to exaggeration and understatement through herding, that is, irrational human mass behavior (Conrad 2005). Here, there should be a balance sheet option to suspend the market value on the basis of current internal ratings that can be verified by the bank supervisor, for trading positions such as loans. The IFRSs are to be geared more strongly to long-term values (Ballwieser et al. 2009).

13.1.3.6 Conclusion

The biggest shortcoming of the recent reforms to the stabilization of the financial system, such as Basel III and the American Dodd Frank Act, is that they increase the capital requirements rather than the causes of the increased risk. They do this in order to absorb the increased risk of speculation following the financial market deregulation and the spreading of derivatives, yet this also greatly increases the costs of borrowed capital. This means that growth losses are accepted and the costs of the financial crisis are once again forced upon the general public.

An alternative option to limit systemic risk would be the internalization of systemic risk into market prices. High capital requirements could be renounced if the systemic risks arising from non-regulated financial contractors are correctly priced or reported. It would be feasible to levy a risk tax on transactions with offshore institutions and other counterparties from unregulated financial markets that create a systemic risk but are not subject to the new regulatory requirements. This could be in the form of a flat-rate penalty tax or on the basis of an analysis of the respective systemic risk. In addition, a valuation discount for the claims against these institutions would be required under accounting law.

This would also reduce the problem of the prisoner's dilemma. The cost of the risk posed by these institutions would be internalized and free-rider benefits reduced. This tax could be collected individually by each state, thus without international financial market regulation. This would be in line with the Basel III regulation described above, which provides additional capital requirements for the risk of default for derivatives that are not settled via central counterparties. However, the problem of market influence by speculation with derivatives remains.

It would generally be better to forbid risky and complex financial products than to further increase regulation complexity and the capital requirements as in Basel III and the American Dodd Frank Act. Real-world problems can arise from the investor behavior whenever there are raw materials that fulfill important economic functions, such as foodstuffs. In the case of commodity trading, the position limits should therefore be reintroduced and the leverage of the derivatives restricted. As with medicines, derivatives should be reviewed by their national regulatory authorities for their systemic risk and transparency before they enter the market. Consumer protection should also be considered. No non-transparent derivatives with unlimited risk such as credit-ladder swaps should be permitted.

Comprehension Questions

1. Name the reasons for the financial crisis.
2. What countermeasures have been implemented since then?
3. Do you think that the measures are sufficient to prevent a new financial crisis?

13.2   Speculation in the International Financial Markets

What Follows Why?
One reason for the financial crisis is called speculation with credit derivatives. To what extent is speculation a part of the financial markets? Is it a normal market economy and what are the economic effects? These questions will be answered below.

For some time now, there has been an intensive discussion about the effects of speculation especially with commodities and agricultural product. In the following we examine the effects of speculation based on the most recent research. The following questions will be addressed: Will futures prices and price volatility be influenced by speculation? Would that create false price signals, and if yes, what effects will that have? In specific will there be demand effects for the spot market prices, which would increase the living costs thus could be seen as unethical?

Learning Goals
You should be able to explain the economic effects of speculation.

13.2.1 What Empirical Evidence Do We Have About Speculation Influencing Markets?

Many empirical studies show a relationship between speculation on futures markets and the price development of goods affected on the cash markets, as well as the volatility of prices for goods. Christopher Gilbert shows, for example, the relationship between index-based investments and the prices for foods, and uses it to explain the exorbitant price increases from 2007 to 2008. This connection, and the peak in food prices from 2010 to 2011, was also shown by Mario Lagi in a comprehensive model that included surveys for merchants and producers. These papers show that in their respective time frames, speculation caused prices to be about 50% above the level that would have been appropriate for the physical demand and supply. Their results have been checked by other researchers from Harvard University and the Federal Reserve Bank of Boston. Many other studies arrive at the same conclusions (Deutsche Bundesbank 2006; Gilbert 2010; Singleton 2011; Lagi et al. 2011b; Chilto 2012). Mayer (2009) points out the influence from various types of speculation on commodity prices.

Pies offers a contradictory argument, namely that the prices for commodities also rose within the same time periods, yet they were not the object of index-fund speculation or even traded on futures markets.[36] It cannot be concluded from this however, that there was no effect from index speculation until long-term correlations between these commodities have been examined, eliminating phenomena such as a price transfer substituting non-indexed commodities for indexed commodities (cross-price elasticity). There are also investors who speculate on increasing commodity prices outside of index funds, thus buying non-indexed commodities forward or investing in long futures.

In a study from 2009 the United States Permanent Subcommittee on Investigations concluded that from 2006 to 2008 investments in index funds inflated grain futures prices in relation to the spot prices on the Chicago stock market.[37] This study was contested[38] by another research team (Stoll and Whaley), which was funded by Gresham Investment Management LLC[39]. Stoll and Whaley test index fund inflows for any influence on futures

---

[36]See Pies, Ingo (2012a), pp. 3.

[37]"This Report finds that there is significant and persuasive evidence to conclude that these commodity index traders, in the aggregate, were one of the major causes of "unwarranted changes"—here, increases—in the price of wheat futures contracts relative to the price of wheat in the cash market. The resulting unusual, persistent, and large disparities between wheat futures and cash prices impaired the ability of participants in the grain market to use the futures market to price their crops and hedge their price risks over time, and therefore constituted an undue burden on interstate commerce." Levin, Carl/Coburn, Tom et al. (2009), p 2.

[38]See Stoll, Hans R. /Whaley, Robert E. (2009), p 65.

[39]The objectivity of this study must be questioned, since financial positions in commodities are key business of Gresham: "Gresham offers several commodity investment programs. Our goal is to provide a responsible way to invest (as opposed to speculate) in the asset class, and to offer our clients the benefits of systematic exposure to a wide range of commodities and commodity groups

prices. In contrast to other studies, they do not find any significant connection between index fund investments and commodity price increases, however, they only take the large positions reported in the COT Report and only the positions of index funds into account.[40] Neither did Scott Irwin and Dwight Sanders determine increased prices or increased volatility on futures markets for commodities as a result of investments in indexed commodity funds. In fact, according to their empirical research, the index investments caused decreased price volatility.[41]

Stoll and Whaley also analyzed the development of commodity prices both in and out of the index, finding a weak correlation of between 0.13 and 0.20 in both cases. They found a similarly weak correlation to index commodities for commodity prices outside of the indexes. From these findings they conclude that the index investments had no effect on the prices.[42] Tang und Xiong calculated however, that there was no correlation (less than 0.1) between indexed commodities in the 1990s and early 2000s. The same was true among non-indexed commodities. In 2009 however, the correlation among indexed commodities increased to over 0.5, while the correlation for non-indexed commodities only increased to 0.2.[43] This result can be traced back to the influence of index investments. The prices for indexed and non-indexed commodities developed differently between 2004 and 2008. The indexed commodities increased evenly in that period then fell, which did not reflect fundamental changes in supply and demand, rather in the flows of investment capital. The other commodities developed very differently.[44] The same increase in demand for various products can have differing effects on prices if the supply elasticity differs. The market power on the supply side would also need to be considered, such as the OPEC cartel on the oil market.

Stoll and Whaley also offer the argument that the shifts in futures positions before the phase-out would have led to significant jumps in prices if the index investors had influence over pricing, which was not the case.[45] We can counter however, that the opposing positions must phase-out and be extended as long as we are not talking about a physical delivery that has been agreed upon. Bass points out that the investors keep their demand constant by rolling over their contracts.[46]

At bottom Stoll und Whaley contradict the Subcomittee and do not consider the functionality of futures markets to have been restricted by index investments because only 3% of the contracts from 2005 to 2009 were physically fulfilled, and thus could not

---

through the use of commodity futures in Diversified Commodity Portfolios (DCP)." http://greshamllc.com/en/pages.php?s=2 (02/10/2014).

[40] See Stoll, Hans R./Whaley, Robert E. (2009), p 66.

[41] See Irwin, Scott H./Sanders, Dwight R. (2010).

[42] See Stoll, Hans R. /Whaley, Robert E. (2009), p 29 and 65.

[43] See Tang, Ke/Xiong, Wei (2012), p 65.

[44] See Tang, Ke/Xiong, Wei (2012), pp 55+ and 64+.

[45] See Stoll, Hans R. /Whaley, Robert E. (2009), p 66.

[46] See Bass, Hans-Heinrich (2011), p 45+.

have influenced the spot market. This also means that the differences from spot prices are not due to index investments.[47] However this does not mean that the futures prices were not positively influenced, however. 97% non-physically fulfilled contracts indicate a large influence of non-commercial goods.

Supporters of speculation offer other causes for the increase in food prices from 2007 to 2008. Irwin and Sanders argue that the greatly increased demand for commodities from China, India and other emerging markets, interruptions in oil production, less demand elasticity in consumers and US monetary policy were all causes of the price increases. Given the negative correlation between the real interest rate and commodity prices, Inamura concludes that too light of a US monetary policy supported the boom in commodity prices.[48] The increased cost of biofuels and weather were given as causes for the increased grain prices.[49] Frenk counters that although the Chinese demand for oil rose by 12% in 2008, Europe and the US entered a recession that brought the international demand for oil down. In fact oil supply increased in the first 6 months of 2008, which makes an increase in oil prices of 50% within the same time period inexplicable.[50] Baffes and Haniotis, like Lagi et al, come to the conclusion from their study that neither the demand from emerging economies nor from biofuel production contributed significantly to the price boom in foods, rather that it was the demand from finance investors.[51] Inamura also considers weather, tensions in the Middle East, and in particular the economic boom in emerging economies (output gap) insufficient to explain the large increase.[52]

In the end the slump in commodity prices after 2008 can only be explained by the lapse in speculation demand resulting from the financial crisis, since all other factors remained constant. The hedge fund manager Masters points out that neither the absolute increases of 2007 and 2010, nor the slump that followed, had been seen before. Such volatility can only be explained by the parallel financial flows, since there were no substantial changes in commodity supply in these time periods.[53]

Inamura found an increasing correlation between commodities and other forms of investment since 2005, and considers it to be an expression of the increased financialization of commodity markets by finance investors. The commodity markets reflect the same liquidity flows in this period as the stock markets.[54] This is indeed an important

---

[47]See Stoll, Hans R. /Whaley, Robert E. (2009), p 67.

[48]See Inamura, Yasunari et al. (2011), p 5.

[49]See Irwin, Scott H./Sanders, Dwight R. (2010), p 4+.

[50]See Frenk, David et al. (2011). p 45.

[51]See Baffes, John/Haniotis, Tassos (2010). "The demand for grains and oilseeds as biofuel feedstocks has been cited as the main cause of the price rise, but there is little direct evidence for this contention. Instead, index-based investment in agricultural futures markets is seen as the major channel through which macroeconomic and monetary factors generated the 2007–2008 food price rises." Lagi, M./Bar-Yam, Yavni/Betrand, K. Z./ Bar-Yarn (2011a).

[52]See Inamura, Yasunari et al. (2011), p 3+.

[53]See Masters, Michael W. (2009), p 4.

[54]See Inamura, Yasunari et al. (2011), p 7.

observation, as the negative correlation is a main reason investors in commodities would diversify and thus reduce the risk of the portfolio as a whole.[55] High futures prices would indicate replenishing stocks and increasing storage capacity. Without high futures prices there would be no sure basis for the calculation of profit from commodity stocks, making it purely speculative.[56] The higher future prices are, the higher the assured profits will be. Krugman therefore sees an influence of futures prices on spot prices only via arbitrage, thus a scarcity in spot offers due to stock holding with a view to selling at higher future prices. He only sees this effect with copper and cotton however, not for agrarian products whose stock holding did not increase.[57] For agrarian markets Pies used wheat to determine a decline in stock keeping until 2008. He admits that the data are incomplete however, since private stocks were not registered. Nonetheless, if storage capacities did not increase there is not necessarily anything we can conclude. If the investment costs for new storage capacity are high, futures prices must exceed spot prices for a longer time in order to make the investment worthwhile.

13.2.2　Critique of Methodology

Within the discussion both sides criticize one another's methodological weaknesses in econometric studies based primarily on Granger. Irwin and Sanders' results are criticized based on the fact that the Granger test is not an appropriate method with highly volatile variables, thus distorting results.[58] The problem is of a more fundamental nature, however. If causal variables are not eliminated, false correlations can show up in Granger tests (spurious regression). The same is true for purely coincidental correlations, which can show up particularly in short time periods of observation.

As we have already shown, many speculation proponents argue that the greatly increased demand for commodities from China, India and other emerging economies, interruptions in oil production, less consumer demand elasticity and US monetary policy were all responsible for the price increases. Increased biofuel production and weather were considered to have caused the price increases.[59] If so many factors were truly affecting prices the Granger test would not have been applicable due to multi-causality. The same is true for the effects of weather, since the required stationarity of variables would not be given.[60] Highly volatile variables such as stock prices or commodities were also

---

[55]Portfolio theory from Markowitz. See Markowitz, Harry (1952).

[56]See Peck, Anne (1985), pp 44–45.

[57]"If high futures prices induce increased storage, this reduces the quantity available to consumers, and it can raise the price. And you can, in fact, argue that something like this has been happening for cotton and copper, where there are apparently large and growing inventories. But for food, it's just not happening: stocks are low and falling." Krugman, Paul (2011).

[58]For a critique of Irwin and Sanders see Frenk, David et al. (2011).

[59]See Irwin, Scott H./Sanders, Dwight R. (2010), p 4+.

[60]See Schulze, Peter M. (2004), p 17+ and Hassler, Uwe (2003), p 813.

determined to have insufficient covariant stationarity, thus the requirement for the regression of time series is not met.[61]

Irwin and Sander have been criticized for using lags of one week and not limiting price influences to one week,[62] as well as for using non-representational data. The same is true for the Stoll and Whaley study. The positions of the index funds are not transparent because the DCOT Swap Dealer Data also contains positions from other market participants. The Commodities Futures Trading Commission (CFTC) estimates in fact that only 41% of the positions for crude oil futures belong to the index funds.[63] This represents a general problem. The quality of the data is also questionable, since it is generally based on questionnaires or is incomplete.[64] OTC derivatives were not even required to be posted in the time periods examined. Only after the financial crisis was it decreed that derivatives had to be registered or dealt via clearing houses.[65]

According to the scientists of the Raiffeisen Association the majority of empirical studies show no verifiable connection between stock volumes and the price increase.[66] The NGO WEED disagrees and lists over 100 empirical studies that are critical of speculation.[67] The economic ethicist Pies examined 35 studies and concluded that no negative effect from commodity speculation could be proven.[68] WEED accuses Pies of

---

[61] See Pagan, A./Schwert, C. (1990); Phillips, P./Loretan, M. (1990); Frenk, David et al. (2011).

[62] See Frenk, David et al. (2011). p 47.

[63] See Frenk, David et al. (2011). p 47 and Masters, M.W./White, A.K. (2008), p 33.

[64] "There have been ongoing complaints that the legacy COT trader designations may be inaccurate ... As one example, speculators may have an incentive to self-classify their activity as commercial hedging to circumvent speculative position limits in some markets. But, the CFTC implements a fairly rigorous process—including statements of cash positions in the underlying commodity—to ensure that commercial traders have an underlying risk associated with futures positions. However, in recent years industry participants began to suspect that these data were contaminated because the underlying risk for many reporting commercials was not a position in the physical commodity... Rather, the reporting commercials were banks and other swap dealers hedging risk associated with over-the-counter (OTC) derivative positions." Irwin, Scott H./ Sanders, Dwight R. (2012), p 258. See also Frenk's critique of the Irwin and Sanders study from 2010. See Frenk, David et al. (2011). p 48.

[65] See Conrad, Christian A. (2013).

[66] "Ganz im Gegenteil kommt die weit überwiegende Mehrzahl der bis dato zu diesem Thema verfassten empirischen Arbeiten—allerdings ebenfalls auf dem Boden der suboptimalen Terminmarktdatensätze—zu dem Ergebnis, dass kein nachweisbare Kausalzusammenhang zwischen Anlagevolumina und Preisanstiegen besteht." Translation: "Quite the opposite, the large majority of papers written on this topic to date—though also based on suboptimal futures market data sets—come to the conclusion that there no causal connection exists between stock volumes and price increases." Petersen, Volker J./Herlinghaus, Axel/Menrad, Michael (2012), p 14.

[67] See http://www2.weed-online.org/uploads/evidence_on_impact_of_commodity_speculation.pdf (Stand 26. November 2013, 04/01/2014).

[68] See Will, Matthias Georg/Prehn, Sören/Pies, Ingo/Glauben, Thomas (2012).

not examining important studies critiquing speculation and having biased criticism against the methodology used in studies critical of speculation.[69] Irwin reviews the evidence from recent studies and argues that "the growing body of literature fails to find compelling evidence that buying pressure from commodity index investment in recent years caused a massive bubble in agricultural future prices."[70] Both positions are in fact supportable using the empirical studies that have been conducted. One part of the studies shows that speculation has influenced commodity prices and the other part proves the opposite. Again we see here the dilemma and weakness of econometric research. There is no proof of causality, as there can be many factors behind a correlation.

The scientific content of the predominantly Granger-based econometric studies must be questioned. There are fundamental method problems here. Because of the risk of false results, the Granger test is not recommended if the variables under study are extremely volatile, which is the case for commodity prices.[71] For highly volatile variables such as stock prices or commodities, a lack of covariance stationarity was found, which does not provide a condition for regressing time series.[72] Due to innumerable influencing factors on supply and demand, we have a strong multi-causality here in which the individual influencing factors cannot be filtered out precisely. If causal variables have not been extracted, Granger tests can show correlations that are not present (spurious regression). The same applies to purely random correlations, which may arise in particular in the case of short observation periods or incorrect time intervals.[73] Also, weather effects such as those that occur in agricultural products are problematic, because then the necessary stationarity of the variables is missing.[74]

Also, the positions of the index funds are not transparent because the DCOT swap dealer data also contains many positions from other market participants. The Commodities Futures Trading Commission (CFTC) estimates that, for example, crude oil futures accounted for only 41% of positions in index funds.[75] So we also have a general problem here. Likewise, the quality of the data is called into question because they are usually based on interviews or not complete.[76] OTC derivatives did not have to be reported during the

---

[69] See Henn, Markus (2013).

[70] See Irwin, Scott H., p. 1.

[71] See Irwin, Scott H./Sanders, Dwight R. (2012), p. 258.

[72] See Pagan, A./Schwert, C. (1990); Phillips, P./Loretan, M. (1990); Frenk, David u.a., (2011).

[73] See Frenk, David u.a. (2011), a.a.O. p. 47.

[74] See Schulze, Peter M. (2004) and Hassler, Uwe (2003), p. 813.

[75] See Frenk, David u.a. (2011), a.a.O., p. 47 and Masters, M.W./White, A.K. (2008), p. 33.

[76] "There have been ongoing complaints that the legacy COT trader designations may be inaccurate . . . . As one example, speculators may have an incentive to self-classify their activity as commercial hedging to circumvent speculative position limits in some markets. But, the CFTC implements a fairly rigorous process—including statements of cash positions in the underlying commodity—to ensure that commercial traders have an underlying risk associated with futures positions. However, in recent years industry participants began to suspect that these data were contaminated because the

investigated periods. Only after the financial crisis was it decreed that they be registered or traded through clearing houses.[77]

Precisely because of such a background, it does not seem to me scientifically founded to derive extreme positions from the existing econometric studies. But this happens again and again, and without logically questioning the results. The absence of a logic-based discussion is a major drawback to current econometric research.

After innumerable studies examining the same thing and coming to different conclusions, it is time to make a change. It is clear that using econometrics proves neither the influence of speculation nor its absence. Additional studies will not change that fact. The two camps of advocates and critics of speculation are still at a draw. Logic should therefore be used as an alternative economic method to analyze the effects of commodity speculation based on known and widely accepted facts.

13.2.3 The Logic of Speculation

Stoll and Whaley argue that investment in commodities is no different than invest in stocks, for example. They fail to note however, that the money flowing into commodities is not productive. No production sites are financed, as may be the case with stocks. Commodity investments do not increase the growth of a national economy. There is also no direct offset for scarcities, such as arbitrage and thus making the most of spatial price differences. An investment in commodities is always in the expectation of future price increases and is therefore speculation. Even if the motivation is to diversify a portfolio, the investor still expects increasing commodity prices. Prices may increase due to scarcity, but there are other causes such as cost increases and inflation. As the utilization of spatial price differences, speculation can balance out future imbalances between supply and demand if the speculation demand leads to a price increase that signals producers to increase their supply. Such a chain of events is not necessarily the case however, since the future scarcity of goods, thus prices different from current prices, is not assured. In order to divert production in the right direction, the speculators must be better informed than the market, which is not generally to be assumed. The opposite is also a possibility, namely that speculation creates a false signal for production.

Speculating at one's own risk is a fundamental part of a market-based system. New market participants entering both sides of the market through speculation by buying or selling has a stabilizing effect on prices because of the increased liquidity. Gary Cohn,

---

underlying risk for many reporting commercials was not a position in the physical commodity.... Rather, the reporting commercials were banks and other swap dealers hedging risk associated with over-the-counter (OTC) derivative positions." Irwin, Scott H./Sanders, Dwight R. (2012), a.a.O., p. 258. See also Frenk's criticism of Irwin and Sanders' 2010 study. See Frenk, David u.a. (2011), a.a.O. p. 48.

[77]See Conrad, Christian A. (2013).

Co-President, Managing Director and CEO of Goldman Sachs New York, argues in favor of allowing non-commercials because where once there were only producers that wanted to sell on futures markets to secure their interests against price fluctuations, now liquidity is available from the other side thanks to non-commercials.[78] With this argument Cohn is forgetting to mention the downstream users of commodities, who are the traditional buyers of commodities and agrarian products on the futures market. In addition, index investors sell differently than speculators because they buy to diversify their portfolios or they want to keep long positions in commodities and risk diversification at a certain proportion to their other stocks. Their profit orientation is also contrary to the downstream users, who want to buy at low prices. Increasing prices attract more investors.[79]

Cheng, Kirilenko and Xiong also show the flip side of liquidity flow. Liquidity flowing in from non-commercials makes the goods dealt on the market fungible, but the 2008 reduction in liquidity put the market under pressure. Emerging markets experienced a similar phenomenon during the Asian crisis of 1997.[80]

Krugman considers speculation to be a zero sum game. Every futures long contract is accompanied by a short contract, which is why he does not see any influence on prices. "Buying a futures contract for oil *does not* reduce the quantity of oil available for consumption; there's no such thing as "virtual hoarding".[81] One must point out however, that the supply and demand on the spot market may not be influenced, but they are on the futures market. Of course a futures contract can only be concluded on the futures market if there is a short position corresponding to the long position, but excess demand will only increase prices until a market participant considers the offset lucrative. In short, if everything else says the same, an additional demand for commodities increases prices on futures markets. Even if futures prices do not influence spot prices with a supply scarcity resulting from increased stock holding, it is still possible for expectations to have an influence. Lagi and others have shown this as ". . . we interviewed participants in the spot market who state unequivocally that they base current prices on the futures market. The use of futures prices as a reference enables speculative bubbles on the futures market to influence actual food prices."[82]

Krugman is correct in that speculation is in principle a zero sum game. What one actors wins, another must lose. In the case of commodity speculation, the speculators can fulfill an important function by buying forward the commodities from downstream users and thus reducing the risk of price changes. In such a case they fill the purpose of insurance, which

---

[78] See Cohn, Gary, Co-President, Managing Director and COO of Goldman Sachs, New York, NY, in: U.p. Government Printing Office (2008), Senate Hearing 110-654, SUMMIT ON ENERGY.

[79] "Traditional Speculators provide liquidity by both buying and selling futures. Index Speculators buy futures and then roll their positions by buying calendar spreads. They never sell. Therefore, they consume liquidity and provide zero benefit to the futures markets." Masters, Michael W. (2009), p. 4.

[80] See Cheng, Ing-Haw,/Kirilenko, Andrei/Xiong, Wie (2012).

[81] See Krugman, Paul (2008).

[82] Lagi, M./Bar-Yam, Yavni/Betrand, K. Z./ Bar-Yarn (2011a), p. 5.

also a central argument of those in favor of unimpeded speculation.[83] With such an argument however, we must remember that a producer can meanwhile be facing up to 4 speculators and thus speculation goes far beyond simple insurance. The speculators may buy and sell amongst one another,[84] which can lead to an increase of futures prices with excess demand. The index funds invested almost exclusively long until the peak of 2008, which created a great deal of excess demand.[85]

13.2.4 Price Distortions and Price Manipulation

Markets can be influenced in many ways by speculation.

An artificial price influence occurs, for example, through short selling on the supply side. When something is sold that either does not exist or is only lent or bought for which there is no real economic use, supply and demand are artificially altered. The price develops differently than it would to influence supply and demand to the desired extent.[86]

As early as 2010, the share of high-speed trading in US equities trading was approx. 60%. Errors in the computer-aided model algorithms can trigger crashes, such as in 2003 for the shares of the US company Corinthian Colleges. Highly fluctuating prices are an expression of a higher risk, which can deter security-oriented market participants. Fundamental long-term value strategies are superseded by short-term mathematical algorithms. Such a connection would be conceivable on the stock market. Apart from a higher market liquidity, no economic advantage is obvious. On the contrary, a ban on high-frequency trading would stabilize the markets.

The impacts of credit default swaps are still contentious. There are the so-called Naked CDS as derivative loan loss insurance without underlying loans. There are those who see a positive effect even in speculative credit default swaps because of the higher liquidity in the market. There are also market participants who believe that the interest rates of the Greek government bonds would be higher if the investors could not insure themselves against a CDS default. However, the Greek Government complained that the betting of hedge funds on Greek bankruptcy over the purchase of CDS would have led to higher margins in Greek government bonds in the European debt crisis. Who is right?

If many hedge funds are speculating against European government bonds, for example, they buy the corresponding CDS as a credit default insurance. This leads to an increase in the CDS spreads, which is not only seen as a reflection of the bond yields but is also seen as

---

[83]See Pies, Ingo/Will, Matthias Georg Will (2013), p. 5+.

[84]There are empirical studies for this as well, which prove a high degree of trade among finance investors. See Domanski, Dietrich/Heath, Alexandra (2007), p. 65. https://www.bis.org/publ/qtrpdf/r_qt0703g.pdf

[85]See Stoll, Hans R. /Whaley, Robert E. (2009), p. 21.

[86]See Masters, Michael W. (2009), p. 17.

a risk indicator by the market participants, thus directly and indirectly driving up the price of the bonds. George Soros also sees the CDS 'very critically'. In his opinion, there is the risk of a "bear raid", i.e. a profitable price influence, at CDS due to the asymmetric risk distribution between the buyer (limited risk of loss, value or premiums of the CDS) and the seller (high risk of loss in the event of bankruptcy). A purchase of CDS' increases the borrowing costs of the borrower and thereby improves its credit rating, which in turn increases the value of the CDS'. According to George Soros, this connection together with the shortselling of the shares caused the collapse of Lehman, AIG and Bear Stearns (Soros 2009).

The risk of a "bear raid" originates from derivatives because their value is determined by real prices. Due to the theoretically unlimited leverage of derivatives, in small-volume markets it may be worthwhile to influence or manipulate the real price on the market in order to be successful with the derivatives position. This was the basis for the arrangements for Libor and gold fixing between major international banks. Even a collectively coordinated behavior for the manipulation of the courses can not be ruled out in smaller markets.

Derivatives such as call options affect the cash price if the option holder can insist on physical delivery. Thus in 2008 Porsche was able to purchase VW with call options cheaper than on the stock market and then increase the VW share secretly to 74%. The option prices did not reflect the scarcity of the VW share, since they had been calculated on the basis of past price fluctuations. They were therefore much too low. The demand surplus then led to a short squeeze and a huge increase of the VW price. Option writers must therefore make sure they are at least partially physically secure and inquire about the commodity.

Short selling should generally be banned because someone is selling something they do not own. There is a lot of room for speculative influence. The damage is suffered by the owners who lent the shares.

In a market economy short selling undermines the system because the owners are liable and not the seller. Funds (including ETF funds) should therefore be banned from lending stocks.

13.2.5 Irrationality and Bubble Creation?

As already stated, according to Eugene Fama's fundamentalist efficiency market hypothesis, speculation-induced deviation of futures prices from fundamental data would not be possible because prices always reflect all information rationally. Rising futures prices would therefore only indicate scarcity in the future.[87] However, speculation would not be worthwhile, because the price difference would only reflect the cost of storage. It is often argued that when bubbles form, other than the fundamentals, other market participants

---

[87]See Gilbert, Christopher L. (2010), p. 10.

form counterparts.[88] This contradicts—as was shown in Sect. 12.2.8.4—the New Behavioral Finance. The empirical investigations of this behavior-oriented research direction confirm the psychologically oriented, non-deterministic explanatory approaches. It turned out that investors perceive and evaluate the information available to them in a very subjective way, and that they do not always maximize the expected benefits in their decisions—contrary to the neoclassical model world.[89] For example, so-called herding can occur, whereby the sociological group orientation of humans dominates. In an uncertain stock-market situation, the investor orients via the other market participants, which the stock market also—at least in the short term—rewarded with rising prices.

Speculation, while exploiting temporal price differentials, can offset future imbalances in supply and demand, for example, where speculative demand leads to a rise in prices that signals producers to increase supply, but this need not be the case as future shortages other than the current prices at arbitrage are uncertain. The speculators must be better informed than the market, but this cannot be assumed. Speculation can therefore also be a non-rational behavior that does not differ from betting and gambling. So the reverse is also conceivable that speculation for the production produces false signals and thus causes bubbles and crashes.

13.2.6 Conclusion

Does speculation has an effect on spot prices which would increase the living costs with unethical effects especially for poor countries? The fact is that financialization has caused new market participants to join commodities and agricultural markets with distinct economic motivations. Because the investors were interested in diversifying their portfolios, massive long positions were built up until the financial crisis. Many billions of dollars thus came into the markets as additional demand. Since the investors did not want the commodities delivered, the additional demand ad a direct influence only on futures markets, not on spot markets. This caused an increase in the secure stock profits that, as long as they were greater than the cost of storage, would lead sooner or later to a scarcity in supply and thus to increased spot market prices. We can therefore assume an influence of futures prices on spot prices if the excess demand on the futures market is high and stays high over a longer time period. If commodity and agriculture producers think futures prices are at a historic high they will sell their production forward, which removes the supply from the future spot market. Increasing prices for end and intermediate goods involving commodities and agriculture product are also possible if the downstream producers secure their positions on futures markets. So we come to the conclusion that speculation influence spot prices of commodities and food prices if it creates a significant excess demand over a

---

[88]See Pies, Ingo (2012b).
[89]See Conrad, Christian (2005).

significant time period. In this case speculation might be seen as unethical, why regulation is needed.

13.3   Summary and Reform Proposals

Many scientists see a distorting market interaction in the restriction of speculation. They see themselves as advocates of liberalized markets, or market-based basic functions. However, the so-called liberalization of the markets around the year 2000 allowed derivatives instruments, which were not market-compliant because they relate to goods or values but do not have to correspond to any real demand or supply. In addition, non-commercial actors were admitted to the market with non-economic but speculative objectives. This has dramatically increased systemic risk.

Only as insurance do derivatives have economic advantages. Derivatives should therefore be permitted only to hedge risks, just before deregulation as a financial instrument, i.e. only in connection with a basic transaction. A corresponding regulation would be an important contribution to the reduction of market influence and systemic risk caused by derivatives. For example, a physical settlement could be prescribed for all derivatives, such as the transfer of the reference security or the corresponding goods. This speculative instrument would be omitted for hedge funds. Speculation would then have to be carried out as before with equity or borrowed capital, thus without the derivatives leverage, which would significantly reduce systemic risk.

Comprehension Questions

1. Explain the economic effects of speculation.
2. Is it a normal market economy phenomenon?
3. In your opinion, should speculation with derivatives be limited? How could this be done and what would be the pros and cons?

References

Agarwal, S., & Ben-David, I. (2011). *The effects of loan officers' compensation on loan approval and performance: Direct evidence from a corporate experiment.* Retrieved from http://citeseerx.ist. psu.edu/viewdoc/summary?doi=10.1.1.365.7234

Andersson, O., Holm, H. J., Tyran, J.-R., & Wengström, E. (2013). *Risking other people's money: Experimental evidence on bonus schemes, competition, and altruism.* IFN Working Paper No. 989. Retrieved from www.ifn.se/wfiles/wp/wp989.pdf

Angner, E. (2006). Economists as experts: Overconfidence in theory and practice. *Journal of Economic Methodology, 13,* 1–24.

Baffes, J., & Haniotis, T. (2010, July). *Placing the 2006/08 commodity price boom into perspective.* Policy Research Working Paper No. 5371. The World Bank. Retrieved from http://www-wds. worldbank.org/external/default/WDSContentServer/IW3P/IB/2010/07/21/000158349_ 20100721110120/Rendered/PDF/WPS5371.pdf

Ballwieser, W., Küting, K., & Schildbach, T. (2009, December 14). Fair Value in der Krise. In *Der Betrieb, 49*, 1. Retrieved from http://www.der-betrieb.de/content/dft,0,341592

Bass, H.-H (2011). Finanzmärkte als Hungerverursacher? *Studie für die Deutsche Welthungerhilfe e. V.,* Bonn 2011. Retrieved from http://www.welthungerhilfe.de/fileadmin/user_upload/Mediathek/ Studie_Nahrungsmittelspekulation_Bass.pdf

Beck, H. (2014). *Behavioral economics: Eine Einführung. 1 Aufl.* Wiesbaden: Springer.

Bell, D. E. (1982). Regret in decision making under uncertainty. *Operations Research, 30*, 961–981.

Blum, U. (2012). Pro Trennbankensystem: Transparente Systematik. *Wirtschaftsdienst, 92*(1), 2.

Boxall, P., Adamowicz, W. L., & Moon, A. (2009). Complexity in choice experiments: Choice of the status quo alternative and implications for welfare measurement. *The Australian Journal of Agricultural and Resource Economics, 53*, 503–519.

Brennan, G., & Buchanan, J. (1985). *The reason of rules.* Cambridge: Cambridge University Press.

Brown, M. E., & Treviño, L. K. (2006). Ethical leadership: A review and future directions. *The Leadership Quarterly, 17*(6), 595–616.

Cai, J., Cherny, K., & Milbourn, T. (2010). *Compensation and risk incentives in banking. compensation and risk incentives in banking and finance* (Research of the Federal Reserve Bank of Cleveland, September 24, 2010). https://www.clevelandfed.org:443/Newsroom and Events/ Publications/Economic Commentary/2010/ec 201013 compensation and risk incentives in banking and finance

Chediak, Felipe/Escudero, Silvio (2004), Ethics ratings: The case of five leading U.S. Investment Banks, in: Berndt, Ralph u.a. (ed.), Competitiveness und Ethik, Herausforderungen an das Management, Schriftenreihe der Graduate School of Business Administration Bd. 11, Zurich, pp. 77–87.

Cheng, I.-H., Kirilenko, A., & Xiong, W. (2012). *Convective risk flows in commodity futures markets.* Working Paper. Princeton University. Retrieved from http://www.princeton.edu/~wxiong/papers/ RiskConvection.pdf

Chilto, B. (2012, February 24). *Speculators and commodity prices—redux.* Retrieved from http:// www.cftc.gov/PressRoom/SpeechesTestimony/chiltonstatement022412

Cohn, G. (2008). Co-President, Managing Director and COO of Goldman Sachs, New York, NY. In U.PP. Government Printing Office (2008), *Senate Hearing 110-654, SUMMIT ON ENERGY.* Retrieved from http://www.gpo.gov/fdsys/pkg/CHRG-110shrg45837/html/CHRG-110shrg45837.htm

Colesa, J. L., Danielb, N. D., & Naveenb, L. (2006). Managerial incentives and risk-taking. *Journal of Financial Economics, 79*(2), 431–468.

Conrad, C. A. (2005a). Kapitalallokation in der Irrational Exuberance – Erkenntnisse aus Theorie und Praxis. In R. Eller et al. (Eds.), *Handbuch asset management* (pp. S387–S406). Stuttgart: Schäffer-Poeschel.

Conrad, C. A. (2005b). *Die Notwendigkeit, die Möglichkeiten und die Grenzen einer internationalen Wettbewerbsordnung – Reformansätze vor dem Hintergrund derzeitiger außenwirtschaftlicher Problemfelder und der Doha-Welthandelsrunde.* Berlin: Duncker & Humblot.

Conrad, C. A. (2010). *Moral und Wirtschaftskrisen – Enron, Subprime & Co.* Hamburg: disserta Verlag.

Conrad, C. A. (2013). Auf dem Weg zu einer besseren Finanzmarktordnung. *Bankarchiv (Journal of Banking and Finance), 61*(April), 233–241.

Conrad, C. A. (2014). Commodity and food speculation, is there a need for regulation? A discussion of the international research. *Applied Economics and Finance, 1*(2), 58–64.

Conrad, C. A. (2015). Incentives, risk and compensation schemes: Experimental evidence on the importance of risk adequate compensation. *Applied Economics and Finance, 2*(2), 50–55.

Conrad, C. A., & Stahl, M. (Eds.). (2000). *Risikomanagement an den internationalen Finanzmärkten*. Stuttgart: Schäffer-Poeschel.

Conrad, C. A., & Stahl, M. (2002). Parallels with the 1920s stock market boom and the monetary policy. *Kredit und Kapital, 35*(4), 533–549.

Conrad, C. A., & Stahl, M. (2003). Geldpolitik und Spekulationsblasen – Das Beispiel der USA. *Österreichisches Bankarchiv, Zeitschrift für das gesamte Bank- und Börsenwesen, 51*, 685–693.

Cooper, M. J., Gulen, H., & Rau, P. R. (2014, October 1). *Performance for pay? The relation between CEO incentive compensation and future stock price performance.* Retrieved from http://ssrn.com/abstract=1572085 or https://doi.org/10.2139/ssrn.1572085

Crotty, J. (2009). Structural causes of the global financial crisis: A critical assessment of the 'new financial architecture'. *Cambridge Journal of Economics, 33*(2009), 563–580. https://doi.org/10.1093/cje/bep023.

Cuomo, A. (2009). *No rhyme or reason: The 'heads i win, tails you lose' bank bonus culture.* Retrieved from workplacebullying.org/multi/pdf/Cuomo.pdf

Dahrendorf, R. (2009). Die verlorene Ehre des Kaufmanns. In *Tagesspiegel.* vom July 12, 2009, from http://www.tagesspiegel.de/wirtschaft/dahrendorf-essay-die-verlorene-ehre-des-kaufmanns/1555814.html

Deutsche Bundesbank. (2006, July). Finanzderivate und ihre Rückwirkung auf die Kassamärkte. *Monatsbericht, 2006*, 55–68.

Deutsche Bundesbank. (2011). *Leitfaden zu den neuen Eigenkapital- und Liquiditätsregeln für Banken*. Frankfurt. Retrieved from https://www.bundesbank.de/Redaktion/DE/Downloads/Veroeffentlichungen/Bundesbank/basel3_leitfaden.pdf?__blob=publicationFile

Doherty, M. E., Mynatt, C. R., Tweney, R. D., & Schiavo, M. D. (1979). Pseudodiagnosticitiy. *Acta Psychologica, 49*, 111–121.

Domanski, D., & Heath, A. (2007, March). Financial investors and commodity markets. *BIS Quarterly Review*, 53–67. Retrieved February 12, 2014, from https://www.bis.org/publ/qtrpdf/r_qt0703g.pdf

Dullien, S. (2012). Bankenregulierung: Schwindende Statik. *Wirtschaftsdienst, 92*(7), 431–434.

Ergenzinger, R., & Krulis-Randa, J. S. (2004). Anforderungen an das Management unter dem Aspekt von Competitiveness und Ethics in der Gegenwart. In R. Berndt et al. (Eds.), *Competitiveness und Ethik, Herausforderungen an das Management, Schriftenreihe der Graduate School of Business Administration* (Vol. 11, pp. 3–16). Zurich: Springer.

Financial Crisis Inquiry Commission. (2010). *The Financial Crisis Inquiry Report: Final Report of the National Commission on the Causes of the Financial and Economic Crisis in the United States*, Washington, DC.

Financial Stability Forum. (2009, April 2). *FSF principles for sound compensation practices.* Retrieved from www.financialstabilityboard.org/wp.../r_0904b.pdf?...

Fox, J. (2009). *The myth of the rational market, a history of risk, reward, and delusion on wall street.* New York: Harper Business.

Frenk, D., et al. (2011). Review of Irwin and Sanders 2010 OECD Report. In Institute for Agriculture and Trade Policy (Ed.), *Excessive Speculation in Agriculture Commodities, Selected writings from 2008-2012*, pp. 43–49. Retrieved from http://www.iadb.org/intal/intalcdi/PE/2011/08247.pdf

Gaumert, U., Götz. S., & Ortgies, J. (2011). Basel III – eine kritische Würdigung. *die bank – Zeitschrift für Bankpolitik und Praxis, 2011*(5). Retrieved from http://www.die-bank.de/betriebswirtschaft/basel-iii-2013-eine-kritische-wurdigung

Giancarlo, H. J. C. (2016). Reconsidering the Dodd-Frank swaps trading regulatory framework. In H. Peirce & B. Klutsey (Eds.), *Reframing financial regulation—Enhancing stability and protecting consumers* (pp. 155–179). Arlington, VA: Mercatus Center, George Mason University.

Gilbert, C. L. (2010). How to understand high food prices. *Journal of Agricultural Economics, 61*, 2. Retrieved from http://econpapers.repec.org/article/blajageco/v_3a61_3ay_3a2010_3ai_3a2_3ap_3a398-425.

Gilla, D., Prowseb, V., & Vlassopoulosc, M. (2013). Cheating in the workplace: An experimental study of the impact of bonuses and productivity. *Journal of Economic Behavior & Organization, 96*, 120–134.

Gold, G., & Feldmann, P. (2007). *A house of cards—From fantasy finance to global crash*. London: Lupus Books.

Götzl, S. (2012). *. . .fokussiert: Baseler Paradoxien*. Retrieved from http://www.gv-bayern.de/Admin/GVB_Module/Druckversion/Druckversion?artikel=73627

Gregg, P., Jewell, S., & Tonks, I. (2012). Executive pay and performance: did bankers' bonuses cause the crisis? *International Review of Finance, Special Issue: Governance, Policy and the crisis: Part I, 12*(1), 89–122.

Hassler, U. (2003). Zeitabhängige Volatilität und instationäre Zeitreihen. *Wirtschaftsdienst, 12*, 811–816. Retrieved from http://core.kmi.open.ac.uk/download/pdf/6697414.pdf.

Henn, M. (2013, May 14). *Kommentar zum Literaturüberblick zur Spekulation mit Agrarrohstoffen von Will et al., WEED*. Retrieved from http://www2.weed-online.org/uploads/kommentar_literaturueberblick_agrarspekulation.pdf

Hofmann, C. (2011). *Basel III – Kontrahentenrisiko*. (Abfrage vom 27.12.2011) Retrieved from http://www.1plusi.de/dokumente/1_plus_i_fachbeitrag_basel_3_Kontrahenten.pdf

Inamura, Y., et al. (2011, March). *Recent surge in global commodity prices—Impact of financialization and globally accommodative monetary conditions*. Bank of Japan Review 2011 E 2. Retrieved from http://www.boj.or.jp/en/research/wps_rev/rev_2011/data/rev11e02.pdf

Irwin, S. H., & Sanders, D. R. (2010). *The impact of index and swap funds on commodity future markets*. OECD Food, Agriculture and Fisheries Working Papers, No. 27. Paris. Retrieved from http://ideas.repec.org/p/oec/agraaa/27-en.html

Irwin, S. H., & Sanders, D. R. (2012). Testing the masters hypothesis in commodity futures markets. *Energy Economics, 34*, 256–269. Retrieved from http://ideas.repec.org/a/eee/eneeco/v34y2012i1p256-269.html.

Jenkins P. (2017, December 18). Why UK bank ringfences don't make everyone safer. *Financial Times*. Retrieved from https://www.ft.com/content/1d529c3c-e1a6-11e7-a8a4-0a1e63a52f9c

Jensen, M., & Meckling, W. (1976). Theory of the firm. Managerial behavior, agency costs, and ownership structure. *Journal of Financial Economics, 3*(4), 305–360.

Kahneman, Daniel/Tversky, Amos (1979), Prospect theory: An analysis of decision under risk, in: Econometrica, Vol. 47, No. 2 pp. 263–292.

Kahneman, D., & Tversky, A. (1981, 30 January). The framing of decisions and the psychology of choice. *Science, 211*, 453–457.

Kahneman, D., & Tversky, A. (1982). The psychology of preferences. *Scientific American, 146*, 160–173.

Kahneman, D., & Tversky, A. (1984). Choices, values and frames. *American Pschologist, 39*(4), 342–350.

Kahneman, D., & Tversky, A. (1986). Rational choice and the framing of decisions. *Journal of Business, 59*(4), 5251–5278.

Kahneman, D., Knetsch, J., & Thaler, R. (1991). Anomalies: The endowment effect, loss aversion and status quo bias. *The Journal of Economic Perspectives, 5*(1), 193–206.

Kern, S. (2010). *US-Finanzmarktreform, Deutsche Bank Research.* Finanzmarkt Spezial, EU-Monitor 77. Retrieved from http://www.db.com/mittelstand/downloads/US_ Finanzmarktreform_12_2010.pdf

Khan, A. (2018). *A behavioral approach to financial supervision, regulation, and central banking.* IMF working paper, No. WP/18/178.

Krahnen, J. N., & Schüwer, U. (2017). Structural reforms in banking: The role of trading. *Journal of Financial Regulation, 3*(1), 66–88. https://doi.org/10.1093/jfr/fjw018.

Krugman, P. (2008, June 21). Calvo on commodities. *New York Times.* Retrieved from http:// krugman.blogs.nytimes.com/2008/06/21/calvo-on-commodities/?_php=true&_type=blogs&_ r=0

Krugman, P. (2009, September 2). How did economists get it so wrong? *New York Times.* https:// www.nytimes.com/2009/09/06/magazine/06Economic-t.html

Krugman, P. (2011, February 7). Speculation and signatures. *New York Times.* http://krugman.blogs. nytimes.com/2011/02/07/signatures-of-speculation/

Lagi, M., Bar-Yam, Y., Bertrand, K. Z., & Bar-Yarn, Y. (2011a). *The food crises: A quantitative model of food prices including speculators and ethanol conversion.* Cambridge: New England Complex Systems Institute. Retrieved from http://necsi.edu/research/social/food_prices.pdf

Lagi, M., Bar-Yam, Y., Bertrand, K. Z., & Bar-Yarn, Y. (2011b). *Economics of food prices and crises.* Cambridge, MA: New England complex System Institute. Retrieved February 12, 2014, from http://arxiv.org/pdf/1109.4859v1.pdf

Langer, E. J. (1975). The illusion of control. *Journal of Personality and Social Psychology, 32*(2), 311–328.

Langer, E. J., & Roth, J. (1975). Heads I win, tails it's chance: The illusion of control as a function of the sequence of outcomes in a purely chance task. *Journal of Personality and Social Psychology, 32*(6), 951–955.

Levin, C., Coburn, T., et al. (2009, June 24). *Excessive Speculation in the Wheat Market, United States Permanent Subcommittee on Investigations (2009), Excessive Speculation in the Wheat Market,* Washington. Retrieved from http://www.gpo.gov/fdsys/pkg/CREC-2008-09-24/pdf/ CREC-2008-09-24-senate.pdf

Lichtenstein, S., Fischhoff, B., & Phillips, L. D. (1982). Calibration of probabilities: The state of art to 1980. In D. Kahneman, P. Slovic, & A. Tversky (Eds.), *Judgment under uncertainty: Heuristics and biases* (pp. 306–334). Cambridge: Cambridge University Press. file:///C:/Eigene% 20Dateien2016/Political%20Economy/Material/ callibration_probabilities_lichtenstein_fischoff_philips.pdf.

Löhr, A. (1997). Die moralische Urteilskraft von Wirtschaftsstudenten: Bemerkungen zum empirischen Forschungsstand. In G. Blickle (Ed.), *Ethik in Organisationen: Konzepte, Befunde, Praxisbeispiele* (pp. 185–208). Göttingen: Verl. für Angewandte Psychologie.

Loomes, G., & Sudgen, R. (1982). Regret theory: An alternative theory of rational choice under uncertainty. *The Economic Journal, 92*(368), 805–824.

Malkiel, B. (2014). *What does the efficient market hypothesis have to say about asset bubbles?* Retrieved from https://www.forbes.com/sites/quora/2014/06/13/what-does-the-efficient-market-hypothesis-have-to-say-about-asset-bubbles/amp/

Markowitz, H. (1952). Portfolio selection. *Journal of Finance, 12,* 77–91. Retrieved from https:// www.math.ust.hk/~maykwok/courses/ma362/07F/markowitz_JF.pdf.

Masters, M. W. (2009). *Testimony of Michael W. Masters Managing Member//Portfolio Manager Masters Capital Management LLC before the Commodity Future Trading Commission.* Retrieved from http://www.cftc.gov/ucm/groups/public/@newsroom/documents/file/hearing080509_mas ters.pdf

Masters, M. W., & White, A. K. (2008). *The accidental hunt brothers: How institutional investors are driving up food and energy prices.* Retrieved from http://www.loe.org/images/content/080919/Act1.pdf

Mayer, J. (2009, October). *The growing interdependence between financial and commodity markets.* UNCTAD Discussion Paper, No. 195. Retrieved from http://unctad.org/en/Docs/osgdp20093_en.pdf

Metcalfe, J. (1998b). Cognitive optimism: Self-deception or memory-based processing heuristic? *Personality and Social Psychology Review, 2*(2), 100–110.

Meyerowitz, B. E., & Chaiken, S. (1987). The effect on message framing on breast-self-examination attitudes, intentions and behavior. *Journal of Personality and Social Psychology, 52*(1987), 500–510.

Miller, S. M. (2016). On simpler, higher capital requirements. In H. Peirce & B. Klutsey (Eds.), *Reframing financial regulation—Enhancing stability and protecting consumers* (pp. 35–59). Arlington, VA: Mercatus Center, George Mason University.

Muolo, P., & Padilla, M. (2008). *Chain of blame: How wall street caused the mortgage and credit crisis.* Hoboken, NJ: Wiley.

Nickerson, R. S. (1998). Confirmation bias: An ubiquitous phenomen in many guises. *Review of General Psychology, 2*(2), 175–220.

Noll, B. (2002). *Wirtschafts- und Unternehmensethik in der Marktwirtschaft.* Stuttgart: Kohlhammer.

Ogger, G. (2001). *Der Börsenschwindel.* Munich: Bertelsmann.

Pagan, A., & Schwert, C. (1990). Testing for covariance stationarity in stock market data. *Economics Letters, 33*(2), 165–170. Retrieved from http://schwerts.com/el90_ps.pdf.

Papaeconomou, P. (2012). *Individual differences & instance based decision making: putting "bounded rationality" to the test.* Retrieved from https://www.era.lib.ed.ac.uk/handle/1842/9942

Peck, A. (1985). The economic role of traditional commodity futures markets. In A. Peck (Ed.), *Future markets: Their economic role* (pp. 1–82). Washington, DC: American Enterprise Institute for Public Policy Research. Retrieved from http://www.farmdoc.illinois.edu/irwin/archive/books/Futures-Economic/Futures-Economic_preface.pdf.

Peirce, H., & Soliman, V. (2016). Rethinking the swaps clearing mandate. In H. Peirce & B. Klutsey (Eds.), *Reframing financial regulation—Enhancing stability and protecting consumers* (pp. 180–224). Arlington, VA: Mercatus Center, George Mason University.

Phillips, P., & Loretan, M. (1990). *Testing covariance stationarity under moment condition failure with an application to common stock returns.* Discussion Paper No. 947. New Haven, CT: Cowles Foundation for Economic Research at Yale University. Retrieved from http://ideas.repec.org/p/cwl/cwldpp/947.html

Pies, I. (2012a). *Wirtschaftsethik konkret: Wie (un)moralisch ist die Spekulation mit Agrarrohstoffen?* Martin-Luther-Universität Halle-Wittenberg: Diskussionspapier No. 2012-15, Halle. Retrieved from http://wcms.uzi.uni-halle.de/download.php?down=25900&elem=2602684

Pies, I. (2012b). Lebensmittelpreise: Die Moral der Agrar-Spekulation. In F.A.Z. Retrieved August 31, 2012, from http://www.faz.net/aktuell/wirtschaft/menschen-wirtschaft/lebensmittelpreise-die-moral-der-agrar-spekulation-11873351.html

Pies, I., Prehn, S., Glauben, T., & Will, M. G. (2013). *Kurzdarstellung Agrarspekulation,* Diskussionspapier No. 2013-2, des Lehrstuhls für Wirtschaftsethik an der Martin-Luther-Universität Halle-Wittenberg, pub. Ingo Pies, Halle. Retrieved from http://wcms.uzi.uni-halle.de/download.php?down=27545&elem=2636563

Ross, S. A. (1973). The economic theory of agency: The principal's problem. *American Economic Review, 63*(2), 134–139.

Ross, L., Lepper, M. R., & Hubbard, M. (1975). Perseverance in self perception and social perception: Biased attributional processes in the debriefing paradigm. *Journal of Personality and Social Psychology, 32*(5), 880–892.

Rubio, V. J., Hernández, J. M., Zaldívar, F., Márquez, O., & Santacreu, J. (2010). Can we predict risk-taking behavior? Two behavioral tests for predicting guessing tendencies in a multiple-choice test. *European Journal of Psychological Assessment, 26*(2), 87–94.

Rubio, V. J, Hernández, J. M., & Santacreu, J. *The objective assessment of risk tendency as a personality dimension.* University Autónoma of Madrid. Retrieved from www.uam.es/proyectosinv/psimasd/assessrisk.pdf

Russo, J. E., & Schoemaker, P. J. H. (1992). Managing overconfidence. *Sloan Management Review, 33,* 7–17.

Sachverständigenrat. (2011). *Verantwortung für Europa wahrnehmen.* Wiesbaden. Retrieved from https://www.sachverstaendigenrat-wirtschaft.de/fileadmin/dateiablage/download/gutachten/ga11_ges.pdf

Samuelson, W., & Zeckhauser, R. (1988b). Status quo bias in decision making. *Journal of Risk and Uncertainty, 1,* 7–59.

Schäfer, D. (2011, November). Banken: Leverage Ratio ist das bessere Risikomaß. In *DIW Wochenbericht No. 46/2011 vom 16.* Retrieved September 14, 2012, from http://www.diw.de/documents/publikationen/73/diw_01.c.388897.de/11-46-3.pdf

Schotter, A., & Weigelt, K. (1992). Behavioral consequenses of corporate incentives and long-term bonuses: An experimental study. *Managemet Sience, 38*(9), 1280–1298.

Schulze, P. M. (2004, August). *Granger-Kausalitätsprüfung – Eine Anwendungsorientierte Darstellung,* Institut für Statistik und Ökonometrie, Johannes Gutenberg-Universität Mainz, Arbeitspapier No. 28. Retrieved from http://www.statoek.vwl.uni-mainz.de/Arbeitspapier_Nr_28_Granger-Kausalitaetspruefung.pdf

Schwarz, N., & Vaughn, L. A. (2002). The availability heuristic revisited: Ease of recall and content of recall as distinct sources of information. In T. Gilovich, D. W. Griffin, & D. Kahneman (Eds.), *Heuristics and biases: The psychology of intuitive judgment* (pp. 103–119). Cambridge: Cambridge University Press.

Sharma, K. (2012, April). *Financial sector compensation and excess risk-taking—A consideration of the issues and policy lessons.* DESA Working Paper No. 115 ST/ESA/2012/DWP/115. Retrieved from www.un.org/esa/desa/papers/.../wp115_2012.pdf

Shiller, R. (2007). *The subprime solution: How today's global financial crisis happened, and what to do about it.* Princeton, NJ: Princeton University Press.

Single, G., & Stahl, M. (2000a). Risikopotential Hedge-Fonds – der Fall LTCM. In C. A. Conrad & M. Stahl (Eds.), *Risikomanagement an den internationalen Finanzmärkten* (pp. 379–391). Stuttgart: Schäffer-Poeschel.

Single, G., & Stahl, M. (2000b). Risikopotential Hedge-Fonds – der Fall LTCM. In C. A. Conrad & M. Stahl (Eds.), *Risikomanagement an den internationalen Finanzmärkten* (pp. 207–221). Stuttgart: Schäffer-Poeschel.

Singleton, K. J. (2011). *Investors flows and the 2008 boom/bust in oil prices.* Stanford. Retreived from http://www.stanford.edu/~kenneths/OilPub.pdf

Soros, G. (2009, March 24). One way to stop bear raids. Credit default swaps need much stricter regulation. *The Wall Street Journal.* Retrieved from https://www.wsj.com/articles/SB123785310594719693

Stahl, M., & Conrad, C. A. (2000a). Strategien zur Risikovermeidung an internationalen Finanzmärkten. In C. A. Conrad & M. Stahl (Eds.), *Risikomanagement an den internationalen Finanzmärkten* (pp. 207–221). Stuttgart: Schäffer-Poeschel.

Stahl, M., & Conrad, C. A. (2000b). Strategien zur Risikovermeidung an internationalen Finanzmärkten. In C. A. Conrad & M. Stahl (Eds.), *Risikomanagement an den internationalen Finanzmärkten* (pp. 379–391). Stuttgart: Schäffer-Poeschel.

Stoll, H. R., & Whaley, R. E. (2009, September). *Commodity index investing and commodity future prices.* Owen Graduate School of Management. Retrieved from http://www.cftc.gov/ucm/groups/public/@swaps/documents/file/plstudy_45_hsrw.pdf

Stulz, R. (2009, March). Six ways companies mismanage risk. *Harvard Business Review*, 86–94.

Sucharow, L. (2013, July). *Wall street in crisis: A Perfect Storm Looming, Labaton Sucharow's, U.S. Financial Services Industry Survey.* Retrieved October 28, 2013, from http://www.secwhistlebloweradvocate.com

Sun, L. (2012). Executive compensation and contract-driven earnings management. *Asian Academy of Management Journal of Accounting and Finance, 8*(2), 111–127.

Taleb, N. N. (2001). *Fooled by randomness.* London: Penguin.

Taleb, N. N. (2007). *The black swan: The impact of the highly improbable.* London: Penguin.

Tang, K., & Xiong, W. (2012). Index investment and the financialization of commodities. *Financial Analyst Journal, 68*(6), 54–74. Retrieved from https://www.princeton.edu/~wxiong/papers/commodity.pdf.

Thaler, R. H. (1981). Some empirical evidence on dynamic inconsistency. *Economic Letters, 8*, 201–207.

Tversky, A., & Kahneman, D. (1974). Judgment under uncertainty: Heuristics and biases. *Science, 185*, 1124–1131.

Ulrich, P. (1993). Unternehmerethos. In G. Enderle et al. (Eds.), *Lexikon der Wirtschaftsethik* (pp. 1165–1175). Freiburg: Herder.

Voinea, G., & Anton, S. (2009). Lessons from the current financial crisis. A risk management approach. *Review of Economic and Business Studies, 3*(2009), 139–147.

Volk, H. (2000). Verunsicherte Mitarbeiter werden schneller krank. *Frankfurter Allgemeine Zeitung vom 18.09.2000, 217*, 37.

von Hayek, F. A. (1974, December 11). *The Pretence of Knowledge, Lecture to the memory of Alfred Nobel.* Retrieved December 31, 2017, from https://www.nobelprize.org/nobel_prizes/economic-sciences/laureates/1974/hayek-lecture.html

Wason, P. C. (1960). On the failure to eliminate hypothesis in a conceptual task. *Quarterly Journal of Experimental Psychology, 12*(3), 129–140.

Weinstein, N. D. (1980). Unrealistic optimism about future life events. *Journal of Personality and Social Psychology, 39*, 806–457.

Will, M. G, Prehn, S, Pies, I., & Glauben, T. (2012). *Is financial speculation with agricultural commodities harmful or helpful? A literature review of current empirical research*, Discussion Paper No. 2012-27, of the Chair in Economic Ethics, Martin-Luther-University Halle-Wittenberg, edited by Ingo Pies, Halle. Retrieved from http://wcms.uzi.uni-halle.de/download.php?down=27388&elem=2633683

Woods, T. E. (2009). *Meltdown: A free-market look at why the stock Market collapsed, the economy tanked, and government bailouts will make things worse.* Washington, DC: Regnery Publishing.

Foreign Trade

14

What Follows Why?

As globalization progresses, international economic relationships are becoming increasingly important to managers. The following chapter will explain the basic determinants of foreign trade, international capital movements and exchange rates.

Learning Goals

You should be able to assess the international influence on their company in their future activities.

14.1 Reasons for Foreign Trade

Unimpeded international foreign trade integrates the various national markets into a world market. The global economy as the sum of all national economies then produces for those of the world market instead of for the demand of the national markets and adapts their production structure accordingly. Foreign trade can be understood as a cross-border exchange of goods. The starting point for any fair and thus repeated exchange is that both parties have advantages. There can be many reasons for the exchange of benefits. In general, transactions are determined by national markets in foreign trade. Here one distinguishes supply and demand, which together form a market price. The immediately obvious motives are lack or scarcity of a good in a country (domestic) and corresponding abundance abroad (raw materials for example). Other reasons for foreign trade may include changes in national demand structures and the absorption of supply-side or demand-side shocks. The following article presents the market mechanisms that cause the integration of the world economy.

Overview of Market Economic Reasons for Foreign Trade

On the supply side	On the demand side
1. Shortage	1. Demand fluctuations
2. Absolute cost advantages	2. Changes in the need structures
3. Relative cost advantages (Ricardo Theorem)	3. Specialization in demand needs
4. Different equipment with production factors	4. Absorption of shocks (Heckscher-Ohlin theorem)
5. Degressive unit costs	
6. Absorption of shocks	
7. Product life cycle hypothesis	
8. Technical progress	

The largest share of world trade is made up of processed products. The main reason here are cost differences in production between countries. Here we distinguish absolute and relative cost differences:

14.1.1 Absolute Cost Differences

Two countries England and Portugal produce two goods of wine and cloth that do not differ in quality. England, with its looms, can produce cloth at a cost less than the sum of manpower and capital, expressed in gold, as opposed to Portugal. Although Portugal does not have looms, it has sun as a natural resource, so it can produce the same amount of wine as England with less labor, expressed in gold pieces. So it's worth it for England to produce only cloth and Portugal only wine.

This specialization and the subsequent exchange of goods creates a welfare gain for both countries.

Absolute cost advantages as a cause of foreign trade have been empirically confirmed: the so-called MacDougall test showed that the relative market share of US exports increases with increasing productivity advantages compared to other countries. Above all, goods are exported in which the relation of labor productivity exceeds that of the wage relation to foreign countries, which can therefore be produced more cheaply in the USA. However, foreign trade is also beneficial in the case of relative cost advantages for both countries. In the so-called comparative cost advantages of Ricardo (1772–1823), the cost

With autarky	Production possibilities using all 10 workers	Cost ratio of production in each country corresponds to the price ratio	Supply according to demand
England (relative cost advantage of cloth)	90 bales of cloth or 60 barrels of wine (1 worker = 9 bales or 3 barrels)	3 bales of cloth against 2 barrels of wine (90/30 = 3)	36 bales of cloth and 18 barrels of wine (4 workers = 9 bales and 6 workers = 3 barrels)
Portugal (relative cost advantage of wine)	120 bales of cloth or 150 barrels of wine (1 worker = 12 bales or 15 barrels)	1.2 bales of cloth against 1.5 barrels of wine (180/150 = 0.8)	48 bales of cloth and 90 barrels of wine (4 workers = 12 bales and 6 workers = 15 barrels)
World in total			84 bales of cloth and 108 barrels of wine

Fig. 14.1   Relative cost advantages with autarky

advantages are not distributed among the countries, but the production costs for the goods differ only within the countries.[1]

14.1.2 Relative Cost Differences

We start from our example above and assume that Portugal has also bought looms, more modern and therefore more productive. Portugal now produces both wine and cloth with less effort, expressed in labor employed, than England. The capital expenditure for the looms is the same in both countries. Each country uses half of its ten workers for the production of wine and cloth (see Fig. 14.1).

The relative exchange price of wine is higher in England than in Portugal. In England you get more cloth for wine. With cloth, it is exactly the opposite. The relative exchange price of cloth is higher in Portugal than in England. In Portugal you get more wine for cloth.

Contrary to the example of the absolute cost advantages, here a country, Portugal, can produce more wine or cloth with the same number of ten workers than England. Nevertheless, England can produce cheaper cloth than wine. England thus has a comparative cost advantage with cloth and a disadvantage with wine. Portugal, on the other hand, has a comparative advantage in wine production and a disadvantage in cloth production. While it would be most efficient if Portugal produced everything, Portugal has only ten workers.

If it comes to foreign trade, then the relative exchange price will settle according to the labor cost ratio or depending on the bargaining position (ie according to the demand elasticities). If the exchange ratio is 0.6 barrels of wine against a bale of cloth, trading is beneficial for both countries. It is worthwhile for Portugal to specialize in the production of wine, and for England, in the production of cloth, owing to the comparative cost

---

[1]See Ricardo, David (1817); Stavenhagen, Gerhard (1969), p. 516; Eltis, Walter (1989) and Bender, Dieter (1992), pp. 427.

With foreign trade	Production possibilities using all 10 workers	with a foreign trade ratio of 0.6 wine / cloth (90/150)	Supply
England	90 bales of cloth	50 bales of cloth against 30 barrels of wine	40 (+4) bales of cloth and 30 (+12) barrels of wine
Portugal	150 barrels of wine	30 barrels of wine against 50 bales of cloth	50 (+2) bales of cloth and 120 (+30) barrels of wine
World total			90 bales of cloth and 150 barrels of wine = welfare gain: + 6 bales of cloth + 42 barrels of wine

Fig. 14.2 Foreign trade with relative cost advantages

advantages of Portugal in wine and England in cloth, for Portugal. In terms of foreign trade, Portugal is able to exchange the most for the production of cloth, and England for the production of cloth (see Fig. 14.2). Each country produces the goods with maximum productivity.

Ricardo's explanatory approach to the relative cost differences criticizes the restrictive model assumptions. For example, countries do not consider the different resource endowments, and there is only one variable factor of production, labor, and the model does not say anything about the distribution of welfare gains between the two countries.

14.1.3 Different Equipment of Production Factors as a Cause of Foreign Trade

We assume that two countries have different production factors (England: a lot of capital and little work, Portugal: little capital and a lot of work). Here, mobile and immobile factors of production can be distinguished.

14.1.3.1 Mobile Production Factors

If we assume substitutional production functions, then production can be replaced by capital in production, and vice versa, but with decreasing productivity (margins) at the same time as the other factor (neoclassic). As a result of the opening of the border, workers are now migrating from Portugal to England, and capital flows from England to Portugal. A current example would be the EU enlargement, which allows laborers from Poland to work in Germany, for example. The scarcity of the respective production factor is compensated for, which is why higher productivity and thus higher production brings welfare gains in every country.[2]

---

[2]See *Ott, Alfred E.* (1989), p. 147ff and *Schumann, Jochen* (1987).

For both countries: $-\Delta Y < +\Delta Y$.

$\Rightarrow$ there is a net welfare gain Work enters the country N ↑ Work immigrates abroad N ↓ Capital flows abroad C ↓ Capital flows into country C ↑.

Distribution effect:

$$\frac{w \downarrow}{i \uparrow} = \frac{\frac{dY}{dN} \downarrow}{\frac{dY}{dC} \uparrow}; \quad \frac{w \downarrow}{i \downarrow} = \frac{\frac{dY}{dN} \uparrow}{\frac{dY}{dC} \downarrow}$$

In addition to this allocation and welfare effect, there is also a distribution effect, since, in line with the reduction in scarcities in the respective countries, productivity also decreases with the increased use of factors and thus factor payments (see Fig. 14.3). Before foreign trade, labor in England was scarce and therefore productivity high, which is why real wages were high—and vice versa for capital. Now labor is pouring from Portugal to England and capital from England to Portugal, which is why productivity and therefore real wages in England are falling with increased labor input and real interest rates are rising with dwindling capital. The mirror image process is taking place in Portugal.

14.1.4 The Rybczynski Theorem

The Rybczynski Theorem addresses the distribution of goods production in a country in foreign trade on the basis of fixed factor ratios and an assumed full employment of production factors. Thus, if England has a compensatory cost penalty at work and therefore introduces labor, the product of high labor intensity (for example, wine) will expand its share of the national product in England.

This theorem arises from the assumption of full employment of the factors of production. If these are to be maintained, as the labor-to-capital ratio has increased in England, relatively more labor-intensive goods (wine) and fewer capital-intensive goods (cloth) will have to be produced so that the imported extra labor has enough capital to be employed,[3] But are there any mechanisms in foreign trade that bring about an adjustment of the factor price costs, without them passing the limit, which is thus used for immobile production factors?

14.1.5 Immobile Factors of Production: The Heckscher-Ohlin Theorem or the Factor Proportion Theorem

Even if the factors of production are immobile, foreign trade brings about an international adjustment of production factor prices and an increase in world welfare, and of every

---

[3] See Rybczynski, T. (1955) and Plümper, Thomas (1996), p. 291.

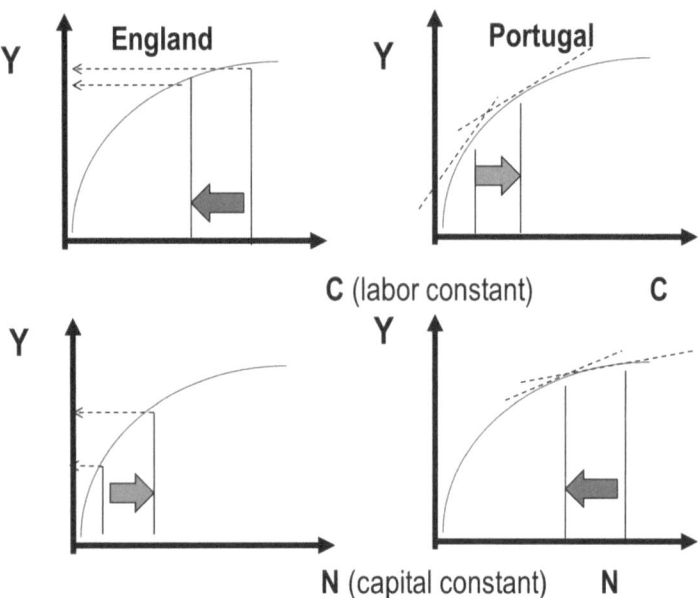

Fig. 14.3 Foreign trade in mobile production factors

country involved in trade, as shown in the example of Portugal and England. We assume that two products are produced, a capital-intensive commodity (C > N) and a labor-intensive commodity (C < N) with fixed factor ratios (wine is labor-intensive: C/N capital intensity = 1/6, cloth is capital-intensive: C/N capital intensity = 6/1) and both countries have the same level of production technology. The prices for the production factor capital amount.

i (Portugal) = 15 pieces of gold per unit of capital > i (England) = 5 pieces of gold per unit of capital and for the production factor work.

w (Portugal) = 4 gold pieces per working unit < w (England) = 12 gold pieces per working unit. So, relative to England in Portugal, due to scarcity, capital is expensive and labor cheap. In England, on the other hand, capital is cheap and labor expensive relative to Portugal (see Fig. 14.4).

The relative price of wine in terms of gold in England is 77 for wine and 42 for a bale cloth. The exchange ratio is therefore 1.8 bales of cloth for a barrel of wine. In Portugal one pays 94 gold pieces for a bale of cloth and 39 gold pieces for a barrel of wine. The exchange ratio is accordingly 0.4 bales of cloth for a barrel of wine.

If there is foreign trade (see Fig. 14.5), the price will settle at 1, depending on the position of the bargain (ie according to the demand elasticities), for a price or exchange ratio. Over time, however, it pays off for Portugal to specialize in wine, owing to the low wages due to the high labor supply and the high cost of capital due to the shortage of capital and, conversely, to England for cloth.

With autarky	Production costs per product	Price ex-change ra-tio	Desired amount	Total cost
England	wine: 77 cloth: 42	1 barrel of wine: 1.8 bales of cloth	50 bales of cloth and 50 barrels of wine	3.850 +2.100 = 5.950
Portugal	wine: 39 cloth: 94	50 bales of cloth and 50 barrels of wine	50 bales of cloth and 50 barrels of wine	1.950 +4.700 = 6.650
World total			100 bales of cloth and 100 barrels of wine	12.600

Fig. 14.4 Production costs with autarky

With foreign trade	Production costs per product	Rate of exchange in foreign trade	Production and production costs	Total cost of the desired amount
England	wine: 77 cloth: 42	1	100 bales of cloth 4,200 gold pieces	50 bales of cloth: 2,100 50 barrels of wine: 2,100 Advantage: 1,750
Portugal	wine: 39 cloth: 94	1	100 barrels of wine 3,900 gold pieces	50 bales of cloth: 1,950 50 barrels of wine: 1,950 Advantage: 2,750
World total				8.100, Advantage: 4.500

Fig. 14.5 Production costs with foreign trade

So we can again record two effects of foreign trade in immobile production factors:

1. **Welfare effect:** Due to the specialization of the countries, each generate a higher social product.
2. **Allocation effect:** England specializes in cloth and Portugal on wine.
3. **Long-term distribution effect:** England will export cloth. Domestic demand is export demand, which is why the price of cloth will rise. The demand for capital will also rise, which is why interest rates will also increase. The share of income from capital assets in the social product will increase. Conversely, the demand for labor and hence the wage will fall, which is why the share of the tighter factor of labor productivity will decrease. The approximation of the factor prices of both countries as a result of foreign trade is called, according to Samuelson, the factor price equalization theorem. Sa-muelson further shows that the reduction in the proportion of the factor z. For example, labor

income can be collected from the social product by collecting duties (Stolper-Samuelson theorem).[4]

A current example would be Germany (a lot of capital, little labor) and China (a lot of labor and little capital). For example, with the factor proportion theorem, it can be said that toys are made in china. Wages will therefore rise in China.

14.1.6 The Leontief Paradox and Neofactor Proportion Theorem

Leontief reviewed Heckscher-Ohlin's factor proportion theorem on the basis of US foreign trade in an input-output analysis. He noted that although the US is one of the richest countries in the world, it imports mainly capital-intensive goods and exports labor-intensive goods. This seems to contradict the factor proportion theorem (hence: Leontief paradox). How can this apparent contradiction be explained?

On the one hand, factor intensity, that is, the ratio of capital employed to production, can change over time (shifting factor intensities). This will be the case when labor costs exceed the threshold value after which the substitution of labor with capital (machines) is worthwhile. A separation of labor-intensive and capital-intensive goods is then no longer possible because labor-intensive products in the US would be produced with a lot of capital. On the other hand, labor in the narrower sense is not a homogeneous factor. Meanwhile, there are more and more products that contradict the neoclassical idea of a combination of almost unskilled workers and capital-consuming machines. For example, creating software, engineering or research is very labor intensive. However, this "intellectual" work effort hides an enormous amount of capital required to qualify the work. One would have to differentiate between physical capital and training capital (human capital). If one considers human capital in the equation, the factor proportion theorem can be used again. One speaks then of the so-called neo-factor proportion theorem, which has been confirmed by empirical investigations. The US and Western Europe have a comparative and absolute advantage in the production of human capital-intensive goods. The trade of these goods takes place, above all, with semi-industrialized developing countries, which are beyond the state of agrarian states. However, the goods composition of this trade flow changes over time. The dynamic product life cycle hypothesis can be derived from this.[5]

---

[4]See *Külp, Bernhard* (1996), *pp. 146*, Stavenhagen, Gerhard (1969), *p. 532f, Bender, Dieter* (1992), *pp. 436; Stolper, Wolfgang/Samuelson, Paul* (1941) *and Ohlin, Bertil* (1933).
[5]See *Leontief, Wassily* (1953); *Külp, Bernhard* (1996), *pp. 146; Bender, Dieter* (1992), *pp. 442.

14.1.7 Product Life Cycle Hypothesis or Theory of the Technological Gap Trade

Due to their high human capital, Western industrialized countries are constantly succeeding in developing new technologies and products (product and process innovations) that temporarily give them a monopoly on the world market with pioneering profits, which is why production with high labor costs is possible (innovation function). With increasing maturity and standardization of the product, it will be possible to relocate production to the semi-industrialized developing and emerging economies, thereby exploiting their labor cost benefits. Direct investment in the western industrialized countries, ie the establishment of production facilities abroad with corresponding know-how transfer, accelerate this process. The innovations are also copied from abroad (imitation function). After all, companies in emerging markets succeed in imitating and not only producing their own products, but even exporting them. The original export product has become an import product for western industrialized countries. The value added takes place abroad, which corresponds to a transfer of know-how and income. Meanwhile, Western industrialized countries have succeeded in developing new products and technologies because of their comparative advantage in human capital. The cycle is repeated. Here, therefore, the different human capital equipment as a prerequisite or advance performance of technical progress is the cause of foreign trade. The product lifecycle hypothesis could also be confirmed empirically using the example of the USA (among others in chip production).[6]

Many companies now plan the product lifecycle according to the time needed for foreign competition to imitate. Some have even decided not to leave the imitation gain to competitors. They are launching their own low-cost product under a different brand just before the competition in Asia could have completed the copy. The product is manufactured in low-wage countries. Should Chinese companies be allowed to take over German high technology companies like Kuka or Putzmeister? Company acquisitions can boost efficiency and are part of a viable competition. From this point of view, it should be allowed within market economies to take over other companies. However, China is violating the GATT principle of reciprocity. Foreign companies are not allowed to acquire a majority stake in Chinese companies. In China, mercantilistic thinking seems to prevail. Like GB in colonialism, countries seem to be trying to reserve the profitable processing on the basis of technical superiority. Against this backdrop, acquisitions should only be allowed for companies from countries that concede the same conditions to foreign companies.

Against the background of the importance of innovation for Western industrialized countries, one can also deduce the need for investment in education and the promotion of individual creativity. For the craft of imitation, collective subordination and memorization will be more necessary than repudiation of already existing ones.

---

[6]See *Bender, Dieter* (1992), *pp. 452 and Franzmeyer, Fritz* (2001), *pp. 276.*

14.1.8 Foreign Trade Due to Specialization

However, most of world trade takes place intersectorally, e.g. within the automotive industry and between the Western industrialized countries, which have similar cost and demand structures as well as capital and work equipment. Why is foreign trade even possible with identical cost and demand structures? This can be explained by the specialization of the manufacturers to different demand needs. For a strong differentiation of the product range or specialization, the national market would not be sufficient. The world marketoffers enough sales potential, however. Foreign trade as cross-border competition forces providers to align themselves with international demand and/or to qualify in market niches. The resulting product variety also corresponds to a welfare gain.

Even degressive, with unit cost curves decreasing with the production volume, there is a welfare gain in the context of an international specialization. As demand increases in accordance with the world market, the production volume increases, and unit costs fall. Production-related economies of large scale can be differentiated as causes of declining unit cost trends due to large fixed cost portions (as they represent, for example, the high development and research costs of the pharmaceutical industry) and learning cost effects.[7]

14.1.9 Conclusion

It has been shown that foreign trade, with the aid of various mechanisms, brings about prosperity gains and a balance of scarcities. Changes in the income distribution were also derived. In the short term, the changes in the international division of labor release a large part of the factors of production, which leads to structural unemployment. The capital employed in a country relative to foreign countries in unprofitable production processes is also devalued. However, in the long term, the welfare gains can also be used to qualify and thus re-employ the workforce at higher productivity and therefore with higher real wages. Product innovations such as mobile phones increase the quality of life and create new demand and thus new jobs.

The distribution of welfare gains between home and abroad is a problem that is tempered by the abundance of goods in international trade. Each country will have goods in which there will be proportionally less and goods that benefit proportionately more from the welfare gains of the division of labor in foreign trade than other countries. The situation is different with regard to the distribution of the welfare gains of foreign trade to the factors of capital and labor. Capital, in contrast to labor, is homogeneous and, given a technical advance, has the same productivity in every country. Capital is mobile in contrast to work and moves internationally very quickly at low transaction costs. It is therefore recommended that the state intervene in the income distribution process between capital

---

[7]See *Bender, Dieter* (1992), *pp. 448.*

and labor through a subsequent taxation of the welfare gain and use the proceeds for an active education policy, ie qualification or retraining of the workforce. Without such a policy, labor would be paid less in line with lower productivity, and the products, whose manufacture would require a certain qualification and allow high pay in accordance with the product life-cycle hypothesis, would be made abroad.

14.2   The Balance of Payments

▶ **Definition** Balance of payments is the statistical summary of all economic transactions between foreign exchange residents and non-residents in the form of monetary flows for a certain period of time.

The time period is normally 1 year. Foreign residents are all persons resident in Germany. Thus, the transactions with the other € states are also recorded. Only the monetary flows between Germany and abroad are recorded. The balance of payments therefore only contains current figures and not stock figures as in the case of commercial balance sheets. Consequently, there are only transaction and no valuation gains.

Before the introduction of the euro, every foreign trade transaction led to a demand for foreign exchange or to a foreign exchange offer. For this reason alone, a counter-position would have to exist for every transaction with foreign countries, since the foreign exchange offer had to be matched by a foreign exchange demand. As eurozone countries now have the same currency as Germany, transactions with these countries have no effect on the exchange rate anymore.

All incoming payments or monetary inflows from abroad are posted to the debit balance sheet, while the outflows are credited (see Fig. 14.6). For this reason, the capital account also offsets the current account. If, for example, we have more goods exports than imported goods, this leads to a monthly net flow from abroad to the domestic market. For the balance of payments to be balanced, an equal flow of domestic capital now has to go abroad, and that can only be a positive balance in capital exports, as these are credited on the credit side.

The current account captures in the first sub-balance sheet the monetary flows that are opposed to exports and imports of goods. The services are described in the overview. Secondary incomes are monetary inflows and outflows, such as Contributions to the EU.

Primary income is the difference between domestic and national product, the balance of primary income, as known from national accounts, with the rest of the world (domestic and foreign income, eg dividends and interest on foreign securities), Labor income of cross-border workers, etc.). The capital account summarizes all short-term and long-term deposits, including direct investment.

▶ **Definition** The direct investments are investments that allow the possibility of influencing the management abroad.

Transactions	Debit incoming payments = foreign currency supply (€-revaluation)	Credit outpayments = foreign currency demand (€-devaluation)
I. Current Account	= €-demand	= €-supply
1. Balance on goods	Export of goods	Import of goods
2. Balance on services	Travel receipts, licenses Banking and insurance services, transport	Travel expenditures
3. Primary income	Incomes from interest, profits, dividends generated from foreign investment incoming payments	and migrant remittances i.e. payments from people living and working overseas outpayments
4. Secondary income	Transfers as monetary flows without counterperformance i.e. insurance benefits (+ net premiums),	Contributions to international organizations, development aid, guest worker transfers etc.
II. Capital account	Transfers of ownership of fixed assets, inheritances, Sale/transfer of patents,	Copyrights, franchises and other transferable contracts, and goodwill, and debt relief

Transactions	Debit incoming payments = foreign currency supply (€-revaluation)	Credit outpayments = foreign currency demand (€-devaluation)
III. Financial Account	*capital imports* *Increase in liabilities*	*export of capital* *Increase in claims*
1. foreign direct investment	Incoming payments	Outpayments
2. portfolio flows	securities	including shares and bonds
3. banking flows	Incoming payments	Outpayments
4.Changes of the monetary reserves of the central bank	Incoming payments	Outpayments
IV. Balancing item	estimated errors	and omissions

Fig. 14.6 Important items of the balance of payments (IMF definition)

An example of this would be the establishment of a foreign production facility or the takeover of foreign companies. The changes in currency reserves are the result of exchange rate intervention by the central bank. The ECB can weaken the exchange rate of the euro when it buys dollars. Then the domestic money supply increases as the ECB spends dollars. This policy was pursued by the Swiss central bank at the time when it wanted to keep the Swiss franc in a fixed exchange rate with the euro in order to provide the Swiss economy with a stable basis for calculating the euro area. However, it had to buy more and more euros, which increased the risk of inflation and the valuation risk of eurobonds too much from the point of view of the central bank. They therefore gave up the fixed exchange rate.

Balancing item is an accrued item which equates the difference between the debit and credit. Sides of the balance of payments at the end of the period. These differences are mainly due to delayed payments and to different measurement concepts.

Conclusion: The balance of payments is always balanced, since it is current values. There are no stocks. What flows in must also flow out again. In the circulation between Germany and abroad, the inflows correspond to the outflows.

The current account is balanced by the capital account: LB balance = KB balance.

Balancing item is an accrued item which equates the difference between the debit and credit.

Sides of the balance of payments at the end of the period. These differences are mainly due to delayed payments and to different measurement concepts.

$$\text{Changes in net foreign assets} = \text{current account balance} + \text{asset transfers.}$$

For the gross domestic product we can write:

$$Y = C + I + Ex - Im$$

Investments also include replacement investments covering depreciation. The following applies: $C = Y - S$

$$\Leftrightarrow Y = (Y - S) + I + Ex - Im$$

$$\Leftrightarrow Ex - Im = S - I$$

Interpretation If more is exported (additional demand from abroad) than imported, goods must be left over from the domestic production because they were not demanded domestically. Then, saving as demand by households consuming less than their income (Y) needs to be greater than the additional demand of companies for capital they use for investment demand. We want to draw more conclusions. There are two possible cases:

$$\Leftrightarrow \text{positive } (Ex - Im) = \text{positive } (S - I)$$

$$\Leftrightarrow S = I + \text{net capital outflow}$$

If there is a current account surplus, capital must go abroad at the same rate, as the balance of payments is always balanced. This corresponds to an increase in claims against foreign countries. Domestic goods have transferred welfare to foreign countries and, in the future, expect a return of welfare plus a reasonable return. In this way, permanent export surpluses cannot be in the interest of the domestic market (example Germany).

$$\Leftrightarrow \text{negative } (Ex - Im) = \text{negative } (S - I)$$

$$\Leftrightarrow \text{Net capital inflow} + S = I$$

If there is a current account deficit, then $S < I$. Thus, the capital from abroad must flow into the country, since the balance of payments is always balanced. Consumed and invested more than produced:

Products $\Rightarrow$ Domestic (import surplus)
Capital $\Rightarrow$ Domestic, equivalent to an increase in liabilities (net capital import)

Example Greece has imported more than it has exported for years after joining the European Union. The savings rate was negative. This means that Greece has consumed more than it has produced. Consequently, the goods had to come from abroad. This import surplus could only be financed by a corresponding influx of capital. The balance of payments was balanced, but Greece's external debt continued to rise. Again, this policy cannot be continued indefinitely. At some point, Greece will have to repay the debts and that will only work if the capital flows out of Greece abroad. The process has to be reversed. Then Greece has to export more than import. Thus, the foreign debt is repaid by a retransfer of welfare.

Question What is good business with foreign countries? Can a country divert long-term welfare from abroad to its own people?

Answer The US has had a negative current account for many years. They imported more than they exported. This was financed by China and Japan through a corresponding export of capital to the USA. They bought dollar investments.

The dollar lost value but in the following years as a result of an expansionary monetary policy it gained in value. Japan and China could not buy the same goods for their dollar deposits as they had previously exported.[8]

Exercises

1. Why is the balance of payments always balanced?
2. Which four sub-balances exist in the balance of payments? Name one transaction each, which is posted here.
3. Derive, why is $Ex - Im = S - I$?
4. How can one determine the changes in net foreign assets from the balance of payments?

---

[8]See WELT ONLINE vom 31.05.2012. https://www.welt.de/wirtschaft/article13726257/USA-ertrinken-in-einem-Meer-von-Schulden.html

14.3 Exchange Rates

Definition of exchange rate (quantity quotation, from 1/1/99)[9]: The exchange rate expresses the amount of foreign currency that is received for a unit of domestic currency (as a fraction: $/€, see Fig. 14.7). Exchange rate = exchange ratio.

Devaluation of the dollar = Appreciation of the euro 1 € = 1$ (in 2003)1 € = 1.5$ (in 2008).

Devaluation of the euro = Appreciation of the dollar 1 € = 1.2$ (in 2010) How much is $ 1 in $?

How can a euro devaluation be explained?

In the quantity quotation, the exchange rate can be represented as the price for one euro (see Fig. 14.8). When a currency loses in value (devaluation), as with any other commodity being traded, either demand must have fallen and/or supply increased. If the demand for euro has fallen, it can only be because fewer goods have been exported or more capital has been imported. If supply has risen, it can only be because imports have gone up or capital exports have fallen. These are the corresponding transactions that result in a corresponding currency movement. What are the effects of a euro devaluation?

Impact of a Devaluation of the Euro

European goods become cheaper, American more expensive, depending on price elasticity (also depends on: substitutes, transport costs, etc.) decrease European imports and exports to the dollar area rise. In the US, exports tend to fall and imports rise. This leads to higher euro and lower dollar demand and, in the case of a deficit current account, to a balancing trend. For example, a Porsche for €100,000 costs only $80T in the US instead of $160,000 if the exchange rate of the Euro from 1.6 $/€ devalued to 0.8 $/€. A weak currency is good for business and bad for consumers.

What influences the exchange rate?

All transactions in the current account, with the financial account dominating the current account (faster and higher volumes).

What influences the capital account?

14.3.1 Interest Rate Parity

Thesis: $i_{home}/i_{foreign} = 1$

According to the interest parity theory, there can be no different rates of return internationally, as yield differentials would be immediately offset by arbitrage. Internationally, interest income is similar to capital movements (interest arbitrage), which cause

---

[9]See Koch, W. A., & Czogalla, C. (2008).

Fig. 14.7 Currency revaluation and depreciation of the euro against the US dollar. © 1998–2016 OnVista Group Source: www.onvista.de, imprint with friendly permission

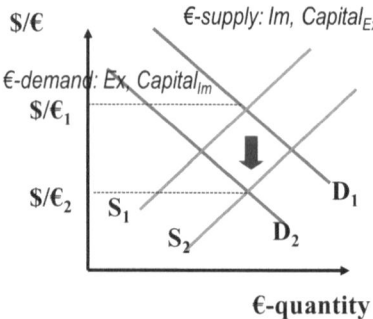

Fig. 14.8 Euro devaluation

exchange rate changes. Future exchange rates (ERt) then correspond to the interest difference related to the period:

$$(ER_t - ER_0)/ER_0 = \Delta\, i_{inl.} - \Delta\, i_{ausl.},$$

$$\Leftrightarrow ER_t = ER_0 + (\Delta i_{inl.} - \Delta i_{ausl.}) ER_0$$

$$\Leftrightarrow ER_t = ER_0 + (\Delta i_{inl.} - \Delta i_{ausl.}) ER_0$$

ER = Exchange Rate

▶ **Definition of Arbitrage** exploiting spatial price differences

▶ **Definition of Speculation** exploitation of temporal price differences

In the EU, there are now 5% more interest rates with unchanged purchasing power of the currency. So an American can buy 5% more goods after 1 year if he puts his money in €. The Americans will exchange $ for € until the 5% interest rate advantage is offset by the euro appreciation (instant arbitrage). He has to pay more and more $ for the € until he gets 5% fewer €, which reduces the purchasing power of his $ by 5%. For example, if the ER is $ 1.3 / € and the US rate is 5% higher than the European rate, which rises from 5% to 10%, the interest rate arbitrage must be unchanged at 1.365 $ / € results:

$$ER_1 = 1,3 + (5\% - 0\%)\, 1,3 = 1365$$

This is the expected exchange rate. He will adjust if there are no other influences on the exchange rate.

What is meant by currency hedging?

Companies hedge their foreign currency receipts through futures. You sell or buy on a given date. The bank gives the company the so-called forward rate with a corresponding premium or discount, which offsets the missed interest differential. In the example where the € interest is 5% higher than the US interest rate, a German exporter would receive $1.235/€ for its $ as its annual forward rate, ie a 5% discount on the spot dollar buying rate. So he gets more $ for the $, because the bank could now swap the $ in € to $1.3/€ and could spend $5 more than $ in a year for 5%, and the exporter could only get $1 a year later. The importer gets 5% fewer $ for €, because he had the € with the higher interest rate for 1 year.

What influences the current account?

14.3.2 Purchasing Power Parity Theory

According to the purchasing power parity theory, an exchange rate can be determined as follows:

$$ER = currency_{foreign}/currency_{home} = p_{foreign}/p_{home}$$

Example: $\$/\text{€} = Price_{USA}/Price_{EU}$
or as relative change of the exchange rate:

$$ER\% = P_{foreign}\% - P_{home}\%$$

Explanation
The purchasing power parity theory supports the thesis that there can be only one price internationally for the same product. If there are price differences, the ER compensates for changes in the purchasing power ratio through arbitrage: if the goods of a country become cheaper, the export increases and the currency is upgraded. Thus the exchange rate reacts at different prices. The exchange rate then corresponds to the price ratio of the goods. The exchange rate is an intermediate price for the exchange of foreign goods.

Example
1 pair of shoes costs $\$100$ in the US and €50 in the EU. Then the exchange rate would have to be $\$100/$ €50, that is $\$2/\text{€}$. Otherwise it would come to arbitrage. If, for example, the price of European shoes doubled to €100, it would be worthwhile importing shoes from the USA until the € ER has depreciated to $\$1/\text{€}$. However, the conditions for the implementation of the purchasing power parity theory are only very limited in practice. Perfect markets and information, above all, no transport costs, identical goods, no price differentiation, flexible trade relations, free trade and transparency are rare. The purchasing power parity theory is therefore only a long-term tendency.

Inflation is the opposite of a return. The currency loses value correspondingly to purchasing power. The currency with the higher inflation must therefore depreciate according to the purchasing power parity theory.

Example: $ER \$/\text{€} \% = P_{\$}\% - P_{\text{€}}\%$

If the exchange rate is 1.2 $\$/\text{€}$ and the US inflation rate is 10% compared to 5% in the EU, according to the purchasing power parity theory, the exchange rate would have to be 1.26 $\$/\text{€}$ in 1 year.

But how can it be explained that international interest rates differ with stable exchange rates?

Greece, for example, paid very high interest rates compared to Germany before entering the euro. The reason was the historically much higher inflation in Greece. The saver has demanded from the Greek government (except for the risk of default) a compensation for the expected inflation. After joining the euro, the Greek state had to pay significantly lower interest rates on its government bonds, which has led politicians to drastically increase public debt.

The difference between the expected rates of inflation therefore corresponds to the interest difference between domestic and foreign (Fisher effect: Inflation↑⇨ nominal interest rate↑). Since the higher interest rates do not lead to more buying power due to the inflation, there are no capital flows. But the change in purchasing power triggered by inflation causes a corresponding currency devaluation with a constant interest differential.

In reality it turns out that the exchange rate fluctuates around purchasing power parity. The greater the deviations, the more worthwhile the arbitrage in foreign trade. In 2008, the dollar was heavily undervalued relative to purchasing power parity, the exchange rate at which American and European goods would have cost the same. At that time, it was worth buying goods in the US and exporting them to the EU. In 2016, the euro is slightly under-valued. It is worth producing goods in the EU and exporting them to the USA.

14.3.3 The Real Exchange Rate as an Indicator of Competitiveness

Real exchange rate

$$ER_{real} = \frac{Price_{ausl.}\,\$}{Price_{inl.}\,€ \cdot ER\,\$/€} \quad or \quad \frac{Price\ index_{Im}}{Price\ index_{Ex}}$$

The real exchange rate serves as a measure to measure the competitiveness of a country. In general, it is a comparison of domestic and foreign goods. If the prices are higher in the country, the domestic has an advantage. Assumption: The US Corvette of GM and the German Porsche are estimated as equal.

$$ER_{real} = \frac{US\text{-}Price\ Corvette_{ausl.}\,\$100,000}{EU\text{-}Price\ Porsche_{inl.}\,€100,000 \cdot 2\$/€} = 0.5$$

You get 0.5 Porsche for 1 Corvette. The consumer thus gets 2 Corvettes for a Porsche. Since he estimates the cars as equivalent, he will buy the Corvette and not the Porshe. The more Porsche I get for a Corvette, the better the competitiveness. On the real exchange rate the prices of the goods act just like the exchange rate. If the real exchange rate rises, this shows that the price relation and thus the competitiveness of the domestic market has improved. The higher the real exchange rate, the more competitive a country is. If the real economy is equal, both foreign and domestic are equally competitive. If the real economy is less than 1, foreign countries are more competitive and if they are larger than one, the domestic market is more competitive. The other side of the coin is the terms of trade (tot) as the reciprocal of the real exchange rate (vice versa). They represent the real exchange ratio of goods between home and abroad.

Terms of Trade

$$\textbf{Terms of trade} = \frac{\text{Price}_{\text{home}} \text{€} \cdot \text{ER } \$/\text{€}}{\text{Price}_{\text{foreign}} \$} \quad \text{or} \quad \frac{\text{Price index}_{\text{Ex}}}{\text{Price index}_{\text{Im}}}$$

Example:

$$\textbf{Terms of trade} = \frac{\text{EU-price Porsche}_{\text{home}} 100 \text{ T€} \cdot 1.5\$/\text{€}}{\text{US-price Corvette}_{\text{foreign}} 100 \text{ T}\$} = 2$$

The terms of trade are the real exchange of goods between home and abroad, how much you get on foreign goods (such as 2 Corvettes or a basket of imported goods) for a unit of domestic goods (for example, Porsche or a basket of export goods).

Central question: How much Corvette do I get for a Porsche?

In this example, I get 2 Corvettes for a Porsche.

An appreciation improves the terms of trade. The terms of trade show which welfare transfer takes place in foreign trade. If the terms of trade are less than one, foreign countries receive relatively more goods from inland than vice versa. So there is a welfare transfer from home to abroad. If the terms of trade are greater than one, it is the other way round and the domestic market gets a welfare gain through foreign trade. At one, foreign trade is welfare-neutral.

If a country can maintain long-term positive terms of trade, it manages to redirect welfare from abroad to the benefit of its own people. If we ask ourselves about the effects of the euro compared to the DM, we can draw the conclusion from both approaches. As countries in the euro area, such as Greece, which tends to have an import surplus, the pressure of appreciation on the euro is lower than that on which the export surplus of Germany alone had an effect. The euro therefore tends to be weaker. This reduces the real exchange rate and thus increases Germany's competitiveness. One could argue that this creates jobs, which is certainly correct, but the German economy managed to offset the appreciation of DM by increasing productivity. At least one cannot say that the Federal Republic has suffered from a lack of labor demand when the DM was the currency. On the contrary, workers were recruited abroad. Ultimately, a weak euro will benefit companies, which will be able to realize more turnover and more profit. This benefits the owners of the companies. Conversely, a weaker euro tends to result in lower terms of trade. So less welfare will be transferred from abroad to Germany. The disadvantage is borne by the population, which has to give up more goods in exchange with imported goods or spending relatively more on vacation abroad. The purchasing power of the population falls. This effect could be offset by significantly higher real wages. But this is not noticeable since the euro entry of Germany. On the contrary, real wages in Germany fell by 0.8% from 2000 to 2008, while in Greece they rose by approx. 40%.[10]

Both sides of the consideration of the break, terms of trade and real exchange rate, stand for different foreign trade strategies. One strategy pursued by, for example, the Federal Republic of Germany, Japan or China is to generate additional demand through export surpluses and thus increase corporate profits and jobs. We have seen that this is only possible if the foreign countries are in the mirror image of the exporting country, because the balance of payments must always be balanced. Conversely, the USA has been showing an import surplus for decades. So you get welfare from abroad. The foreign countries work for them, so that they can afford more than they are able to produce. This also applied to Greece, especially after the euro accession. Ultimately, you can answer the question clearly. There is no point in getting only export surpluses. At some point a benefit from abroad must be transferred back to the exporting country. Otherwise, the exporting country loses welfare without getting anything in return. Export surpluses are also normally offset by an appreciation of the currency of the exporting country and a devaluation of the currency of the importing country. However, this was not possible for the euro countries due to the same currency.

Exercises

1. Calculate the projected euro-dollar exchange rate in 1 year, assuming no change in purchasing power, starting from a price of 1.50 $/€, if euro interest rates are 3% and dollar interest rates are 6%.

2. If the exchange rate is 1.3 $/€ and the US inflation rate is 10% compared to 5% in the EU, then according to the purchasing power parity theory, how would the exchange rate be in 1 year?

3. Excavators of the US company Caterpillar cost $150T, those of the German company Liebherr €200T. Use these prices to proxy the terms of trade and the real exchange rate and interpret the change:

    (a) for an exchange rate of 1.3 $/€ and a year later at 1.10 $/€. Which conclusions can be drawn from this.

    (b) with an ER of 1.3 $/€ and a year later for a US inflation rate of 6% and an EMU inflation rate of 3%.

---

[10]See   http://www.handelsblatt.com/politik/international/realloehne-griechen-mit-groesstem-plus-der-eu-staaten/5753996.html and http://www.boeckler.de/7029_1256.htm (12.10.2016).

14.4   Economic Policy in the Open Economy

In the following, we want to analyze how the state spending policy (fiscal policy) and monetary policy affect the balance of payments. To do this, we must first derive the external economic mechanisms of action.

14.4.1 Effect Chains of External Transactions

1. Ceteris paribus—nothing else changes
2. Underutilization with rising costs
3. Constant share of income is spent on imports

A. Real track (Current Account)

1. **Income import mechanism**

In the income-import mechanism, an increase in income has a positive effect on import demand. If we have more income, we will automatically buy more imported goods as well, since most of our daily necessities are produced abroad, such as television. A constant share of income is spent on imports. To buy these goods you need foreign money. The demand for foreign currency is rising, there is a devaluation.

$$\text{IM}❷ \uparrow = \text{IM} \left(❶Y_{\text{home}} \uparrow, P_{\text{home}}, P_{\text{foreign}}\right) \uparrow$$

→Demand for foreign currency ❸devaluation, ER ↓

2. **Money Price Mechanism**

The monetary price mechanism is based on the equation of quantity. A higher money supply leads to a higher price level with the same amount of goods and the speed of circulation v. This affects the current account. As domestic prices rise, exports will tend to fall and imports will rise. The demand for foreign currency is rising, there is a devaluation.

$$❶M \uparrow v = Y P \uparrow ❷ \quad \textit{quantity equation}$$

$$❷EX \downarrow = EX \left(❶P_{\text{home}} \uparrow, P_{\text{foreign}}, Y_{\text{foreign}}\right) \quad \downarrow$$
$$- \qquad +$$

$$❷IM \uparrow = IM \left(❶P_{\text{home}} \uparrow, P_{\text{foreign}}, Y_{\text{foreign}}\right) \quad \uparrow$$
$$+ \qquad -$$

$$\to \text{❸devaluation, ER} \downarrow$$

$$V = \text{money velocity}$$

3. Income or Demand Price Mechanism

In the income or demand price mechanism, domestic prices are rising due to increased incomes or, more generally, to increased aggregate demand. It has the same impact on the current account as the monetary price mechanism.

$$\mathbf{Y}_{\text{home}} \uparrow \Rightarrow \mathbf{P}_{\text{home}} \uparrow$$

$$\text{❷EX} = \text{EX}\left(\text{❶P}_{\text{home}} \uparrow, \text{P}_{\text{foreign}}, \text{Y}_{\text{foreign}}\right) \downarrow$$
$$ - +$$

$$\text{❷IM} = \text{IM}\left(\text{❶P}_{\text{home}} \uparrow, \text{P}_{\text{foreign}}, \text{Y}_{\text{home}}\right) \uparrow$$
$$ + -$$

$$\to \text{❸devaluation, ER} \downarrow$$

B. Monetary Track (Capital Account)

The financial account has an impact on domestic and foreign interest rates. As shown, changes in real interest rates lead to arbitrage and thus to capital movements. The interest rates, as well as the money supply, which indirectly influences interest rates, are determined by the central bank or are formed on the capital market. If interest rates rise in Germany, there will be a capital inflow, ie a capital import. If they fall, the reverse occurs. Money goes abroad. The reverse effects arise with foreign interest. If this rises with an unchanged domestic interest rate, there will be more capital exports and fewer capital imports.

Capital- or money-interest-mechanism

M $\uparrow \to$ i $\downarrow \to$ devaluation (net capital export)
M $\downarrow \to$ i $\uparrow \to$ revaluation (net capital import)
Financial account:

$$\text{EX}_{\text{Cap}} - \text{IM}_{\text{Cap}} = \text{EX}_{\text{Cap}}\left(\underset{-}{i_{\text{home}}}, \underset{+}{i_{\text{foreign}}}\right) - \text{IM}_{\text{Cap}}\left(\underset{+}{i_{\text{home}}}, \underset{-}{i_{\text{foreign}}}\right)$$

$$\text{Capital export} \Rightarrow \text{devaluation (ER} \downarrow)$$

$$\text{Capital export} \Rightarrow \text{revaluation (ER} \downarrow)$$

$$\text{Cap} = \text{Capital}$$

From this we can now deduce the effects of monetary and fiscal policy on foreign trade transactions.

14.4.2 Expansive Monetary Policy in the Open Economy

The money supply is increased and the interest rate lowered, but only when there is a rise in the amount of money do interest rates fall. According to the equation of quantity, prices rise as more money is matched by the same amount of goods. Lower interest rates increase investment. There is thus an increase in demand. Income and production rise. Due to the fall in interest rates, more capital will tend to be exported abroad. There is an increased demand for foreign exchange and thus a devaluation. The current account is impacted by higher domestic prices and higher incomes. More tends to be imported than exported. There is a devaluation.

$$M \uparrow \rightarrow i \downarrow, P_{home} \uparrow, I\,(i) \uparrow, Y_{home} \uparrow,$$

1. **Financial Account**

$$\left(EX_{Kap} - IM_{Kap}\right) \uparrow = \uparrow EX_{Kap}\,(i_{inl} \downarrow) - IM_{Kap} \downarrow (i_{inl} \downarrow) \rightarrow \text{Devaluation}$$

2. **Current Account**

$$(Ex - Im) \downarrow = EX\,(P_{inl} \uparrow) \downarrow - IM\,(P_{inl} \uparrow) \uparrow - IM \uparrow (Y_{inl} \uparrow) \rightarrow \text{Devaluation}$$

After the financial crisis, all countries pursued an expansionary monetary policy. The US was the first to resort to an extremely expansionary monetary policy by buying government bonds on the capital market. The ECB implemented this so-called quantitative easing under Draghi after the European sovereign debt crisis.

In the US, the policy of expansionary monetary policy has resulted in a strong dollar devaluation, impacted above all by Japan and China due to their large holdings of American government bonds. It shows here that the strategy of achieving export surpluses over decades can lead to a loss of welfare, because neither Japan nor China, after devaluing the US dollar with their American government bonds, could buy the goods they had in turn made available to the US. On the one hand, it strengthened the competitiveness first of the US and then of the EU as Draghi adopted the same policy.

14.4.3 Debt-Financed Expansionary Fiscal Policy in the Open Economy

$$\text{Cap}^D \text{ (Capital Demand)}, G \text{ (Government Expenditure)} \left(Y^D\right) \uparrow$$

$$\rightarrow i \uparrow, P_{inl} \uparrow, Y_{inl} \uparrow$$

1. **Financial account**

$$\left(EX_{Cap} - IM_{Cap}\right) \downarrow = \downarrow EX_{Cap} \left(i_{home} \uparrow\right) - IM_{Cap} \uparrow \left(i_{home} \uparrow\right) \rightarrow \text{Revaluation}$$

2. **Current account**

$$\left(Ex - Im\right) \downarrow = EX \left(P_{home} \uparrow\right) \downarrow - IM \left(P_{home} \uparrow\right) \uparrow - IM \left(Y_{home} \uparrow\right) \rightarrow \text{Devaluation}$$

Conclusion
Balancing the balance of payments and the foreign exchange market is taking place in credit-financed, expansive fiscal policy, as the devaluation resulting from the import surplus is offset by a revaluation as a result of net capital imports. However, foreign debt is rising, causing new problems, as the example of Greece shows.

Example
Greece operated a credit-financed expansionary fiscal policy after joining the European Union. What effects has this had?

As we have already said, a move to the euro must result in a renunciation of autonomous economic, wage and fiscal policies. The economic, wage and financial policies of the countries must not differ greatly, because too many cost increases (differences in competitiveness) or economic differences can no longer be offset by changes in exchange rates. The Greek government was able to benefit from sharply lower interest rates following the euro accession after joining the euro, like Germany after the reunification, when it used a credit-financed expansionary fiscal policy. A lot of money flowed into construction projects (including Olympics) and in the pay of public servants. Domestic demand rose sharply, along with economic growth.

At first glance, therefore, Greece's euro participation was a success story. The economy grew and employment increased. Wages also increased on account of the demand and the Greeks enjoyed their better life in the euro. Due to economic growth, some people may not have been surprised that interest rates in Greece were higher than in Germany. German and French banks in particular invested large sums in Greek government bonds. The interest differential was partially recognized as a present value and led to high bonuses in investment banking, as in the financial crisis. The high demands of the German and French financial system against Greece subsequently made a rescue of Greece seem inevitable (too big to fail). The consequence of increased wages and prices was less and less competitive for Greece. Tax receipts fell and unemployment rose, as did the debt problem, while growth slowed and unemployment increased. As a result of dwindling competitiveness, exports continued to fall, whereas imports rose. The current account deficit increased. Had Greece still had its national currency, the weakness of competition would have been offset by a devaluation. This was no longer possible in the euro. This also affected other euro countries. A particular problem of Greece was the high level of tax evasion, which aggravated the debt problem.

It is a demand problem from the point of view of the Greek economy, but from an economic point of view it is a supply problem. Without an offer that suits the interests of the buyers, Greece cannot sell anything and therefore cannot finance its needs. The Greek unemployed also have needs, that is to say, demand that they can no longer pay without employment. With too of high wages compared to other countries and productivity, they can not generate an offer to pay for their demand. There is a lot of demand here, but there is no production to pay for it. So Greece is unproductive and cannot service its debts.

Conclusion

After the reasons for foreign trade, the balance of payments showed us the accounting of the cross-border flows of money and goods. The exchange rate shows the exchange ratio and, determines together with the price level the exchange ratio of goods (ToT) and the competitiveness (ER real). The chain of effects showed us the dynamic interdependencies of an open economy.

Comprehension Questions

Using the impact chains of foreign trade transactions, show the impact of Greece's expansionary, credit-financed fiscal policy of recent years. What would Greece have to do to repay the debt?

References

Bender, D. (1992). Außenhandel. In D. Bender et al. (Eds.), *Vahlens Kompendium der Wirtschaftstheorie und Wirtschaftspolitik* (5th ed., pp. 419–477). München: Vahlen.

Eltis, W. (1989). David Ricardo (1772-1823). In J. Joachim Starbatty (Ed.), *Klassiker des ökonomischen Denkens II* (pp. 188–207). München: Beck.

Franzmeyer, F. (2001). Europäische Regionalpolitik: Zwischen Solidarität und Effizienz. In R. Ohr & T. Theurl (Eds.), *Kompendium Europäische Wirtschaftspolitik* (pp. 271–307). München: Vahlen.

Koch, W. A., & Czogalla, C. (2008). *Grundlagen und Probleme der Wirtschaftspolitik*. Köln: Wirtschaftsverlag Bachem.

Külp, B. (1996). Heckscher-Ohlin-Theorem. In T. Plümper (Ed.), *Lexikon der Internationalen Wirtschaftsbeziehungen*. München: Oldenbourg.

Leontief, W. (1953). Domestic production and foreign trade: The American capital position re-examined. *Proceedings of the American Philosophical Society, 97*, 331–349.

Ohlin, B. (1933). *Interregional and international trade*. Cambridge, MA: The MIT Press.

Ott, A. E. (1989). *Grundzüge der Preistheorie* (3rd ed.). Göttingen: Vandenhoeck.

Plümper, T. (1996). *Lexikon der Internationalen Wirtschaftsbeziehungen*. München: Oldenbourg.

Ricardo, D. (1817). *The principles of political economy and taxation*. London: John Murray 1817 (Deutsch: Grundsätze der Volkswirtschaft und Besteuerung, Jena 1905).

Rybczynski, T. (1955). Factor endowments and relative commodity prices. *Economica, 22*, 336–341.

Schumann, J. (1987). *Grundzüge der mikroökonomischen Theorie*. Berlin: Springer.

Stavenhagen, G. (1969). *Geschichte der Wirtschaftstheorie*. Göttingen: Vandenhoeck.

Stolper, W., & Samuelson, P. (1941). Protection and real wages. *Review of Economic Studies, 9*, 58–73.

Solutions to the Exercises 15

To Chap. 5: Market and Competition

Competition functions

Assign the examples below to the respective competition functions.

1. ⇒ Innovation and imitation function
2. ⇒ Steering function
3. ⇒ Liberty function
4. ⇒ Control function
5. ⇒ first allocation function and adaption function
6. ⇒ Sanction function
7. ⇒ Adaption function (and steering function)
8. ⇒ second allocation function
9. ⇒ distribution function, incentive function und innovation function
10. ⇒ distribution, incentive function und innovation function
11. ⇒ incentive function (distribution function)

To Chap. 8: Political Failure

Solution Voting Rules Berlin versus Bonn (Fig. 15.1)

To Chap. 9: Competition Policy

International Competition Policy

© The Editor(s) (if applicable) and The Author(s), under exclusive license to Springer   545
Fachmedien Wiesbaden GmbH, part of Springer Nature 2020
C. A. Conrad, *Political Economy*,
https://doi.org/10.1007/978-3-658-30884-1_15

	1. rank (priority)	2. rank (priority)	3. rank (priority)
A:Bonn and Berlin	146 x 3 = 438	222 x 2 = 444	289 Σ 1.171
B: Berlin	222 x 3 = 666	265 x 2 = 530	170 Σ 1.366
C: Bonn	289 x 3 = 867	170 x 2 = 340	198 Σ 1.405

Fig. 15.1   Solution transfer task voting rules

3. (a)

$$\text{Normal value} = \text{retail price China } €10 + \text{export costs } €1 = €11$$

$$\text{Anti} - \text{dumping duty} = \text{normal value} - \text{selling price EU} = €11 - €5$$
$$= €6 \text{ (percentage : 120\%)}$$

(b)

$$\text{Calculated normal value} = \text{unit cost} + \text{overhead costs} + \text{profit margin} + \text{export costs}$$
$$= €15 + €1.50 + €0.825 + €2$$
$$= €19.325$$

$$\text{Antidumping duty} = \text{normal value} - \text{sales price EU} = €19.325 - €12.00$$
$$= €7.325 \text{ (in percentage : 61\%)}$$

Exercise Subvention Race (Prisoner's Dilemma) (Fig. 15.2)

There are four combinations: If a and all n governments decide not to subsidize, then for all governments, after deducting the social and political costs of unemployment (−2), there will be an increase in wealth caused by optimal resource allocation (especially imports, +4). The payout of 2 (4 − 2). (Combination 1–1) However, no government will be willing to subsidize its industry without being certain that all other governments will do so as well. If only one does not choose to subsidize, whereas the other governments subsidize, he will bear the social and political costs of his refusal to subsidize (−2), without any benefit for him in the form of a welfare benefit

− For a to receive the maximum payout, a has to subsidize, but all other governments will have subsidies. In this case, a can bypass his political social costs. The welfare gained by

Fig. 15.2 Solution subsidy race

a\n	Not subsidize [1]	subsidize [2]
Not subsidize [1]	(4-2 =) 2, 2	(0-X) (– 2), 0
subsidize [2]	4, 2	0, 0

the state through imports that have become cheaper abroad within the non-subsidized market +4. The state thus participates in the public good without contributing anything (free-rider position or Free rider behavior; combination 2–1).

– All states will therefore take the Free Rider position, which automatically leads to the suboptimal combination 2–2 (dominant strategy), in which no subsidy-free market as a public good comes about. The Nash equilibrium is thus combined [2,2]. It is thus the game-theoretical situation of a prisoner's lemma.

To Chap. 13: Monetary Policy
Inflation

1. The price index for 2010 is calculated by comparing the prices to the volumes and prices of the base year:

Price index for 2010 =
$$\frac{P(\text{car 2010}) \times \text{quantity (car 2000)} + P(\text{bread 2010}) \times \text{amount (bread 2000)}}{P \text{ (car 2000)} \times \text{quantity (car 2000)} + P \text{ (bread 2000)} \times \text{amount (bread 2000)}}$$

$$= \frac{60.000€ \times 100 + 20€ \times 500.000}{50.000€ \times 100 + 10€ \times 500.000}$$
$$= 1,6$$

The price index is thus 1.6, which means that the price increase rate between 2000 and 2010 was 60%.

ECB tasks (Fig. 15.3)

1. in growth rates, quantity-equation:

$Y + P = M + V$

$M = Y + P - V$

$M = 2\% + 1.8\% - (0) = 3.8\%$

2.

The marginal allotment rate is 3.05%

Weighted average interest:

Bank	Interest rate Interest tender	Money quantity	Quantity tender	Money quantity x allotment rate 0,5
A	3.07	10 (10)	3.06	15 (25%; 7.5)
B	3.06	10 (10)	3.06	5 (8,3%; 2.5)
C	3.05	10 (2.5)	3.06	10 (16.7%; 5)
D	3.05	10 (2.5)	3.06	15(25%; 7.5)
E	3.03	5 (0)	3.06	15(25%; 7.5)
				60(30)

Fig.15.3 Solution EZB-exercise

$$(3.07\% \times 10 + 3.06\% \times 10 + 3.05\% \times 5) : 25 = 3.062\%$$

To Chap. 14: Foreign Trade
To 14.1.1

Give four reasons for foreign trade. See the explanations in the book

2. Explain in your own words the difference between foreign trade due to absolute and relative cost advantages.

Absolute cost advantages, one country can produce one product at a lower cost than another country.

Relative cost advantages, one country can produce both products more cheaply than another country. Every country can produce a product more cheaply in the country most cheaply with relatively less work. When it produces this product, welfare effects are created.

3. What effect does different foreign input trade make on factoring?

(a) for mobile production factors: The scarcity of the respective production factor is compensated, which is why in each country a higher productivity and thus a higher production sets as a welfare gain. Factor prices (interest and wages) are the same.
(b) for immobile production factors

• see explanations in the book

4. Give two examples each of the production life cycle phase and foreign trade due to specialization:

– Production life cycle phase:

A new German high-tech machine will be "copied" by the Chinese two years after it was launched, which will then launch a similar machine at a lower price.

ABS at Daimler was the unique selling point, and this system was then adapted by foreign carmakers.

– Foreign trade due to specialization:

Germany has specialized in manufacturing high-tech vehicles and machines.
Switzerland has specialized in the production of fine mechanical pocket knives and watches.

To 14.2
See the explanations in the book.

To 14.3
1.

$$ER_t = ER_0 + (\Delta\, i_{inl.} - \Delta\, i_{ausl.})\, ER_0$$

$$ER_t = 1,5 - 3\% \times 1,5 = 1,455\ \$/€.$$

2. (a)

$$ER\ \$/€\% = P_{ausl.}.\% - P_{inl.}\%$$

$$ER\ \$/€\% = 10\% - 5\% = 5\%$$

So the ER $/€ will be 1.3 + 1.3 × 5% in 1 year, which is $1.365 $/€.
(b)

$$ER\ \$/€\% = P_{ausl.}.\% - P_{inl.}\%$$

$$ER\ \$/€\% = 5\% - 10\% = -5\%$$

So the ER $/€ 1.3 will be 1.3 × (−5%), which is $1.235 $/€.
3.
for an exchange rate of $1.3 $/€

$$\text{Terms of trade} = \frac{\text{EU-price digger Liebherr}_{inl.}\ 200\ T€ \cdot 1,3\ \$/€}{\text{US-price digger Caterpillar}_{ausl.}\ 150\ T\$} = 1,733$$

Reciprocal value as real exchange rate = 0.58

Since the real ER is 0.58 < 1, the US is more competitive with the Caterpillars than Germany with the Liebherr excavators. Conversely, we get 1.733 Caterpillar for an equivalent Liebherr, so more goods in real terms in exchange with the US, which means a welfare gain for Germany.

(b) and a year later at 1.10 \$/€.

$$\text{Terms of trade} = \frac{\text{EU-price digger Liebherr}_{\text{inl.}} 200 \text{ T€} \cdot 1.1 \text{ \$/€}}{\text{US-price digger Caterpillar}_{\text{ausl.}} 150 \text{ T\$}} = 1.467$$

Reciprocal value as real exchange rate = 0.68

The ToT decreased by around 15%, that is, the EU gets 15% fewer goods in real terms in exchange with the US than before. The welfare gain has fallen. The real ER increased by around 17%, which also means the EU's competitiveness against the US.

(b) with a GDP of \$1.3/€ for a US inflation rate of 6% and an EMU inflation rate of 3%.

$$\text{US price Caterpillar} = 150 \text{ T \$} + 150 \text{ T \$} \times 6\% = 159 \text{ T \$ EU price Liebherr}$$
$$= 200 \text{ T €} + 200 \text{ T €} \times 3\% = 206 \text{ T €}$$

(The exchange rate adjustment takes place later with a delay, since the arbitrage has yet to take place.)

$$\text{Terms of trade} = \frac{\text{EU-price digger Liebherr}_{\text{inl.}} 200 \text{ T€} \cdot 1.3 \text{ \$/€}}{\text{US-price digger Caterpillar}_{\text{ausl.}} 150 \text{ T\$}} = 1.733$$

Reciprocal value as real exchange rate = 0.58

$$\text{Terms of trade} = \frac{\text{EU-price digger Liebherr}_{\text{inl.}} 206 \text{ T€} \cdot 1.3 \text{ \$/€}}{\text{US-price digger Caterpillar}_{\text{ausl.}} 159 \text{ T\$}} = 1.684$$

Reciprocal value as real exchange rate = 0.59

The ToT decreased by around 3%, that is, the EU gets 3% fewer goods in real terms in exchange with the US than before. The welfare gain has fallen. The real ER increased by around 2%, which also means the EU's competitiveness against the US.

To 14.4

$$1.\text{Cap}^D \uparrow, G \uparrow \left(\text{d.h.} Y^D \uparrow\right) \rightarrow i \uparrow, P_{\text{home}} \uparrow, Y_{\text{home}} \uparrow$$

1. Financial account

$$\left(EX_{Cap} - IM_{Cap}\right) \downarrow = \downarrow EX_{Cap} \left(i_{home} \uparrow\right) - IM_{Cap} \uparrow \left(i_{home} \uparrow\right) \text{ thus net capital import}$$

2. Currrent Account

$$(Ex - Im) \downarrow = EX \left(P_{home} \uparrow\right) \downarrow - IM \left(P_{home} \uparrow\right)$$
$$\uparrow - IM \left(Y_{home} \uparrow\right) \text{ thus current account deficit}$$

The current account deficit in a credit-financed expansionary fiscal policy is compensated by capital imports, but external debt rises. Greece would have to reverse the process, reducing capital demand (reducing public debt, for example by raising taxes, combating tax evasion, Greece's finance ministers: half would be sufficient for debt servicing) and reducing government spending and/or increased competitiveness (with lower domestic prices, like wages) fall or devaluation of the currency, with exit from the euro) achieve an export surplus, which allows a capital export. But this also means that the Greeks have to save more (so that goods are left for export) and that, first of all, the gross domestic product falls in Greece.

Index